Holy Spirit and Salvation

Holy Spirit and Salvation

The Sources of Christian Theology

Edited by Veli-Matti Kärkkäinen

WESTMINSTER
JOHN KNOX PRESS
LOUISVILLE · KENTUCKY

1st edition
Published by Westminster John Knox Press
Louisville, Kentucky

10 11 12 13 14 15 16 17 18 19—10 9 8 7 6 5 4 3 2 1

Book design by Drew Stevens
Cover design by Eric Walljasper, Minneapolis, MN
Cover art: Painting No. 0528 *(oil on canvas) by Alberto Magnelli (1888–1971)*
Private Collection / Peter Willi / The Bridgeman Art Library Nationality /
©2009 Artists Rights Society (ARS), New York / ADAGP, Paris.

Library of Congress Cataloging-in-Publication Data

Holy Spirit and salvation : the sources of Christian theology / Veli-Matti Kärkkäinen, editor.
  p.   cm. — (The sources of Christian theology)
Includes bibliographical references and index.
ISBN 978-0-664-23136-1 (alk. paper)
1. Holy Spirit. 2. Salvation—Christianity. I. Kärkkäinen, Veli-Matti.
BT121.3.H64 2010
231'.309—dc22

2009028353

Contents

Series Introduction

The Sources of Christian Theology is a series of books to provide resources for the study of major Christian doctrines. The books are edited by expert scholars who provide an extended introductory discussion of the important dimensions of the doctrine. The main focus of each volume is on selections of source materials. These are drawn from major Christian theologians and documents that convey essential elements of theological formulations about each doctrine. The editor provides context and backgrounds in short introductory materials prior to the selections. A bibliography for further study is included.

There is no substitute in theological study for a return to the "sources." This series provides a wide array of source materials from the early church period to the present time. The selections represent the best Christian theological thinking and display the range of ways in which Christian persons have thought about the issues posed by the major aspects of Christian faith.

We hope that those interested in the study of Christian theology will find these volumes rich and valuable resources. They embody the efforts of Christian thinkers to move from "faith" to "understanding."

Donald K. McKim
Westminster John Knox Press

Introduction to Pneumatology

First Words: Overcoming the Forgetfulness of the Spirit
In recent years, one of the most exciting developments in theology has been an unprecedented interest in the Holy Spirit.[1] The reverberations can be felt across a broad range of academic studies, in the renewal of spirituality, and in new movements such as green pneumatology or liberation pneumatology. The resurgence of pneumatology may have to do, in part, with the better knowledge of the rich spiritual and pneumatological traditions of the Eastern Orthodox churches, who have accused their Western counterparts of "forgetfulness of the Spirit." The worldwide spread of Pentecostals and charismatics has turned our attention to the practical and at times spectacular manifestations of the Spirit.

Until recently it was commonplace to introduce pneumatological treatises with a lament over the Spirit's neglect.[2] There were several reasons for this "oblivion of the Spirit," such as the naming of the Holy Spirit as the "bond" of love by the Augustinian tradition.[3] While based on biblical hints, this labeling also contributed to a nonpersonal conception of the Spirit. Other reasons for the omission of the Spirit include the biblical perception that the Holy Spirit is never self-referential but rather turns our attention to the Son and through the Son to the Father. Yet another reason for the junior role of the Spirit in the Trinitarian understanding of the Christian God may have to do with ecclesial concerns. As early as the charismatic revival movement, beginning from the second century, Montanists all the way through Reformation "Enthusiasts" to modern-day Pentecostals started to claim the authority of the Spirit in favor of human leaders of the church—or as it was often perceived, over the written Word of God. Thus, a need was felt to control the Spirit.

Finally, behind the question of a forgetfulness of the Spirit is the ecumenically divisive debate about the *filioque* clause in the creed; the clause

---

1. For a brief account, see Veli-Matti Kärkkäinen, *Pneumatology: The Holy Spirit in Ecumenical, International, and Contextual Perspectives* (Grand Rapids: Baker Academic, 2002), chap. 1.

2. Somewhat sensationally, the Holy Spirit has been claimed to be the "Cinderella" of theology. See Jürgen Moltmann, *The Spirit of Life: A Universal Affirmation* (Minneapolis: Fortress Press, 1993), 1; and Alister McGrath, *Christian Theology: An Introduction* (Cambridge, MA: Blackwell, 1994), 240. Already in the 1960s Hendrikus Berkhof (*The Doctrine of the Holy Spirit* [Atlanta: John Knox Press, 1964], 10) lamented that even in the Anglo-Saxon literature one could discover little of substance on the topic of pneumatology.

3. For an insightful discussion, see Bernd Jochen Hilberath, "Identity through Self-Transcendence: The Holy Spirit and the Communion of Free Persons," in *Advents of the Spirit: An Introduction to the Current Study of Pneumatology*, ed. Bradford E. Hinze and D. Lyle Dabney (Milwaukee: Marquette University Press, 2001), 263–65.

was the official reason for the split of the church of Christ in 1054 between the East and West. The Latin phrase simply means "and from the Son," making the derivation of the Spirit in the Trinity dual, from both Father and Son.[4] Why this addition to the creed? The Bible does not clarify the interrelations of Father, Son, and Spirit, including the procession of the Spirit. On the one hand, Jesus says that he himself will send the Spirit (John 16:7; called here *Parakletos*) who proceeds from the Father (John 15:26). On the other hand, Jesus prays to the Father for him to send the Spirit (John 14:16), and the Father will send the Spirit in Jesus' name (John 14:26). Because of the lack of clarity in the biblical record, the Christian West added the Spirit's dual procession, *filioque* (Latin: "[and] from the Son"), to the Niceno-Constantinopolitan Creed that originally said that the Holy Spirit "proceeds from the Father." The Christian East objects vigorously to this addition, claiming that it was a one-sided addition without ecumenical consultation, that it compromises the monarchy of the Father as the source of divinity, and that it subordinates the Spirit to Jesus with theological corollaries in ecclesiology, the doctrine of salvation, and so on. As a mark of the desire to resolve this theological and ecumenical impasse, there is a growing consensus among Western theologians, both Roman Catholic and Protestant, about the need to delete the addition and thus return to the original form of the creed. An alternative to *filioque,* "from the Father *through* the Son," would be also acceptable to the Christian East.[5]

The rediscovery of the role of the Spirit in theology raises the question of the proper place for pneumatology in Christian theology. Traditionally, pneumatology has not received a separate locus in Christian systematic theologies. Unlike the doctrine of the Trinity or the church, the discussion of the Spirit has not been allowed to stand on its own. Pneumatological topics have most often been incorporated into the doctrines of Trinity, revelation, and salvation (soteriology). Or pneumatology has been connected with the doctrine of the church, following the ancient creedal practice of connecting the Holy Spirit with the church. These are all important and relevant loci for the discussion of the ministry of the Spirit. Yet not having its own space, as it were, has tended to put the doctrine of the Holy Spirit in the shadow of other doctrinal loci.

Theologically responsible ways of trying to rehabilitate the place of pneumatology in theology either assign a separate chapter to the Spirit

---

4. While some of the historical details are somewhat debated, the standard view is that this addition was first accepted by the Council of Toledo in 589 and ratified by the 809 Aachen Synod.

5. For details, see Veli-Matti Kärkkäinen, *The Trinity: Global Perspectives* (Louisville, KY: Westminster John Knox Press, 2007), 56–59. Even in contemporary theology there are a few theologians who for some reason support the *filioque* clause, Karl Barth being the most well known in his fear of not missing the biblical insistence on the Spirit as the Spirit of the Son.

in the presentation of Christian doctrine or make a conscious attempt to connect the Spirit with all main topics of theology. The latter is the procedure adopted by the Lutheran Wolfhart Pannenberg, who in his monumental three-volume *Systematic Theology*[6] connects the Spirit with each of the main loci of theology. In this approach, the Holy Spirit, far more than a "gap-filler," is a necessary part of the theological structure itself.

The Tapestry of Biblical Testimonies

The Bible, of course, does not present a "systematic" theology of the Holy Spirit—any more than it does of, say, Christology or the church. The Bible speaks of the Spirit in terms of symbols, images, metaphors, and stories.[7] The basic biblical terms, the Old Testament *ruach* and the New Testament *pneuma*, carry similar ambiguity: "breath," "air," "wind," or "soul." Some of the metaphors used of the Spirit are wind, fire, dove, and paraclete. The Old Testament[8] contains about one hundred references to the "Spirit of God" (Gen. 1:2; Isa. 11:2). Among the many facets of the role of the Spirit in God's creation, probably nothing is more central than the idea of the Spirit as the principle of life, the life force. The same Spirit of God that participated in creation over the chaotic primal waters (Gen. 1:2) gave life to the human being (Gen. 2:7) and sustains life in the whole cosmos:

> When you [Yahweh] send forth your spirit [*ruach*], they are created;
> and you renew the face of the ground.
>
> (Ps. 104:30)

Similarly, when Yahweh

> take[s] away their breath [*ruach*], they die
> and return to their dust.
>
> (Ps. 104:29)

As a charismatic power, *ruach* can come mightily upon a human being (Judg. 14:6; 1 Sam. 16:13) and "clothe" him or her to equip for powerful works, including release from threatening powers (Judg. 3:10; 6:34) or to give prophetic visions (Ezek. 3:12; 8:3; 11:1). The Spirit can bring about the craftsman's skill (Exod. 31:3) or any outstanding ability (Dan. 6:3).

The prophetic books see an integral connection between the Messiah and the Spirit; the messianic figure is anointed and empowered by the Spirit of God (Isa. 11:1–8; 42:1–4; 49:1–6). God gives a new Spirit to heal and restore his people (Ezek. 18:31; Joel 2:28–32). In the Wisdom

---

6. Wolfhart Pannenberg, *Systematic Theology*, 3 vols., trans. Geoffrey W. Bromiley (Grand Rapids: Wm. B. Eerdmans Publishing Co., 1991–1998).

7. The main source in this section is George T. Montague, *The Holy Spirit: Growth of a Biblical Tradition* (Peabody, MA: Hendrickson, 1994); for shorter, less technical discussions, see idem, "The Fire in the Word: The Holy Spirit in Scripture," in *Advents of the Spirit*, 35–62.

8. A very helpful outline of Old Testament perspectives is offered by E. Kamlah, "Spirit," in *Dictionary of New Testament Theology*, ed. Colin Brown (Grand Rapids: Zondervan, 1978), 3:690–92.

literature, wisdom can be correlated or identified with the word/*Logos* or the Spirit (Prov. 8:22–31).

In the New Testament[9] Gospels, an authentic Spirit Christology comes to the fore. Jesus' birth (Matt. 1:18–25; Luke 1:35); baptism (Matt. 3:16; Mark 1:10; Luke 3:22; John 1:33); testing in the wilderness (Matt. 4:1; Mark 1:12; Luke 4:1); and ministry with healings, exorcisms, and other miracles (Matt. 12:28; Luke 4:18; 11:20) are functions of the Spirit. According to the Pauline tradition, Jesus was raised to new life by the Spirit (Rom. 1:4). Indicative of the eschatological ministry of the Spirit is Jesus' role as the baptizer in the Spirit (Matt. 3:11; Mark 13:11).

The transforming power of the Spirit is evident in the origins and life of the earliest Christian communities. In the aftermath of the Day of Pentecost, with a powerful outpouring of the Spirit (Acts 2:1–3)—fulfilling the prophecy of Joel (2:28–29)—the reception of the Spirit often took place with visible signs (Acts 4:31; 8:15–19; etc.); indeed, those signs were taken as the evidence of the work of God (Acts 8:12–25; 10:44–48; 19:1–7). Often at pivotal moments in the life of an individual or the church, the Holy Spirit was seen as the source of an extraordinary power (Acts 9:17; 11:15–18; etc.). Another means by which the Spirit helped the early church in its mission was to give a special authority to the leadership of the community (Acts 4:31; 5:1–10; 6:10; etc.) The Spirit also directed the work of missionaries (Acts 8:29, 39; 10:19).

Similarly to the Gospels, Paul[10] has a thick Spirit Christology. The Spirit is the Spirit of Christ (Rom. 8:9; Gal. 4:6; Phil. 1:19). Therefore, it is only through the Spirit that the believer is able to confess that "Jesus is Lord" (1 Cor. 12:1–3). The *Abba* prayer wells up from the Spirit of sonship in believers (Rom. 8:15). To be "in Christ" and "in the Spirit" are virtually synonymous; therefore, the Spirit cannot be experienced apart from Christ (1 Cor. 12:3). Paul can even go so far as to say that Christ became "a life-giving Spirit" (1 Cor. 15:45). Along with the soteriological aspect of Paul's teaching on the Spirit, also crucial for Paul is the charismatic endowment and gifting (1 Cor. 1:4–7; Gal. 3:5). Another role of the Spirit is the experience of illumination and divine revelation in the face of affliction (1 Thess. 1:6; 1 Cor. 2:10–12; 2 Cor. 3:14–17). For Paul, the Spirit of the new age has already broken into the old. Paul refers to the Spirit as an *arrabon*, a down-payment of the glory to come (2 Cor. 1:22; 5:5; Eph. 1:13–14), and as the first installment of the believer's inheritance in the kingdom of God (Rom. 8:15–17; 14:17; 1 Cor. 6:9–11; 15:42–50; Gal. 4:6–7).

---

9. A very helpful guide to New Testament perspectives is offered by James D. G. Dunn, "Spirit," in *Dictionary of New Testament Theology*, ed. Colin Brown (Grand Rapids: Zondervan, 1978), 3:693–709.

10. A massive study on Pauline pneumatological traditions is Gordon Fee, *God's Empowering Presence: The Holy Spirit in the Letters of Paul* (Peabody, MA: Hendrickson, 1994).

In addition to charismatic, prophetic, and eschatological dimensions, a moral transformation by means of the Spirit is also to be expected (1 Cor. 6:9–11). There is a constant struggle, even warfare, between "spirit" and "flesh" (Rom. 8:1–17; Gal. 5:16–26). Therefore, the believer has a responsibility to live his or her life in the power of the Spirit, "walking in the Spirit," being led by the Spirit (Rom. 8:4–6, 14; Gal. 5:16, 18, 25). As far as there is advancement, the fruit of the Spirit will become evident (Gal. 5:22–23).

The pneumatology of the Johannine literature is highly distinctive. That tradition picks up the Old Testament images of the Spirit related to the life-giving power of water and breath as is evident in the metaphors of rebirth (John 3:5–8), spring of life (John 4:14; 6:63; 7:38–39), and new creation (John 20:22; cf. Gen. 2:7; Ezek. 37:9). The Epistles speak of anointing (1 John 2:20, 27), another significant Old Testament aspect. The Johannine Jesus has been given the Spirit "without measure" (John 3:34). John also ties Jesus' gift of the Spirit more closely to Jesus' death (6:51–58, 62–63; 19:34). One of the most distinctive features of Johannine pneumatology is the introduction of the Spirit as the "other Advocate" (14:16), obviously implying that Jesus is the first (1 John 2:1). The term *parakletos* (from *para* + *kalein*) means "one called alongside to help," thus an advocate or defense attorney or a guide into truth (John 14:26). In the book of Revelation, the Spirit plays a crucial role in inspiration and vision (1:10; 4:2; 14:13; 17:3; 19:10; 21:10; 22:17). The Apocalypse mentions "seven spirits" (1:4; 4:5) or the spirits of Jesus (3:1; 5:6), phrases typical of apocalyptic literature.

To summarize briefly the rest of the New Testament testimonies to the Spirit, the following remarks are in order: The Pastoral Epistles seem to be shy about the Spirit's manifested ministry in the church and link it closely with longstanding gifting to the ministry as well as to inspiration of Scripture (2 Tim. 1:7; 3:16). Titus 3:5 connects the Holy Spirit with regeneration. While the book of Hebrews obviously knows about the charismatic vitality evident in earlier times (2:4), inspiration of Scripture (3:7; 9:8; 10:15) is a main theme. Significantly, the book also connects the Spirit with Christ's self-offering on the cross (9:14), thus expanding the domain of the Gospels' Spirit Christology. The Letters of Peter similarly connect the Spirit with inspiration (1 Pet. 1:11; 2 Pet. 1:21). First Peter (4:14) also makes the important connection between the Spirit and our suffering as Christians.

The New Testament also speaks of spirits vis-à-vis the Spirit of God. It recognizes the reality of a battle going on between the kingdom of God and evil spirits, a perspective depicted especially in the Synoptic Gospels (Mark 3:23–27 par.). Since there are both good spirits and bad, the church and individual Christians need to be able to discern the spirits (1 Cor. 12:10; 14:12; 2 Cor. 11:4).

A few theological observations are in order on the nature of pneumatologies of the Bible. As needed in Christology, we need to speak of pneumatologies in the plural. Both diversity and plurality are hallmarks.

While common themes appear, such as the Spirit's role as the provider of life or Messiah/Spirit Christologies, there is no attempt among the biblical witnesses to reduce the sphere or the ministry of the Spirit. Reflecting the diverse imagery used of the Spirit, the work of the Spirit has a gentle and subtle facet as well as the rushing-wind or stormy side. There is the silent, hidden side as well as the audible, visible, and tangible aspect; the salvific, soteriological ministry as well as the gifting and empowering energies; and so forth.

A theologically and historically significant observation can be gleaned from the pneumatologies of the last part of the Christian Bible, the Catholic Epistles. While the charismatic, dynamic, and surprising elements of the Spirit's ministry are either absent or marginal, the tasks such as inspiration of Scripture and gifting to the ministry ("ordination"), which lean toward structures and institutionalization, take the upper hand. This is exactly what happened soon after the first centuries when church structures, established ministries such as the episcopacy, and the Christian canon were formed.

Given the richness, diversity, and pluriformity of biblical testimonies to the Spirit, it is no surprise that a rich tapestry of pneumatologies emerged during church history, culminating in the mosaic of contemporary times. To this development of pneumatological traditions we turn next.

The Historical Growth of Pneumatological Traditions

According to Catholic Yves Congar, in the beginning the church saw itself subject to the activity of the Spirit and filled with the Spirit's gifts; no opposition yet existed between "hierarchical" and "charismatic" ministries in the church.[11] Doctrinal development of the Spirit advanced slowly; christological and Trinitarian deliberations took prominence.[12] What pushed the church toward a more accurate understanding of the Spirit was the emergence of heretical Christian movements. For example, Irenaeus wrote much on the Spirit (and the Trinity) in his *Against Heresies*. A significant challenge to the understanding of the ministry of the Spirit came from the second-century charismatic, prophetic movement called Montanism. It raised questions such as, How does one discern a true prophecy of the Spirit? and What is the role of Scripture and of prophets in the church? Montanists were expelled from the church and labeled heretics as superseding ecclesial authority.

---

11. Yves Congar, *I Believe in the Holy Spirit*, trans. David Smith, 3 vols. (New York: Crossroad, 1996), 1:65.

12. Three reliable, accessible sources on the historical growth of pneumatological traditions are Stanley M. Burgess, *Holy Spirit: Ancient Christian Traditions* (Peabody, MA: Hendrickson, 1984); idem, *The Holy Spirit: Eastern Christian Traditions* (Peabody, MA: Hendrickson, 1989); and idem, *The Holy Spirit: Medieval Roman Catholic and Reformation Traditions* (Peabody, MA: Hendrickson, 1997).

The Cappadocian Fathers (Basil the Great, Gregory of Nazianzen, Gregory of Nyssa) and Athanasius in the Christian East were the first ones to develop a doctrine of the Spirit. For some time the contours were fluid: not only was the question of the deity of the Spirit unsettled, but there were also times when the Son and Spirit were confused with each other. The Fathers' prime need was to secure an orthodox doctrine of salvation and liturgy. If the deifying Spirit was not really divine as the heretic Macedonius (d. ca. 362) and the Pneumatomachoi ("enemies of the Spirit") argued, that jeopardized our salvation. In the liturgy, if the Spirit were not divine, then the church's doxology to the triune God would be blasphemous.

The first decisive step in the church's doctrinal understanding concerning the Spirit was reached at the Nicene-Constantinopolitan Creed in 381. According to the creed, the Spirit is the "Lord and life-giver, proceeding from the Father, object of the same worship and the same glory with the Father and the Son."[13]

In the Christian West, Hilary of Poitiers and especially St. Augustine made a lasting contribution to Trinitarian doctrine and pneumatology. Both separately from and building on the tradition of the Eastern pneumatologists, Augustine robustly calls the Spirit "God." His formulations of the Spirit as Gift and as Love have been embraced by tradition.

The doctrinal and creedal tradition of the patristic era laid the foundation for everything in subsequent centuries. Generally speaking, developments in the millennium-long medieval period can be roughly classified under three different categories: (1) The prophetic-apophatic approach of Montanists and, say, Ephraim the Syrian was taken up by visionaries such as Pseudo-Dionysius the Areopagite and Joachim of Fiore. (2) The doctrinal work of both Eastern and Western doctors was taken to its analytic heights by the angelic doctor Thomas Aquinas and Anselm of Canterbury. (3) The mystical-poetic narratives of the Spirit of *The Passion of the Holy Martyrs Perpetua and Felicitas* and the like were creatively and intensely enriched by a number of medieval mystical female theologians, such as Catherine of Siena and Hildegard of Bingen, as well as their male counterparts, such as Bernard of Clairvaux. On the doctrinal domain, the Thomistic teaching on grace and the Spirit's role in salvation both built on the work of Aquinas and gave it a new twist that came to dominate Catholic theology until contemporary times. Again, diversity is the rule.

Mainline Protestants, both Lutheran and Reformed, followed the debates about the Spirit only to the degree to which they dealt with questions related to the inspiration of Scripture (particularly John Calvin); to the doctrine of faith, righteousness, and sacraments (particularly Martin Luther); as well as—in a more polemic context—to challenges raised by

---

13. The Nicene-Constantinopolitan Creed, in R. P. C. Hanson, *The Search for the Christian Doctrine of God: The Arian Controversy 318–381* (Edinburgh: T. & T. Clark, 1988), 815–16.

the Radical Reformation. Anabaptists and others were pejoratively named the "Enthusiasts," because in the eyes of both Luther and Calvin, they were alleged to substitute for the written Word and sacraments of the church an inner spiritual experience and unmediated revelations from the Spirit. The Catholic Reformers such as Ignatius of Loyola, John of Avila, and John of the Cross produced spiritually and mystically uplifting accounts of and guides to the Spirit.

While the aftermath of the Reformation on the way to the nineteenth-century theology of modernity again betrays a diversity of developments, this work will highlight two main pneumatological venues. First is the rich tapestry of various Protestant revival movements, such as Puritanism, pietism, Methodist and holiness movements, Quakerism, and evangelicalism, whose intent was to revive the "religion of the heart." In the Great Awakenings of the eighteenth and nineteenth centuries in Wales and in the United States, this search for renewal reached its zenith.

Second, in the aftermath of the Enlightenment out of which modernity evolved, the nineteenth century brought about what is called "modern theology," most ably represented by the father of Protestant theology, F. D. E. Schleiermacher. The turn to the subject and the immanentism of modern Protestant theology radically revised theological canons in general and the conception of the Spirit in particular. The liberals did not spend much ink on traditional doctrines such as the Trinity, which they saw as virtually unnecessary, but were rather much more concerned about what they saw as flaws in tradition, particularly the radical discontinuity between the divine and human spirits. The pervasive influence of liberal pneumatology can be discerned in the work of Paul Tillich, whose third volume of *Systematic Theology* (1963) is one of the first contemporary pneumatologies to attempt to transcend the dividing line between the Spirit and spirit. For Tillich the Spirit of God is the life-giving principle that makes human life and the life of the whole creation meaningful and specific.

More traditional theologies of the Spirit on the eve of the twentieth century were presented by the neo-Calvinist school under the tutelage of the Dutch Abraham Kuyper and Herman Bavinck. Another formative Reformed school of thought, on the American side of the Atlantic Ocean and more conservative, was carried on by the Princeton orthodoxy. In association with other conservatives, such as the Baptist A. H. Strong, Princeton theologians attempted a major rebuttal to what they saw as the dangers of liberalism. Whereas liberalism has replaced God as the center of theological task for human subject, this new orthodoxy harkened back to reaffirming the radical distinction between the Spirit of God and the human spirit.

At the turn of the last century of the second millennium a number of these developments came to compete with each other alongside new developments. One major development that emerged and helped shape pneumatology and Christian spirituality in a dramatic way was the rise of pentecostal/charismatic movements. At the danger of oversimplifying an extremely complex and complicated set of developments, the following overview of twentieth-century pneumatologies describes three major streams within European and North American contexts. After discussing these three pneumatological streams, we will look at the rapidly spreading cultural diversification of testimonies and interpretations coming from the Global South, that is, Africa, Asia, and Latin America.

Three Pneumatological Streams: Eastern, Western, and Pentecostal/Charismatic

One way to begin to frame developments and orientations in contemporary pneumatology is to highlight three distinctive ways of approaching the Spirit: that of the Christian East (Orthodox churches), the Christian West (Roman Catholic and Protestant churches), and the new pentecostal/charismatic movements.

In a general sense, it can be said that whereas Orthodox theology has more consciously built on pneumatological foundations, Western theology has emphasized Christology. In the most distinctive doctrine of the Christian East—namely, understanding salvation as "deification"—the role of the Holy Spirit comes to the fore. Union with God is the goal of the Christian life; in this view *theosis*, divinization, is attributed to the Spirit and Christ. Orthodox theologians of the past generation, such as Vladimir Lossky, deepened the church's understanding of mystical theology and a pneumatological understanding of revelation and salvation.

In the twentieth-century pneumatologies of the Christian West, the decisive turn for the Roman Catholic camp came with the Second Vatican Council (1962–1965). The most significant document, *Lumen Gentium*, opens with a Trinitarian statement in which pneumatology has a secure place in ecclesiology. The document insists that the Holy Spirit sanctifies and leads the people of God not only through the sacraments and church ministries but also through special charisms bestowed freely on all the faithful in a variety of ways. A number of Roman Catholic theologians both prepared the agenda of the council and elaborated on the leads given by it. The seminal three-volume work by the French Dominican Yves Congar, *I Believe in the Holy Spirit*, has already reached the status of a pneumatological classic.

On the Protestant side, the previous century has led to such a proliferation of views that—unlike among Orthodox and Roman Catholic theologians—the denominational boundaries mean much less. By any account, the most well-known and widely debated contemporary pneumatology comes from the German Reformed theologian Jürgen Moltmann. His *Spirit of Life: A Universal Affirmation* relates the discussion to pressing contemporary themes such as the environment, justice, and equality. Moltmann is in search of a "holistic," "all-encompassing," or "comprehensive" approach to the Spirit, a pneumatology that does not exclude any area of life. The leading theme is the role of the Spirit of God in giving birth and sustaining life. In his *God the Spirit*,[14] Michael Welker, another Reformed German theologian, presents a unique approach to the doctrine of the Spirit. On the basis of biblical materials Welker critiques "metaphysical," "speculative," or "abstract" pneumatologies in favor of a "concrete" and "realistic" view. God's Spirit makes it possible to know the creative power of God, which brings the diversity of all that is creaturely into rich, fruitful, life-sustaining relations.

The pneumatology of the Lutheran Wolfhart Pannenberg derives its main agenda from his overall theological orientation, namely, the idea of theology as a public discipline rather than an exercise in individual piety. His doctrine of the Spirit is integrated with his ambitious theological program, which seeks to integrate science, philosophy, the public sphere, and theology. Pneumatology is interwoven with every major locus of Pannenberg's systematics, especially with God, creation, human beings, Christology, the church, and eschatology. Taking his cue from the biblical teaching depicting the Spirit as the life-giving principle to which all creatures owe life, movement, and activity, Pannenberg asks how this biblical view of life can be reconciled with modern biology.

The third stream is formed by pentecostal/charismatic movements, the rapidly growing segment of Christianity that has already outnumbered Protestantism. Drawing from Methodist/holiness movements, the Protestant Reformation, mystical/charismatic movements in the Catholic Church, as well as "Black" or African American spirituality, Pentecostalism has offered a grassroots challenge to established churches and theologies by highlighting the importance of charismatic spirituality. Often ridiculed for emotionalism, Pentecostals introduced a dynamic, enthusiastic type of spirituality and worship life to the contemporary church, emphasizing the possibility of experiencing God mystically. Gifts of the Spirit, from speaking in tongues to prophesying and prayer for healing, were enthusiastically embraced. What is especially significant about pentecostal and charismatic movements is their international and intercultural presence. For the most part, Pentecostals have not produced much theological literature until very recently. In contrast, the charismatic theologians within traditional churches, particularly the Roman Catholic charismatics, have engaged the theological task from the beginning. An example of a Protestant theologian with strong charismatic leanings is the Canadian Baptist Clark Pinnock, whose *Flame of Love: A Theology of the Holy Spirit*[15]

---

14. Michael Welker, *God the Spirit* (Minneapolis: Fortress Press, 1994).

15. Clark Pinnock, *Flame of Love: A Theology of the Holy Spirit* (Downers Grove, IL: InterVarsity Press, 1996).

endeavors to construct a full-scale systematic theology from a pneumato
logical perspective. The result is an exciting mixture of theology, spirituality, and insights about the Spirit.

Challenges to Mainstream Pneumatologies

Several feminist theologians have challenged traditional ways of interpreting pneumatology.[16] These theologians focus on the feminine or maternal
characteristics of the Holy Spirit to counterbalance masculine pronouns
for Father and Son. Applying feminine images to the Spirit is biblically
legitimate since in the Bible the role of the Spirit involves activities more
usually associated with maternity and femininity in general: inspiring,
helping, supporting, enveloping, bringing to birth. Of all the Trinitarian
persons, the Holy Spirit is more often related to intimacy. Several feminists, such as Sallie McFague and Elizabeth Johnson, have suggested a
metaphorical understanding of God-language to combat the literalism
(and thus patriarchalism) of traditional theology.

Several contemporary theologians have reflected on the relationship between the environment and the Spirit in response to charges that
Christianity is to be blamed for the impending ecocrisis. Mark I. Wallace's
Fragments of the Spirit: Nature, Violence, and the Renewal of Creation[17]
argues that there is a profound change in the spiritual sensibilities of our
culture: many people sense that we live in the "age of the Spirit." Wallace,
the feminist Elizabeth Johnson, and others claim that a reverence for the
Spirit in all life forms is the most promising response to the threat of global
ecological collapse.

Other alternative and complementary approaches to pneumatology can
be found in contemporary theology, such as the politically oriented *God's
Spirit: Transforming a World in Crisis* by Geiko Müller-Fahrenholz[18] and
Work in the Spirit by Miroslav Volf,[19] which relate pneumatological discussion to political realities and to work. A distinctive feature of Volf's volume
is that it also interacts with Marxist understanding of work and society.

Pneumatological Insights from the Global South

Theology always takes root in and is shaped by its particular context.
Therefore, each cultural and religious setting tends to promote distinctive
ideas of God and the Spirit. This is no less true of Western traditions than
of traditions from Africa, Asia, and Latin America.

---

16. For a brief consideration, see Kärkkäinen, *Pneumatology*, 164–69.

17. Mark I. Wallace, *Fragments of the Spirit: Nature, Violence, and the Renewal of Creation* (New York: Continuum, 1996).

18. Geiko Müller-Fahrenholz, *God's Spirit: Transforming a World in Crisis*, trans. John Cumming (New York: Continuum, 1995).

19. Miroslav Volf, *Work in the Spirit: Toward a Theology of Work* (Eugene, OR: Wipf & Stock, 2001).

In the African worldview,[20] spiritual and physical beings are seen as real entities that interact with one another in time and space. Therefore, African Christians reject both the secularist worldview as well as missionaries' "Western" conceptions of reality and spirit. In many African cultures, the spirits live in close relation to God. Among the spirits, the ancestors, who live closer to the living community, are a central feature of all African religiosity. At the same time, the African worldview is also thoroughly religious; there is a genuine "this-worldly" orientation to much of African Christianity, with the expectation that the Spirit of God intervenes, whether regarding spiritual, physical, psychological, communal, or environmental needs.

A this-worldly orientation is perhaps one reason that pentecostal/charismatic movements are becoming the main face of African Christianity. Even those churches that do not identify themselves formally with pentecostal/charismatic movements often reflect the kind of spirituality that has been associated with those movements. African Pentecostalism is in constant interaction with the African spirit world in much the same way that Latin American Pentecostalism conceptually encounters folk Catholicism and Brazilian spiritism and Korean Pentecostals have made use of shamanistic traditions in the culture.

It is often said that whereas African theology begins with a shout of joy, in Latin America theological reflection starts from a cry of despair. The theme of liberation is the driving force in much of Latin American liberation theology, including the immigrant theologies written by Hispanic theologians in the United States. The Belgian-born Brazilian priest and theologian José Comblin's *The Holy Spirit and Liberation*[21] is a landmark work in this genre. Furthermore, like those in most societies of Africa and Asia, Latin American people value community and communalism. It is impossible even to begin to understand pneumatological contributions from Latin America without taking into consideration several other formative influences, such as the importance of folk religions and their influence on Catholic piety and the rapidly growing pentecostal/charismatic movements and their spiritualities in both Roman Catholic and Protestant communities.

Similarly to that of Africa—but manifesting itself in a unique way—the Asian worldview is highly spiritualistic and hungry for spiritual experiences. Multireligiosity, religious pluralism, and poverty form the biggest challenges and opportunities for the majority of Asians. Appropriate to this background, the pneumatological contributions from Asian Christians often reflect themes of religious diversity and the struggle for justice

---

20. See further, A. H. Anderson, *Moya: The Holy Spirit from an African Perspective* (Pretoria: University of South Africa Press, 1994).

21. José Comblin, *The Holy Spirit and Liberation* (Maryknoll, NY: Orbis Books, 1989).

and peace. A significant number of Asian Christian pneumatologies come from the hands of theologians who reside in the United States, such as the Indian-born Roman Catholic Raimundo Panikkar, the Korean-born Methodist Jung Young Lee, and the Japanese-born Presbyterian Kosuke Koyama.

Last Words: Comparison between Traditional and Contemporary Pneumatologies

This last section reflects on what is new and what kinds of themes are emerging in the beginning of the third millennium vis-à-vis the past. Jürgen Moltmann puts many of the contemporary developments in perspective in a helpful way:

> In both Protestant and Catholic theology and devotion, there is a tendency to view the Holy Spirit solely as the Spirit of redemption. Its place is in the church, and it gives men and women the assurance of the eternal blessedness of their souls. This redemptive Spirit is cut off both from bodily life and from the life of nature. It makes people turn away from "this world" and hope for a better world beyond. They then seek and experience in the Spirit of Christ a power that is different from the divine energy of life, which according to the Old Testament ideas interpenetrates all the living. The theological textbooks therefore talk about the Holy Spirit in connection with God, faith, the Christian life, the church and prayer, but seldom in connection with the body and nature.[22]

In the past the doctrine of the Spirit was mainly—though of course not exclusively—connected with topics such as the doctrines of salvation, the inspiration of Scripture, issues of ecclesiology, as well as individual piety. With regard to the doctrine of salvation, the Spirit represented the "subjective" side whereas Christology formed the objective basis. The Spirit was regarded as the agent of the benefits of salvation achieved at the cross of Christ. With regard to Scripture, the Spirit played a crucial role in both inspiration and illumination of the Word of God. In various Christian traditions, from mysticism to pietism to classical liberalism and beyond, the Spirit's work was seen mainly in relation to animating and refreshing one's inner spiritual life. While ecclesiology was often built—especially in the Christian West—on christological foundations, the Spirit was invoked to animate and energize already existing structures. At times the Spirit was connected with various ministries in the church, as well as with its prayer life and with sacraments—a connection made as a rule in the Christian East. After all, in the ancient creeds, the Spirit is part of the third article, that of the church and the end times.

In other words, the role of the Spirit in traditional theology was quite reserved and limited. It is this reductionism that has elicited a number of

---

22. Moltmann, *Spirit of Life*, 8.

new proposals. While not leaving behind these emphases, today the Spirit is also connected with other theological topics, such as creation, God, Christology, and eschatology. There is an attempt to give the Spirit a more integral and central role. Political, social, environmental, liberationist, and other "public" issues are being invoked by the theologians of the Spirit in the beginning of the third millennium. The Old Testament idea of the Spirit of God as the Spirit of Life has gained a new significance. Furthermore, contemporary theology includes a stress on spirituality. In contrast to traditional pneumatologies, often perceived as dry and abstract, there is a new appreciation of the experience and spirituality of the Spirit.

Finally, contemporary pneumatology also expresses a desire to connect the Spirit with ethics and life, which is, after all, a thoroughly biblical idea. Contemporary theology both acknowledges and desires to relate pneumatology to particular contexts, for example, allowing women to express their experience of the Spirit in a unique way. Contemporary pneumatology gives voices to the poor and oppressed and to testimonies from Africa, Asia, and Latin America in a way never before done in the history of reflection on the Spirit. Last, but not least, contemporary theologies show an enthusiastic desire to connect the Spirit of God with the spirits of religions, in other words, to do theology of religions from a pneumatological perspective.

Abbreviations

The following abbreviations are used for texts frequently cited.

ANF   *The Ante-Nicene Fathers: Translations of the Writings of the Fathers down to A.D. 325.* 9 vols. Ed. Alexander Roberts, James Donaldson, et al. Edinburgh, 1885–1897, http://www.ccel.org.

BC   *Book of Concord: The Confessions of the Evangelical Lutheran Church.* Trans. and ed. Theodore G. Tappert with Jaroslav Pelikan, Robert W. Fischer, and Arthur C. Piepkorn. Philadelphia: Fortress Press, 1959.

Inst.   John Calvin, *Institutes of the Christian Religion.* Trans. Henry Beveridge. London, 1599, http://www.ccel.org.

LW   *Luther's Works.* American ed. (Libronix Digital LIbrary), 55 vols. Ed. Jaroslav Pelikan and Helmut T. Lehman. Minneapolis: Fortress Press, 2002.

NPNF[1]   *A Select Library of the Nicene and Post-Nicene Fathers of the Christian Church.* First Series. 14 vols. Ed. Philip Schaff. Edinburgh, 1886–1889, http://www.ccel.org.

NPNF[2]   *A Select Library of the Nicene and Post-Nicene Fathers of the Christian Church.* Second Series. 14 vols. Ed. Philip Schaff and Henry Wace. Edinburgh, 1890–1900, http://www.ccel.org.

ST   St. Thomas Aquinas, *Summa Theologica.* Trans. Fathers of the English Dominican Province. Benziger Bros. ed., 1947, http://www.ccel.org.

TDNT   *Theological Dictionary of the New Testament.* 10 vols. Ed. G. Kittel and G. Friedrich. Trans. G. W. Bromiley. Grand Rapids, 1964–1976.

PART I

History of Pneumatological Traditions

CHAPTER 1

The Earliest Pneumatologies

Introduction: The Developing Theology of the Spirit before Nicea

"Long before the Spirit was a theme of doctrine, He was a fact in the experience of the community." This remark by the New Testament theologian Eduard Schweizer, a noted pneumatologist, is a key to retrieving the way Christian theology came slowly into a fuller understanding of the Holy Spirit alongside the Father and Son.[1] For the Apostolic Fathers and the Apologists as well as other theologians prior to the Council of Nicea (325), such as Tertullian, Irenaeus, and Origen, christological and Trinitarian debates stood at the forefront of reflection and discussion. The question of the divinity of the Holy Spirit and the corollary issue of how the Spirit relates to Father and Son emerged only later. Similarly to those concerning Christology, the doctrinal fights were less about theoretical problems—even though the conversations were often carried on at a quite sophisticated level—and more about liturgy, sacramentology, and salvation. The fact that the Spirit was being mentioned alongside the Father and Son in doxologies and prayers of the church as well as in baptismal liturgies and that it took the divine Spirit to help humanity be connected with the benefits of Christ's salvific work were the main reasons behind the development of pneumatological doctrine. This is but the application of the ancient rule *lex orandi lex credendi* (the law of prayer [is or becomes] the law of believing).

The New Testament theologian James D. G. Dunn has argued that, from the beginning, two ecclesiological "streams" have flowed alongside each other: one was charismatic and enthusiastic; the other, more conventional and traditional. The former might have been the "mainstream" during the first postbiblical century and exercised considerable influence beyond that time.[2] The Roman Catholic Yves Congar has argued that indeed in the

---

1. Eduard Schweizer, "πνεῦμα," *TDNT* 6:396.
2. See, e.g., James D. G. Dunn, *Unity and Diversity in the New Testament: An Inquiry into the Character of Earliest Christianity* (London: SCM Press/Philadelphia: Trinity Press International, 1991), chap. 9.

beginning the church saw itself subject to the activity of the Spirit and filled with the Spirit's gifts. Towards the end of the first century, Clement of Rome was also obliged to give rules for the church at Corinth as to the right use of charisms, implying that spiritual gifts were active at that time. According to Congar, no opposition yet existed between "hierarchical" and "charismatic" ministries in the church. By definition, ministry as well as the whole church itself were considered charismatic. Furthermore, according to Congar, there was no opposition yet between the growth of tradition (doctrinal development) and charisms, such as visions and warnings from the Spirit.[3] Very soon, however, there arose what Schweizer calls "the official strand," an understanding and practice of the ministry in which the one who is rightly instituted into office is now guaranteed the Spirit of God, rather than the other way around (i.e., that the one whom God appoints by endowment with the Spirit is ordained to the ministry).[4]

The Apostolic Fathers

Confusion about the Nature and Role of the Spirit

The task of the Apostolic Fathers was more about a faithful transmission of tradition than a constructive reworking, as was the case with later patristic thinkers. Similarly to the New Testament, they do not go much beyond the economic language of faith. Illustrative of the lack of sophistication of terminology is the less-than-precise usage of the term *Spirit* when judged in light of later creedal and theological orthodoxy, as well as the occasional confusion between the Son (Word) and Spirit in general.[5] As long as the Spirit was not differentiated from the Son as a separate hypostatic entity, it was difficult to say if the Spirit was the power or influence of the Father (filling or empowering the Son) or something less than a person. Until the end of the third century or so, confusion remained about the mutual relationship and distinction between the Son and Spirit for the simple reason that the New Testament does not make it clear. In the earliest postbiblical writings, such as the second-century *2 Clement*, it is not uncommon to find a blurring of the distinction between Son and Spirit. Speaking of those who abuse the flesh, it says that "such a one then shall not partake

---

3. Yves Congar, *I Believe in the Holy Spirit* (New York: Herder & Herder, 1997), 65–68.

4. Schweizer, "πνεῦμα," *TDNT* 6:451. See also Bernd Jochen Hilberath, "Pneumatologie," in *Handbuch der Dogmatik*, ed. Theodor Schneir et al. (Dusseldorf: Patmos, 1992), 1:491–92.

5. I am reminded of the remark by Wolfhart Pannenberg: "The NT statements do not clarify the interrelations of the three but they clearly emphasize the fact that they are interrelated" (*Systematic Theology*, vol. 1, trans. Geoffrey W. Bromiley [Grand Rapids: Wm. B. Eerdmans Publishing Co., 1991], 269).

of the spirit, which is Christ."[6] Other such examples can be found in *The Shepherd of Hermas*. At times, it is not clear whether the writing considered the Son to be an angel or more ancient than the angels. Occasionally, there is the blurring of the distinction between Son and Spirit and in one instance even a conflation of the two with the saying that "the Spirit is the Son of God."[7]

Even in later second-century theologians such as Theophilus of Antioch and Irenaeus, the Trinitarian pattern is still in the making. Both of them define the triad in terms of God, Word, and Wisdom.[8] To make things more complicated, Theophilus equated the Spirit with the Word while Irenaeus did so with Wisdom, illustrating the profound difficulties related to the development of a defined pneumatological doctrine in early theology.[9]

Two *"Epistles of Clement"*

As with many earlier writings, there are many historical questions about these works, including the authorship of *The First Epistle to the Corinthians* attributed to Clement of Rome, claimed to be the third bishop of Rome (after the apostles), and the *Second Epistle of Clement*, also known as Pseudo-Clement, an anonymous homily. Written in the first half of the second century (at least the first letter), both letters have only few references to the Holy Spirit; the latter, indeed only one.

From Clement of Rome, *The First Epistle to the Corinthians* 45, ANF 1:17.[10]

Look carefully into the Scriptures, which are the true utterances of the Holy Spirit. Observe that nothing of an unjust or counterfeit character is written in them.

From Pseudo-Clement, *The Second Epistle of Clement* 14, ANF 7:521.

I do not, however, suppose ye are ignorant that the living Church is the body of Christ. . . . Now the Church, being spiritual, was manifested in the flesh of Christ, *thus* signifying to us that, if any of us

6. *The Second Epistle of Clement*, 14 (*ANF* 7:521). For such examples in Justin Martyr, see J. N. D. Kelly, *Early Christian Creeds*, 3rd ed. (London: Longman, 1972), 148.

7. *The Shepherd of Hermas*, similitude 9.1 (*ANF* 2:44).

8. Theophilus of Antioch, *Theophilus to Autolycus: Book II*, 15 (*ANF* 2:101); Irenaeus, *Against Heresies* 4.20.3 (*ANF* 1:488).

9. For the early history of the doctrine of the Spirit, see further, Veli-Matti Kärkkäinen, *Pneumatology: The Holy Spirit in Ecumenical, International, and Contextual Perspectives* (Grand Rapids: Baker Academic, 2002), esp. 37–46.

10. Citations from *ANF, NPNF,* and *Early Christian Fathers* are from Christian Classics Ethereal Library (public domain) unless otherwise indicated.

keep her in the flesh and do not corrupt her, he shall receive her again in the Holy Spirit: for this flesh is the copy of the spirit. Such life and incorruption this flesh can partake of, when the Holy Spirit is joined to it. No one can utter or speak "what the lord hath prepared" for his elect.

Ignatius of Antioch

Ignatius, the bishop of Antioch, appeals to the Holy Spirit for the unity of the church and for the right episcopal ministry.

From Ignatius of Antioch, *Letter to the Philadelphians* 7, ANF 1:83–84.

For though some would have deceived me according to the flesh, yet the Spirit, as being from God, is not deceived. For it knows both whence it comes and whither it goes, and detects the secrets [of the heart]. For, when I was among you, I cried, I spoke with a loud voice: Give heed to the bishop, and to the presbytery and deacons. . . . But the Spirit proclaimed these words: Do nothing without the bishop; keep your bodies as the temples of God; love unity; avoid divisions; be the followers of Jesus Christ, even as He is of His Father. . . . But the Spirit made an announcement to me, saying as follows: Do nothing without the bishop; keep your bodies as the temples of God; love unity; avoid divisions.

The Didache

Also known by the name *The Teaching of the Twelve Apostles*, written in the early second century, the *Didache* gives guidance about many kinds of issues such as morality, baptism, and the charismatic ministry of itinerant ministers alongside the local ones. The importance of the Trinitarian baptismal formula is stressed.

From *The Teaching of the Twelve Apostles, Commonly Called the Didache* 7.1–3, in *Early Christian Fathers*, ed. Cyril C. Richardson, 174, http://www.ccel.org (hereafter *ECF*).

Now about baptism: this is how to baptize. Give public instruction on all these points, and then "baptize" in running water, "in the name of the Father and of the Son and of the Holy Spirit." [2]If you do not have running water, baptize in some other. [3]If you cannot in cold, then in warm. If you have neither, then pour water on the head three times "in the name of the Father, Son, and Holy Spirit."

While this Christian manual assumes the ministry of the charismatic and ecstatic ministers, it also gives specific instructions as to how to deal with them and how to assess their claims to the Spirit.

From *Didache* 11.7–12 (*ECF*, 176–77).

[7]While a prophet is making ecstatic utterances, you must not test or examine him. For "every sin will be forgiven," but this sin "will not be forgiven." [8]However, not everybody making ecstatic utterances is a prophet, but only if he behaves like the Lord. It is by their conduct that the false prophet and the [true] prophet can be distinguished. [9]For instance, if a prophet marks out a table in the Spirit, he must not eat from it. If he does, he is a false prophet. [10]Again, every prophet who teaches the truth but fails to practice what he preaches is a false prophet. [11]But every attested and genuine prophet who acts with a view to symbolizing the mystery of the Church, and does not teach you to do all he does, must not be judged by you. His judgment rests with God. For the ancient prophets too acted in this way. [12]But if someone says in the Spirit, "Give me money, or something else," you must not heed him. However, if he tells you to give for others in need, no one must condemn him.

The Shepherd of Hermas

This mid-second-century document, claimed to be oracles of "the Shepherd" to Hermas, narrates mystical and prophetic utterances, including transportations and visions in the Spirit, and thus opens a window into early Christian spirituality and experiences of the Spirit. One of the topics the writing deals with is the difference between an evil and a good spirit (the Holy Spirit) as well as the importance of not grieving the Holy Spirit. Grieving can be done, for example, with a negative attitude such as grief.

From *The Shepherd of Hermas* 2.10.1–2,[11] ANF 2:26–27.

10.1. . . . "You are senseless, O man. Do you not perceive that grief is more wicked than all the spirits, and most terrible to the servants of God, and more than all other spirits destroys man and crushes out the Holy Spirit, and yet, on the other hand, she saves him?". . .

   10.2. "Hear, then," says he, "foolish man, how grief crushes out the Holy Spirit, and on the other hand saves. When the doubting

---

11. In *ANF* 2 the writing is titled *The Pastor of Hermas*. I am using the more common title.

man attempts any deed, and fails in it on account of his doubt, this grief enters into the man, and grieves the Holy Spirit, and crushes him out. Then, on the other hand, when anger attaches itself to a man in regard to any matter, and he is embittered, then grief enters into the heart of the man who was irritated, and he is grieved at the deed which he did, and repents that he has wrought a wicked deed. This grief, then, appears to be accompanied by salvation, because the man, after having done a wicked deed, repented. Both actions grieve the Spirit: doubt, because it did not accomplish its object; and anger grieves the Spirit, because it did what was wicked. Both these are grievous to the Holy Spirit—doubt and anger. Wherefore remove grief from you, and crush not the Holy Spirit which dwells in you, lest he entreat God against you, and he withdraw from you. For the Spirit of God which has been granted to us to dwell in this body does not endure grief nor straitness. Wherefore put on cheerfulness, which always is agreeable and acceptable to God, and rejoice in it. For every cheerful man does what is good, and minds what is good, and despises grief; but the sorrowful man always acts wickedly. First, he acts wickedly because he grieves the Holy Spirit, which was given to man a cheerful Spirit. Secondly, grieving the Holy Spirit, he works iniquity, neither entreating the Lord nor confessing to Him.

The document urges Christians to test the Spirit and prophets by their works.

From *The Shepherd of Hermas* 2.11, ANF 2:27–28.

Try the man who has the Divine Spirit by his life. First, he who has the Divine Spirit proceeding from above is meek, and peaceable, and humble, and refrains from all iniquity and the vain desire of this world, and contents himself with fewer wants than those of other men, and when asked he makes no reply; nor does he speak privately, nor when man wishes the spirit to speak does the Holy Spirit speak, but it speaks only when God wishes it to speak. When, then, a man having the Divine Spirit comes into an assembly of righteous men who have faith in the Divine Spirit, and this assembly of men offers up prayer to God, then the angel of the prophetic Spirit, who is destined for him, fills the man; and the man being filled with the Holy Spirit, speaks to the multitude as the Lord wishes. Thus, then, will the Spirit of Divinity become manifest. Whatever power therefore comes from the Spirit of Divinity belongs to the Lord. Hear, then," says he, "in regard to the spirit which is earthly, and empty, and powerless, and foolish. First, the man who seems to have the

Spirit exalts himself, and wishes to have the first seat, and is bold, and impudent, and talkative, and lives in the midst of many luxuries and many other delusions, and takes rewards for his prophecy; and if he does not receive rewards, he does not prophesy. Can, then, the Divine Spirit take rewards and prophesy? It is not possible that the prophet of God should do this, but prophets of this character are possessed by an earthly spirit."

The Apologists

The second-century Apologists made a conscious effort to make Christian faith understandable especially to the learned audience of the empire. Because of their focus on Christology, especially *Logos* Christology, pneumatology does not play a crucial role, and they are less attuned with the mystical, enthusiastic spirituality of the Apostolic Fathers. The place where the Spirit comes to the fore in Justin Martyr, the most important of the Apologists, relates to the Trinity. One of the pneumatological themes that occurs frequently in Justin's *Apologies* is the role of the Spirit in prophecy and Scriptures; hence the frequent designation "Spirit of prophecy."

From Justin Martyr, *First Apology* 33, *ANF* 1:174.

It is wrong, therefore, to understand the Spirit and the power of God as anything else than the Word, who is also the first-born of God, as the foresaid prophet Moses declared; and it was this which, when it came upon the virgin and overshadowed her, caused her to conceive, not by intercourse, but by power. And the name Jesus in the Hebrew language means Σωτήρ (Saviour) in the Greek tongue. Wherefore, too, the angel said to the virgin, "Thou shalt call His name Jesus, for He shall save His people from their sins." And that the prophets are inspired by no other than the Divine Word, even you, as I fancy, will grant.

Another Apologist, Tatian, highlighted the anthropological implications of pneumatology. In his remarkable apologetic statement in *Address to the Greeks*, chapter 13, "The Theory of the Soul's Immortality," and subsequent paragraphs, he contends that only in union with the Divine Spirit can a mortal human person share in immortality of God.

From Tatian, *Address to the Greeks* 13, ANF 2:70–71.

The soul is not in itself immortal, O Greeks, but mortal. Yet it is possible for it not to die. If, indeed, it knows not the truth, it dies, and is dissolved with the body, but rises again at last at the end of the world with the body, receiving death by punishment in immortality. But, again, if it acquires the knowledge of God, it dies not, although for a time it be dissolved. In itself it is darkness, and there is nothing luminous in it. And this is the meaning of the saying, "The darkness comprehendeth not the light." For the soul does not preserve the spirit, but is preserved by it, and the light comprehends the darkness. The Logos, in truth, is the light of God, but the ignorant soul is darkness. On this account, if it continues solitary, it tends downward towards matter, and dies with the flesh; but, if it enters into union with the Divine Spirit, it is no longer helpless, but ascends to the regions whither the Spirit guides it: for the dwelling-place of the spirit is above, but the origin of the soul is from beneath. Now, in the beginning the spirit was a constant companion of the soul, but the spirit forsook it because it was not willing to follow. Yet, retaining as it were a spark of its power, though unable by reason of the separation to discern the perfect, while seeking for God it fashioned to itself in its wandering many gods, following the sophistries of the demons. But the Spirit of God is not with all, but, taking up its abode with those who live justly, and intimately combining with the soul, by prophecies it announced hidden things to other souls. And the souls that are obedient to wisdom have attracted to themselves the cognate spirit; but the disobedient, rejecting the minister of the suffering God, have shown themselves to be fighters against God, rather than His worshippers.

Pneumatologies of the Third-Century Fathers

Several important Fathers at the end of the second and during the third century made contributions to the developing doctrine and spirituality of the Holy Spirit. Among those selected for this presentation are Irenaeus, Tertullian, Clement of Alexandria, Origen, Novatian, Hippolytus, and Cyprian.

Irenaeus

Irenaeus, the bishop of Lyons in Gaul, disciple of Polycarp of Smyrna, and follower of the apostle John, is the most significant theologian of the latter part of the second century. One of the most famous statements of Irenaeus concerns God's creation of the world and humanity using his "two hands," the Son and Spirit.

The Spirit and the Son in Creation and Salvation

From Irenaeus, *Against Heresies* 4.20.1, 3, *ANF* 1:487–88.

4.20.1. For with Him were always present the Word and Wisdom, the Son and the Spirit, by whom and in whom, freely and spontaneously, He made all things, to whom also He speaks, saying, "Let Us make man after Our image and likeness"; He taking from Himself the substance of the creatures [formed], and the pattern of things made, and the type of all the adornments in the world. . . .

4.20.3. I have also largely demonstrated, that the Word, namely the Son, was always with the Father; and that Wisdom also, which is the Spirit, was present with Him, anterior to all creation.

The same triune God who has created everything also sent the Son into the world so that the humanity may be united through the Spirit with divinity. This is one of the seminal formulations of *theosis*, deification.

From Irenaeus, *Against Heresies* 4.20.5–6, *ANF* 1:488–89.

4.20.5. Now this is His Word, our Lord Jesus Christ, who in the last times was made a man among men, that He might join the end to the beginning, that is, man to God. Wherefore the prophets, receiving the prophetic gift from the same Word, announced His advent according to the flesh, by which the blending and communion of God and man took place . . . causing us to serve Him in holiness and righteousness all our days, in order that man, having embraced the Spirit of God, might pass into the glory of the Father . . .

4.20.6. Men therefore shall see God, that they may live, being made immortal by that sight, and attaining even unto God . . . that God should be seen by men who bear His Spirit [in them], and do always wait patiently for His coming.

Whereas in later theology, especially in the Christian West, soteriology came to be linked predominantly with Christology, in Irenaeus there is a healthy balance between a christological and pneumatological understanding of salvation.

From Irenaeus, *Against Heresies* 5.1.1, *ANF* 1:527.

Since the Lord thus has redeemed us through His own blood, giving His soul for our souls, and His flesh for our flesh, and has also poured out the Spirit of the Father for the union and communion of God and man, imparting indeed God to men by means of the Spirit, and, on the other hand, attaching man to God by His own incarnation, and bestowing upon us at His coming immortality durably and truly, by means of communion with God,—all the doctrines of the heretics fall to ruin.

The Spirit and the Church

Irenaeus makes a significant contribution to a developing doctrine of the church by making the presence of the Spirit the hallmark of its being.

From Irenaeus, *Against Heresies* 4.24.1, *ANF* 1:458.

Our faith; which, having been received from the Church, we do preserve, and which always, by the Spirit of God, renewing its youth, as if it were some precious deposit in an excellent vessel, causes the vessel itself containing it to renew its youth also. For this gift of God has been entrusted to the Church, as breath was to the first created man, for this purpose, that all the members receiving it may be vivified; and the [means of] communion with Christ has been distributed throughout it, that is, the Holy Spirit, the earnest of incorruption, the means of confirming our faith, and the ladder of ascent to God. . . . For where the Church is, there is the Spirit of God; and where the Spirit of God is, there is the Church, and every kind of grace; but the Spirit is truth. Those, therefore, who do not partake of Him, are neither nourished into life from the mother's breasts, nor do they enjoy that most limpid fountain which issues from the body of Christ; but they dig for themselves broken cisterns out of earthly trenches, and drink putrid water out of the mire, fleeing from the faith of the Church lest they be convicted; and rejecting the Spirit, that they may not be instructed.

During Irenaeus's time the signs and works of the Spirit seem to be quite common in the church.

From Irenaeus, *Against Heresies* 5.6.1, *ANF* 1:531.

In like manner we do also hear many brethren in the Church, who possess prophetic gifts, and who through the Spirit speak all kinds of languages, and bring to light for the general benefit the hidden things of men, and declare the mysteries of God, whom also the apostle terms "spiritual," they being spiritual because they partake of the Spirit . . . and because they have become purely spiritual.

Hippolytus

It is fitting to introduce the pneumatology of Hippolytus following that of his teacher Irenaeus. This presbyter of Rome, however, is much less known than his esteemed mentor or some other early third-century theologians to be presented here, such as Tertullian and Origen. Hippolytus wrote in Greek; Latin soon became the language of the Christian West. According to Hippolytus, the Holy Spirit is being transmitted in the church from generation to generation to help the church carry on with apostolic tradition and combat all heretical views.

From Hippolytus, *Refutation of All Heresies* 1, preface, *ANF* 5:10.

But none will refute these, save the Holy Spirit bequeathed unto the Church, which the Apostles, having in the first instance received, have transmitted to those who have rightly believed. But we, as being their successors, and as participators in this grace, high-priesthood, and office of teaching, as well as being reputed guardians of the Church, must not be found deficient in vigilance, or disposed to suppress correct doctrine. Not even, however, labouring with every energy of body and soul, do we tire in our attempt adequately to render our Divine Benefactor a fitting return; and yet withal we do not so requite Him in a becoming manner, except we are not remiss in discharging the trust committed to us, but careful to complete the measure of our particular opportunity, and to impart to all without grudging whatever the Holy Ghost supplies, not only bringing to light, by means of our refutation, matters foreign (to our subject), but also whatsoever things the truth has received by the grace of the Father, and ministered to men. These also, illustrating by argument and creating testimony by letters, we shall unabashed proclaim.

Against the Errors of the Enthusiastic Montanist Movement
Conservative in his theology, Hippolytus highly appreciated tradition and vehemently opposed all heresies, including the enthusiastic Montanist movement with its claim to prophecy and spiritual tradition apart from the episcopal office and church structures. The following quotations come from Hippolytus's *Refutation of All Heresies*, which also attacks Gnosticism and Monarchianism (a Trinitarian heresy that considered "Father," "Son," and "Spirit" to be names or modes of an undifferentiated deity).

> From Hippolytus, *Refutation of All Heresies* 8.12, ANF 5:123–24.
> Chapter XII.—The Montanists; Priscilla and Maximilla Their Prophetesses . . .

But there are others who themselves are even more heretical in nature (than the foregoing). . . . These have been rendered victims of error from being previously captivated by (two) wretched women, called a certain Priscilla and Maximilla, whom they supposed (to be) prophetesses. And they assert that into these the Paraclete Spirit had departed; and antecedently to them, they in like manner consider Montanus as a prophet. And being in possession of an infinite number of their books, (the Phrygians) are overrun with delusion; and they do not judge whatever statements are made by them, according to (the criterion of) reason; nor do they give heed unto those who are competent to decide; but they are heedlessly swept onwards, by the reliance which they place on these (impostors). And they allege that they have learned something more through these, than from law, and prophets, and the Gospels. But they magnify these wretched women above the Apostles and every gift of Grace, so that some of them presume to assert that there is in them a something superior to Christ. These acknowledge God to be the Father of the universe, and Creator of all things, similarly with the Church, and (receive) as many things as the Gospel testifies concerning Christ. They introduce, however, the novelties of fasts, and feasts, and meals of parched food, and repasts of radishes, alleging that they have been instructed by women. And some of these assent to the heresy of the Noetians, and affirm that the Father himself is the Son, and that this (one) came under generation, and suffering, and death. Concerning these I shall again offer an explanation, after a more minute manner; for the heresy of these has been an occasion of evils to many. We therefore are of opinion, that the statements made concerning these (heretics) are sufficient, when we shall have briefly proved to all that the majority of their books are silly, and their attempts (at reasoning) weak, and worthy of no consideration. But it is not necessary for those who possess a sound mind to pay attention (either to their volumes or their arguments).

The Holy Spirit in Ordination and the Charisms of the Church

In his *The Apostolic Tradition*, as early as the preface, Hippolytus refers to "On Charismatic Gifts," a work lost to us; scholars wonder whether that work was originally part of a larger work, perhaps a two-volume work including *The Apostolic Tradition*. Be that as it may, the work that has been retained contains much about the Spirit and the Spirit's gifts, relatively speaking.

> From Hippolytus, *The Apostolic Tradition* 1.1, in *The Apostolic Tradition of Hippolytus*, ed. and trans. Burton Scott Easton (Cambridge: Cambridge University Press, 1934), 33 (hereafter Easton).

We have duly completed what needed to be said about "Gifts," describing those gifts which God by His own counsel has bestowed on men, in offering to Himself His image which had gone astray. But now, moved by His love to all His saints, we pass on to our most important theme, "The Tradition," our teacher. And we address the churches, so that they who have been well trained, may, by our instruction, hold fast that tradition which has continued up to now and, knowing it well, may be strengthened. This is needful, because of that lapse or error which recently occurred through ignorance, and because of ignorant men. And [the] Holy Spirit will supply perfect grace to those who believe aright, that they may know how all things should be transmitted and kept by them who rule the church.

Highly interesting and significant is the account of the ordination of the bishop, an event that seems to be highly pneumatological from the election to the consecration and gifting, as the next excerpt shows.

> From Hippolytus, *The Apostolic Tradition* 2, 3, 4, and 6 (Easton, 33–37).

2. Let the bishop be ordained after he has been chosen by all the people.... The bishops shall lay their hands upon him.... Then one of the bishops who are present shall, at the request of all, lay his hand on him who is ordained bishop, and shall pray as follows, saying:

3. God and Father of our Lord Jesus Christ, Father of mercies and God of all comfort, ... Pour forth now that power, which is thine, of thy royal Spirit, which thou gavest to thy beloved Servant Jesus Christ, which he bestowed on his holy apostles, who established the church in every place, the church which thou hast sanctified unto unceasing glory and praise of thy name. Thou who knowest the hearts of all, grant to this thy servant, whom thou hast chosen to be bishop, [to feed thy holy flock] and to serve as thy high priest

without blame, ministering night and day, to propitiate thy countenance without ceasing and to offer thee the gifts of thy holy church. And by the Spirit of high-priesthood to have authority to remit sins according to thy commandment, to assign the lots according to thy precept, to loose every bond according to the authority which thou gavest to thy apostles, and to please thee in meekness and purity of heart, offering to thee an odour of sweet savour. Through thy Servant Jesus Christ our Lord, through whom be to thee glory, might, honour, with [the] Holy Spirit in [the] holy church, both now and always and world without end. Amen.

4. And when he is made bishop, all shall offer him the kiss of peace, for he has been made worthy. . . . And then he shall proceed immediately: We give thee thanks, O God, through thy beloved Servant Jesus Christ . . . whom thou didst send from heaven into the womb of the Virgin, and who, dwelling within her, was made flesh, and was manifested as thy Son, being born of [the] Holy Spirit and the Virgin. Who, fulfilling thy will, and winning for himself a holy people, spread out his hands when he came to suffer, that by his death he might set free them who believed on thee. . . . And we pray thee that thou wouldest send thy Holy Spirit upon the offerings of thy holy church; that thou, gathering them into one, wouldest grant to all thy saints who partake to be filled with [the] Holy Spirit, that their faith may be confirmed in truth, that we may praise and glorify thee. Through thy Servant Jesus Christ, through whom be to thee glory and honour, with [the] Holy Spirit in the holy church, both now and always and world without end. Amen. . . .

6. . . . Glory be to thee, with [the] Holy Spirit in the holy church, both now and always and world without end. [Amen.]

Pneumatic gifts seems to include healing—even though one should not lay hands on another before there is evidence of the working of the gift in the person's life—as well as teaching.

From Hippolytus, *The Apostolic Tradition* 15; 35.3 (Easton, 41, 54).

15. If anyone says, "I have received the gift of healing," hands shall not be laid upon him: the deed shall make manifest if he speaks the truth." . . .

35.3. If a [specially gifted] teacher should come, let none of you delay to attend the place where the instruction is given, for grace will be given to the speaker to utter things profitable to all, and thou wilt hear new things, and thou wilt be profited by what the Holy Spirit will give thee through the instructor; so thy faith will be strengthened by what thou hearest, and in that place thou wilt learn thy duties at home; therefore let everyone be zealous to go to the church, the place where the Holy Spirit abounds.

Novatian

Martyred as sectarian and founder of Novatianism, a separatist holiness movement, the priest Novatian was for a time a self-appointed antipope. Novatian is also the first Latin writer of the Roman Church. While still a member of the church, he penned the important *Treatise Concerning the Trinity*. While the doctrine of the Spirit is still evolving, as the first shorter quotation illustrates, this document gives us a glimpse of the early developments in early Trinitarian theology and pneumatology.

From Novatian, *Treatise Concerning the Trinity* 16, ANF 5:625–26.

The Paraclete has received from Christ what He may declare. But if He has received from Christ what He may declare to us, Christ is greater than the Paraclete, because the Paraclete would not receive from Christ unless He were less than Christ. But the Paraclete being less than Christ, moreover, by this very fact proves Christ to be God, from whom He has received what He declares: so that the testimony of Christ's divinity is immense, in the Paraclete being found to be *in this economy* less than Christ, and taking from Him what He gives to others; seeing that if Christ were only man, Christ would receive from the Paraclete what He should say, not the Paraclete receive from Christ what He should declare.

Most of the treatise is devoted to the affirmation of the deity of the Father and Son; only towards the end of the writing are there statements about the third member of the Trinity, Spirit's ministry of the Spirit in salvation, the Christian life, and the church.

From Novatian, *Treatise Concerning the Trinity* 39, ANF 5:640–41.

Chapter XXIX. *Argument.*—He Next Teaches Us that the Authority of the Faith Enjoins, After the Father and the Son, to Believe Also on the Holy Spirit, Whose Operations He Enumerates from Scripture.

Moreover, the order of reason, and the authority of the faith in the disposition of the words and in the Scriptures of the Lord, admonish us after these things to believe also on the Holy Spirit, once promised to the Church, and in the appointed occasions of times given. For He was promised by Joel the prophet, but given by Christ. "In the last days," says the prophet, "I will pour out of my Spirit upon

my servants and my handmaids." And the Lord said, "Receive ye
the Holy Ghost: whose sins ye remit, they shall be remitted; and
whose ye retain, they shall be retained." But this Holy Spirit the Lord
Christ calls at one time "the Paraclete," at another pronounces to be
the "Spirit of truth." And He is not new in the Gospel, nor yet even
newly given; for it was He Himself who accused the people in the
prophets, and in the apostles gave them the appeal to the Gentiles.
For the former deserved to be accused, because they had contemned
the law; and they of the Gentiles who believe deserve to be aided by
the defence of the Spirit, because they earnestly desire to attain to the
Gospel law. Assuredly in the Spirit there are different kinds of offices,
because in the times there is a different order of occasions; and yet,
on this account, He who discharges these offices is not different, nor
is He another in so acting, but He is one and the same, distributing
His offices according to the times, and the occasions and impulses
of things. Moreover, the Apostle Paul says, "Having the same Spirit;
as it is written, I believed, and therefore have I spoken; we also
believe, and therefore speak." He is therefore one and the same Spirit
who was in the prophets and apostles, except that in the former He
was occasional, in the latter always. But in the former not as being
always in them, in the latter as abiding always in them; and in the
former distributed with reserve, in the latter all poured out; in the
former given sparingly, in the latter liberally bestowed; not yet manifested before the Lord's resurrection, but conferred after the resurrection. For, said He, "I will pray the Father, and He will give you
another Advocate, that He may be with you for ever, even the Spirit
of truth." And, "When He, the Advocate, shall come, whom I shall
send unto you from my Father, the Spirit of truth who proceedeth
from my Father." And, "If I go not away, that Advocate shall not
come to you; but if I go away, I will send Him to you." And, "When
the Spirit of truth shall come, He will direct you into all the truth."
And because the Lord was about to depart to the heavens, He gave
the Paraclete out of necessity to the disciples; so as not to leave
them in any degree orphans, which was little desirable, and for-
sake them without an advocate and some kind of protector. For this
is He who strengthened their hearts and minds, who marked out
the Gospel sacraments, who was in them the enlightener of divine
things; and they being strengthened, feared, for the sake of the Lord's
name, neither dungeons nor chains, nay, even trod under foot the
very powers of the world and its tortures, since they were henceforth
armed and strengthened by the same Spirit, having in themselves
the gifts which this same Spirit distributes, and appropriates to the
Church, the spouse of Christ, as her ornaments. This is He who
places prophets in the Church, instructs teachers, directs tongues,

gives powers and healings, does wonderful works, offers discrimination of spirits, affords powers of government, suggests counsels, and orders and arranges whatever other gifts there are of *charismata*; and thus make the Lord's Church everywhere, and in all, perfected and completed.

Tertullian

This North African theologian, allegedly a lawyer by training, is noted for many things, first and foremost for his contributions to the Trinity terminology and his association with the first "pentecostal" movement of postapostolic times, Montanism. While he later disassociated himself from Montanism, there is a debate among the scholars as to how much that enthusiastic movement's influence can be found in his writings. The Trinity is a treasured topic for Tertullian—the doctrine that distinguishes Christian faith from Judaism (*Against Praxeas* 31, *ANF* 3:627)—and occupies a major part of one of his greatest works, *Against Praxeas*. Praxeas was a heretic who was claimed to teach modalism, according to which the Father, Son, and Spirit only consist of names or "modes" rather than "persons"; *persona* was one of the terms Tertullian introduced into Trinitarian discourse. In order to make his Trinitarian teaching more easily understandable, Tertullian also employs familiar metaphors taken from nature.

The Spirit in the Trinity

From Tertullian, *Against Praxeas* 7–9, *ANF* 2:601–4.

7. Thus does He [Father] make Him [Son] equal to Him: for by proceeding from Himself He became His first-begotten Son, because begotten before all things. . . . *The Father* took pleasure evermore in Him, who equally rejoiced with a reciprocal gladness in the Father's presence. . . . The Son likewise acknowledges the Father, speaking in His own person, under the name of Wisdom: "The Lord formed Me as the beginning of His ways, with a view to His own works; before all the hills did He beget Me." For if indeed Wisdom in this passage seems to say that She was created by the Lord with a view to His works, and to accomplish His ways, yet proof is given in another Scripture that "all things were made by the Word, and without Him was there nothing made"; as, again, in another place (it is said), "By His word were the heavens established, and all the powers thereof by His Spirit"—that is to say, by the Spirit (or Divine Nature) which was in the Word . . .

8. . . . "For what man knoweth the things which be in God, but the Spirit which is in Him?" But the Word was formed by the Spirit, and

(if I may so express myself) the Spirit is the body of the Word. The Word, therefore, is both always in the Father. . . .

9. Bear always in mind that this is the rule of faith which I profess; by it I testify that the Father, and the Son, and the Spirit are inseparable from each other, and so will you know in what sense this is said. Now, observe, my assertion is that the Father is one, and the Son one, and the Spirit one, and that They are distinct from Each Other. . . . For the Father is the entire substance, but the Son is a derivation and portion of the whole, as He Himself acknowledges: "My Father is greater than I." In the Psalm His inferiority is described as being "a little lower than the angels." Thus the Father is distinct from the Son, being greater than the Son, inasmuch as He who begets is one, and He who is begotten is another; He, too, who sends is one, and He who is sent is another; and He, again, who makes is one, and He through whom the thing is made is another. Happily the Lord Himself employs this expression of the person of the Paraclete, so as to signify not a division or severance, but a disposition (of mutual relations in the Godhead); for He says, "I will pray the Father, and He shall send you another Comforter . . . even the Spirit of truth," thus making the Paraclete distinct from Himself, even as we say that the Son is also distinct from the Father; so that He showed a third degree in the Paraclete, as we believe the second degree is in the Son, by reason of the order observed in the *Economy*.

The Spirit in the Sacraments

In Tertullian's *Baptism*, the North African theologian developed a profound pneumatological sacramentology. He begins by linking the sacramental nature of baptism to primeval waters in creation, including the creation of the first human being.

From Tertullian, *Baptism* 3–4, ANF 3:670–72.

3. The first thing, O man, which you have to venerate, is the *age* of the waters in that their substance is ancient; the second, their *dignity*, in that they were the seat of the Divine Spirit, more pleasing *to Him*, no doubt, than all the other then existing elements. . . . Water was the first to produce that which had life, that it might be no wonder in baptism if waters know how to give life. For was not the work of fashioning man himself also achieved with the aid of waters? . . .

4. But it will suffice to have *thus* called at the outset those points in which withal is recognised that primary principle of baptism . . . that the Spirit of God, who hovered over (the waters) from the beginning, would continue to linger over the waters of the baptized. . . . All waters, therefore, in virtue of the pristine privilege of their

origin, do, after invocation of God, attain the sacramental power of sanctification; for the Spirit immediately supervenes from the heavens, and rests over the waters, sanctifying them from Himself; and being thus sanctified, they imbibe at the same time the power of sanctifying. . . . After the waters have been in a manner endued with medicinal virtue through the intervention of the angel, the spirit is corporeally washed in the waters, and the flesh is in the same spiritually cleansed. . . . Not that *in* the waters we obtain the Holy Spirit; but in the water . . . we are cleansed, and prepared *for* the Holy Spirit. In this case also a type has preceded; for thus was John beforehand the Lord's forerunner, "preparing His ways." Thus, too, does the angel, the witness of baptism, "make the paths straight" for the Holy Spirit, who is about to come upon us, by the washing away of sins, which faith, sealed in (the name of) the Father, and the Son, and the Holy Spirit, obtains. For if "in *the mouth of* three witnesses every word shall stand":—while, through the benediction, we have the same (three) as witnesses of our faith whom we have as sureties of our salvation too—how much more does the number of the divine names suffice for the assurance of our hope likewise! Moreover, after the pledging both of the attestation of faith and the promise of salvation under "three witnesses," there is added, of necessity, mention of the Church; inasmuch as, wherever there are three, (that is, the Father, the Son, and the Holy Spirit,) there is the Church, which is a body of three.

Based on biblical images of the deluge and the dove, Tertullian continues his explanation of the spiritual meaning of the rite of baptism as well as its pneumatological ramifications.

From Tertullian, *Baptism* 6–7, ANF 3:672–73.

6. After this, when we have issued from the font, we are thoroughly anointed with a blessed unction,—(a practice derived) from the old discipline, wherein on entering the priesthood, *men* were wont to be anointed with oil from a horn, ever since Aaron was anointed by Moses. Whence Aaron is called "Christ," from the "chrism," which is "the unction"; which, when made spiritual, furnished an appropriate name to the Lord, because He was "anointed" with the Spirit by God the Father. . . .

7. In the next place the hand is laid on us, invoking and inviting the Holy Spirit through benediction. Shall it be granted possible for human ingenuity to summon a spirit into water, and, by the application of hands from above, to animate their union into one body with another spirit of so clear sound; and shall it not be possible for God,

in the case of His own organ, to produce, by means of "holy hands," a sublime spiritual modulation? . . . Then, over our cleansed and blessed bodies willingly descends from the Father that Holiest Spirit. Over the waters of baptism, recognising as it were His primeval seat, He reposes: (He who) glided down on the Lord "in the shape of a dove" [Luke 3:22], in order that the nature of the Holy Spirit might be declared by means of the creature (the emblem) of simplicity and innocence, because even in her bodily structure the dove is without literal gall. And accordingly He says, "Be ye simple as doves" [Matt. 10:16]. Even this is not without the supporting evidence of a preceding figure. For just as, after the waters of the deluge, by which the old iniquity was purged—after the baptism, so to say, of the world—a *dove* was the herald which announced to the earth the assuagement of celestial wrath, when she had been sent her way out of the ark, and had returned with the olive-branch, a sign which even among the nations is the fore-token of *peace*; so by the self-same law of heavenly effect, to earth—that is, to our flesh—as it emerges from the font, after its old sins flies the *dove* of the Holy Spirit, bringing us the peace of God, sent out from the heavens where is the Church, the typified ark. But the world returned unto sin; in which point baptism would ill be compared to the deluge. And so it is destined to fire; just as the man too is, who after baptism renews his sins: so that this also ought to be accepted as a sign for our admonition.

Charisms and Spiritual Manifestations

To talk about spiritual manifestations in Tertullian is a notorious task for the reason mentioned above: his association with Montanism. A related issue is that there is no definite knowledge of the chronology of Tertullian's life. Thus we do not know how much of what he describes is meant to be a statement about the church life in general, which are the views of the mature Tertullian, and how much of his writings are linked with his Montanist period. The first two examples that follow come from his *A Treatise on the Soul*, the first psychological study from a Christian perspective, which is variously dated between 203 and 209. Assuming that his formal break with the Church happened around 207–211, but that his great interest in the movement began earlier, it is hard to find the *Sitz im Leben* of this writing. Similar kinds of narratives about the presence of the charismatic manifestations can also be found elsewhere in his writings—for example, in his main work, the five-volume *Against Marcion*, dated around 207–208. In this portion of his psychological discussion, in this case focusing on the composition of human persons, Tertullian shares an experience of a sister he calls Montanist. What makes this narrative significant is that Tertullian is not purporting to discuss charisms and spiritual manifestations, let alone prove their existence—he simply assumes them in his church—but rather uses the experience as a teaching aid in his anthropological reflection.

From Tertullian, *A Treatise on the Soul* 9, ANF 3:188.

As for ourselves, indeed, we inscribe on the soul the lineaments of corporeity, not simply from the assurance which reasoning has taught us of its corporeal nature, but also from the firm conviction which divine grace impresses on us by revelation. For, seeing that we acknowledge spiritual *charismata*, or gifts, we too have merited the attainment of the prophetic gift, although coming after John (the Baptist). We have now amongst us a sister whose lot it has been to be favoured with sundry gifts of revelation, which she experiences in the Spirit by ecstatic vision amidst the sacred rites of the Lord's day in the church: she converses with angels, and sometimes even with the Lord; she both sees and hears mysterious communications; some men's hearts she understands, and to them who are in need she distributes remedies. Whether it be in the reading of Scriptures, or in the chanting of psalms, or in the preaching of sermons, or in the offering up of prayers, in all these religious services matter and opportunity are afforded to her of seeing visions. It may possibly have happened to us, whilst this sister of ours was rapt in the Spirit, that we had discoursed in some ineffable way about the soul. After the people are dismissed at the conclusion of the sacred services, she is in the regular habit of reporting to us whatever things she may have seen in vision (for all her communications are examined with the most scrupulous care, in order that their truth may be probed). "Amongst other things," says she, "there has been shown to me a soul in bodily shape, and a spirit has been in the habit of appearing to me; not, however, a void and empty illusion, but such as would offer itself to be even grasped by the hand, soft and transparent and of an ethe-rial colour, and in form resembling that of a human being in every respect." This was her vision, and for her witness there was God; and the apostle most assuredly foretold that there were to be "spiritual gifts" in the church.

The Passion of the Holy Martyrs Perpetua and Felicitas

While Tertullian in his *A Treatise on the Soul* mentions the names of Per-petua and Felicitas, who suffered martyrdom in the reign of Septimius Severus about the year 202 CE, few if any contemporary scholars believe the narrative itself comes from the pen of Tertullian. It might, however, be possible that he was a kind of editor or at least transmitter of the story. His-torical and biographical details aside, this *hagiography* offers a fascinating description of the kind of eschatologically loaded, charismatic spirituality typical of Montanism and other enthusiastic movements of the time and throughout church history, even all the way to the contemporary pentecostal/charismatic phenomenon. The preface sets the tone for the testimony document.

From *The Passion of the Holy Martyrs Perpetua and Felicitas*, preface, ANF 3:699.

For "in the last days, saith the Lord, I will pour out of my Spirit upon all flesh; and their sons and their daughters shall prophesy. And upon my servants and my handmaidens will I pour out of my Spirit; and your young men shall see visions, and your old men shall dream dreams." And thus we—who both acknowledge and reverence, even as we do the prophecies, modern visions as equally promised to us, and consider the other powers of the Holy Spirit as an agency of the Church for which also He was sent, administering all gifts in all, even as the Lord distributed to every one as well needfully collect them in writing, as commemorate them in reading to God's glory; that so no weakness or despondency of faith may suppose that the divine grace abode only among the ancients, whether in respect of the condescension that raised up martyrs, or that gave revelations; since God always carries into effect what He has promised, for a testimony to unbelievers, to believers for a benefit.

In the midst of narratives about visions and raptures comes an account of Perpetua's baptism, an occasion in which the Spirit confirmed to her the impending suffering and martyrdom.

From *The Passion of the Holy Martyrs Perpetua and Felicitas* 1.2, ANF 3:699–700.

2. "While" says she [Perpetua], "we were still with the persecutors, and my father, for the sake of his affection for me, was persisting in seeking to turn me away, and to cast me down from the faith . . . we were baptized, and to me the Spirit prescribed that in the water *of baptism* nothing else was to be sought for bodily endurance. After a few days we are taken into the dungeon, and I was very much afraid, because I had never felt such darkness. O terrible day! O the fierce heat of the shock of the soldiery, because of the crowds! I was very unusually distressed by my anxiety for my infant.

Cyprian

With Tertullian, Cyprian is the leading North African patristic theologian, surpassed in influence only by his famous later counterpart St. Augustine. Widely regarded as the "father of ecclesiology," Cyprian made a lasting contribution to the Christian understanding of the church. His *The Unity of the Catholic Church* is the first major outline of the doctrine of the church, from which we have the famous saying *extra ecclesiam nulla salus* ("no salvation outside the church"; 6, *ANF* 5:423). One of the schismatics Cyprian addresses in this work is Novatius. While insisting on the church's unity and episcopal ministry, Cyprian is in no way a stranger to charismatic manifestations. Indeed, his ecclesiology is a careful attempt to incorporate the charismatic life and give it room within the church structure. Cyprian's defense of the unity of the church, as guarded by the episcopal office in succession to the ministry of Peter, is Trinitarian.

The Unity of the Church

From Cyprian, *The Unity of the Catholic Church* 4, 6, *ANF* 5:422, 423.

And although to all the apostles, after His resurrection, He gives an equal power, and says, "As the Father hath sent me, even so send I you: Receive ye the Holy Ghost: Whose soever sins ye remit, they shall be remitted unto him; and whose soever sins ye retain, they shall be retained;" yet, that He might set forth unity, He arranged by His authority the origin of that unity, as beginning from one. Assuredly the rest of the apostles were also the same as was Peter, endowed with a like partnership both of honour and power; but the beginning proceeds from unity. Which one Church, also, the Holy Spirit in the Song of Songs designated in the person of our Lord, and says, "My dove, my spotless one, is but one. She is the only one of her mother, elect of her that bare her." Does he who does not hold this unity of the Church think that he holds the faith? Does he who strives against and resists the Church trust that he is in the Church, when moreover the blessed Apostle Paul teaches the same thing, and sets forth the sacrament of unity, saying, "There is one body and one spirit, one hope of your calling, one Lord, one faith, one baptism, one God?" . . .

6. . . . He who breaks the peace and the concord of Christ, does so in opposition to Christ; he who gathereth elsewhere than in the Church, scatters the Church of Christ. The Lord says, "I and the Father are one;" and again it is written of the Father, and of the Son, and of the Holy Spirit, "And these three are one." And does any one believe that this unity which thus comes from the divine strength and coheres in celestial sacraments, can be divided in the

Church, and can be separated by the parting asunder of opposing wills? He who does not hold this unity does not hold God's law, does not hold the faith of the Father and the Son, does not hold life and salvation.

An imperative for preserving unity and a charitable attitude to other Christians comes from the nature of the Holy Spirit as charitable.

From Cyprian, *The Unity of the Catholic Church* 9, ANF 5:424.

Therefore also the Holy Spirit came as a dove, a simple and joyous creature, not bitter with gall, not cruel in its bite, not violent with the rending of its claws, loving human dwellings, knowing the association of one home; when they have young, bringing forth their young together; when they fly abroad, remaining in their flights by the side of one another, spending their life in mutual intercourse, acknowledging the concord of peace with the kiss of the beak, in all things fulfilling the law of unanimity. This is the simplicity that ought to be known in the Church, this is the charity that ought to be attained, that so the love of the brotherhood may imitate the doves, that their gentleness and meekness may be like the lambs and sheep.

Salvation, Sacraments, and Prayer
The following citation speaks of the Spirit's ministry of sanctification.

From Cyprian, *The Lord's Prayer* 12, ANF 5:450.

But by whom is God sanctified, since He Himself sanctifies? Well, because He says, "Be ye holy, even as I am holy," we ask and entreat, that we who were sanctified in baptism may continue in that which we have begun to be. And this we daily pray for; for we have need of daily sanctification, that we who daily fall away may wash out our sins by continual sanctification. And what the sanctification is which is conferred upon us by the condescension of God, the apostle declares, when he says, "neither fornicators, nor idolaters, nor adulterers, nor effeminate, nor abusers of themselves with mankind, nor thieves, nor deceivers, nor drunkards, nor revilers, nor extortioners, shall inherit the kingdom of God. And such indeed were you; but ye are washed; but ye are justified; but ye are sanctified in the name of our Lord Jesus Christ, and by the Spirit of our God." He says that we are sanctified in the name of our Lord Jesus Christ, and by the Spirit of our God. We pray that this sanctification may abide in us and because our Lord and Judge warns the man that was healed and quickened by Him, to sin no more lest a worse thing happen unto him, we make this supplication in our constant prayers, we ask this day and night, that the sanctification and quickening which is received from the grace of God may be preserved by His protection.

Similarly, in his *The Dress of Virgins*, Cyprian highlights the ministry of the Spirit in sanctification and relates it to the sacraments.

From Cyprian, *The Dress of Virgins* 22, *ANF* 5:436.

All indeed who attain to the divine gift and inheritance by the sanctification of baptism, therein put off the old man by the grace of the saving laver, and, renewed by the Holy Spirit from the filth of the old contagion, are purged by a second nativity. But the greater holiness and truth of that repeated birth belongs to you, who have no longer any desires of the flesh and of the body. Only the things which belong to virtue and the Spirit have remained in you to glory.

Clement of Alexandria

Clement, the Greek theologian, is routinely mentioned as the first theologian of Alexandria, one of the three centers of Christian learning alongside Athens and Rome during the patristic era. Clement of Alexandria made a significant contribution to theology in general and apologetic theology in particular.

True Knowledge of God
In his major work, the eight-volume *Miscellanies* (one volume of which was lost), this great apologist is attempting to furnish the materials for the construction of a true *gnosis*, a Christian philosophy. Freely acknowledging general revelation of God among the pagans, Clement makes faith in the Christian sense a function of the Holy Spirit.

From Clement of Alexandria, *Miscellanies* 5.13, *ANF* 2:465.

For there was always a natural manifestation of the one Almighty God, among all right-thinking men; and the most, who had not quite divested themselves of shame with respect to the truth, apprehended the eternal beneficence in divine providence. In fine, then, Xenocrates the Chalcedonian was not quite without hope that the notion of the Divinity existed even in the irrational creatures. And Democritus, though against his will, will make this avowal by the consequences of his dogmas; for he represents the same images as issuing, from the divine essence, on men and on the irrational animals. Far from destitute of a divine idea is man, who, it is written in Genesis, partook of inspiration, being endowed with a purer essence than the other animate creatures. Hence the Pythagoreans say that mind comes to man by divine providence, as Plato and Aristotle avow; but we assert that the Holy Spirit inspires him who has believed. The Platonists hold that mind is an effluence of divine dispensation in the soul, and they place the soul in the body. For it is expressly said by Joel, one of the twelve prophets, "And it shall come to pass after these things, I will pour out of My Spirit on all flesh, and your sons and your daughters shall prophesy" [Joel 2:28]. But it is not as a portion of God that the Spirit is in each of us. But how this dispensation takes place, and what the Holy Spirit is, shall be shown by us in the books on prophecy, and in those on the soul. But "incredulity is good at concealing the depths of knowledge," according to Heraclitus; "for incredulity escapes from ignorance."

The goal of another significant work of the Alexandrian theologian, *Exhortation to the Greeks*, is to show the supremacy of Christian wisdom over the errors and abominable licentiousness of pagan religions. One of the themes developed in this work, in line with Christian theology in general, is the inspiration of Scripture by the Holy Spirit.

From Clement of Alexandria, *Exhortation
to the Greeks* 8–9, ANF 2:194–95.

8. Jeremiah the prophet, gifted with consummate wisdom, or rather the Holy Spirit in Jeremiah, exhibits God. "Am I a God at hand," he says, "and not a God afar off? Shall a man do ought in secret, and I not see him? Do I not fill heaven and earth? Saith the Lord" [Jer. 23:23–24]. . . . And again by Isaiah, "Who shall measure heaven with a span, and the whole earth with his hand?" [Isa. 40:12] . . . What the Holy Spirit says by Hosea, I will not shrink from quoting: "Lo, I am He that appointeth the thunder, and createth spirit; and His hands have established the host of heaven." And once more by Isaiah . . .

9. I could adduce ten thousand Scriptures of which not "one tittle shall pass away," without being fulfilled; for the mouth of the Lord the Holy Spirit hath spoken these things.

Perfect Salvation

Clement's work *Paedagogus*, or *Christ the Educator*, is meant to be a manual for Christian formation for those who have left behind paganism. In the following quotation, he lays out a Trinitarian theology of salvation in a remarkably powerful way. In keeping with Greek theology, the language of union—often called *theosis* in the Christian East—is employed, as well as the emphasis on the perfection of salvation.

From Clement of Alexandria, *Paedagogus* 1.6, *ANF* 2.215–17.

Straightway, on our regeneration, we attained that perfection after which we aspired. For we were illuminated, which is to know God. . . . For at the moment of the Lord's baptism there sounded a voice from heaven, as a testimony to the Beloved, "Thou art My beloved Son, to-day have I begotten Thee" [Luke 3:22]. . . . He is perfected by the washing—of baptism—alone, and is sanctified by the descent of the Spirit? Such is the case. The same also takes place in our case, whose exemplar Christ became. Being baptized, we are illuminated; illuminated, we become sons; being made sons, we are made perfect; being made perfect, we are made immortal. "I," says He, "have said that ye are gods, and all sons of the Highest" [John 10:34]. This work is variously called grace, and illumination, and perfection, and washing: washing, by which we cleanse away our sins; grace, by which the penalties accruing to transgressions are remitted; and illumination, by which that holy light of salvation is beheld, that is, by which we see God clearly. Now we call that perfect which wants nothing. For what is yet wanting to him who knows God? For it were truly monstrous that that which is not complete should be called a gift (or act) of God's grace. Being perfect, He consequently bestows perfect gifts. As at His command all things were made, so on His bare wishing to bestow grace, ensues the perfecting of His grace. For the future of time is anticipated by the power of His volition.

Further release from evils is the beginning of salvation. We then alone, who first have touched the confines of life, are already perfect; and we already live who are separated from death. . . . As, then, those who have shaken off sleep forthwith become all awake within; or rather, as those who try to remove a film that is over the eyes, do not supply to them from without the light which they do not possess, but removing the obstacle from the eyes, leave the pupil free; thus also we who are baptized, having wiped off the sins which obscure the light of the Divine Spirit, have the eye of the spirit free, unimpeded, and full of light, by which alone we contemplate the Divine, the Holy Spirit flowing down to us from above. This is the eternal adjustment of the vision, which is able to see the eternal light, since like loves like; and that which is holy, loves that from which holiness proceeds, which has appropriately been termed light. . . . We are washed from all our sins, and are no longer entangled in evil. This is the one grace of illumination, that our characters are not the same as before our washing. And since knowledge springs up with illumination, shedding its beams around the mind, the moment we hear, we who were untaught become disciples. Does this, I ask, take place on the advent of this instruction? You cannot tell the time. For instruction leads to faith, and faith with baptism is trained by the Holy Spirit. For that faith is the one universal salvation of humanity, and that there is the same equality before the righteous and loving God, and the same fellowship between Him and all.

Spirit, Church, and Sacraments

Using one of the ancient symbols of the church going back to Cyprian, that of the mother, the Alexandrian theologian paints a beautiful picture of Christian community.

From Clement of Alexandria, *Paedagogus* 1.5, ANF 2:214.

The mother draws the children to herself; and we seek our mother the Church. Whatever is feeble and tender, as needing help on account of its feebleness, is kindly looked on, and is sweet and pleasant, anger changing into help in the case of such. . . . Thus also the Father of the universe cherishes affection towards those who have fled to Him; and having begotten them again by His Spirit to the adoption of children, knows them as gentle, and loves those alone, and aids and fights for them; and therefore He bestows on them the name of child. . . . The spirit of those that are children in Christ, whose lives are ordered in endurance, rejoice. . . . That which is signified by the prophet may be interpreted differently,—namely, of our rejoicing for salvation, as Isaac. He also, delivered from death, laughed, sporting and rejoicing with his spouse, who was the type of the Helper of our salvation, the Church, to whom the stable name of endurance is given; for this cause surely, because she alone remains to all generations, rejoicing ever, subsisting as she does by the endurance of us believers, who are the members of Christ. And the witness of those that have endured to the end, and the rejoicing on their account, is the mystic sport, and the salvation accompanied with decorous solace which brings us aid.

The spiritual meaning of the Eucharist is explained by this Greek theologian in a way that reflects a profound Spirit Christology. In line with Greek theology, the ultimate gift flowing from the Eucharist is immortality.

From Clement of Alexandria, *Paedagogus* 2.2, ANF 2:242–43.

The natural, temperate, and necessary beverage, therefore, for the thirsty is water. This was the simple drink of sobriety, which, flowing from the smitten rock, was supplied by the Lord to the ancient Hebrews. It was most requisite that in their wanderings they should be temperate. Afterwards the sacred vine produced the prophetic cluster. This was a sign to them, when trained from wandering to their rest; representing the great cluster the Word, bruised for us. For the blood of the grape—that is, the Word—desired to be mixed with water, as His blood is mingled with salvation.

And the blood of the Lord is twofold. For there is the blood of His flesh, by which we are redeemed from corruption; and the spiritual, that by which we are anointed. And to drink the blood of Jesus, is to become partaker of the Lord's immortality; the Spirit being the energetic principle of the Word, as blood is of flesh. Accordingly, as wine is blended with water, so is the Spirit with man. And the one, the mixture of wine and water, nourishes to faith; while the other, the Spirit, conducts to immortality. And the mixture of both—of the water and of the Word—is called Eucharist, renowned and glorious grace; and they who by faith partake of it are sanctified both in body and soul. For the divine mixture, man, the Father's will has mystically compounded by the Spirit and the Word. For, in truth, the spirit is joined to the soul, which is inspired by it; and the flesh, by reason of which the Word became flesh, to the Word.

Origen

One of the most significant early theologians—though not without controversy because of contested views, such as those on universalism—Origen was not only trained widely in the philosophies of his time but also received catechesis in the school of Clement of Alexandria. Similarly to his teacher, this Greek theologian was highly appreciative of the interaction between philosophy and the Christian faith and worldview. Yet at the same time, Origen acknowledges the critical role of the Holy Spirit in the appropriation and right understanding of apostolic teaching.

From Origen, *First Principles*, preface, 3, *ANF* 4:239.

Now it ought to be known that the holy apostles, in preaching the faith of Christ, delivered themselves with the utmost clearness on certain points which they believed to be necessary to every one, even to those who seemed somewhat dull in the investigation of divine knowledge; leaving, however, the grounds of their statements to be examined into by those who should deserve the excellent gifts of the Spirit, and who, especially by means of the Holy Spirit Himself, should obtain the gift of language, of wisdom, and of knowledge: while on other subjects they merely stated the fact that things were so, keeping silence as to the manner or origin of their existence; clearly in order that the more zealous of their successors, who should be lovers of wisdom, might have a subject of exercise on which to display the fruit of their talents,—those persons, I mean, who should prepare themselves to be fit and worthy receivers of wisdom.

The Equality of the Spirit in the Trinity under Consideration

With all his superb intellectual skills, Origen was not always a consistent thinker, as evident for example in his *Commentary on John* (2.6; *ANF* 10:328), in which he seems to make the Spirit not only derivative from the Son but also to have been made by the Logos. This is, of course, a radically subordinationist idea and as such reflects the great difficulty that early Christian theology encountered in trying to hammer out Trinitarian canons. An indication of the fact that the formulation in the commentary is not just a fleeting deviation from the affirmation of the full deity of the Spirit is the second passage, from Origen's main work, *First Principles*, which again comes back to the problem of the Spirit's origin. It is remarkable that this passage from the preface to that work claims to summarize the apostolic tradition.

From Origen, *First Principles*, preface, 4, *ANF* 4:204.

First, That there is one God, who created and arranged all things, and who, when nothing existed, called all things into being—God from the first creation and foundation of the world. . . . *Secondly*, That Jesus Christ Himself, who came (into the world), was born of the Father before all creatures. . . . Then, *Thirdly*, the apostles related that the Holy Spirit was associated in honour and dignity with the Father and the Son. But in His case it is not clearly distinguished whether He is to be regarded as born or innate, or also as a Son of God or not: for these are points which have to be inquired into out of sacred Scripture according to the best of our ability, and which demand careful investigation. And that this Spirit inspired each one of the saints, whether prophets or apostles; and that there was not one Spirit in the men of the old dispensation, and another in those who were inspired at the advent of Christ, is most clearly taught throughout the Churches.

One of the ways early Christian theology tried to clarify the distinctions, yet unity, among the Father, Son, and Spirit, was to relate them to different spheres of operation. Reflecting the typical Greek theology's and Eastern Church's understanding of salvation in terms of union, Origen surmises that the Holy Spirit only works among the faithful, whereas the Father and Son work everywhere in the created order.

From Origen, *First Principles* 1.3.5, 7, ANF 4:253–54.

5. Nevertheless it seems proper to inquire what is the reason why he who is regenerated by God unto salvation has to do both with Father and Son and Holy Spirit, and does not obtain salvation unless with the co-operation of the entire Trinity; and why it is impossible to become partaker of the Father or the Son without the Holy Spirit. And in discussing these subjects, it will undoubtedly be necessary to describe the special working of the Holy Spirit, and of the Father and the Son. I am of opinion, then, that the working of the Father and of the Son takes place as well in saints as in sinners, in rational beings and in dumb animals; nay, even in those things which are without life, and in all things universally which exist; but that the operation of the Holy Spirit does not take place at all in those things which are without life, or in those which, although living, are yet dumb; nay, is not found even in those who are endued indeed with reason, but are engaged in evil courses, and not at all converted to a better life. In those persons alone do I think that the operation of the Holy Spirit takes place, who are already turning to a better life, and walking along the way which leads to Jesus Christ, i.e., who are engaged in the performance of good actions, and who abide in God. . . .

7. Finally, also, at the time of the flood, when all flesh had corrupted their way before God, it is recorded that God spoke thus, as of undeserving men and sinners: "My Spirit shall not abide with those men for ever, because they are flesh." By which, it is clearly shown that the Spirit of God is taken away from all who are unworthy. In the Psalms also it is written: "Thou wilt take away their spirit, and they will die, and return to their earth. Thou wilt send forth Thy Spirit, and they shall be created, and Thou wilt renew the face of the earth"; which is manifestly intended of the Holy Spirit, who, after sinners and unworthy persons have been taken away and destroyed, creates for Himself a new people, and renews the face of the earth, when, laying aside, through the grace of the Spirit, the old man with his deeds, they begin to walk in newness of life. And therefore the expression is competently applied to the Holy Spirit, because He will take up His dwelling, not in all men, nor in those who are flesh, but in those whose land has been renewed. Lastly, for this reason was the grace and revelation of the Holy Spirit bestowed by the imposition of the apostles' hands after baptism. Our Saviour also, after the resurrection, when old things had already passed away, and all things had become new, Himself a new man, and the first-born from the dead, His apostles also being renewed by faith in His resurrection, says, "Receive the Holy Spirit." . . . In this manner, then, is the working of the power of God the Father and of the Son extended without

distinction to every creature; but a share in the Holy Spirit we find possessed only by the saints. And therefore it is said, "No man can say that Jesus is Lord, but by the Holy Ghost."

The Sanctifying Spirit

Origen develops a profound Trinitarian theology of salvation as union with God, highlighting the work of the Spirit as sanctifier.

From Origen, *First Principles* 1.3.8, *ANF* 4:255–56.

Having made these declarations regarding the Unity of the Father, and of the Son, and of the Holy Spirit, let us return to the order in which we began the discussion. God the Father bestows upon all, existence; and participation in Christ, in respect of His being the word of reason, renders them rational beings. From which it follows that they are deserving either of praise or blame, because capable of virtue and vice. On this account, therefore, is the grace of the Holy Ghost present, that those beings which are not holy in their essence may be rendered holy by participating in it. Seeing, then, that firstly, they derive their existence from God the Father; secondly, their rational nature from the Word; thirdly, their holiness from the Holy Spirit,—those who have been previously sanctified by the Holy Spirit are again made capable of receiving Christ, in respect that He is the righteousness of God; and those who have earned advancement to this grade by the sanctification of the Holy Spirit, will nevertheless obtain the gift of wisdom according to the power and working of the Spirit of God. And this I consider is Paul's meaning, when he says that to "some is given the word of wisdom, to others the word of knowledge, according to the same Spirit." And while pointing out the individual distinction of gifts, he refers the whole of them to the source of all things, in the words, "There are diversities of operations, but one God who worketh all in all." Whence also the working of the Father, which confers existence upon all things, is found to be more glorious and magnificent, while each one, by participation in Christ, as being wisdom, and knowledge, and sanctification, makes progress, and advances to higher degrees of perfection; and seeing it is by partaking of the Holy Spirit that any one is made purer and holier, he obtains, when he is made worthy, the grace of wisdom and knowledge, in order that, after all stains of pollution and ignorance are cleansed and taken away, he may make so great an advance in holiness and purity, that the nature which he received from God may become such as is worthy of Him who gave it to be pure and perfect, so that the being which exists may be as worthy as He who called it into existence. For, in this way, he who is such as his Creator wished him to be, will receive from God power always to exist, and to abide for ever. That this may be the case, and that those whom He has created may be unceasingly and inseparably present with Him, Who IS, it is the business of wisdom to instruct and train them, and to bring them to perfection by confirmation of His Holy Spirit and unceasing sanctification, by which alone are they capable of receiving God. In this way, then, by the renewal of the ceaseless working of Father, Son, and Holy Spirit in us, in its various stages of progress, shall we be able at some future time perhaps, although with difficulty, to behold the holy and the blessed life, in which (as it is only after many struggles that we are able to reach it) we ought so to continue, that no satiety of that blessedness should ever seize us; but the more we perceive its blessedness, the more should be increased and intensified within us the longing for the same, while we ever more eagerly and freely receive and hold fast the Father, and the Son, and the Holy Spirit. But if satiety should ever take hold of any one of those who stand on the highest and perfect summit of attainment, I do not think that such an one would suddenly be deposed from his position and fall away, but that he must decline gradually and little by little, so that it may sometimes happen that if a brief lapsus take place, and the individual quickly repent and return to himself, he may not utterly fall away, but may retrace his steps, and return to his former place, and again make good that which had been lost by his negligence.

The Manifold Gifts of the Spirit

Following many early theologians, Origen appeals to the truthfulness of Christian faith not only in reference to its divine origin but also with regard to divine attestation evidenced in signs and wonders as well as in right lifestyle. These arguments he mounts in his main apologetical work, the multivolume *Against Celsus*, a defense of the Christian faith in opposition to a Greek philosopher named Celsus, whose work titled *The True Word*, or *The True Discourse*, we only know from the quotations in Origen's book.

From Origen, *Against Celsus* 1.2, ANF 4:397–98.

Now this is our answer to his allegations, and our defence of the truths contained in Christianity, that if any one were to come from the study of Grecian opinions and usages to the Gospel, he would not only decide that its doctrines were true, but would by practice establish their truth, and supply whatever seemed wanting, from a Grecian point of view, to their demonstration, and thus confirm the truth of Christianity. We have to say, moreover, that the Gospel has a demonstration of its own, more divine than any established by Grecian dialectics. And this diviner method is called by the apostle the "manifestation of the Spirit and of power": of "the Spirit," on account of the prophecies, which are sufficient to produce faith in any one who reads them, especially in those things which relate to Christ; and of "power," because of the signs and wonders which we must believe to have been performed, both on many other grounds, and on this, that traces of them are still preserved among those who regulate their lives by the precepts of the Gospel.

Origen paints a colorful picture of the many gifts the Spirit is granting to Christians and to the church.

From Origen, *First Principles* 2.7.3, ANF 4:284–85.

In the Holy Spirit . . . is contained every kind of gifts. For on some is bestowed by the Spirit the word of wisdom, on others the word of knowledge, on others faith; and so to each individual of those who are capable of receiving Him, is the Spirit Himself made to be that quality, or understood to be that which is needed by the individual who has deserved to participate. These divisions and differences not being perceived by those who hear Him called Paraclete in the Gospel, and not duly considering in consequence of what work or act He is named the Paraclete, they have compared Him to some common spirits or other, and by this means have tried to disturb the Churches of Christ, and so excite dissensions of no small extent among brethren; whereas the Gospel shows Him to be of such power and majesty, that it says the apostles could not yet receive those things which the Saviour wished to teach them until the advent of the Holy Spirit, who, pouring Himself into their souls, might enlighten them regarding the nature and faith of the Trinity. But these persons, because of the ignorance of their understandings, are not only unable themselves logically to state the truth, but cannot even give their attention to what is advanced by us; and entertaining unworthy ideas of His divinity, have delivered themselves over to errors and deceits, being depraved by a spirit of error, rather than instructed by the teaching of the Holy Spirit, according to the declaration of the apostle, "Following the doctrine of devils, forbidding to marry, to the destruction and ruin of many, and to abstain from meats, that by an ostentatious exhibition of stricter observance they may seduce the souls of the innocent."

4. We must therefore know that the Paraclete is the Holy Spirit, who teaches truths which cannot be uttered in words, and which are, so to speak, unutterable, and "which it is not lawful for a man

to utter," i.e., which cannot be indicated by human language. The phrase "it is not lawful" is, we think, used by the apostle instead of "it is not possible"; as also is the case in the passage where he says, "All things are lawful for me, but all things are not expedient: all things are lawful for me; but all things edify not." For those things which are in our power because we may have them, he says are lawful for us. But the Paraclete, who is called the Holy Spirit, is so called from His work of consolation, *paraclesis* being termed in Latin *consolatio*. For if any one has deserved to participate in the Holy Spirit by the knowledge of His ineffable mysteries, he undoubtedly obtains comfort and joy of heart. For since he comes by the teaching of the Spirit to the knowledge of the reasons of all things which happen—how or why they occur—his soul can in no respect be troubled, or admit any feeling of sorrow; nor is he alarmed by anything, since, clinging to the Word of God and His wisdom, he through the Holy Spirit calls Jesus Lord. And since we have made mention of the Paraclete, and have explained as we were able what sentiments ought to be entertained regarding Him; and since our Saviour also is called the Paraclete in the Epistle of John, when he says, "If any of us sin, we have a Paraclete with the Father, Jesus Christ the righteous, and He is the propitiation for our sins"; let us consider whether this term Paraclete should happen to have one meaning when applied to the Saviour, and another when applied to the Holy Spirit. Now Paraclete, when spoken of the Saviour, seems to mean intercessor. For in Greek, Paraclete has both significations—that of intercessor and comforter. On account, then, of the phrase which follows, when he says, "And He is the propitiation for our sins," the name Paraclete seems to be understood in the case of our Saviour as meaning intercessor; for He is said to intercede with the Father because of our sins. In the case of the Holy Spirit, the Paraclete must be understood in the sense of comforter, inasmuch as He bestows consolation upon the souls to whom He openly reveals the apprehension of spiritual knowledge.

CHAPTER 2

*Patristic Views of the Spirit
after Nicea: Greek and
Other Eastern Fathers*

Introduction: The Spirit in the Post-Nicene Fathers

Trinitarian and christological debates both continued and were tentatively resolved in the several creedal pronouncements in the fourth and fifth centuries. Building on the statement of the Council of Nicea (325), the Council of Constantinople (381) offered a definitive statement about the Trinity, including the Holy Spirit. The way the role of the Spirit in the Trinity was being clarified and the Spirit "elevated" to the same status as the Son (even when the two still tended to be regarded in some way or another as "inferior" to the Father, as the source) was the slow growth of pneumatological doctrine and its insistence on the deity of the Spirit.

The Greek-speaking theologians who will be presented first in this survey came from the two centers of the Christian East: Alexandria (Athanasius and the three Cappadocians, Basil of Caesarea, Gregory of Nyssa, and Gregory of Nazianzen) and Antioch (Theodore of Mopsuestia and John Chrysostom). The main Latin-speaking theologians, whose contributions will be presented in the last section on patristic views of the Spirit, were Hilary of Poitiers, Ambrose, and St. Augustine.

Key theologians in the development of pneumatological doctrine were the Eastern theologians, especially those from Alexandria. Athanasius directed his *The Letters to Serapion on the Holy Spirit* (355–60) against the *tropicii* (Tropici), a group that was not willing to give the same divine status to the Spirit as to the Son. This work, as well as Basil the Great's *On the Holy Spirit* (376) (directed against the Pneumatomachoi), are landmark works in affirming the deity of the Spirit and thus equality with the Son. Other Cappadocians affirmed the same.

The Shared Trinitarian Faith:
One God with Three Persons

Eastern Christian traditions, of course, include others than those mentioned above, such as the East Syrian (Assyrian) Church and several non-Chalcedonian churches, Armenian, Coptic, Ethiopian, and Jacobite (West Syrian) Churches. This survey hardly includes them except for the Egyptian Pseudo-Macarius and the Jacobite Ephrem the Syrian, who had a profound influence in the Eastern Church and beyond.

The development of pneumatological canons can be seen by a simple comparison of the length of the statements. Whereas at the Council of Nicea in 325 the statement on the third person of the Trinity is very short, "And [we believe] in the Holy Ghost,"[1] in the Creed of Constantinople I (381)[2] the consubstantiality of the Spirit was officially confirmed: "And [we believe] in the Holy Ghost, the Lord and Giver-of-Life, who proceedeth from the Father, who with the Father and the Son together is worshipped and glorified, who spake by the prophets."[3]

Cyril of Jerusalem

Towards a Biblically Based Doctrine and Symbology of the Holy Spirit
Similarly to many Fathers, in his *Catechetical Lectures* the archbishop of Jerusalem stresses the importance of Scripture as the source for developing the doctrine and spirituality of the Holy Spirit.

From Cyril, *Catechetical Lectures* 4.16–17, NPNF[2] 7:23.

16. Believe thou also in the Holy Ghost, and hold the same opinion concerning Him, which thou hast *received to hold* concerning the Father and the Son, and follow not those who teach blasphemous things of Him. But learn thou that this Holy Spirit is One, indivisible, of manifold power; having many operations, yet not Himself divided; Who knoweth the mysteries, Who *searcheth all things, even the deep things of God*: Who descended upon the Lord Jesus Christ in form of a dove; Who wrought in the Law and in the Prophets; Who now also at the season of Baptism sealeth thy soul; of Whose

1. *NPNF*[2] 14:3.
2. Known as the Nicene-Constantinopolitan Creed, the basic outline of which was drafted at the Council of Nicea in 325.
3. *NPNF*[2] 14:163.

holiness also every intellectual nature hath need: against Whom *if any dare to blaspheme, he hath no forgiveness, neither in this world, nor in that which is to come*: "Who with the Father and the Son together" is honoured with the glory of the Godhead: of Whom also *thrones, and dominions, principalities, and powers* have need. For there is One God, the Father of Christ; and One Lord Jesus Christ, the Only-begotten Son of the Only God; and One Holy Ghost, the sanctifier and deifier of all, Who spake in the Law and in the Prophets, in the Old and in the New Testament.

17. Have thou ever in thy mind this seal, which for the present has been lightly touched in my discourse, by way of summary, but shall be stated, should the Lord permit, to the best of my power with the proof from the Scriptures. For concerning the divine and holy mysteries of the Faith, not even a casual statement must be delivered without the Holy Scriptures; nor must we be drawn aside by mere plausibility and artifices of speech. Even to me, who tell thee these things, give not absolute credence, unless thou receive the proof of the things which I announce from the Divine Scriptures. For this salvation which we believe depends not on ingenious reasoning, but on demonstration of the Holy Scriptures.

In addition to this summary statement, Cyril also expands considerably the doctrine of the Holy Spirit in lectures 16 and 17. As mentioned in the previous citation, he emphasizes the role of Scripture. Indeed, what these lectures purport to offer is merely a careful scrutiny and exposition of biblical pneumatology. A skillful orator, the archbishop elaborates on the nature and ministry of the Spirit by taking up the biblical image of water.

From Cyril, *Catechetical Lectures* 16.11–12, NPNF[2] 7:117–18.

11. Let then thus much suffice concerning those outcasts; and now let us return to the divine Scriptures, and let us *drink waters out of our own cisterns* [that is, the holy Fathers], *and out of our own springing wells.* Drink we of *living water, springing up into everlasting life*; *but this spake* the Saviour *of the Spirit, which they that believe on Him should receive.* For observe what He says, *He that believeth on Me* (not simply this, but), *as the Scripture hath said* (thus He hath sent thee back to the Old Testament), *out of his belly shall flow rivers of living water*, not rivers perceived by sense, and merely watering the earth with its thorns and trees, but bringing souls to the light. And in another place He says, *But the water that I shall give him, shall be in him a well of living water springing up into everlasting life,*—a new kind of water living and springing up, springing up unto them who are worthy.

12. And why did He call the grace of the Spirit water? Because by water all things subsist; because water brings forth grass and living things; because the water of the showers comes down from heaven; because it comes down one in form, but works in many forms. For one fountain watereth the whole of Paradise, and one and the same rain comes down upon all the world, yet it becomes white in the lily, and red in the rose, and purple in violets and hyacinths, and different and varied in each several kind: so it is one in the palm-tree, and another in the vine, and all in all things; and yet is one in nature, not diverse from itself; for the rain does not change itself, and come down first as one thing, then as another, but adapting itself to the constitution of each thing which receives it, it becomes to each what is suitable. Thus also the Holy Ghost, being one, and of one nature, and indivisible, divides to each His grace, *according as He will*: and as the dry tree, after partaking of water, puts forth shoots, so also the soul in sin, when it has been through repentance made worthy of the Holy Ghost, brings forth clusters of righteousness. And though He is One in nature, yet many are the virtues which by the will of God and in the Name of Christ He works.

The Gentle Nature of the Spirit

Contrasting with the rude and violent nature of evil spirits, Cyril describes the gentle nature of the Holy Spirit as the Spirit comes to the life of the Christian.

From Cyril, *Catechetical Lectures* 16.16, *NPNF*[2] 7:119.

First, His coming is gentle; the perception of Him is fragrant; His burden most light; beams of light and knowledge gleam forth before His coming. He comes with the bowels of a true guardian: for He comes to save, and to heal, to teach, to admonish, to strengthen, to exhort, to enlighten the mind, first of him who receives Him, and afterwards of others also, through him. And as a man, who being previously in darkness then suddenly beholds the sun, is enlightened in his bodily sight, and sees plainly things which he saw not, so likewise he to whom the Holy Ghost is vouchsafed, is enlightened in his soul, and sees things beyond man's sight, which he knew not; his body is on earth, yet his soul mirrors forth the heavens. He sees, like Esaias, *the Lord sitting upon a throne high and lifted up*; he sees, like Ezekiel, *Him who is above the Cherubim*; he sees like Daniel, *ten thousand times ten thousand, and thousands of thousands*; and the man, who is so little, beholds the beginning of the world, and knows the end of the world, and the times intervening, and the successions of kings,—things which he never learned: for the True Enlightener is present with him. The man is within the walls of a house; yet the power of his knowledge reaches far and wide, and he sees even what other men are doing.

The Spirit in the Sacraments and Salvation
Speaking to baptismal candidates, the archbishop of Jerusalem develops a pneumatological sacramentology and soteriology.

From Cyril, *Catechetical Lectures* 3.3–5, NPNF[2] 7:14–15.

3. Each one of you is about to be presented to God before tens of thousands of the Angelic Hosts: the Holy Ghost is about to seal your souls: ye are to be enrolled in the army of the Great King. Therefore make you ready, and equip yourselves, by putting on I mean, not bright apparel, but piety of soul with a good conscience. Regard not the Laver as simple water, but rather regard the spiritual grace that is given with the water. For just as the offerings brought to the heathen altars, though simple in their nature, become defiled by the invocation of the idols, so contrariwise the simple water having received the invocation of the Holy Ghost, and of Christ, and of the Father, acquires a new power of holiness.

4. For since man is of twofold nature, soul and body, the purification also is twofold, the one incorporeal for the incorporeal part, and the other bodily for the body: the water cleanses the body, and the Spirit seals the soul; that we may draw near unto God, *having our heart sprinkled* by the Spirit, *and our body washed with pure water.* When going down, therefore, into the water, think not of the bare element, but look for salvation by the power of the Holy Ghost: for without both thou canst not possibly be made perfect. It is not I that say this, but the Lord Jesus Christ, who has the power in this matter: for He saith, *Except a man be born anew* (and He adds the words) *of water and of the Spirit, he cannot enter into the kingdom of God.* Neither doth he that is baptized with water, but not found worthy of the Spirit, receive the grace in perfection; nor if a man be virtuous in his deeds, but receive not the seal by water, shall he enter into the kingdom of heaven. A bold saying, but not mine, for it is Jesus who hath declared it: and here is the proof of the statement from Holy Scripture. Cornelius was a just man, who was honoured with a vision of Angels, and had set up his prayers and alms-deeds as a good memorial before God in heaven. Peter came, and the Spirit was poured out upon them that believed, and they spake with other tongues, and prophesied: and after the grace of the Spirit the Scripture saith that Peter *commanded them to be baptized in the name of*

Jesus Christ; in order that, the soul having been born again by faith, the body also might by the water partake of the grace.

5. But if any one wishes to know why the grace is given by water and not by a different element, let him take up the Divine Scriptures and he shall learn. For water is a grand thing, and the noblest of the four visible elements of the world. Heaven is the dwelling-place of Angels, but the heavens are from the waters: the earth is the place of men, but the earth is from the waters: and before the whole six days' formation of the things that were made, *the Spirit of God moved upon the face of the water*. The water was the beginning of the world, and Jordan the beginning of the Gospel tidings: for Israel deliverance from Pharaoh was through the sea, and for the world deliverance from sins *by the washing of water with the word* of God. Where a covenant is made with any, there is water also.

An Emerging Spirit Christology

Giving an exposition on the baptism of Jesus, Cyril begins to lay the foundation for a Spirit Christology that comes to full fruition in the work of the later Greek Fathers, especially of the Cappadocians. In this Spirit Christology, the benefits of the mutual working of the Son and Spirit in the great act of salvation are addressed to us for our salvation and participation in the divine life.

From Cyril, *Catechetical Lectures* 3.11–14, *NPNF*² 7:16–17.

3.11. Jesus sanctified Baptism by being Himself baptized. If the Son of God was baptized, what godly man is he that despiseth Baptism? But He was baptized not that He might receive remission of sins, for He was sinless; but being sinless, He was baptized, that He might give to them that are baptized a divine and excellent grace. For *since the children are partakers of flesh and blood, He also Himself likewise partook of the same*, that having been made partakers of His presence in the flesh we might be made partakers also of His Divine grace: thus Jesus was baptized, that thereby we again by our participation might receive both salvation and honour. . . .

12. . . . Having gone down dead in sins, thou comest up quickened in righteousness. For if thou hast been *united with the likeness of the Saviour's death*, thou shalt also be deemed worthy of His Resurrection. For as Jesus took upon Him the sins of the world, and died, that by putting sin to death He might rise again in righteousness; so thou by going down into the water, and being in a manner buried in the waters, as He was in the rock, art raised again *walking in newness of life*.

13. Moreover, when thou hast been deemed worthy of the grace, He then giveth thee strength to wrestle against the adverse powers. For as after His Baptism He was tempted forty days (not that He was unable to gain the victory before, but because He wished to do all things in due order and succession), so thou likewise, though not daring before thy baptism to wrestle with the adversaries, yet after thou hast received the grace and art henceforth confident in *the armour of righteousness*, must then do battle, and preach the Gospel, if thou wilt.

14. Jesus Christ was the Son of God, yet He preached not the Gospel before His Baptism. If the Master Himself followed the right time in due order, ought we, His servants, to venture out of order? *From that time Jesus began to preach*, when *the Holy Spirit had descended upon Him in a bodily shape, like a dove*; not that Jesus might see Him first, for He knew Him even before He came in a bodily shape, but that John, who was baptizing Him, might behold Him. For *I*, saith he, *knew Him not: but He that sent me to baptize with water, He said unto me, Upon whomsoever thou shalt see the Spirit descending and abiding on Him, that is He*. If thou too hast unfeigned piety, the Holy Ghost cometh down on thee also, and a Father's voice sounds over thee from on high—not, "*This is My Son*," but, "This has now been made My son;" for the "*is*" belongs to Him alone, because *In the beginning was the Word, and the Word was with God, and the Word was God*.

Athanasius

Born around 300 at Alexandria, Athanasius was educated in the catechetical school of Clement and Origen. First serving as deacon of Bishop Alexander, Athanasius made a significant contribution at Nicea against the Arians. Soon thereafter he was appointed bishop while still a young man.

Combating Pneumatological Errors and Opponents

Athanasius's *Letters to Serapion Concerning the Holy Spirit* is the first doctrinal formulation of the Spirit in the history of theology, written around 357 during the bishop's third exile in the desert, even antedating the famous work of St. Basil *On the Holy Spirit*. It is written against the Tropici, Christians who, while affirming the full divinity of the Son, did not confess the divinity of the Holy Spirit. The first part of the letter considers scriptural passages used by the opponents in their denial of the Spirit's divinity (1.1–14). The second part (1.15–33) then refutes the main arguments of the Tropici, one of which is that the Spirit is a "son" (or "brother") of the Son (1.15). Athanasius argues for the indivisibility of the Trinity (1.17) and resorts to biblical "symbols" that he believes are "sufficient and adequate" (1.19). By elaborating on those biblical symbols, Athanasius affirms both the unity and *perichoresis*, the mutual interpenetration and mutual indwelling, of all three members of the Trinity, including the Spirit. The claim of the Tropici that the Spirit is a creature is thus combated.

From Athanasius, *Letters to Serapion Concerning the Holy Spirit*, 1.19–20, in *Athanasius*, trans. and ed. Khaled Anatolios (London: Routledge, 2004), 217–19 (hereafter Anatolios).

19. Thus, the Father is called "Fountain" and "Light"..., "the fountain of living water" (Jer 2:13).... But, in relation to the fountain, the Son is spoken of as the river: for "the river of God is filled with waters" (Ps 65:10). Relative to the light, he is called radiance, as Paul says: "who is the radiance of his glory, and the reflection of his being (*hypostaseos*)" (Heb 1:3). Thus, the Father being light, while the Son is his radiance (for we cannot shrink from saying the same things about them many times), we can also see in the Son the Spirit, in whom we are enlightened: "that he may give you the Spirit of wisdom and revelation in the knowledge of him," it says, "enlightening the eyes of your heart" (Eph 1:17). But when we are enlightened by the Spirit, it is Christ who in the Spirit enlightens us.... So, again, while the Father is fountain, and the Son is called river, we are said to drink of the Spirit. For it is written that "we have all been given to drink of one Spirit" (1 Cor 12:13). But when we are given to drink of the Spirit, we drink Christ; for "they drank from the spiritual rock that followed them, and that rock was Christ" (1 Cor 10:4). And again, while Christ is the true Son, we are made into sons when we receive the Spirit: "For you have not received," it says, "the Spirit of slavery that leads back to fear. But you have received the Spirit of sonship" (Rom 8:15). But when we are made sons by the Spirit, it is clearly in Christ that we receive the title of "children of God": "For to those who did accept him, he gave power to become children of God" (Jn 1:12). Then again, while the Father, as Paul says, is the "only wise one" (Rom 16:27), the Son is his wisdom: "Christ, the power of God and the wisdom of God" (1 Cor 1:24). But, the Son being wisdom, when we receive the Spirit of wisdom, we attain Christ and become wise in him.... But when we are made alive in the Spirit, Christ himself is said to live in us: "I have been crucified with Christ," it says, "I live, yet it is no longer I who live, but Christ lives in me" (Gal 2:19–20).... So also, Paul said that the works that he accomplished in the power of the Spirit were the works of Christ: "I will not presume to speak of anything except what Christ has accomplished through me, for the sake of the obedience of the Gentiles, by word

and work, in the power of signs and wonders, in the power of the Holy Spirit" (Rom 15:18–19).

20. Such being the correlation (*sustoichia*) and the unity of the Holy Trinity, who would dare to separate the Son from the Father, or the Spirit from the Son or from the Father himself? Or who would be so presumptuous as to say that the Trinity is unlike (*anomion*) and heterogenous (*heterophyē*) with respect to itself, or that the Son is of a different being (*allotrioousion*) than the Father, or that the Spirit is foreign to the Son? But how can this be? If one were to enquire and ask again: How can it be that when the Spirit is in us, the Son is said to be in us, and when the Son is in us, the Father is said to be in us? Or, how is it really a Trinity if the three are depicted (*semainetai*) as one? Or how is it that when one is in us, the Trinity is said to be in us? Let such an enquirer begin by separating the radiance from the light, or wisdom from the one who is wise, or else let him say himself how these things can be. But if this cannot be done, then how much more is it the presumption of insane people to enquire into these things with respect to God?

Athanasius finds a number of names for the Spirit in Scripture that illustrate the Spirit's manifold ministry, such as "the Spirit of holiness and of renewal," "life-giving," "anointing," and "seal." In a remarkable statement, Athanasius also attributes to the Spirit the participation of all creatures with God, which also makes possible *theosis*.

From Athanasius, *Letters to Serapion Concerning the Holy Spirit* 1.22–24 (Anatolios, 221–24).

22. . . . Moreover, the Spirit is and is called the Spirit of holiness and of renewal. For Paul writes: "He was established as Son of God in power according to the Spirit of holiness, through resurrection from the dead, Jesus Christ, our Lord" (Rom 1:4). And again he says: "But you were sanctified, you were justified in the name of our Lord Jesus Christ and in the Spirit of our God" (1 Cor 6:11). And when writing to Titus, he said: "But when the kindness and love of God our Savior appeared, not because of righteous deeds that we had done but because of his mercy, he saved us through the bath of rebirth and the renewal of the holy Spirit, whom he richly poured out on us through Jesus Christ our Savior, so that we may be justified by his grace and become heirs in hope of eternal life" (Titus 3:4–7). As for creatures, however, they are sanctified and renewed, for "You will send forth your spirit and they will be created and you will renew the face of the earth" (Ps 104:30). Paul also says, "For it is impossible for those who

have once been enlightened and have tasted the heavenly gift and have attained participation in the Holy Spirit" (Heb 6:4).

23. But how can that which is not sanctified by another and which does not participate in holiness but is itself participated the one in which all of creation is sanctified itself be one of the all? How can it belong among those who participate in it? It would be necessary, then, for those who say this to say also that the Son, through whom all things come into being, is himself one of the "all." The Spirit is called "life-giving." For it says, "The one who raised Jesus Christ from the dead will also give life to your mortal bodies, through his Spirit that dwells in you" (Rom 8:11). While the Lord is life itself and, as Peter said, "the author of life" (Acts 3:15), the Lord himself said, "The water which I will give to him will become in him a fount of water welling up to eternal life. . . . He said this concerning the Spirit that those who believed in him were to receive." But, as we have said, creatures are granted life through the Spirit. So then how can that which does not participate in life but is itself participated and in fact grants life to creatures have any kinship with things that come into being? Or how can the Spirit be in any way one of the creatures which are granted life in the Spirit by the Word? The Spirit is spoken of as "anointing" and is "seal." So John writes: "As for you, the anointing that you received from him remains in you, and you have no need of someone to teach you. But his anointing," his Spirit, "teaches you about everything" (1 Jn 2:27). In the prophet Isaiah, it is written: "The Spirit of the Lord is upon me, because he has anointed me" (Isa 61:1). Paul says, "Having believed in him you have been sealed for the day of redemption" (cf. Eph 1:13). But, as for creatures, they are sealed and anointed by the Spirit and taught everything by the Spirit. Now, if the Spirit is "anointing" and "seal," as the one in whom the Word anoints and seals all things, what kind of likeness or commonality of identity (*idiotēs*) can there be between the unction and seal and those who are anointed and sealed? So, on this account also, the Spirit is not among all things, for the seal cannot be from among the things that are sealed; neither can the unction be from among the things that are anointed, but rather belongs (*idion*) to the anointing and sealing Word. The unction has the fragrance and breath of the one who anoints and those who are anointed, when they partake of this unction, say: "We are the fragrance of Christ" (2 Cor 2:15). The seal possesses the form of Christ who seals, while those who are sealed participate in it, and become conformed to it, as the apostle says: "My children, for whom I am again in labor, until Christ is formed in you" (Gal 4:19). When we are sealed in this way, we properly become sharers in the divine nature, as Peter says

(2 Pet 1:4), and so the whole creation participates of the Word, in the Spirit.

24. Moreover, all things are said to be participants of God through the Spirit. For it says, "Do you not know that you are the temple of God and that the Spirit of God dwells in you? If anyone destroys the temple of God, God will destroy that one. For the temple of God, which you are, is holy" (1 Cor 3:16, 17). But if the Holy Spirit were a creature, there would not be for us any participation of God in the Spirit. Indeed, if we were merely united to a creature, we would still be foreigners to the divine nature, having no participation in it. But now that we are called participants of Christ and participants of God, it is thereby shown that the unction and seal which is in us is not of a created nature but of the nature of the Son, who unites us to the Father through the Spirit that is in him. This is what John teaches, when he writes, as has been cited above, "This is how we know that we remain in God and he in us, in that he has given us his Spirit" (1 Jn 4:13). But if we become sharers in the divine nature through participation in the Spirit, one would have to be crazy to say that the Spirit is of a created nature and not of the nature of God, for that is how those in whom the Spirit is become divinized. But if the Spirit divinizes, it is not to be doubted that it is of the nature of God himself.

And for a still clearer negation of this heresy, the psalmist sings in the one-hundred-and-third psalm, as we have previously quoted: "You will take away their spirit and they will perish and return to their dust. You will send forth your spirit and they will be created, and you will renew the face of the earth" (Ps 104:29–30). And Paul writes to Titus: "Through the bath of regeneration and the renewal of the Holy Spirit, which he poured out richly upon us through Jesus Christ" (Titus 3:5–6). But if the Father creates and renews all things through the Son and in the Holy Spirit, what likeness or kinship can there be between creatures and the Creator? Or how can it at all be the case that the one in whom everything is created is a creature?

Baptism of Jesus in Water and Spirit

From Athanasius, *Defense against the Arians* 1.12.46–48, NPNF[2] 4:332–35.

The Lord Himself hath said by His own mouth in the Gospel according to John, "I have sent them into the world, and for their sakes do I sanctify Myself, that they may be sanctified in the truth" [John 17:18–19]. In saying this He has shown that He is not the sanctified, but the Sanctifier; for He is not sanctified by other, but Himself sanctifies Himself, that we may be sanctified in the truth. He who sanctifies Himself is Lord of sanctification. How then does this take place? What does He mean but this? "I, being the Father's Word, I give to Myself, when becoming man, the Spirit; and Myself, become man, do I sanctify in Him, that henceforth in Me, who am Truth (for 'Thy Word is Truth'), all may be sanctified" [John 17:17].

47. If then for our sake He sanctifies Himself, and does this when He is become man, it is very plain that the Spirit's descent on Him in Jordan was a descent upon us, because of His bearing our body. And it did not take place for promotion to the Word, but again for our sanctification, that we might share His anointing, and of us it might be said, "Know ye not that ye are God's Temple, and the Spirit of God dwelleth in you?" [1 Cor. 6:19]. For when the Lord, as man, was washed in Jordan, it was we who were washed in Him and by Him. And when He received the Spirit, we it was who by Him were made recipients of It. And moreover for this reason, not as Aaron or David or the rest, was He anointed with oil, but in another way above all His fellows, "with the oil of gladness" [Ps. 45:7], which He Himself interprets to be the Spirit, saying by the Prophet, "The Spirit of the Lord is upon Me, because the Lord hath anointed Me" [Luke 4:18]; as also the Apostle has said, "How God anointed Him with the Holy Ghost" [Acts 10:38]. When then were these things spoken of Him but when He came in the flesh and was baptized in Jordan, and the Spirit descended on Him? And indeed the Lord Himself said, "The Spirit shall take of Mine" [John 16:13]; and "I will send Him" [John 16:7]; and to His disciples, "Receive ye the Holy Ghost" [John 20:22]. And notwithstanding, He who, as the Word and Radiance of the Father, gives to others, now is said to be sanctified, because now He has become man, and the Body that is sanctified is His. From Him then we have begun to receive the unction and the seal, John saying, "And ye have an unction from the Holy One" [1 John 2:20]; and the Apostle, "And ye were sealed with the Holy Spirit of promise" [Eph. 1:14]. Therefore because of us and for us are these words. What advance then of promotion, and reward of virtue or generally of conduct, is proved from this in our Lord's instance? . . . And if, as the Lord Himself has said, the Spirit is His, and takes of His, and He sends It, it is not the Word, considered as the Word and Wisdom, who is anointed with the Spirit which He Himself gives, but the flesh assumed by Him which is anointed in Him and by Him; that the sanctification coming to the Lord as man, may come to all men from Him.

48. . . . Surely as, before His becoming man, He, the Word, dispensed to the saints the Spirit as His own, so also when made man, He sanctifies all by the Spirit and says to His Disciples, "Receive ye the Holy Ghost" [John 20:22]. And He gave to Moses and the other seventy; and through Him David prayed to the Father, saying, "Take

not Thy Holy Spirit from me" [Ps. 51:11]. On the other hand, when made man, He said, "I will send to you the Paraclete, the Spirit of truth" [John 15:26]; and He sent Him, He, the Word of God, as being faithful. Therefore "Jesus Christ is the same yesterday, to-day, and for ever" [Heb. 13:8], remaining unalterable, and at once gives and receives, giving as God's Word, receiving as man. It is not the Word then, viewed as the Word, that is promoted; for He had all things and has them always; but men, who have in Him and through Him their origin of receiving them. For, when He is now said to be anointed in a human respect, we it is who in Him are anointed; since also when He is baptized, we it is who in Him are baptized. But on all these things the Saviour throws much light, when He says to the Father, "And the glory which Thou gavest Me, I have given to them, that they may be one, even as We are one" [John 17:22].

Divine Union

Further explaining the Johannine Jesus' sayings of the mutual indwelling of the Father and Son, Athanasius elaborates on the significance of this union for our union with the Triune God in the Spirit.

From Athanasius, *Defense against the Arians* 3.25.25, NPNF² 4:407.

The Saviour, then, saying of us, "As Thou, Father, art in Me, and I in Thee, that they too may be one in Us" [John 17:21], does not signify that we were to have identity with Him; for this was shewn from the instance of Jonah; but it is a request to the Father, as John has written, that the Spirit should be vouchsafed through Him to those who believe, through whom we are found to be in God, and in this respect to be conjoined in Him. For since the Word is in the Father, and the Spirit is given from the Word, He wills that we should receive the Spirit, that, when we receive It, thus having the Spirit of the Word which is in the Father, we too may be found on account of the Spirit to become One in the Word, and through Him in the Father. And if He say, "as we" [John 17:22], this again is only a request that such grace of the Spirit as is given to the disciples may be without failure or revocation. For what the Word has by nature, as I said, in the Father, that He wishes to be given to us through the Spirit irrevocably; which the Apostle knowing, said, "Who shall separate us from the love of Christ" [Rom. 8:35] for "the gifts of God" and "grace of His calling are without repentance" [Rom. 11:29]. It is the Spirit then which is in God, and not we viewed in our own selves; and as we are sons and gods because of the Word in us, so we shall be in the Son and in the Father, and we shall be accounted to have become one in Son and in Father, because that Spirit is in us, which is in the Word which is in the Father. When then a man falls from the Spirit for any wickedness, if he repent upon his fall, the grace remains irrevocably to such as are willing; otherwise he who has fallen is no longer in God (because that Holy Spirit and Paraclete which is in God has deserted him), but the sinner shall be in him to whom he has subjected himself, as took place in Saul's instance; for the Spirit of God departed from him and an evil spirit was afflicting him. God's enemies hearing this ought to be henceforth abashed, and no longer to feign themselves equal to God. But they neither understand (for "the irreligious," he saith, "does not understand knowledge") nor endure religious words, but find them heavy even to hear.

The Power of the Spirit

While we do not know if Athanasius wrote *Life of Antony*, a hagiography—biography of a holy person, in this case a monk by the name Antony—its influence on the post-Nicene church's spirituality, especially the ascetic life, has been significant. Therefore, leaving the question of its authenticity to continuing historical debates, the work's contribution to emerging pneumatological doctrine and spirituality is being discussed in the context of St. Athanasius.

Among other topics, *Life of Antony* discusses widely the role of evil spirits and demons and how those could be combated. Various types of miracles, including healings, are attributed to Antony.

From Athanasius, *Life of Antony* 48, 49, *NPNF*[2] 4:209.

48. When therefore he [Antony] had retired and determined to fix a time, after which neither to go forth himself nor admit anybody, Martinian, a military officer, came and disturbed Antony. For he had a daughter afflicted with an evil spirit. But when he continued for a long while knocking at the door, and asking him to come out and pray to God for his child, Antony, not bearing to open, looked out from above and said, "Man, why dost thou call on me? I also am a man even as you. But if you believe on Christ whom I serve, go, and according as you believe, pray to God, and it shall come to pass" [Acts 3:12]. Straightway, therefore, he departed, believing and calling upon Christ, and he received his daughter cleansed from the devil. Many other things also through Antony the Lord did, who saith, "Seek and it shall be given unto you" [Luke 11:9]. For many of the sufferers, when he would not open his door, slept outside his cell, and by their faith and sincere prayers were healed.

49. But when he saw himself beset by many, and not suffered to withdraw himself according to his intent as he wished, fearing because of the signs which the Lord wrought by him, that either he

should be puffed up, or that some other should think of him above what he ought to think, he considered and set off to go into the upper Thebaid, among those to whom he was unknown.

The Cappadocians

The Cappadocians wrote against the Pneumatomachoi, the fighters of the Spirit who undermined the Nicean orthodoxy and thus echoed Arian misgivings about the equality of the Son with the Father. The Cappadocians never call the Spirit "God," since the Bible does not do so, yet in more than one way they affirm the equality of the Spirit with the Son and the Father in the Trinity. The closest St. Basil comes to affirm this is to say "that the Holy Spirit partakes of the fullness of divinity" (*On the Holy Spirit* 18.46), and he also calls the Spirit "Lord" based on biblical teaching (*On the Holy Spirit* 21.52). Biblical, liturgical, and sacramental (water baptism) grounds are used as well as the weight of tradition, that is, *lex orandi lex credendi*. Basil lists a number of his predecessors whom he finds supporting his teaching, such as Irenaeus, Clement of Rome, Origen, and many more (*On the Holy Spirit* 29.71–74).

St. Basil the Great

Basil, who had received training in rhetoric and logic, offers a highly sophisticated and detailed rebuttal of the arguments set forth by the Pneumatomachoi, analyzing the pronouns used both in the beginning (*On the Holy Spirit* 2.4–5.12) and end of the treatise (*On the Holy Spirit* 25.58–27.68). While focusing on the Holy Spirit, Basil's treatise is indeed a powerful Trinitarian exposition in which the status of the Son in relation to the Father is dealt with in quite an extensive manner (*On the Holy Spirit* 6.13–7.21). While he never says directly, "the Holy Spirit is God," he affirms the Spirit's divinity. One of his lasting contributions—and an idea that also was contested by opponents—is the introduction of a new doxological formula: "Glory to the Father with the Son together with the Holy Spirit" replacing the older one "Glory to the Father through the Son in the Holy Spirit." Therefore, it was appropriate to glorify the Spirit along with the Father and Son (*On the Holy Spirit* 19.48). He acknowledged that this new phrase was considered to be a novelty and against the tradition (*On the Holy Spirit* 1.3, 13), yet he still believed it was in keeping with biblical teaching and tradition. Those who opposed the equality of the Spirit in the Trinity were not only in error but were also "transgressors" (*On the Holy Spirit* 11.27).

"The Law of Prayer is the Law of Believing"
Because the Spirit is holy, only a purified mind may behold the Spirit.

From Basil, *On the Holy Spirit* 9.23, *NPNF*[2] 8:15–16.

Only then after a man is purified from the shame whose stain he took through his wickedness, and has come back again to his natural beauty, and as it were cleaning the Royal Image and restoring its ancient form, only thus is it possible for him to draw near to the Paraclete. And He, like the sun, will by the aid of thy purified eye show thee in Himself the image of the invisible, and in the blessed spectacle of the image thou shalt behold the unspeakable beauty of the archetype. Through His aid hearts are lifted up, the weak are held by the hand, and they who are advancing are brought to perfection. Shining upon those that are cleansed from every spot, He makes them spiritual by fellowship with Himself. Just as when a sunbeam falls on bright and transparent bodies, they themselves become brilliant too, and shed forth a fresh brightness from themselves, so souls wherein the Spirit dwells, illuminated by the Spirit, themselves become spiritual, and send forth their grace to others. Hence comes foreknowledge of the future, understanding of mysteries, apprehension of what is hidden, distribution of good gifts, the heavenly citizenship, a place in the chorus of angels, joy without end, abiding in God, the being made like to God, and, highest of all, the being made God. Such, then, to instance a few out of many, are the conceptions concerning the Holy Spirit, which we have been taught to hold concerning His greatness, His dignity, and His operations, by the oracles of the Spirit themselves.

In keeping with the *lex orandi lex credendi* rule, Basil, with other Cappadocians, derived even the most sophisticated Trinitarian and pneumatological formulae from liturgy and soteriology. The following quote from a short letter to a deaconess makes this clear.

From Basil, *Letter 15*, *NPNF*[2] 8:186.

You have professed your faith in Father, Son and Holy Ghost. Do not abandon this deposit; the Father—origin of all; the Son—Only begotten, begotten of Him, very God, Perfect of Perfect, living image, shewing the whole Father in Himself; the Holy Ghost, having His subsistence of God, the fount of holiness, power that gives life, grace that maketh perfect, through Whom man is adopted, and the mortal made immortal, conjoined with Father and Son in all things in glory and eternity, in power and kingdom, in sovereignty and godhead; as is testified by the tradition of the baptism of salvation.

Not only is there order, *taxis*, of the Trinity with regard to the role of the Father, Son, and Spirit; there is also an epistemological order in that the knowledge of God proceeds from "the Spirit of knowledge" via the Son to the Father and back.

From Basil, *On the Holy Spirit* 18.47, NPNF² 8:29.

"No man knoweth the Father save the Son." And so "no man can say that Jesus is the Lord but by the Holy Ghost." For it is not said through the Spirit, but by the Spirit, and "God is a spirit, and they that worship Him must worship Him in spirit and in truth," as it is written "in thy light shall we see light," namely by the illumination of the Spirit, "the true light which lighteth every man that cometh into the world." It results that in Himself He shows the glory of the Only begotten, and on true worshippers He in Himself bestows the knowledge of God. Thus the way of the knowledge of God lies from One Spirit through the One Son to the One Father, and conversely the natural Goodness and the inherent Holiness and the royal Dignity extend from the Father through the Only-begotten to the Spirit.

On the Nature of the Holy Spirit
The Spirit as incorporeal and unlimited.

From Basil, *On the Holy Spirit* 9.22, NPNF² 8:15.

Let us now investigate what are our common conceptions concerning the Spirit, as well those which have been gathered by us from Holy Scripture concerning It as those which we have received from the unwritten tradition of the Fathers. First of all we ask, who on hearing the titles of the Spirit is not lifted up in soul, who does not raise his conception to the supreme nature? It is called "Spirit of God," "Spirit of truth which proceedeth from the Father," "right Spirit," "a leading Spirit." Its proper and peculiar title is "Holy Spirit," which is a name specially appropriate to everything that is incorporeal, purely immaterial, and indivisible. So our Lord, when teaching the woman who thought God to be an object of local worship that the incorporeal is incomprehensible, said "God is a spirit." On our hearing, then, of a spirit, it is impossible to form the idea of a nature circumscribed, subject to change and variation, or at all like the creature. We are compelled to advance in our conceptions to the highest, and to think of an intelligent essence, in power infinite, in magnitude unlimited, unmeasured by times or ages, generous of Its good gifts, to whom turn all things needing sanctification, after whom reach all things that live in virtue, as being watered by Its inspiration and helped on toward their natural and proper end; perfecting all other things, but Itself in nothing lacking; living not as needing restoration, but as Supplier of life; not growing by additions; but straightway full, self-established, omnipresent, origin of sanctification, light perceptible to the mind, supplying, as it were, through Itself, illumination to every faculty in the search for truth; by nature unapproachable, apprehended by reason of goodness, filling all things with Its power, but communicated only to the worthy; not shared in one measure, but distributing Its energy according to "the proportion of faith"; in essence simple, in powers various, wholly present in each and being wholly everywhere; impassively divided, shared without loss of ceasing to be entire, after the likeness of the sunbeam, whose kindly light falls on him who enjoys it as though it shone for him alone, yet illumines land and sea and mingles with the air. So, too, is the Spirit to every one who receives it, as though given to him alone, and yet It sends forth grace sufficient and full for all mankind, and is enjoyed by all who share It, according to the capacity, not of Its power, but of their nature.

The Spirit's nature and works are described in ways characteristic of God.

From Basil, *On the Holy Spirit* 19.49, NPNF[2] 8:30–31.

And His operations, what are they? For majesty ineffable, and for numbers innumerable. How shall we form a conception of what extends beyond the ages? What were His operations before that creation whereof we can conceive? How great the grace which He conferred on creation? What the power exercised by Him over the ages to come? He existed; He pre-existed; He co-existed with the Father and the Son before the ages. It follows that, even if you can conceive of anything beyond the ages, you will find the Spirit yet further above and beyond. And if you think of the creation, the powers of the heavens were established by the Spirit, the establishment being understood to refer to disability to fall away from good. For it is from the Spirit that the powers derive their close relationship to God, their inability to change to evil, and their continuance in blessedness. Is it Christ's advent? The Spirit is forerunner. Is there the incarnate presence? The Spirit is inseparable. Working of miracles, and gifts of healing are through the Holy Spirit. Demons were driven out by the Spirit of God. The devil was brought to naught by the presence of the Spirit. Remission of sins was by the gift of the Spirit, for "ye were washed, ye were sanctified, . . . in the name of the Lord Jesus Christ, and in the holy Spirit of our God." There is close relationship with God through the Spirit, for "God hath sent forth the Spirit of His Son into your hearts, crying Abba, Father." The resurrection from the dead is effected by the operation of the Spirit, for "Thou sendest forth thy spirit, they are created; and Thou renewest the face of the earth." If here creation may be taken to mean the bringing of the departed to life again, how mighty is not the operation of the Spirit, Who is to us the dispenser of the life that follows on the resurrection, and attunes our souls to the spiritual life beyond?

A Trinitarian Pneumatology of Salvation
Salvation is the work of the Trinity.

From Basil, *On the Holy Spirit* 10.26, NPNF[2] 8:17.

And in what way are we saved? Plainly because we were regenerate through the grace given in our baptism. How else could we be? And after recognising that this salvation is established through the Father and the Son and the Holy Ghost, shall we fling away "that form of doctrine" which we received? . . . For if to me my baptism was the beginning of life, and that day of regeneration the first of days, it is plain that the utterance uttered in the grace of adoption was the most honourable of all. Can I then, perverted by these men's seductive words, abandon the tradition which guided me to the light, which bestowed on me the boon of the knowledge of God, whereby I, so long a foe by reason of sin, was made a child of God? But, for myself, I pray that with this confession I may depart hence to the Lord, and them I charge to preserve the faith secure until the day of Christ, and to keep the Spirit undivided from the Father and the Son, preserving, both in the confession of faith and in the doxology, the doctrine taught them at their baptism.

From Basil, *On the Holy Spirit* 15.36, NPNF[2] 8:22.

Through the Holy Spirit comes our restoration to paradise, our ascension into the kingdom of heaven, our return to the adoption of sons, our liberty to call God our Father, our being made partakers of the grace of Christ, our being called children of light, our sharing in eternal glory, and, in a word, our being brought into a state of all "fulness of blessing," both in this world and in the world to come, of all the good gifts that are in store for us, by promise hereof, through faith, beholding the reflection of their grace as though they were already present, we await the full enjoyment.

The Spirit and Eschatology
The Spirit's role in the eschaton is highlighted here.

From Basil, *On the Holy Spirit* 16.40, NPNF[2] 8:25.

Moreover by any one who carefully uses his reason it will be found that even at the moment of the expected appearance of the Lord from heaven the Holy Spirit will not, as some suppose, have no functions to discharge: on the contrary, even in the day of His revelation, in which the blessed and only potentate will judge the world in righteousness, the Holy Spirit will be present with Him. For who is so ignorant of the good things prepared by God for them that are worthy, as not to know that the crown of the righteous is the grace of the Spirit, bestowed in more abundant and perfect measure in that day, when spiritual glory shall be distributed to each in proportion as he shall have nobly played the man? . . . They, then, that were sealed by the Spirit unto the day of redemption, and preserve pure and undiminished the first fruits which they received of the Spirit, are they that shall hear the words "well done thou good and faithful servant; thou hast been faithful over a few things, I will make thee ruler over many things" [Matt. 25:23]. In like manner they which have grieved the Holy Spirit by the wickedness of their ways, or have not wrought for Him that gave to them, shall be deprived of what they have received, their grace being transferred to others.

Gregory of Nyssa

St. Basil's brother Gregory, the bishop of Nyssa, wrote *On the Holy Trinity of the Godhead of the Holy Spirit to Eustathius* and *On the Holy Spirit against the Followers of Macedonius* (381), in which he defends the Cappadocian conviction of the equality of the Spirit in the Trinity. Macedonius was a sectarian leader with Arian and Eunomian tendencies, deposed from the See of Constantinople, 360 CE, who compromised the divinity and full equality of the Spirit with the Father.

The Spirit Equal to the Father and Son
While Gregory never uses the term *homoousios* of the Spirit, in many ways he confirms the equality of the Spirit with the Father and Son and lists attributes pertaining to God.

From Gregory of Nyssa, *On the Holy Spirit against the
Followers of Macedonius,*[4] *NPNF*[2] 5:323.

The Holy Spirit is . . . because of qualities that are essentially holy, that
which the Father, essentially Holy, is; and such as the Only-begotten
is, such is the Holy Spirit; then, again, He is so by virtue of life-giving,
of imperishability, of unvariableness, of everlastingness, of justice, of
wisdom, of rectitude, of sovereignty, of goodness, of power, of capacity to give all good things, and above them all life itself, and by being
everywhere, being present in each, filling the earth, residing in the
heavens, shed abroad upon supernatural Powers, filling all things
according to the deserts of each, Himself remaining full, being with
all who are worthy, and yet not parted from the Holy Trinity. He ever
"searches the deep things of God," ever "receives" from the Son, ever
is being "sent," and yet not separated, and being "glorified," and yet
He has always had glory.

The Unity of the Works of the Trinity
The unity of the three persons in their outward works in the world occurs
in a manner different from the way several human beings collaborate.
Gregory materially affirms the Augustinian rule according to which the
works of the Trinity *ad extra* are indivisible.

From Gregory of Nyssa, *On "Not Three Gods," NPNF*[2] 5:334.

Thus, since among men the action of each in the same pursuits is
discriminated, they are properly called many, since each of them is
separated from the others within his own environment, according to
the special character of his operation. But in the case of the Divine
nature we do not similarly learn that the Father does anything by
Himself in which the Son does not work conjointly, or again that the
Son has any special operation apart from the Holy Spirit; but every
operation which extends from God to the Creation, and is named
according to our variable conceptions of it, has its origin from the
Father, and proceeds through the Son, and is perfected in the Holy
Spirit. For this reason the name derived from the operation is not
divided with regard to the number of those who fulfil it, because the
action of each concerning anything is not separate and peculiar, but
whatever comes to pass, in reference either to the acts of His providence for us, or to the government and constitution of the universe,
comes to pass by the action of the Three, yet what does come to pass

---

4. There are no subdivisions (chapters or paragraphs) marked in the document; hence, only pages
in *NPNF*[2] 5 are given.

is not three things. We may understand the meaning of this from one single instance. From Him, I say, Who is the chief source of gifts, all things which have shared in this grace have obtained their life. When we inquire, then, whence this good gift came to us, we find by the guidance of the Scriptures that it was from the Father, Son, and Holy Spirit. Since then the Holy Trinity fulfils every operation . . . not by separate action according to the number of the Persons, but so that there is one motion and disposition of the good will which is communicated from the Father through the Son to the Spirit (for as we do not call those whose operation gives one life three Givers of life, neither do we call those who are contemplated in one goodness three Good beings, nor speak of them in the plural by any of their other attributes); so neither can we call those who exercise this Divine and superintending power and operation towards ourselves and all creation, conjointly and inseparably, by their mutual action, three Gods.

Spirit Christology

With Athanasius and other Cappadocians, Gregory of Nyssa develops a Spirit Christology. Going back to the Old Testament custom of anointing the king with oil, Gregory draws theological lessons from the metaphor of Christ as king and the Spirit as unction.

From Gregory of Nyssa, *On the Holy Spirit*, NPNF[2] 5:321.

For as between the body's surface and the liquid of the oil nothing intervening can be detected, either in reason or in perception, so inseparable is the union of the Spirit with the Son; and the result is that whosoever is to touch the Son by faith must needs first encounter the oil in the very act of touching; there is not a part of Him devoid of the Holy Spirit. Therefore belief in the Lordship of the Son arises in those who entertain it, by means of the Holy Ghost; on all sides the Holy Ghost is met by those who by faith approach the Son. If, then, the Son is essentially a King, and the Holy Spirit is that dignity of Kingship which anoints the Son, what deprivation of this Kingship, in its essence and comparing it with itself, can be imagined?

Salvation as Deification

In *On the Baptism of Christ*, in keeping with the soteriology of the East, Gregory applies this Spirit Christology to salvation and the sacraments and explains our deification in terms of the incarnation and the Spirit's ministry. His careful pneumatological and Trinitarian reflection on sacramental theology is profound.

From Gregory of Nyssa, *On the Baptism of Christ*, NPNF[2] 5:518–20.

Christ . . . is baptized by John that He might cleanse him who was defiled, that He might bring the Spirit from above, and exalt man to heaven, that he who had fallen might be raised up and he who had cast him down might be put to shame. And marvel not if God showed so great earnestness in our cause: for it was with care on the part of him who did us wrong that the plot was laid against us; it is with forethought on the part of our Maker that we are saved. . . . But Christ, the repairer of his evil-doing, assumes manhood in its fulness, and saves man, and becomes the type and figure of us all, to sanctify the first-fruits of every action, and leave to His servants no doubt in their zeal for the tradition. Baptism, then, is a purification from sins, a remission of trespasses, a cause of renovation and regeneration. . . . And this gift it is not the water that bestows (for in that case it were a thing more exalted than all creation), but the command of God, and the visitation of the Spirit that comes sacramentally to set us free. But water serves to express the cleansing. For since we are wont by washing in water to render our body clean when it is soiled by dirt or mud, we therefore apply it also in the sacramental action, and display the spiritual brightness by that which is subject to our senses. . . . "Except a man be born of water and of the Spirit, he cannot enter into the kingdom of God" [John 3:5]. Why are both named, and why is not the Spirit alone accounted sufficient for the completion of Baptism? Man, as we know full well, is compound, not simple: and therefore the cognate and similar medicines are assigned for healing to him who is twofold and conglomerate:—for his visible body, water, the sensible element,—for his soul, which we cannot see, the Spirit invisible, invoked by faith, present unspeakably. For "the Spirit breathes where He wills, and thou hearest His voice, but canst not tell whence He cometh or whither He goeth" [John 3:8]. He blesses the body that is baptized, and the water that baptizes. Despise not, therefore, the Divine laver, nor think lightly of it, as a common thing, on account of the use of water. For the power that operates is mighty, and wonderful are the things that are wrought thereby. For this holy altar, too, by which I stand, is stone, ordinary in its nature, nowise different from the other slabs of stone that build our houses and adorn our pavements; but seeing that it was consecrated to the service of God, and received the benediction, it is a holy table, an altar undefiled, no longer touched by the hands of all, but of the priests alone, and that with reverence. The bread again is at first common bread, but when the sacramental action consecrates it, it is called, and becomes, the Body of Christ. So with the sacramental oil; so with the wine: though before the benediction they are of little value, each of them, after the sanctification bestowed by the Spirit, has its several operation. The same power of the word, again, also makes the priest venerable and honourable, separated, by the new blessing bestowed upon him, from his community with the mass of men. While but yesterday he was one of the mass, one of the people, he is suddenly rendered a guide, a president, a teacher of righteousness, an instructor in hidden mysteries; and this he does without being at all changed in body or in form; but, while continuing to be in all appearance the man he was before, being, by some unseen power and grace, transformed in respect of his unseen soul to the higher condition. . . . And the wood of the Cross is of saving efficacy for all men, though it is, as I am informed, a piece of a poor tree, less valuable than most trees are. So a bramble bush showed to Moses the manifestation of the presence of God: so the remains of Elisha raised a dead man to life; so clay gave sight to him that was blind from the womb. And all these things, though they were matter without soul or sense, were made the means for the performance of the great marvels wrought by them, when they received the power of God. Now by a similar train of reasoning, water also, though it is nothing else than water, renews the man to spiritual regeneration, when the grace from above hallows it.

Gifts and Strength of the Spirit

The Spirit also brings about charisms and the strength for the Christian walk. Yet purity of life is a prerequisite for an appropriate use and reception of these gifts.

From Gregory of Nyssa, *On the Christian Mode of Life*, in *The Fathers of the Church* (Washington, DC: Catholic University of America Press, 1947–), 58:141–42.[5]

Do not acquiesce in His gifts, thinking that because of the wealth and ungrudging grace of the Spirit nothing else is needed for perfection. When these riches come to you be modest in thought, ever submissive and thinking of love as the foundation of the treasure of grace for the soul, struggle against all passion until you come to the height of the goal of reverence which the apostle himself came first and to which he leads his disciples through prayer and teaching, showing to those who love the Lord the change for the better and the grace which results from love, when he says . . . "If any man is in Christ, he is a new creature, the former things have passed away" [2 Cor. 5:17]. The "new creation" is the apostolic rule. And what this

5. There are no subdivisions (chapters or paragraphs) marked in the document; hence, only pages in *Fathers of the Church* are given here.

is he makes abundantly clear in another section, saying: "In order that I might present to myself the church in all her glory, not having spot or wrinkle or any such thing, but that she might be holy and without blemish" [Eph. 1:4]. A new creature he called the indwelling of the Holy Spirit in a pure and blameless soul removed from evil and wickedness and shamefulness. For, when the soul hates sin, it closely, unites itself with God, as far as *it* can, in the regimen of virtue;—having been transformed in life, it receives the grace of the Spirit to itself, becomes entirely new again and is recreated.

Gregory of Nazianzus

In the Eastern Orthodox tradition, only three persons are called "theologians": St. John the Evangelist, Gregory of Nazianzus (or Nazianzen), and Symeon the New Theologian. A one-time bishop and presider of the Council of Constantinople for a while, Nazianzen's five sermons known as *The Theological Orations* helped clarify significantly Trinitarian issues against Arians, Eunomians, and other who contested orthodoxy. The final oration, the fifth one, is devoted to the Holy Spirit. In keeping with the ancient and contemporary Eastern teaching, he regarded the Father as the "monarchy" in the Trinity; yet at the same time he believed it to be "a Monarchy that is not limited to one Person" (29.2) and that therefore the inferiority of either the Son or the Spirit does not follow.

The Way of the Knowledge of God
Historically, a fuller pneumatological understanding should come gradually, by way of progressive revelation.

From Gregory of Nazianzus, *On the Holy Spirit* 26, NPNF[2] 7:326.

The Old Testament proclaimed the Father openly, and the Son more obscurely. The New manifested the Son, and suggested the Deity of the Spirit. Now the Spirit Himself dwells among us, and supplies us with a clearer demonstration of Himself. For it was not safe, when the Godhead of the Father was not yet acknowledged, plainly to proclaim the Son; nor when that of the Son was not yet received to burden us further (if I may use so bold an expression) with the Holy Ghost; lest perhaps people might, like men loaded with food beyond their strength, and presenting eyes as yet too weak to bear it to the sun's light, risk the loss even of that which was within the reach of their powers; but that by gradual additions, and, as David says, Goings up, and advances and progress from glory to glory, the Light of the Trinity might shine upon the more illuminated. For this reason it was, I think, that He *gradually* came to dwell in the Disciples, measuring Himself out to them according to their capacity to receive Him, at the beginning of the Gospel, after the Passion, after the Ascension, making perfect their powers, being breathed upon them, and appearing in fiery tongues. And indeed it is by little and little that He is declared by Jesus, as you will learn for yourself if you will read more carefully. I will ask the Father, He says, and He will send you another Comforter, even the spirit of Truth.

While using all the logical and rhetorical skills, the theologian of the church of the East followed the ancient *lex orandi lex credendi* rule, according to which theological knowledge is gained primarily from the liturgy and the Spirit's role in salvation, that is, deification. Speaking of the Triune God in general and the Holy Spirit in particular, Gregory writes the following.

From Gregory of Nazianzus, *On the Holy Spirit* 28, NPNF[2] 7:327.

For if He is not to be worshipped, how can He deify me by Baptism? but if He is to be worshipped, surely He is an Object of adoration, and if an Object of adoration He must be God; the one is linked to the other, a truly golden and saving chain. And indeed from the Spirit comes our New Birth, and from the New Birth our new creation, and from the new creation our deeper knowledge of the dignity of Him from Whom it is derived.

Therefore, nothing less than our salvation, deification, is at stake in the right understanding of the status and nature of the Spirit.

Gregory attacks the Pneumatomachoi aggressively.

From Gregory of Nazianzus, *On the Holy Spirit* 5, NPNF[2] 7:319.

And of the Greeks those who are more inclined to speak of God, and who approach nearest to us, have formed some conception of Him, as it seems to me, though they have differed as to His Name, and have addressed Him as the Mind of the World, or the External Mind, and the like. But of the wise men amongst ourselves, some have conceived of him as an Activity, some as a Creature, some as God; and some have been uncertain which to call Him, out of reverence for Scripture, they say, as though it did not make the matter clear either way. And therefore they neither worship Him nor treat Him with dishonour, but take up a neutral position, or rather a very miserable one, with respect to Him. And of those who consider Him to be God, some are orthodox in mind only, while others venture to be so with the lips also.

The Preeminence of the Spirit as Divine

Gregory does not tire in mounting evidence of various names and works assigned to the Spirit that speak for his deity and equality with the Son.

From Gregory of Nazianzus, *On the Holy Spirit* 29, NPNF[2] 7:327.

Indeed I tremble when I think of the abundance of the titles, and how many Names they outrage who fall foul of the Spirit. He is called the Spirit of God, the Spirit of Christ, the Mind of Christ, the Spirit of The Lord, and Himself The Lord, the Spirit of Adoption, of Truth, of Liberty; the Spirit of Wisdom, of Understanding, of Counsel, of Might, of Knowledge, of Godliness, of the Fear of God. For He is the Maker of all these, filling all with His Essence, containing all things, filling the world in His Essence, yet incapable of being comprehended in His power by the world; good, upright, princely, by nature not by adoption; sanctifying, not sanctified; measuring, not measured; shared, not sharing; filling, not filled; containing, not contained; inherited, glorified, reckoned with the Father and the Son; held out as a threat; the Finger of God; fire like God; to manifest, as I take it, His consubstantiality; the Creator-Spirit, Who by Baptism and by Resurrection creates anew; the Spirit That knoweth all things, That teacheth, That bloweth where and to what extent He listeth; That guideth, talketh, sendeth forth, separateth, is angry or tempted; That revealeth, illumineth, quickeneth, or rather is the very Light and Life; That maketh Temples; That deifieth; That perfecteth so as even to anticipate Baptism, yet after Baptism to be sought as a separate gift; That doeth all things that God doeth; divided into fiery tongues; dividing gifts; making Apostles, Prophets, Evangelists, Pastors, and Teachers; understanding manifold, clear, piercing, undefiled, unhindered, which is the same thing as Most wise and varied in His actions; and making all things clear and plain; and of independent power, unchangeable, Almighty, all-seeing, penetrating all spirits that are intelligent, pure, most subtle (the Angel Hosts I think); and also all prophetic spirits and apostolic in the same manner and not in the same places; for they lived in different places; thus showing that He is uncircumscript.

The following passage from Gregory's treatise *On Pentecost* exalts the greatness of the Holy Spirit in a most profound way.

From Gregory of Nazianzus, *Oration* 41, *On Pentecost* 11, NPNF[2] 7:382.

The Holy Ghost, then, always existed, and exists, and always will exist. He neither had a beginning, nor will He have an end; but He was everlastingly ranged with and numbered with the Father and the Son. For it was not ever fitting that either the Son should be wanting to the Father, or the Spirit to the Son. For then Deity would be shorn of Its Glory in its greatest respect, for It would seem to have arrived at the consummation of perfection as if by an after-thought. Therefore He was ever being partaken, but not partaking; perfecting, not being perfected; sanctifying, not being sanctified; deifying, not being deified; Himself ever the same with Himself, and with Those with Whom He is ranged; invisible, eternal, incomprehensible, unchangeable, without quality, without quantity, without form, impalpable, self-moving, eternally moving, with free-will, self-powerful, All-powerful (even though all that is of the Spirit is referable to the First Cause, just as is all that is of the Only-begotten); Life and Lifegiver; Light and Lightgiver; absolute Good, and Spring of Goodness; the Right, the Princely Spirit; the Lord, the Sender, the Separator; Builder of His own Temple; leading, working as He wills; distributing His own Gifts; the Spirit of Adoption, of Truth, of Wisdom, of Understanding, of Knowledge, of Godliness, of Counsel, of Fear (which are ascribed to Him) by Whom the Father is known and the Son is glorified; and by Whom *alone* He is known; one class, one service, worship, power, perfection, sanctification.

The theologian argues with the force of logic for the eternity of all three members.

From Gregory of Nazianzus, *On the Holy Spirit* 4, NPNF[2] 7:318–19.

4. If ever there was a time when the Father was not, then there was a time when the Son was not. If ever there was a time when the Son was not, then there was a time when the Spirit was not. If the One was from the beginning, then the Three were so too. If you throw down the One, I am bold to assert that you do not set up the other Two. For what profit is there in an imperfect Godhead? Or rather, what Godhead can there be if It is not perfect? And how can that be perfect which lacks something of perfection? And surely there is something lacking if it hath not the Holy, and how would it have this if it were without the Spirit? For either holiness is something different from Him, and if so let some one tell me what it is conceived to be; or if it is the same, how is it not from the beginning, as if it were better for God to be at one time imperfect and apart from the Spirit?

Even then the question was raised about whether praying to and worshiping the Spirit is appropriate. Gregory responds in a clever way by showing that indeed prayer to the Spirit means that Spirit is praying in us and helping us pray.

From Gregory of Nazianzus, On the Holy Spirit 12, NPNF² 7:321.

But, he says, who in ancient or modern times ever worshipped the Spirit? Who ever prayed to Him? Where is it written that we ought to worship Him, or to pray to Him, and whence have you derived this tenet of yours? We will give the more perfect reason hereafter, when we discuss the question of the unwritten; for the present it will suffice to say that it is the Spirit in Whom we worship, and in Whom we pray. For Scripture says, God is a Spirit, and they that worship Him must worship Him in Spirit and in truth. And again,—We know not what we should pray for as we ought; but the Spirit Itself maketh intercession for us with groanings which cannot be uttered; and I will pray with the Spirit and I will pray with the understanding also;—that is, in the mind and in the Spirit. Therefore to adore or to pray to the Spirit seems to me to be simply Himself offering prayer or adoration to Himself. And what godly or learned man would disapprove of this, because in fact the adoration of One is the adoration of the Three, because of the equality of honour and Deity between the Three?

Miracles and Charisms

No stranger to miracles, Gregory talks about three significant events in his and his family's life in which the Spirit intervened, saving and protecting. First he tells vividly about the miraculous healings of his father and then his mother, and finally about his own survival in a storm. The occasion for recalling these miracles is extraordinary: they are all to be found in what is one of his most moving passages, in the funeral sermon *Oration 18, On the Death of His Father*, preached in the presence of St. Basil.

From Gregory of Nazianzus, Oration 18, On the Death
of His Father 28–29, NPNF² 7:263–64.

One of the wonders which concern him was that he suffered from sickness and bodily pain. But what wonder is it for even holy men to be distressed, either for the cleansing of their clay, slight though it may be, or a touchstone of virtue and test of philosophy, or for the education of the weaker, who learn from their example to be patient instead of giving way under their misfortunes? Well, he was sick, the time was the holy and illustrious Easter, the queen of days, the brilliant night which dissipates the darkness of sin, upon which with abundant light we keep the feast of our salvation, putting ourselves to death along with the Light once put to death for us, and rising again with Him who rose. This was the time of his sufferings. . . . The skill of physicians, the prayers, most earnest though they were, of his friends, and every possible attention were alike of no avail. He himself in this desperate condition, while his breath came short and fast, had no perception of present things, but was entirely absent, immersed in the objects he had long desired, now made ready for him. We were in the temple, mingling supplications with the sacred rites, for, in despair of all others, we had betaken ourselves to the Great Physician, to the power of that night, and to the last succour, with the intention, shall I say, of keeping a feast, or of mourning; of holding festival, or paying funeral honours to one no longer here? O those tears! which were shed at that time by all the people. O voices, and cries, and hymns blended with the psalmody! From the temple they sought the priest, from the sacred rite the celebrant, from God their worthy ruler, with my Miriam to lead them and strike the timbrel not of triumph, but of supplication; learning then for the first time to be put to shame by misfortune, and calling at once upon the people and upon God; upon the former to sympathize with her distress, and to be lavish of their tears, upon the latter, to listen to her petitions, as, with the inventive genius of suffering, she rehearsed before Him all His wonders of old time.

29. What then was the response of Him who was the God of that night and of the sick man? A shudder comes over me as I proceed with my story. And though you, my hearers, may shudder, do not disbelieve: for that would be impious, when I am the speaker, and in reference to him. The time of the mystery was come, and the reverend station and order, when silence is kept for the solemn rites; and then he was raised up by Him who quickeneth the dead, and by the holy night. At first he moved slightly, then more decidedly; then in a feeble and indistinct voice he called by name one of the servants who was in attendance upon him, and bade him come, and bring his clothes, and support him with his hand. He came in alarm, and gladly waited upon him, while he, leaning upon his hand as upon a staff, imitates Moses upon the mount, arranges his feeble hands in prayer, and in union with, or on behalf of, his people eagerly celebrates the mysteries, in such few words as his strength allowed, but, as it seems to me, with a most perfect intention. What a miracle! In the sanctuary without a sanctuary, sacrificing without an altar, a priest far from the sacred rites: yet all these were present to him in the power of the spirit, recognised by him, though unseen by those who were there. Then, after adding the customary words of thanksgiving, and after blessing the people, he retired again to his bed, and after taking a little food, and enjoying a sleep, he recalled

his spirit, and, his health being gradually recovered, on the new day of the feast, as we call the first Sunday after the festival of the Resurrection, he entered the temple and inaugurated his life which had been preserved, with the full complement of clergy, and offered the sacrifice of thanksgiving. To me this seems no less remarkable than the miracle in the case of Hezekiah, who was glorified by God in his sickness and prayers with an extension of life, and this was signified by the return of the shadow of the degrees, according to the request of the king who was restored, whom God honoured at once by the favour and the sign, assuring him of the extension of his days by the extension of the day.

Pseudo-Macarius (of Egypt)

Before moving to considering post-Nicene Western Fathers, two Eastern Fathers apart from the Greek Fathers discussed above will be presented. The late-fourth-century (?) Pseudo-Macarius is not only highly venerated in Eastern Christian spirituality but has also been acknowledged by Westerners, such as Franciscans, Jesuits, and pietists, as well as John Wesley, who translated Marcarius's *Homilies* into English. The ascetic and hermit St. Macarius lived in the desert community of Skete and was known for profound spiritual insight and charity, including miracles.

Spiritual Exercises as a Means of Acquiring the Spirit
In keeping with the ascetic spirituality of the Christian East, Macarius believes that human effort and suffering is needed for the reception of the Spirit.

> From Pseudo-Macarius, *The Fifty Spiritual Homilies* 9.7, 10, 12, in Pseudo-Macarius, *The Fifty Spiritual Homilies and The Great Letter*, trans., ed., and intro. George A. Maloney (New York: Paulist Press, 1992), 85–87 (hereafter Maloney).

7. We have offered . . . examples from Holy Scripture to show that the power of divine grace is in man and the gift of the Holy Spirit which is given to the faithful soul comes forth with much contention, with much endurance, patience, trials, and testings. Through such, man's free will is put to the test by all sorts of afflictions. And, when man does not grieve the Spirit in any way but is in harmony with grace by keeping all the commandments, then he is regarded as worthy to receive freedom from all passions. He also receives the full adoption of the Spirit, which is always a mystery, along with spiritual riches and wisdom which are not of this world, of which true Christians are made participators. For this reason such persons differ in all

things from other men who have the spirit of this world, for they are endowed with prudence, understanding, and wisdom. . . .

10. But one cannot possess his soul and the love of the heavenly Spirit unless he cuts himself off from all the things of this world and surrenders himself to seek the love of Christ. His mind must be freed of all crass and material concerns so that he may be totally taken up with only one aim, namely, to direct all these things according to the commandments so that his whole concern, striving, attention, and preoccupation of soul may be centered on the search for transcendent values as the soul may strive to be adorned with the Gospel virtues and the heavenly Spirit and may become a participator in the purity and sanctification of Christ. . . .

12. For how lovely it is when a spiritual person consecrates himself totally to the Lord and clings to him alone. He walks in his commands, never forgetting. Reverently honoring the overshadowing presence of the Spirit of Christ, he becomes one spirit with him and one being, just as the Apostle says: "He that is joined to the Lord is one Spirit" (1 Cor 6:17). But if anyone gives himself over to cares or glory or dignities, or is concerned with human honors and diligently sets his heart on these, and if he is full of worldly thoughts or is disturbed or held in bondage to anything of this world, should he want to leap over such, flee from them, and get rid of such dark passions in which he is held captive by the demonic forces, he will be unable to do so. The reason is that he loves and does the will of the dark powers. He does not totally despise the pursuits of evil.

Struggle and self-denial are also the way to acquiring the "armor of the Spirit."

From Pseudo-Macarius, *The Fifty Spiritual Homilies* 27.13 (Maloney, 179–80).

It is written: "Having begun in the Spirit, do you now finish in the flesh?" (Gal 3:3). Again it says: "Put on the whole armor of the Spirit so that you may be able to stand against the attacks of the devil" (Eph 4:30). These texts speak of two different levels: one where a person was after he put on the armor and the other where he is when he wars against the principalities and powers: namely, in light or in darkness. Again it is written: "That you may be able to quench the fiery darts of the wicked one" (Eph 6:16). And again: "Sadden not the Holy Spirit of God" (Eph 4:30). And again: "It is impossible that those who once were enlightened and tasted the gift of God and were made participators of the Holy Spirit and fell away, be renewed" (Heb 6:4). See, there are those who have been enlightened and have tasted the Lord and still fall. You see that a man possesses the free will to live in harmony with the Spirit and also has the free will to grieve him. Surely he takes up arms to go into the battle and struggle against the enemies. Surely he was enlightened so as to war against the darkness.

The Spirit of Union and Deification
In the Christian East, salvation is perceived in terms of union with God, or deification, which is brought about by the Holy Spirit.

From Pseudo-Macarius, *The Great Letter* (Maloney, 269–70).

Indwelling Spirit
Such a person shows himself to be a pure dwelling place for the adorable and Holy Spirit from whom he receives the immortal peace of Christ, through whom he is joined and united with the Lord. Such a person, accepting the Spirit's grace and joined to the Lord, becomes one Spirit with him (1 Cor 6:17). He performs easily, not only works of virtue, never ceasing to battle against the enemy in order to become stronger than the devil in his wiles, but also more importantly, he takes upon himself the sufferings of the Savior. He delights more in these than the devotees of this life delight in human honors and glory and kingdoms. For Christians, through their continued conversion and the gift of the Holy Spirit to maturity—by the grace that is given to them—prefer above the glory, pleasures, and all that is delightful, the greater desire to be held in contempt for the sake of Christ, to bear all insults and ignominy through faith in God.

From Pseudo-Macarius, *The Great Letter* (Maloney, 257).

Mystical Union
For such a soul, wounded by love for Christ, dies to any other desire in order, I speak boldly, to possess that most beautiful intellectual and mystical communion with Christ according to the immortal quality of divinizing fellowship. Truly, such a soul is blessed and happy, when conquered by spiritual passion, it has worthily become espoused to God the Word. Let her say, "My soul will exalt in the Lord, who has clothed me in the garments of salvation and has wrapt me in the cloak of integrity like a bridegroom wearing his crown, like a bride adorned in her jewels" (Is 61:10). For the King of Glory, ardently desiring her beauty, has deigned to regard her, not only as the temple of God, but also as the daughter of the king and also the queen. Indeed, she is the temple of God, since she is inhabited by the Holy Spirit. She is also the daughter of the king since she has been adopted by the Father of lights. She is also queen as endowed with the divinity of the glory of the Only-Begotten Son.

Contrasting the economy of the law and that of grace, Macarius elaborates on the significance of the baptism with the Spirit

From Pseudo-Macarius, *The Fifty Spiritual Homilies* 47.1–2 (Maloney, 232–33).

1. The glory of Moses which he received on his countenance was a figure of the true glory. . . . With them [Moses and the Jews] was a baptism sanctifying the flesh, but with us there is a baptism of the Holy Spirit and fire. For John preached this: "He shall baptize you in the Holy Spirit and fire" (Mt 3:11).

2. They had an inner and an outer tabernacle, and into the latter the priests went continually, performing the services. But into the former the high priest alone went once a year with the blood, the Holy Spirit signifying that the way into the holiest was not yet made manifest (Heb 9:6ss). Here, however, those who are deemed worthy enter into "the tabernacle not made with hands, whither the fore-runner has entered for us" (Heb 6:20), namely, Christ. It is written in the Law that the priest should receive two doves and should kill one, but sprinkle the living one with its blood and should let it loose to fly away freely (Lv 14:4, 22). But that which was done was a figure and shadow of the truth. For Christ was sacrificed and his blood, sprinkling us, made us grow wings. For he gave to us the wings of the Holy Spirit to fly unencumbered into the air of the Godhead.

The Spirit of Love

Echoing the theology of love of St. Augustine, but certainly independently from him, Pseudo-Macarius contrasts the love of the world and love of God, the latter of which is the function of the Spirit, the Spirit of Love.

From Pseudo-Macarius, *The Fifty Spiritual Homilies* 18.2, 5 (Maloney, 142–44).

2. Therefore, one who has found and possesses within himself the heavenly treasure of the Spirit fulfills all the commands justly and practices all the virtues without blame, purely without forcing and with a certain ease. Let us, therefore, beg God, seeking and pray-ing him to gift us with the treasure of the Spirit in order that we may be empowered to walk in all of his commands without blame and purely, and to fulfill every justice asked of the Spirit with purity and perfection by means of the heavenly treasure which is Christ. For he who is indigent and poor and a beggar in the world cannot acquire anything. His destitution restrains him. But he who pos-sesses the treasure, as I said, easily acquires whatever possessions he wishes without much effort. The soul that is naked and stripped of the fellowship of the Spirit and lives under the terrible poverty of

sin is unable, even if it wished to do so, to produce the fruit of the Spirit of righteousness in truth, unless it becomes a participator of the Spirit. . . .

5. So also it is with those who are rich in the Holy Spirit. They truly possess the fellowship of the Spirit within themselves. And when they speak words of truth or deliver any spiritual conference and wish to edify persons, they speak out of the same wealth and treasure which indwells within them and out of this they edify persons who listen to their spiritual discourses. And they do not fear lest they run short since they possess within themselves the heavenly treasure of goodness from which they draw to feed those who hunger for spiritual food. But the poor man, who does not possess the riches of Christ nor have within himself a spiritual wealth which can bring forth a stream of goodness in words and deeds and of divine ideas and ineffable mysteries, even if, I say, he wishes to speak a word of truth and refresh his listeners, he does not possess in himself the Word of God in power and in truth. He repeats things he memorized or borrowed from some writings or from what he has heard from spiritual persons and these he organizes and teaches. Yes, he may even seemingly entertain some, and certainly some profit from his sermons. But when he has delivered his discourse, each word returns to its source from which it came. Then he again remains naked and poor, not possessing the treasure of the Spirit as his own from which he draws to help and refresh others, but he himself first of all is not refreshed nor does he rejoice in the Spirit.

Pseudo-Macarius explains the meaning of new birth and salvation as a miracle even bigger than the miracles evident in Jesus' ministry.

From Pseudo-Macarius, *The Fifty Spiritual Homilies* 12.17–18 (Maloney, 104).

17. And what indeed can be so surprising if those who came to the Lord and were intimately associated with him received his power as we see when the Apostles preached the Word of God and the Spirit fell upon those believers? Cornelius received power from the Word of God when he heard it. How much more in the case of the Lord speaking with Mary or Zacchaeus or to the sinful woman who let her hair down and wiped the feet of the Lord, or with the Samaritan woman or the good thief—did not power go out and the Holy Spirit mingle with the souls? Now those who pursue God in love, having abandoned everything else, and who persevere in prayer, are taught secretly things they had not known before. For truth itself comes to them according to their desire and it teaches them. "I am the truth"

(Jn 14:6). Even the Apostles themselves, before the crucifixion, staying close to the Lord, saw great miracles, namely, how lepers were cleansed and the dead raised to life. But they did not yet know how the divine power operates or ministers in the heart. They did not yet know that they had to be reborn spiritually and be joined with the heavenly soul and become a new creature. Because of the signs that he performed, they loved the Lord. But the Lord told them: "Why do you marvel at such signs? I give you a great inheritance which the whole world does not possess."

18. However, these words were strange to them until he arose from the dead and ascended with his body into heaven for us. And then the Spirit, the Comforter, entered and mingled with them. The Truth in person shows himself to the faithful. And the heavenly Man walks with you and forms one fellowship. Whoever, therefore, dedicate themselves to different forms of service and eagerly perform all such activities, motivated by zeal, faith, and love of God, that very service, after a while, leads them to a knowledge of truth itself. For the Lord appears to their souls and teaches them how the Holy Spirit operates. Glory and adoration to the Father and the Son and the Holy Spirit forever. Amen.

Ephraim the Syrian

Also known as Ephrem (or Ephraem)—named by Pope Benedict XV in 1920 as a "Doctor of the Church"—Ephraim is the leading Syrian spiritual writer. While nothing like scholarly consensus exists about much of his biography, his literary career is impressive and highly influential, including Bible commentaries, sermons, and hymns.

Symbols of the Trinity

Poetic and symbolic in his writings, Ephraim the Syrian did not care much about the more intellectual approach of theologians and philosophers. Nature and the makeup of the human being as the image of God were for him a great source of spiritual knowledge and inspiration.

From Ephrem the Syrian, *Eighty Rhythms upon the Faith, against the Disputers*, 18.1–2, in *Selected Works of S. Ephrem the Syrian*, ed. J. B. Morris (Oxford: John Henry Parker; London: F. & J. Rivington, 1847), 165–67 (hereafter Morris).

1. The threefold Names are sown in a threefold way, in the spirit and in the soul and in the body, as in the mystery. When our trinity was perfected by the Threefold One, it reigned unto the ends [of the earth].

2. If the spirit suffer, it is wholly sealed with the Father; and if the soul suffer, it is wholly blended with the Son; and if the body confess and be burned, it communicateth wholly with the Holy Ghost. And if the little bird drew in its wings and refused to use the silly mystery of the Cross, the air would then refuse her, and not bear her up; but her wings praise the Rood. And if a ship spreadeth her sails for the sea, in the mystery of the Rood and from the yoke of wood, she maketh a bosom for the wind; when she hath spread forth the Rood, then is the course spread clearly out for her voyage.

Baptism and Chrismation

Ephraim has a highly sacramental and symbolic theology of water baptism which he presents in a mystical Spirit Christology paradigm. He speaks a great deal of the spiritual significance of Jesus' baptism as the paradigm for the faithful.

> From Ephrem, *Hymns for the Feast of the Epiphany* 19.1–3, 6, 7, 12, in
> *Selections from Hymns and Homilies of Ephraim the Syrian and from the*
> *Demonstration of Aphrahat the Persian Sage*, ed. and intro. John Gwynn
> [with several translators], http://www.ccel.org, *NPNF*[2] 13:279–80.

1. O John, who sawest the Spirit,—that abode on the head of the Son,—to show how the Head of the Highest—went down and was baptized—and came up to be Head on earth!—Children of the Spirit ye have thus become,—and Christ has become for you the Head:— ye also have become His members.

2. Consider and see how exalted ye are;—how instead of the river Jordan—ye have glorious Baptism, wherein is peace;—spreading her wings to shade your bodies.—In the wilderness John baptized:—in Her pure flood of Baptism,—purely are ye baptized therein.

3. Infants think when they see its glory,—that by its pomp its might is enhanced.—But it is the same, and within itself—is not divided.—But the might which never waxes less or greater—in us is little or again great;—and he in whom is great understanding,— great in him is Baptism. . . .

6. How beautiful is Baptism—in the eye of the heart; come, let us gaze on it!—Like as by a seal ye have been moulded;—receive ye its image,—that nought may be lacking to us of our image!—For the sheep that are white of heart—gaze on the glory that is in the water:—in your souls reflect ye it!

7. Water is by nature as a mirror,—for one who in it examines *himself.*—Stir up thy soul, thou that discernest,—and be like unto it!—For it in its midst reflects thy image;—from it, on it, find an example;—gaze in it on Baptism,—and put on the beauty that is hidden therein! . . .

12. Our Lord when he was baptized by John—sent forth twelve fountains;—and they issued forth and cleansed by their streams—the defilement of the peoples.—His worshippers are made white like His garments,—the garments in Tabor and the body in the water.—Instead of the garments the peoples are made white,—and have become for Him a clothing of glory.

Ephraim describes vividly the baptism of Christ and its spiritual meaning.

From Ephrem, *Hymns for the Feast of the Epiphany* 8.16–20, NPNF[2] 13:278.

16. In the beginning the Spirit that brooded—moved on the waters; they conceived and gave birth—to serpents and fishes and birds.—The Holy Spirit has brooded in Baptism,—and in mystery has given birth to eagles,—Virgins and Prelates;—and in mystery has given birth to fishes,—celibates and intercessors; and in mystery of serpents,—lo! the subtle have become simple as doves!

17. Lo! the sword of our Lord in the waters!—that which divides sons and fathers:—for it is the living sword that makes—division, lo! of the living from the dying.—Lo! they are baptized and they become—Virgins and saints,—who have gone down, been baptized, and put on—the One Only begotten.—Lo! many have come boldly to Him!

18. For whoso have been baptized and put on Him—the Only begotten the Lord of the many,—has filled thereby the place of many,—for to him Christ has become a great treasure:—for He became in the wilderness—a table of good meats,—and He became at the marriage feast—a fountain of choice wines.—He has become *such* to all in all things,—by helps and healings and promises.

19. Elisha was the equal of the Watchers—in his doings, glorious and holy.—The camp of the Watchers was round about him;—thus let Baptism be unto you,—a camp of guardians,—for by means of it there dwells in the heart—the hope of them that are below—and the Lord of them that are above.—Sanctify for Him your bodies,—for where He abides, corruption comes not near.

20. They are no more, the waters of that sea—which by its billows preserved the People,—and by its billows laid low the peoples.—Of contrary effect are the waters in Baptism.—In them, lo! the people have life;—in them, lo! the People perishes:—for all that are not baptized,—in the waters that give life to all,—they are dead invisibly.

From Ephrem the Syrian, *Eighty Rhythms upon the Faith* 74.2–3 (Morris, 343).

2. The Spirit also clothed Apostles and sent them forth to the four quarters of the world upon labours. By heat all things are ripened, as by the Spirit all things are hallowed! . . .

3. Heat looseneth the evil bridle, yea, the chilly silence of the frost upon the lips, and penetrateth the mouth, yea, and the tongue, as did the tongues of the Spirit which settled on the Disciples. The Holy Spirit by His Heat applied by the tongues chased silence away from the Disciples.

A Holistic Salvation

When speaking of the work of the Savior in the Gospels, Ephraim outlines a view of salvation in a way contemporary soteriology speaks of holistic salvation, in terms of touching all areas of life from spiritual to moral to physical.

From Ephrem, *On the Sinful Woman* 1–3, NPNF[2] 13:336–37.

1. Hear and be comforted, beloved, how merciful is God. To the sinful woman He forgave her offences; yea, He upheld her when she was afflicted. With clay He opened the eyes of the blind, so that the eyeballs beheld the light. To the palsied He granted healing, who arose and walked and carried his bed. And to us He has given the pearls; His holy Body and Blood. He brought His medicines secretly; and with them He heals openly. And He wandered round in the land of Judea, like a physician, bearing his medicines. Simon invited Him to the feast, to eat bread in his house. The sinful woman rejoiced when she heard that He sat and was feasting in Simon's house; her thoughts gathered together like the sea, and like the billows her love surged. She beheld the Sea of Grace, how it had forced itself into one place; and she resolved to go and drown all her wickedness in its billows.

2. She bound her heart, because it had offended, with chains and tears of suffering; and she began weeping (with herself): "What avails me this fornication? What avails this lewdness? I have defiled the innocent ones without shame; I have corrupted the orphan; and without fear I have robbed the merchants of merchandise, and my rapacity was not satisfied. I have been as a bow in war, and have slain the good and the bad. I have been as a storm on the sea, and have sunk the ships of many. Why did I not win me one man, who might have corrected my lewdness? For one man is of God, but many are of Satan."

3. These things she inwardly said; then began she to do outwardly. She washed and put away from her eyes the dye that blinded them that saw it. And tears gushed forth from her eyes over that deadly eyepaint. She drew off and cast from her hands the enticing bracelets of her youth. She put off and cast away from her body the tunic of fine linen of whoredom, and resolved to go and attire herself in the tunic the garment of reconciliation. She drew off and cast from her feet the adorned sandals of lewdness; and directed the steps of her going in the path of the heavenly Eagle. She took up her gold in her palm and held it up to the face of heaven, and began to cry secretly, to Him who hears openly: "This, O Lord, that I have gained from iniquity, with it will I purchase to myself redemption. This which was gathered from orphans, with it will I win the Lord of orphans."

CHAPTER 3

Hilary of Poitiers

Contemporary to Athanasius in the Greek-speaking church, Hilary in the Western church helped consolidate the deity of the Spirit. Yet he does not do so theoretically but, similarly to other Fathers, in close connection with and deriving from spirituality, especially soteriology. For Hilary, the evidence of the Spirit's deity is the biblical statement that Christ (whose deity had been strongly affirmed by this time) lives in us through the Spirit of God, which implies the similarity of nature among all three Trinitarian members. The same approach is evident in the second citation, in which Hilary draws from the biblical Great Commission passage the equality of the Spirit with the Father and Son. These are profound applications of the ancient rule *lex orandi lex credendi*.

The Deity of the Spirit

From Hilary of Poitiers, *On the Trinity* 7.21–23, NPNF[2] 9:143–44.

21. For wishing to teach the unity of nature in the case of the Father and the Son, he [Apostle Paul] speaks thus *But ye are not in the flesh but in the Spirit, if indeed the Spirit of God is in you. But if any have not the Spirit of Christ, he is none of His. But if Christ is in you, the body indeed is dead through sin, but the Spirit is life through righteousness. But if the Spirit of Him Who raised up Christ from the dead dwelleth in you; He Who raised up Christ from the dead shall also quicken your mortal bodies, because of His Spirit Who dwelleth in you* [Rom. 8:9–11]. We are all spiritual if the Spirit of God dwells in us. But this Spirit of God is also the Spirit of Christ, and though the Spirit of Christ is in us, yet His Spirit is also in us Who raised Christ from the dead, and He Who raised Christ from the dead shall quicken our mortal bodies also on account of His Spirit that dwelleth in us. We are quickened therefore on account of the Spirit of Christ that dwelleth in us, through Him Who raised Christ from the dead. And since the Spirit of Him Who raised Christ from the dead dwells in us, and yet the Spirit of Christ is in us, nevertheless the Spirit Which is in us

cannot but be the Spirit of God. Separate, then, O heretic, the Spirit of Christ from the Spirit of God, and the Spirit of Christ raised from the dead from the Spirit of God Which raises Christ from the dead; when the Spirit of Christ that dwelleth in us is the Spirit of God, and when the Spirit of Christ Who was raised from the dead is yet the Spirit of God Who raises Christ from the dead.

22. And now I ask whether thou thinkest that in the Spirit of God is signified a nature or a property belonging to a nature. For a nature is not identical with a thing belonging to it, just as neither is a man identical with what belongs to a man, nor fire with what belongs to fire itself, and in like manner God is not the same as that which belongs to God.

23. For I am aware that the Son of God is revealed under the title *Spirit of God* in order that we may understand the presence of the Father in Him, and that the term *Spirit of God* may be employed to indicate Either, and that this is shewn not only on the authority of prophets but of evangelists also, when it is said, *The Spirit of the Lord is upon Me; therefore He hath anointed Me* [Luke 4:18]. And again, *Behold My Servant Whom I have chosen, My beloved in Whom My soul is well pleased, I will put My Spirit upon Him* [Isa. 42:1]. And when the Lord Himself bears witness of Himself, *But if I in the Spirit of God cast out devils, then has the kingdom of God come upon you* [Matt. 12:28]. For the passages seem without any doubt to denote either Father or Son, while they yet manifest the excellence of nature.

Anticipating the more fully developed reflections of St. Augustine, Hilary pays attention to the biblical statement that God is Spirit, on the one hand, and that there is also the Spirit, the third member of the Trinity. He offers insightful reflections on this issue and thereby clarifies both the unity and distinctions of Father and Spirit.

From Hilary of Poitiers, *On the Incarnation* 2.31–32, *NPNF*[2] 9:60–61.

31. But the words of the Gospel, *For God is Spirit*, need careful examination as to their sense and their purpose. For every saying has an antecedent cause and an aim which must be ascertained by study of the meaning. We must bear this in mind lest, on the strength of the words, *God is Spirit* [John 4:24], we deny not only the Name, but also the work and the gift of the Holy Ghost. The Lord was speaking with a woman of Samaria, for He had come to be the Redeemer for all mankind. After He had discoursed at length of the living water, and of her five husbands, and of him whom she then had who was not her husband, the woman answered, *Lord, I perceive that Thou*

art a prophet. Our fathers worshipped in this mountain; and ye say that in Jerusalem is the place where men ought to worship. The Lord replied, *Woman, believe Me, the hour cometh when neither in this mountain, nor in Jerusalem, shall ye worship the Father. Ye worship that which ye know not; we worship that which we know; for salvation is from the Jews. But the hour cometh, and now is, when the true worshippers shall worship the Father in the Spirit and in truth; for the Father seeketh such to worship Him. For God is Spirit, and they that worship Him must worship in the Spirit and in truth, for God is Spirit* [John 4:19–24]. We see that the woman, her mind full of inherited tradition, thought that God must be worshipped either on a mountain, as at Samaria, or in a temple, as at Jerusalem; for Samaria in disobedience to the Law had chosen a site upon the mountain for worship, while the Jews regarded the temple founded by Solomon as the home of their religion, and the prejudices of both confined the all-embracing and illimitable God to the crest of a hill or the vault of a building. God is invisible, incomprehensible, immeasurable; the Lord said that the time had come when God should be worshipped neither on mountain nor in temple. For Spirit cannot be cabined or confined; it is omnipresent in space and time, and under all conditions present in its fulness. Therefore, He said, they are the true worshippers who shall worship in the Spirit and in truth. And these who are to worship God the Spirit in the Spirit shall have the One for the means, the Other for the object, of their reverence: for Each of the Two stands in a different relation to the worshipper. The words, *God is Spirit* [John 4:24], do not alter the fact that the Holy Spirit has a Name of His own, and that He is the Gift to us. The woman who confined God to hill or temple was told that God contains all things and is self-contained: that He, the Invisible and Incomprehensible must be worshipped by invisible and incomprehensible means. The imparted gift and the object of reverence were clearly shewn when Christ taught that God, being Spirit, must be worshipped in the Spirit, and revealed what freedom and knowledge, what boundless scope for adoration, lay in this worship of God, the Spirit, in the Spirit.

32. The words of the Apostle are of like purport; *For the Lord is Spirit, and where the Spirit of the Lord is, there is liberty.* To make his meaning clear he has distinguished between the Spirit, Who exists, and Him Whose Spirit He is Proprietor and Property, *He* and *His* are different in sense. Thus when he says, *The Lord is Spirit* he reveals the infinity of God; when He adds, *Where the Spirit of the Lord is, there is liberty,* he indicates Him Who belongs to God; for He is the Spirit of the Lord, and *Where the Spirit of the Lord is, there is liberty* [2 Cor.

3:17]. The Apostle makes the statement not from any necessity of his own argument, but in the interests of clearness. For the Holy Ghost is everywhere One, enlightening all patriarchs and prophets and the whole company of the Law, inspiring John even in his mother's womb, given in due time to the Apostles and other believers, that they might recognise the truth vouchsafed them.

Spirit Christology
In several places in his treatise *On the Trinity*, Hilary develops a Spirit Christology in which the Christ is not only the Giver but also the Receiver of the Spirit.

From Hilary of Poitiers, *On the Trinity* 2.26–27, NPNF² 9:59.

26. . . . An Angel blesses Mary and promises that she, a virgin, shall be the mother of the Son of God. Conscious of her virginity, she is distressed at this hard thing; the Angel explains to her the mighty working of God, saying, *The Holy Ghost shall come from above into thee, and the power of the Most High shall overshadow thee* [Luke 1:35]. The Holy Ghost, descending from above, hallowed the Virgin's womb, and breathing therein (for *The Spirit bloweth where it listeth* [John 3:8]), mingled Himself with the fleshly nature of man, and annexed by force and might that foreign domain. And, lest through weakness of the human structure failure should ensue, the power of the Most High overshadowed the Virgin, strengthening her feebleness in semblance of a cloud cast round her, that the shadow, which was the might of God, might fortify her bodily frame to receive the procreative power of the Spirit. Such is the glory of the conception.

27. The Angel tells Joseph that the Virgin shall bear a Son, and that Son shall be named Emmanuel, that is, *God with us* [Matt. 1:23]. The Spirit foretells it through the prophet, the Angel bears witness; He that is born is God with us. . . . An Angel brings to the shepherds the news that Christ the Lord is born, the Saviour of the world. A multitude of the heavenly host flock together to sing the praise of that childbirth; the rejoicing of the Divine company proclaims the fulfilment of the mighty work. Then *glory to God in heaven, and peace on earth to men of good will* [Luke 2:14] is announced. And now the Magi come and worship Him wrapped in swaddling clothes; . . . Thus the Magi stoop to reverence the infirmities of Infancy; its cries are saluted by the heavenly joy of angels; the Spirit Who inspired the prophet, the heralding Angel, the light of the new star, all minister around Him. In such wise was it that the Holy Ghost's descent and the overshadowing power of the Most High brought Him to His birth.

From Hilary of Poitiers, *On the Trinity* 15–16, NPNF[2] 9:186.

15. . . . The Man Christ Jesus was born perfect, and made in the form of a servant by the assumption of the body, which the Virgin conceived? For the Virgin conceived, what she conceived, from the Holy Ghost alone, and though for His birth in the flesh she supplied from herself that element, which women always contribute to the seed planted in them, still Jesus Christ was not formed by an ordinary human conception. In His birth, the cause of which was transmitted solely by the Holy Ghost, His mother performed the same part as in all human conceptions: but by virtue of His origin He never ceased to be God.

16. This deep and beautiful mystery of His assumption of manhood the Lord Himself reveals in the words, *No man hath ascended into heaven, but He that descended from heaven, even the Son of Man which is in heaven* [John 3:13]. "Descended from heaven" refers to His origin from the Spirit: for though Mary contributed to His growth in the womb and birth all that is natural to her sex, His body did not owe to her its origin. The "Son of Man" refers to the birth of the flesh conceived in the Virgin; "Who is in heaven" implies the power of His eternal nature: an infinite nature, which could not restrict itself to the limits of the body, of which it was itself the source and base. By the virtue of the Spirit and the power of God the Word, though He abode in the form of a servant, He was ever present as Lord of all, within and beyond the circle of heaven and earth. So He descended from heaven and is the Son of Man, yet is in heaven: for the Word made flesh did not cease to be the Word. As the Word, He is in heaven, as flesh He is the Son of Man. As Word made flesh, He is at once from heaven, and Son of Man, and in heaven, for the power of the Word, abiding eternally without body, was present still in the heaven He had left: to Him and to none other the flesh owed its origin. So the Word made flesh, though He was flesh, yet never ceased to be the Word.

The Spirit as Gift

Again, in keeping with later tradition, especially the Augustinian, one of the key designations for the Spirit in Hilary's thinking is Gift, as was already evident in the previous citation.

From Hilary of Poitiers, *On the Trinity* 2.29, NPNF[2] 9:60.

Concerning the Holy Spirit I ought not to be silent, and yet I have no need to speak; still, for the sake of those who are in ignorance, I cannot refrain. There is no need to speak, because we are bound to confess Him, proceeding, as He does, from Father and Son. For my own part, I think it wrong to discuss the question of His existence. He does exist, inasmuch as He is given, received, retained; He is joined with Father and Son in our confession of the faith, and cannot be excluded from a true confession of Father and Son; take away a part, and the whole faith is marred. If any man demand what meaning we attach to this conclusion, he, as well as we, has read the words of the Apostle, *Because ye are sons of God, God hath sent the Spirit of His Son into our hearts, crying, Abba, Father* [Rom. 8:15–16], and *Grieve not the Holy Spirit of God, in Whom ye have been sealed* [Eph. 4:30], and again, *But we have received not the spirit of this world, but the Spirit which is of God, that we may know the things that are given unto us by God* [1 Cor. 2:12], and also *But ye are not in the flesh but in the Spirit, if so be that the Spirit of God is in you. But if any man hath not the Spirit of Christ, he is not His* [Rom. 8:9], and further, *But if the Spirit of Him that raised up Jesus from the dead dwelleth in you, He that raised up Christ from the dead shall quicken also your mortal bodies for the sake of His Spirit which dwelleth in you* [Rom. 8:11].

The Work of the Spirit in Salvation, Enlightenment, and Gifts
Hilary elaborates on spiritual gifts.

From Hilary of Poitiers, *On the Trinity* 2.33–35, NPNF² 9:61.

33. Let us hear from our Lord's own words what is the work of the Holy Ghost within us. He says, *I have yet many things to say unto you, but ye cannot bear them now* [John 16:12]. For *it is expedient for you that I go: if I go I will send you the Advocate* [John 16:7]. And again, *I will ask the Father and He shall send you another Advocate, that He may be with you for ever, even the Spirit of truth* [John 14:16]. *He shall guide you into all truth, for He shall not speak from Himself, but whatsoever things He shall hear He shall speak, and He shall declare unto you the things that are to come. He shall glorify Me, for He shall take of Mine* [John 16:13–14]. These words were spoken to show how multitudes should enter the kingdom of heaven; they contain an assurance of the goodwill of the Giver, and of the mode and terms of the Gift. . . .

34. The next step naturally is to listen to the Apostle's account of the powers and functions of this Gift. He says, *As many as are led by the Spirit of God, these are the children of God. For ye received not the Spirit of bondage again unto fear, but ye received the Spirit of adoption whereby we cry, Abba, Father* [Rom. 8:14–15], and again,

For no man by the Spirit of God saith anathema to Jesus, and no man can say, Jesus is Lord, but in the Holy Spirit [1 Cor. 12:3]; and he adds, *Now there are diversities of gifts, but the same Spirit, and diversities of ministrations, but the same Lord, and diversities of workings, but the same God, Who worketh all things in all. But to each one is given the enlightenment of the Spirit, to profit withal. Now to one is given through the Spirit the word of wisdom, to another the word of knowledge according to the same Spirit, to another faith in the same Spirit, to another gifts of healings in the One Spirit, to another workings of miracles, to another prophecy, to another discerning of spirits, to another kinds of tongues, to another interpretation of tongues. But all these worketh the One and same Spirit* [1 Cor. 12:4–11]. Here we have a statement of the purpose and results of the Gift; and I cannot conceive what doubt can remain, after so clear a definition of His Origin, His action and His powers.

35. Let us therefore make use of this great benefit, and seek for personal experience of this most needful Gift. For the Apostle says, in words I have already cited, *But we have not received the spirit of this world, but the Spirit which is of God, that we may know the things that are given unto us by God* [1 Cor. 2:12]. . . . This gift is with us unto the end of the world, the solace of our waiting, the assurance, by the favours which He bestows, of the hope that shall be ours, the light of our minds, the sun of our souls. This Holy Spirit we must seek and must earn, and then hold fast by faith and obedience to the commands of God.

Ambrose

The Holy Spirit in Biblical Symbols and Types

A skillful Bible expositor, the former lawyer and governor, then bishop of Milan (who took that position only eight days after his baptism), Ambrose majored in allegorical treatment of the Old Testament texts, as the excerpts from his major pneumatological work, the three-volume *The Holy Spirit*, beautifully illustrate. These three books, as St. Ambrose himself acknowledges, are sequel to his main doctrinal work, *On the Christian Faith*. Basically *The Holy Spirit* is an exposition of biblical testimonies to the Spirit, the first two books focusing on the Old Testament. The first excerpt offers a poetic oration on water and river as symbols of the Spirit.

From Ambrose, *The Holy Spirit* 1.16.176–79, *NPNF*[2] 10:113–14.

176. But lest perchance any one should speak against as it were the littleness of the Spirit, and from this should endeavour to establish a difference in greatness, arguing that water seems to be but a small part of a Fount, although examples taken from creatures seem by no means suitable for application to the Godhead; yet lest they should judge anything injuriously from this comparison taken from creatures, let them learn that not only is the Holy Spirit called Water, but also a River, as we read: "From his belly shall flow rivers of living water. But this He said of the Spirit, Whom they were beginning to receive, who were about to believe in Him" [John 7:38–39].

177. So, then, the Holy Spirit is the River, and the abundant River, which according to the Hebrews flowed from Jesus in the lands, as we have received it prophesied by the mouth of Isaiah. This is the great River which flows always and never fails. And not only a river, but also one of copious stream and overflowing greatness, as also David said: "The stream of the river makes glad the city of God" [Ps. 46:4].

178. For neither is that city, the heavenly Jerusalem, watered by the channel of any earthly river, but that Holy Spirit, proceeding from the Fount of Life, by a short draught of Whom we are satiated, seems to flow more abundantly among those celestial Thrones, Dominions and Powers, Angels and Archangels, rushing in the full course of the seven virtues of the Spirit. For if a river rising above its banks overflows, how much more does the Spirit, rising above every creature, when He touches the as it were low-lying fields of our minds, make glad that heavenly nature of the creatures with the larger fertility of His sanctification.

179. And let it not trouble you that either here it is said "rivers," or elsewhere "seven Spirits," for by the sanctification of these seven gifts of the Spirit, as Isaiah said, is signified the fulness of all virtue; the Spirit of wisdom and understanding, the Spirit of counsel and strength, the Spirit of knowledge and godliness, and the Spirit of the fear of God. One, then, is the River, but many the channels of the gifts of the Spirit. This River, then, goes forth from the Fount of Life.

The Deity of the Spirit

Ambrose affirms the deity of the Spirit in more than one way and thus joins in the orthodoxy of the time. The following, longer citation, offers an interesting argumentation. The reasoning for the divinity of the Spirit is based in the first place on an allegorical reading of OT material regarding anointing with oil, related to the Holy Spirit and Christ.

From Ambrose, *The Holy Spirit* 1.9.100–107, NPNF[2] 10:106–7.

100. Now many have thought that the Holy Spirit is the ointment of Christ. And well it is said ointment, because He is called the oil of gladness, the joining together of many graces giving a sweet fragrance. But God the Almighty Father anointed Him the Prince of priests, Who was, not like others anointed in a type under the Law, but was both according to the Law anointed in the body, and in truth was full with the virtue of the Holy Spirit from the Father above the Law.

101. This is the oil of gladness, of which the prophet says: "God, even Thy God, hath anointed Thee with the oil of gladness above Thy fellows" [Heb. 1:9]. Lastly, Peter says that Jesus was anointed with the Spirit, as you read: "Ye know that word which went through all Judea beginning from Galilee after the baptism which John preached, even Jesus of Nazareth, how God anointed Him with the Holy Spirit" [Acts 10:37–38]. The Holy Spirit is, then, the oil of gladness.

102.[1] And well did he say oil of gladness, lest you should think Him a creature; for it is the nature of this sort of oil that it will by no means mingle with moisture of another kind. Gladness, too, does not anoint the body, but brightens the inmost heart, as the prophet said: "Thou hast put gladness in my heart" [Ps. 4:7]. So as he loses his pains who wishes to mix oil with moister matter, because since the nature of oil is lighter than others, when the others settle, it rises and is separated. How do those wretched pedlars think that the oil of gladness can by their tricks be mingled with other creatures, since of a truth corporeal things cannot be mingled with incorporeal, nor things created with uncreated?

102. And well is that called oil of gladness wherewith Christ was anointed; for neither was usual nor common oil to be sought for Him, wherewith either wounds are dressed or heat assuaged; since the salvation of the world did not seek alleviation for His wounds, nor the eternal might of His wearied Body demand refreshment.

103. Nor is it wonderful if He have the oil of gladness, Who made those about to die rejoice, put off sadness from the world, destroyed the odour of sorrowful death. And so the Apostle says: "For we are the good odour of Christ to God" [2 Cor. 2:15]; certainly showing that he is speaking of spiritual things. But when the Son of God Himself says: "The Spirit of the Lord is upon Me, because He hath anointed Me" [Luke 4:18], He points out the ointment of the Spirit. Therefore the Spirit is the ointment of Christ.

---

1. There are two paragraphs no. 102 in the text I follow.

104. Or since the Name of Jesus is as ointment poured out, if they wish to understand Christ Himself, and not the Spirit of Christ to be expressed under the name of ointment, certainly when the Apostle Peter says that the Lord Jesus was anointed with the Holy Spirit, it is without doubt plain that the Spirit also is called ointment.

105. But what wonder, since both the Father and the Son are said to be Spirit. Of which we shall speak more fully when we begin to speak of the Unity of the Name. Yet since most suitable place occurs here, that we may not seem to have passed on without a conclusion, let them read that both the Father is called Spirit, as the Lord said in the Gospel, "for God is Spirit" [John 4:24]; and Christ is called Spirit, for Jeremiah said: "The Spirit before our face, Christ the Lord."

106. So, then, both the Father is Spirit and Christ is Spirit, for that which is not a created body is spirit, but the Holy Spirit is not commingled with the Father and the Son, but is distinct from the Father and from the Son. For the Holy Spirit did not die, Who could not die because He had not taken flesh upon Him, and the eternal Godhead was incapable of dying, but Christ died according to the flesh.

107. For of a truth He died in that which He took of the Virgin, not in that which He had of the Father, for Christ died in that nature in which He was crucified. But the Holy Spirit could not be crucified, Who had not flesh and bones, but the Son of God was crucified, Who took flesh and bones, that on that cross the temptations of our flesh might die. For He took on Him that which He was not that He might hide that which He was; He hid that which He was that He might be tempted in it, and that which He was not might be redeemed, in order that He might call us by means of that which He was not to that which He was.

In several places Ambrose's writings affirm the deity of the Spirit by following the typical *lex orandi lex credendi* formula, as the following excerpt shows. The Spirit's incorporeality and immutability follow from his salvific work among corporeal and changing human beings, implying that the Spirit, similarly to the Father and Son, is divine. (A similar kind of argumentation can be found in *The Holy Spirit* 1.10, *NPNF*[2] 10:108, where Ambrose speaks of the forgiveness of sins as an evidence of the Spirit's deity since that is a task also performed by the Father and Son.)

From Ambrose, *The Holy Spirit* 1.5.62–64, *NPNF*[2] 10:101–2.

62. The Holy Spirit is not, then, of the substance of things corporeal, for He sheds incorporeal grace on corporeal things; nor, again, is He of the substance of invisible creatures, for they receive His sanctification, and through Him are superior to the other works of the

universe. Whether you speak of Angels, or Dominions, or Powers, every creature waits for the grace of the Holy Spirit. For as we are children through the Spirit, because "God sent the Spirit of His Son into our hearts crying, Abba, Father; so that thou art now not a servant but a son" [Rom. 8:15]; in like manner, also, every creature is waiting for the revelation of the sons of God, whom in truth the grace of the Holy Spirit made sons of God. Therefore, also, every creature itself shall be changed by the revelation of the grace of the Spirit, "and shall be delivered from the bondage of corruption into the liberty of the glory of the children of God" [Rom. 8:21].

63. Every creature, then, is subject to change, not only such as has been changed by some sin or condition of the outward elements, but also such as can be liable to corruption by a fault of nature, though by careful discipline it be not yet so; for, as we have shown in a former treatise, the nature of Angels evidently can be changed. It is certainly fitting to judge that such as is the nature of one, such also is that of others. The nature of the rest, then, is capable of change, but the discipline is better.

64. Every creature, therefore, is capable of change, but the Holy Spirit is good and not capable of change, nor can He be changed by any fault, Who does away the faults of all and pardons their sins. How, then, is He capable of change, Who by sanctifying works in others a change to grace, but is not changed Himself.

The Unity of the Trinity

One of the ways Ambrose argues for both the deity of the Spirit and the unity of the Trinity is to highlight the mutual working of Father, Son, and Spirit in bringing about creation.

From Ambrose, *The Holy Spirit* 2.5.32–35, *NPNF*² 10:118–19.

32. But who can doubt that the Holy Spirit gives life to all things; since both He, as the Father and the Son, is the Creator of all things; and the Almighty Father is understood to have done nothing without the Holy Spirit; and since also in the beginning of the creation the Spirit moved upon the water.

33. So when the Spirit was moving upon the water, the creation was without grace; but after this world being created underwent the operation of the Spirit, it gained all the beauty of that grace, wherewith the world is illuminated. And that the grace of the universe cannot abide without the Holy Spirit the prophet declared when he said: "Thou wilt take away Thy Spirit, and they will fail and be turned again into their dust. Send forth Thy Spirit, and they shall be made, and Thou wilt renew all the face of the earth" [Ps. 104:29–

30]. Not only, then, did he teach that no creature can stand without the Holy Spirit, but also that the Spirit is the Creator of the whole creation.

34. And who can deny that the creation of the earth is the work of the Holy Spirit, Whose work it is that it is renewed? For if they desire to deny that it was created by the Spirit, since they cannot deny that it must be renewed by the Spirit, they who desire to sever the Persons must maintain that the operation of the Holy Spirit is superior to that of the Father and the Son, which is far from the truth; for there is no doubt that the restored earth is better than it was created. Or if at first, without the operation of the Holy Spirit, the Father and the Son made the earth, but the operation of the Holy Spirit was joined on afterwards, it will seem that that which was made required His aid, which was then added. But far be it from any one to think this, namely, that the divine work should be believed to have a change in the Creator, an error brought in by Manicheus.

35. But do we suppose that the substance of the earth exists without the operation of the Holy Spirit, without Whose work not even the expanse of the sky endures? For it is written: "By the Word of the Lord were the heavens established, and all the strength of them by the Spirit of His Mouth" [Ps. 33:6]. Observe what he says, that all the strength of the heavens is to be referred to the Spirit. For how should He Who was moving before the earth was made, be resting when it was being made?

No less important is the role of the Spirit in new creation. Along with the Father and Son, the Spirit works to bring about new birth and sanctification.

From Ambrose, *The Holy Spirit* 2.12.62–64, NPNF[2] 10:122–23.

62. So, then, the Father creates in good works, and the Son also, for it is written: "But as many as received Him, to them gave He power to become the sons of God, even to them who believe on His Name; who were born not of blood, nor of the will of the flesh, nor of the will of man, but of God" [John 1:12–13].

63. In like manner the Lord Himself also testifies that we are born again of the Spirit according to grace, saying: "That which is born of the flesh is flesh, because it is born of flesh; and that which is born of the Spirit is spirit, because God is Spirit. Marvel not that I said unto you, Ye must be born again. The Spirit breatheth where He willeth, and thou hearest His voice, but knowest not whence He cometh or whither He goeth, so is every one who is born of the Spirit" [John 3:6–8].

64. It is then clear that the Holy Spirit is also the Author of the grace of the Spirit, since we are created according to God, that we may be made the sons of God. So when He has taken us into His kingdom by the adoption of holy regeneration, do we deny Him that which is His? He has made us heirs of the new birth from above; do we claim the heritage and reject its Author? But the benefit cannot remain when its Author is shut out; the Author is not without the gift, nor the gift without the Author. If you claim the grace, believe the power; if you reject the power, do not ask for the grace. He who has denied the Spirit has at the same time denied the gift. For if the Author be of no account how can His gifts be precious? Why do we grudge the gifts we ourselves receive, diminish our hopes, repudiate our dignity, and deny our Comforter?

Spirit Christology

In a remarkable statement in the third book of his *The Holy Spirit*, Ambrose lays the foundation for a robust Spirit Christology by arguing that the Spirit not only sent prophets and apostles but also the Son. Not only is the Spirit sent by the Son, but also the Son is sent by the Spirit, along with the Father.

From Ambrose, *The Holy Spirit* 3.1.1–6, 8, NPNF[2] 10:135–36.

1. In the former book we have shown by the clear evidence of the Scriptures that the apostles and prophets were appointed, the latter to prophesy, the former to preach the Gospel, by the Holy Spirit in the same way as by the Father and the Son; now we add what all will rightly wonder at, and not be able to doubt, that the Spirit was upon Christ; and that as He sent the Spirit, so the Spirit sent the Son of God. For the Son of God says: "The Spirit of the Lord is upon Me, because He hath anointed Me, He hath sent Me to preach the Gospel to the poor, to proclaim liberty to the captives, and sight to the blind" [Luke 4:18]. And having read this from the Book of Isaiah, He says in the Gospel: "To-day hath this Scripture been fulfilled in your ears" [Luke 4:21]; that He might point out that it was said of Himself.

2. Can we, then, wonder if the Spirit sent both the prophets and the apostles, since Christ said: "The Spirit of the Lord is upon Me"? And rightly did He say "upon Me," because He was speaking as the Son of Man. For as the Son of Man He was anointed and sent to preach the Gospel.

3. But if they believe not the Son, let them hear the Father also saying that the Spirit of the Lord is upon Christ. For He says to John: "Upon whomsoever thou shalt see the Spirit descending from heaven and abiding upon Him, He it is Who baptizeth with the Holy

Spirit" [John 1:33]. God the Father said this to John, and John heard and saw and believed. He heard from God, he saw in the Lord, he believed that it was the Spirit Who was coming down from heaven. For it was not a dove that descended, but the Holy Spirit as a dove; for thus it is written: "I saw the Spirit descending from heaven as a dove" [John 1:32].

4. As John says that he saw, so, too, wrote Mark; Luke, however, added that the Holy Spirit descended in a bodily form as a dove; you must not think that this was an incarnation, but an appearance. He, then, brought the appearance before him, that by means of the appearance he might believe who did not see the Spirit, and that by the appearance He might manifest that He had a share of the one honour in authority, the one operation in the mystery, the one gift in the bath, together with the Father and the Son; unless perchance we consider Him in Whom the Lord was baptized too weak for the servant to be baptized in Him.

5. And he said fittingly, "abiding upon Him," because the Spirit inspired a saying or acted upon the prophets as often as He would, but abode always in Christ.

6. Nor, again, let it move you that he said "upon Him," for he was speaking of the Son of Man, because he was baptized as the Son of Man. For the Spirit is not upon Christ, according to the Godhead, but in Christ; for, as the Father is in the Son, and the Son in the Father, so the Spirit of God and the Spirit of Christ is both in the Father and in the Son, for He is the Spirit of His mouth. For He Who is of God abides in God, as it is written: "But we received not the spirit of this world, but the Spirit which is of God" [1 Cor. 2:12]. And He abides in Christ, Who has received from Christ; for it is written again: "He shall take of Mine": and elsewhere: "The law of the Spirit of life in Christ Jesus made me free from the law of sin and death." He is, then, not over Christ according to the Godhead of Christ, for the Trinity is not over Itself, but over all things: It is not over Itself but in Itself. . . .

8. So both the Father and the Spirit sent the Son; the Father sent Him, for it is written: "But the Paraclete, the Holy Spirit, Whom the Father will send in My Name." The Son sent Him, for He said: "But when the Paraclete is come, Whom I will send unto you from the Father, even the Spirit of Truth." If, then, the Son and the Spirit send each other, as the Father sends, there is no inferiority of subjection, but a community of power.

Another unique and creative way of developing the mutual relationship between the Spirit and Son is to speak of the Spirit as "Finger" and the Son as "Right Hand"!

From Ambrose, *The Holy Spirit* 3.13.11, *NPNF*[2] 10:137.

So, too, the Spirit is also called the Finger of God, because there is an indivisible and inseparable communion between the Father, the Son, and the Holy Spirit. For as the Scripture called the Son of God the Right Hand of God, as it is said: "Thy Right Hand, O Lord, is made glorious in power. Thy Right Hand, O Lord, hath dashed in pieces the enemy"; so the Holy Spirit is called the Finger of God, as the Lord Himself says: "But if I by the Finger of God cast out devils." For in the same place in another book of the Gospel He named the Spirit of God, as you find: "But if I by the Spirit of God cast out devils."

Augustine

The Spirit in the Trinity

While the Eastern Fathers, as explained above, did not dare to call the Spirit God even when they fully affirmed the Spirit's divinity, Augustine does, for example, in the preamble to chapter 6 in book 1 of *The Trinity*: "That the Holy Spirit is Very God, Equal with the Father and the Son," and in 1.6.13: "but also very God; and therefore absolutely equal with the Father and the Son, and in the unity of the Trinity consubstantial and co-eternal."

From Augustine, *The Trinity* 1.6.13, *NPNF*[1] 3:23.

Concerning the Holy Spirit, of which those who have discussed the subject before ourselves have most fully availed themselves, that He too is God, and not a creature. But if not a creature, then not only God (for men likewise are called gods), but also very God; and therefore absolutely equal with the Father and the Son, and in the unity of the Trinity consubstantial and co-eternal.

Augustine carefully considers the relationships among the three Trinitarian persons.

From Augustine, *On Christian Doctrine* 1.5, *NPNF*[1] 2:524.

The Father is not the Son nor the Holy Spirit; the Son is not the Father nor the Holy Spirit; the Holy Spirit is not the Father nor the Son: but the Father is only Father, the Son is only Son, and the Holy Spirit is only Holy Spirit. To all three belong the same eternity, the same unchangeableness, the same majesty, the same power. In the

Father is unity, in the Son equality, in the Holy Spirit the harmony of unity and equality; and these three attributes are all one because of the Father, all equal because of the Son, and all harmonious because of the Holy Spirit.

Augustine, *Letter 169 to Bishop Evodius*, NPNF[1] 1:540.

Therefore let us with steadfast piety believe in one God, the Father, and the Son, and the Holy Spirit; let us at the same time believe that the Son is not [the person] who is the Father, and the Father is not [the person] who is the Son, and neither the Father nor the Son is [the person] who is the Spirit of both the Father and the Son. Let it not be supposed that in this Trinity there is any separation in respect of time or place, but that these Three are equal and co-eternal, and absolutely of one nature: and that the creatures have been made, not some by the Father, and some by the Son, and some by the Holy Spirit, but that each and all that have been or are now being created subsist in the Trinity as their Creator; and that no one is saved by the Father without the Son and the Holy Spirit, or by the Son without the Father and the Holy Spirit, or by the Holy Spirit without the Father and the Son, but by the Father, the Son, and the Holy Spirit, the only one, true, and truly immortal (that is, absolutely unchangeable) God.

As is well known, Augustine was instrumental in the consolidation of the *filioque* clause (Latin: "and from the Son") according to which the Spirit proceeds from both the Father and the Son. While the Western Church adopted this view into the creeds, the East has vehemently opposed it. The *filioque* became the official doctrinal reason for the tragic 1054 split between the Christian East and West—coupled, of course, with ecclesiastical and other reasons. Augustine saw this view taught in the Bible, as his first comment in the commentary on John indicates.

From Augustine, *Tractates on the Gospel of John* 9.7, NPNF[1] 7:65.

For the Holy Spirit is not that of the Father only, nor of the Son only, but the Spirit of the Father and of the Son. For it is written, "If any man love the world, the Spirit of the Father is not in him." And again, "Whoso hath not the Spirit of Christ is none of His." The same, then, is the Spirit of the Father and of the Son. Therefore, the Father and the Son being named, the Holy Spirit also is understood, because He is the Spirit of the Father and of the Son.

From Augustine, *The Trinity* 15.26.47, *NPNF*[1] 3:225.

And the Son is born of the Father; and the Holy Spirit proceeds from the Father principally, the Father giving the procession without any interval of time, yet in common from both [Father and Son]. But He would be called the Son of the Father and of the Son, if—a thing abhorrent to the feeling of all sound minds—both had *begotten* Him. Therefore the Spirit of both is not begotten of both, but proceeds from both.

The Holy Spirit as Love and Gift

While Augustine, with other theologians, knows a number of names for the third person of the Trinity, three stand out in his theology, namely, *Holy* Spirit, Spirit as *Love*, and Spirit as *Gift*. The first nomenclature he considers is Holy Spirit.

From Augustine, *The Trinity* 5.11.12, *NPNF*[1] 3:93.

Neither can the Trinity in any wise be called the Son, but it can be called, in its entirety, the Holy Spirit, according to that which is written, "God is a Spirit"; because both the Father is a spirit and the Son is a spirit, and the Father is holy and the Son is holy. Therefore, since the Father, the Son and the Holy Spirit are one God, and certainly God is holy, and God is a spirit, the Trinity can be called also the Holy Spirit. But yet that Holy Spirit, who is not the Trinity, but is understood as in the Trinity, is spoken of in His proper name of the Holy Spirit relatively, since He is referred both to the Father and to the Son, because the Holy Spirit is the Spirit both of the Father and of the Son. . . . Therefore the Holy Spirit is a certain unutterable communion of the Father and the Son; and on that account, perhaps, He is so called, because the same name is suitable to both the Father and the Son. For He Himself is called specially that which they are called in common; because both the Father is a spirit and the Son a spirit, both the Father is holy and the Son holy.

As is well known, for Augustine the Spirit is the bond of love between the Father and Son. While acknowledging the fact that any of the members of the Trinity could be called Love, on the basis of biblical passages such as 1 John 4:7–19 and Rom. 5:5 he comes to the conclusion that the Spirit particularly can be called Love.

From Augustine, *The Trinity* 15.17.31, *NPNF*[1] 3:216–17.

But where the Holy Spirit is called Love, is to be found by careful scrutiny of the language of John the apostle, who, after saying, "Beloved, let us love one another, for love is of God" [1 John 4:7], has gone on to say, "And every one that loveth is born of God, and knoweth God. He that loveth not, knoweth not God; for God is love." Here, manifestly, he has called that love God, which he said was of God; therefore God of God is love. But because both the Son is born of God the Father, and the Holy Spirit proceeds from God the Father, it is rightly asked which of them we ought here to think is the rather called the love that is God. For the Father only is so God as not to be of God; and hence the love that is so God as to be of God, is either the Son or the Holy Spirit. But when, in what follows, the apostle had mentioned the love of God, not that by which we love Him, but that by which He "loved us, and sent His Son to be a propitiator for our sins" [1 John 4:10], and thereupon had exhorted us also to love one another, and that so God would abide in us,—because, namely, he had called God Love; immediately, in his wish to speak yet more expressly on the subject, "Hereby," he says, "know we that we dwell in Him, and He in us, because He hath given us of His Spirit" [1 John 4:13]. Therefore the Holy Spirit, of whom He hath given us, makes us to abide in God, and Him in us; and this it is that love does. Therefore He is the God that is love. Lastly, a little after, when he had repeated the same thing, and had said "God is love" [1 John 4:8], he immediately subjoined, "And he who abideth in love, abideth in God, and God abideth in him" [1 John 4:16]; whence he had said above, "Hereby we know that we abide in Him, and He in us, because He hath given us of His Spirit" [1 John 4:13]. He therefore is signified, where we read that God is love. Therefore God the Holy Spirit, who proceedeth from the Father, when He has been given to man, inflames him to the love of God and of his neighbor, and is Himself love. For man has not whence to love God, unless from God; and therefore he says a little after, "Let us love Him, because He first loved us" [1 John 4:19]. The Apostle Paul, too, says, "The love of God is shed abroad in our hearts by the Holy Ghost, which is given unto us" [Rom. 5:5].

From Augustine, *Tractates on the Gosepl of John* 105, *NPNF*[1] 7:396.

The Holy Spirit is also understood, because He is the Spirit of the Father and Son, as the substantial and consubstantial love of both.

Being Love, the Spirit is also a Gift.

From Augustine, *The Trinity* 15.18.32, *NPNF*[1] 3:217.

Love, therefore, which is of God and is God, is specially the Holy Spirit, by whom the love of God is shed abroad in our hearts, by which love the whole Trinity dwells in us. And therefore most rightly is the Holy Spirit, although He is God, called also the gift of God.

From Augustine, *The Trinity* 15.18.33, *NPNF*[1] 3:217.

Is this too to be proved, that the Holy Spirit is called in the sacred books the gift of God? If people look for this too, we have in the Gospel according to John the words of our Lord Jesus Christ, who says, "If any one thirst, let him come to me and drink: he that believeth on me, as the Scripture saith, out of his belly shall flow rivers of living water" [John 7:38]. And the evangelist has gone on further to add, "And this He spake of the Spirit, which they should receive who believe in Him."

The Holy Spirit as Uncreated Grace

While the soteriology of the Christian West is often—rightly!—blamed by Eastern theologians for its lack of pneumatological orientation, this is not to say that for theologians such as St. Augustine, the Spirit does not play an important role in salvation and soteriology is only a function of Christology. Indeed, for Augustine the Holy Spirit is the uncreated grace (*gratia increata*) given to humans. Thus, grace and justification are understood as the actual effect of the Holy Spirit. The first passage from chapter 5 in *The Spirit and the Letter*—in which the bishop most clearly presents his mature theology of salvation in pneumatological terms—titled "True Grace is the Gift of the Holy Ghost, Which Kindles in the Soul the Joy and Love of Goodness," teaches that the human person is able to advance in the Christian life when aided by the grace that comes from Holy Spirit. The two subsequent passages further elaborate on the importance of the Spirit for growth in the Christian life.

From Augustine, *The Spirit and the Letter* 5; *NPNF*[1] 5:84–85.

We, however, on our side affirm that the human will is so divinely aided in the pursuit of righteousness, that (in addition to man's being created with a free-will, and in addition to the teaching by which he is instructed how he ought to live) he receives the Holy Ghost, by whom there is formed in his mind a delight in, and a love of, that supreme and unchangeable good which is God, even now while he is still "walking by faith" and not yet "by sight"; in order that by this gift to him of the earnest, as it were, of the free gift, he may conceive an ardent desire to cleave to his Maker, and may burn to enter upon the participation in that true light, that it may go well with him from Him to whom he owes his existence. A man's free-will, indeed, avails for nothing except to sin, if he knows not the way of truth; and even after his duty and his proper aim shall begin to become known to him, unless he also take delight in and feel a love for it, he neither does his duty, nor sets about it, nor lives rightly. Now, in order that such a course may engage our affections, God's "love is shed abroad in our hearts" [Rom. 5:5], not through the free-will which arises from ourselves, but "through the Holy Ghost, which is given to us."

The Spirit as Gift brings about both justification to a person, who without the Spirit is unable to exercise free will given in original creation, as well as continuing sanctification.

From Augustine, *The Spirit and the Letter* 6, NPNF[1] 5:85.

For that teaching which brings to us the command to live in chastity and righteousness is "the letter that killeth," unless accompanied with "the spirit that giveth life" [2 Cor. 3:6]. . . . But, when the Holy Ghost withholds His help, which inspires us with a good desire instead of this evil desire (in other words, diffuses love in our hearts), that law, however good in itself, only augments the evil desire by forbidding it. Just as the rush of water which flows incessantly in a particular direction, becomes more violent when it meets with any impediment, and when it has overcome the stoppage, falls in a greater bulk, and with increased impetuosity hurries forward in its downward course. In some strange way the very object which we covet becomes all the more pleasant when it is forbidden. And this is the sin which by the commandment deceives and by it slays, whenever transgression is actually added, which occurs not where there is no law.

From Augustine, *The Spirit and the Letter* 7, NPNF[1] 5:85.

To lead a holy life is the gift of God,—not only because God has given a free-will to man, without which there is no living ill or well; nor only because He has given him a commandment to teach him how he ought to live; but because through the Holy Ghost He sheds love abroad in the hearts of those whom he foreknew, in order to predestinate them; whom He predestinated, that He might call them; whom He called, that he might justify them; and whom he justified, that He might glorify them.

This salvific and sanctifying grace was hidden in the Old Testament and now revealed in the New Testament, where the Spirit is called the "Finger of God."

From Augustine, *The Spirit and the Letter* 27–28, NPNF[1] 5:95.

27. This grace hid itself under a veil in the Old Testament, but it has been revealed in the New Testament according to the most perfectly ordered dispensation of the ages, forasmuch as God knew how to dispose all things. And perhaps it is a part of this hiding of grace, that in the Decalogue, which was given on Mount Sinai, only the portion which relates to the Sabbath was hidden under a prefiguring precept. The Sabbath is a day of sanctification; and it is not without significance that, among all the works which God accomplished, the first sound of sanctification was heard on the day when He rested from all His labours. On this, indeed, we must not now enlarge. But at the same time I deem it to be enough for the point now in question, that it was not for nothing that the nation was commanded on that day to abstain from all servile work, by which sin is signified; but because not to commit sin belongs to sanctification, that is, to God's gift through the Holy Spirit. . . .

28. "Now the Lord is that Spirit: and where the Spirit of the Lord is, there is liberty" [2 Cor. 3:17]. Now this Spirit of God, by whose gift we are justified, whence it comes to pass that we delight not to sin,—in which is liberty; even as, when we are without this Spirit, we delight to sin,—in which is slavery, from the works of which we must abstain;—this Holy Spirit, through whom love is shed abroad in our hearts, which is the fulfilment of the law, is designated in the gospel as "the finger of God." Is it not because those very tables of the law were written by the finger of God, that the Spirit of God by whom we are sanctified is also *the finger of God*, in order that, living by faith, we may do good works through love? Who is not touched by this congruity, and at the same time diversity? For as fifty days are reckoned from the celebration of the Passover (which was ordered by Moses to be offered by slaying the typical lamb, to signify, indeed, the future death of the Lord) to the day when Moses received the law written on the tables of stone by the finger of God, so, in like manner, from the death and resurrection of Him who was led as a lamb to the slaughter, there were fifty complete days up to the time when the finger of God—that is, the Holy Spirit—gathered together in one perfect company those who believed.

The Spirit and Grace Can Be Had Only in the Church

In Augustine's theology in general and in pneumatology in particular, the church plays a critical role. The Holy Spirit can only be received in the church.

From Augustine, *Baptism* 3.16.21, *NPNF*[1] 4:442–43.

But when it is said that "the Holy Spirit is given by the imposition of hands in the Catholic Church only, I suppose that our ancestors meant that we should understand thereby what the apostle says, "Because the love of God is shed abroad in our hearts by the Holy Ghost which is given unto us" [Rom. 5:5]. For this is that very love which is wanting in all who are cut off from the communion of the Catholic Church; and for lack of this, "though they speak with the tongues of men and of angels, though they understand all mysteries and all knowledge, and though they have the gift of prophecy, and all faith, so that they could remove mountains, and though they bestow all their goods to feed the poor, and though they give their bodies to be burned, it profiteth them nothing." But those are wanting in God's love who do not care for the unity of the Church; and consequently we are right in understanding that the Holy Spirit may be said not to be received except in the Catholic Church. For the Holy Spirit is not only given by the laying on of hands amid the testimony of temporal sensible miracles, as He was given in former days to be the credentials of a rudimentary faith, and for the extension of the first beginnings of the Church. For who expects in these days that those on whom hands are laid that they may receive the Holy Spirit should forthwith begin to speak with tongues? But it is understood that invisibly and imperceptibly, on account of the bond of peace, divine love is breathed into their hearts, so that they may be able to say, "Because the love of God is shed abroad in our hearts by the Holy Ghost which is given unto us." But there are many operations of the Holy Spirit, which the same apostle commemorates in a certain passage at such length as he thinks sufficient, and then concludes: "But all these worketh that one and the selfsame Spirit, dividing to every man severally as He will" [1 Cor. 12:11].

Hence, it is also understandable that the grace of God, brought about by the Holy Spirit, the Gift of God, can only be received in the church. Thus, the church is also the locus of forgiveness.

From Augustine, *Enchiridion on Faith, Hope and Love* 65, NPNF[1] 3:258.

But even crimes themselves, however great, may be remitted in the Holy Church.... [It is the] Church in which the sins are remitted ...; and outside the Church sins are not remitted. For the Church alone has received the pledge of the Holy Spirit, without which there is no remission of sins—such, at least, as brings the pardoned to eternal life.

From Augustine, *Sermon on the Mount* 21.28, NPNF[1] 6:328.

And thus sins, because they are not forgiven out of the Church, must be forgiven by that Spirit, by whom the Church is gathered together into one. In fact, if any one out of the Church repent him of his sins, and for this so great sin whereby he is an alien from the Church of God, has an heart impenitent, what doth that other repentance profit him? Seeing by this alone he speaketh a word against the Holy Ghost, whereby he is alienated from the Church, which hath received this gift, that in her remission of sins should be given in the Holy Ghost? Which remission though it be the work of the Whole Trinity, is yet understood specially to belong to the Holy Spirit. For He is the Spirit of the adoption of sons, "in whom we cry Abba, Father;" that we may be able to say to Him, "Forgive us our debts" [Luke 11:4]. And, "Hereby we know" as the Apostle John says, "that Christ dwelleth in us, by His Spirit which He hath given us" [1 John 4:13]. "The Spirit Itself beareth witness with our spirit that we are the children of God" [Rom. 8:16]. For to Him appertains the fellowship, by which we are made the one body of the One only Son of God. Whence it is written, "If there be therefore any consolation in Christ, if any comfort of love, if any fellowship of the Spirit" [Phil. 2:1].

Referring to Cyprian, to whom we owe the ancient rule *extra ecclesiam nulla salus* ("outside the church there is no salvation"), Augustine thus concludes that those who separate themselves from the church, by that act also are also separated from grace and the Holy Spirit.

From Augustine, *Baptism* 4.23.3, NPNF[1] 4:475.

He [Cyprian] says "that the Church, and the Spirit, and baptism, are mutually incapable of separation from each other, and therefore" he wishes that "those who are separated from the Church and the Holy Spirit should be understood to be separated also from baptism." But if this is the case, then when any one has received baptism in the

Catholic Church, it remains so long in him as he himself remains in the Church, which is not so. For it is not restored to him when he returns, just because he did not lose it when he seceded. But as the disaffected sons have not the Holy Spirit in the same manner as the beloved sons, and yet they have baptism; so heretics also have not the Church as Catholics have, and yet they have baptism. "For the Holy Spirit of discipline will flee deceit," and yet baptism will not flee from it. And so, as baptism can continue in one from whom the Holy Spirit withdraws Himself, so can baptism continue where the Church is not. But if "the laying on of hands" were not "applied to one coming from heresy," he would be as it were judged to be wholly blameless; but for the uniting of love, which is the greatest gift of the Holy Spirit, without which any other holy thing that there may be in a man is profitless to his salvation, hands are laid on heretics when they are brought to a knowledge of the truth.

CHAPTER 4

Medieval Pneumatologies:
Eastern Traditions

Introduction to Medieval Pneumatologies

Attempting to do any kind of justice to a time period that stretches over a millennium—from the end of the patristic era at the beginning of the sixth century to the time of the Protestant and Catholic Reformations—requires tremendous selectivity.[1] What is more, we have at our disposal sources not only from two main traditions, the Christian East and Christian West, but also genres as different as the prophetic-apophatic approaches of Pseudo-Dionysius the Areopagite or Joachim of Fiore to the highly analytic-doctrinal treatises of Thomas Aquinas and Anselm of Canterbury to the mystical-poetic narratives of women theologians such as Catherine of Siena and Hildegard of Bingen.

Any kind of generalization sweeping over such a long time span and diversity of approaches is just that, a generalization. Yet most scholars would agree that while the Holy Spirit did not of course disappear from the theological radar screen, neither was there much new doctrinal initiative except for the scholastic *summas*. Nevertheless, even the main works of Aquinas built not only on Augustinian but also on other patristic resources. In many ways, the doctrinal refinements in pneumatology merely attempted to clarify the points left open or disputed in patristic theology.

What is noteworthy and certainly something to be presented in a source book like this is the proliferation of views and experiences of the Spirit. The first group of pneumatological and soteriological traditions comes from the branch of the church that after the split of the Christian church in 1054 as a result of the *filioque* debate came to be known as the Christian East. This branch includes not only the "major" Eastern Orthodox Church but also a number of other Eastern traditions, such as the Assyrian Church,

---

1. For a helpful guide, see Stanley M. Burgess, *The Holy Spirit: Eastern Christian Traditions* (Peabody, MA: Hendrickson, 1989); idem, *The Holy Spirit: Medieval Roman Catholic and Reformation Traditions* (Peabody, MA: Hendrickson, 1997).

three Non-Chalcedonian churches, Armenian, Coptic, Ethiopian, and the Jacobite or West Syrian Church. In this survey, the smaller Eastern churches are only marginally represented.

Following the Eastern Christian testimonies, the experiences and theologies of the Spirit in the Christian West will be grouped under two subheadings. The first category is the rich and variegated mystical spirituality of the (High) Middle Ages represented by a number of female saints such as Hildegard of Bingen, Catherine of Siena, Birgitta of Sweden, among others, as well as two male mystics, Bernard of Clairvaux and St. Bonaventure (chap. 5). The second category consists of "scholastic" or "mainstream" theologians of the Christian West headed by the Venerable Bede and followed by the two luminaries, the Angelic Doctor, Thomas Aquinas, and Anselm of Canterbury (chap. 6). Some medieval theologians such as Richard of St. Victor represent both traditions.

The Spirit in Medieval Eastern Christian Traditions

Pseudo-Dionysius the Areopagite

A fitting opening testimony to the post-patristic Eastern Orthodox pneumatologies is offered by the body of writings of the fifth- or sixth-century anonymous mystic whose works are attributed to Dionysius the Areopagite, mentioned in Acts 17:34 as having been baptized by St. Paul in the aftermath of the apostle's famous speech at Mars Hill, the Areopagus, in Athens. There is no way for us to know the author of these writings; scholars wonder if it could be a late fifth- or early sixth-century Syrian monk with Platonic leanings. Notwithstanding lack of historical knowledge, the writings attributed to the Areopagite exercised a powerful influence surpassed by few writings both in the Christian East and West throughout the medieval period. The opening paragraph of his *Mystical Theology* sets the tone for a proper Trinitarian spirituality in awe and mystery.

> From Dionysius the Areopagite, *Mystical Theology* 1, in *Dionysius the Areopagite:*
> *On the Divine Names and the Mystical Theology*, ed. Clarence Edwin Rolt
> (London: SPCK, 1920), http://www.ccel.org, 192–93 (hereafter Rolt).

TRINITY, which exceedeth all Being, Deity, and Goodness! Thou that instructeth Christians in Thy heavenly wisdom! Guide us to that topmost height of mystic lore which exceedeth light and more than exceedeth knowledge, where the simple, absolute, and unchangeable mysteries of heavenly Truth lie hidden in the dazzling obscurity of the secret Silence, outshining all brilliance with the intensity of their darkness, and surcharging our blinded intellects with the utterly impalpable and invisible fairness of glories which exceed all beauty! . . . For, by the unceasing and absolute renunciation of thyself and all things, thou shalt in pureness cast all things aside, and be released from all, and so shalt be led upwards to the Ray of that divine Darkness which exceedeth all existence.

In his other main work, *The Divine Names*, Pseudo-Dionysius further elucidates the approach of this apophatic theology that takes as its bases Scripture and the power of the Holy Spirit.

From Pseudo-Dionysius the Areopagite,
The Divine Names 1.1 (Rolt, 51–53).

And here also let us set before our minds the scriptural rule that in speaking about God we should declare the Truth, not with enticing words of man's wisdom, but in demonstration of the power which the Spirit stirred up in the Sacred Writers, whereby, in a manner surpassing speech and knowledge, we embrace those truths which, in like manner, surpass them, in that Union which exceeds our faculty, and exercise of discursive, and of intuitive reason. We must not then dare to speak, or indeed to form any conception, of the hidden super-essential Godhead, except those things that are revealed to us from the Holy Scriptures. For a super-essential understanding of It is proper to Unknowing, which lieth in the Super-Essence Thereof surpassing Discourse, Intuition and Being; acknowledging which truth let us lift up our eyes towards the steep height, so far as the effluent light of the Divine Scriptures grants its aid, and, as we strive to ascend unto those Supernal Rays, let us gird ourselves for the task with holiness and the reverent fear of God. For, if we may safely trust the wise and infallible Scriptures, Divine things are revealed unto each created spirit in proportion to its powers, and in this measure is perception granted through the workings of the Divine goodness, the which in just care for our preservation divinely tempereth unto finite measure the infinitude of things which pass man's understanding. For even as things which are intellectually discerned cannot be comprehended or perceived by means of those things which belong to the senses, nor simple and imageless things by means of types and images, nor the formless and intangible essence of unembodied things by means of those which have bodily form, by the same law of truth the boundless Super-Essence surpasses Essences, the Super-Intellectual Unity surpasses Intelligences, the One which is beyond thought surpasses the apprehension of thought, and the Good which is beyond utterance surpasses the reach of words. Yea, it is an Unity which is the unifying Source of all unity and a Super-Essential Essence, a Mind beyond the reach of mind and a Word beyond utterance, eluding Discourse, Intuition, Name, and every kind of being. It is the Universal Cause of existence while Itself existing not, for It is beyond all Being and such that It alone could give, with proper understanding thereof, a revelation of Itself.

Maximus the Confessor

One-time aide to the Byzantine emperor Heraclius, the seventh-century theologian and monk Saint Maximus the Confessor (also known as Maximus the Theologian and Maximus of Constantinople) is highly regarded also in the Christian West. He was a key opponent to heretical christological views of monothelism and monoenergism that claimed, respectively, that Jesus had only one will and one activity. In keeping with the apophatic theology of the Christian East, Maximus considers the knowledge of God in the context of mystical seeing, purity of life, and deification.

Union with God as the Goal of the Knowledge of God

From Maximus the Confessor, *Four Hundred Texts on Love*,
First Century, 87, 88, 90, in *Maximus Confessor: Selected Writings*,
Classics of Western Spirituality, trans. and notes by George C. Berthold
(New York: Paulist Press, 1985), 41 (hereafter Berthold).

87. When the mind is pure and takes on ideas of things it is moved to a spiritual contemplation. But when it has become impure by carelessness, it imagines mere ideas of other things, so that receiving human ideas it turns back to shameful and evil thoughts.

88. When in time of prayer no ideas of the world ever disturb the mind, then know that you are not outside the limits of detachment. . . .

90. Just as the beauty of visible things attracts the eye of sense, so also the knowledge of invisible things attracts the pure mind to itself.

Liturgy is the pinnacle of the Eastern church's life; it is there that true knowledge of God is also imparted.

From Maximus the Confessor, *The Church's*
Mystagogy 23, 24 (Berthold, 204, 207).

23. . . . And consider how the soul . . . comes as into a church to an inviolable shelter of peace in the natural contemplation in the Spirit, and how free of any fighting or disorder it enters it together with reason and before the Word and our great and true High Priest of God. There it learns, by symbols of the divine readings which take place, the principles of beings and the marvelous and grand mystery of divine Providence revealed in the Law and the Prophets, and it receives in each, by the beautiful instruction divinely given in them through the holy angels who spiritually communicate to it the true understanding. . . .

24. . . . By the prayer through which we are made worthy to call God our Father we receive the truest adoption in the grace of the Holy Spirit. By the "One is holy" and what follows, we have the grace and familiarity which unites us to God himself.

The Holy Spirit as God's Kingdom

In one of the most unusual statements about the Holy Spirit, Maximus considers the Spirit as the kingdom of God!

From Maximus the Confessor, *Commentary*
on the Our Father 4 (Berthold, 106–7).

4. . . . For the name of God the Father who subsists essentially is the only-begotten Son, and the kingdom of God the Father who subsists essentially is the Holy Spirit. Indeed, what Matthew here calls kingdom another evangelist elsewhere calls Holy Spirit: "May your Holy Spirit come and purify us." . . . It is right, then, that after the elimination of anger and lust there comes, according to the prayer, the victory of the kingdom of God the Father for those who, having rejected them, are worthy to say, "thy kingdom come," that is to say, the Holy Spirit, for by the principle and path of meekness they have already become temples of God by the Spirit.

Hence, it is understandable the Spirit is present everywhere in the world, even among those who do not know God.

From Maximus the Confessor, *First Century on Various Texts* 72–73, in
The Philokalia: The Complete Text, vol. 2, comp. St. Nikodimos of the Holy Mountain
and St. Makarios of Corinth; trans. and ed. G. E. H. Palmer, Philip Sherrard,
Kallistos Ware, and Holy Transfiguration Monastery et al. (London; Boston:
Faber & Faber, 1979), 180–81 (hereafter *Philokalia*).

72. The Holy Spirit is not absent from any created being, especially not from one which in any way participates in intelligence. For being God and God's Spirit, He embraces in unity the spiritual knowledge of all created things, providentially permeating all things with His power, and vivifying their inner essences in accordance with their nature. In this way he makes men aware of things done sinfully against the law of nature, and renders them capable of choosing principles which are true and in conformity with nature. Thus we find many barbarians and nomadic peoples turning to a civilized way of life and setting aside the savage laws which they had kept among themselves from time immemorial.

73. The Holy Spirit is present unconditionally in all things, in that He embraces all things, provides for all, and vivifies the natural seeds within them. He is present in a specific way in all who are under the Law, in that He shows them where they have broken the commandments and enlightens them about the promise given concerning Christ. In all who are Christians He is present also in yet another way in that He makes them sons of God. But in none is He fully present as the author of wisdom except in those who have understanding, and who by their holy way of life have made themselves fit to receive His indwelling and deifying presence.

The Holy Spirit as Grace

Following the tradition of the East, not only is Maximus's understanding of salvation Trinitarian but also his understanding of grace is thoroughly pneumatological.

From Maximus the Confessor, *Four Hundred Texts on Love*, Fourth Century, 77–78 (Berthold, 84).

77. Who enlightened you with the faith of the holy, adorable, and consubstantial Trinity? Or who made known to you the incarnate dispensation of one of the holy Trinity? Or who taught you about the principles of incorporeal beings and those concerning the origin and end of the visible world, or about the resurrection from the dead and eternal life, or about the glory of the kingdom of heaven and the awful judgment? Was it not the grace of Christ dwelling in you, which is the pledge of the Holy Spirit? What is greater than this grace, or what is better than this wisdom and knowledge? Or what is loftier than these promises? . . .

78. God who has promised you everlasting happiness and placed in your heart the pledge of the Spirit has enjoined you to tend to your behavior so that the inner man, freed from the passions, might begin here and now to enjoy this happiness.

Spiritual Gifts and Love

From Maximus the Confessor, *First Century on Various Texts*, 96–97 (*Philokalia*, 186–87).

96. St. Paul refers to the different energies of the Holy Spirit as different gifts of grace, stating that they are all energized by one and the same Holy Spirit (cf. 1 Cor. 12:11). The "manifestation of the Spirit" (1 Cor. 12:7) is given according to the measure of every man's faith through participation in a particular gift of grace. Thus every believer is receptive to the energy of the Spirit in a way that corresponds to his degree of faith and the state of his soul; and this energy grants him the capacity needed to carry out a particular commandment.

97. One person is given the quality of wisdom, another the quality of spiritual knowledge, another the quality of faith, and someone else one of the other gifts of the Spirit enumerated by St Paul (cf. 1 Cor. 12:8–11). In the same way, one person receives through the Spirit, according to the degree of his faith, the gift of that perfect and direct love for God which is free from all materiality; another through the same Spirit receives the gift of perfect love for his neighbour; another receives something else from the same Spirit. In each, as I have said, the gift that conforms with his state is energized. For every capacity for fulfilling a commandment is called a gift of the Spirit.

Symeon the New Theologian

Along with St. John the Evangelist and Gregory of Nazianzus, one of the three Cappadocians, Symeon has acquired the name "theologian" in the Christian East. Living at the turn of the second millennium, he served as the abbot of the St. Mamas monastery. His main work, *The Discourses*, is a manual for monks and at the same time a profound guide to spirituality and theology. Pneumatological themes abound in those writings, and several of them are specifically devoted to the topics of the Spirit and salvation (6, 10, 16, 20, 24, and so forth).

The Qualities of the Spiritual Person

Symeon's discourses give examples of several saints whose spirituality and experiences in the Spirit stand out as powerful examples for others. Discourse 6, chapter 6, shares about the spiritual experience "of our holy father," without any specific designation (unless it is Symeon the Pious as mentioned in the beginning of the discourse).

From Symeon the New Theologian, *Discourses* 6.6, in
Symeon the New Theologian, The Discourses, trans. C. J. deCatanzaro
(New York: Paulist Press, 1980), 124–25 (hereafter deCatanzaro).

Just as a cistern is filled by running water, so our holy father partook
of the fullness of our Master Jesus Christ and was filled by the grace
of His Spirit, which is "living water" (*Jn. 4:10*). A man may take water
from a cistern that overflows and runs down on the outside till his
thirst is quenched. Similarly we have seen and have received from
our holy father that which overflowed and constantly poured over;
we drank of it and washed our faces with it, even our hands and feet,
and bathed our entire bodies (*Jn. 13:9f*) and our very souls with that
immortal water. What a strange and wonderful mystery, brethren!

In the following passage Symeon lists the qualities of the saint.

Symeon the New Theologian, *Discourses*
10.2 (deCatanzaro, 163).

The whole praise and blessedness of the saints consists of these two
elements—their orthodox faith and praiseworthy life, and the gift of
the Holy Spirit and His spiritual gifts. A third point follows on them.
When a man lives rightly, as a friend of God, with orthodox faith,
and when God bestows His gifts on him and glorifies him through
the gift of the Spirit, there follows the praise of the whole Church of
the faithful and on the part of all its teachers and their pronounce-
ment of his blessedness.

The Nature and Metaphors of the Holy Spirit

Most of the time when speaking of theology in general and pneumatology
in particular, the mystical theologian employs a number of metaphors and
illustrations. In speaking of the Spirit and the Spirit's work, Symeon also
uses metaphors that have not been used much elsewhere, such as the lamp
and the key of the door.

Symeon the New Theologian, *Discourses*
33.1–6 (deCatanzaro, 340–44).

2. Just as it is no use to him who walks in darkness to have many and
very beautiful lamps all extinguished (*cf. Mt. 25:8*), for they cannot
help him to see either himself or any one else, so he who appears to
have all virtues in him (even if it were possible) (*cf. Lk. 8:18*), but
has not the light of the Holy Spirit in him, can neither see his own
actions properly nor have sure knowledge whether they are pleasing
to God. . . .

4. I will tell you yet again, the door is the Son, for, says He, "I am the door" (*Jn. 10:7, 9*). The key of the door is the Holy Spirit, for He says, "Receive the Holy Spirit. If you forgive the sins of any, they are forgiven; if you retain the sins of any, they are retained" (*Jn. 20:22–23*).

5. But that the Holy Spirit first opens our minds and teaches us the things concerning the Father and Son, He Himself again said, "When He, the Spirit of truth comes, who proceeds from the Father, He will bear witness to Me (*Jn. 15:25*), and will guide you into all the truth" (*Jn. 16:13*). Do you see how through the Spirit, or, rather, in the Spirit, the Father and the Son are made known inseparably? . . .

6. The Holy Ghost is spoken of as a key because through Him and in Him we are first enlightened in mind. We are purified and illuminated with the light of knowledge; we are baptized from on high and born anew (*cf. Jn. 3:3, 5*) and made into children of God.

Salvation as Union

Under the title "God as the Light of the Soul," Symeon describes the blessings of union with God and God's Spirit, which is *theosis.*

From Symeon the New Theologian, *Discourses*
15.3 (deCatanzaro, 195–96).

Let no one deceive you! God is light (*1 John 1:5*), and to those who have entered into union with Him He imparts of His own brightness to the extent that they have been purified. When the lamp of the soul, that is, the mind, has been kindled, then it knows that a divine fire has taken hold of it and inflamed it. How great a marvel! Man is united to God spiritually and physically, since the soul is not separated from the mind, neither the body from the soul. By being united in essence man also has three hypostases by grace. He is a single god by adoption with body and soul and the divine Spirit, of whom he has become a partaker. Then is fulfilled what was spoken by the prophet David, "I have said, ye are gods, and ye are all the sons of the Most High" (*Ps. 82:6*), that is, sons of the Most High according to the image of the Most High and according to His likeness (*Gen. 1:26*). We become the divine offspring of the Divine Spirit (*Jn. 3:8*), to whom the Lord rightly said and continues to say, "Abide in Me, that you may bring forth much fruit" (*Jn. 15:4, 8*). . . . It is evident that just as the Father abides in His own Son (*Jn. 14:10*) and the Son in His Father's bosom (*Jn. 1:18*) by nature, so those who have been born anew through the divine Spirit (*Jn. 3:3, 5*) and by His gift have become the brothers of Christ our God and sons of God and gods by adoption, by grace abide in God and God in them (*1 John 4:12ff.*).

On Means to Acquiring the Spirit
In the Christian East, not only among the Desert Fathers but also more widely, ascetic exercises, prayers, tears, as well as other similar spiritual exercises are considered to be the proper means of acquiring the Spirit. While these have nothing to do with "merit"—a term unknown in Eastern soteriological conversations—they demonstrate the willingness and desire of the person to grow in Christian faith and practice.

From Symeon the New Theologian, *Discourses*
1.5 (deCatanzaro, 45–46).

My dear brethren in Christ, let us then be eager to employ all means, including mutual love, to serve God. . . . Thus I too in my lowliness may rejoice as I see your continual progress in the life that is in accordance with God, as you increase in faith, in purity, in the fear of God, in reverence, in compunction and tears. By these the inward man is purified and is filled with divine light, and wholly becomes the possession of the Holy Spirit in a contrite soul and a downcast mind. My joy will be a blessing for you and an increase of imperishable and blessed life in Christ Jesus our Lord, to whom be glory forever. Amen.

Gregory Palamas

A spiritual father and theologian, the fourteenth-century monk Gregory Palamas of Mount Athos, also bishop of Thessalonica, is one of the most highly venerated teachers in the Eastern Church. He made lasting contributions to the doctrine of the Trinity by consolidating the now standard distinction in the East between the "essence" and "energies" of God (the roots of which go back to the famous, or better, infamous, hesychastic movement of the eleventh century under the leadership of Symeon the New Theologian), the Eastern doctrine of salvation as *theosis*, and the like. Vehemently opposing Barlaam, the main opponent embraced by the Roman Catholics, Gregory trusted in prayer, especially the Jesus prayer, as the means to attain true spiritual knowledge as opposed to secular knowledge. His main work is *The Triads*, which emerged in various stages in debate with Barlaam and his counterwritings.

Salvation as Deification and Participation in God's Energies
No other post-patristic Father has expounded so powerfully and convincingly the meaning and implications of the Christian East's distinctive vision of salvation as *theosis* or deification than Gregory Palamas. In these expositions, one can easily discern the underlying theological

anthropology of the East, in which the human being as *image of God* is believed to be able to receive the deifying grace of the Holy Spirit.

From *The Triads of Gregory Palamas*, ed., with intro. John Meyendorff, trans. Nicholas Gendle (New York: Paulist Press, 1983), 33 (hereafter Meyendorff).

So, when the saints contemplate this divine light within themselves, seeing it by the divinising communion of the Spirit, through the mysterious visitation of perfecting illuminations—then they behold the garment of their deification, their mind being glorified and filled by the grace of the Word, beautiful beyond measure in His splendour. . . . How can this be accomplished corporeally, now that He Himself is no longer corporeally present after His ascension to the heavens? It is necessarily carried out in a spiritual fashion, for the mind becomes supercelestial, and as it were the companion of Him who passed beyond the heavens for our sake, since it is manifestly yet mysteriously united to God, and contemplates supernatural and ineffable visions, being filled with all the immaterial knowledge of a higher light.

Often deification is described in terms of "seeing the Light," which is spiritual seeing beyond just the knowledge of God.

From Gregory Palamas, *Triads* (Meyendorff, 57–60).

This light is not the essence of God, for that is inaccessible and incommunicable; it is not an angel, for it bears the marks of the Master. Sometimes it makes a man go out from the body or else, without separating him from the body, it elevates him to an ineffable height. At other times, it transforms the body, and communicates its own splendour to it when, miraculously, the light which deifies the body becomes accessible to the bodily eyes. . . . But hesychasts know that the purified and illuminated mind, when clearly participating in the grace of God, also beholds other mystical and supernatural visions—for in seeing itself, it sees more than itself: It does not simply contemplate some other object, or simply its own image, but rather the glory impressed on its own image by the grace of God. This radiance reinforces the mind's power to transcend itself, and accomplish that union with those better things which is beyond understanding. By this union, the mind sees God in the Spirit in a manner transcending human powers. . . . Thus we set forth as a summary the words of Isaac, the faithful interpreter of these things: "Our soul," he affirms, "possesses two eyes, as all the Fathers tell us. . . . Yet the sight which is proper to each 'eye' is not for the same use: with one eye, we behold the secrets of nature, that is to say, the power of God, His wisdom and providence towards us, things comprehensible by virtue of the greatness of His governance. With the other eye, we contemplate the glory of His holy nature, since it pleases God to introduce us to the spiritual mysteries."

Eastern spirituality not only speaks liberally about the union between God and the human being. In the following quotation, Gregory claims astonishingly that the union can be so strong as to make a human person "light and spirit"!

From Gregory Palamas, *Triads* (Meyendorff, 66).

Paul therefore *was* light and spirit, to which he was united, by which he had received the capacity of union, having gone out from all beings, and become light by grace, and nonbeing by transcendence, that is by exceeding created things. As St. Maximus says, he who is in God has left behind him "all that is after God . . . all the realities, names and values which are after God will be outside those who come to be in God by grace." But in attaining this condition, the divine Paul could not participate absolutely in the divine essence, for the essence of God goes beyond even nonbeing by reason of transcendence, since it is also "more-than-God."

The Deifying Spirit

Thus, in the Christian East, the Holy Spirit is often called the "deifying Spirit."

From Gregory Palamas, *Triads* (Meyendorff, 89–90).

The deifying gift of the Spirit thus cannot be equated with the superessential essence of God. It is the deifying energy of this divine essence, yet not the totality of this energy, even though it is indivisible in itself. Indeed, what created thing could receive the entire, infinitely potent power of the Spirit, except He who was carried in the womb of a Virgin, by the presence of the Holy Spirit and the overshadowing of the power of the Most High? He received "all the fulness of the Divinity." . . . Thus the deifying gift of the Spirit is a mysterious light, and transforms into light those who receive its richness.

Pursuit of Spiritual Life and Spiritual Gifts

In addition to a more positive anthropology, Eastern spirituality also emphasizes asceticism, prayers, and other spiritual exercises as a way to a deeper spirituality. These are not considered merits (indeed, in the Christian East, the Augustinian-Pelagian type of debates are totally unknown) but rather proper and necessary responses to the grace of God. Pursuing the ways of the Spirit and the will of God also leads to the acquiring of charisms.

From Gregory Palamas, *Triads* (Meyendorff, 52–53).

When the soul pursues this blessed activity, it deifies the body also; which, being no longer driven by corporeal and material passions—although those who lack experience of this think that it is always so driven—returns to itself and rejects all contact with evil things. Indeed, it inspires its own sanctification and inalienable divinisation, as the miracle-working relics of the saints clearly demonstrate. What of Stephen, the first martyr, whose face, even while he was yet living, shone like the face of an angel? Did not his body also experience divine things? Is not such an experience and the activity allied to it common to soul and body? . . .

Indeed every man of sense knows well that most of the charisms of the Spirit are granted to those worthy of them at the time of prayer. "Ask and it shall be given," the Lord says. This applies not only to being ravished "even to the third heaven," but to all the gifts of the Spirit. The gift of diversity of tongues and their interpretation which Paul recommends us to acquire by prayer, shows that certain charisms operate through the body. . . . The same is true of the word of instruction, the gift of healing, the performing of miracles and Paul's laying-on of hands by which he communicated the Holy Spirit.

In the case of the gifts of instruction and of tongues and their interpretation, even though these are acquired by prayer, yet it is possible that they may operate even when prayer is absent from the soul. But healings and miracles never take place unless the soul of the one exercising either gift be in a state of intense mental prayer and his body in perfect tune with his soul. In short, the transmission of the Spirit is effected not only when prayer is present in the soul, a prayer which mystically accomplishes the union with the perpetual source of these benefits; not only when one is practising mental prayer, since it is not recorded that the apostles uttered any audible words at the moment of laying on their hands.

Gregory of Sinai

The fourteenth-century saint Gregory of Sinai is named so after Mount Sinai, on which he took the monastic vows. Known for his piety and especially his ceaseless prayer life, he was also a spiritual director. Following the tradition of the Christian East, Gregory of Sinai emphasizes the active nature of faith as opposed to a lazy faith.

Saving Faith

From St. Gregory of Sinai, *Texts on Commandments and Dogmas*, vol. 5, par. 28, in *Writings from the Philokalia on Prayer of the Heart*, trans. E. Kadloubovsky and G. E. H. Palmer (London: Faber & Faber, n.d.), 43 (hereafter Kadloubovsky & Palmer).

28. Faith, full of grace, supported by the keeping of commandments would by itself lead to salvation, if we kept it in full force and did not prefer dead and inactive faith to living and active faith in Christ. It behoves a believer to establish the image of faith in his heart and to organise his life according to active faith in Christ. But nowadays ignorance teaches the pious a faith manifested in words, dead and unfeeling, instead of the faith of grace.

While mainline Protestant Christianity is very reserved about making distinctions between various levels of sanctification, in the Christian East such gradations are typical since they do not hesitate to talk about the divine-human *synergia* (cooperation) in salvation.

From St. Gregory of Sinai, *Texts on Commandments and Dogmas*, 41–44, 54, 56 (Kadloubovsky & Palmer, 45–47).

41. If our nature is not kept immaculate by the Spirit, or is not purified as it should be, then body and soul cannot be one with Christ, now and in the future resurrection. For the all-embracing and all-uniting force of the Spirit is not wont to sew the old cloak of the passions on to the new garment of grace.

42. He will share in Christ's glory who, through being formed in Christ, has received renewal by the Spirit and has preserved it, and so has attained to ineffable deification. No one, there, will be one with Christ or be a member of Christ, if he has not become even here a receiver of grace and has not, thereby, become 'transformed by the renewing of' his 'mind' (Rom. xii. 2). . . .

44. By many mansions the Saviour meant the different degrees of existence in the other world. The kingdom is one, but within it there are many divisions, according to the difference in knowledge and virtue of those who enter therein, and to their degree of deification. For 'there is one glory of the sun, and another glory of the moon, and another glory of the stars; for one star differeth from another star in glory' [1 Cor. 15:41], as says the divine Apostle, though all

shine alike in the firmament. He is akin to the angels, as it were incorporeal and free from corruption, who has cleansed his mind by tears, has resurrected his soul even here by the Spirit and, having subjugated his body to reason, has made it radiant with light, like a flame. . . .

54. It is said that in the life to come the angels and saints shall never cease to progress in increasing their gifts, striving for greater and ever greater blessings. No slackening or change from virtue to sin is admitted in that life. . . .

56. In the future, a man shall have the degree of deification corresponding to his present perfection in spiritual stature.

The Patriarch Callistus of Xanthopoulous and Ignatius of Xanthopoulous

Student of Gregory of Sinai, Callistus of Xanthopoulous became Patriarch of Constantinople. From him we know much of his spiritual father's life. His closest fellow worker was Ignatius, with whom he penned a highly treasured *Directions to Hesychasts*. The following passages from that manual reflect, on the one hand, a high theology of the sacraments, in this case water baptism, and, on the other hand, the need for the faithful to pursue a spiritual life worthy of this high calling.

From Callistus and Ignatius of Xanthopoulous, *Directions to Hesychasts* 5–7 (Kadloubovsky & Palmer, 166–69).

5. *The glory of the grace of holy baptism, what dims and what restores it*
When we are being baptised, our soul, purified by the Spirit, becomes brighter than the sun; not only are we then able to look at the glory of God, but we ourselves take on something of its radiance. As polished silver, illumined by the rays of the sun, radiates light not only from its own nature but also from the radiance of the sun, so a soul, purified by the Divine Spirit, becomes more brilliant than silver; it both receives the ray of Divine glory, and from itself reflects the ray of this same glory. . . . Have you heard now the words of the Spirit? Have you realised the power of this sacrament? Have you understood the travail of our complete spiritual regeneration after we leave the holy font, its fruits, its fullness and the honours of victory? Do you see how much it lies in our power to increase or to diminish this supernatural grace, that is, to show it forth or to obscure it? What obscures it is the storm of worldly cares, and the ensuing darkness of passions. . . . Conversely, grace is manifested by that which is reflected from

the Divine commandments, in the souls of those who walk not in the flesh, but in the Spirit; for it is said: "Walk in the Spirit, and ye shall not fulfil the lust of the flesh" (Gal. v. 16). Grace leads such souls towards salvation and raises them, as by a ladder, to the very summit of perfection, to its very highest degree—love, which is God.

6. *In holy baptism we freely receive Divine grace. When we cover it over with passions, we cleanse it again by obedience to commandments*

In the Divine womb, that is, in the holy font, we freely receive perfect Divine grace. If after this we cover it over with the fog of passions, either through abuse of temporal things, or through excess of cares for worldly activities, it is possible, even after this, to regain possession of it, to restore its supernatural brightness and to see quite vividly its manifestation, by repentance and the fulfilment of commandments whose action is Divine. Grace manifests in proportion to each man's zeal in remaining faithful to faith, but above all through the help and benevolence of our Lord Jesus Christ.

7. *A man living in God should follow all the commandments, but devote the greater part of his activity to the foremost of them as the parents of others*

As we have said, the principle and root of all activity natural to us is to live in accordance with the saving commandments, while the fruit and the end (expected from this) is to recapture the perfect grace of the Holy Spirit, granted us from the first through baptism, which still remains in us . . . although, being buried under passions, it reveals itself only through our fulfilling the commandments given by God. Therefore it behoves us to try with all zeal to fulfil all these commandments, and by this purification to reveal the grace of the Spirit existing in us, making it manifest and clearly seen. . . . For in this way, with God's help, we shall attain without stumbling both the aim of the right action we have undertaken in the beginning, and the end of our strivings, that is, the manifestation in us of the grace of the Holy Spirit.

The Spirit in Medieval Western Christian Traditions 1: The Mystics

Veni Spiritus Creator

A fitting way to introduce the medieval pneumatological and soteriological discourses in the Christian West is to listen to the perhaps most famous hymn ever written to the Spirit, known as "Veni Spiritus Creator." While scholarly consensus is lacking, an old tradition attributes this hymn to Gregory the Great, often named "the last Latin Father" (after Ambrose, Jerome, and Augustine), the sixth-century pope and great advocate of the office of the primacy.

From Robert C. Broderick, ed., *The Catholic Encyclopedia*
(Nashville: Thomas Nelson, 1975), 598–99.

Creator-Spirit, all-Divine,
Come, visit every soul of Thine,
And fill with Thy celestial flame
The hearts which Thou Thyself didst frame.

O gift of God, Thine is the sweet
Consoling name of Paraclete—
And spring of life and fire and love
And unction flowing from above.

The mystic sevenfold gifts are Thine,
Finger of God's right hand divine;
The Father's promise sent to teach
The tongue a rich and heavenly speech.

Kindle with fire brought from above
Each sense, and fill our hearts with love;
And grant our flesh, so weak and frail,
The strength of Thine which cannot fail.

Drive far away our deadly foe.
And grant us Thy true peace to know;
So we, led by Thy guidance still,
May safely pass through every ill.

To us, through Thee, the grace be shown
To know the Father and the Son;
And Spirit of Them both, may we
Forever rest our faith in Thee.

To Sire and Son be praises meet,
And to the Holy Paraclete;
And may Christ send us from above
That Holy Spirit's gift of love.

Hildegard of Bingen

The year 1998 was the nine-hundredth birthday of the twelfth-century Benedictine Hildegard of Bingen. This multitalented woman was a theologian, herbalist, composer, visionary, and prophet. A prolific author, she produced hundreds of letters; *Scivias*, a theological "summa"; songs; and other writings.

> From Hildegard of Bingen, *Scivias*, trans. Columba
> Hart and Jane Bishop (New York: Paulist Press, 1990),
> bk. 2, vision 1, 150 (hereafter Hart & Bishop).

O you who are wretched earth, and, as a woman, untaught in all learning of earthly teachers and unable to read literature with philosophical understanding, you are nonetheless touched by My light, which kindles in you an inner fire like a burning sun; cry out and relate and write these My mysteries that you see and hear in mystical visions. So do not be timid, but say those things you understand in the Spirit as I speak them through you.

> From Hildegard of Bingen, *Scivias*
> 1.1 (Hart & Bishop, 67).

And behold, He Who was enthroned upon that mountain cried out in a strong, loud voice saying, "O human, who are fragile dust of the earth and ashes of ashes! Cry out and speak of the origin of pure salvation until those people are instructed, who, though they see the inmost contents of the Scriptures, do not with to tell them or preach them, because they are lukewarm and sluggish in serving God's justice. Unlock for them the enclosure of mysteries that they, timid as they are, conceal in a hidden and fruitless field. Burst forth into a fountain of abundance and overflow with mystical knowledge. . . . For you have received your profound insight not from humans, but from the lofty and tremendous Judge on high, where this calmness will shine strongly with glorious light among the shining ones."

Catherine of Siena

With her predecessor Hildegard, the fourteenth-century Catherine of Siena is one of the leading Western female mystics. Catherine claimed to receive her first vision at the age of six. Her contemporaries believed she had the gift of healing, and she was also believed to have experienced a "mystical death." Catherine devoted her life in the service of all needy.

The Trinity
Firmly Trinitarian, basically following the Augustinian canons, Catherine had much to say about the Trinity and the Spirit's role alongside Father and Son. While every human being is fashioned in a way that reflects the Trinity, the Mother of God does so particularly.

> From Catherine of Siena, prayer 18, in *The Prayers of Catherine of Siena*, ed. Suzanne Noffke, OP (New York: Paulist Press, 1983), 158–59 (hereafter Noffke, 1983).

You, O Mary, have been made a book in which our rule is written today. In you today is written the eternal Father's wisdom; in you today our human strength and freedom are revealed. I say that our human dignity is revealed because if I look at you, Mary, I see that the Holy Spirit's hand has written the Trinity in you by forming within you the incarnate Word, God's only-begotten Son. He has written for us the Father's wisdom, which this Word is; he has written power for us, because he was powerful enough to accomplish this great mystery; and he has written for us his own—the Holy Spirit's—mercy, for by divine grace and mercy alone was such a great mystery ordained and accomplished.

Salvation history and the Spirit's role therein has a Trinitarian structure.

From Catherine of Siena, *The Dialogue*, trans. and ed. Suzanne Noffke
(New York: Paulist Press, 1980), 140, 288. (hereafter Noffke, 1980).

But by sending into the world my Truth, the incarnate Word, I saw to it that he should take away the wildness and uproot the thorns of original sin. And I made it a grade watered by the blood of Christ crucified, and planted there the seven gifts of the Holy Spirit after rooting out deadly sin. All this happened only after my only-begotten Son's death. It was prefigured in the Old Testament when Elisha was asked to raise up the young man who was dead. . . . He breathed sharply seven times into the boy's mouth and the boy took seven breaths as a sign that he had come back to life.

The Spirit as Love—and as Mother
It is not common in tradition to speak of the Holy Spirit as Mother, yet neither is it something totally unknown.

From Catherine of Siena, *Dialogue* 141 (Noffke, 1980, 292).

Such a soul has the Holy Spirit as a mother who nurses her at the breast of divine charity. The Holy Spirit has set her free, releasing her, as her lord, from the slavery of selfish love. For where the fire of my charity is, the water of selfishness cannot enter to put out this sweet fire in the soul. This servant, the Holy Spirit, whom I in my providence have given her, clothes her, nurtures her, inebriates her with tenderness and the greatest wealth.

The Spirit as the "Waiter" and a "Strong Hand"
In some of the most moving passages of the Trinity, the visionary of Siena imagines the Trinity as servants at the Eucharist table.

From Catherine of Siena, *The Letters of St. Catherine of Siena*,
ed. Suzanne Noffke, OP, vol. 1 (Binghamton, NY: Center for Medieval and Early Renaissance Studies, 1988), 52, 161 (hereafter Noffke, 1988).

I beg you, for love of Christ crucified, to respond with joy and longing to the invitation to this sweet glorious wedding feast, for it is a wedding feast full of joy, sweetness, and every delight. At this wedding feast we leave uncleanness behind and are freed from suffering and guilt. [God] feeds us at the table of the Lamb, who is there as our food and our waiter. For you see, the Father is for us a table bearing everything there is (except sin, which is not in him). The Word,

God's Son, is made our food, roasted over the blazing fire of charity. And that very charity, the Holy Spirit, is our waiter, who with his hands has given and continues to give us God. He is constantly serving us every grace and gift, spiritual as well as material. How foolish, then, for . . . anyone else to stay away from such delight!

Catherine of Siena, *Letters* 47 (Noffke, 1988, 145).

I found myself in desire at the table of the Lamb, and he said to this miserable wretch: "I am table and I am food." The hand of the Holy Spirit was dispensing this food, sweetly serving those who truly relished it.

Here is another striking metaphor Catherine employs of the Spirit.

Catherine of Siena, *Letters* 55 (Noffke, 1988, 171–72).

Oh gentle fire of love! You have given us as servant, as laborer, the most merciful free-flowing Holy Spirit, Who is love itself! He is the strong hand that held the Word nailed fast to the cross. He crushed this tender body and made it yield blood powerful enough to give us life and to secure every stone into the building. [So] every virtue is of value to us and gives life when it has Christ as its foundation and is steeped in his blood. May our hearts burst with love at seeing his blood do what water could not! Who now could wish for more? . . . Let these stones, our hardened hearts, melt in the heat!

The Purifying Spirit

Catherine of Siena, *Prayers* 7 (Noffke, 1983, 58–59).

You are a fire always burning. Yet, though you always consume all that the soul possesses apart from you, you never consume the things that are pleasing to you. Burn with the fire of your Spirit and consume, root out from the bottom up, every fleshly love and affection from the hearts of the new plants you have kindly seen fit to set into the mystic body of holy Church. . . . Fill them with your love's true fervor and make them zealous for faith and virtue.

Joachim of Fiore

Widely considered the most significant apocalyptic prophet of the Middle Ages in the Christian West, Joachim of Fiore was a man of visions and spiritual experiences par excellence. The abbot of a Cistercian monastery later in his life, Joachim divided history into three periods, those of the Father, of the Son, and finally of the Spirit, the end-time apocalyptic pouring out of the Spirit ushering in the end. The last era, that of the Spirit, started with St. Benedictine, whom Joachim admired greatly. As a prophet and mystic, Joachim was no stranger to visions. At times, those visions helped him grasp more fully key doctrines such as the Trinity. This happened on Pentecost Sunday.

> From Joachim of Fiore, preface to *Ten-Stringed Psalter*, quoted in
> *Apocalyptic Spirituality: Treatises and Letters of Lactantius, Also of Montier-en-Der,*
> *Joachin of Fiore, the Spiritual Franciscans, Savonarola*, trans. Bernard McGinn
> (New York: Paulist Press, 1979), 99 (hereafter McGinn).

In the meantime, when I had entered the church to pray to Almighty God before the holy altar, there came upon me an uncertainty concerning belief in the Trinity as though it were hard to understand. . . . When that happened, I prayed with all my might. I was very frightened and was moved to call on the Holy Spirit whose feast day it was to deign to show me the holy mystery of the Trinity. The Lord has promised us that the whole understanding of truth is to be found in the Trinity. I repeated this and began to pray the psalms to complete the number I had intended. Without delay at this moment the shape of a ten-stringed psaltery appeared in my mind.

Fond of typologies and cycles, Joachim speaks of the highest order of the "elect," namely, the monastic order, which is above the orders of the married and the clergy, and attributes it to the Holy Spirit.

> From Joachim of Fiore, *The Book of Concordance,*
> bk. 2, pt. 1, chap. 5 (McGinn, 125).

The monastic order, according to a certain proper form in which the Holy Spirit, who is the author of good things, has shown his full authority, started with Saint Benedict, a man quite famous for his miracles, his work, and his sanctity. This order will bear fruit in the last times.

Meister Eckhart

The thirteenth-century Johannes Eckhart, routinely known as Meister Eckhart (from the German academic title "Master), was not only a leading mystic of the Western Middle Ages but also a widely controversial theologian who fell under papal condemnation for centuries to come.

Grace as Gift

> From Meister Eckhart, "Grace," in *Light, Life, and Love:*
> *Selections from the German Mystics of the Middle Ages,*
> ed. W. R. Inge (1904), n.p., http://www.ccel.org.

Grace never comes in the intelligence or in the will. If it could come in the intelligence or in the will, the intelligence and the will would have to transcend themselves. On this a master says: There is something secret about it; and thereby he means the spark of the soul, which alone can apprehend God. The true union between God and the soul takes place in the little spark, which is called the spirit of the soul. Grace unites not to any work. It is an indwelling and a living together of the soul in God.

Every gift of God makes the soul ready to receive a new gift, greater than itself.

Yea, since God has never given any gift, in order that man might rest in the possession of the gift, but gives every gift that He has given in heaven and on earth, in order that He might be able to give one gift, which is Himself, so with this gift of grace, and with all His gifts He will make us ready for the one gift, which is Himself.

Sanctification as Union—The Highest Goal of the Spiritual Life
In his sermon on sanctification, the Meister elevates sanctification as the highest goal of spiritual life and makes it virtually synonymous with union.

> From Meister Eckhart, *Sermon on Sanctification*, in
> *Meister Eckhart's Sermons*, trans. Claud Field (London:
> H. R. Allenson, 1909?), 41–47,[1] http://www.ccel.org.

I have read many writings both of heathen philosophers and inspired prophets, ancient and modern, and have sought earnestly to discover what is the best and highest quality whereby man may approach most nearly to union with God, and whereby he may most resemble the ideal of himself which existed in God, before God created men. And after having thoroughly searched these writings as far as my reason may penetrate, I find no higher quality than sanctification or separation from all creatures. . . .

Various teachers have praised love greatly, as St Paul does, when he saith, "to whatever height I may attain, if I have not love, I am

---

1. The online edition does not allow accurate distinctions between individual pages since it gives two consecutive page numbers at a time.

nothing." But I set sanctification even above love; in the first place because the best thing in love is that it compels me to love God. . . .

Everything settles in its own appropriate place; now God's proper place is that of oneness and holiness; these come from sanctification; therefore God must of necessity give Himself to a sanctified heart.

Birgitta of Sweden

The most well-known Scandinavian mystic, the fourteenth-century Birgitta (or Bridget) of Sweden received her first vision at the age of seven. A person of many visions, ecstatic experiences, and other spiritual experiences, this mother of eight children (including St. Catherine of Sweden, once a noblewoman) retired towards the end of her life to a simple life of prayer, finally travelling to Rome.

A Lady of Spiritual Authority
Similar to several other spiritual women, Birgitta was a person of miracles, divine oracles, and visions that confirmed God's call.

From *The Life of Blessed Birgitta (by Prior Peter and Master Peter)*, 38, 40, in *Birgitta of Sweden: Life and Selected Writings*, ed. Marguerite Tjader Harris, trans. Albert Ryle Kezel (New York: Paulist Press, 1990), 82–83 (hereafter Harris).

38. Moreover, it also happened very often that to the same Birgitta were revealed the most secret thoughts and doubts of those came to her and even of certain other persons who were absent—things that they themselves had never at all made public by word or by sign. . . .

40. What more is there? For the testimony to so many virtues, to such great holiness and excellence, to such flowing and abundant grace divinely shining in her is all disclosed in the books of the *Heavenly Revelations*, which were divinely given to her, and in the *Book of Questions*, which was also given to her divinely, through an infusion from the Holy Spirit, in a wonderful manner and, as it were, in a single hour, while she was riding her horse and journeying to her villa in Vadstena, as is more fully recorded at the beginning of that same *Book of Questions*. Testimony is also provided by visual experiences, for very often these things were seen by us ourselves and by many others in various parts of the world.

A Prayer Warrior
Here is a vivid testimony to the persistence and power of prayers of Birgitta for her beloved son, Lord Charles, a knight.

From Birgitta of Sweden, *The Seventh Book of Revelation*, 60, 62 (Harris, 186).

60. By her charitable prayers and pious works his mother has perseveringly knocked at the gate of mercy on his behalf; and, for more than thirty years, she has shed many thousands of tears that God might deign to pour the Holy Spirit into his heart so that this same son of hers might willingly offer his goods, his body, and his soul to God's service. . . .

62. And the Virgin Mother of God has given to him, out of her own virtue, whatever he lacks in those spiritual weapons and garments that are proper for knights who must, in the kingdom of heaven, enter the presence of the highest Emperor.

Testimonies to her prayer life abound.

From Birgitta of Sweden, *The Seventh Book of Revelation*, 4, 5 (Harris, 212).

4. For when I see blowing on the hearts of human beings the dangerous winds of the devil's temptations and wicked suggestions, at once I have recourse to my Lord and my God, my Son Jesus Christ, helping them with my prayers and obtaining from him 5. his outpouring of some holy infusions of the Holy Spirit into their hearts to prop them up and savingly confirm them that they may be kept spiritually uninjured by the diabolic wind of temptations lest the devil prevail against human beings, breaking their souls and plucking them up by the stem in accord with his wicked desire.

Julian of Norwich

Another famous fourteenth-century mystic woman, England's Julian of Norwich, reveals her many visions and spiritual experiences in her *Revelations of Divine Love*, also known as *Showings*, which she claimed to have received when she was illiterate. This claim, like so much of her life, is not well known to later generations. Many of her visions were focused on the suffering of Jesus.

From Julian of Norwich, *Revelations of Divine Love*, chap. 16, 28, http://www.ccel.org (no information about translator or editor).

After this Christ shewed a part of His Passion near His dying. I saw His sweet face as it were dry and bloodless with pale dying. And later, more pale, dead, languoring; and then turned more dead unto blue; and then more brown-blue, as the flesh turned more deeply dead. For His Passion shewed to me most specially in His blessed face (and chiefly in His lips): there I saw these four colours, though it were afore fresh, ruddy, and pleasing, to my sight. This was a pitiful change to see, this deep dying. And also the [inward] moisture clotted and dried, to my sight, and the sweet body was brown and black, all turned out of fair, life-like colour of itself, unto dry dying.

A mystic, Julian received spiritual knowledge that included the Trinity in a spiritual vision of the suffering of Jesus.

From Julian of Norwich, *Revelations*, chap. 23, p. 29.

And in these three words: *It is a Joy, a bliss, an endless satisfying to me*, were shewed three heavens, as thus: For the joy, I understood the pleasure of the Father; and for the bliss, the worship of the Son; and for the endless satisfying, the Holy Ghost. The Father is pleased, the Son is worshipped, the Holy Ghost is satisfied. And here saw I, for the Third Beholding in His blissful Passion: that is to say, *the Joy and the Bliss that make Him to be well-satisfied in it.*

Bernard of Clairvaux

A contemporary of Hildegard of Bingen, Bernard of Clairvaux contributed significantly to the revival of both monastic (especially Cistercian order) and popular spirituality in the twelfth century. He is best known for his great commentary *On the Song of Songs*. While at times doctrinally suspect and socially as well as emotionally troubled, his contribution to union-with-Christ mysticism is unsurpassed.

The Spirit as Bond and Kiss
While Bernard held the Augustinian view of the Spirit as the bond of love, he also used the quite daring image of the Spirit as the kiss of the Father and Son and between the Bride and the church.

From Bernard of Clairvaux, *On the Song of Songs* Sermon 8, in *The Works of Bernard of Clairvaux*, vol. 2, trans. Kilian Walsh, OCSO, and Irene M. Edmonds (Kalamazoo, MI: Cistercian Publications, 1976), 2:46–50 (hereafter Walsh).

2. . . . The bride, although otherwise so audacious, does not dare to say: "Let him kiss me with his mouth," for she knows that this is the prerogative of the Father alone. What she does ask for is something less: "Let him kiss me with the kiss of his mouth." Do you wish to see the newly-chosen bride receiving this unprecedented kiss, given

not by the mouth but by the kiss of the mouth? Then look at Jesus in the presence of his Apostles: "He breathed on them," according to St John, "and he said: 'Receive the Holy Spirit'" [John 20:22]. That favor, given to the newly-chosen Church, was indeed a kiss. That? you say. That corporeal breathing? O no, but rather the invisible Spirit, who is so bestowed in that breath of the Lord that he is understood to proceed from him equally as from the Father, truly the kiss that is common both to him who kisses and to him who is kissed. Hence the bride is satisfied to receive the kiss of the Bridegroom, though she be not kissed with his mouth. For her it is no mean or contemptible thing to be kissed by the kiss, because it is nothing less than the gift of the Holy Spirit. . . .

3. He it is then who inspires the daring spirit of the bride, he it is whom she trustingly petitions to come to her under the guise of a kiss. . . . But the bride has no doubt that if he will reveal himself to anybody, it will be to her. Therefore, she dares to ask for this kiss, actually for that Spirit in whom both the Father and the Son will reveal themselves to her. For it is not possible that one of these could be known without the other. . . .

4. But one of you may interpose and say: "Therefore knowledge of the Holy Spirit is not necessary, because when he said eternal life consisted of the knowledge of the Father and Son, he did not mention the Holy Spirit." True enough; but where there is perfect knowledge of the Father and the Son, how can there be ignorance of the goodness of both, which is the Holy Spirit? For no man has a complete knowledge of another until he finds out whether his will be good or evil. . . . The Holy Spirit indeed is nothing else but the love and the benign goodness of them both. . . .

5. . . . And it is certain that he makes this revelation through the kiss, that is, through the Holy Spirit, a fact to which St Paul bears witness: "These are the very things that God has revealed to us through the Spirit." It is by giving the Spirit, through whom he reveals, that he shows us himself; he reveals in the gift, his gift is in the revealing. Furthermore, this revelation which is made through the Holy Spirit, not only conveys the light of knowledge but also lights the fire of love, as St Paul again testifies: "The love of God has been poured into our hearts by the Holy Spirit which has been given us." . . .

6. . . . You must walk by the Spirit and not according to your personal opinions, for the Spirit teaches not by sharpening curiosity but by inspiring charity. . . .

Thus the Father, when he kisses the Son, pours into him the plenitude of the mysteries of his divine being, breathing forth love's deep delight.

Spiritual Experience

As any mystic, Bernard considers spiritual experience an important way to the knowledge of spiritual things. Bernard speaks of the importance of experience especially in his lengthier commentary on the phrase: "Let him kiss me with the kiss of his mouth" (Song 1:2) which takes several sermons (nos. 3–9).

From Bernard of Clairvaux, *On the Song of Songs* Sermon 3 (Walsh, 2:16).

Today the text we are to study is the book of our own experience. You must therefore turn your attention inwards, each one must take note of his own particular awareness of the things I am about to discuss. I am attempting to discover if any of you has been privileged to say from his heart: "Let him kiss me with the kiss of his mouth." Those to whom it is given to utter these words sincerely are comparatively few, but any one who has received this mystical kiss from the mouth of Christ at least once, seeks again that intimate experience, and eagerly looks for its frequent renewal. I think that nobody can grasp what it is except the one who receives it.

The Way of Salvation and Holiness

While he speaks of salvation in other works as well, in the commentary on the Song of Songs Bernard also shows us the way of salvation. In keeping with mystical spirituality, there is progress toward perfection.

From Bernard of Clairvaux, *On the Song of Songs*, Sermon 3 (Walsh, 2:16–19).

II.2. I should like however to point out to persons like this that there is an appropriate place for them on the way of salvation. They may not rashly aspire to the lips of a most benign Bridegroom, but let them prostrate with me in fear at the feet of a most severe Lord. Like the publican full of misgiving, they must turn their eyes to the earth rather than up to heaven. Eyes that are accustomed only to darkness will be dazzled by the brightness of the spiritual world, overpowered by its splendor, repulsed by its peerless radiance and whelmed again in a gloom more dense than before. . . . Perhaps you think the Word of God is not a medicine? Surely it is, a medicine strong and pungent, testing the mind and the heart. . . .

II.3. Though you have made a beginning by kissing the feet, you may not presume to rise at once by impulse to the kiss of the mouth; there is a step to be surmounted in between, an intervening kiss on the hand for which I offer the following explanation. If Jesus says to me: "Your sins are forgiven" [Matt. 9:2], what will it profit me if I do not cease from sinning. . . .

II.4. I am now able to see what I must seek for and receive before I may hope to attain to a higher and holier state. I do not wish to be suddenly on the heights, my desire is to advance by degrees.

III.4. The impudence of the sinner displeases God as much as the modesty of the penitent gives him pleasure. You will please him more readily if you live within the limits proper to you, and do not set your sights at things beyond you. . . .

III.5. Once you have had this twofold experience of God's benevolence in these two kisses, you need no longer feel abashed in aspiring to a holier intimacy. Growth in grace brings expansion of confidence. You will love with greater ardor, and knock on the door with greater assurance, in order to gain what you perceive to be still wanting to you. "The one who knocks will always have the door opened to him" [Matt. 7:7]. . . .

From Bernard of Clairvaux, *On the Song of Songs*, Sermon 4 (Walsh, 2:21).

We said, as you remember, that these kisses were given to the feet, the hand and the mouth, in that order. The first is the sign of a genuine conversion of life, the second is accorded to those making progress, the third is the experience of only a few of the more perfect.

Union as the Goal
In mystical spirituality, union with God is the desired goal of salvation and Christian progress.

From Bernard of Clairvaux, *The Steps of Humility and Pride* 7.21 (Walsh, 49).

The union of the Holy Spirit with the human will give birth to charity. See now this perfect soul, its two powers, the reason and the will, without spot or wrinkle, the reason instructed by the Word of Truth, the will inflamed by Truth's Spirit; sprinkled with the hyssop of humility, fired with the flame of charity; cleansed from spot by humility, smoothed of wrinkle by charity; the reason never shrinking from the truth, the will never striving against reason; and this blessed soul the Father binds to himself as his own glorious bride.

Bonaventure

According to Stanley M. Burgess, "While Thomas Aquinas supplied the great medieval theological synthesis for Western Christianity, Bonaventure provided one of the most important spiritual syntheses."[2] Franciscan theologian and biographer of St. Francis of Assisi, Bonaventure happened to be a student in Paris at the same time with Thomas Aquinas, and served as a close assistant to the pope in addition to teaching theology. His most famous work is *The Soul's Journey into God.*

Perichoresis

Both a great theologian and a great mystic, Bonaventure describes in a most profound way the meaning of the ancient Trinitarian rule of *perichoresis*, mutual indwelling, in the framework of his leading theological idea, that of God as self-diffusive love.

From Bonaventure, *The Soul's Journey into God*, 6.2,
in Bonaventure, *The Soul's Journey into God; The Tree of Life;
The Life of St. Francis*, trans. and ed. Ewert Cousins (New York:
Paulist Press, 1978), 104 (hereafter Cousins).

. . . then you can see
that through the highest communicability of the good,
there must be
a Trinity of the Father and the Son and the Holy Spirit.
From supreme goodness,
it is necessary that there be in the Persons
supreme communicability;
from supreme communicability, supreme consubstantiality;
from supreme consubstantiality, supreme configurability;
and from these supreme coequality
and hence supreme coeternity;
finally, from all of the above, supreme mutual intimacy,
by which one is necessarily in the other
by supreme interpenetration
and one acts with the other
in absolute lack of division
of the substance, power and operation
of the most blessed Trinity itself.

Spirit Christology

Bonaventure anchors his doctrine of the Trinity in salvation history and develops a biblical Spirit Christology.

2. Stanley M. Burgess, *The Holy Spirit: Medieval Roman Catholic and Reformation Traditions* (Peabody, MA: Hendrickson, 1997), 70.

From Bonaventure, *The Tree of Life* 3 (Cousins, 127).

3. Finally, *the fulness of time* (Gal. 4:4) had come. Just as man was formed from the earth on the sixth day by the power and wisdom of the divine hand, so at the beginning of the sixth age, the Archangel Gabriel was sent to the Virgin. When she gave her consent to him, the Holy Spirit came upon her like a divine fire inflaming her soul and sanctifying her flesh in perfect purity. But the *power of the Most High overshadowed* her (Luke 1:35) so that she could endure such fire. By the action of that power, instantly his body was formed, his soul created, and at once both were united to the divinity in the Person of the Son, so that the same Person was God and man, with the properties of each nature maintained.

From Bonaventure, *The Tree of Life* 9 (Cousins, 133).

Jesus, Heavenly Baptist

9. When the Savior reached the age of thirty, wishing to work out our salvation, he began first to act before he taught (cf. Acts 1:1). And beginning with baptism as the doorway of the sacraments and the foundation of virtues, he wished to be baptized by John, in order to show us an example of perfect justice and to "confer regenerative power on water by contact with his most pure flesh." You also, accompany him faithfully; and once regenerated in him, explore his secrets so that "on the banks of the Jordan you may discern the Father in the voice, the Son in the flesh and the Holy Spirit in the dove, and when the heaven of the Trinity is opened to you," you will be taken up into God.

Jesus, the receiver of the Spirit, becomes the giver of the Spirit, as Bonaventure's Pentecost exposition tells us.

From Bonaventure, *The Tree of Life* 39 (Cousins, 163).

Jesus, Giver of the Spirit

39. When seven weeks had passed since the resurrection, on the fiftieth day, when the disciples were gathered in one place with the women and Mary the mother of Jesus, suddenly there came a sound from heaven as of a violent wind blowing (Acts 1:14, 2:1). The Spirit descended upon the group of a hundred and twenty persons (Acts 1:15) and appeared in the form of tongues of fire to give speech to the mouth, light to the intellect and ardor to the affection. They were all filled with the Holy Spirit and began to speak in different languages (Acts 2:4), as the prompting of the Holy Spirit dictated, who

taught them all truth and inflamed them with all love and strengthened them in every virtue. For aided by his grace, illumined by his teaching and strengthened by his power, although they were few and simple, "they planted the Church with their own blood" throughout the world, partly by their fiery words, partly by their perfect example, partly by their astonishing miracles. Purified, illumined and perfected by the power of the same Holy Spirit, the Church became lovable to her Spouse and his attendants for being exceedingly beautiful and adorned with a wonderful variety (Ps. 44:15).

The Grace of the Holy Spirit

Chapter 5 in his *Breviloquium* is devoted to the discussion of the grace of the Spirit, in which Bonaventure follows his contemporary Thomas Aquinas's key ideas, making a distinction yet not a separation between the Spirit and grace. This discussion presents and explains many of the main concepts of classic Catholic soteriology.

> From St. Bonaventure, *Works of St. Bonaventure: Breviloquium*,
> 5.1.1, 2, 4–6; 5.2.2, 3–5; 5.3.1, 4, 6, trans. Dominic V. Monti, OFM
> (St. Bonaventure, NY: Franciscan Institute Publications, 2005), 169–81.

Chapter 1: Grace: A Gift Divinely Given

1. Now that we have examined the Incarnation of the Word, which is the origin and wellspring of every gratuitous gift, we must say something about the grace of the Holy Spirit. . . .

2. Considering grace as a divinely given gift, we must maintain the following points. First, as a gift, grace is bestowed and infused directly by God. For truly, together with grace and in it, we receive the Holy Spirit, the uncreated gift, the *good and perfect gift coming down from the Father of lights* through the Incarnate Word. . . . At the same time grace is a gift by which the soul is perfected and becomes the bride of Christ, the daughter of the eternal Father, and the temple of the Holy Spirit. . . . Finally, grace is a gift that purifies, illumines, and perfects the soul; that vivifies, reforms, and strengthens it; that elevates it, likens it, and joins it to God, and thereby makes it acceptable to God. This is a gift of such kind that it is rightly and properly called 'the grace that makes pleasing' [*gratia gratum faciens*].

4. Again, the one who enjoys God possesses God. Hence, it follows that together with that grace which, by its God-conforming nature, leads to the enjoyment of God, there is also bestowed the uncreated gift, the Holy Spirit. Whoever possesses it possesses God's own self.

5. . . . And no one possesses and is possessed by God without loving God and being loved by God in a particular and incomparable

manner, as in the case of a bride and groom where each loves and is loved by the other. And no [one] is loved in this way without being adopted as a child entitled to an eternal inheritance. Therefore, the "grace which makes pleasing" makes the soul the temple of God, the bride of Christ, and the daughter of the eternal Father. And since this cannot occur except through a supremely gracious condescension of the part of God, it could not be caused by some naturally implanted habit, but only by a free gift divinely infused. This is most evident if we consider what it truly means to be God's temple and God's child, and to be joined to God as in wedlock by the bond of love and grace.

6. Thus it is called "the grace that makes pleasing" [*gratis gratum faciens*] because it makes the one who possesses it acceptable in God's sight. For not only is it given freely by God, it also conforms to God and leads to God as an end, so that the work that came from God might return to God. In this way, it achieves, in the manner of an intelligible circle, the fulfillment of all rational spirits.

Chapter 2: Grace: An Aid to Meritorious Good

2. With regard to God's grace assisting human beings to perform meritorious acts, we should maintain that, in this case, the word "grace" may be used in several senses: general, particular, and proper.

a. Speaking very generally, "grace" refers to the assistance generously and freely granted by God to a creature for any of its activities whatsoever. Without this support, we could do nothing; in fact, we could not even continue to exist.

b. Speaking more particularly, "grace" refers to the assistance that God gives human beings so that they might prepare themselves for receiving the gift of the Holy Spirit, which is the condition by which we are able to perform meritorious deeds. This is called "gratuitously given grace" [*gratia gratis data*]. Without it, we could not do sufficiently what lies within us to prepare ourselves for salvation.

c. But in its most proper sense, "grace" refers to that assistance that God gives us for the actual acquisition of merit. This gift is called "the grace that makes pleasing," without which no one may acquire merit, advance in good, or attain eternal salvation. This grace, as the root of merit, precedes all our merits. Hence, it is said to "go before the unwilling, that they may will, and it follows the willing that they may not will in vain." Therefore no one can merit this grace in the full sense of the word [*de condigno*]. And yet "grace itself merits to be increased by God in this life and that increase merits perfection" in our homeland and everlasting glory by that same God; who alone has power to infuse, augment, and perfect that grace according to the cooperation of our will. . . .

3. Again, since the rational spirit is turned in upon itself, if it is ever to prepare itself for the gift of heavenly grace, particularly in our state of fallen nature, it requires the gift of another "gratuitously given" grace. . . .

For, since "the cause is superior to the effect," no spirit can make itself better or perform a work that pleases God, unless it is itself beforehand pleasing to God; for God looks with favor first on the person, and only then on that person's offering. Merit, therefore, is rooted entirely in the "grace that makes pleasing" which alone makes us worthy in the sight of God; this is why no one can merit this grace as a matter of right [*de condigno*], but only in congruous sense [*de congruo*].

4. But once we possess this grace, it merits its own increase if we make good use of it here below, and this merit is a just claim [*de digno*]. Certainly, God alone is the fontal principle by which grace is poured into us. But if we consider how grace is increased, God is the sole source in terms of infusion, but grace itself is also a source in terms of merit and worthiness. Furthermore, our free choice is a source [of the increase of grace] by virtue of its cooperating and meriting, to the extent that free will cooperates with grace and makes what belongs to grace its own.

5. In this way, not only does free will merit through grace a just title [*de digno*] to an increase of grace in the present life, but also an absolute right [*de condigno*] to its perfecting in our homeland.

Chapter 3: Grace: A Remedy for Sin
1. Considering grace as a remedy for sin, the following things must be held. Although free choice is "the greatest power under God," on its own it is liable to rush headlong into sin. Furthermore, it cannot rise from sin in any way without the assistance of the divine grace that is called "the grace that makes pleasing." However, this grace, even though it is a sufficient remedy for sin, is not poured into the soul of an individual without the consent of that person's free choice. Thus, we may conclude that four things concur for the justification of a sinner: the infusion of grace, the expulsion of guilt, contrition, and an act of free choice. Therefore, sin is expelled by God's grace not by virtue of free will, and yet not without the consent of free will.

4. Furthermore, God restores us in a manner that does not impair the established laws of nature. Thus, God grants this grace to free will in such a way that grace does not force it, but leaves the will free to consent.

6. What Augustine tells us is therefore true, that "the one who created you without you, will not justify you without you." Yet it is also

true that *it depends not on human will or exertion, but on the God who shows mercy*. And so it is true that we cannot pride ourselves on our own merits, for anything God crowns in us is nothing but his own gift. For God reserves to himself the generous distribution of the favors of grace, teaching us human beings not to be ungrateful or to boast in ourselves as if we had not received, but instead to *boast in the Lord*. Nevertheless, it is also true that, although free will by itself could neither fulfill the law nor gain grace, it is inexcusable if it does not do what it can. For "grace given gratuitously" is always at hand to rouse it, and with its aid the will can exert itself to the full. When this is done, it may possess "the grace that makes pleasing" and when this has been obtained, it may fulfill the law and God's will.

CHAPTER 6

The Spirit in Medieval Western Christian Traditions 2: The Scholastics

The Venerable Bede

Called the "Father of English History" and "the most learned man in Western Europe" of his time, at the end of the seventh and the beginning of the eighth century Bede devoted his intellectual skills not only to recording the history of his homeland but also especially to a faithful commentary on Scripture. Bede's *Commentary on the Acts of the Apostles* gives insight into the theology of the Spirit held by this deacon and (later) priest from northern England.

The Day of Pentecost
Bede considers in his commentary on the book of Acts the spiritual meaning of the Day of Pentecost.

> From *The Venerable Bede, Commentary on the Acts of the Apostles*, trans., with intro. Lawrence T. Martin (Kalamazoo, MI: Cistercian Publications, 1989), 27–29 (hereafter Martin).

[Acts] 2:1 . . . Now whoever desires to be filled with the Holy Spirit must transcend the abode of the flesh by contemplation of the mind. For just as the forty days during which the Lord kept company with his disciples after the resurrection designate the church of this present pilgrim-state as it rises with Christ, so also the fiftieth day, upon which the Holy Spirit was received, appropriately represents the perfection of the blessed rest in which the temporal labor of the church will be rewarded with an eternal denarius. . . .

[Acts] 2:2 And suddenly there came a sound from heaven, as of a violent wind coming, and so forth. . . . *For because he caused the disciples to be internally inflamed with zeal, and skilled in words, externally there showed tongues of fire. The elements, therefore, were put to use in signification, so that those who in their bodies perceived fire and sound might indeed be taught in their hearts by invisible fire and by a voice without sound.*

[Acts] 2:3a And there appeared to them, it says, parted tongues as of fire. Now the Holy Spirit appeared in fire and in tongues because all those whom he fills he makes simultaneously to burn and to speak—to burn because of him, and to speak about him. And at the same time he indicated that the holy church, when it had spread to the ends of the earth, was to speak in the languages of all nations.

[Acts] 2:3b And it settled upon each of them. That [fire] which is said to have settled [on them] was a token of royal power. Or certainly [by this] was indicated that his resting place is among the saints.

[Acts] 2:4 And they began to speak in a variety of languages. The church's humility recovers the unity of languages which the pride of Babylon had shattered. Spiritually, however, the variety of languages signifies gifts of a variety of graces. Truly therefore, it is not inconsistent to understand that the Holy Spirit first gave to human beings the gift of languages, by which human wisdom is both learned and taught extrinsically, so that he might thereby show how easily he can make men wise through the wisdom of God, which is within them. . . .

[Acts] 2:13 Others, however, said in mockery that they were full of new wine. These mockers nevertheless mystically bore witness to truths, for they [the disciples] were not filled with the old wine which ran short in the marriage of the church, but with the new wine of spiritual grace. For now new wine had come in new skins, since the apostles reechoed *the wonderful works of God* not *in the oldness of the letter but in the newness of the Spirit.*

[Acts] 2:15 For these men are not drunk, as you suppose, since it is the third hour of the day. In order to proclaim to the world the glory of the indivisible Trinity, the Holy Spirit descended appropriately at the third hour. And since it was said above, *They were persevering in prayer*, they quite rightly received the Holy Spirit at the hour of prayer, so that it might be shown to readers that it is not easy to receive the grace of the Holy Spirit unless the mind is raised from material things by concentration on the things which are above. . . .

[Acts] 2:17 I will pour forth of my spirit on all flesh. The word effusion shows the lavishness of the gift, for the grace of the Holy Spirit was not to be granted, as formerly, only to individual prophets and priests, but to everyone in every place, regardless of sex, state of life, or position.

A Trinitarian Spirit Christology

Bede summarizes in a masterful way the soteriological and theological implications of a Spirit Christology in an authentic Trinitarian framework.

From *Venerable Bede, Commentary* (Martin, 102–3).

[Acts] 10:38a How God anointed him with the Holy Spirit and with power. Another text says: *Inasmuch as God anointed him.* John preached Jesus inasmuch as God anointed him with the Holy Spirit at the time when he said, *He will baptize you in the Holy Spirit;* and again, *I saw the Spirit descending as a dove upon him.* Jesus was anointed *not with oil, but with the gift of grace, which is signified by the visible oil with which the church anoints those who are baptized. Yet, Christ was not anointed with the Holy Spirit at the time when it descended as a dove upon him at his baptism, for at that time he condescended to prefigure his body, that is, his church, in which the baptized principally receive the Holy Spirit. Rather he must be understood to have been anointed with a mystical and invisible anointing when the Word of God was made flesh, that is, when human nature, without any preceding merits from good works, was joined to God the Word in the womb of the Virgin, so as to become one person with him. Because of this we confess that he was born of the Holy Spirit and of the virgin Mary. . . .*

[Acts] 10:44 The Holy Spirit fell down upon everyone who was listening to his message. Lest there might be any hesitation about conferring baptism upon the gentiles, support was supplied by the testimony of the Holy Spirit, who in an unexpected sequence of events acted in advance of the waters of the baptismal bath, which are ordinarily the means of sanctification. This is reported to have happened once in testimony to the faith of the gentiles, but never in the case of the Jews.

Anselm of Canterbury

Italian by birth, Anselm spent most of his life in Normandy at Bec as a Benedictine monk until at the age of sixty he became archbishop of Canterbury. No stranger to controversies, both political and ecclesiastical, this eleventh-century philosopher-theologian is widely regarded as a pioneer scholastic theologian. The following citations from his *Monologion* on the nature and workings of the Spirit are typical of his highly analytic theology.

The Spirit in the Trinity

From Anselm of Canterbury, *Monologion* 28, in *Anselm of Canterbury*, vol. 1, ed. and trans. Jasper Hopkins and Herbert Richardson (New York: Edwin Mellen, 1974), 42–43.

This Spirit exists in an unqualified sense; compared to it created things do not exist. Therefore, from the foregoing considerations it is seen to follow that this Spirit, which exists in such a marvellously unique and uniquely marvellous way of its own, in a certain sense alone exists—while by comparison to it other things, whatever they are seen to be, do not exist. For if we take a close look, only this Spirit will be seen to exist in an unqualified sense and completely and absolutely; and everything else will be seen almost not to exist and scarcely to exist. On account of its immutable eternity this Spirit can be said unqualifiedly to exist; it cannot be said, in accordance with some alteration, to have existed or to be going to exist. Nor is it, through being changeable, anything which at some time it was not or will not be; nor does it fail to be something which it once was or will be. Rather, whatever it is it is once, at once, and without limitation. Since, I say, it is this kind of being, it is rightly said to exist in an unqualified sense and absolutely and completely.

In Defense of the "Filioque"

Anselm is a Western theologian. He finds compelling theological reasons to repudiate the Eastern Church's opposition to the double procession of the Holy Spirit from the Father and Son.

> From Anselm of Canterbury, *The Procession of the Holy Spirit* 1, in
> *Anselm of Canterbury*, vol. 3, ed. and trans. Jasper Hopkins and
> Herbert Richardson (New York: Edwin Mellen, 1974), 183, 191–92.

That the Holy Spirit proceeds from the Son, as we Latins confess, is denied by the Greeks. They also reject our Latin teachers whom we follow with respect to this doctrine.

Someone will argue: Suppose that when the Son exists from the Father, then since the Father and the Holy Spirit are one God it follows that the Son exists from the Holy Spirit. . . .

To this objection I reply: Assuredly, the Son and the Holy Spirit exist from the Father—but in different ways. For the one [exists from the Father] by being begotten, and the other [exists from the Father] by proceeding, so that for this reason they are distinct from each other—as I have said. Hence, when the one is begotten, the other who is distinct from Him by virtue of the fact that He is not likewise begotten but proceeds cannot be begotten with Him. And when the one proceeds, the other who is distinct from Him by virtue of the fact that He does not likewise proceed but is begotten cannot proceed together with Him. Hence, God's unity does not necessitate the above consequence, because [that consequence] is opposed by the plurality which arises from the begottenness and the procession. For even if the Son and the Holy Spirit were not more than one for some *other* reason, they would be different for *this* reason alone. But when I say that from the fact of the Father's being one God with the Son or with the Holy Spirit it follows that either the Son exists from the Holy Spirit or the Holy Spirit exists from the Son, I do not generate here a plurality which opposes the consequence of unity. For I do not say that both alternates are true but only that one or the other is. . . . But the Son is not begotten from the Holy Spirit. For if the Son were begotten from the Holy Spirit, He would be the son of the Holy Spirit, and the Holy Spirit would be His father. But the one is neither the father nor the son of the other. Therefore, the Son is not begotten from the Holy Spirit. And it is no less clear that the Son does not proceed from the Holy Spirit. For [in that case] He would be the spirit of the Holy Spirit—a doctrine clearly denied when the Holy Spirit is said and is believed to be the spirit of the Son. For the Son cannot be the spirit of His own spirit. Therefore, the Son does not proceed from the Holy Spirit. Hence, the Son in no way exists from the Holy Spirit. And so it follows by irrefutable reasoning that the Holy Spirit exists from the Son, even as He also exists from the Father.

Thomas Aquinas

The "Angelic Doctor" and "Prince of the Scholastics," this thirteenth-century Dominican theologian, alongside the bishop of Hippo, is the greatest theologian of Christian history and certainly its greatest *summa* writer. While a great systematician and rationalist, Aquinas was no stranger to spirituality, including hymns; the following hymn is attributed to him.

From Daniel Joseph Donahoe, *Early Christian Hymns*, series 2 (Middletown, CT: Donahoe, 1911), 156–59.

Warming Fire, whose virtue giveth
To the world its life and light,
Every form on earth that liveth,
And in ocean's depths, receiveth
Quickening from thy gracious might;
Moving power of every creature,
Life of life, sweet guide and teacher,
Thou art motion, thou art rest,
All and each, O Spirit Blest.

Come, O Holy Ghost, Creator,
And thy sevenfold gifts bestow,
Thou, the world's high renovator,
Source of blessing, war's abater,
Bring thy dower of love below.
Unto holy souls a treasure
Is thy joy; but thy displeasure,
And the anger of thy face
Send confusion to the base.

O'er the waters' wild elation
Breathed thy spirit all divine,
In the birth-time of creation;
Then uprose in animation
Strength, and power, and love benign;
But when man, with soul new-gifted,
Fell in crime, thy hand uplifted,
And restored him to high place
With thy vivifying grace. . . .

Happy, then, in your salvation
O ye ransomed people, sing;
To the Spirit shout laudation;
Bowing low, let every nation
Hymns of praise and blessing bring.
Lift on high your "Holy! Holy!"
Out of hearts, sincere and lowly;
Lay your sorrows at his feet,
Seek his love and mercy sweet.

Unto thee, thou Fount of Graces,
Comes for cure each wounded soul;
Grant the strength that lifts and braces,
Pour the balm that sin effaces,
By thy bounties make us whole;
Bring to kings thy inspiration,
Lead to justice every nation,
So that all the world may be
Blessed with peace and unity.

The Procession of the Holy Spirit

In his discussion of the doctrine of the Trinity, Aquinas clarifies the question of the origin and procession of the Holy Spirit.

From St. Thomas Aquinas, *ST* 1.36.1.[1]

[While it can be said that] . . . "Holy Ghost" is not the proper name of one divine person or no name which is common to the three persons is the proper name of any one person, I answer that, While there are two processions in God, one of these, the procession of love, has no proper name of its own. . . . Hence the relations also which follow from this procession are without a name: for which reason the Person proceeding in that manner has not a proper name. But as some names are accommodated by the usual mode of speaking to signify the aforesaid relations, as when we use the names of procession and spiration, which in the strict sense more fittingly signify the notional acts than the relations; so to signify the divine Person, Who proceeds by way of love, this name "Holy Ghost" is by the use of scriptural speech accommodated to Him. . . .

[Therefore] . . . the expression Holy Spirit, if taken as two words, is applicable to the whole Trinity: because by "spirit" the immateriality of the divine substance is signified. . . . And by adding the word "holy" we signify the purity of divine goodness. But if Holy Spirit be taken as one word, it is thus that the expression, in the usage of the Church, is accommodated to signify one of the three persons, the one who proceeds by way of love, for the reason above explained.

The Holy Spirit as Love and Gift
Following the Augustinian tradition, Thomas names the Holy Spirit as Love and Gift.

From Aquinas, *ST* 1.37.1.

Gregory says (Hom. xxx, in Pentecost.): "The Holy Ghost Himself is Love." . . . The name Love in God can be taken essentially and personally. If taken personally it is the proper name of the Holy Ghost; as Word is the proper name of the Son. To see this we must know that . . . there are two processions in God, one by way of the intellect, which is the procession of the Word, and another by way of the will, which is the procession of Love. . . . Hence, we are obliged to employ circumlocution as regards the person Who proceeds, and the relations following from this procession which are called "procession" and "spiration," as stated above [1.27.4], and yet express the origin rather than the relation in the strict sense of the term. Nevertheless we must consider them in respect of each procession simply. For as

---

1. Part 1, question 36, article 1 (and so throughout).

when a thing is understood by anyone, there results in the one who understands a conception of the object understood, which conception we call word; so when anyone loves an object, a certain impression results, so to speak, of the thing loved in the affection of the lover; by reason of which the object loved is said to be in the lover; as also the thing understood is in the one who understands; so that when anyone understands and loves himself he is in himself, not only by real identity, but also as the object understood is in the one who understands, and the thing loved is in the lover. As regards the intellect, however, words have been found to describe the mutual relation of the one who understands the object understood, as appears in the word "to understand"; and other words are used to express the procession of the intellectual conception—namely, "to speak," and "word." Hence in God, "to understand" is applied only to the essence; because it does not import relation to the Word that proceeds; whereas "Word" is said personally, because it signifies what proceeds; and the term "to speak" is a notional term as importing the relation of the principle of the Word to the Word Himself. On the other hand, on the part of the will, with the exception of the words "dilection" and "love," which express the relation of the lover to the object loved, there are no other terms in use, which express the relation of the impression or affection of the object loved, produced in the lover by fact that he loves—to the principle of that impression, or "vice versa." And therefore, on account of the poverty of our vocabulary, we express these relations by the words "love" and "dilection": just as if we were to call the Word "intelligence conceived," or "wisdom begotten."

It follows that so far as love means only the relation of the lover to the object loved, "love" and "to love" are said of the essence, as "understanding" and "to understand"; but, on the other hand, so far as these words are used to express the relation to its principle, of what proceeds by way of love, and "vice versa," so that by "love" is understood the "love proceeding," and by "to love" is understood "the spiration of the love proceeding," in that sense "love" is the name of the person and "to love" is a notional term, as "to speak" and "to beget."

Grace and Justification
When speaking of grace, Thomas sets himself the question "Whether grace is a quality of the soul?" and gives an affirmative answer.

From Aquinas, *ST* 1–2.110.2.[2]

As stated above [1–2.110.1], there is understood to be an effect of God's gratuitous will in whoever is said to have God's grace. Now it was stated [1–2.109.1] that man is aided by God's gratuitous will in two ways: first, inasmuch as man's soul is moved by God to know or will or do something, and in this way the gratuitous effect in man is not a quality, but a movement of the soul; for "motion is the act of the mover in the moved." Secondly, man is helped by God's gratuitous will, inasmuch as a habitual gift is infused by God into the soul; and for this reason, that it is not fitting that God should provide less for those He loves, that they may acquire supernatural good, than for creatures, whom He loves that they may acquire natural good. Now He so provides for natural creatures, that not merely does He move them to their natural acts, but He bestows upon them certain forms and powers, which are the principles of acts, in order that they may of themselves be inclined to these movements, and thus the movements whereby they are moved by God become natural and easy to creatures, according to Wis. 8:1: "she . . . ordereth all things sweetly." Much more therefore does He infuse into such as He moves towards the acquisition of supernatural good, certain forms or supernatural qualities, whereby they may be moved by Him sweetly and promptly to acquire eternal good; and thus the gift of grace is a quality.

While owing to Augustine, Thomas is thus also critical of the bishop's view of the identification of grace with the Spirit given to the heart of the believer. While for Augustine, God/Spirit is not only the giver but also the gift, that is, the personal presence of God in the heart of the believer, for Thomas grace (and love) springs from the Holy Spirit, who then sets the soul in motion acquiring the justifying grace, as will be explained in the following section. In the following citation, Thomas answers affirmatively the question of whether grace/charity is created in the soul.

From Aquinas, *ST* 2–2.23.2.

[In response to what] . . . Augustine says (De Trin. xv, 17): "It was said: God is Charity, even as it was said: God is a Spirit." Therefore charity is not something created in the soul, but is God Himself. . . .

[Thomas] answer[s] that . . . if we consider the matter aright, this would be, on the contrary, detrimental to charity. For when the Holy Ghost moves the human mind the movement of charity does

---

2. 1–2 in the following refers to the first part of the second part; similarly 2–2 refers to the second part of the second part.

not proceed from this motion in such a way that the human mind be merely moved, without being the principle of this movement, as when a body is moved by some extrinsic motive power. For this is contrary to the nature of a voluntary act, whose principle needs to be in itself, as stated above [1–2.6.1]: so that it would follow that to love is not a voluntary act, which involves a contradiction, since love, of its very nature, implies an act of the will.

Likewise, neither can it be said that the Holy Ghost moves the will in such a way to the act of loving, as though the will were an instrument, for an instrument, though it be a principle of action, nevertheless has not the power to act or not to act, for then again the act would cease to be voluntary and meritorious, whereas it has been stated above [1–2.114.4] that the love of charity is the root of merit: and, given that the will is moved by the Holy Ghost to the act of love, it is necessary that the will also should be the efficient cause of that act.

Thomas makes a distinction between operating and cooperating grace.

From Aquinas, *ST* 1–2.111.2.

As stated above [1–2.110.2] grace may be taken in two ways; first, as a Divine help, whereby God moves us to will and to act; secondly, as a habitual gift divinely bestowed on us.

Now in both these ways grace is fittingly divided into operating and cooperating. For the operation of an effect is not attributed to the thing moved but to the mover. Hence in that effect in which our mind is moved and does not move, but in which God is the sole mover, the operation is attributed to God, and it is with reference to this that we speak of "operating grace." But in that effect in which our mind both moves and is moved, the operation is not only attributed to God, but also to the soul; and it is with reference to this that we speak of "cooperating grace." Now there is a double act in us. First, there is the interior act of the will, and with regard to this act the will is a thing moved, and God is the mover; and especially when the will, which hitherto willed evil, begins to will good. And hence, inasmuch as God moves the human mind to this act, we speak of operating grace. But there is another, exterior act; and since it is commanded by the will, as was shown above [1–2.17.9] the operation of this act is attributed to the will. And because God assists us in this act, both by strengthening our will interiorly so as to attain to the act, and by granting outwardly the capability of operating, it is with respect to this that we speak of cooperating grace. Hence after the aforesaid words Augustine subjoins: "He operates that we may will; and when we will, He cooperates that we may perfect." And thus if grace is taken for God's gratuitous motion whereby He moves us to meritorious good, it is fittingly divided into operating and cooperating grace.

But if grace is taken for the habitual gift, then again there is a double effect of grace, even as of every other form; the first of which is "being," and the second, "operation"; thus the work of heat is to make its subject hot, and to give heat outwardly. And thus habitual grace, inasmuch as it heals and justifies the soul, or makes it pleasing to God, is called operating grace; but inasmuch as it is the principle of meritorious works, which spring from the free-will, it is called cooperating grace.

While ultimately the initiative lies in God's work, proper preparation is needed for the reception of grace.

From Aquinas, *ST* 1–2.112. 2.

As stated above [1–2.111.2], grace is taken in two ways: first, as a habitual gift of God. Secondly, as a help from God, Who moves the soul to good. Now taking grace in the first sense, a certain preparation of grace is required for it, since a form can only be in disposed matter. But if we speak of grace as it signifies a help from God to move us to good, no preparation is required on man's part, that, as it were, anticipates the Divine help, but rather, every preparation in man must be by the help of God moving the soul to good. And thus even the good movement of the free-will, whereby anyone is prepared for receiving the gift of grace is an act of the free-will moved by God. And thus man is said to prepare himself, according to Prov. 16:1: "It is the part of man to prepare the soul"; yet it is principally from God, Who moves the free-will. Hence it is said that man's will is prepared by God, and that man's steps are guided by God.

In Catholic theology, differently from the theology of the Lutheran Confessions, justification is a change of status rather than merely a declaration of righteousness. At the same time, in the remission of sins, that is, justification of the sinner, grace is being infused into the soul.

From Aquinas, *ST* 1–2.113.1.

And it is thus we are now speaking of the justification of the ungodly, according to the Apostle (Rom. 4:5): "But to him that worketh not, yet believeth in Him that justifieth the ungodly," etc. And because movement is named after its term "whereto" rather than from its term "whence," the transmutation whereby anyone is changed by the remission of sins from the state of ungodliness to the state of justice, borrows its name from its term "whereto," and is called "justification of the ungodly."

From Aquinas, ST 1–2.113.2.

By sinning a man offends God as stated above [1–2.75.5] . Now an offense is remitted to anyone, only when the soul of the offender is at peace with the offended. Hence sin is remitted to us, when God is at peace with us, and this peace consists in the love whereby God loves us. Now God's love, considered on the part of the Divine act, is eternal and unchangeable; whereas, as regards the effect it imprints on us, it is sometimes interrupted, inasmuch as we sometimes fall short of it and once more require it. Now the effect of the Divine love in us, which is taken away by sin, is grace, whereby a man is made worthy of eternal life, from which sin shuts him out. Hence we could not conceive the remission of guilt, without the infusion of grace.

While justification of the sinner is the act of God, human cooperation is called forth. This "movement of the soul" towards God is nothing else than faith.

From Aquinas, ST 1–2.113.4.

As stated above [1–2.113] a movement of free-will is required for the justification of the ungodly, inasmuch as man's mind is moved by God. Now God moves man's soul by turning it to Himself according to Ps. 84:7 (Septuagint): "Thou wilt turn us, O God, and bring us to life." Hence for the justification of the ungodly a movement of the mind is required, by which it is turned to God. Now the first turning to God is by faith, according to Heb. 11:6: "He that cometh to God must believe that He is." Hence a movement of faith is required for the justification of the ungodly.

"Gratuitous Graces": Charisms

Thomas introduces *ST* 2–2.171 by saying, "After treating individually of all the virtues and vices that pertain to men of all conditions and estates, we must now consider those things which pertain especially to certain men," that is, the discussion of gratuitous graces such as prophecy and miracles (questions 171–82). He distinguishes three aspects in graces and then applies that typology first to the grace of prophecy.

From Aquinas, *ST* 2–2.171, intro. and 1.

[Introduction] With regard to gratuitous graces, which are the first object to be considered, it must be observed that some of them pertain to knowledge, some to speech, and some to operation. Now all things pertaining to knowledge may be comprised under "prophecy," since prophetic revelation extends not only to future events relating to man, but also to things relating to God, both as to those which are to be believed by all and are matters of "faith," and as to yet higher mysteries, which concern the perfect and belong to "wisdom." Again, prophetic revelation is about things pertaining to spiritual substances, by whom we are urged to good or evil; this pertains to the "discernment of spirits." Moreover it extends to the direction of human acts, and this pertains to "knowledge," as we shall explain further on [2–2.177].

[Question 1.] . . . Prophecy first and chiefly consists in knowledge, because, to wit, prophets know things that are far [*procul*] removed from man's knowledge. Wherefore they may be said to take their name from [*phanos*], "apparition," because things appear to them from afar. Wherefore, as Isidore states (Etym. vii, 8), "in the Old Testament, they were called Seers, because they saw what others saw not, and surveyed things hidden in mystery." . . .

Since, however, it is written (1 Cor. 12:7): "The manifestation of the Spirit is given to every man unto profit," and further on (1 Cor. 14:12): "Seek to abound unto the edification of the Church," it follows that prophecy consists secondarily in speech, in so far as the prophets declare for the instruction of others, the things they know through being taught of God.

In response to the question "Whether there is a gratuitous grace of working miracles?" the Doctor has the following to say.

From Aquinas, *ST* 2–2.178.1.

As stated above [2–2.177.1], the Holy Ghost provides sufficiently for the Church in matters profitable unto salvation, to which purpose the gratuitous graces are directed. Now just as the knowledge which a man receives from God needs to be brought to the knowledge of others through the gift of tongues and the grace of the word, so too the word uttered needs to be confirmed in order that it be rendered credible. This is done by the working of miracles, according to Mk. 16:20, "And confirming the word with signs that followed": and reasonably so. For it is natural to man to arrive at the intelligible truth through its sensible effects. Wherefore just as man led by his natural reason is able to arrive at some knowledge of God through His natural effects, so is he brought to a certain degree of supernatural knowledge of the objects of faith by certain supernatural effects which are called miracles. Therefore the working of miracles belongs to a gratuitous grace.

Peter Abelard: Pentecost Hymn

While theologically and pedagogically it is appropriate to make a distinction between the mystics and "scholastics" of the medieval period, that divide should never be taken categorically: the angelic Doctor Thomas had a powerful mystical experience toward the end of his life as a result of which his unsurpassed intellectual powers seemed to be of little value. Peter Abelard, the twelfth-century Parisian theologian and master of letters, penned a number of hymns, one of which is to be sung on the day of Pentecost.

From Sister Jane Patricia, *The Hymns of Abelard in English Verse* (Lanham, MD: University Press of America, 1986), 84–85.

The Holy Spirit comes to share
His burning altar in our heart.
Accept, of God, your temples there;
With virtues dedicate their art.
These are the sevenfold gifts you as God possess,
Binding seven demons of wickedness.
These your gifts are goodness and holiness.

The *fear* of God can set us free,
But wickedness must first abate.
The poor on earth with such a key
May enter rich in heaven's gate.
You, Master, give us this; give to us graciously.
Give the guilty less than the penalty.
Yours the glory, yours be the victory.

And give us force of *holiness*;
Let not temptation overwhelm.
The mild and merciful possess
This grace and all the earthly realm.
And, Master, give us this.

Let *knowledge* fall on us as well,
Through which we know the grace of tears.
Your pardon casts its holy spell
When we have paid up all arrears.
And, Master, give us this.

With holy *might* your strength is shed
On those who thirst for righteousness.
The fulness of the very bread
Is vigor pilgrim souls express.
And, Master, give us this.

And give us highest *counsel*, Lord;
Hereto your mercy will suffice.
So may you then allow reward;
For this you ask, not sacrifice.
And, Master, give us this.

In *understanding* you are known
As God within the Trinity.
The pure in heart can see alone
The kingdom's high sublimity.
And, Master, give us this.

You give us *wisdom* finally,
In which the Sons of God take rest.
The name of father makes them free
To sanctify what there is blest.
And, Master, give us this.

By force of the apostles' prayers
Whom you renewed at Pentecost,
Give us the graces such as theirs,
And strengthen us lest we be lost.
These are the sevenfold gifts you as God possess,
Binding seven demons of wickedness.
These your gifts are goodness and holiness.

CHAPTER 7

Reformation
Pneumatologies

Introduction to Reformation Pneumatologies

A fitting introduction to Reformation pneumatologies is offered by the Roman Catholic Yves Congar in his celebrated *I Believe in the Holy Spirit*:

> Luther and Calvin . . . kept to the classical teaching of Nicea and Constantinople (381) and even to the Creed *Quicumque* with regard to the Trinity. Both had to fight on two fronts. On the one hand, they had to combat entrenched "Catholic" positions which were rightly or wrongly identified with a need to regard the "Church," or rather the "hierarchy," as absolute. On the other hand, they had to fight against "enthusiasts" who appealed to the Spirit in their claim that they were furthering the reforming movement. The enthusiasts whom Luther had to resist were the *Schwärmer* Storch, Müntzer and Karlstadt, and those whom Calvin opposed were the Anabaptists. Both Reformers kept to a middle road, or rather a synthesis, and each in his own way insisted on a close relationship between an external "instrument" of grace—Scripture—and the activity of the Spirit.[1]

The above quotation identifies the three main theological and spiritual movements of the Reformation period.[2] First, we will take a look at the magisterial Reformation, in other words, the mainstream Protestant Reformation represented by Martin Luther, Ulrich Zwingli, and Jean Calvin. Second, some leading Roman Catholic theologians from the time of the Reformation will be studied, namely, Ignatius of Loyola, John of Avila, and John of the Cross. Third, two leading radical Reformers' views of the Spirit and salvation will be discussed, those of Thomas Müntzer and Menno Simons.

---

1. Yves Congar, *I Believe in the Holy Spirit*, trans. David Smith [three volumes in one] (New York: Crossroad, 1997), 138.

2. For a helpful guide, see Stanley M. Burgess, *Medieval Roman Catholic and Reformation Traditions* (Peabody, MA: Hendrickson, 1997).

The Protestant Magisterial Reformation

Martin Luther

"The concept of the Holy Spirit completely dominates Luther's theology. In every decisive matter, whether it be the study of Luther's doctrine of justification, his doctrine of the sacraments, his ethics, or any other fundamental teaching, we are forced to take into consideration his concept of the Holy Spirit."[3] While an overstatement in my opinion, this opening paragraph in the classic study by Regin Prenter, *Spiritus Creator*, reminds us of the important role of pneumatology in the Reformer's theological vision. In light of the fact that the main source for Luther's theology of the Holy Spirit can be found in his Pentecost sermons, it is appropriate to begin the discussion of his pneumatology by presenting his Pentecost Day hymn of 1524.

The Day of the Pentecost

From James F. Lambert, *Luther's Hymns* (Philadelphia: General Council Publication House, 1917), 72.

Come, Holy Ghost, God and Lord!
Be all Thy graces now outpoured
On each believer's mind and heart;
Thy fervent love to them impart.
Lord, by the brightness of thy light,
Thou in the faith dost men unite
Of ev'ry land and ev'ry tongue;
This to Thy praise, O Lord, our God, be sung.
Hallelujah! Hallelujah!

Thou holy Light, Guide Divine,
Oh, cause the Word of life to shine!
Teach us to know our God aright
And call Him Father with delight.
From ev'ry error keep us free;
Let none but Christ our Master be
That we in living faith abide,
In Him, our Lord, with all our might confide.
Hallelujah! Hallelujah!

---

3. Regin Prenter, *Spiritus Creator: Luther's Concept of the Holy Spirit*, trans. John M. Jensen (Philadelphia: Muhlenberg Press, 1953), ix.

Thou holy Fire, Comfort true,
Grant us the will Thy work to do
And in Thy service to abide;
Let trials turn us not aside.
Lord, by Thy power prepare each heart
And to our weakness strength impart,
That bravely here we may contend,
Through life and death to Thee, our God, ascend.
Hallelujah! Hallelujah!

The Spirit in the Trinity

While agreeing with tradition, Luther developed the doctrine of the Trinity in a novel way by speaking of God as self-giving love, an idea that goes back to Bernard of Clairvaux, Richard of Saint Victor, and others.

From Martin Luther, "Large Catechism," Creed, art. 3, par. 64–65, *BC*, 419.

God . . . created us . . . to redeem and sanctify us. Moreover, having bestowed upon us everything in heaven and on earth, he has given us his Son and his Holy Spirit, through whom he brings us to himself. . . . We could never come to recognize the Father's favor and grace were it not for the Lord Christ, who is a mirror of the Father's heart. Apart from him we see nothing but an angry and terrible Judge. But neither could we know anything of Christ, had it not been revealed by the Holy Spirit.

The Sanctifying Spirit

Similarly to Augustine and Christian tradition in general, Luther took the designation *Holy* Spirit to mean the sanctifying work, as the famous passage from the Large Catechism clearly puts it.

From Luther, "Large Catechism," pt. 2: Creed, art. 3, par. 35–37, *BC*, 419.

To this article [the third article of the creed], as I have said, I cannot give a better title than "Sanctification." In it is expressed and portrayed the Holy Spirit and his office, which is that he makes us holy. Therefore, we must concentrate on the term "Holy Spirit," because it is so precise that we can find no substitute for it. . . . God's Spirit alone is called Holy Spirit, that is, he who has sanctified and still sanctifies us. As the Father is called Creator and the Son is called Redeemer, so on account of his work the Holy Spirit must be called Sanctifier, the One who makes holy. How does this sanctifying take place? Answer: Just as the Son obtains dominion by purchasing us through his birth, death, and resurrection, etc., so the Holy Spirit effects our sanctification through the following: the communion of saints or Christian church, the forgiveness of sins, the resurrection of the body, and the life everlasting. In other words, he first leads us into his holy community, placing us upon the bosom of the church, where he preaches to us and brings us to Christ.

The sanctifying work of the Spirit is also the way to connect the Spirit to salvation and to the church.

From Luther, "The Sermons on Catechism," *LW* 51:166.

The third article is about the Holy Spirit, who is one God with the Father and the Son. His office is to make holy or to vivify. Here again one must understand the words, "Holy Spirit," what "Holy Spirit" means, for there is the human spirit, evil spirits, and the Holy Spirit. Here he is called the "Holy Spirit." Why is he so called? Because he sanctifies. And therefore I believe in the Holy Spirit, because he has sanctified me and still sanctifies me. How does this happen? In this way; just as the Son accepts and receives his lordship through his death, so the Holy Spirit sanctifies through the following parts. In the first place he has led you into the holy, catholic church and placed you in the bosom of the church. But in that church he preserves [you] and through it he preaches and brings you [to Christ] through the Word. Christ gained his lordship through death; but how do I come to it? If [his] work remains hidden, then it is lost. So, in order that Christ's death and resurrection may not remain hidden, the Holy Spirit comes and preaches, that is, the Holy Spirit leads you to the Lord, who redeems you. So if I ask you, What does this article mean? answer: I believe that the Holy Spirit sanctifies me. So, as the Father is my creator and Christ is my Lord, so the Holy Spirit is my sanctifier. For he sanctifies me through the following works: through "the forgiveness of sins, the resurrection of the body, and the life everlasting."

The Christian church is your mother, who gives birth to you and bears you through the Word. And this is done by the Holy Spirit who bears witness concerning Christ. . . . The Holy Spirit . . . sanctifies by leading you into the holy church and proclaiming to you the Word which the Christian church proclaims.

Analogies of the Spirit

As a preacher, Luther was fond of using various analogies and metaphors of the Holy Spirit. One of them has to do with "movement" or "motion."

From Luther, *Galatians Commentary* (1519) on 4:6, *LW* 27:290.

We . . . have our being in God, move and live in Him (Acts 17:28). We have our being because of the Father, who is the "Substance" of the Godhead. We are moved by the image of the Son, who, moved by a divine and eternal motion, so to speak, is born of the Father. We live according to the Spirit, in whom the Father and the Son rest and live, as it were. But these matters are too sublime to belong here.

In his lectures on Genesis, Luther uses a delightful picture from the domestic animal world.

From Luther, *Lectures on Genesis*, chap. 1–5, on 1:2, *LW* 1:9.

The Father creates heaven and earth out of nothing through the Son, whom Moses calls the Word. Over these the Holy Spirit broods. As a hen broods her eggs, keeping them warm in order to hatch her chicks, and, as it were, to bring them to life through heat, so Scripture says that the Holy Spirit brooded, as it were, on the waters to bring to life those substances which were to be quickened and adorned. For it is the office of the Holy Spirit to make alive.

Word and Spirit

One of the key emphases in Luther's theology is that not only are the Spirit and Word related but that the Spirit is given through external means of grace rather than, as the "Enthusiasts" argued, through the "direct" access to the Spirit that they claimed.

From Luther, "Schmalcald Articles," pt. 3, art. 8, par. 3–12; *BC*, 312–13.

In these matters, which concern the external, spoken Word, we must hold firmly to the conviction that God gives no one his Spirit or grace except through or with the external Word which comes before. Thus we shall be protected from the enthusiasts—that is, from the spiritualists who boast that they possess the Spirit without and before the Word and who therefore judge, interpret, and twist the Scriptures or spoken Word according to their pleasure. Münzer did this, and many still do it in our day who wish to distinguish sharply between the letter and the spirit without knowing what they say or teach. . . . Even so, the enthusiasts of our day condemn the external Word, yet they do not remain silent but fill the world with their chattering and scribbling, as if the Spirit could not come through the Scriptures or the spoken word of the apostles but must come through their own writings and words. . . .

[7] Even those who have come to faith before they were baptized and those who came to faith in Baptism came to their faith through the external Word which preceded. Adults who have attained the age of reason must first have heard, "He who believes and is baptized will be saved" (Mark 16:16), even if they did not at once believe and did not receive the Spirit and Baptism until ten years later. . . . [10] Accordingly, we should and must constantly maintain that God will not deal with us except through his external Word and sacrament. Whatever is attributed to the Spirit apart from such Word and sacrament is of the devil. . . . [12] John the Baptist was not conceived without the preceding word of Gabriel, [13] nor did he leap in his mother's womb until Mary spoke.

Consequently, preaching of the Word in the church is of primary importance.

> From Luther, "Large Catechism," Creed, art. 3 par. 45, *BC*, 416.

For where Christ is not preached, there is no Holy Spirit to create, call, and gather the Christian church, and outside it no one can come to the Lord Christ.

That the Spirit is given through the Word is also a highly encouraging and consoling truth to Christians in distress. Expositing Psalm 118:6, Luther writes the following.

> From Luther, *Selected Psalms III*, *LW* 14:62.

"In my sore distress He came to me through His eternal Word and Spirit. I scarcely know that I have been troubled." We must not, as the sectarians do, imagine that God comforts us immediately, without His Word. Comfort does not come to us without the Word, which the Holy Spirit effectively calls to mind and enkindles in our hearts, even though it has not been heard for ten years.

Justification by Faith
Without the Holy Spirit, which is given through Word, the fallen human person is not able to turn to God or believe in him.

> From Luther, "Small Catechism," Creed, art. 3, *BC*, 345.

I believe that by my own reason or strength I cannot believe in Jesus Christ, my Lord, or come to him. But the Holy Spirit has called me through the Gospel, enlightened me with his gifts, and sanctified and preserved me in true faith, just as he calls, gathers, enlightens, and sanctifies the whole Christian church on earth and preserves it in union with Jesus Christ in the one true faith.

From Luther, "Large Catechism," Creed, art. 3, par. 38–39, BC, 415.

Neither you nor I could ever know anything of Christ, or believe in him and take him as our Lord, unless these were first offered to us and bestowed on our hearts through the preaching of the Gospel by the Holy Spirit. The work is finished and completed, Christ has acquired and won the treasure for us by his sufferings, death, and resurrection, etc. But if the work remained hidden and no one knew of it, it would have been all in vain, all lost. In order that this treasure might not be buried but put to use and enjoyed, God has caused the Word to be published and proclaimed, in which he has given the Holy Spirit to offer and apply to us this treasure of salvation. [39] Therefore to sanctify is nothing else than to bring us to the Lord Christ to receive this blessing, which we could not obtain by ourselves.

The following succinct statement makes clear that justification means both the "favor" of God, that is, forgiveness, and the "gift" (*donum*) of God, the reception of Christ's own righteousness or Christ's presence—the key to the Reformer's understanding of salvation.

From Luther, Lectures on Romans, on 5:5, LW 25:306.

But "the grace of God" and "the gift" are the same thing, namely, the very righteousness which is freely given to us through Christ.

In his polemical writing from 1521 *Against Latomus*, Luther elaborates on this theme.

From Luther, Against Latomus (1521), LW 32:229–30.

Now we finally come to the point. A righteous and faithful man doubtless has both grace and the gift. Grace makes him wholly pleasing so that his person is wholly accepted, and there is no place for wrath in him any more, but the gift heals from sin and from all his corruption of body and soul. It is therefore most godless to say that one who is baptized is still in sin, or that all his sins are not fully forgiven. For what sin is there where God is favorable and wills not to know any sin, and where he wholly accepts and sanctifies the whole man? However, as you see, this must not be attributed to our purity, but solely to the grace of a favorable God. Everything is forgiven through grace, but as yet not everything is healed through the gift. The gift has been infused, the leaven has been added to the mixture. It works so as to purge away the sin for which a person has already been forgiven, and to drive out the evil guest for whose expulsion permission has been given. In the meantime, while this is happening, it is called sin, and is truly such in its nature; but now it is sin without wrath, without the law, dead sin, harmless sin, as long as one perseveres in grace and his gift. As far as its nature is concerned, sin in no way differs from itself before grace and after grace; but it is indeed different in the way it is treated. . . . A person neither pleases, nor has grace, except on account of the gift which labors in this way to cleanse from sin. God saves real, not imaginary, sinners, and he teaches us to mortify real rather than imaginary sin.

In the following citation from a short tract, Luther makes a distinction between two kinds of righteousness, namely "alien" and "our" righteousness. This distinction is critical for the understanding of the Reformer's soteriology. In this short passage he lays out clearly his view of justification, which can also be expressed with the idea of union with Christ. Clearly here, Luther himself goes beyond the typical forensic (or declarative) understanding of justification, more prevalent in the Confessional Books of Lutheranism.

From Luther, *Two Kinds of Righteousness*, LW 31:297, 299.

There are two kinds of Christian righteousness, just as man's sin is of two kinds.

The first is alien righteousness, that is the righteousness of another, instilled from without. This is the righteousness of Christ by which he justifies through faith, as it is written in I Cor. 1[:30]: "Whom God made our wisdom, our righteousness and sanctification and redemption." . . . This righteousness, then, is given to men in baptism and whenever they are truly repentant. Therefore a man can with confidence boast in Christ and say: "Mine are Christ's living, doing, and speaking, his suffering and dying, mine as much as if I had lived, done, spoken, suffered, and died as he did." Just as a bridegroom possesses all that is his bride's and she all that is his—for the two have all things in common because they are one flesh [Gen. 2:24]—so Christ and the church are one spirit [Eph. 5:29–32]. . . .

Through faith in Christ, therefore, Christ's righteousness becomes our righteousness and all that he has becomes ours; rather, he himself becomes ours. Therefore the Apostle calls it "the righteousness of God" in Rom. 1[:17]: For in the gospel "the righteousness of God

is revealed . . . ; as it is written, 'The righteous shall live by his faith.'"
Finally, in the same epistle, chapter 3[:28], such a faith is called "the
righteousness of God": "We hold that a man is justified by faith."
This is an infinite righteousness, and one that swallows up all sins
in a moment, for it is impossible that sin should exist in Christ. On
the contrary, he who trusts in Christ exists in Christ; he is one with
Christ, having the same righteousness as he. It is therefore impossible that sin should remain in him. This righteousness is primary; it
is the basis, the cause, the source of all our own actual righteousness.
For this is the righteousness given in place of the original righteousness lost in Adam. It accomplishes the same as that original righteousness would have accomplished; rather, it accomplishes more.

As a result of Christ's righteousness—of Christ's presence—being given to
us, renewal of sanctification happens in a daily process.

From Luther, *Two Kinds of Righteousness*, LW 31:299–300.

Therefore this alien righteousness, instilled in us without our works
by grace alone—while the Father, to be sure, inwardly draws us to
Christ—is set opposite original sin, likewise alien, which we acquire
without our works by birth alone. Christ daily drives out the old
Adam more and more in accordance with the extent to which faith
and knowledge of Christ grow. For alien righteousness is not instilled
all at once, but it begins, makes progress, and is finally perfected at
the end through death.

The second kind of righteousness is our proper righteousness,
not because we alone work it, but because we work with that first and
alien righteousness. This is that manner of life spent profitably in
good works, in the first place, in slaying the flesh and crucifying the
desires with respect to the self, of which we read in Gal. 5[:24]. . . .

This righteousness is the product of the righteousness of the
first type, actually its fruit and consequence, for we read in Gal.
5[:22]: "But the fruit of the spirit [i.e., of a spiritual man, whose very
existence depends on faith in Christ] is love, joy, peace, patience,
kindness, goodness, faithfulness, gentleness, self-control." . . . This
righteousness goes on to complete the first for it ever strives to do
away with the old Adam and to destroy the body of sin. Therefore
it hates itself and loves its neighbor; it does not seek its own good,
but that of another, and in this its whole way of living consists. For
in that it hates itself and does not seek its own, it crucifies the flesh.
Because it seeks the good of another, it works love. Thus in each
sphere it does God's will, living soberly with self, justly with neighbor, devoutly toward God.

This righteousness follows the example of Christ in this respect [1 Pct. 2:21] and is transformed into his likeness [2 Cor. 3:18]. It is precisely this that Christ requires. Just as he himself did all things for us, not seeking his own good but ours only—and in this he was most obedient to God the Father—so he desires that we also should set the same example for our neighbors.

Commenting on Rom. 8:16, Luther elaborates on the testimony of the Spirit in the heart of the believer.

From Luther, *Lectures on Romans*, LW 25:359.

For it is the Spirit Himself. In his sermon on the Annunciation, blessed Bernard, who was filled with the same Holy Spirit, very clearly shows that this testimony is the faith of our heart in God, saying: "I believe that this testimony consists of three parts. For it is necessary first of all to believe that you cannot have the remission of sins except through the kindness of God. Second, that you could not possess any good work unless God Himself gave it to you. And last, that you cannot earn eternal life by any of your works, unless it is given to you by grace." But this is not yet enough, but we must consider it as a kind of beginning and foundation of faith. For if you believe that your sins are not taken away except by Him, you do well. But you must still add: That you do believe this; not that you could do this yourself, but the Spirit must cause you to believe this, "because through Him you are given the forgiveness of sins. This is the testimony which the Holy Spirit produces in our hearts, saying: 'Your sins are forgiven you.' For in this way the apostle believes that a man is justified by faith." . . . "Thus also concerning eternal life it is not enough to believe that He gives it to you freely, but it is also necessary to have the testimony of the Spirit that you will come to eternal life by God's favor."

The Christian Church

As the following citation from the Larger Catechism testifies, Luther puts forth a pneumatological view of the church as the community of saints.

From Luther, "Large Catechism," Creed, art. 3, par. 47–53, *BC*, 416–17.

The Creed calls the holy Christian church a *communio sanctorum*, "a communion of saints." . . . [It is] a community composed only of saints, or, still more clearly, "a holy community." . . . It is called together by the Holy Spirit in one faith, mind, and understanding. It possesses a variety of gifts, yet is united in love without sect or schism. Of this community I also am a part and member, a participant and co-partner in all the blessings it possesses. I was brought to it by the Holy Spirit and incorporated into it through the fact that I have heard and still hear God's Word, which is the first step in entering it. Before we had advanced this far, we were entirely of the devil, knowing nothing of God and of Christ. Until the last day the Holy Spirit remains with the holy community or Christian people. Through it he gathers us, using it to teach and preach the Word. By it he creates and increases sanctification, causing it daily to grow and become strong in the faith and in the fruits of the Spirit.

The Christian Walk and Daily Repentance

From Luther, *Lectures on Romans* (1515), on Rom. 8:14, *LW* 25:356.

For all who are led by the Spirit of God are sons of God. "To be led by the Spirit of God" is to put to death our flesh, that is, the old Adam, and to do it freely, promptly, and gladly, that is, to despise and renounce all that is not God, even ourselves, and thus "not to fear death or the friends of death, the fierce race of penalties," and likewise "to give up the empty pleasures of the world and its corrupt and sordid prizes," and freely to relinquish all good things and embrace evils in their place. This is not characteristic of our nature, but is a work of the Spirit of God in us.

The same Spirit also strengthens and encourages Christians in need.

From Luther, *Lectures on Romans* (1515), on Rom. 8:26, *LW* 25:365–66.

Therefore, when everything is hopeless for us and all things begin to go against our prayers and desires, then those unutterable groans begin. And then "the Spirit helps us in our weakness" (Rom. 8:26). For unless the Spirit were helping, it would be impossible for us to bear this action of God by which He hears us and accomplishes what we pray for. . . . Therefore these people who do not have the Spirit flee and do not want the works of God to be done but want to form themselves. But those who have the Spirit are helped by Him. Thus they do not lose hope but have confidence, even though they are aware of what goes contrary to what they have so sincerely prayed for. For the work of God must be hidden and never understood, even when it happens. But it is never hidden in any other way than under that which appears contrary to our conceptions and ideas. Hence Gabriel says to the Virgin: "The Holy Spirit will come upon you," that is, He will come upon you in a way which is above what you think, "and the power of the Most High will overshadow you"

(Luke 1:35), that is, you will not understand, and therefore do not ask how it will come to pass.

Ulrich Zwingli

While of course inspired and influenced by Luther's groundbreaking reform work, Zwingli and Calvin also launched a distinctive Reformed renewal of the church. Differently from Luther, Zwingli was thoroughly shaped by humanism, and rather than consulting his own painful pilgrimage, he began a more intellectual reform.

Spiritual Authority
The following statement from *The Defense of the Reformed Faith* is a good example of the Reformation insistence on the supreme authority of Scripture, which Zwingli—alongside Luther—saw compromised by Catholics with their appeal to church authority and the radical Reformers with their appeal to spiritual experience.

> From *Huldrych Zwingli Writings: The Defense of the Reformed Faith*, vol. 1, trans. E. J. Furcha (Allison Park, PA: Pickwick Publications, 1984), 46, 57.

Whether the Spirit of God is with you is demonstrated above all, by whether his word is your guide, and by whether you do nothing except what is clearly stated in the word of God so that scripture is your master and not you, masters of scripture. . . . Whenever we give heed to the word, we acquire pure and clear knowledge of the will of God and are drawn to him by his Spirit and transformed into his likeness.

A Reformed theologian, Zwingli elaborates on the right understanding of election.

> From Ulrich Zwingli, *On Providence and Other Essays*, ed. William John Hinke (Durham, NC: Labyrinth Press, 1983), 43–44.

For thus it is written in Acts [13:48]: "And as many as were ordained to eternal life believed." Those, therefore, that believe are ordained to eternal life. But no one, save he who believes, knows who truly believe. He is already certain that he is elect of God. For, according to the apostle's word [2 Cor. 1:22], he has the seal of the Spirit, by which, pledged and sealed, he knows that he has become truly free, a son of the family, and not a slave. For the Spirit cannot deceive. If He tells us that God is our Father, and we confidently and fearlessly call Him Father, untroubled because we shall enter upon the eternal inheritance, then it is certain that God's Spirit has been shed abroad in our hearts. It is therefore settled that he is elect who has this security and certainty, for they who believe are ordained to eternal life. Yet many are elect who as yet have no faith.

The Spirit's Work in Salvation

In keeping with his pneumatological approach to Scripture and the Word, Zwingli insists on the necessity of the Spirit in spiritual awakening.

From Zwingli, *Defense of the Reformed Faith*, 61.

I have amply shown earlier that one cannot learn the word and mind of God from any person except through the one Spirit of God; in him alone a person is assured, firm and certain. . . . Note, beloved brothers, certainty of the word of God does not come from human judgments but rather from God, so that when a person has such a clear faith that he trusts God in all things, indeed, gives full credence to him alone, he fully knows that God is truthful. . . . Should he find it in his gospel, i.e. in the teaching which flows from God's Spirit and grace, he does not just accept it at that point, but he is so clearly informed and illumined beforehand that he accepts nothing except that in which God has guided him through Christ. . . . For God's Spirit informs our spirit that we are sons of God, Rom. 8:16. How are we to know that we are sons of God except God assure us in our hearts through the spirit of his grace? Or how are we, who are full of lies, to know the truth, except it be by the breath of his Spirit? In short, nothing is true except that which God shows us.

Building on the brief Pauline tradition, Zwingli here lays out a rough outline of an *ordo salutis*, including water baptism as the rite of initiation.

From Zwingli, *Defense of the Reformed Faith*, 109–10.

Paul . . . speaks thus to Titus, "But after that the kindness and love of God our Saviour toward man appeared, not by works of righteousness which we have done, but according to his mercy he saved us, by the washing of regeneration, and renewing of the Holy Ghost; which he shed on us abundantly through Jesus Christ our Saviour" [Titus 3:4–6]. Who does not see that there is attributed here to the washing of regeneration that which really and truly belongs only to the divine Spirit? For though Paul said first that we were renewed by the washing of regeneration, yet, that he might be the more clearly understood, he immediately added an explanatory "and," meaning "and by the washing of the renewing of the Holy Ghost." Or does not the regeneration belong really and truly to the Holy Ghost? When, therefore, baptism is called the washing of regeneration, does not the sacrament receive truly the name of the regeneration of the Spirit? But how graceful it is when not the symbol is called the washing, but the internal working and renewing of the divine Spirit which is indicated by the sacrament is called the washing! Thus the names of the things and their symbols are in turn borrowed from each other.

The thirteenth article of the *Reformed Faith* explains salvation by faith in a way that sounds quite surprising to those steeped in the Protestant formulations; it does so in terms of deification, an idea not unknown to Luther, as we observed above. With its strong pneumatological flavor, this statement reads very much like those of Eastern Christianity.

From Zwingli, *Defense of the Reformed Faith*, 57.

That a person is drawn to God by God's Spirit and deified, becomes quite clear from scripture. "No one comes to Christ unless the heavenly Father draw him," Jn. 6:44. "And when the Spirit of truth comes, he shall teach all truth," Jn. 16.13. . . . For wherever the Spirit of Christ is, there you need not worry how the good is to be done. Here you recognize the smallness and weakness of your faith in that you do not let go of the bench [i.e., your reason] and give your hand confidently to God, allowing him to lead you. For you cling to the elements of this world which is human reason. But if you desire to be God's, you must submit freely to him; let him govern and direct your life, food, counsel and all things; then God lives in you. And though you might fall into sin because of your weakness, God allows it so that your faith and confidence in him may be renewed and strengthened.

Against Catholic suspicions of a lack of emphasis on good works in the Reformed insistence on faith as the root of Christian life, Zwingli here speaks of the importance of good works in terms of Christ's presence in the believer and the fruit of the Spirit.

From Zwingli, *Defense of the Reformed Faith*, 149.

The testament of the gospel is inscribed upon human hearts and works in us by the Spirit of God. From this follows: Where there is faith, there the Spirit of God is also, and where he is there one may find good works.

Faith and Sacraments

One of the well-known main differences between the Lutheran and Reformed Reformations has to do with sacraments. Advocating a "symbolic" understanding of sacraments, Zwingli took pains in explaining the primacy of faith rather than any religious rite as the root of salvation. Herein Zwingli appeals to St. Augustine, the theologian most often invoked by all three magisterial Reformers.

From Zwingli, *On Providence*, 113–15.

In this passage of Augustine [*Trinity*, bk. 15, chap. 26] we have to consider three things. First, since he says that the Holy Ghost was not given by the disciples, that they only prayed for it, much less is it true that the bestowal of the Holy Ghost is bound up with the sacraments administered by the clergy. Secondly, that the bestowal of the Holy Ghost was not bound up with the laying on of hands, which I do not deny is a sacrament. For since they only prayed that the Holy Ghost might be given to those upon whom they laid hands, they had no power to promise this by laying on of hands. Finally, when Augustine says, "In which preeminently the baptized receive the Holy Ghost," he is speaking symbolically (for he does not use the word "preeminently" to indicate a certainty that they who receive baptism necessarily also receive the Holy Ghost, but in a sense like that of "to wit," "namely," etc.,—in the sense, "the church, namely the one in which the baptized receive the Holy Ghost"). Thus receiving the Holy Ghost is not the effect of baptism, but baptism is the effect of having received the Holy Ghost. . . . For Augustine's remark that Christ received the Holy Ghost before His baptism, and that the apostles do not give the Holy Ghost, shows that there is no intimate connection of the Holy Ghost with the minister or the sacrament. From this it follows at once that the language is used symbolically and not in its simple sense when that which belongs to the Spirit is attributed to the sacraments. And this will be made plainer by the second quotation.

Speaking of the grace received from the sacrament of the Eucharist, Zwingli emphasizes the importance of faith brought about by the Spirit.

From Zwingli, *On Providence*, 190, 254–55.

Although the gift and bounty of the divine goodness are extolled therein [in the Eucharist], they are not brought to us by the power of the symbols, except in so far as the symbols and the words of the preacher proclaim them. For it is alone the Spirit that draws the mind to that fountain by which the soul, that has pined away through despair over its sins, is refreshed and renewed in youth. . . . Only those repented whom the Spirit illumined within so that they recognized that this was the Saviour, and whom the Father drew to come to Him and accept Him. Since, furthermore, externals can do nothing more than proclaim and represent (and when faith is brought into activity by them, certainly a faith is thus brought into activity which was there before), and since faith is a gift of the Holy Spirit, it is clear that the Spirit operated before the external symbols were introduced. . . .

None but the Holy Spirit giveth faith, which is confidence in God, and no external thing giveth it. Yet the sacraments do work faith, historical faith; for all festivals, trophies, nay, monuments and statues, work historical faith: that is, call to mind that a certain thing once took place, the memory of which is thus refreshed, as was the case with the festival of the Passover, among the Hebrews. . . . In this way, then, the Lord's Supper worketh faith, that is, signifies as certain that Christ was born and suffered. But to whom does it signify this? To the believer and the unbeliever alike. For it signifies to all that which belongs to the meaning of the sacrament, namely, that Christ suffered, whether they receive it or not, but that He suffered for us it signifies to the pious believer only. For no one knows or believes that Christ suffered for us, save those whom the Spirit within has taught to recognize the mystery of divine goodness. For such alone receive Christ. Hence nothing gives confidence in God except the Spirit.

John Calvin

The Deity of the Spirit
One of the initial tasks Calvin sets in the first part of his *Institutes* is to prove the deity of the Son and Spirit. He does so mostly using biblical materials. The starting point is the Spirit's role in creation. The reference in the first line to "the same sources" means "practical knowledge" as derived from the Bible rather than "idle speculation" (1.13.13).

From John Calvin, *Inst.* 1.13.14–15, http://www.ccel.org.

14. In asserting the divinity of the Spirit, the proof must be derived from the same sources. And it is by no means an obscure testimony which Moses bears in the history of the creation, when he says that the Spirit of God was expanded over the abyss or shapeless matter; for it shows not only that the beauty which the world displays is maintained by the invigorating power of the Spirit, but that even

before this beauty existed the Spirit was at work cherishing the confused mass. . . .

But, as I observed, the best proof to us is our familiar experience. For nothing can be more alien from a creature, than the office which the Scriptures ascribe to him, and which the pious actually feel him discharging,—his being diffused over all space, sustaining, invigorating, and quickening all things, both in heaven and on the earth. The mere fact of his not being circumscribed by any limits raises him above the rank of creatures, while his transfusing vigour into all things, breathing into them being, life, and motion, is plainly divine. Again, if regeneration to incorruptible life is higher, and much more excellent than any present quickening, what must be thought of him by whose energy it is produced? Now, many passages of Scripture show that he is the author of regeneration, not by a borrowed, but by an intrinsic energy; and not only so, but that he is also the author of future immortality. In short, all the peculiar attributes of the Godhead are ascribed to him in the same way as to the Son. . . . Most clearly, therefore does Paul ascribe divine power to the Spirit, and demonstrate that he dwells hypostatically in God.

15. Nor does the Scripture, in speaking of him, withhold the name of God. . . . Now it ought not to be slightly overlooked, that all the promises which God makes of choosing us to himself as a temple, receive their only fulfilment by his Spirit dwelling in us. . . . And the Apostle says at one time that we are the temple of God, and at another time, in the same sense, that we are the temple of the Holy Spirit.

The Life-Giving Spirit
Commenting on Ps. 104:29, Calvin highlights the life-giving role of the Spirit in a way rediscovered enthusiastically in the contemporary pneumatologies of Moltmann, Pannenberg, and others.

From John Calvin, on Ps. 104:29, *Calvin's Commentaries: Psalms 93–119*, vol. 4, trans. James Anderson (Grand Rapids: Christian Classics Ethereal Library, n.d.), http://www.ccel.org.

We continue to live, so long as he sustains us by his power; but no sooner does he withdraw his life-giving spirit than we die. Even Plato knew this, who so often teaches that, properly speaking, there is but one God, and that all things subsist, or have their being only in him. . . . He [the psalmist] again declares, that the world is daily *renewed*, because *God sends forth his spirit*. In the propagation of living creatures, we doubtless see continually a new creation of the world. In now calling *that* God's spirit, which he before represented as the spirit of living creatures, there is no contradiction. God sendeth forth that spirit which remains with him whither he pleases; and as soon as he has sent it forth, all things are created. In this way, what was his own he makes to be ours. . . . He [the prophet] termed that the *spirit of God* which proceeds from him. By the way, he instructs us, that it is ours, because it is given us, that it may quicken us. The amount of what is stated is, that when we see the world daily decaying, and daily renewed, the life-giving power of God is reflected to us herein as in a mirror. All the deaths which take place among living creatures, are just so many examples of our nothingness, so to speak; and when others are produced and grow up in their room, we have in that presented to us a renewal of the world. Since then the world daily dies, and is daily renewed in its various parts, the manifest conclusion is, that it subsists only by a secret virtue derived from God.

The Spirit's Proceeding from the Father and Son

Calvin sticks with the teaching of the Christian West by affirming the *filioque*, the proceeding of the Spirit from both Father and Son. He sees it taught in the Bible, especially in Romans 8.

From Calvin, *Inst.* 1.3.18.

18. . . . To the Father is attributed the beginning of action, the fountain and source of all things; to the Son, wisdom, counsel, and arrangement in action, while the energy and efficacy of action is assigned to the Spirit. Moreover, though the eternity of the Father is also the eternity of the Son and Spirit, since God never could be without his own wisdom and energy; and though in eternity there can be no room for first or last, still the distinction of order is not unmeaning or superfluous, the Father being considered first, next the Son from him, and then the Spirit from both. For the mind of every man naturally inclines to consider, first, God, secondly, the wisdom emerging from him, and, lastly, the energy by which he executes the purposes of his counsel. For this reason, the Son is said to be of the Father only; the Spirit of both the Father and the Son. This is done in many passages, but in none more clearly than in the eighth chapter to the Romans, where the same Spirit is called indiscriminately the Spirit of Christ, and the Spirit of him who raised up Christ from the dead. And not improperly. For Peter also testifies (1 Pet. 1:21), that it was the Spirit of Christ which inspired the prophets, though the Scriptures so often say that it was the Spirit of God the Father.

The Inner Testimony of the Spirit

Chapter 7 of the first book of the *Institutes* is titled "The Testimony of the Spirit Necessary to Give Full Authority to Scripture. . . ." Here Calvin argues against his understanding of the Catholic doctrine of Scripture, in which the ultimate authority of the Bible rests on the church, by setting forth his own pneumatological understanding of biblical authority.

From Calvin, Inst. 1.7.4–5; 1.8.1.

4. . . . Our conviction of the truth of Scripture must be derived from a higher source than human conjectures, Judgments, or reasons; namely, the secret testimony of the Spirit. . . . The testimony of the Spirit is superior to reason. For as God alone can properly bear witness to his own words, so these words will not obtain full credit in the hearts of men, until they are sealed by the inward testimony of the Spirit. The same Spirit, therefore, who spoke by the mouth of the prophets, must penetrate our hearts, in order to convince us that they faithfully delivered the message with which they were divinely entrusted. . . .

5. Let it therefore be held as fixed, that those who are inwardly taught by the Holy Spirit acquiesce implicitly in Scripture; that Scripture, carrying its own evidence along with it, deigns not to submit to proofs and arguments, but owes the full conviction with which we ought to receive it to the testimony of the Spirit.

Hence, the saving power of Scripture is the function of the authority of God brought about by the Holy Spirit, as stated succinctly in the following brief summary.

From Calvin, Inst. 1.8.13.

Then only, therefore, does Scripture suffice to give a saving knowledge of God when its certainty is founded on the inward persuasion of the Holy Spirit. Still the human testimonies which go to confirm it will not be without effect, if they are used in subordination to that chief and highest proof, as secondary helps to our weakness.

While insisting on the inner testimony of the Spirit, Calvin is in no way implying drifting away from the written Scripture—as he, with Luther, accused the Enthusiasts of doing—but rather the opposite: the Spirit and the Word are integrally related and go hand in hand.

From Calvin, Inst. 1.9.3.

The letter therefore is dead, and the law of the Lord kills its readers when it is dissevered from the grace of Christ, and only sounds in the ear without touching the heart. But if it is effectually impressed on the heart by the Spirit; if it exhibits Christ, it is the word of life converting the soul, and making wise the simple. Nay, in the very same passage, the apostle calls his own preaching the ministration of the Spirit (2 Cor. 3:8), intimating that the Holy Spirit so cleaves to his own truth, as he has expressed it in Scripture, that he then only exerts and puts forth his strength when the word is received with due honour and respect.

There is nothing repugnant here to what was lately said (chap. 7) that we have no great certainty of the word itself, until it be confirmed by the testimony of the Spirit. For the Lord has so knit together the certainty of his word and his Spirit, that our minds are duly imbued with reverence for the word when the Spirit shining upon it enables us there to behold the face of God; and, on the other hand, we embrace the Spirit with no danger of delusion when we recognise him in his image, that is, in his word. Thus, indeed, it is. God did not produce his word before men for the sake of sudden display, intending to abolish it the moment the Spirit should arrive; but he employed the same Spirit, by whose agency he had administered the word, to complete his work by the efficacious confirmation of the word. In this way Christ explained to the two disciples (Luke 24:27), not that they were to reject the Scriptures and trust to their own wisdom, but that they were to understand the Scriptures. In like manner, when Paul says to the Thessalonians, "Quench not the Spirit" [1 Thess. 5:19], he does not carry them aloft to empty speculation apart from the word; he immediately adds, "Despise not prophesying" [1 Thess. 5:20].

The Work of the Spirit in the Christian's Life

Having established the close relationship between the Spirit and the Word, Calvin goes on to apply it to the work of God in bringing about faith in God, beginning from illumination of the heart.

From Calvin, *Inst.* 2.5.5.

5. . . . God works in his elect in two ways: inwardly, by his Spirit; outwardly, by his Word. By his Spirit illuminating their minds, and training their hearts to the practice of righteousness, he makes them new creatures, while, by his Word, he stimulates them to long and seek for this renovation. In both, he exerts the might of his hand in proportion to the measure in which he dispenses them. The Word, when addressed to the reprobate, though not effectual for their amendment, has another use. It urges their consciences now, and will render them more inexcusable on the day of judgment.

The fact that the Holy Spirit is instrumental in turning the heart of the elect does not mean setting aside the part played by the human person, though never apart from grace. The citation in Calvin's text refers to Augustine.

From Calvin, Inst. 2.5.14–15.

14. . . . [Augustine] reminds us that the agency of man is not destroyed by the motion of the Holy Spirit, because nature furnishes the will which is guided so as to aspire to good. . . . The very idea of help implies that we also do something, we must not understand it as if he were attributing to us some independent power of action. . . .

15. Meanwhile, we deny not the truth of Augustine's doctrine, that the will is not destroyed, but rather repaired, by grace—the two things being perfectly consistent—viz. that the human will may be said to be renewed when its vitiosity and perverseness being corrected, it is conformed to the true standard of righteousness and that, at the same time, the will may be said to be made new, being so vitiated and corrupted that its nature must be entirely changed. There is nothing then to prevent us from saying, that our will does what the Spirit does in us, although the will contributes nothing of itself apart from grace. . . . But though every thing good in the will is entirely derived from the influence of the Spirit, yet, because we have naturally an innate power of willing, we are not improperly said to do the things of which God claims for himself all the praise.

Through the Spirit, the benefits of Christ's salvific work are communicated to us. The Spirit also unites us with Christ.

From Calvin, Inst. 3.1.1.

To communicate to us the blessings which he received from the Father, he [Christ] must become ours and dwell in us. Accordingly, he is called our Head, and the first-born among many brethren, while, on the other hand, we are said to be ingrafted into him and clothed with him, all which he possesses being, as I have said, nothing to us until we become one with him. And although it is true that we obtain this by faith, yet since we see that all do not indiscriminately embrace the offer of Christ which is made by the gospel, the very nature of the case teaches us to ascend higher, and inquire into the secret efficacy of the Spirit, to which it is owing that we enjoy Christ and all his blessings. I have already treated of the eternal essence and divinity of the Spirit (Book 1 chap. 13 sect. 14, 15); let us at present attend to the special point, that Christ came by water and blood, as the Spirit testifies concerning him, that we might not lose the benefits of the salvation which he has purchased. For as there are said to be three witnesses in heaven, the Father, the Word, and the Spirit, so there are also three on the earth, namely, water, blood, and Spirit. It is not without cause that the testimony of the Spirit is twice mentioned, a testimony which is engraven on our hearts by way of seal, and thus seals the cleansing and sacrifice of Christ. For which reason, also, Peter says, that believers are "elect" "through sanctification of the Spirit, unto obedience and sprinkling of the blood of Jesus Christ" (1 Pet. 1:2). By these words he reminds us, that if the shedding of his sacred blood is not to be in vain, our souls must be washed in it by the secret cleansing of the Holy Spirit.

From the beginning to the end the communication of salvation is the work of the Holy Spirit, culminating in sealing as a token of the eschatological final redemption.

From Calvin, *Inst.* 3.2.36.

But if the illumination of the Spirit is the true source of understanding in the intellect, much more manifest is his agency in the confirmation of the heart. . . . The Spirit performs the part of a seal, sealing upon our hearts the very promises, the certainty of which was previously impressed upon our minds. It also serves as an earnest in establishing and confirming these promises. Thus the Apostle says, "In whom also, after that ye believed, ye were sealed with that holy Spirit of promise, which is the earnest of our inheritance" (Eph. 1:13, 14). You see how he teaches that the hearts of believers are stamped with the Spirit as with a seal, and calls it the Spirit of promise, because it ratifies the gospel to us. In like manner he says to the Corinthians, "God has also sealed us, and given the earnest of the Spirit in our hearts" (2 Cor. 1:22). And again, when speaking of a full and confident hope, he founds it on the "earnest of the Spirit" (2 Cor. 5:5).

Spiritual Gifts and the Fruit of the Spirit
In his exposition on Gal. 5:22–26, Calvin discusses the fruit of the Spirit.

From John Calvin, *Commentary on Galatians 5:22, 25,* in *Calvin's Commentaries: Galatians and Ephesians,* trans. William Pringle (Grand Rapids: Christian Classics Ethereal Library, n.d.), http://www.ccel.org.

Joy does not here, I think, denote that "joy in the Holy Ghost" (Romans 14:17) of which he speaks elsewhere, but that cheerful behavior towards our fellow-men which is the opposite of moroseness. *Faith* means truth, and is contrasted with cunning, deceit, and falsehood, as *peace* is with quarrels and contentions. *Long-suffering* is gentleness of mind, which disposes us to take everything in good part, and not to be easily offended. The other terms require no explanation, for the dispositions of the mind must be learned from the outward conduct. . . .

25. *If we live in the Spirit.* According to his usual custom, the apostle draws from the doctrine a practical exhortation. The death of the flesh is the life of the Spirit. If the Spirit of God lives in us, let him govern our actions. There will always be many persons daring enough to make a false boast of living in the Spirit, but the apostle challenges them to a proof of the fact. As the soul does not remain idle in the body, but gives motion and rigour to every member and part, so the Spirit of God cannot dwell in us without manifesting himself by the outward effects. By the *life* is here meant the inward power, and by the *walk* the outward actions. The metaphorical use of the word *walk*, which frequently occurs, describes works as evidences of the spiritual life.

Calvin's view of spiritual gifts in his own time is cautious and reserved. Yet he argues that with the coming of Christ there are more gifts than during the time of the prophets.

> From John Calvin, *Commentary on Joel 2:28*, in *Calvin's Commentaries: Twelve Minor Prophets: Amos, Joel, Obadiah*, vol. 2, trans. John Owen (Grand Rapids: Christian Classics Ethereal Library, n.d.), http://www.ccel.org.

The Prophet, no doubt, promises here something greater than what the fathers under the Law had experienced. The gift of the Spirit, we know, was enjoyed even by the ancients; but the Prophet promises not what the faithful had before found; but, as we have said, something greater . . . and God did not pour out his Holy Spirit so abundantly and so largely under the law as after the manifestation of Christ. Since, then, the gift of the Spirit was more copiously given to the Church after the advent of Christ, the Prophet uses here an unwonted expression—that God would pour out his Spirit.

Another circumstance is added, *upon all flesh.* Though the Prophets, as we know, had formerly their colleges, yet they were but few in number. As then the gift of prophecy was rare among the Jews, the Prophets in order to show that God would deal more bountifully to his new Church when restored, says, that he would pour out his Spirit upon all flesh. He then intimates that all in common would be partakers of the gift of the Spirit, and of its rich abundance, while under the law a few had but a sparing taste of it. We now then perceive the design of the Prophet; it was to make a manifest difference between the state of the ancient people and the state of the new Church, of the restoration of which he now speaks. The comparison is, that God would not only endow a few with his Spirit, but the whole mass of the people, and then that he would enrich his faithful with all kinds of gifts, so that the Spirit would seem to be poured forth in full abundance: *I will then pour out my Spirit upon all flesh.* We hence learn how absurdly the Greek interpreter has rendered this, "I will pour out from my Spirit:" for he diminishes this promise by saying, "From my Spirit," as though God promised here some small portion of his Spirit; while, on the contrary the Prophet speaks of abundance, and intended to express it. Prophesy then shall your sons and your daughters, he says, so that he does not exclude women.

In commenting on the 1 Corinthians 12 discussion of charisms, Calvin emphasizes their use for the upbuilding of the church.

From John Calvin, *Commentary on 1 Corinthians 12:4–7*, in *Calvin's Commentaries: Corinthians*, trans. John Pringle, vol. 1 (Grand Rapids: Christian Classics Ethereal Library, n.d.), http://www.ccel.org.

4. *Now there are diversities of gifts.* The symmetry of the Church consists, so to speak, of a manifold unity, that is, when the variety of gifts is directed to the same object, as in music there are different sounds, but suited to each other with such an adaptation, as to produce concord. Hence it is befitting that there should be a distinction of gifts as well as of offices, and yet all harmonize in one. . . .

One Spirit. This passage ought to be carefully observed in opposition to fanatics, who think that the name Spirit means nothing essential, but merely the gifts or actions of divine power. Here, however, Paul plainly testifies, that there is *one* essential power of God, whence all his works proceed. The term Spirit, it is true, is sometimes transferred by metonymy to the gifts themselves. Hence we read of the Spirit of knowledge—of judgment—of fortitude—of modesty. Paul, however, here plainly testifies that judgment, and knowledge, and gentleness, and all other gifts, proceed from *one* source. For it is the office of the Holy Spirit to put forth and exercise the power of God by conferring these gifts upon men, and distributing them among them. . . . *The administrations*, says Paul, *are different*, but there is only one God whom we must serve, whatever *administration* we discharge. . . .

7. *But the manifestation of the Spirit is given to every man. . . . The manifestation of the Spirit* may be taken in a passive as well as in an active sense—in a *passive* sense, because wherever there is prophecy,

or knowledge, or any other gift, the Spirit of God does there *manifest* himself—in an *active* sense, because the Spirit of God, when he enriches us with any gift, unlocks his treasures, for the purpose of *manifesting to* us those things that would otherwise have been concealed and shut up. The second interpretation suits better. The view taken by Chrysostom is rather harsh and forced—that this term is used, because unbelievers do not recognize God, except by visible miracles.

The Spirit in the Sacraments

One of the long-lasting theological contributions of the Geneva Reformer is his pneumatological framing of the sacraments.

From Calvin, Inst. 4.14.9.

The sacraments duly perform their office only when accompanied by the Spirit, the internal Master, whose energy alone penetrates the heart, stirs up the affections, and procures access for the sacraments into our souls. If he is wanting, the sacraments can avail us no more than the sun shining on the eyeballs of the blind, or sounds uttered in the ears of the deaf. Wherefore, in distributing between the Spirit and the sacraments, I ascribe the whole energy to him, and leave only a ministry to them; this ministry, without the agency of the Spirit, is empty and frivolous, but when he acts within, and exerts his power, it is replete with energy. . . . But if it is true, as has been explained, that . . . in our hearts it is the work of the Holy Spirit to commence, maintain, cherish, and establish faith, then it follows, both that the sacraments do not avail one iota without the energy of the Holy Spirit. . . .

From Calvin, Inst. 4.17.10.

But though it seems an incredible thing that the flesh of Christ . . . should be food to us, let us remember how far the secret virtue of the Holy Spirit surpasses all our conceptions, and how foolish it is to wish to measure its immensity by our feeble capacity. Therefore, what our mind does not comprehend let faith conceive—viz. that the Spirit truly unites things separated by space. That sacred communion of flesh and blood by which Christ transfuses his life into us, just as if it penetrated our bones and marrow, he testifies and seals in the Supper, and that not by presenting a vain or empty sign, but by there exerting an efficacy of the Spirit by which he fulfils what he promises.

The Catholic Reformation

Ignatius Loyola

The year 1990 saw the 450th anniversary of the founding of the Society of Jesus, and the following year, the 500th anniversary of its most famous pioneer, Ignatius of Loyola, contemporary to the pioneer of the Protestant Reformation, Martin Luther. Ironically, the heyday of the Protestant Reformation, the year 1521, happened to be the time of Loyola's conversion and dedication to the service of God and the Catholic Church. Visionary mystic, profound thinker, founder of a religious order, prolific author, reformer of faith, and missionary catalyst—these are but few of his most obvious descriptors. His *Spiritual Exercises* is one of the classics in spirituality.

Trinitarian Spirituality
Ignatius is well known for his deep Trinitarian spirituality and love of the Trinity.

From Ignatius of Loyola, *Spiritual Diary* 48, 109–10, in
Spiritual Exercises and Selected Works, ed. George E. Ganss, SJ, et al.
(New York: Paulist Press, 1991), 244–45, 253 (hereafter Ganss).

[48] Later while I was preparing the altar and vesting, words came to me: "Eternal Father, confirm me! Eternal Son, confirm me. Eternal Holy Spirit, confirm me. Holy Trinity, confirm me. My One and Only God, confirm me." I said this many times, with great vehemence, devotion, and tears; and I felt it very deeply. . . .

[109]—When I had finished Mass and unvested, during my prayer at the altar there was so much sobbing and effusion of tears, all terminating in the love of the Holy Trinity, that I seemed to have no desire to leave. For I was feeling so much love and so much spiritual sweetness.

[110]—Then several times near the fire I experienced interior love for the Holy Trinity and impulses to weep. Later . . . whenever I remembered the Holy Trinity I felt an intense love and sometimes motions toward weeping. All these visitations terminated in the Name and Essence of the Holy Trinity.

Ignatius's experience of the presence of the Holy Spirit is extraordinary and profound.

From Ignatius of Loyola, *Spiritual Diary* 14, 18 (Ganss, 241–42).

[14]—The Holy Spirit . . .

In the midst of my accustomed prayer, without deliberations, while offering or asking God our Lord that the oblation made be accepted by his Divine Majesty, I had abundant devotion and tears. Later, speaking with the Holy Spirit in view of saying his Mass, with the same devotion or tears I seemed to see him or perceive him in dense brightness or in the color of a flame of fire burning in an unusual way. Through all of this the election made was confirmed in me.

[18]—A little later still when I was about to leave for Mass, while giving myself to a short prayer, I experienced an intense devotion, and tears came over me as I somehow perceived interiorly or saw the Holy Spirit. This, so to speak, made the election seem a finished matter. And yet I was unable to see either of the other two divine Persons.

The Church of the Spirit

A faithful servant of the church, Ignatius held tightly to the principle of the Spirit working in the Catholic Church.

From Ignatius of Loyola, *Spiritual Exercises* 365 (Ganss, 213).

The Thirteenth. To keep ourselves right in all things, we ought to hold fast to this principle: What I see as white, I will believe to be black if the hierarchical Church thus determines it. For we believe that between Christ our Lord, the Bridegroom, and the Church, his Spouse, there is the one same Spirit who governs and guides us for the salvation of our souls. For it is by the same Spirit and Lord of ours who gave the ten commandments that our holy Mother Church is guided and governed.

John of Avila

Of Jewish descent and a contemporary of Ignatius and great admirer of his order, John of Avila barely escaped the Inquisition and became a famous preacher and catalyst of spiritual reform, including the Catholic clergy. The following quotations are taken from a collection of sermons titled *The Holy Ghost.*

Preparation for the Reception of the Holy Spirit

John speaks often of the right preparation for the reception of the Holy Spirit.

From Blessed John of Avila, *The Holy Ghost*
(Chicago: Scepter, 1959), 9, 11–12.

I have chosen no text for this sermon, because our text is nothing more than that we should prepare ourselves to be the dwelling-place of the Holy Ghost, and that we should ask the Holy Ghost with great fervour to condescend to come to us. . . .

The *first* requirement for the coming of the Holy Ghost to our souls is that we should be aware of His power, and that we should believe that he can accomplish marvels. However sad a soul may be, He is sufficient to console it; however worthless, he can make it valuable; however, lukewarm, He can fire it; however weak, He can strengthen it; however lacking in piety, He can inflame it with ardent devotion. What is the way to bring the Holy Ghost to us? It is to be aware of His might. And it has been said of the might of the Holy Ghost: "*For great is the power of God alone: and he is honoured by the humble.*"

The *second* requirement for the Holy Ghost to be willing to come into our hearts (so that we may not be rejected or found wanting) is to have the will to receive Him as our guest, sincerely and anxiously to desire His coming. "Oh, if only the Holy Ghost would come! Oh, if that Comforter would only visit me and console my soul!"

Like any great preacher, the one from Avila uses striking images to make his case.

From John of Avila, *Holy Ghost*, 19–20.

Give the Holy Ghost to eat, and give Him your heart: He eats flesh; but see that it is mortified flesh. How would it be if you gave your guest a live bird? "What is this?"—he would say to you—"Take it away. That bird is not fit to eat."

Raise your heart often to heaven and beg that it may be fired with love. Your flesh must be dead and some time dead, punished and mortified, subjugated with fasts and scourgings; it must be dead to the world. Guard your heart carefully! Raise your thoughts and desires to God! Become as a golden eagle through these thoughts and exercises: soar upwards and do not rest until you have reached the Holy Ghost. . . . Do not let your thoughts dwell on things corrupt or perishable or noisome, but on heaven. "*Where thy treasure is, there is thy heart*" [Luke 12:34] and more especially during this season.

Seek seclusion throughout this week in preparation for the Holy Ghost! Be on your guard!

The Possession of the Spirit as the Mark of the Christian

Following the apostle Paul, John of Avila makes the possession of the Spirit the mark of being a Christian.

From John of Avila, *Holy Ghost*, 46–47, 66–67.

"He who has not the Spirit of Christ is none of His" [Rom. 8:9] . . . He who lives by his own spirit, does not belong to Christ. You are not to live according to your own intellect, your own will, or your own judgment; you are to live in the Spirit of Christ. You must have received the Spirit of Christ. What does the Spirit of Christ mean? The heart of Christ. He who does not possess the heart of Christ, does not belong to Christ. . . .

"Since Jesus Christ is the door, where will this door lead to?" "To the Holy Ghost." *I am the door* [John 10:7]. He who enters through Me will come into the presence of the Holy Ghost . . . Vine and branches are nourished with the same sap; Head and body are sustained by the same holiness: the spirit of Christ and the spirit of those who are incorporated in Him, is all one. He is the vine, and His members are the branches. *I am the door:* he who wishes to receive the Holy Ghost let him enter through Me!

The Power of Pentecost

John describes vividly the power of the Holy Spirit.

From John of Avila, *Holy Ghost*, 81.

The blessed apostles were filled to overflowing with the fire of the Holy Ghost; they were filled with this celestial grace, so that it might be understood ever after that no one should speak or preach of the Holy Ghost unless he be filled, and filled to overflowing, with this heavenly gift, with this holy fire. When the apostles spoke and told of the marvels and wonders that witnessed to God's greatness and published them abroad, they were glowing with fervour and filled with grace sent them by Our Lord. The Holy Ghost came in tongues of fire so that they might understand that the tongues of those who speak of the wonders of God must speak words of fire, words of burning love. These tongues when talking of God and His greatness must not speak words that are insipid like the water, empty like wind, nor words that are of the earth.

John of the Cross

The "Mystical Doctor" and the spiritual director of the "discalded" (bare-foot, because they did not wear shoes) Carmelite Order is a leading mystical Catholic writer who, alongside his closest spiritual colleague Teresa of Avila, brought about a spiritual reform in the latter part of the sixteenth century.

Union with God
A mystic, John searches out union with God.

From John of the Cross, prologue to *The Living Flame of Love*,
versions A⁴ and B, trans. and intro. Jane Ackerman (Binghamton, NY: Medieval
& Renaissance Texts & Studies, 1995), 70 (hereafter Ackerman).

2. And one need not marvel that God may bestow such elevated and extraordinary gifts on the souls whom He chooses to favor. If we consider that He is God, and that He bestows them as God with infinite love and goodness, it will not seem unreasonable to us; for He said that *on him who loved Him would come the Father, Son, and Holy Spirit, and They would make their abode in him* [John 14:23] which had to be by making the person live and dwell in the Father, Son, and Holy Spirit in the life of God, as the soul would have us understand in these stanzas.

3. . . . . Similarly fire, having entered wood, may have transformed it into itself and may be now united with it, but as the fire burns more intensely and is in it longer, the wood becomes increasingly more incandescent and inflamed until it flashes fire and sends out tongues of flame.

The first stanza and its explanation elaborate on the work of the Holy Spirit in union.

From John of the Cross, *Living Flame*, 1.1, 3, 9 (Ackerman 74, 76, 80).

Stanza 1
O living flame of love
that tenderly wounds
my soul in its deepest center;
now that you are not contrary,
finish then if you wish,
rend the veil of this sweet encounter!

4. I am following version A throughout this work.

1. The soul now feels itself completely inflamed in divine union, its palate now bathed in glory and love. Flowing forth no less than rivers of glory from even the most intimate part of its being, abounding now in joys, the soul feels flow *from its womb rivers of living water* [John 7:38] which the Son of God said would flow forth in such souls. It seems to it that it is so close to blessedness that only a thin veil separates it, by such intensity is it transformed in God, so sublimely is it possessed by Him, and with such sumptuous wealth of gifts and virtues is it adorned. And it sees that each time that delicate flame of love which burns in it assails it, the flame does so as though it were glorifying the soul with gentle and powerful glory. This occurs to such a degree that each time the flame absorbs the soul and assails it, it seems that is going to give the soul eternal life and is going to tear the veil of mortal life, very little lacking. Due to that little, it has not yet completely been glorified in its substance. The soul therefore now says with great desire to the flame—which is the Holy Spirit—to rend mortal life through that sweet encounter, in which the flame truly communicates to the soul what it seems each time to be going to give to it and do when it encounters it, which is to glorify it entirely and perfectly. And so, the soul says: O living flame of love! . . .

3. This *flame of love* is the spirit of the soul's Bridegroom, Who is the Holy Spirit and Whom the soul already senses in itself, not only as a fire which has consumed and transformed it in gentle love, but as a fire which, more than that, burns in the soul and flares up, as I mentioned. The flame bathes the soul in glory and refreshes it with disposition for divine life. This is the operation of the Holy Spirit in the soul transformed in love. The acts that the Spirit performs interiorly are to blaze up in inflammations of love, in which the will of the soul loves sublimely, being united and having become one love with that flame. . . .

9. This feast of the Holy Spirit occurs in the substance of the soul, where neither the center of the senses nor the devil can reach. And so the more interior the feast, the more secure, substantial, and delightful it is, because the more interior it is, the more pure; and the greater the purity, the more abundantly, frequently, and universally does God communicate Himself.

The Holy Spirit as love unites the believer with God, which, as the second citation reveals, makes the whole human being enjoy this blessed unity.

From John of the Cross, *Living Flame*, 1.13–14 (Ackerman 82, 84).

13. Love unites the soul with God, and the more degrees of love the soul attains, the more deeply does it enter into God and does it cen-

ter itself in Him. Thus we can say that for however many degrees of love of God there are, that many centers—each one deeper than the next—there are in the soul in God, which are *the many mansions* [John 14:2] which He said *there were in his Father's house.*

From John of the Cross, *Living Flame*, 2.22 (Ackerman, 126).

22. Concerning this benefit of the soul, the union of the spirit at times overflows in the body, and the whole sensitive substance and all its members, bones, and marrow take delight, not so sluggishly as commonly occurs but with a feeling of great delight and glory which is sensed down to the last joints of the feet and hands. The body is aware of so much glory in the substance of the soul that it praises God in its own way, feeling Him in its bones, its praise resembling what David says, *All my bones will say: God, who will there be like You?* [Ps. 35:10]. Because all that can be said of this, concerning the body as concerning the spirit, [is] *that the touch tastes of eternal life's* and all debt repays.

Love Awakened
One of the many roles of the Holy Spirit is to remove spiritual dryness and slumber.

From St. John of the Cross, *The Spiritual Canticle*, 17.2, 4, 5, in *The Collected Works of St. John of the Cross*, trans. Kieran Kavanaugh, OCD, and Otilio Rodriquez, OCD (Washington, DC: Institute of Carmelite Studies, 1973), 479–80 (hereafter Kavanaugh).

2. . . . spiritual dryness also hampers the interior satisfaction and sweetness of which she spoke. Dreading this, she does two things here:

First, she impedes dryness by closing the door to it through continual prayer and devotion.

Second, she invokes the Holy Spirit; He it is Who will dispel this dryness and sustain and increase her love for the Bridegroom. He also moves the soul to the interior exercise of the virtues, so that the Son of God, her Bridegroom, may rejoice and delight more in His bride. She invokes the Holy Spirit because her entire aim is to please her Bridegroom. . . .

4. South wind come, you that waken love.

The south wind is a delightful breeze: it causes rain, makes the herbs and plants germinate, opens the flowers, and scatters their fragrance. Its effects are the opposite of those of the north wind. The soul, by this breeze, refers to the Holy Spirit, who awakens love. When this divine breeze strikes her, it wholly enkindles and refreshes her, and quickens and awakens the will, and elevates the previously fallen appetites that were asleep to the love of God; it does so in such a way that she can easily add, you that waken love, both His love and hers.

What she asks of the Holy Spirit is expressed in the following verse:

5. Breathe through my garden,

This garden is the soul. As the soul above calls herself a "vineyard in flower," because the flower of the virtues within her supply sweet-tasting wine, here she calls herself a garden, because the flowers of perfections and virtues planted within her come to life and begin to grow.

One of the many metaphors for the Spirit is "spiced wine," another dramatic picture of the refreshing work of the Spirit in the soul.

From St. John of the Cross, *Spiritual Canticle* 25.7 (Kavanaugh, 508).

7. "The spiced wine." This spiced wine is another much greater favor which God sometimes grants to advanced souls, in which He inebriates them in the Holy Spirit with a wine of sweet, delightful, and fortified love. Accordingly, she calls this love, "spiced wine." As this wine is seasoned and strengthened with many diverse, fragrant, and fortified spices, so this love, which God accords to those who are already perfect, is fermented and established in them and spiced with the virtues they have gained. Prepared with these precious spices, this wine gives such strength and abundance of sweet inebriation in these visits granted by God to the soul that they cause her to direct toward Him, efficaciously and forcefully, flowings or outpourings of praise, love, and reverence, etc., which we have mentioned. And she does this with admirable desires to work and suffer for Him.

The Radical Reformers

As the name indicates, the Radical Reformers and Anabaptists considered the reforms of mainline Protestantism wanting and desired to go even further with regard to both church structures and independence as well as the insistence of each individual Christian's responsibility in faith and discipleship. While the umbrella term "Radical Reformation" is just that, an umbrella—bringing together various types of reform movements, from politically active to neutral ones or from highly charismatic and prophetic to more ethically and discipleship-oriented ones—it is also a helpful nomenclature to distinguish that group from Roman Catholics, the magisterial Reformers, as well as the British (or Anglican) Reformation. Two main figures' contributions to Spirit and salvation will be presented here: that of Thomas Müntzer, at one time deeply influenced by Luther; and of Menno Simons, an Anabaptist pioneer. Not only are these two figures representative examples, their writings are also easily available in English.

Thomas Müntzer

Present at the famous disputation between Luther and Johann Eck in 1519 and at times quite close to Luther, Müntzer drifted away from both Luther and his theology and started advocating a sectarian, pneumatic understanding of the church and an unmediated theology of salvation. Spiritualist and apocalyptic in his later life, Müntzer influenced many quarters of the left-wing reformation because of his itineraries, at times forced upon him because of excommunications.

Spiritual Authority and Insight

Like any spiritual reformer, Müntzer assumed great spiritual authority to himself and as a consequence took the right to harshly criticize the teachers of the church, both past and contemporary, for skewed interpretation of the Bible and doctrines, as the citation from his *Protestation or Proposition* against Luther reveals. Discerning the "inner word" and holiness of life are prerequisites for listening to the Word of God.

> From Thomas Müntzer, *The Second Chapter of Daniel*, in *The Collected Works of Thomas Müntzer*, ed. and trans. Peter Matheson (Edinburgh: T. & T. Clark, 1988), 240.

Hence Paul [is] . . . speaking there [in Rom. 10] of the inward word which is to be heard in the abyss of the soul through the revelation of God. Now anyone who has not become conscious and receptive to this through the living witness of God, Romans 8, may have devoured a hundred thousand Bibles, but he can say nothing about God which has any validity. . . . The holy spirit must direct him to consider earnestly the pure and straight-forward meaning of the law, Psalm 18. Otherwise his heart will be blind and he will dream up for himself a wooden Christ and lead himself astray. . . . Similarly, if a man is to receive the revelation of God he must cut himself off from all distractions and develop an earnest concern for the truth.

True Faith

One crucial theme in the Radical Reformation's challenge to others was the charge of a lack of true, genuine faith and instead a shallow, formal reliance on human traditions and rites. In his *On Counterfeit Faith* Müntzer calls for sincere repentance and personal faith.

From Müntzer, *On Counterfeit Faith*, in *Collected Works*, 218–19.

Our poor, wretched, pitiable, lamentable Christian people cannot be helped because they do not recognise what is wrong with them; because they use the mere form of true faith as a fig leaf and declined to abandon their counterfeit faith they are impervious to advice assistance. The same fault is common to all; none will recognise when they first came to faith; they are on the same level as the pagans, Jews, and all unbelievers. On the contrary, each dons his and preens himself about his faith and his good deeds, although really knows nothing about the source or foundation of either. For this reason our crude and clumsy forefathers handed over the world (themselves only excepted) to the devil.

Menno Simons

Menno Simons was a primary Anabaptist leader of the Low Countries during the time of the emergence of the Protestant Reformation. Consequently, his followers became known as Mennonites (*Mennisten*). Ordained into priesthood and having come under the influence of the "Sacramentists" led by Melchior Hoffman, who among other things argued against the established view of Christ's real presence in the Eucharist, Simons started advocating a reform of the church even more radical than that of Luther and Zwingli. Menno's reformation, however, avoided the extremes of many other Radical Reformers, and while persecuted, the emerging Anabaptist movement was established on a solid foundation.

The Holy Spirit in the Trinity

The following citations set forth a solid confession of the Trinity.

From Menno Simons, *A Solemn Confession of the Triune, Eternal, and True God, Father, Son, and Holy Ghost*, in *The Complete Writings of Menno Simons*, trans. Leonard Verguin (Scottdale, PA: Herald Press, 1956), 491, 495–96.

We believe and confess with the holy Scriptures that there is an only, eternal, and true God, who is a Spirit. . . . Besides this only, eternal, living, Almighty sovereign God and Lord we know no other; and since He is a Spirit so great, terrible, and invisible, He is also ineffable, incomprehensible, and indescribable, as may be deduced and understood from the Scriptures. . . .

. . . We believe and confess the Holy Ghost to be a true, real, and personal Holy Ghost, as the fathers called Him; and that in a divine fashion, even as the Father is a true Father and the Son a true Son. Which Holy Ghost is a mystery to all mankind, incomprehensible, ineffable, and indescribable (as we have shown above of the Father and the Son); divine with His divine attributes, proceeding from the Father through the Son, although He ever remains with God and in God, and is never separated from the being of the Father and the Son.

Against Accusations

In various places, Menno Simons had to offer an apology or explanation against misjudgments and accusations. Here are some examples from his *Reply to Gellius Faber*, a formally Catholic priest who was widely suspected of teaching Lutheran doctrine. To Faber's 78-page-long book of accusations, Menno drafted one of his most extensive writings.

From Menno Simons, *Reply to Gellius Faber*, in *Complete Writings*, 759–61.

[1] *In the first place Gellius accuses us, saying, They (he means us) falsely adorn and deck themselves with the sanctity of the church. For since the Holy Spirit (which sanctifies the church both by the remission of sins, the mortification of the old man with all its lusts, and also by the restraint or annihilation of the sins in the flesh) is given through faith, therefore I cannot see how they can receive the Holy Spirit, together with true sanctification and be the holy church, seeing they angrily contend among themselves about the deity of the Holy Spirit (who, besides other evidence, sufficiently proves His deity in the work of sanctification), as well as about many other principal articles of the faith.*

Reply. . . . I never entertained the thought that God's Holy and eternal Spirit was not God in God, and God with God. Yet, Gellius would accuse us, who are not guilty, of denying the sanctification, grace, fruit, and power of the Holy Spirit, because some, who have been expelled by us, have erred in this respect, and probably still err; although he sees with his eyes and feels with his hands the sanctification and power of the Holy Spirit in our people, namely, that they restrain the old man with his lusts and destroy the sins in their flesh, a thing which he calls the sanctification of the Holy Spirit, as has been heard. Behold, thus he reviles those who have not merited it and so he accuses the non-guilty. Whether this is not the Pharisaic, envious, and defaming spirit, which put an evil construction on all that was good in Christ and His disciples, and incited the thoughtless populace against them, this I will leave to him to reflect.

[2] *In the second place he accuses us, saying, They have a proud faith; one half of which is founded upon the merits of Christ, and the other half upon their own merits....*

Reply. ... Our doctrine and publications abundantly testify that we ... seek justification in the righteous and crucified Christ Jesus alone....

[4] *In the fourth place he accuses us, saying, If they are the church, the spiritual bride of Christ, pure, holy, and unblamable, then let them prove the unity of the Spirit, especially concerning the twelve articles which are the foundation of the church, and let not one be the Menno, the other of Adam Pastor, the third of Obbe, and the four etc. For although they ban one another as much they please, it is still evident that they are all Anabaptists....*

Reply. I hope that we, by the grace of God, are so wedded to the Bridegroom, Christ Jesus, that we are prepared to sacrifice our lives for the sake of hearing His holy voice. We do not boast of our sanctity but of our great weakness, although we are slandered thus by Gellius. I trust also that we who are grains of one loaf agree not only as to the twelve articles (as he counts them), but also as to all the articles of the Scripture, such as regeneration, repentance, baptism, Holy Supper, expulsion, etc., which Christ Jesus (whom we together with Isaiah, Peter, and Paul confess foundation of the churches—and not the twelve articles as he has preached by His own blessed mouth, and left and taught us in clear words).

Neither are we so divided as he says, for the followers of Dirck agree, and I trust through the grace of God, we will ever continue so.

New Birth and Discipleship

Along with Müntzer and other radical Reformers, Menno's constant concern was that people who called themselves Christians were not truly newborn. He sounded a strong call for sincere repentance, personal experience of new birth, and submission of one's life to wholehearted devotion of discipleship and suffering. His tract *The New Birth* gives a representative example of his preaching.

From Menno Simons, *The New Birth*, in *Complete Writings*, 89–94.

In order that you may comfort yourselves no longer with ... false and vain hopes contrary to all Scriptures and to your eternal damnation, and may not vainly boast in the ... riches and glory of the children of God in the kingdom of Christ ... which do not as yet belong to you since you are altogether earthly, carnal, and devilishly minded . . . therefore I have undertaken through the merciful grace of the Lord as much as is in my power to point out very briefly . . . who are and who are not in possession of the grace of God, the afore-mentioned gifts, merits, and promises of Christ.

Tell me, dearly beloved, where and when did you read in the Scriptures, the true witness of the Holy Ghost and criterion of your consciences, that the unbelieving, disobedient, carnal man, the adulterous, immoral, drunken, avaricious, idolatrous, and pompous man has one single promise of the kingdom of Christ and His church, yes, part or communion in His merits, death, and blood? I tell you the truth, nowhere and never do we read it in the Scriptures. . . . Except ye be converted, and become as little children, ye shall not enter into the kingdom of heaven [Matt. 18:3]. And, Except a man be born again, he cannot see the kingdom of God [John 3:5]. . . . But if you wish to be saved, by all means and first of all, your earthly, carnal, ungodly life must be reformed. . . . The first birth of man is out of the first and earthly Adam, and therefore its nature is earthly and Adam-like. . . . If now you desire to have your wicked nature cleared up, and desire to be free from eternal death and damnation . . . then you must be born again. For the regenerate are in grace and have the promise as you have heard.

The regenerate, therefore, lead a penitent and new life, for they are renewed in Christ and have received a new heart and spirit. Once they were earthly-minded, now heavenly; once they were carnal, now spiritual. . . . Their minds are like the mind of Christ, they gladly walk as He walked; they crucify and tame their flesh with all its evil lusts.

In baptism they bury their sins in the Lord's death and rise with Him to a new life. They circumcise their hearts with the Word of the Lord; they are baptized with the Holy Ghost into the spotless, holy body of Christ, as obedient members of His church, according to the true ordinance and Word of the Lord. They put on Christ and manifest His spirit, nature, and power in all their conduct. They fear God with all the heart and seek in all their thoughts, words, and works, nothing but the praise of God and the salvation of their beloved brethren. . . .

These regenerated people have a spiritual king over them who rules them by the unbroken sceptre of His mouth, namely, with His Holy Spirit and Word. He clothes them with the garment of righteousness of pure white silk. He refreshes them with the living water of His Holy Spirit and feeds them with the Bread of Life.

CHAPTER 8

Post-Reformation Renewal Movements

Introduction

Speaking of a number of Protestant renewal movements that arose in the aftermath of the Reformation, such as Puritanism, pietism, holiness movements, and evangelicalism, Donald Bloesch gives an apt description:

> A burgeoning interest in the spiritual life is reflected in the rise of movements of spiritual purification after the Reformation in the late sixteenth through the nineteenth and early twentieth centuries. . . . These are convergent rather than divergent currents of renewal, and they often overlap. Yet each one has distinctive emphases, and this is why I treat them separately. Though emerging in the past they continue in new forms. A common strand in all these movements is the emphasis on heart religion. It is not enough to subscribe to the tenets of the faith. One must have a palpable experience of the object of faith if one is to be regarded as a true believer. A purely theoretical knowledge of Christ must give way to an existential knowledge, often called the knowledge of acquaintance. Many of these people manifested an appreciation for the mystics of the faith, though they generally steered clear of mystics who gravitated toward pantheism. The need to prepare the heart for the gift of grace as well as the role of disciplines of devotion that enable us to remain in the state of grace are also conspicuous in these ventures of renewal. The Puritans, Pietists and Evangelicals were united in affirming the Reformation doctrine of salvation by grace alone (*sola gratia*) and justification by faith alone (*sola fide*), though they wished to unite these themes with the biblical call to holiness. An exclusive emphasis on faith alone was treated with grave reservations by many of the revival leaders, including John Wesley. Faith must prove itself in a life of outgoing love.[1]

The Wesley brothers and Methodism, the Great Awakening pioneers of the eighteenth and nineteenth centuries in Wales and in the United States, as well as the Quakers, are other examples of renewal movements owing to Reformation that will be discussed under the wide umbrella concept of post-Reformation renewal movements.

---

1. Donald Bloesch, *The Holy Spirit: Works and Gifts* (Downers Grove, IL: InterVarsity Press, 2000), 111–12.

Puritanism

Puritanists were seeking for the renewal of the Christian life and church within or originating in Anglicanism. Up until contemporary times their influence on Anglicanism and beyond has been substantial. Unlike some other Protestant reformation movements, Puritans not only emphasized "heart faith" but also the role of sacraments and rites. Some leading Puritanists such as John Owen and Thomas Goodwin were shapers of the Congregationalist wing of Puritanism.

Richard Sibbes

Richard Sibbes, a priest in the Church of England, was one of the greatest Puritans of the first generation at the turn of the seventeenth century. His preaching and theological writings have significantly influenced Puritanism in the whole English-speaking world beyond his own homeland. In keeping with emerging Puritan spirituality, he spoke extensively of the role of the Spirit in salvation and the life of each Christian.

The Spirit in the Life of Christ
A profound Bible expositor, commenting on 2 Cor. 3:17, Sibbes has this to say of the work of the Spirit in the life of Christ.

From Richard Sibbes, *Treatises and Sermons from the Epistles
to the Corinthians*, vol. 4 of *The Complete Works of Richard Sibbes*,
ed. Alexander B. Grosart (Edinburgh: James Nichol,
1862–1864), 205–7 (hereafter Grosart).

Verse 17. "Now the Lord is that Spirit: and where the Spirit of the Lord is, there is liberty." "The Lord is that Spirit" that takes away the veil that is spoken of before. He sets down what Christ is by what he doth; Christ is "that Spirit," because he gives the Spirit. And then a sweet effect of the Spirit of Christ, "Where the Spirit of Christ is, there is liberty." The Spirit here is not taken for the person of God, as if the Holy Ghost had said, "The Lord is a Spirit," and not a bodily thing, though that be a truth. . . . "The Lord is that Spirit"; that is, the Lord Jesus Christ, who is the Lord of his church by marriage, office, etc., "is that Spirit"; that is, he (1) Hath the Spirit in himself eminently; and

(2) Dispenseth and giveth the Spirit unto others; all receiving the

Spirit from him as the common root and fountain of all spiritual gifts. . . .

. . . He was "that Spirit," as *having the Holy Ghost in himself as man*. The Holy Ghost filled the human nature and made it spiritual. The Spirit is all in all in the human nature of Christ; and whatsoever he doth, he doth, as it were, being full of the Spirit, in himself. He gives the Spirit as God, and receives it as man. So he both gives and receives. The Spirit proceedeth from the Father and the Son as God, but the Spirit sanctified Christ as man, as it did in the virgin's womb. The Holy Ghost sanctified that blessed mass of his body. It sanctified him, and filled him with all graces and gifts; whereupon it is said, "He received the Spirit without measure," John iii. 34; that is, in abundance. Christ hath the Spirit in himself in a more eminent excellent manner than all others; and it must needs be so for these reasons:

(1) *From the near union between the human nature and the divine.* They are one person. Therefore there is more Spirit in Christ than in all creatures put together; than in all the angels, and all men, because divine nature is nearer to Christ than it is to the angels or to any creature.

(2) Christ hath the Spirit without measure, *both in regard of extension and intension*, as we say. He hath all graces in all degrees. . . . All others have it in their measure and proportion.

(3) *The Spirit doth rest upon Christ invariably.* In other men than the Spirit, it ebbs and flows; it is sometimes more and sometimes less. There be spiritual desertions, not only in regard of comfort, but in regard of grace, though not totally. But the Spirit rests on Christ eternally full measure; and therefore you have it thus in Tm. xi. 2, "The Spirit of the Lord shall rest upon him, the Spirit of wisdom and understanding, the Spirit of counsel and might," etc. . . .

. . . He hath his name from anointing, "Christ." He was anointed; is, separated and ordained to the office of mediatorship, by anointing, properly, that is, with any material oil, but with the Spirit. . . .

Quest. When did this fulness of the Spirit come upon Christ? When had he it?

Ans. 1. There was a fulness of the Spirit poured out upon Christ *in the union of the human nature with the divine.* Union and unction went together. There was anointing of the Spirit, together with the union of the Spirit.

Ans. 2. There was a more full manifestation of the Spirit *in his baptism.* When the Holy Ghost fell on him in the shape of a dove, then he received the Spirit. He was to enter into the ministry of the gospel. "The Spirit of the Lord God was upon him," because he had anointed him to preach good tidings unto the meek, etc., Isa. lxi. 1.

Ans. 3. But the fullest degree of declaration and manifestation of the Spirit upon Christ was *after his resurrection*; after he had satisfied fully for our salvation. Then the stop of his glory was taken away. For to work our salvation, there was a keeping back of the glory of Christ from his human nature, that he might be abased to suffer for us. When he had fully suffered for us, that stay of his glory, his abasement, was taken away, and then nothing appeared but all glory and Spirit in Christ. All things were put under his feet, and he was set upon his throne as a glorious king. His priestly office appeared in his death, his prophetical office before his death. But then he appeared to be King and Lord of all in the resurrection. Thus we see how Christ is that Spirit; that is, he is full of the Spirit in regard of himself.

"Like Son, Like Us"

The implication of this Spirit Christology for us is that whatever the Father is doing in the life of the Son through his Spirit is being given to us in Christ through the Spirit.

> From Richard Sibbes, "Description of Christ, Matt. XII, 18," in
> *Works of Richard Sibbes*, vol. 1, ed. Alexander B. Grosart (Edinburgh:
> Banner of Truth Trust, 1973), 17–19 (hereafter Grosart, 1973).

I answer, Christ is both God and man. Christ, as God, gives the Spirit to his human nature; so he communicates his Spirit. The Spirit is his Spirit as well as the Father's. The Spirit proceeds from them both. Christ, as man, receives the Spirit. God the Father and the Son put the Spirit upon the manhood of Christ; so Christ both gives and receives the Spirit in diverse respects. As God, he gives and sends the Spirit. The spiration and breathing of the Spirit is from him as well as from the Father, but as man he received the Spirit.

And this is the reason of it: next under the Father, Son, and Holy Ghost, Christ the Mediator, was to be the spring and original of all comfort and good. Therefore, Christ's nature must not only be sanctified and ordained by the Spirit; but he must receive the Spirit to enrich it, for whatsoever is wrought in the creature is by the Spirit. Whatsoever Christ did as man, he did by the Spirit. Christ's human nature, therefore, must be sanctified, and have the Spirit put upon it. God the Father, the first person in Trinity, and God the Son, the second, they work not immediately, but by the Holy Ghost, the third person. Therefore, whatsoever is wrought upon the creature, it comes from the Holy Ghost immediately. So Christ received the Holy Ghost as sent from the Father and the Son. Now as the Holy Spirit is from the Father and the Son, so he works from the Father and the Son. He sanctifieth and purifieth, and doth all from the Father and the Son, and knits us to the Father and the Son; to the Son first, and then to the Father. Therefore it is said, "The grace of our Lord Jesus Christ, the love of God the Father, and the communion of the Holy Ghost," 2 Cor. xiii. 14; because all the communion we have with God is by the Holy Ghost. And the communion that Christ as man had with God was by the Holy Ghost; and all the communion that God hath with us, and we with God, is by the Holy Ghost: for the Spirit is the bond of union between Christ and us, and between God and us. God communicates himself to us by his Spirit, and we communicate with God by his Spirit. God doth all in us by his Spirit, and we do all back again to God by the Spirit. Because Christ, as a head, as the second Adam, was to be the root of all that are saved, as the first Adam was the root of all that are damned, he was therefore to receive the Spirit, and to have it put upon him in a more excellent and rich manner: for we must know that all things are first in Christ, and then in us. . . . We have not the Holy Ghost immediately from God, but we have him as sanctifying Christ first, and then us; and whatsoever the Holy Ghost doth in us, he doth the same in Christ first, and he doth in us because in Christ. . . . The Holy Ghost fetcheth all from Christ in his working and comfort, and he makes Christ the pattern of all; for whatsoever is in Christ, the Holy Ghost, which is the Spirit of Christ, works in us as it is in Christ. Therefore, in John i. 13, it is said, "of his fulness we receive grace for grace"—that is, grace answerable to his grace. There are three things that we receive answerable to Christ by the Spirit.

We receive grace—that is, the favour of God answerable to the favour God shews his Son.

The Spirit's Work with the Gospel

A passionate preacher, Sibbes issues serious warnings to those who are about to miss the call of the gospel through the Spirit.

From Sibbes, "The Ungodly's Misery" (Grosart, 1973, 1:391–92).

How the Spirit works with the gospel. Now the Spirit works with the gospel by degrees. 1. It bringeth some to be willing to hear the gospel, who yet presently neglect and disregard the same. 2. Others are more obedient for a time, "as the stony ground," Mat. xiii. 5, but because they opened not their hearts to the working of the Spirit only, but will be ruled partly by carnal wisdom, and partly by the Spirit, it leaves them at last altogether. 3. But some there are who give up themselves wholly to the government of Christ, to be ruled in all things by his blessed Spirit, highly esteeming the treasures of heaven, and comforts of a better life, above all the fading outward felicities which this world can afford; who would not gain any earthly thing, hurt their consciences, or once defile themselves with unfruitful works of darkness; fearing lest they should in anything dishonour Christ, or grieve his good Spirit; and to such only hath the gospel come in power.

John Owen

Widely considered the most significant Puritan alongside Jonathan Edwards, John Owen wore many hats, that of the pastor, chaplain to Oliver Cromwell, vice-chancellor of Oxford University, and finally the leader for the Independents through the two decades of persecution until the end of his life in 1683.

"Of Communion with God the Father, Son and Holy Ghost"
This is the title of one of his finest devotional works, written in a homiletical style, in which he considers the union between the human person and the triune God. While the whole Trinity is present in the communion, and grace is a gift from Father, Son, and Spirit, Owen discerns the following kind of differentiation.

> From John Owen, *Of Communion with God the Father, Son and Holy Ghost* (repr. Edinburgh: Banner of Truth Trust, 1965), 17, http://www.ccel.org.

It remaineth only to intimate, in a word, *wherein this distinction lies,* and what is the ground thereof. Now, this is, that the Father doth it by the way of *original authority*; the Son by the way of communicating from a *purchased treasury*; the Holy Spirit by the way of *immediate efficacy*.

1st. The Father communicates all grace by the way of *original authority*: He quickeneth whom he will, John v. 21. . . .

2dly. The Son, by the way of making out a *purchased treasury*. . . .

3dly. The Spirit doth it by the way of *immediate efficacy*, Rom. viii. 11, "But if the Spirit of him that raised up Jesus from the dead dwell in you, he that raised up Christ from the dead shall also quicken your mortal bodies by his Spirit that dwelleth in you." Here are all three comprised, with their distinct concurrence unto our quickening. Here is the Father's authoritative quickening,—"He raised Christ from the dead, and he shall quicken you"; and the Son's mediatory quickening,—for it is done in "the death of Christ"; and the Spirit's immediate efficacy,—"He shall do it by the Spirit that dwelleth in you." He that desires to see this whole matter farther explained, may consult what I have elsewhere written on this subject. And thus is the distinct communion whereof we treat both proved and demonstrated.

The specific role of the Holy Spirit in this communion is explained in the following.

From Owen, *Of Communion*, 222, 228, 229.

The foundation of all our communion with the Holy Ghost consisting in his *mission*, or sending to be our comforter, by Jesus Christ. . . . This is the sum:—the presence of the Holy Ghost with believers as a comforter, sent by Christ for those ends and purposes for which he is promised, is better and more profitable for believers than any *corporeal* presence of Christ can be, now he hath fulfilled the one sacrifice for sin which he was to offer. . . .

The most frequent adjunct of the communication of the Spirit is this, that he is given and received as of gift: "He will give his Holy Spirit to them that ask him" [Luke 11:13]. That which is of gift is free. The Spirit of grace is given of grace: and not only the Spirit of sanctification, or the Spirit to sanctify and convert us, is a gift of free grace, but in the sense whereof we speak, in respect of consolation, he is of gift also. . . .

Hence is the sin against the Holy Ghost . . . unpardonable, and hath that adjunct of rebellion put upon it that no other sin hath,— namely, because he comes not, he acts not, in his own name only, though in his own also, but in the name and authority of the Father and Son, from and by whom he is sent; and therefore, to sin against him is to sin against all the authority of God, all the love of the Trinity, and the utmost condescension of each person to the work of our salvation. It is, I say, from the authoritative mission of the Spirit that the sin against him is peculiarly unpardonable;—it is a sin against the recapitulation of the love of the Father, Son, and Spirit. And from this consideration, were that our present business, might the true nature of the sin against the Holy Ghost be investigated. . . . Hence is that great weight, in particular, laid upon our *not grieving the Spirit*, Eph. iv. 30,—because he comes to us in the name, with the love, and upon the condescension, of the whole blessed Trinity.

Spiritual Gifts

In his main work on pneumatology, titled *A Discourse Concerning the Holy Spirit* (or briefly just *Pneumatologia*), Owen wanted to steer a middle course between rationalistic approaches that tended to downplay spiritual experience (Socinians being one such example) and enthusiastic movements that placed too much emphasis on the Spirit in his opinion (such as the Quakers). The end result is one of the most comprehensive treatises into the Spirit ever written. Interestingly enough, Owen begins his study under the heading "General Principles Concerning the Holy Spirit and His Work" (chap. 1) by speaking of spiritual gifts and their proper use based on 1 Corinthians 12. With his usual orderliness, he presents an outline of the nature and use of charisms in the church.

From John Owen, *A Discourse Concerning the Holy Spirit* (Edinburgh: Banner of Truth Trust, 1965), bk. 1, chap. 1, 20–21, http://www.ccel.org.

Treating, therefore, περί τῶν πνεματικῶν, of these spiritual things or gifts in the church, he first declares their *author*, from whom they come, and by whom they are wrought and bestowed. Him he calls the "Spirit," verse 4; the "Lord," verse 5; "God," verse 6; and to denote the *oneness* of their author, notwithstanding the diversity of the things themselves, he calls him the *same Spirit*, the *same Lord*, the *same God*. The words may be understood two ways: First, That the whole Trinity, and each person distinctly, should be intended in them;—for consider the immediate *operator* of these gifts, and it is the "Spirit" or the Holy Ghost, verse 4; consider them as to their *procurement* and immediate authoritative collation, and so they are from Christ, the Son, the "Lord," verse 5; but as to their *first original* and fountain, they are from "God," even the Father, verse 6: and all these are one and the same. But rather the Spirit alone is intended, and hath this threefold denomination given unto him; for as he is particularly denoted by the name of the "Spirit," which he useth that we may know whom it is that eminently he intendeth, so he calls him both "Lord" and "God," as to manifest his *sovereign authority* in all his works and administrations, so to ingenerate a due reverence in their hearts towards him with whom they had to do in this matter. And no more is intended in these three verses but what is summed up, verse 11, "But all these worketh that one and the self-same Spirit, dividing to every man severally as he will."

Secondly, With respect unto their *general nature*, the apostle distributes them into "gift," χαρίσματα, verse 4; "administrations," διακόνιαι, verse 5; "operations," ἐνεργήματα, verse 6;—which division, with the reasons of it, will in our progress be farther cleared.

Thirdly, He declares the *general end* of the Spirit of God in the communication of them, and the use of them in the church: Verse 7, "But the manifestation of the Spirit is given to every man to profit withal." Φανέρωσις τοῦ Πνεύματος . . . "the revelation of the Spirit"; that is, the gifts whereby and in whose exercise he manifests and reveals his own presence, power, and effectual operation. And the Spirit of God hath no other aim in granting these his enlightening gifts, wherein he manifests his care of the church, and declares the things of the gospel unto any man, but that they should be used to the profit, advantage, and edification of others. . . .

Fourthly, The apostle *distributes* the spiritual gifts then bestowed on the church, or some members of it, into *nine particular heads* or instances: as,—1. Wisdom; 2. Knowledge, 1 Cor. xii. 8, or the word of wisdom and the word of knowledge; 3. Faith; 4. Healing, verse 9; 5. Working of miracles; 6. Prophecy; 7. Discerning of spirits; 8. Kinds of tongues; 9. Interpretation of tongues, verse 10. And all these were extraordinary gifts, in the manner of the communication and exercise, which related unto the then present state of the church.

The Spirit's Work in Creation and Providence
Following the ancient rule of *opera Trinitatis ad extra sunt indivisa*, Owen carefully considers the distinctions and unity of the work of the Trinity in the world and the Spirit's role therein.

From Owen, *Discourse*, bk. 1, chap. 4, 93–99.

That all *divine operations* are usually ascribed unto *God absolutely*. So it is said God made all things; and so of all other works, whether in nature or in grace. . . . Whereas the *order of operation* among the distinct persons depends on the *order of their subsistence* in the blessed Trinity, in every great work of God, the *concluding, completing, perfecting acts* are ascribed unto the Holy Ghost. This we shall find in all the instances of them that will fall under our consideration. Hence, the immediate actings of the Spirit are the most hidden, curious, and mysterious, as those which contain the perfecting part of the works of God. . . . The work of the *old creation* had two parts:—1. That which concerned the *inanimate part* of it in general, with the influence it had into the production of animated or living but brute creatures. 2. The *rational* or *intelligent part* of it, with the law of its obedience unto God, [and] the especial uses and ends for which it was made. In both these sorts we shall inquire after and consider the especial works of the Holy Spirit. . . . Now, the forming and perfecting of *this host* of heaven and earth is that which is assigned peculiarly to the Spirit of God; and hereby the work of creation was completed and finished. . . . For the heavens: Job xxvi. 13, "By his Spirit he hath garnished the heavens." . . . And thus was it also in the earth. God first out of nothing created the *earth*. . . . The whole material mass of earth and water . . . was first created . . . the "Spirit of God moved upon the face of the waters" [Gen. 1:2]. . . . This, therefore, was the work of the Holy Spirit of God in reference unto the *earth* and the *host* thereof. . . . And as at the first creation, so in the course of providence, this work of cherishing and nourishing the creatures is assigned in an especial manner unto the Spirit: Ps. civ. 30, "Thou sendest forth thy Spirit, they are created; and thou renewest the face of the earth."

The Spirit's Work in New Creation

From Owen, *Discourse*, bk. 2, chap. 5, 189–90, 192–93, 195, 201.

First, Unto the work of the Holy Spirit *towards the church* some things are *supposed*, from whence it proceeds, which it is built upon and resolved into. It is not an original but a perfecting work. Some things it supposeth, and bringeth all things to perfection; and these are,—1. The *love*, grace, counsel, and eternal purpose of the Father; 2. The whole work of the *mediation* of Jesus Christ, (which things I have handled elsewhere;)—for it is the peculiar work of the Holy Spirit to make those things of the Father and Son effectual unto the souls of the elect, to the praise of the glory of the grace of God. . . . Secondly, From the *nature* and *order* of this work of God it is, that after the *Son* was actually exhibited in the flesh, according to the promise, and had fulfilled what he had taken upon him to do in his own person, the great promise of carrying on and finishing the whole work of the grace of God in our salvation concerns the *sending of the Holy Spirit* to do and perform what he also had undertaken. . . . Here lay the foundation of the Christian church: The Lord Christ had called his apostles to the great work of building his church, and the propagation of his gospel in the world. . . . And this he would not do, nor did, any otherwise but by sending the Holy Spirit unto them; on whose presence and assistance alone depended the whole success of their ministry in the world. It was "through the Holy Ghost that he gave commandments unto them," Acts i. 2. . . . Thirdly, It is the Holy Spirit who supplies the *bodily absence* of Christ, and by him doth he accomplish all his promises to the church. Hence, some of the ancients call him "Vicarium Christi," "The vicar of Christ," or him who represents his person, and dischargeth his promised work. . . . Fourthly, As he represents the *person* and supplies the room and place of Jesus Chest, so he worketh and effecteth whatever the Lord Christ hath *taken upon himself* to work and effect towards his disciples. . . . Fifthly, Whereas the Holy Spirit is the *Spirit of grace*, and the immediate efficient cause of all grace and gracious effects in men, wherever there is mention made of *them* or any fruits of them, it is to be looked on as a *part of his work*, though he be not expressly named, or it be not particularly attributed unto him. . . . But for grace, I think all men will grant that, as to our participation of it, it is of the Holy Spirit, and of him alone.

Having laid down the great outline of the Spirit's work in new creation, Owen considers in more detail the specific soteriological works of the Spirit in regeneration. Here Owen also reflects his Congregationalist, non-sacramental theological orientation.

From Owen, *Discourse*, bk. 3, chap. 1, 207–9; 216–17, 219–22, 224.

First, *Regeneration* in Scripture is everywhere assigned to be the *proper and peculiar work* of the Holy Spirit. . . . And because there is in it [regeneration] a communication of a new spiritual life, it is called a "vivification" or "quickening," with respect unto the state wherein all men are before this work is wrought in them and on them. . . . Regeneration doth not consist in a participation of the ordinance of *baptism* and a profession of the doctrine of *repentance*. This is all that some will allow unto it, to the utter rejection and over-throw of the grace of our Lord Jesus Christ: . . . The apostle Paul doth plainly distinguish between the outward ordinances, with what belongs unto a due participation of them, and the work of regenera-tion itself. . . . Regeneration doth not consist in a *moral reformation* of life and conversation. . . . Now . . . we grant that this spiritual reno-vation of nature will infallibly produce a moral reformation of life; so if they will grant that this moral reformation of life doth proceed from a spiritual renovation of our nature, this difference will be at an end. And this is that which the ancients intend by first receiving the Holy Ghost, and then all graces with him . . . 2 Cor. v. 17, "If any man be in Christ he is a new creature." This new creature is that which is intended, that which was before described, which being born of the Spirit is spirit. This is produced in the souls of men by a creating act of the power of God, or it is not a *creature*. . . . This *new creature*, there-fore, doth not consist in a *new course of actions*, but in renewed fac-ulties, with *new dispositions, power,* or *ability* to them and for them. Hence it is called the "divine nature": 2 Pet. i. 4, "He hath given unto us exceeding great and precious promises, that by these ye might be partakers of the divine nature." . . . There is a work of God in us preceding all our good works towards him; for before we can work any of them, in order of nature, we must be the workmanship of God, created unto them, or enabled spiritually for the performance of them. Again: This *new man*, whereby we are born again, is said to be *created in righteousness and true holiness*. . . . Thirdly, the work of the Holy Spirit in regeneration doth not consist, in *enthusiastical raptures, ecstasies, voices,* or any thing of the like kind.

Thomas Goodwin

With John Owen, Thomas Goodwin aligned himself with the Congregationalist wing of Puritanism and thus moved in 1634 from Cambridge, where he served as vicar, to London. Five years later he had to move to Holland because of persecution. A prolific author, his *The Work of the Holy Ghost in Our Salvation* is a treasure-house of pneumatology and soteriology.

The Equal Status of the Spirit in the Trinity
Goodwin argues from the works of the Holy Spirit for full equal status of the Spirit with Son and Father.

> From Thomas Goodwin, *The Work of the Holy Ghost in
> Our Salvation*, vol. 6 of *The Works of Thomas Goodwin* (Edinburgh:
> James Nichol, 1863 [no info. about trans. or ed.]), 3–4.

There is a general omission in the saints of God, in their not giving the Holy Ghost that glory that is due to his person, and for his great work of salvation in us, insomuch that we have in our hearts almost lost this third person. We give daily in our thoughts, prayers, affections, and speeches, an honour to the Father and the Son; but who almost directs the aims of this praise (more than in that general way of doxology we use to close our prayers with, "All glory be," etc.) unto God the Holy Ghost? He is a person in the Godhead equal with the Father and the Son; and the work he doth for us in its kind is as great as those of the Father or the Son. . . . The Holy Ghost is indeed the last in order of the persons, as proceeding from the other two, yet in the participation of the Godhead he is equal with them both; and in his work, though it be last done for us, he is not behind them, nor in the glory of it inferior to what they have in theirs. And indeed he would not be God, equal with the Father and the Son, if the work alloted to him, to shew he is God, were not equal unto each of theirs.

Interestingly, Goodwin argues for the "visibility" of the coming of the Holy Spirit, in some sense parallel to the coming of the Word.

> From Goodwin, *Work of the Holy Ghost*, 8–9.

That a signal coming should be appointed to him, to the performance of his work, as well as unto Christ to perform his. This coming of his you have inculcated again and again in these chapters, in these words, "When he is come," and the like. Which imported that, although he was given to work regeneration in men afore, even under the Old Testament (as Neh. ix. 20, "He gave them his good Spirit," and many other places, [show]), that yet to let all the world of believers take notice his coming, and his work, he must have a coming in state, in a solemn and visible manner, accompanied with visible effects, as well as Christ had, and whereof all the Jews should be, and were witnesses (thus Acts, chaps. ii. iv.), and it was also apparent throughout the primitive times, in outward signs and miracles, extraordinary gifts and conversions. . . . And, lastly, on purpose to honour his visible coming, he had answerably an extraordinary work left to him, upon that his visible coming: the conversion of the whole Gentile world; and the raising and building of the churches of the New Testament was reserved of his glory. To believe in the Holy Ghost, and the holy catholic church, you know how near they stand together in the Creed. His invisible coming at Pentecost was the visible consecration and dedication of that great temple, the mystical body of Christ, to be reared under the gospel.

The Spirit's Work in Our Salvation

From Goodwin, *Work of the Holy Ghost*, 17–19.

But let us consider particularly his works . . . in regeneration, which is his prime work in us. He is the author of all the principles or habits of grace, of that whole new creature, of that workmanship created to good works, the spiritual man, which is called *spirit*; that divine nature, which is the mass and lump of all things pertaining to life and godliness; that which is born of the Spirit, John iii. 6. . . . Let us go over the particular actings of the soul, which are as a drawing out of those created principles, whether at or in our first conversion or afterwards; and we shall find that each and every particular thereof are attributed to this Spirit.

. . . Hast thou seen thy sinful condition, and been humbled, as to hell, for it? It is the Spirit's proper work, for which he was sent. . . . This is the first work . . . that the Holy Spirit beginneth with, in conversion, viz., a conviction of a state of sin and unbelief. . . . It is the Spirit who also "witnesseth to us that we are the sons of God"; and by the opposition it will follow that if the Holy Ghost be the Spirit of adoption spoken of, that he also was that Spirit of bondage. . . . It is this Spirit which works repentance upon this discovery of sin, and turns our hearts from sin to God effectually. . . . The work of faith is of his operation; and therefore he is styled.

From Thomas Goodwin, *An Exposition of the First
Chapter of the Epistle to the Ephesians*, vol. 1 in *The Works of
Thomas Goodwin* (Edinburgh: James Nichol, 1863), 237.

[Now I] shall keep to the text. It is called a seal; reason every seal
hath an impress upon it. *What is the impress of the immediate seal of
the Spirit that it stampeth upon a man's heart?*

To help you to understand this, I must have recourse to that 2
Tim. ii. 19, "The foundation of God standeth sure, having this seal,
The Lord knoweth who are his"; that is, God knoweth whom he hath
loved from everlasting. Here is God's seal. Well, what is the seal of the
Spirit? It is the impress of this seal from everlasting; he cometh and
stampeth upon heart, The Lord knoweth thee to be his. It beareth the
image of lasting love, (it is news with a witness,) of God's everlasting
love to a man, to him in particular; that is the motto, the impress
about this seal. . . . The particular seal of the Spirit is, God knoweth
thee to be his.

The Builder of the Church

While it is customary of speak of the church as the body of Christ, it is
quite rare to hear talk about the Holy Spirit as the "builder" of the universal church.

From Goodwin, *Work of the Holy Ghost*, 13–14.

Let us now consider the operations of the Holy Ghost in and upon
the church . . . the body of Christ.

1. He was the first founder of the church of the New Testament.
The apostle, writing to the Ephesians . . . sets before them, chap.
ii., an infinitely far greater and more glorious temple, whereof they
themselves, he tells them, were a part, even the church universal of
the New Testament, consisting of Jew and Gentile. . . . And now, let
us think what a mighty and vast work this of forming and building
the universal church is, whereof this Holy Spirit is the former and
effecter. There was a perfect pattern and platform of the whole and
every member thereof in God's breast, an *idea* also in . . . which this
Spirit will bring in the end the whole unto, and frame each living
stone in the building to bear a due, suitable, and comely proportion in the whole, and each to other. . . . And this Spirit, who is the
dedolator, the architectonical master-workman, hath in his eye every
degree of grace he works in every of these members' hearts who is a
stone in this building, according to the pattern which the Father and
Christ have in their *idea* and model, of every particular, as also of the
whole, and exactly frames each and the whole unto their mind, and
misseth not the least of the set proportion in the pattern, which, in

so long, so various, and multifarious a work to do (as this therefore must be supposed), what infinite wisdom and power doth it require, and argues him to be God, that is in God, as the spirit of a man within him, and "searcheth the deep things of God."

John Bunyan

John Bunyan is undoubtedly the most popular religious writer in the English language, the highly acclaimed author of *Pilgrim's Progress*. Life for this seventeenth-century man of low socioeconomic status was challenging and at times disturbing, taking him from war to persecution to various disputes, all the while plagued with severe mental problems, among other things.

Sin against the Holy Spirit
In his now-classic spiritual autobiography, *Grace Abounding to the Chief of Sinners*, this Puritan preacher gives us a vivid account of his spiritual struggle as he finally found light at the end of the long tunnel darkened by constant fear of sinning against the Holy Spirit.

From John Bunyan, *Grace Abounding to the Chief of Sinners*, nos. 103, 148, 174, 180, 196, 204–8, 229–30, http://www.ccel.org.

103. In these days, when I have heard others talk of what was the sin against the Holy Ghost, then would the tempter so provoke me to desire to sin that sin, that I was as if I could not, must not, neither should be quiet until I had committed that. . . .

148. I feared therefore that this wicked sin of mine might be that sin unpardonable. . . .

174. Once as I was walking to and fro in a good man's shop, bemoaning of myself in my sad and doleful state, afflicting myself with self-abhorrence for this wicked and ungodly thought; lamenting, also, this hard hap of mine, for that I should commit so great a sin; greatly fearing I would not be pardoned; praying, also, in my heart, that if this sin of mine did differ from that against the Holy Ghost, the Lord would show it me. . . . This lasted, in the savour of it, for about three or four days, and then I began to mistrust and to despair again. . . .

180. About this time I took an opportunity to break my mind to an ancient Christian, and told him all my case; I told him, also, that I was afraid that I had sinned the sin against the Holy Ghost; and he told me he thought so too. Here, therefore, I had but cold comfort; but, talking a little more with him, I found him, though a good man,

a stranger to much combat with the devil. Wherefore, I went to God again, as well as I could, for mercy still. . . .

196. Now began my heart again to ache and fear I might meet with disappointment at the last. . . .

204. But one morning, when I was again at prayer, and trembling under the fear of this, that no word of God could help me, that piece of a sentence darted in upon me, "My grace is sufficient" (2 Cor. 12:9). At this methought I felt some stay, as if there might be hopes. . . .

205. By these words I was sustained, yet not without exceeding conflicts, for the space of seven or eight weeks; for my peace would be in and out, sometimes twenty times a day; comfort now, and trouble presently; peace now, and before I could go a furlong as full of fear and guilt as ever heart could hold. . . .

206. Therefore I still did pray to God, that He would come in with this scripture more fully on my heart; to wit, that He would help me to apply the whole sentence, for as yet I could not. . . . Wherefore, one day, as I was in a meeting of God's people, full of sadness and terror, for my fears again were strong upon me . . . these words did, with great power, suddenly break in upon me, "My grace is sufficient for thee, my grace is sufficient for thee, my grace is sufficient for thee," three times together; and, oh! methought that every word was a mighty word unto me; as my, and grace, and sufficient, and for thee; they were then, and sometimes are still, far bigger than others be.

207. At which time my understanding was so enlightened, that I was as though I had seen the Lord Jesus look down from heaven through the tiles upon me, and direct these words unto me. This sent me mourning home, it broke my heart, and filled me full of joy, and laid me low as the dust; only it stayed not long with me, I mean in this glory and refreshing comfort, yet it continued with me for several weeks, and did encourage me to hope. But so soon as that powerful operation of it was taken off my heart, that other about Esau returned upon me as before; so my soul did hang as in a pair of scales again, sometimes up and sometimes down, now in peace, and anon again in terror. . . .

208. Thus I went on for many weeks, sometimes comforted, and sometimes tormented; and, especially at some times, my torment would be very sore. . . .

229. But one day, as I was passing in the field, and that too with some dashes on my conscience, fearing lest yet all was not right, suddenly this sentence fell upon my soul, "Thy righteousness is in heaven"; and methought withal, I saw, with the eyes of my soul, Jesus Christ at God's right hand; there, I say, is my righteousness; . . . I also saw, moreover, that it was not my good frame of heart that made my righteousness better, nor yet my bad frame that made my righteousness

worse; for my righteousness was Jesus Christ Himself, the same yesterday, and to-day, and for ever (Heb. 13.8). . . .

230. Now did my chains fall off my legs indeed, I was loosed from
my affliction and irons, my temptations had fled away. . . . Here,
therefore, I lived for some time, very sweetly at peace with God
through Christ; Oh, methought, Christ! Christ! there was nothing
but Christ that was before my eye.

Charles Haddon Spurgeon

Charles Haddon Spurgeon was the best-known preacher in England in
the nineteenth century. At the age of only twenty, he became pastor of the
famous New Park Street Church in London, where he preached for five
decades to audiences numbering over ten thousand. His sermon collec-
tions, such as the hailed *The Treasury of David*, are voluminous.

"The Holy Ghost—The Great Teacher"
In a sermon titled "The Holy Ghost—The Great Teacher," Spurgeon, having lamented the state of spiritual knowledge in his times, argued for the
necessity of the Holy Spirit as the Christian's Guide and Teacher, based on
Jesus' promise of sending the Comforter.

From Charles Haddon Spurgeon, "The Holy Ghost—
The Great Teacher," Sermon 50, http://www.spurgeon.org/sermons/
2902.htm, n.p., accessed July 13, 2007.

This generation hath gradually, and almost imperceptibly, become
to a great extent a godless generation. . . . Even among professing
Christians, while there is a great amount of religion, there is too little
godliness: there is much external formalism, but too little inward
acknowledgment of God, too little living on God, living with God,
and relying upon God. . . . In many places dedicated to Jehovah the
name of Jesus is too often kept in the background; the Holy Spirit
is almost entirely neglected; and very little is said concerning his
sacred influence. . . . May God send us a Christ-exalting, Spirit-
loving ministry—men who shall proclaim God the Holy Ghost in all
his offices and shall extol God the Saviour as the author and finisher
of our faith. . . . Now . . . we require a guide to conduct us into all
truth. The difficulty is that truth is not so easy to discover. There is
no man born in this world by nature who has the truth in his heart.
. . . Truth itself is no easy thing to discover. . . . We also need a guide,
because *we are so prone to go astray.* . . .

This person is "he, the Spirit," the "Spirit of truth;" not an influence or an emanation, but actually a person. "When the Spirit of truth is come, he shall guide you into all truth." Now, we wish you to look at this guide to consider how adapted he is to us. In the first place, he is *infallible*; he knows everything and cannot lead us astray. . . . Again, we rejoice in this Spirit because he is *ever-present*. . . . There is no college for holy education like that of the blessed Spirit, for he is an ever-present tutor, to whom we have only to bend the knee, and he is at our side, the great expositor of truth. . . . But there is one thing about the suitability of this guide which is remarkable. I do not know whether it has struck you—the Holy Spirit can "guide us *into* a truth." Now, man can guide us *to* a truth, but it is only the Holy Spirit who can "guide us *into* a truth."

"Holiness Demanded"
Echoing the Puritan call for holiness of life, Spurgeon's sermon from 1862 issues a powerful invitation.

From Charles H. Spurgeon, "Holiness Demanded," Sermon 2902, http://www.spurgeon.org/sermons/2902.htm, n.p., accessed July 13, 2007.

There has been a desperate attempt made by certain Antinomians to get rid of the injunction which the Holy Spirit here means to enforce. They have said that this is the imputed holiness of Christ. Do they not know, when they so speak, that, by an open perversion, they utter that which is false? . . . The righteousness of Christ is not to be followed; it is bestowed upon the soul in the instant when it lays hold of Christ Jesus. This is another kind of holiness. It is, in fact, as every one can see who chooses to read the connection, practical, vital holiness which is the purport of this admonition. It is conformity to the will of God, and obedience to the Lord's command. It is, in fine, the Spirit's work in the soul, by which a man is made like God, and becomes a partaker of the divine nature, being delivered from the corruption which is in the world through lust. . . . This holiness is a thing of growth. It may be in the soul as the grain of mustard-seed, and yet not developed; it may be in the heart as a wish and a desire, rather than anything that has been fully realized,—a groaning, a panting, a longing, a striving. As the Spirit of God waters it, it will grow till the mustard-seed shall become a tree. Holiness, in a regenerate heart, is but an infant; it is not matured,—perfect it is in all its parts, but not perfect in its development. Hence, when we find many imperfections and many failings in ourselves, we are not to conclude that, therefore, we have no interest in the grace of God.

Pietism

Pietism is Puritanism's counterpart among Lutheran and Reformed churches in the aftermath of the Reformation. While its heyday was the seventeenth and eighteenth centuries, its influence, similarly to that of Puritanism, continues even until contemporary times. Unlike Protestant orthodoxy with its detailed schemes of *ordo salutis*, personal faith, often termed new birth, was an experience that pietists sought.

Johannes Arndt

Often named the father of pietism, Arndt was a staunch defender of Lutheran orthodoxy at the turn of the sixteenth century. In addition, he also called for personal embrace and experience of faith, so much so that Albert Schweitzer named him the "prophet of interior Protestantism."[2]

New Life in the Spirit
In response to his question, "How man is once again renewed to eternal life in Christ," Arndt responds by outlining what happens in new birth.

From Johann Arndt, *True Christianity*, trans. and ed.
Peter Erb (New York: Paulist Press, 1979), 37–38.

The new birth is a work of God the Holy Spirit, by which a man is made a child of grace and blessedness from a child of wrath and damnation, and from a sinner a righteous man through faith, word, and sacrament by which our heart, thoughts, mind, understanding, will, and affections are made holy, renewed, and enlightened as a new creature in and according to Jesus Christ. The new birth contains two chief aspects in itself: justification and sanctification or renewal (Tit. 3:5).

There is a twofold birth of a Christian man: the carnal, sinful, damnable, and accursed birth that comes from Adam, by which the seeds of the serpent, the image of Satan, and the earthly bestial quality of man is continued, and the spiritual, holy, blessed, gracious, new birth that comes out of Christ, by which the seed of God and the heavenly, godly man is perpetuated in a spiritual manner.

2. Peter Erb, introduction to Johann Arndt, *True Christianity,* trans. and ed. Peter Erb (New York: Paulist Press, 1979), 1.

As a result, each Christian man has two birth lines in himself, the fleshly line of Adam and the spiritual line of Christ, which comes out of grace. Just as Adam's old birth is in us, so also must Christ's new birth be in us. This is the new and the old man, the old and the new birth, the old and the new Adam, the earthly and the heavenly image, the old and the new Jerusalem, flesh and spirit, Adam and Christ in us, the internal and the external man.

Note how we are newborn out of Christ. Just as the old birth in a fleshly manner was continued from Adam, so the new birth in a spiritual manner is continued from Christ and this occurs through the Word of God. The Word of God is the seed of the new birth (1 Pet. 1:23 . . .; Jas. 1:18 . . .). This Word awakens faith and faith clings to this Word and grasps in the Word Jesus Christ together with the Holy Spirit. Through the Holy Spirit's power and activity, man is newborn. The new birth occurs first through the Holy Spirit (Jn 3:4). This is what the Lord calls "to be born of the Spirit."

Mystical Union
At times a mystic, Arndt speaks freely of the union of the believer with Christ in the Spirit.

From Arndt, *True Christianity*, 252–56.

Chapter Five. *Concerning the indwelling of the Holy Spirit*
How great a relationship, community, and union of the highest and eternal God with man is established is clearly witnessed by three chief works of grace: first, the creation of man to God's image (Gen. 1:26), second, the incarnation of the Son of God, third, the sending of the Holy Spirit. Through these great works, the Lord God revealed and made clear the purpose for which man was created, redeemed and made holy, namely, that he might enjoy communion with God in which the highest and only blessedness of man consists. Therefore, *the Word became flesh and dwelt with us* (Jn. 1:14).

Therefore, the Holy Spirit was sent down from heaven so that he might establish this communion and union of God with man.

1. We have great need of the Spirit of God so that we might be freed and loosed from the spirit of this world. We have great need of the spirit of wisdom (Is. 11:2) so that we might love the highest good. The spirit of understanding is very necessary for us so that we might be able to wisely carry out the responsibilities of our calling. [Likewise, we need] the spirit of counsel so that we might bear the cross in patience, the spirit of strength and of power so that we might conquer the world and the Devil, the spirit of understanding so that we might shun vices and evils, the spirit of childlike fear so

that we might be pleasing to God, the spirit of grace and of prayer so that we might call upon God in all our needs and be able to praise his grace and goodness in all his works (Zech. 12:10). . . .

5. We are also purified with this oil of joy against the world and the Devil's foolishness and raging. So that we might not suffer, *the heavenly Father poured into our hearts His love through the Holy Spirit* (Rom. 5:5). . . .

7. Finally, because we must have a life-giving spirit against death, God our Father sanctified our bodies as the temples and dwelling places of the Holy Spirit. . . .

Chapter Six. *The union of God with man occurs by healing repentance or conversion to God as true regret and sorrow for sins and by faith.*
. . . Healing repentance . . . brings about spiritual remarriage and union . . . alone fruitfully; that it seeks without ceasing the Lord God alone. . . .

Chapter Seven. *The union of Christ with the believing soul occurs through the spiritual wedding and marriage.*
If the bridegroom comes, the holy soul rejoices and looks closely and eagerly toward his presence. By his joyous, enlivening, and holy arrival he drives out darkness and night and the heart has sweet joy, the waters of meditation flow in upon it, the soul melts for love, the spirit rejoices, the affections and the desires become fervid, love is ignited, the mind rejoices, the mouth gives praise and honor, man takes vows, and all the powers of the soul rejoice in and because of the bridegroom. It rejoices, I say, because it has found what it loves and because he whom it loves has taken it up to himself as his bride. Oh what a love! Oh what a fiery desire! Oh what a loving conversation! Oh how chaste a kiss! If the Holy Spirit comes, if the Consoler overshadows [the soul], if the Highest enlightens [it], if the Word of the Father is there, wisdom speaks and loves and receives it in joy.

Jacob Böhme

Also known by the last name Behmen, Jacob grew up as a Lutheran and was greatly influenced by pietism. A shoemaker by profession, he had a number of mystical experiences, including a significant spiritual vision in 1600 that he claimed revealed the spiritual structure of the world, as well as the relationship between God and man, and good and evil. Ten years later he began publishing those visions with his first work, *Aurora*.

Spiritual Seeing

Closely following the spirituality of some Eastern Christian Fathers and later mystics, Jacob claims a spiritual vision for spiritual people.

From Jacob Böhme, *The Incarnation of Jesus Christ*, trans.
John Rolleston Earle, pt. 2.7.1–3, 7–8, http://www.heiligeteksten.nl/the%20
incarnation%20of%20christ-%20bohme.htm, accessed July 13, 2007.

1. EXTERNAL Reason says: How can a man in this world see into God, as into another world, and say what God is? . . .

2. Answer: So far external Reason reacheth; and further it cannot explore, so that it might rest. And if I were still involved in that art, I should also speak in like manner. . . . But I would have the scoffer and earthly man asked, whether heaven is blind, as well as hell and God himself? Whether in the divine world there is also a seeing? Whether the Spirit of God can see, both in the world of love and light, and also in the fierceness in the world of wrath, in the centre? . . .

3. He that is holy sees with God's eyes what God has in view, and that the Spirit of God sees in the new birth by true human eyes, by the image of God. This Spirit is to the wise man a seeing and also a doing; not to the old Adam, he must be a servant to it, he must practically work out what the new man sees in God. . . . The spirit of Christ sees through and in us what he wills; and what he wills, that we see and know in him, and out of him we know nothing of God. He does divine works and sees what and when he pleases. . . .

7. If then anyone says: I see nothing divine; let him consider that flesh and blood along with the subtlety of the devil is a hindrance and veil to him. . . .

8. Is then the Holy Spirit to be supposed blind when he dwells in man? Or do I write this for my glorification? Not so, but for the reader's guidance, that he may desist from his error, proceed from the path of reviling and blasphemy into a holy divine existence, that he also may see with divine eyes the wonders of God, so that God's will may be done.

A Christian Theosophy?

Drawing from various influences, such as Neoplatonist and alchemical writers as well as the Religious Society of Friends and Theosophy, Böhme's Mariology and theology of the incarnation clearly reflect his revisionist Christian cosmology and spirituality.

From Böhme, *Incarnation of Jesus Christ*, 1.10.4–7.

4. And we are able to recognize, that, as the first Adam put his imagination into earthliness and became earthly, and did this moreover contrary to the purpose of God, the purpose of God had nevertheless to stand. For now God established his purpose in Adam's child, and introduced his imagination into the corrupt image, and made it pregnant with his divine power and essentiality, and turned the soul's will round from earthliness to God; so that Mary became pregnant with such a child as Adam was to become pregnant with. This the individual's own power could not accomplish, but sank down into sleep as into the magia; whereupon out of Adam was made the woman, who should not have been made, but Adam should have made himself pregnant in the matrix of Venus, and brought forth magically. As, however, this could not be, Adam was divided, and his own will of great power was broken and shut up in death. As he would not place his imagination in the Spirit of God, his great power had to come to a standstill in death and suffer the Spirit of God to place His imagination in it, and do with him what He pleased.

5. Therefore the Spirit of God raised up to him life out of this death, and became the spirit of this life, in order that the image and likeness of God (which from eternity had been known in God's wisdom) might at last be born and endure. For it stood before the times of the world and even from eternity in the virgin mirror in the wisdom of God, and that in two forms: namely, according to the first Principle of the Father in fire, and in the second Principle of the Son in light, and yet was only manifest in the light, and in the fire just as if in a magia, that is, in a possibility. As the astral heaven imprints by its power a figure in the mind of man, in his sleep so was represented the image in the centre of the nature of fire, quite invisibly; but in wisdom, in the mirror of the Deity, it has appeared as a figure, like a shadow, yet without material being, but has had being in the essence of the spirit. . . . Therefore, when the first image imaginated into the severe might and in consequence became earthly and dead, the Spirit of God led its will and life into death, and retook from death the first life into himself, in order that the first life might stand in complete obedience before Him, and He alone be the willing and also the doing.

6. Thus, we know that God has entered into the half-dead image, that is, into Mary, and into the very same virgin form which was shut up in death, in which Adam was to become pregnant and bring forth an image according to himself in virgin chastity. In this shut up and half-dead virgin matrix, the Word or heart of God, viz. the centre of the Holy Trinity, has, without infringement of its being, become

an image of man. And seeing the first living virgin matrix in Adam would not be obedient to God, it became thus, when raised again from death, obedient to him, and gave itself up humbly and willingly to God's will. . . .

7. And so are we to understand regarding the incarnation of Christ. When God's Spirit raised up again in Mary the virgin life, which in the earthly essence lay shut up in death and wrath, then this life turned itself only unto God's will and love, and gave itself up to the Spirit of God. Thus it became pregnant with a true virgin image, which was to have been in the case of Adam, but was not realized; for one imagination received the other.

Philip Jacob Spener

Influenced by Luther, Philip Jacob Spener set out to further spiritual renewal by championing Bible study, biblical sermons, lay participation, and the importance of the Christian life over against what he saw as formal, scholastic pursuits. His *Pia Desideria* or "Heartfelt Desire for God-Pleasing Reform" is the classic statement of pietism, often considered the birth mark of the movement. First published in 1675 by Spener, it is both a devotional work and a textbook on church renewal and against deadness and moral laxity in the churches of the time. In keeping with the spirit of the Old Testament prophets, Spener both deplored the spiritual state of the people of God and called them to repentance and reform. In the first citation, he targets ministers who should know better what the essence of Christian life and spirituality is.

From Philip Jacob Spener, *Pia Desideria*, ed. Theodore G. Tappert (Philadelphia: Fortress Press, 1964), 46.

But greater scandal is caused when . . . people . . . get the notion that what they see in their preachers must be real Christianity and that they ought not hold it against them. Most distressing of all, however, is the fact that the lives of many such preachers and the absence in them of the fruits of faith indicate that they are themselves wanting in faith. What they take to be faith and what is the ground of their teaching is by no means that true faith which is awakened through the Word of God, by the illumination, witness, and sealing of the Holy Spirit, but is a human fancy. To be sure, as others have acquired knowledge in their fields of study, so these preachers, with their own human efforts and without the working of the Holy Spirit, have learned something of the letter of the Scriptures, have comprehended and assented to true doctrine, and have even known how to preach it to others, but they are altogether unacquainted with the true, heavenly light and the life of faith.

In keeping with the "inner religion" of pietism, Spener outlines here "proposals for correcting conditions," as he puts it, especially regarding renewed preaching.

From Spener, *Pia Desideria*, 116–17.

Our whole Christian religion consists of the inner man or the new man, whose soul is faith and whose expressions are the fruits of life, and all sermons should be aimed at this. . . . One should therefore emphasize that the divine means of Word and sacrament are concerned with the inner man. Hence it is not enough that we hear the Word with our outward ear, but we must let it penetrate to our heart, so that we may hear the Holy Spirit speak there, that is, with vibrant emotion and comfort feel the sealing of the Spirit and the power of the Word. Nor is it enough to be baptized, but the inner man, where we have put on Christ in Baptism, must also keep Christ on and bear witness to him in our outward life. Nor is it enough to have received the Lord's Supper externally, but the inner man must truly be fed with that blessed food. Nor is it enough to pray outwardly with our mouth, but true prayer, and the best prayer, occurs in the inner man, and it either breaks forth in words or remains in the soul, yet God will find and hit upon it. Nor, again, is it enough to worship God in an external temple, but the inner man worships God best in his own temple, whether or not he is in an external temple at the time. So one could go on.

Count Nicholaus Zinzendorf and Moravianism

While obviously an overstatement, what G. W. Forell says of the most famous Moravian pietist is worth hearing: "The most influential German theologian between Luther and Schleiermacher was Nicholaus Ludwig Count von Zinzendorf . . . who, by the way, never studied theology."[3] In the spirit of pietism, Zinzendorf argues for the necessity of personal faith; as the first citation indicates, he even ties the right to pray the Lord's Prayer to the experience of "new birth."

3. George W. Forell, introduction to Nicholaus Ludwig Count von Zinzendorf, *Nine Public Lectures on Important Subjects in Religion,* trans. and ed. George W. Forell (Iowa City: University of Iowa Press, 1973), vii.

From Nicholaus Ludwig Count von Zinzendorf, *Nine Public
Lectures on Important Subjects in Religion*, trans. and ed.
George W. Forell (Iowa City: University of Iowa Press, 1973), 4–5.

I seldom pray the Lord's Prayer in public gatherings. . . . The reason is this: the listeners are so apt to join in the prayer, and at the same time they all have the idea that the prayer is directed to the first person in the Godhead; and yet the Saviour has declared in the most positive and preemptory manner that no one can invoke His Father but the children of God. Thus, whoever prays the Lord's Prayer and is not a child of God, takes the name of the Lord his God in vain and incurs the judgment of the Second Commandment. . . . To be permitteed to pray it is one of the greatest gifts of grace, a privilege which one first obtains through the deep fundamental solidity of his own salvation, through one's everlasting pardoning, through the eternal absolution of all sins. . . . Where is there more prating about the mystery of the Trinity than in the schools, by men who do not love their Saviour? . . . Who gave them the commission to talk at random among the so-called Christians concerning the Trinity, concerning the Father, concerning the Holy Spirit, etc.? For they have not yet experienced the Saviour and His blood, the guarantee of their inheritance, the point of redemption. . . . Yet we cannot have the joyful confidence, the courage to cry, "Abba! Father!" (Gal. 4:6) until the Holy Spirit has cried it in our hearts. The cantor in the church cannot make us sing it, nor the minister in the pulpit make us pray it; rather, it is the Holy Spirit. The Bible assures us that He must do it; He cries in the heart, "Abba! dear Father!" then it will do. "Because you are children, God has sent the Spirit of His Son into your hearts" (Gal. 4:6).

Zinzendorf explains the role of the Spirit in new birth and drawing people to Jesus.

From Zinzendorf, *Nine Public Lectures*, 29–30.

The new begetting, when the Spirit from God comes into our heart, when Jesus Christ with His five wounds is formed in us, when we are allotted to Him in heaven above—this is a divine moment. We see this in John, who in his mother's womb was filled with the Holy Spirit. . . . The Holy Spirit portrays Jesus to souls; He preaches His wounds. To one this happens distinctly, to another indistinctly. . . . And just for this reason we are not to be very concerned about the bride which the Holy Spirit courts in this world for Jesus Christ; the proxy-marriage in the name of Jesus Christ takes its course, and no devil can obstruct it, let him do what he will. No worldly circumstance, no absolute prohibition of the Gospel in any country, no drought and famine of the divine Word can thwart it. He is sure of His souls; they are souls which live and move and have their being in Him. They live no longer, but rather He lives in them.

Johann Christoph Blumhardt and
Christoph Friedrich Blumhardt

The elder Blumhardt, Johann Christoph (1805–1880), a Reformed pastor and one-time missions executive, was confronted in 1842 with a pastoral challenge, namely, how to deal with one of his parishioners, a young woman by the name Gottlieben Dittus. She obviously suffered from a disorder and believed she had psychic visitations. Johann Christoph concluded it was a demon possession. The son of Johann Christoph, Christoph Friedrich, happened to be born right at the time his father was dealing with Gottlieben's demons. Having left a parish pastorate because of disillusionment with the church and academic theology, he became a well-known evangelist and faith healer. That career, however, came to an end in the aftermath of a successful crusade in Berlin in 1888 as Christoph concluded that it is not healing but cleansing that really matters in the Christian life.

The first citation by Johann Christoph Blumhardt is titled "The Holy Spirit and His Gifts."

From Vernard Eller, ed., *Thy Kingdom Come. A Blumhardt Reader* (Grand Rapids: Wm. B. Eerdmans Publishing Co., 1980), 34–35.

The Holy spirit is the Spirit of Truth. Consequently, he preaches to us in our hearts—especially in reminding us of what Jesus said, renewing this in our minds and making it ever dearer to us. . . . The Spirit, as master teacher, grants us inward revelation; we "see" what otherwise is only heard and thought. We understand profoundly, even when, now and then, words fail. Thus should the Holy Spirit be our teacher.

Our basic prayer always should be for the coming of the Holy Spirit. Of course, this is a tremendous request in itself; and it will cost us pains to put into a few words all that this petition signifies. As a very minimum, I would say, there lies in this prayer a desire to stand inwardly right before God and to come into true community with him. This is something which is mediated and accomplished by God through the Spirit. . . . No one can even call Jesus Lord except through the Holy Spirit; so, to a certain extent, this idea also is expressed in our basic prayer, that God might give us an understanding of spiritual things, might let us understand his ways, his ideas about us, his plans for us.

All we have said thus far represents only the preliminary stages of our prayer, for in the phrase, "Pray for the Holy Spirit," much more is being asked. At the time Jesus commanded this prayer, the disciples had not yet had the experience of Pentecost; and in that coming of the Spirit lay the salvation of all.

The one thing with which the disciples were to concern themselves was prayer for the coming of that Spirit—for themselves, for the world, for all flesh. After the Lord departed from them, that was to be their one task. We know that they did pray. Daily they were united together, praying for the promised Spirit. Together with their praying, they worked until the time was fulfilled. And on the feast of Pentecost the glorious gift and grace and power came; and they were all wonderfully filled. From that moment they truly became new men. The heavens opened, and the Lord brought the disciples into a unity with the things of heaven. Powers from above descended and covered everything upon earth. And through these powers, everything shall henceforth be overcome, and the powers of darkness shall be trampled underfoot.

The elder Blumhardt is especially well known for his inclusive view of salvation that encompassed spiritual renewal, healing of the body, as well as social and political redemption.

From Eller, Thy Kingdom Come, 18–21.

The Redemption of the Body

The Spirit must embody itself. It *must enter into our earthly life*; it must happen that deity be born in flesh so that it can overcome this earthly world. God is active Spirit only when he gets something of our material underfoot; before that, he is mere idea. The Spirit would govern life.

It is a *divine-natural law that body and soul hang together*; and whoever would work on one part must take the other into consideration as well. Whoever would divide body and soul may be said to commit murder.

It seems to be the first concern of the human spirit that the body quickly become well; whereas, in silence the soul should thank God that, in its illness, the body had more rest than in its health—indeed, that it again feels more life and power than it did in healthy days. But many people become almost angry over such a consolation; they are so unaccustomed to being still and considering their lives that they forcibly push themselves back into the turbulence of activity. Yet precisely in this way do they stand in the way of their own health at the very moment God would put them under spiritual restraint, because he does not want them given over to destruction. . . .

As long as our spiritual piety does not present itself as true for the body, as right for the body, as freeing the body for God—as long as this piety is not free of human customs, insofar as these are perverted and out of harmony with divine laws—so long we remain only pious cripples. We must learn to be genuine creations of God through which life can stream out in all directions, as is the intention for all creation.

Therefore, we do not pray, "Do miracles," but rather "Let things go the way of truth." God should do miracles—but only when they are an aspect of the spiritual rectification of mankind. There must be a ground for them, a ground in the kingdom of God renewing and enlightening us from the divine side. It is *from this base* that miracles should take place; and then—yea, then—we shall shout aloud for joy, when, from within, things get set right. But at that point, *outward* miracles can disappear. . . . I do not wish to see a single miracle in anyone that is not the consequence of that person's inner rectification.

Political Redemption

Only revelation brings progress; and that is what makes it so important that finally revelation come into the body politic. That would be a real step forward for the world, because until now it has not happened. God has not yet truly entered into the history of the nations. There are only more and more human histories—as, for example, the Boer War. Only after such an incident can the Spirit of God give more light to individuals . . . so that they can see further. Yet, through revelation, enlightenment also must come into politics.

In several respects these are threatening times; and it is necessary that we keep faith and, in particular, that we not accept the belief that war or anything of the sort would improve our situation. . . . We need no swords or cannon. We should live and let live. So have mercy upon us, O Lord our God, that finally, finally, thou wilt create the kingdom of peace which thou hast promised.

Methodism

John Wesley

A former Anglican minister, John Wesley is the founder of the Methodist tradition. What started from a "Holy Club" at Oxford University, England, and developed on both sides of the Atlantic became the worldwide movement that it is today, with a stated focus on holiness and pursuit of perfection. After returning to his homeland, England, from Savannah, Georgia, Wesley had the famous Aldersgate experience on May 24, 1738, which became a defining moment in his spiritual search and theological development. On that occasion, Wesley received a deep spiritual conviction of belonging to Christ and having been adopted in the sonship of God.

"Holy Ghost, My Comforter"
Not only a theologian, pastor, evangelist, and leader, Wesley is also well known for a great number of hymns, as is his brother Charles. Here is a hymn of the Holy Spirit.

From John Wesley, "Holy Ghost, My Comforter," no. 753, in
A Collection of Hymns for the Use of the People Called Methodists
(1876), http://www.ccel.org (accessed Jan. 10, 2008).

1. HOLY Ghost! my Comforter!
   Now from highest heaven appear,
   Shed thy gracious radiance here.
2. Come to them who suffer dearth,
   With thy gifts of priceless worth,
   Lighten all who dwell on earth!
3. Thou the heart's most precious guest,
   Thou of comforters the best,
   Give to us, the o'er-laden, rest.
4. Come! in thee our toil is sweet,
   Shelter from the noon-day heat,
   From whom sorrow flieth fleet.
5. Blessed Sun of grace! o'er all
   Faithful hearts who on thee call
   Let thy light and solace fall.
6. What without thy aid is wrought,
   Skilful deed or wisest thought,
   God will count but vain and nought.
7. Cleanse us, Lord, from sinful stain,

O'er the parched heart O rain!
Heal the wounded of its pain.
8. Bend the stubborn will to thine,
Melt the cold with fire divine,
Erring hearts to right incline.
9. Grant us, Lord, who cry to thee,
Steadfast in the faith to be,
Give thy gift of charity.
10. May we live in holiness,
And in death find happiness,
And abide with thee in bliss!

The Spirit and Justifying Faith

Much of Wesley's theology comes to us in the forms of sermons, hymns, and pamphlets. Here is an exposition from one of his sermons on justification and its relation to sanctification.

> From John Wesley, "Justification by Faith," sermon no. 5, in
> *Sermons on Several Occasions*, II.1, II.5, http://www.ccel.org.

II. 1. But what is it to be "justified?" What is "justification?" This was the Second thing which I proposed to show. And it is evident, from what has been already observed, that it is not the being made actually just and righteous. This is "sanctification"; which is, indeed, in some degree, the immediate fruit of justification, but, nevertheless, is a distinct gift of God, and of a totally different nature. The one implies what God does for us through his Son; the other, what he works in us by his Spirit. So that, although some rare instances may be found, wherein the term "justified" or "justification" is used in so wide a sense as to include "sanctification" also; yet, in general use, they are sufficiently distinguished from each other, both by St. Paul and the other inspired writers. . . .

5. The plain scriptural notion of justification is pardon, the forgiveness of sins. It is that act of God the Father, hereby, for the sake of the propitiation made by the blood of his Son, he "showeth forth his righteousness (or mercy) by the remission of the sins that are past." This is the easy, natural account of it given by St. Paul, throughout this whole epistle. So he explains it himself, more particularly in this and in the following chapter. . . . To him that is justified or forgiven, God "will not impute sin" to his condemnation. He will not condemn him on that account, either in this world or in that which is to come. His sins, all his past sins, in thought, word, and deed, are covered, are blotted out, shall not be remembered or mentioned against him, any more than if they had not been.

In his sermon on the Holy Spirit, Wesley looks at the role of the Third Person of the Trinity in the life of the believer.

From Wesley, "On the Holy Spirit," sermon no. 141,
in *Sermons on Various Occasions*, III.

III. Here I shall . . . only consider what the Holy Spirit is to every believer, for his personal sanctification and salvation. It is not granted to every one to raise the dead, and heal the sick. What is most necessary is, to be sure, as to ourselves, that we are "passed from death unto life"; to keep our bodies pure and undefiled, and let them reap that health which flows from a magnanimous patience, and the serene joys of devotion. The Holy Spirit has enabled men to speak with tongues, and to prophesy; but the light that most necessarily attends it is a light to discern the fallacies of flesh and blood, to reject the irreligious maxims of the world, and to practice those degrees of trust in God and love to men, whose foundation is not so much in the present appearances of things, as in some that are yet to come. . . .

But I think the true notion of the Spirit is, that it is some portion of, as well as preparation for, a life in God, which we are to enjoy hereafter. The gift of the Holy Spirit looks full to the resurrection; for then is the life of God completed in us.

Then, after man has passed through all the *penalties* of sin, the drudgery and vanity of human life, the painful reflections of an awakened mind, the infirmities and dissolution of the body, and all the sufferings and mortifications a just God shall lay in his way; when, by this means, he is come to know God and himself, he may safely be entrusted with true life, with the freedom and ornaments of a child of God; for he will no more arrogate anything to himself. Then shall the Holy Spirit be fully bestowed, when the flesh shall no longer resist it, but be itself changed into an angelical condition, being clothed upon with the incorruption of the Holy Spirit; when the body which, by being born with the soul, and living through it, could only be called an animal one, shall now become spiritual, whilst by the Spirit it rises into eternity. . . .

Well may a man ask his own heart, whether it is able to admit the Spirit of God. For where that divine Guest enters, the laws of another world must be observed. . . . The fruits of this Spirit must not be mere moral virtues, calculated for the comfort and decency of the present life; but holy dispositions, suitable to the instincts of a superior life already begun. . . .

For now we obtain but some part of his Spirit, to model and fit us for incorruption, that we may, by degrees, be accustomed to receive and carry God within us; and, therefore, the Apostle calls it, "the earnest of the Spirit"; that is, a part of that honour which is promised us by the Lord. If, therefore, the earnest, abiding in us, makes us spiritual even now, and that which is mortal is, as it were, swallowed up of immortality; how shall it be when, rising again, we shall see him face to face? when all our members shall break forth into songs of triumph, and glorify Him who hath raised them from the dead, and granted them everlasting life? For if this earnest or pledge, embracing man into itself, makes him now cry, "Abba, Father"; what shall the whole grace of the Spirit do, when, being given at length to believers, it shall make us like unto God, and perfect us through the will of the Father? . . .

I will conclude all with that excellent Collect of our Church:—"O God, who in all ages hast taught the hearts of thy faithful people, by sending to them the light of thy Holy Spirit; grant us by the same Spirit to have a right judgment in all things, and evermore to rejoice in his holy comfort, through the merits of Jesus Christ our Saviour; who liveth and reigneth with thee, in the unity of the same Spirit, one God, world without end. Amen."

The Witness of the Spirit

In the sermon by that title, Wesley explains a particular work of the Spirit in the life of the justified person, namely the witness of the Spirit.

> From Wesley, "The Witness of the Spirit," sermon no. 10,
> Discourse I in *Sermons on Several Occasions*, I.1, 6, 7, 9.

I. 1. Let us first consider, what is the witness or testimony of our spirit. But here I cannot but desire all those who are for swallowing up the testimony of the Spirit of God, in the rational testimony of our own spirit, to observe, that in this text the Apostle is so far from speaking of the testimony of our own spirit *only*, that it may be questioned whether he speaks of it *at all*,—whether he does not speak *only* of the testimony of God's Spirit. It does not appear but the original text may fairly be understood thus. The Apostle had just said, in the preceding verse, "Ye have received the Spirit of adoption, whereby we cry, Abba, Father" [Rom. 8:15]; and immediately subjoins, *Auto to pneuma* (some copies read *to auto pneuma*) *symmartyrei toi pneumati hemon, hoti esmen tekna Theou*, which may be translated, The same Spirit beareth witness to our spirit that we are the children of God [Rom. 8:16] (the preposition *syn* only denoting that he witnesses this *at the same* time that he enables us to cry Abba, Father.) But I contend not; seeing so many other texts, with the experience of all real Christians, sufficiently evince, that there is in every believer, both the testimony of God's Spirit, and the testimony of his own, that he is a child of God. . . .

I. 6. Now this is properly the testimony of our own spirit; even the testimony of our conscience, that God hath given us to be holy of heart, and holy in outward conversation. It is a consciousness of our having received, in and by the Spirit of adoption, the tempers mentioned in the Word of God as belonging to his adopted children; even a loving heart toward God and toward all mankind; hanging with childlike confidence on God our Father, desiring nothing but him, casting all our care upon him, and embracing every child of man with earnest, tender affection:—A consciousness that we are inwardly conformed, by the Spirit of God, to the image of his Son, and that we walk before him in justice, mercy, and truth, doing the things which are pleasing in his sight.

I. 7. But what is that testimony of God's Spirit, which is superadded to, and conjoined with, this? How does he "bear witness with our spirit that we are the children of God?" It is hard to find words in the language of men to explain "the deep things of God." Indeed, there are none that will adequately express what the children of God experience. But perhaps one might say, (desiring any who are taught of God to correct, to soften or strengthen the expression.) The testimony of the Spirit is an inward impression on the soul, whereby the Spirit of God directly witnesses to my spirit, that I am a child of God; that Jesus Christ hath loved me, and given himself for me; and that all my sins are blotted out, and I, even I, am reconciled to God. . . .

I. 9. Then, and not till then,—when the Spirit of God beareth that witness to our spirit, "God hath loved thee, and given his own Son to be the propitiation for thy sins; the Son of God hath loved thee, and hath washed thee from thy sins in his blood,"—"we love God, because he first loved us"; and, for his sake, we love our brother also. And of this we cannot but be conscious to ourselves: We "know the things that are freely given to us of God." We know that we love God and keep his commandments; and "hereby also we know that we are of God." This is that testimony of our own spirit, which, so long as we continue to love God and keep his commandments, continues joined with the testimony of God's Spirit, "that we are the children of God."

Wesley considers the question of how to distinguish a true witness of the Spirit from one's own pretension.

From Wesley, "The Witness of the Spirit," sermon no. 10, II.1–3.

II. 1. How this joint testimony of God's Spirit and our spirit may be clearly and solidly distinguished from the presumption of a natural mind, and from the delusion of the devil, is the next thing to be considered. . . .

II. 2. And, First, how is this testimony to be distinguished from the presumption of a natural mind? It is certain, one who was never convinced of sin, is always ready to flatter himself, and to think of himself, especially in spiritual things, more highly than he ought to think. And hence, it is in no wise strange, if one who is vainly puffed up by his fleshly mind, when he hears of this privilege of true Christians, among whom he undoubtedly ranks himself, should soon work himself up into a persuasion that he is already possessed thereof. Such instances now abound in the world, and have abounded in all ages. How then may the real testimony of the Spirit with our spirit, be distinguished from this damning presumption?

II. 3. I answer, the Holy Scriptures abound with marks, whereby the one may be distinguished from the other. They describe, in the plainest manner, the circumstances which go before, which accompany, and which follow, the true, genuine testimony of the Spirit of God with the spirit of a believer. Whoever carefully weighs and attends to these will not need to put darkness for light. He will perceive so wide a difference, with respect to all these, between the real and the pretended witness of the Spirit, that there will be no danger, I might say, no possibility, of confounding the one with the other.

Christian Perfection

While Wesley speaks of Christian perfection everywhere in his sermons, Bible expositions, and other places, the short tract *A Plain Account of Christian Perfection* (usually dated 1777 because that is believed to be the time of the last revision) sets forth the doctrine in a wonderfully clear way. Often he describes it as perfect love, the pursuit of which consumed his attention from early on, as the first brief excerpt from the beginning of the tract reveals. The following statement is a classical catechism-type statement about perfection.

From John Wesley, *A Plain Account of Christian Perfection*, in *The Works of John Wesley*, vol. 11, ed. Thomas Jackson (1872), 366–446, http://www.ccel.org (accessed Jan. 9, 2008).

17. On Monday, June 25, 1744, our First Conference began; six Clergymen and all our Preachers being present. The next morning we seriously considered the doctrine of sanctification, or perfection. The questions asked concerning it, and the substance of the answers given, were as follows:

"QUESTION. What is it to be sanctified?"

"ANSWER. To be renewed in the image of God, 'in righteousness and true holiness.'"

"Q. What is implied in being a perfect Christian?"

"A. The loving God with all our heart, and mind, and soul. (Deut. 6:5.)"

"Q. Does this imply, that all inward sin is taken away?"

"A. Undoubtedly; or how can we be Said to be 'saved from all our uncleannesses?' (Ezek. 36:29.)"

As mentioned, one of the standard ways of speaking of perfection is with the notion of perfect love for God.

From Wesley, *A Plain Account*, 19.

"QUESTION. What is Christian perfection?"

"ANSWER. The loving God with all our heart, mind, soul, and strength. This implies, that no wrong temper, none contrary to love, remains in the soul; and that all the thoughts, words, and actions, are governed by pure love."

"Q. Do you affirm, that this perfection excludes all infirmities, ignorance, and mistake?"

"A. I continually affirm quite the contrary, and always have done so."

"Q. But how can every thought, word, and work be governed by pure love, and the man be subject at the same time to ignorance and mistake?"

"A. I see no contradiction here: 'A man may be filled with pure love, and still be liable to mistake.' Indeed I do not expect to be freed from actual mistakes, till this mortal puts on immortality. I believe this to be a natural consequence of the soul's dwelling in flesh and blood. For we cannot now think at all, but by the mediation of those bodily organs which have suffered equally with the rest of our frame. And hence we cannot avoid sometimes thinking wrong, till this corruptible shall have put on incorruption."

From John Wesley, *The Journal of John Wesley*, ed. Percy Livingstone Parker (Chicago: Moody Press, 1951), chap. 15, http://www.ccel.org.

"By Christian perfection, I mean 1) loving God with all our heart. Do you object to this? I mean 2) a heart and life all devoted to God. Do you desire less? I mean 3) regaining the whole image of God. What objection to this? I mean 4) having all the mind that was in Christ. Is this going too far? I mean 5) walking uniformly as Christ walked. And this surely no Christian will object to. If anyone means anything more or anything else by perfection, I have no concern with it. But if this is wrong, yet what need of this heat about it, this violence, I had almost said, fury of opposition, carried so far as even not to lay out anything with this man, or that woman, who professes it?"

Sin in the Christian

How does the idea of perfection relate to sin in the believer's life? In one of his sermons, titled "On Sin in Believers," Wesley considers carefully this problem.

From Wesley, "On Sin in Believers," sermon no. 13,
in *Sermons on Various Occasions.*

I. 1. Is there then sin in him that is in Christ? Does sin *remain* in one that believes in him? Is there any sin in them that are born of God, or are they wholly delivered from it? . . .

II. . . . 2. By sin, I here understand inward sin; any sinful temper, passion, or affection; such as pride, self-will, love of the world, in any kind or degree; such as lust, anger, peevishness; any disposition contrary to the mind which was in Christ.

3. The question is not concerning *outward sin*; whether a child of God *commits sin* or no. We all agree and earnestly maintain, "He that committeth sin is of the devil." We agree, "Whosoever is born of God doth not commit sin." Neither do we now inquire whether inward sin will *always* remain in the children of God; whether sin will continue in the soul as long as it continues in the body: Nor yet do we inquire whether a justified person may *relapse* either into inward or outward sin; but simply this, Is a justified or regenerate man freed from *all sin* as soon as he is justified? Is there then no sin in his heart? nor ever after, unless he fall from grace?

4. We allow that the state of a justified person is inexpressibly great and glorious. He is born again, "not of blood, nor of the flesh, nor of the will of man, but of God" [John 1:13]. He is a child of God, a member of Christ, an heir of the kingdom of heaven. "The peace of God, which passeth all understanding, keepeth his heart and mind in Christ Jesus" [Phil. 4:7]. His very body is a "temple of the Holy Ghost" [1 Cor. 6:19], and an "habitation of God through the Spirit" [Eph. 2:22]. He is "created anew in Christ Jesus" [2 Cor. 5:17]: He is *washed*, he is *sanctified*. His heart is purified by faith; he is cleansed "from the corruption that is in the world"; "the love of God is shed abroad in his heart by the Holy Ghost which is given unto him." And so long as he "walketh in love," (which he may always do,) he worships God in spirit and in truth. He keepeth the commandments of

God, and doeth those things that are pleasing in his sight; so exercising himself as to "have a conscience void of offence, toward God and toward man": And he has power both over outward and inward sin, even from the moment he is justified. . . .

V. 1. The sum of all is this: There are in every person, even after he is justified, two contrary principles, nature and grace, termed by St. Paul the *flesh* and the *Spirit*. Hence, although even babes in Christ are *sanctified*, yet it is only in part. In a degree, according to the measure of their faith, they are spiritual; yet, in a degree they are carnal. Accordingly, believers are continually exhorted to watch against the flesh, as well as the world and the devil. And to this agrees the constant experience of the children of God. While they feel this witness in themselves, they feel a will not wholly resigned to the will of God. They know they are in him; and yet find an heart ready to depart from him, a proneness to evil in many instances, and a backwardness to that which is good. The contrary doctrine is wholly new; never heard of in the church of Christ, from the time of his coming into the world, till the time of Count Zinzendorf; and it is attended with the most fatal consequences. It cuts off all watching against our evil nature, against the Delilah which we are told is gone, though she is still lying in our bosom. It tears away the shield of weak believers, deprives them of their faith and so leaves them exposed to all the assaults of the world, the flesh, and the devil.

2. Let us, therefore, hold fast the sound doctrine "once delivered to the saints," and delivered down by them with the written word to all succeeding generations: That although we are renewed, cleansed, purified, sanctified, the moment we truly believe in Christ, yet we are not then renewed, cleansed, purified altogether; but the flesh, the evil nature, still *remains* (though subdued) and wars against the Spirit. So much the more let us use all diligence in "fighting the good fight of faith" [1 Tim. 6:12]. So much the more earnestly let us "watch and pray" [Mark 14:38] against the enemy within. The more carefully let us take to ourselves, and "put on, the whole armor of God" [Eph. 6:11–13]; that, although "we wrestle" both "with flesh, and blood, and with the principalities, and with powers, and wicked spirits in high places," we may be able to withstand in the evil day, and having done all, to stand.

Charles Wesley

The younger brother of John Wesley, Charles is most well known for his hymns. The first one is meant to be read before reading the Scripture, and the second one aptly describes "inward religion."

From *John and Charles Wesley: Selected Prayers, Hymns, Journal Notes, Sermons, Letters and Treatises*, ed. Frank Whaling, Classics of Western Spirituality (New York: Paulist Press, 1981), 187–88 and 188–89.

1. Come, Holy Ghost, our hearts inspire, Let us thine influence prove,
   Source of the old prophetic fire, Fountain of life and love.

2. Come, Holy Ghost (for moved by thee The prophets wrote and spoke);
   Unlock the truth, thyself the key, Unseal the sacred book.

3. Expand thy wings, celestial dove, Brood o'er our nature's night;
   On our disordered spirits move, And let there now be light.

4. God through himself we then shall know, If thou within us shine;
   And sound, with all thy saints below, The depths of love divine.

    1. Author of faith, eternal Word,
       Whose spirit breathes the active flame,
       Faith, like its finisher and Lord,
       Today as yesterday the same;

    2. To thee our humble hearts aspire,
       And ask the gift unspeakable;
       Increase in us the kindled fire,
       In us the work of faith fulfill.

    3. By faith we know thee strong to save
       (Save us, a present Savior thou!)
       Whate'er we hope, by faith we have,
       Future and past subsisting now.

    4. To him that in thy name believes
       Eternal life with thee is given;
       Into himself he all receives—
       Pardon, and holiness, and heaven.

    5. The things unknown to feeble sense,
       Unseen by reason's glimmering ray,
       With strong commanding evidence
       Their heavenly origin display.

6. Faith lends its realizing light,
   The clouds disperse, the shadows fly;
   Th'Invisible appears in sight,
   And God is seen by mortal eye.

John William Fletcher

Swiss by birth, John Fletcher, a British Anglican priest, fully supported John Wesley's work, including his idea of perfection, yet he never left his own church even though Wesley would have considered him his designated successor.

"Christian Perfection Defined"
Under this rubric, Fletcher presents an understanding of perfection that is fully in keeping with his famous Methodist colleague.

> From John Fletcher, *Fletcher on Perfection*, ed. Michael R.
> Williams (Salem, OH: Schmul Publishing, 2000), 9.

We call Christian perfection the maturity of grace and holiness, which established, adult believers attain to under the Christian dispensation. By this means we distinguish that maturity of grace, both from the ripeness of grace which belongs to the dispensation of the Jews below us, and from the ripeness of glory which belongs to departed saints above us. Hence it appears that, by *Christian perfection*, we mean nothing but the cluster and maturity of the graces which compose the Christian character in the church militant.

In other words, Christian perfection is a spiritual constellation made up of these gracious stars: perfect repentance, perfect faith, perfect humility, perfect meekness, perfect self-denial, perfect resignation, perfect hope, perfect charity for our visible enemies (as well as for our earthly relations) and above all, perfect love for our invisible God, through the explicit knowledge of our Mediator Jesus Christ. As this last star is always accompanied by all the others, as Jupiter is by his satellites, we frequently use (as St. John) the phrase *perfect love* instead of the word *perfection*. We understand by it the pure love of God shed abroad in the heart of established believers by the Holy Ghost, which is abundantly given them under the fullness of the Christian dispensation.

George Whitefield

The English preacher of the American "Great Awakening," Whitefield is considered another founder of Methodism—one with a Calvinistic orientation—along with the Wesley brothers. He is best known for his powerful sermons, and is undoubtedly one of the greatest evangelists of all times.

Whitefield speaks of walking with God as a function of having been led by the Spirit.

> From George Whitefield, "Walking with God," sermon no. 1, in *Selected Sermons of George Whitefield*, http://www.ccel.org, n.p. (accessed Jan. 10, 2008).

And *First, walking with God* implies, that the prevailing power of the enmity of a person's heart be taken away by the blessed Spirit of God. Perhaps it may seem a hard saying to some, but our own experience daily proves what the scriptures in many places assert, that the carnal mind, the mind of the unconverted natural man, nay, the mind of the regenerate, so far as any part of him remains unrenewed, is enmity, not only an enemy, but enmity itself, against God; so that it is not subject to the law of God, neither indeed can it be. Indeed, one may well wonder that any creature, especially that lovely creature man, made after his Maker's own image, should ever have any enmity, much less a prevailing enmity, against that very God in whom he lives, and moves, and hath his being. But alas! so it is.

In a remarkable sermon titled "The Indwelling of the Spirit, the Common Privilege of All Believers," this evangelist attempts passionately to convince his audience of the continuing ministry of the Spirit among believers without being taken back by the fear of enthusiasm.

> From Whitefield, "The Indwelling of the Spirit, the Common Privilege of All Believers," sermon no. 38, in *Selected Sermons*.

John 7:37–39—"In the last day, that great [day] of the feast, Jesus stood and cried, saying, If any man thirst, let him come unto me, and drink. He that believeth on me, as the scripture hath said, out of his belly shall flow rivers of living water. (But this spake he of the Spirit, which they that believe on him should receive."

Nothing has rendered the cross of Christ of less effect; nothing has been a greater stumbling-block and rock of offense to weak minds, than a supposition, now current among us, that most of what is contained in the gospel of Jesus Christ, was designed only for our Lord's first and immediate followers, and consequently calculated but for one or two hundred years. . . . As this is true of the doctrines of the gospel in general, so it is of the operation of God's Spirit upon the hearts of believers in particular; for we no sooner mention the necessity of our receiving the Holy Ghost in these last days, as well as formerly, but we are looked upon by some, as enthusiasts and madmen; and by others, represented as willfully deceiving the people, and undermining the established constitution of the church.

Judge ye then, whether it is not high time for the true ministers of Jesus, who have been made partakers of this heavenly gift, to lift up their voices like a trumpet; and if they would not have those souls perish, for which the Lord Jesus has shed his precious blood, to declare, with all boldness, that the Holy Spirit is the common privilege and portion of all believers in all ages; and that we as well as the first Christians, must receive the Holy Ghost, before we can be truly called the children of God.

For this reason . . . I have chosen the words of the text. They were spoken by Jesus Christ, when he was at the feast of tabernacles. . . . At the last day of this feast, it was customary for many pious people to fetch water from a certain place, and bring it on their heads. . . . And that we might know what our Savior meant by this living water, the Evangelist immediately adds, "But this spake he of the Spirit, which they that believe on him should receive" [John 7:39].

First, I am to show, what is meant by the word Spirit. By the Spirit, is evidently to be understood the Holy Ghost, the third person in the ever-blessed Trinity, consubstantial and co-eternal with the Father and the Son, proceeding from, yet equal to them both. For, to use the words of our Church in this day's office, that which we believe of the glory of the Father, the same we believe of the Son, and of the Holy Ghost, without any difference or inequality.

I proceed,

Secondly, To prove that the Holy Ghost is the common privilege of all believers.

But, here I would not be understood of to receiving the Holy Ghost, as to enable us to work miracles, or show outward signs and wonders. I allow our adversaries, that to pretend to be inspired, in this sense, is being wise above what is written. . . . For the world being now become nominally Christian . . . there need not outward miracles, but only an inward co-operation of the Holy Spirit with the word, to prove that Jesus is the Messiah which was to come into the world.

Besides, if it was possible for thee, O man, to have faith, so as to be able to remove mountains, or cast out devils; nay, couldst thou speak with the tongue of men and angels, yea, and bid the sun stand still in the midst of heaven; what would all these gifts of the Spirit avail thee, without being made partaker of his sanctifying graces? Saul had the spirit of government for a while, so as to become another man, and yet probably was a cast-away. And many, who cast out devils, in Christ's name, at the last will be disowned by him. If therefore, thou hadst only the gifts, and was destitute of the graces of the Holy Ghost, they would only serve to lead thee with so much the more solemnity to hell.

Here then we join issue with our adversaries, and will readily grant, that we are not in this sense to be inspired, as were our Lord's first Apostles. But unless men have eyes which see not, and ears that hear not, how can they read the latter part of the text, and not confess that the Holy Spirit, in another sense, is the common privilege of all believers, even to the end of the world? . . .

A great noise hath been made of late, about the word enthusiast, and it has been cast upon the preachers of the gospel, as a term of reproach; but every Christian, in the proper sense of the word, must be an enthusiast; that is, must be inspired of God or have God, by his Spirit, in him. . . . Indeed, I will not say, all our letter-learned preachers deny this doctrine in express words; but however, they do in effect; for they talk professedly against inward feelings, and say, we may have God's Spirit without feeling it, which is in reality to deny the thing itself. And had I a mind to hinder the progress of the gospel, and to establish the kingdom of darkness, I would go about, telling people, they might have the Spirit of God, and yet not feel it.

The Quakers

George Fox

What now is called formally "Religious Society of Friends (Quakers)" and more briefly "Friends" had its beginning in seventeenth-century England. Originally, they called themselves just "Friends of Truth," claiming the friendship of Jesus, as they thought of themselves as friends of Jesus (John 15:15). In time they came to be known simply as "Friends." The name "Quaker" was a nickname given by others because of spiritual manifestations such as shaking. The most well-known writing of the movement, the journal of its founder George Fox, has been placed among the greatest religious autobiographies such as St. Augustine's *Confessions* and Saint Teresa's *Life*. Here the founder of Quakerism gives a vivid account of his deep and at times mystical religious experiences. Similarly to the mystics of the past, he had divine visitations, experienced a number of mighty spiritual experiences, and claimed to have spiritual gifts such as discernment. The formative spiritual experience for Fox—which also gave basic shape to Quakerism as a movement—was enlightenment with divine light.

From George Fox, *An Autobiography*, ed. Rufus M. Jones,
http://www.ccel.org, chap. 2, n.p. (accessed Jan. 11, 2008).

Now the Lord God opened to me by His invisible power that every man was enlightened by the divine Light of Christ, and I saw it shine through all; and that they that believed in it came out of condemnation to the Light of life, and became the children of it; but they that hated it, and did not believe in it were condemned by it, though they made a profession of Christ. This I saw in the pure openings of the Light without the help of any man; neither did I then know where to find it in the Scriptures; though afterwards, searching the Scriptures, I found it. For I saw, in that Light and Spirit which was before the Scriptures were given forth, and which led the holy men of God to give them forth, that all, if they would know God or Christ, or the Scriptures aright, must come to that Spirit by which they that gave them forth were led and taught.

At times, Fox exercised the gift of spiritual discernment.

From Fox, *An Autobiography*, chap. 7.

The Lord had given me a spirit of discerning, by which I many times saw the states and conditions of people, and could try their spirits. For not long before, as I was going to a meeting, I saw some women in a field, and I discerned an evil spirit in them; and I was moved to go out of my way into the field to them, and declare unto them their conditions. At another time there came one into Swarthmore Hall in the meeting time, and I was moved to speak sharply to her, and told her she was under the power of an evil spirit; and the people said afterwards she was generally accounted so. There came also at another time another woman, and stood at a distance from me, and I cast mine eye upon her, and said, "Thou hast been an harlot"; for I perfectly saw the condition and life of the woman. The woman answered and said that many could tell her of her outward sins, but none could tell her of her inward. Then I told her her heart was not right before the Lord, and that from the inward came the outward. This woman came afterwards to be convinced of God's truth, and became a Friend.

William Penn

Whereas George Fox is the spiritual founder of the Friends, William Penn, the namesake of Pennsylvania, is the visionary behind the sociopolitical freedom and liberty among the Friends. At the same time, Penn also helped defend and clarify the most well-known—and undoubtedly, most widely debated—idea of "light," the belief that within every believer God continues to speak (based on John 1:9).

From William Penn, *Primitive Christianity Revived* (Philadelphia: Miller & Burlock, 1857), chap. 1, §§3–4; chap. 2, §§1, 4.

§3. There are divers ways of speaking they have been led to use, by which they declare and express what this *principle* is, about which I think fit to precaution the reader—viz., they call it, *The light of Christ within man, or, light within,* which is their ancient, and most general and familiar phrase. . . .

§4. It is to this principle of Light, Life, and Grace, that this People refer all: for they say it is the great Agent in Religion; *that,* without which, there is no *Conviction,* so no *Conversion,* or *Regeneration*; and consequently no entering into the Kingdom of God. That is to say, there can be no true sight of sin, nor sorrow for it, and therefore no forsaking or overcoming of it, or Remission or Justification from it. A necessary and powerful Principle indeed, when either Sanctification nor Justification can be had without it. . . .

[chap. 2] §1. I shall begin with the evidence of the blessed Scriptures of Truth, for this *divine principle,* and that under the name of *light,* the first and most common word used by them, to express and denominate this principle by, as well as most apt and proper in this dark state of the world. . . .

Among many, nomenclatures such as "Light of God" are equated with the Holy Spirit, a claim contested by many but strongly defended by Penn.

From Penn, *Primitive Christianity Revived,* chap. 5, §§1, 2.

§1. But some may say, *We could willingly allow to the Spirit and grace of God, which seemed to be the peculiar blessing of the new and second covenant, and the fruit of the coming of Christ, all that which you ascribe to the light within; but except it appeared to us that this light were the same in nature with the Spirit and grace of God, we cannot easily bring ourselves to believe what you say in favour of the light within.*

Answ. This *objection*, at first look, seems to carry weight with it: but upon a just and serious review, it will appear to have more words than matter, show than substance: yet because it gives occasion to solve scruples, that may be flung in the way of the simple, I shall attend it throughout. I say, then, if it appear that the *properties* ascribed to the *light within* are the same with those that are given to the *Holy Spirit* and *grace of God*; and that those several terms or epithets, are only to express the divers manifestations or operations of one and the same principle, then it will not, it cannot be denied, but this light within, is *divine* and *efficacious*, as we have asserted it. Now, that it is of the same nature with the Spirit and grace of God, and tends to the same end, which is to bring people to God, let the *properties* of the *light* be compared with those of the Spirit and grace of God. I say, they are the same, in that, *First*, the light proceeds from the *One Word*, and *One Life* of that *One Word*, which was *with* God and was God. John i. 4: In him was life; and the life was the light of men. And John i. 9: That was the true Light, which lighteth every man that cometh into the world. Secondly, it is *universal*, it lighteth *every* man. Thirdly, *it giveth the knowledge of God and fellowship with* him. Rom. i. 19: Because that which may be known of God is manifest in them; for God hath shewed it unto them . . . *Fourthly*, it manifesteth and reproveth evil, John iii. 20: For every one that doeth evil hateth the light, neither cometh to the light, lest his deeds should be reproved . . . *Fifthly*, it is made the rule and guide of Christian walking, Psalm xliii. 3: O send out thy light and thy truth: let them lead me; let them bring me unto thy holy hill, and to thy tabernacles. . . . *Sixthly*, it is the path for God's people to go in, Psalm cxix. 105: Thy word is a lamp unto my feet, and a light unto my path. . . . *Lastly*, it is the armour of the children of God against Satan, Psalm xxvii. 1: The Lord is my light and my salvation; whom shall I fear? The Lord is the strength of my life; of whom shall I be afraid? . . .

§2. Now let all this be compared with the *properties* of the *Holy Spirit*, and their agreement will be very manifest. *First, it proceedeth from God*, because it is the Spirit of God, Rom. vi. 11 . . . Secondly, it is *universal*. It *strove* with the old world, Gen. vi. 3: And the Lord said, My Spirit shall not always strive with man, for that he also is flesh: yet his days shall be an hundred and twenty years. Then to be sure with the new One: *Every one hath a measure of it given to profit withal*, 1 Cor. xii. 7. *Thirdly, it revealeth God*, Job xxxii. 8. . . . *Fourthly, it reproveth sin*, John xvi. 8: And when he is come, he will reprove the world of sin, and of righteousness, and of judgment. *Fifthly*, it is a rule and a guide for the children of God to walk by, Rom. viii. 14. . . . *Sixthly*, it is also the *path* they are to walk in, Rom. viii. 1. . . .

Lastly, this is not all; it is likewise the *spiritual weapon* of a true Christian. Eph. vi. 17: Take the helmet of salvation, and the sword of the Spirit, which is the word of God. After this, I hope none will deny that this Light and this Spirit must be of one and the same nature, that work *one and the same effect*, and tend evidently to *one and the same holy end*.

|

Jonathan Edwards
and the Great Awakening

|

Considered by many to be one of the greatest preachers and churchmen in American history, Jonathan Edwards was instrumental also in the first Great Awakening.

Spirit Christology

In the following excerpt Edwards ties in a remarkable way the work of the Spirit to that of Christ.

From Jonathan Edwards, "Work of Redemption," #402,
in *Works of Jonathan Edwards Online*, vol. 13, *The Miscellanies*, ed.
Harry S. Stout, Kenneth P. Minkema, Caleb J. D. Maskell (2005–),
http://edwards.yale.edu/archive (hereafter Stout et al.).

The sum of all that Christ purchased is the Holy Ghost. . . . The great thing purchased by Jesus Christ for us is communion with God, which is only in having the Spirit; 'tis participation of Christ's fullness, and having grace for grace, which is only in having of that Spirit which he has without measure; this is the promise of the Father, Luke 24:49. He purchased God's love, favor and delight, which is still the Holy Ghost, for us; Galatians 3:2 . . . and 3:13–14 . . . "Good things" and "the Holy Spirit" are synonymous; Matthew 7:11. . . . Therefore 'tis called the "Spirit of promise" (Ephesians 1:13), because it is the great subject of the promises, the sum of the gospel promises. Christ purchased for us grace and many spiritual blessings in this world, but they are all comprised in that, in having the indwelling of the Holy Ghost. Christ purchased glory for us in another world, that we should be like God, that we should be perfect in holiness and happiness; which still is comprised in that, in having the indwelling of the Holy Ghost. The Spirit is that river of water of life, which in heaven proceeds from the throne of God and the Lamb (Revelations

22:1). Therefore the Holy Ghost that believers have here, is said to be the earnest of the inheritance, or purchased possession (Ephesians 1:14). The earnest is some of the same given before hand; the purchased possession is only a fullness of that Spirit. As the persons of the Trinity are equal among themselves, so there seems to [be] an exact equality in each person's concern in the work of redemption, and in our concern with them in that great affair; and the glory of it equally belongs to each of them. The benefits and blessedness of redemption are wholly and entirely from each of them: it is wholly originally from the Father; the Son is the medium of it all; the Holy Ghost immediately possesses us of it all, or rather is the sum of it all—he possesses us of it by coming and dwelling in us himself. Thus "of him, and through him, and to him" (or in him) "are all things," Romans 11:36.

The Spirit's Work in the Believer
Edwards makes a distinction between the two kinds of work of the Spirit in the regenerate and unregenerate lives.

> From Edwards, "Spirit's Operation, Conviction, Conversion," #471,
> in *Works of Jonathan Edwards Online*, vol. 13 (Stout et al.)

Difference between [the] Spirit's operation in converted and unconverted men. The Spirit of God influences and operates upon the minds of both natural and regenerate men; but doubtless there is a great difference, not only in the works he does or the effects he produces, but also in the manner of his operation: for wicked men are sensual and have not the Spirit; those that are none of Christ's have not the Spirit of Christ. And the difference seems to be this: the Holy Ghost influences the godly as dwelling in them as a vital principle, or as a new supernatural principle of life and action. But in unregenerate men, he operates only by assisting natural principles to do the same work which they do of themselves, to a greater degree. . . . But the Spirit of God, when he convinces and awakens a sinner, assists it to do it, to do it to a greater degree by his assistance, [and] frees it in a measure from its clog and hindrance by sin. But in the sanctifying work of the Holy Ghost, not only remaining principles are assisted to do their work to a greater degree, but those principles are restored that were utterly destroyed by the fall; [so that] the mind habitually exerts those acts that the dominion of sin had made the soul wholly destitute of, as much as a dead body is destitute of vital acts. And then there is this other difference: the Spirit of God in the souls of his saints exerts its own proper nature; that is to say, it communicates and exerts itself in the soul, in those acts which are its proper, natural and essential acts in itself *ad intra*, or within the Deity from all eternity. The proper nature of the Spirit of God, the act which is its nature and wherein its being consists, is (as we have shewn) divine love. Therefore the Holy Ghost influences the minds of the godly by living in the godly. The Spirit of God may operate upon a mind and produce effects in it, and yet not communicate itself in its nature in the soul. The Spirit of God operates in the minds of the godly by only being in them, uniting itself to their souls, and living in 'em and acting itself.

While always advocating personal conversion and holiness, Edwards was not thereby ignorant of the communal aspects of the Spirit's work.

From Edwards, "Holy Ghost," #330, in *Works of Jonathan Edwards Online*, vol. 13 (Stout et al.).

It appears that the Holy Spirit is the holiness, or excellency and delight of God, because our communion with God and with Christ consists in our partaking of the Holy Ghost (2 Corinthians 13:14; 1 Corinthians 6:17; 1 John 3:24, 4:13). The oil that was upon Aaron's head ran down to the skirts of his garments [Ps. 133]; the Spirit which Christ our Head has without measure is communicated to his church and people. The sweet perfumed oil signified Christ's excellency and sweet delight, Philippians 2:1. Communion, we know, is nothing else but the common partaking with others of good: communion with God is nothing else but a partaking with him of his excellency, his holiness and happiness.

Sin against the Holy Spirit

From Edwards, "Sin against the Holy Ghost," #475, 1–3, in *Works of Jonathan Edwards Online*, vol. 13 (Stout et al.).

There seem to be three things essential to this sin, viz. conviction, malice, and presumption (presumption in expressing that malice). Christ says (Matthew 12:31–32), "Blasphemy against the Holy Ghost shall not be forgiven unto men. And whosoever speaketh a word against the Son of man, it shall be forgiven him: but whosoever speaketh against the Holy Ghost, [it shall not be forgiven him], neither in this world, neither in the world to come." Here I would observe,

1. In order to a man's speaking against or reviling the Holy Ghost in the sense of this text, he must have some knowledge of him. If a man only hears the name "Holy Ghost," having no notion what is meant by it, and reviles he knows not what, he don't blaspheme the

Holy Ghost in the sense of the text: or if he has only such a notion, that he is one of the persons in the Godhead, and speaks against him as he does against the other persons, having no notion in his mind of anything that is a distinction of nature or work. . . . Therefore when men blaspheme the Holy Ghost, they express spite against something that they have an idea or notion of in their minds, that is particularly pertaining to and distinguishing of this divine Person. . . . Christ, in mentioning the blasphemy against the Holy Ghost, has respect to their laying all that he did as acting by the Holy Ghost, to an unclean spirit; he has not only a respect to this particular instance of casting out devils, for they did not only mean that this, but that all was from the devil. He rather takes occasion to mention it now, because such a miracle was a powerful argument to convince them . . . and they were now convinced by the strength of it, as he saw, who knew their thoughts (as it is said, v. 25); and they shewed their conviction by what they said, as we observed before. . . .

2. In order to a man's blaspheming the Holy Ghost in the sense in which Christ speaks, his so doing must be attended with conviction; he must be sensible that he does it; he must be sensible that the thing he reviles is God's Spirit, or at least that it is from God. He must have conviction that God is God, and must have a malice against him, and must from malice against him express his contempt or despite of some gracious or holy spiritual operation of his; or, in a word, he must revile the grace of God that he has light to know is His. A man is not said to blaspheme or revile another in the sense that the expression is used in this text, if he don't know who he is: if a man meets another that is his father, and reviles him, he don't revile his father if he don't know that it is his father. . . .

3. By speaking against the Holy Ghost, I understand any way outwardly and presumptuously declaring malice by reproaching and blaspheming. A having malice inwardly is not sufficient, though it be against convictions of conscience. But when a person has with his malice also the presumption as to appear in it, [when] he has that spirit of contempt that he is not restrained by any fear or awe, but is so horribly daring as outwardly to express his malice by reproaching; then he commits the unpardonable sin against the Holy Ghost. Generally words and actions go together.

CHAPTER 9

Nineteenth-Century
Pneumatologies

Introduction

Before venturing into the twentieth-century pneumatological traditions, we will briefly survey some representative movements of the previous century. While much more could be said, the pneumatological theologies and narratives will be limited to the following: modern Protestant theologies (F. D. E. Schleiermacher, G. W. F. Hegel), the neo-Calvinist movement (A. Kuyper), and the so-called Reformed orthodoxy closely allied with Princeton Seminary (B. Warfield, C. Hodge, A. A. Hodge, and A. H. Strong). Studying these materials will help us transition to the twentieth-century developments.

Friedrich D. E. Schleiermacher, appropriately named the "father of modern Protestant theology," is the ablest and by any standard the most influential shaper of the classical liberal tradition. Widely influenced by pietism, romanticism, and the philosophies of his time, Schleiermacher produced a highly appealing view of religion and theology for the post-Enlightenment world. His contemporary Georg W. F. Hegel—perhaps the greatest philosopher since the masters of the ancient world such as Plato—stood in the line of the greatest medieval writers, even though radically different in content. Hegel mastered the skill of commenting on almost any topic, whether philosophy or politics or religion. His philosophical system based on the dialectic of idealism is the most creative interpretation of the Spirit ever produced by the human mind.

The neo-Calvinist school's views of the Spirit and salvation will be presented through the lens of its premier theologian, the Dutch Abraham Kuyper. While he did not say everything said by this end-of-the-nineteenth-century Reformed school, he outlined its main orientations. The views of another great theologian in the domain, Herman Bavinck, Kuyper's successor as professor of theology at the Free University of Amsterdam, would have been discussed had his last volume of the four-volume *Reformed Dogmatics*, titled *Holy Spirit, Church, and New Creation*, been available in English at the time of this writing.

The last part of this section will look at another formative Reformed school of thought, that on the American side of the Atlantic Ocean, the Princeton orthodoxy represented by three of its ablest theologians, B. B. Warfield and the two Hodges, Charles (father) and Archibald (son), as well as the fundamentalism of some like-minded thinkers such as the Baptist Strong. A vigorous antithesis and rebuttal of liberal theologies, this group of theologians formed the backbone of American fundamentalism and conservativism, out of which also emerged the currently highly influential evangelicalism (to be studied in what follows).

Modern Protestant Theologies

Friedrich Schleiermacher

Religion as the "Feeling" of Absolute Dependency
While Immanuel Kant located religion in the realm of morality, and Hegel, in rational knowledge, for liberal theology the locus of religion and theology was to be found in the "feeling"—a term not to be confused with the contemporary "thin" understanding of feeling as emotion, but rather in a "thick" feeling of "absolute dependency," as Schleiermacher called it, a recognition of being referred to something "beyond." In his early work *On Religion: Speeches to Its Cultural Despisers*, he sets forth this kind of understanding of religion.

From Friedrich Schleiermacher, *On Religion: Speeches to Its Cultural Despisers*, trans. John Oman (London: K. Paul, Trench, Trubner & Co., 1893), 36, http://www.ccel.org.

It is true that religion is essentially contemplative. . . . But this contemplation is not turned, as your knowledge of nature is, to the existence of a finite thing, combined with and opposed to another finite thing. It has not even, like your knowledge of God—if for once I might use an old expression—to do with the nature of the first cause, in itself and in its relation to every other cause and operation. The contemplation of the pious is the immediate consciousness of the universal existence of all finite things, in and through the Infinite, and of all temporal things in and through the Eternal. Religion is to seek this and find it in all that lives and moves, in all growth and change, in all doing and suffering. It is to have life and to know life in immediate feeling, only as such an existence in the Infinite and Eternal. . . . Religion is not knowledge and science, either of the world or of God. Without being knowledge, it recognizes knowledge and science. In itself it is an affection, a revelation of the Infinite in the finite, God being seen in it and it in God.

The Christian Life as Partaking of the Spirit

Unlike *On Religion*, which was a kind of apologetic work aimed at those outside the household of faith, *The Christian Faith* sets forth an exposition of dogmatics assuming and based on a knowledge of Christian vocabulary. In keeping with his revised understanding of theology as a reflection on the Christian experience, Schleiermacher proposes the basis for the Christian life as the union of human with the Divine Spirit.

From F. D. E. Schleiermacher, *The Christian Faith*, ed. H. R. Mackintosh and J. S. Stewart (London/New York: T. & T. Clark, 1999), §123.1, 569.

§123. First Theorem.—The Holy Spirit is the union of the Divine Essence with human nature in the form of the common Spirit animating the life in common of believers.

1. When in connexion with the doctrines of Christ we were discussing the union in Him of the divine with the human, we put entirely aside the question whether or not this divine, apart from its union with human nature, was something special, as being the second Person in the Godhead, and something relatively distinct in the Divine Essence. So here too, in proposing a similar formula for the Holy Spirit, we must (although the Trinity is now completely before us) in the same way leave this consideration out of account. What we have to treat here is simply this relation between the highest Essence and human nature, in so far as in its operations it meets us within our Christian self-consciousness.

Thus, the Christian life is simply partaking of the Holy Spirit.

From Schleiermacher, *Christian Faith*, §124.1–2, 574–77.

§124. *Second Theorem.—Every regenerate person partakes of the Holy Spirit, so that there is no living fellowship with Christ without an indwelling of the Holy Spirit, and vice versa.*

1. Up to this point the question as to how redemption is realized in the human soul has been answered by saying that it happens through being taken up into living fellowship with Christ. Now the demand is made that everyone must partake of the Holy Spirit. . . .

For being taken up into living fellowship with Christ includes at the same time being conscious both of our sonship with God and of the Lordship of Christ; and both in Scripture are ascribed to the indwelling of the Holy Spirit. We therefore cannot imagine how one could exist were the other absent. . . .

Membership in this common life therefore means at the same time being set within the sphere of operation of the sole Founder. Thus we find expressed the belief that such an outpouring of the Spirit would only have been possible after the appearance of the Son of God, and on the basis of His personal influence; and this carries with it the implication that our participation in that Spirit and our own bond with the living influence of Christ are one and the same thing.

On the other side, the same thing holds good. If we begin with Christ and hold to the proposition that the union of the Divine with His human personality was at the same time an enrichment of human nature as a whole, it follows not only in general that even after His departure this union must continue, but also (since this continuation is to proceed from the union itself) that wherever it exists there must be a bond with Christ, and *vice versa*. And since after the departure of Christ the enlarged range of connexion with Him can only proceed from the fellowship of believers, these three facts—being drawn by that union into the fellowship of believers, having a share in the Holy Spirit, and being drawn into living fellowship with Christ—must simply mean one and the same thing.

2. In this connexion it is very natural to ask what is the relation between the two expressions used by the same apostle, that Christ liveth in us, and that we are led by the Spirit? When the same Apostle says that those who are led by the Spirit are God's children, either he is contradicting (and that no one can believe) him who says that those who have received Christ are God's children, or else here too these two things, the life of Christ in us and the leading of the Holy Spirit in us, are one, both within that third thing, being children of God. Either there are two different kinds of children of God (which we should all deny as much as Paul or John), or else these two things are the same. If we are to answer the question from the connexion in which the expressions are used in the Church, we notice to begin with that the second is peculiar and characteristic in a higher degree than the first, and has therefore obtained a larger place in the language of the Schools and in the usage of devotional religion which attributes special value to what is easily understood. On the other hand, the first is very far from prominent in the language of the Schools, and has won a special place in the devotional vocabulary usually known as mystical. Now, if we consider that the Holy Spirit is

also called the Spirit of Christ, it follows at once that we say more particularly in one context that the Spirit of Another lives in us, and in a different context that the Other Himself lives in us, without intending to mean anything different by the two phrases. Indeed, in any case nothing different could be meant. If we add the thought of the union of the Divine and the human in Christ, obviously the human can be in us only as a rightly apprehended picture or representation, but the Divine as a powerful impulse, even although in us it does not, as in Him, exclusively determine our whole personality, but only works in and along with His rightly apprehended picture, which again can only take shape in our minds in the measure of truth and perfection in which the Divine glorifies it before our thought. But just this is the work of the Holy Spirit—to bring Christ into memory and glorify Him in us. Thus however they are regarded, the two things are one and the same.

The same result is reached if we compare the content of the two expressions with reference to the effects they indicate. If we conceive ourselves as perfectly within the living fellowship of Christ, then all our actions can be regarded as His. But the Holy Spirit also, when leading us through the knowledge of Christ into all truth, cannot possibly lead us to any other actions than those in which Christ can be recognized; the fruits of the Spirit are therefore nothing but the virtues of Christ. To recognize in our souls any leading of the divine Spirit which could not be brought into connexion with what Christ's words and life have conveyed to us as His way of acting, is to open the door to every sort of visionary fanaticism that the Protestant Church from the very start has most steadily opposed. The leading of the Holy Spirit is never other than a divine incitement to realize the standard of what Christ, in virtue of the being of God in Him, humanly was and did. And the life of Christ in us is nothing but activity in behalf of the Kingdom of God which embraces men all together in the grasp of the love flowing from Him; that is, it is the power of the Christian common spirit.

From this it is also clear how, if to believe in Christ and to have Christ living in one are the same thing, it may be said on the one hand that the Holy Spirit produces faith, and on the other hand that the Holy Spirit comes through faith. For through the activity of those who already have a share in the Spirit, He effects faith in others who are brought by them to recognize what is divine and saving in Christ; in these, thereby, the Holy Spirit becomes the moving principle. And so, since the Divine Essence was bound up with the human person of Christ, but is now (His directly personal influence having ceased) no longer personally operative in any individual, but henceforward manifests itself actively in the fellowship of believers as their common spirit, this is just the way in which the work of redemption is continued and extended in the Church.

The Spirit and the Christian Community

Schleiermacher's pneumatological soteriology in *The Christian Faith*, evident in the previous citations, is part of his wider topic on the Christian community, the church. While the critics of the father of modern Protestant theology (particularly by Karl Barth) are suspicious that for him the Holy Spirit was not divine but rather merely "common [human or social] spirit," it is also true that Schleiermacher elevates the role of the Spirit in ecclesiology in a way that is yet to be fully appreciated. Schleiermacher describes the Christian church with the term "common spirit," uniting Christians with Christ and with one another.

From Schleiermacher, *Christian Faith*, §123.2–3, 570–73.

[§123]2. If now . . . we return to the point that in the Church from the beginning, and therefore already in the New Testament, all the powers at work in the Christian Church—and not merely the miraculous gifts, which in this connexion are quite accidental—are traced to the Holy Spirit; and if we ask what is thus supposed to have been present from the very start, the following admissions have to be made.

First, these powers are not to be found outside of the Christian Church, and hence they neither arise from the general constitution of human nature (which would make Christ superfluous) nor from any other divine arrangement. . . . Third, the Holy Spirit is not something that, although divine, is not united with the human nature, but only somehow influences it from without. For whatever enters us from without does so only through the senses and never becomes more than an occasion for our action. What action is to follow on this occasion is determined from within, and only this, and not the former region of the senses, is the sphere of the Holy Spirit. That occasions are given us from without does not preclude the unity of our self-consciousness and self-determination. But this unity would at once be dissolved if determinations were given from without. . . . There is indeed no way of imagining how the Spirit's gifts could be within us, and He Himself remain without. . . .

3. . . . Now if the Holy Spirit is an effective spiritual power in the souls of believers, we must either represent Him as bound up with their human nature, or we shall have to surrender the unity of their being, if on the one hand they are such that in them human nature shows itself in operation, and on the other, such that in them

the Holy Spirit is acting in separation from human nature. To adopt such a view would produce so entire a dualism within human life that it could never be maintained. The theory of a definite activity of the Holy Spirit has indeed been carried to this extreme, not, however, when this supposed activity was still taking place, but only long after it had ceased. All that remains to explain is the fact that this union is realized in the form of a common spirit. Now everything (even in human nature viewed apart from redemption) that as spiritual power is absolutely the same in all individuals of a race and is incapable of any individualizing modification, and above all, reason, we regard as something not varied according to the individual, but as in all and in each the same.

As a consequence of this union, the church is "the perfect image of the Redeemer."

From Schleiermacher, *Christian Faith*, §125.1, 578–79.

§125. *Third Theorem.—The Christian Church, animated by the Holy Spirit, is in its purity and integrity the perfect image of the Redeemer, and each regenerate individual is an indispensable constituent of this fellowship.*

1. Fixing our attention on the Redeemer in the maturity of His human life, we see in the totality of His powers an organism adequate to the impulses proceeding from the being of God within Him. The individual as regenerate can never in this respect be regarded even as an image of Him, because the condition of varied sinfulness in which divine grace found him does not permit of an exact correspondence in the relationship of his psychical capacities to the impulses of the Spirit. But if the Christian Church is a true common life, a unified or, as we say, a moral personality though not indeed an inherited or natural one, it cannot on this latter account be the same as a personality arising from the person-forming activity of Nature, for in the two cases growth and decay are related in very different fashion; but none the less it can and must be an image of such a personality. For since the Divine Essence is one and everywhere self-identical, then, even if its mode of being in the individual, Christ, and in the common life is not the same, it follows that the impulses proceeding from it must be the same in both cases. Hence the modes both of comprehension and of action are the same in the Church as in the Redeemer, because there are present in every member, and therefore in the whole, the very same powers which in Christ's case were taken up into unity with the divine principle.

Georg W. F. Hegel

Examining in the same chapter two thinkers as diverse as Schleiermacher and Hegel may give rise to the misunderstanding that these two share materially similar kinds of views. The only reason these two giants are treated together is that they stand between the Reformation and the twentieth century as representatives of the best of the Enlightenment heritage in their passion to revise Christian understanding of reality and theology. Hegel, of course, made his main contribution as a philosopher, and the relation of his world-embracing system to Christian theology is a complicated question. The only thing that interests us here, however, is the way he developed the idea of the Spirit, insofar as it relates to Christian pneumatological discourse.

Faith

In his *Early Theological Writings* from the last decade of the eighteenth century, Hegel is drawn to the mystical milieu of the Gospel of John. Considering the union of the divine and human in Jesus' incarnation, Hegel speaks of faith as the "relation of spirit to spirit." Faith, however, is only the beginning of the relationship, the culminating point of which is friendship.

> From G. W. F. Hegel, "The Divine in a Particular Shape," *Early Theological Writings (1793–1800)*, in *G. W. F. Hegel: Theologian of the Spirit*, ed. Peter C. Hodgson, The Making of Modern Theology, Nineteenth and Twentieth Century Texts (Minneapolis: Fortress Press, 1997), 64–65 (hereafter Hodgson).

Spirit alone recognizes spirit. They [the Jews] saw in Jesus only the human being, the Nazarene, the carpenter's son whose brothers and kinsfolk lived among them. . . . The Jewish multitude was bound to shatter his attempt to give them the consciousness of something divine, for faith in something divine, something great, cannot make its home in a hut. The lion has no room in a nut[shell], the infinite spirit none in the prison of a Jewish soul, the whole of life none in a withering leaf. The hill and the eye which sees it are object and subject, but between humanity and God, between spirit and spirit, there is no such cleft of objectivity and subjectivity; one is to the other an other only in that one recognizes the other; both are one.

. . . "God is spirit, and they that worship him must worship him in spirit and in truth" [John 4:24]. How could anything but a spirit know a spirit? The relation of spirit to spirit is a feeling of harmony, is their unification; how could heterogeneity be unified? Faith in the divine is only possible if in believers themselves there is a divine element which rediscovers itself, its own nature, in that on which it believes, even if it be unconscious that what it has found is its own nature. In all human beings there is light and life; they are the property of the light. They are not illumined by a light in the way in which a dark body is when it borrows a brightness not its own; on the contrary, their own inflammability takes fire and they burn with a flame that is their own. . . . This faith, however, is only the first stage in the relationship with Jesus. In its culmination this relationship is conceived so intimately that his friends are one with him. See John 12:36: "Until you yourselves have light, believe in the light, so that you may become the children of light."

Incarnation

In his most famous work, *The Phenomenology of the Spirit*, Hegel sets forth his speculative theory of incarnation, which resembles the classical Christian idea but also goes far beyond it.

From Hegel, *The Phenomenology of the Spirit (1807)* (Hodgson, 119).

Spirit has in it two sides that are represented above as two reverse propositions: the one is this, that *substance* divests or empties itself of itself and becomes self-consciousness [i.e., divine becoming human]; the other is the reverse, that *self-consciousness* divests itself of itself and makes itself into an objective thing [*Dingheit*] or a universal self [i.e., human becoming divine]. Both sides have in this way encountered each other, and through this encounter their true union [has] come about. The divestment of substance and its coming into self-consciousness expresses its transition into its opposite, the unconscious transition of *necessity*, or in other words, that substance is *in itself* self-consciousness. Conversely, the divestment of self-consciousness expresses that it is *in itself* the universal being or essence, or because the self is pure being-for-itself that remains at home with itself in its opposite—that substance is self-consciousness *for itself*, and just for this reason is spirit. Of this Spirit, which has abandoned the form of substance and enters into determinate existence in the shape of self-consciousness, it may be said—if we wish to employ relationships derived from natural generation—that it has an *actual mother* but an *implicit* father. For *actuality* or self-consciousness and *implicitness* as substance are its two moments, through whose reciprocal divestment, each becoming the other, spirit comes into determinate existence as their unity.

Trinity

While Hegel's philosophical system comes to maturity in his *Encyclopedia of the Philosophical Sciences*, his work *Lectures on the Philosophy of Religions* brings to culmination his Trinitarian vision as part of the reflections on religion. In the Godhead, there are three moments of divine reality, something similar to the Christian doctrine of the Trinity. "Eternal" or "Essential Being," "the idea of God of and in itself," is something similar to the Father or immanent Trinity; "Representation" or "the form of appearance, that of particularization, of being for others," echoes the Christian idea of the incarnate Son; and finally, the "form of return from appearance to itself," or "absolute self-consciousness" or "absolute presence-to-self," resembles the Holy Spirit, which manifests itself in community and cultus. In Hegel's world-embracing system, thus, the final goal of all historical happening and the process of the Spirit is God returning to himself in humanity. This takes place in the religious life in which humanity comes to know God as God knows himself. This is the final reconciliation within reality.

Its particular relation to the spirit makes Christianity "the consummate religion."

From Hegel, *Lectures on the Philosophy of Religion (1824)* (Hodgson, 205–6).

This is the *consummate religion*, the religion that is the being of spirit for itself, the religion in which religion has become objective to itself. We have called religion the consciousness of God, the consciousness of the absolute being [*Wesen*]—and that is the concept of this religion. Consciousness is inward differentiation, spirit that differentiates itself. Now, therefore, God is [present] as consciousness, or the consciousness of God means that finite consciousness has its essential being, this God, as its object; and it knows the object as its essential being, it objectifies it for itself. In the consciousness of God there are two sides: the one side is God, the other is that where consciousness as such stands. With the consciousness of God we arrive directly at one side, which is what we have called religion. This content is now itself an object. It is the whole that is an object to itself, or religion has become objective to itself. It is *religion* that has become objective to itself—religion as the consciousness of God, or the self-consciousness of God as the return of consciousness into itself.

This religion is precisely what we have called *spirituality*. "Spirit" means precisely not what immediately is, but what is objectively for itself. Spirit is *for* spirit in such a way that the two are distinct. They are defined by their contrast: the one as universal, the other as particular; the one as inner, the other as outer; the one as infinite spirit, the other as finite spirit. This distinction *is* religion, and at the same time religion is the sublation of this distinction, i.e., the self-consciousness of freedom—a spirituality which was there for *us* in all the preceding formative stages of religion, but which is now the *object*. The single self-consciousness finds the consciousness of its essential being in it; hence it is free in this object, and it is just this freedom that *is* spirituality—and this, we say, is religion. . . . The freedom of self-consciousness is the content of religion, and this content is itself the object of the Christian religion, i.e., spirit is its own object. This absolute being distinguishes itself at one and the same time into absolute power and subject; it communicates itself in what is distinguished from it while at the same time remaining undivided, so that the other is also the whole—all this, along with its return to itself, is the concept of religion. [It] constitutes the totality of spirituality, it is the very nature of spirituality. This concept is the absolute idea, which has previously been [an object] for us in our study of religion, and [is] now itself the object [for itself]; spirit is identical with spirit.

"Community Spirit"

The third element in the Trinitarian movement of the Spirit is the emergence of the community. As is well known, Hegel believed that it is in Protestant communities that the "turn to inwardness" is best expressed, over against Catholicism, which stops at the "objectifying representation of the Son."

From Hegel, *Lectures on the Philosophy of Religion (1824)* (Hodgson, 244).

C. The Third Element: Community Spirit

This is the transition from externality, from appearance, to inwardness. What it is concerned with is subjectivity, the certainty felt by the subject of its own infinite, nonsensible essentiality, the certainty with which it knows itself to be infinite, to be eternal, immortal. Beyond that there is the subject's being filled with the truth, and the fact that this truth is in self-consciousness *as* self-consciousness, that it is not external but is there as the inward truth of thought, as the representation of inwardness as such. At first, subjectivity and the knowledge of its essence is the knowledge of a sensibly present content. This is obviously nonspiritual, transitory; yet it is not merely transitory, but essentially *transitional*—it is a door where one cannot tarry, a form that is destined to be sublated, a form that is defined not merely as past but as belonging eternally to the spiritual nature of God. This is the turning to the inward path, and in this third realm we find ourselves on the soil of spirit as such—this is the *community*, the *cultus, faith*

We have defined the manifestation of God first as revelatory and second as appearance. The third [moment of manifestation] is knowledge or faith, for faith is also knowledge, but in a distinctive form. This third [moment] we now have to consider.

It consists, then, in the divine content being posited as *self-conscious* knowledge of this content, posited in the element of self-consciousness, of inwardness. On the one hand it is the knowledge that the content is the truth, and [on the other hand] that it is the truth of finite spirit as such—that is to say, the knowledge of it belongs to finite spirit so that finite spirit has its freedom in this knowledge, and is itself the process of casting off its particular individuality and of liberating itself in this content.

Hegel names the transition from the sensible appearance to the internal spiritual state in the aftermath of the departure of Jesus "the outpouring of the Spirit."

From Hegel, *Lectures on the Philosophy of Religion (1824)* (Hodgson, 248–49).

This transition is what is termed the *outpouring of the Spirit*. It could occur only after the Christ who had become flesh had withdrawn, after his sensible, immediate presence had ceased; then for the first time the Spirit issued forth. What the Spirit alone produces is something else, has another form.

We have arrived, then, at the issuing forth of the Spirit in the community. . . . The third [moment] is that the Spirit defines itself as the unity of the first two. . . . This third [moment] consists in what was already there in the Son—namely, that spirit is objective for itself, that it objectifies itself as the unity of the first and the second [moments], so that the second [moment], otherness, is sublated in eternal love. But this love expresses initially [i.e., in God made flesh] a relationship, a knowing, a seeing of the one in the other, such that the two extremes remain independent; it expresses an identity in which the two extremes are not absorbed. Now, on the contrary, it is love [itself] that is defined as what is objective; this is the Spirit.

It is possible, in the form of a [particular] religion, to advance basically no further than the representation of the Son and those about him. This is perhaps the case principally in Catholicism, with the result that Mary, the Mother of God, and the saints are exalted, the Spirit being also recognized as spirit, but only entering into the picture, as it were, rather than dwelling in the church and abiding in its decrees. As a result the second [moment] is brought to the fore in its sensible form for sensible imagination, rather than being spiritualized, and spirit does not essentially become an object.

The Neo-Calvinist School

Abraham Kuyper

A Dutch Christian minister and theologian who towards the end of his productive life was appointed prime minister of the Netherlands in the beginning of the twentieth century, Abraham Kuyper was also a journalist, founder of the antirevolutionary party, and instrumental in the founding of the Free University of Amsterdam. The preface to the magisterial *The Work of the Holy Spirit* makes it clear that Kuyper aligns himself with Calvin.

Common Grace
One of Kuyper's greatest contributions was the development of the Reformed idea of "common grace," which he conceived pneumatologically. (Unfortunately, only fragments of Kuyper's three-volume work on common grace have been translated from Dutch to English.)

From Abraham Kuyper, "Common Grace," in *Abraham Kuyper: A Centennial Reader*, ed. James D. Bratt (Grand Rapids: Wm. B. Eerdmans Publishing Co., 1998), 181.

Naturally . . . we have to distinguish between the two very distinct operations of common grace. Though "common grace" impacts the whole of our human life, it does not impact all aspects of this life in the same way. One common grace aims at the *interior*, another at the *exterior* part of our existence. The former is operative wherever civic virtue, a sense of domesticity, natural love, the practice of human virtue, the improvement of the public conscience, integrity, mutual loyalty among people, and a feeling for piety leaven life. The latter is in evidence when human power over nature increases, when invention upon invention enriches life, when international communication is improved, the arts flourish, the sciences increase our understanding, the conveniences and joys of life multiply, all expressions of life become more vital and radiant, forms become more refined, and the general image of life becomes more winsome.

While distinctions should be made for the sake of theological clarity, the Dutch theologian also emphasizes that there is but one grace—one work—of God. In other words, Kuyper attempts to help theology in general and Reformed tradition in particular to find an integral connection between the work of Christ and Spirit in creation, election, redemption, and new creation. Interestingly enough, he finds resources for such a wider perspective also in the Old Testament history, as the following citiation illustrates.

From Kuyper, "Common Grace," 184–85, 169.

It must again get through to the Reformed mind that the work of creation and the work of redemption—and to that extent also the work of common and of special grace—find a higher unity in Christ only because the eternal Son of God is behind both starting points, and that the Father together with the Son and the Holy Spirit as the triune God has himself posed this starting point and the point at which the two operations diverge.

That there is in fact a connection between the *saving* grace which is *special* and the *restraining* grace which is *common* cannot be doubted. This is immediately evident from the undeniable fact that, without common grace, the elect would not have been born, would not have seen the light of day. Had Adam and Eve died the day they sinned, Seth would not have been born from them, nor Enoch from Seth, and no widely ramified race of peoples and nations would ever have originated on earth. On that basis alone all special grace assumes *common grace*. . . . From whatever angle one looks at this issue, then, special grace presupposes *common grace*. Without the latter the former cannot function.

Ordo Salutis

In the long line of the Reformed tradition, Kuyper presents in his pneumatology a fairly typical *ordo salutis*, order of salvation.

From Abraham Kuyper, *The Work of the Holy Spirit*, trans. Henri De Vries (Grand Rapids: Wm. B. Eerdmans Publishing Co., 1946), 295–97, http://www.ccel.org.

For a correct idea of the entire work of grace in its different phases let us notice the following successive stages or milestones:

1. *The implanting of the new life principle*, commonly called *regeneration* in the limited sense, or the implanting of the faith-*faculty*. . . .

2. *The keeping of the implanted principle of life*, while the sinner still continues in sin, so far as his consciousness is concerned. Persons who received the life-principle early in life are no more dead, but live. Dying before actual conversion, they are not lost, but saved. In early life they often manifest holy inclinations; sometimes truly marvelous . . .

3. The *call* by the Word and the Spirit, internal and external. Even this is a divine act, commonly performed through the service of the Church. It addresses itself not to the deaf but to the hearing, not to the dead but to the living, altho [*sic*] still slumbering. It proceeds from the Word and the Spirit, because not only the faith-*faculty*, but faith itself—i.e., the *power* and *exercise* of the faculty—are gifts of grace. . . .

4. This call of God produces *conviction of sin and justification*, two acts of the same exercise of faith. . . .

5. This exercise of faith results in *conversion*; at this stage in the way of grace the child of God becomes clearly *conscious* of the implanted life. . . . Conversion does not become a fact so long as the sinner only *sees* his lost condition, but when he *acts* upon this principle; for then the old man begins to die and the new man begins to rise, and these are the two parts of all real conversion. . . . There is this difference, however, that in regeneration and faith's first exercise he was *passive*, while in conversion grace enabled him to be *active*. One is converted and one converts himself; the one is incomplete without the other.

6. Hence conversion merges itself in *sanctification*. This is also a divine act, and not human; not a growing toward Christ, but an absorbing of His life through the roots of faith. . . .

7. Sanctification is finished and closed in the *complete redemption* at the time of death. In the severing of body and soul divine grace completes the dying to sin. Hence in death a work of grace is performed which imparts to the work of regeneration its fullest unfolding. If until then, considering ourselves out of Christ, we are still lost in ourselves and lying in the midst of death, the article of death ends all this. Then faith is *turned into sight*, sin's excitement is disarmed, and we are forever beyond its reach.

Lastly, our *glorification* in the last day, when the inward bliss will be manifest in outward glory, and by an act of omnipotent grace the soul will be reunited with its glorified body, and be placed in such heavenly glory as becomes the state of perfect felicity.

An Inclusive View of Salvation and Grace

Typical of Kuyper, his exposition of the work of grace with regard to salvation is inclusive and challenges a typical misunderstanding according to which grace would merely help the sinner return, as it were, to the original state of blessedness.

From Kuyper, *Work of the Holy Spirit*, 48–49.

The subsequent activity of the Holy Spirit lies in the realm of grace. In nature the Spirit of God appears as creating, in grace as re-creating. We call it *re*-creation, because God's grace creates not something inherently new, but a new life in an old and degraded nature.

But this must not be understood as tho [*sic*] grace restored only what sin had *destroyed*. For then the child of God, born anew and sanctified, must be as Adam was in Paradise before the fall. Many understand it so, and present it as follows: In Paradise Adam became diseased; the poison of eternal corruption entered his soul and penetrated his whole being. Now comes the Holy Spirit as the physician, carrying the remedy of grace to heal him. He pours the balm into his wounds, He heals his bruises and renews his youth; and thus man, born again, healed, and renewed, is, according to their view, precisely what the first man was in the state of rectitude. Once more the provisions of the covenant of works are laid upon him. By his good works he is again to inherit eternal life. Again he may fall like Adam and become a prey of eternal death.

But this whole view is wrong. Grace does not place the ungodly in a state of *rectitude*, but *justifies* him—two very different things. He that stands in a state of rectitude has certainly an original righteousness, but this he may lose; he may be tried and fail as Adam failed. He must vindicate his righteousness. Its inward consistency must discover itself. He who is righteous to-day may be unrighteous to-morrow.

But when God justifies a sinner He puts Him in a totally different state. The righteousness of Christ becomes his. And what is this righteousness? Was Jesus in a state of rectitude only? In no wise. His righteousness was tested, tried, and sifted; it was even tested by the consuming fire of God's wrath. And this righteousness converted from "*original rectitude*" into "*righteousness vindicated*" was imputed to the ungodly.

Therefore the ungodly, when justified by grace, has nothing to do with Adam's state *before the fall*, but occupies the position of Jesus *after the resurrection*. He possesses a good that can not be lost. He works no more for wages, but the inheritance is his own. His works, zeal, love, and praise flow not from his own poverty, but from the overflowing fulness of the life that was obtained for him. As it is often expressed: For Adam in Paradise there was first work and then the Sabbath of rest; but for the ungodly justified by grace the Sabbath rest comes first, and then the labor which flows from the energies of that Sabbath. In the beginning the week closed with the Sabbath; for us the day of the resurrection of Christ opens the week which feeds upon the powers of that resurrection.

Hence the great and glorious work of re-creation has two parts: First, the removing of corruption, the healing of the breach, the death to sin, the atonement for guilt. Second, the reversing of the first order, the changing of the entire state, the bringing in and establishing of a new order.

The Spirit in the World and Cosmos

While Kuyper's main pneumatological work, *The Work of the Holy Spirit*, majors in soteriological aspects of the Spirit's work, it is by no means limited to these aspects. The following two citations illustrate this more inclusive orientation, first with regard to the sustenance of life, second, with regard to the general gifting of human beings.

From Kuyper, *Work of the Holy Spirit*, 43–45, 39.

Let us not be understood to say that God comes into contract with the creature only in the regeneration of His children, which would be untrue. . . . And this puts the work of the Holy Spirit in a light quite different from that in which for many years the Church has looked upon it. The general impression is that His work refers to the life of grace only, and is confined to regeneration and sanctification. This is due more or less to the well-known division of the Apostolic Creed by the Heidelberg Catechism, question 29, "How are these articles divided?" which is answered: "Into three parts—of God the Father and our creation, of God the Son and our redemption, and of God the Holy spirit and our sanctification." . . . And yet, inadmissible as this view may be, it is more reverent and God-fearing than the crude superficialities of the current views that confine the Spirit's operations entirely to the elect, beginning only at their regeneration.

From the whole Scripture teaching we therefore conclude that the Holy Spirit has a work in connection with mechanical arts and official functions—in every special talent whereby some men excel in such art or office. This teaching is not simply that such gifts and talents are not of man but from God like all other blessings, but that they are not the work of the Father, nor of the son, but of the Holy Spirit.

Speaking in Tongues

Unlike many Reformed theologians of his own time, Kuyper analyzes carefully the phenomenon and contemporary meaning of the appearance of speaking in tongues at the Day of Pentecost and its relation to the speaking in tongues that the New Testament designates as one of the regular gifts in the church.

From Kuyper, *Work of the Holy Spirit*, 133–35.

The third sign following the outpouring of the Holy Spirit consisted in extraordinary sounds that proceeded from the lips of the apostles—sounds foreign to the Aramaic tongue, never before heard from their lips. . . . The question how to interpret this wonderful sign has occupied the thinking minds of all times. Allow us to offer a solution, which we present in the following observations:

In the first place—This phenomenon of spiritual speaking in extraordinary sounds is not confined to Pentecost nor to the second chapter of the Acts. On the contrary, the Lord told His disciples, even before the ascension, that they should speak with new tongues—Mark xvi. 8. And from the epistles of St. Paul it is evident that this prophecy did not refer to Pentecost alone; for we read in 1 Cor. xii. 10 that in the apostolic Church, spiritual gifts included that of tongues; that some spoke in . . . kinds of tongues or sounds. . . . That the gift of tongues mentioned by St. Paul and the sign of which St. Luke speaks in Acts ii are substantially one and the same can not be doubted. In the first place Christ's prophecy is general: "They shall speak, with new tongues." Secondly, both phenomena are said to have made irresistible impressions upon unbelievers. Thirdly, both are treated as spiritual gifts. And lastly, to both is applied the same name.

Yet there was a very *perceptible difference* between the two: the miracle of tongues on the day of Pentecost was intelligible to a large number of hearers of different nationalities; while in the apostolic churches it was understood only by a few who were called interpreters. Connected with this is the fact that the miracle on Pentecost made the impression of speaking at once to different hearers in different tongues so that they were edified. However, this is no fundamental difference. Altho in the apostolic churches there were but few interpreters, yet there were some who understood the wonderful speech.

There was, moreover, a marked difference between the men thus endowed: some understood what they were saying; others did not. For St. Paul admonishes them, saying: "Let him that speaketh in an unknown tongue, pray that he may interpret" (1 Cor. xiv. 13). Yet even without this ability, the speaking with tongues had an edifying effect upon the speaker himself; but it was an edification not understood, the effect of an unknown operation in the soul.

From this we gather that the miracle of tongues consisted in the uttering of extraordinary sounds which from existing data could be explained neither by the speaker nor by the hearer; and to which another grace was sometimes added, viz., that of interpretation. Hence three things were possible: that the speaker alone understood what he said; or, that others understood it and not himself; or, that both speaker and hearers understood it. This understanding has reference to one or more persons.

On the ground of this we comprise these miracles of tongues in one class; with this distinction, however, that on the day of Pentecost the miracle appeared *perfect*, but later on *incomplete*. As there is in the miracles of Christ in raising the dead a perceptible increase of power: first, the raising up of one just dead (the daughter of Jairus), then, of one about to be buried (the young man of Nam), and lastly, of one already decomposing (Lazarus); so there is also in the miracle of tongues a difference of power—not *increasing*, but *decreasing*. The mightiest operation of the Holy Spirit is seen first, then those less powerful. It is precisely the same as in our own heart: first, the mighty fact of regeneration; after that, the less marked manifestations of spiritual power. Hence on Pentecost there was the miracle of tongues in its perfection; later on in the churches, in weaker measure.

Reformed Orthodoxy

Charles Hodge

For half a century, Charles Hodge was professor of theology at Princeton Seminary and, with B. B. Warfield, the most noted defender of Calvinism and Reformed theology in their conservative forms. His main work is his three-volume *Systematic Theology*.

The Inspiration of Scripture
One of the key values of Reformed orthodoxy was to defend the divine inspiration by the Holy Spirit of Scripture.

From Charles Hodge, *Systematic Theology*, 3 vols.
(New York: Charles Scribner's Sons, 1917), 1:156–57, 163.

A third point included in the Church doctrine of inspiration is, that the sacred writers were the organs of God, so that what they taught, God taught. It is to be remembered, however, that when God uses any of his creatures as his instruments, He uses them according to their nature. . . . Men are intelligent voluntary agents; and as such were made the organs of God. The sacred writers were not made unconscious or irrational. The spirits of the prophets were subject to the prophets. (1 Cor. xiv. 32.) They were not like calculating machines which grind out logarithms with infallible correctness. . . . The Church has never held what has been stigmatized as the mechanical theory of inspiration. The sacred writers were not machines. Their self-consciousness was not suspended; nor were their intellectual powers superseded. Holy men spake as they were moved by the Holy Ghost. It was men, not machines; not unconscious instruments, but living, thinking, willing minds, whom the Spirit used as his organs. Moreover, as inspiration did not involve the suspension or suppression of the human faculties, so neither did it interfere with the free exercise of the distinctive mental characteristics of the individual. All this is involved in the fact that God uses his instruments according to their nature . . . nevertheless, and none the less, they spoke as they were moved by the Holy Ghost, and their words were his words. . . . This is the fourth element of the Church doctrine on this subject. It means, first, that all the books of Scripture are equally inspired. All alike are infallible in what they teach, and secondly, that inspiration extends to all the contents of these several books. It is not confined to moral and religious truths, but extends to the statements of facts, whether scientific, historical, or geographical. It is not confined to those facts the importance of which is obvious, or which are involved in matters of doctrine. It extends to which any sacred writer asserts to be true.

The Spirit and Grace

Utilizing the classical terminological apparatus of Christian tradition, Hodge offers a highly nuanced discussion of the relationship between grace, Spirit, and truth.

From Hodge, *Systematic Theology*, 2:654–55, 660–61.

A work of grace is the work of the Holy Spirit; the means of grace are the means by which, or in connection with which, the influence of the Spirit is conveyed or exercised. By common grace, therefore, is meant that influence of the Spirit, which . . . [is] granted to all who hear the truth. By sufficient grace is meant such kind and degree of the Spirit's influence as is sufficient to lead men to repentance, faith, and a holy life. By efficacious grace is meant such an influence of the Spirit as is certainly effectual in producing regeneration mid conversion. By preventing grace is intended that operation of the Spirit on the mind which precedes and excites its efforts to return to God. By the *gratia gratum faciens* is meant the influence of the Spirit which renews or renders gracious. Cooperating grace is that influence of the Spirit which aids the people of God in all the exercises of the divine life. By habitual grace is meant Holy Spirit as dwelling in believers; or, that permanent, immanent mind due to his abiding presence and power. . . . By grace, therefore, in this connection is meant the influence of the Spirit of God on the minds of men. This is an influence of the Holy Spirit distinct from, and accessary to the influence of the truth. There is a natural relation between truth, whether speculative, aesthetic, moral, or religious, and the mind of man. . . .

An inward teaching by the Spirit is absolutely necessary to give the truth effect. This distinction between the outward teaching of the Word and the inward teaching of the Spirit is kept up throughout the Scriptures. . . .

3. The Scriptures therefore teach that there is an influence of the Spirit required to prepare the minds of men for the reception of the truth. The truth is compared to light, which is absolutely necessary to vision; but if the eye be closed or blind it must be opened or restored before the light can produce its proper impression. . . .

4. Accordingly the great promise of the Scriptures especially in reference to the Messianic period was the effusion of the Holy Spirit. "Afterward," said the prophet Joel, "I will pour out my Spirit upon all flesh" (ii. 28). The effects which the Spirit was to produce prove that something more, and something different from the power of the truth was intended. The truth however clearly revealed and however imbued with supernatural energy could not give the power to prophesy, or to dream dreams or to see visions. The Old Testament abounds with predictions and promises of this gift of the Holy Ghost, which was to attend and to render effectual the clearer revelation of the things of God to be made by the Messiah. Isaiah xxxii. 15, . . . Isaiah xliv. 3, . . . [and] Ezekiel xxxix. 29.

Union and Renewal of Life

In keeping with the Reformed understanding of the central role of the Holy Spirit in the life of the Christian who lives in union with his or her Savior, Hodge speaks of sanctification and renewal.

From Charles Hodge, *The Way of Life* (London:
Banner of Truth Trust, 1959), 224–25, 227, 229.

The Scriptures . . . teach, that believers are so united to Christ, that
they are not only partakers of the merit of his death, but also of his
Holy Spirit, which dwells in them as a principle of life, bringing
them more and more into conformity with the image of God, and
working in them both to will and to do, according to his own good
pleasure. . . . Being united to Christ in his death, they are partakers
of his life, and in virtue of this union they bring forth fruit unto God.
They are henceforth led by the Spirit which dwells in them; and this
Spirit is a source of life, not only to the soul, but also to the body;
for if the Spirit of him that raised Christ from the dead dwell in us,
he that raised up Christ from the dead shall also quicken our bodies by his Spirit that dwelleth in us. The doctrine of sanctification,
therefore, as taught in the Bible, is, that we are made holy not by the
force of conscience, or of moral motives, nor by acts of discipline,
but by being united to Christ so as to become reconciled to God, and
partakers of the Holy Ghost. Christ is made unto us sanctification as
well as justification. He not only frees from the penalty of the law,
but he makes holy. . . .

The effects ascribed to this union, as already stated, are an interest
in the merits of Christ, in order to our justification, and the indwelling of his Spirit, in order to our sanctification. Its nature is variously
illustrated. It is compared to that union which subsists between a
representative and those for whom he acts. . . .

As union with Christ is the source of spiritual life, the means by
which that life is to be maintained and promoted are all related to
this doctrine, and derive from it all their efficacy.

Archibald Alexander Hodge

The son of Charles Hodge, Archibald Alexander Hodge was the principal theologian of Princeton seminary from 1878 to 1886. His *Outlines of
Theology*, from which many of the following quotations are drawn, is a
milestone defense of conservative Christian doctrines.

The Holy Spirit as Person
A. A. Hodge offers here a detailed argumentation for the personal nature
of the Spirit.

From A. A. Hodge, *Outlines of Theology*, rev. and enlarg.
(Grand Rapids: Wm. B. Eerdmans, 1949), 174–76.

31. *How can it be proved that all the attributes of personality are ascribed to the Holy Ghost in the Scriptures?*

The attributes of personality are such as intelligence, volition, separate agency. Christ uses the pronouns, I, thou, he, when speaking of the relation of the Holy Spirit to himself and the Father: "I will send him" [John 16:7]. "He will testify of me" [John 15:26]. "Whom the Father will send in my name" [John 14:26]. Thus he is sent; he testifies; he takes of the things of Christ, and shows them to us. He teaches and leads to all truth. He knows, because he searches the deep things of God. He works all supernatural gifts, dividing to every man as he wills. . . .

32. *How may his personality be argued from the offices which he is said in the Scriptures to execute?*

The New Testament throughout all its teachings discovers the plan of redemption as essentially involving the agency of the Holy Ghost in applying the salvation which it was the work of the Son to accomplish. He inspired the prophets and apostles; he teaches and sanctifies the church; he selects her officers, qualifying them by the communication of special gifts at his will. He is the advocate, every Christian is his client. He brings all the grace of the absent Christ to us, and gives it effect in our persons in every moment of our lives. His personal distinction is obviously involved in the very nature of these functions which he discharges. . . .

34. *How may his personality be proved by what is said of the sin against the Holy Ghost?*

In Matt. xii. 31, 32; Mark iii. 28, 29; Luke xii. 10, this sin is called "blasphemy against the Holy Ghost." Now, blasphemy is a sin committed against a person, and it is here distinguished from the same act as committed against the other persons of the Trinity.

35. *How can such expressions as "giving" and "pouring out the Spirit" be reconciled with his personality?*

These and other similar expressions are used figuratively to set it forth our participation in the gifts and influences of the Spirit. It is one of the most natural and common of all figures to designate the gift by the name of the giver. Thus we are said "to put on Christ," "to be baptized into Christ," etc. . . .

40. *How can such expressions as, "he shall not speak of himself" be reconciled with his divinity?*

This and other similar expressions are to be understood as referring to the official work of the Spirit; just as the Son is said in his official character to be sent by and to be subordinate to the Father. The object of the Holy Ghost, in his official work in the hearts of men, is not to reveal the relations of his own person to the other persons of the Godhead, but simply to reveal the mediatorial character and work of Christ.

Justification and Sanctification

The relationship between justification and sanctification is explained with reference to the work of the Spirit.

From Hodge, *Outlines of Theology*, 522.

6. *What is the relation which justification and sanctification sustain to each other?*

In the order of nature, regeneration precedes justification, although as to time they are always necessarily contemporaneous. The instant God regenerates a sinner he acts faith in Christ. The instant he acts faith in Christ he is justified, and sanctification, which is the work of carrying on and perfecting that which is begun in regeneration, is accomplished under the conditions of those new relations into which he is introduced by justification. In justification we are delivered from all the penal consequences of sin, and brought into such a state of reconciliation with God, and communion of the Holy Ghost, that we are emancipated from the bondage of legal fear, and endued with that spirit of filial confidence and love which is the essential principle of all acceptable obedience. Our justification, moreover, proceeds on the ground of our federal union with Christ by faith, which is the basis of that vital and spiritual union of the soul with him from whom our sanctification flows.

Sanctification is the work of the Holy Spirit.

From Hodge, *Outlines of Theology*, 523.

10. *What do the Scriptures teach as to the agency of the truth in the work of sanctification?*

The whole process of sanctification consists in the development and confirmation of the new principle of spiritual life implanted in the soul in regeneration, conducted by the Holy Ghost in perfect conformity to, and through the operation of the laws and habits of action natural to the soul as an intelligent, moral and free agent. Like the natural faculties both of body and mind, and the natural habits which modify the actions of those faculties, so Christian graces, or spiritual habits, are developed by exercise; the truths of the gospel being the objects upon which these graces act, and by which they are both excited and directed. Thus the divine loveliness of God presented in the truth, which is his image, is the object of our complacent love; his goodness of our gratitude; his promises of our trust; his judgments of our wholesome awe, and his commandments variously exercise us in the thousand forms of filial obedience.

Benjamin Warfield

Benjamin Breckinridge Warfield was professor of New Testament exegesis and literature at Princeton Seminary from 1887 until his death in 1921 and the leading defender of Reformed orthodoxy.

The Inspiration of Scripture
One of the dearest doctrines to the Princeton theologian was the authority and inspiration of Scripture. In 1881 Warfield coauthored with A. A. Hodge an essay on the inspiration and authority of Scripture that became a magna carta of conservative Christianity for many generations.

From Benjamin B. Warfield, "The Authority & Inspiration of the Scriptures" (orig. pub. *Westminster Teacher*, Sept. 1889), http://www.ondoctrine.com/2war0801.htm, n.p. (accessed Jan. 28, 2008).

Now it goes, of course, without saying, that the apostles were not given this supreme authority as legislators to the Church without preparation for their high functions, without previous instruction in the mind of Christ, without safeguards thrown about them in the prosecution of their task, without the accompanying guidance of the Holy Spirit. And nothing is more noticeable in the writings which they have given the Church than the claim which they pervasively make that in giving them they are acting only as the agents of Christ, and that those who wrote them wrote in the Spirit of Christ. Every Scripture of the Old Testament is inspired by God (2 Tim. iii. 16), and . . . we cannot fail to perceive that the apostles claim to be attended in their work of giving law to God's Church by prevailing superintending grace from the Holy Spirit. This is what is called inspiration. It does not set aside the human authorship of the books. But it puts behind the human also a divine authorship. It ascribes to the authors such an attending influence of the Spirit in the process of writing, that the words they set down become also the words of God; and the resultant writing is made not merely the expression of Paul's or John's or Peter's will for the churches, but the expression of God's will. . . .

The Leading of the Holy Spirit

Another famous essay of Warfield is titled "The Leading of the Spirit" (a chapter in *The Power of God unto Salvation* [Philadelphia: Presbyterian Board of Publication and Sabbath–School Work, 1903]), which is based on Rom. 8:14.

From Warfield, *The Power of God unto Salvation*, 152–59.

There is certainly abundant reason why we should seek to learn what the Scriptures mean by "spiritual leading." There are few subjects so intimately related to the Christian life, of which Christians appear to have formed, in general, conceptions so inadequate, where they are not even positively erroneous. The sober-minded seem often to look upon it as a mystery into which it would be well not to inquire too closely. And we can scarcely expect those who are not gifted with sobriety to guide us in such a matter into the pure truth of God. The consequence is that the very phrase, "the leading of the Spirit," has come to bear, to many, a flavor of fanaticism. Many of the best Christians would shrink with something like distaste from affirming themselves to be "led by the Spirit of God"; and would receive with suspicion such an averment on the part of others, as indicatory of an unbalanced religious mind. It is one of the saddest effects of extravagance in spiritual claims that, in reaction from them, the simple-minded people of God are often deterred from entering into their privileges. . . .

"As many as are led by the Spirit of God," says the apostle, "these are sons of God." We have here in effect a definition of the sons of God. . . . Thus, the leading of the Spirit is presented as the very characteristic of the children of God. This is what differentiates them from all others. All who are led by the Spirit of God are thereby constituted the sons of God; and none can claim the high title of sons of God who are not led by the Spirit of God. The leading of the Spirit thus appears as the constitutive fact of sonship. . . . This leading of the Spirit is not some peculiar gift reserved for special sanctity and granted as the reward of high merit alone. It is the common gift poured out on all God's children to meet their common need, and is the evidence, therefore, of their common weakness and their common unworthiness. . . . When we consider this Divine work within our souls with reference to the end of the whole process we call it sanctification; when we consider it with reference to the process itself, as we struggle on day by day in the somewhat devious and always thorny pathway of life, we call it spiritual leading. Thus the "leading of the Holy Spirit" is revealed to us as simply a synonym for sanctification when looked at from the point of view of the pathway itself, through which we are led by the Spirit as we more and more advance toward that conformity to the image of His Son, which God has placed before us as our great goal.

It is obvious at once then how grossly it is misconceived when it is looked upon as a peculiar guidance granted by God to His eminent servants in order to insure their worldly safety, worldly comfort, even worldly profit. The leading of the Holy Spirit is always for good; but it is not for all goods, but specifically for spiritual and eternal good. . . .

Accordingly, we observe next that the spiritual leading of which Paul speaks is not something sporadic, given only on occasion of some special need of supernatural direction, but something continuous, affecting all the operations of a Christian man's activities throughout every moment of his life. . . . It is easy to estimate, then, what a perversion it is of the "leading of the Spirit" when this great saving energy of God, working continually in the sinner, is forgotten, and the name is accorded to some fancied sporadic supernatural direction in the common offices of life.

Cessationism

One of the more polemical writings of Warfield is titled *Counterfeit Miracles*, in which he argues along the lines of what is called cessationism, the belief that the miracles ceased after the closing of the canon in the fourth century because external "proofs" were no longer needed alongside Scripture. The following citations come from his article titled "The Cessation of the Charismata."

From Benjamin B. Warfield, "The Cessation of the Charismata," http://www.ondoctrine.com/2war0101.htm, n.p. (accessed Jan. 28, 2008).

When our Lord came down to earth He drew heaven with Him. The signs which accompanied His ministry were but the trailing clouds of glory which He brought from heaven, which is His home. The number of the miracles which He wrought may easily be underrated. It has been said that in effect He banished disease and death from Palestine for the three years of His ministry. If this is exaggeration it is pardonable exaggeration. Wherever He went, He brought a blessing. . . . His own divine power by which He began to found His church He continued in the Apostles whom He had chosen to complete this great work. They transmitted it in turn, as part of their own miracle-working and the crowning sign of their divine commission, to others, in the form of what the New Testament calls spiritual gifts in the sense of extraordinary capacities produced in the early Christian communities by direct gift of the Holy Spirit.

The number and variety of these spiritual gifts were considerable. Even Paul's enumerations, the fullest of which occurs in the twelfth chapter of I Corinthians, can hardly be read as exhaustive scientific catalogues. . . .

How long did this state of things continue? It was the characterizing peculiarity of specifically the Apostolic Church, and it belonged therefore exclusively to the Apostolic age—although no doubt this designation may be taken with some latitude. These gifts were not the possession of the primitive Christian as such; nor for that matter of the Apostolic Church or the Apostolic age for themselves; they were distinctively the authentication of the Apostles. They were part of the credentials of the Apostles as the authoritative agents of God in founding the church. Their function thus confined them to distinctively the Apostolic Church, and they necessarily passed away with it. Of this we may make sure on the ground both of principle and of fact; that is to say both under the guidance of the New Testament teaching as to their origin and nature, and on the credit of the testimony of later ages as to their cessation. . . .

The writings of the so-called Apostolic Fathers contain no clear and certain allusions to miracle-working or to the exercise of the charismatic gifts, contemporaneously with themselves. These writers inculcate the elements of Christian living in a spirit so simple and sober as to be worthy of their place as the immediate followers of the Apostles. . . . Irenaeus . . . adds a mention of two new classes of miracles—those of speaking with tongues and of raising the dead, to both of which varieties he is the sole witness during these centuries. . . . Tertullian in like manner speaks of exorcisms, and adduces one case of a prophetically gifted woman (Apol., xxviii; De Anima, ix); and Minucius Felix speaks of exorcism (Oct., XXVi). Origen professes to have been an eye-witness of many instances of exorcism, healing, and prophecy, although he refuses to record the details lest he should rouse the laughter of the unbeliever (Cent. Cels., I, ii; III, xxiv; VII, iv, lxvii). Cyprian speaks of gifts of visions and exorcisms. And so we pass on to the fourth century in an ever-increasing stream.

There is . . . a deeper principle recognizable here, of which the actual attachment of the charismata of the Apostolic Church to the mission of the Apostles is but an illustration. This deeper principle may be reached by us through the perception, more broadly, of the inseparable connection of miracles with revelation, as its mark and credential; or, more narrowly, of the summing up of all revelation, finally, in Jesus Christ. Miracles do not appear on the page of Scripture vagrantly, here, there, and elsewhere indifferently, without assignable reason. They belong to revelation periods, and appear only when God is speaking to His people through accredited messengers, declaring His gracious purposes. Their abundant display in the Apostolic Church is the mark of the richness of the Apostolic age in revelation; and when this revelation period closed, the period of miracle-working had passed by also, as a mere matter of course. . . . Because Christ is all in all, and all revelation and redemption alike are summed up in Him, it would be inconceivable that either revelation or its accompanying signs should continue after the completion of that great revelation with its accrediting works, by which Christ has been established in His rightful place as the culmination and climax and all-inclusive summary of the saving revelation of God, the sole and sufficient redeemer of His people.

Augustus Hopkins Strong

The most noted Baptist theologian of the turn of the twentieth century, Augustus H. Strong served four decades as president and professor of systematic theology at Rochester Theological Seminary. His magnum opus is the widely used three-volume *Systematic Theology*, in which he outlines a Reformed Baptist dogmatics.

The Spirit in the Trinity
Strong explicates his method of doing theology in general and Trinitarian theology in particular in a way indicative of his theological method, which is based on the primacy of Scripture and his view of authority.

From Augustus Hopkins Strong, *Systematic Theology: The Doctrine of God*, vol. 1 (Philadelphia: Judson Press, 1907), 343, http://www.ccel.org.

We therefore only formulate truth which is concretely expressed in Scripture, and which is recognized by all ages of the church in hymns and prayers addressed to Father, Son, and Holy Spirit, when we assert that in the nature of the one God there are three eternal distinctions, which are best described as persons, and each of which is the proper and equal object of Christian worship. We are also warranted in declaring that, in virtue of these personal distinctions or modes of subsistence, God exists in the relations, respectively, first, of Source, Origin, Authority, and in this relation is the Father; . . .

Secondly, of Expression, Medium, Revelation, and in this relation is the Son; thirdly, of Apprehension, Accomplishment, Realization, and in this relation is the Holy Spirit.

Ordo Salutis

In accordance with his theological method, Strong's exposition of calling following election in the typical Reformed *ordo salutis* is based primarily on Scripture.

> From Augustus Hopkins Strong, *Systematic Theology: The Doctrine of Salvation*, vol. 3 (Philadelphia: Judson Press, 1907), 790–91, http://www.ccel.org.

> Calling is that act of God by which men are invited to accept, by faith, the salvation provided by Christ.—The Scriptures distinguish between; (a) *The general, or external, call* to all men through God's providence, word, and Spirit . . . ; (b) *The special, efficacious call* of the Holy Spirit to the elect.

"Union with Christ" is one aspect of the typical Reformed order of salvation.

> From Strong, *Systematic Theology*, 3:795.

> The Scriptures declare that, through the operation of God, there is constituted a union of the soul with Christ different in kind from God's natural and providential concursus with all spirits, as well as from all unions of mere association or sympathy, moral likeness, or moral influence,—a union of life, in which the human spirit, while then most truly possessing its own individuality and personal distinctness, is interpenetrated and energized by the Spirit of Christ, is made inscrutably but indissolubly one with him and so becomes a member and partaker of that regenerated, believing and justified humanity of which he is the head.

The Baptist theologian continues by going into a more detailed description of this union, again supporting his views with a number of scriptural passages, which have not been copied here.

> From Strong, *Systematic Theology*, 3:798.

> (e) All believers are one in Christ. . . .
> (f) The believer is made partaker of the divine nature. . . .
> (g) The believer is made one spirit with the Lord. . . .

In the following he explains the nature of the union.

From Strong, *Systematic Theology*, 3:800–801.

(a) An organic union,—in which we become members of Christ and partakers of his humanity. . . .

(b) A vital union,—in which Christ's life becomes the dominating principle within us. This union is a vital one, in distinction from any union of mere juxtaposition or external influence.

(c) A spiritual union,—that is, a union whose source and author is the Holy Spirit. By a spiritual union we mean a union not of body but of spirit,—a union, therefore, which only the Holy Spirit originates and maintains.

(d) An indissoluble union,—that is, a union which, consistently with Christ's promise and grace, can never be dissolved.

(e) An inscrutable union,—mystical, however, only in the sense of surpassing in its intimacy and value any other union of souls which we know.

Strong considers various understandings of "The Efficient Cause of Regeneration" and argues for the last one, which focuses on the agency of the Holy Spirit.

From Strong, *Systematic Theology*, 3:814, 818–19.

Three views only need be considered,—all others are modifications of these. The first view puts the efficient cause of regeneration in the human will; the second, in the truth considered as a system of motives; the third, in the immediate agency of the Holy Spirit. . . .

The immediate agency of the Holy Spirit, as the efficient cause of regeneration.

In ascribing to the Holy Spirit the authorship of regeneration, we do not affirm that the divine Spirit accomplishes his work without any accompanying instrumentality. We simply assert that the power which regenerates is the power of God, and that although conjoined with the use of means, there is a direct operation of this power upon the sinner's heart which changes its moral character. We add two remarks by way of further explanation:

(a) The Scriptural assertions of the indwelling of the Holy Spirit and of his mighty power in the soul forbid us to regard the divine Spirit in regeneration as coming in contact, not with the soul but only with the truth. The phrases, "to energize the truth," "to intensify the truth," "to illuminate the truth," have no proper meaning;

since even God cannot make the truth more true. If any change is wrought, it must be wrought, not in the truth, but in the soul. . . .

Of faith and witness of the Spirit, Strong has the following to say, among other things.

From Strong, *Systematic Theology*, 3:844–45.

(c) That the ground of faith is the external word of promise. The ground of assurance, on the other hand, is the inward witness of the Spirit that we fulfil the conditions of the Promise (Rom. 4:20, 21; 8:16; Eph.1:13; 1 John 4:13; 5:10). This witness of the Spirit is not a new revelation from God, but a strengthening of faith so that it becomes conscious and indubitable. True faith is possible without assurance of salvation. But if [James Waddel] Alexander's view were correct, that the object of saying faith is the proposition: "God, for Christ's sake, now looks with reconciling love on me, a sinner," no one could believe, without being at the same time assured that he was a saved person. Upon the true view, that the object of saving faith is not a proposition, but a person, we can perceive not only the simplicity of faith, but the possibility of faith even where the soul is destitute of assurance or of joy. Hence those who already believe are urged to seek for assurance (Heb. 6:11; 2 Peter 1:10).

Here Strong utilizes the typical terminological distinctions of Reformed orthodoxy when explaining the divine and human agencies in salvation.

From Strong, *Systematic Theology*, 3:872.

The agency through which God effects the sanctification of the believer is the indwelling Spirit of Christ . . . [whereas] the mediate or instrumental cause of sanctification, as of justification, is faith.

PART II

Contemporary Theologies
of the Spirit and Salvation

Introduction to Twentieth-Century
Pneumatologies

Not surprisingly, the pneumatologies of the twentieth century and the beginning of the third millennium reflect the diversity, plurality, and pluriformity characteristic of all contemporary theologies. In addition to diversity, there is also an unprecedented pneumatological interest, perhaps even an enthusiasm. The rich flow of academic publications alongside various scholarly events devoted to the Holy Spirit are but the tip of the iceberg in the current pneumatological renaissance. There is also a general hunger for the Holy Spirit and for spiritual experiences among Christian churches and believers.

While pneumatological and soteriological traditions are being revisited, reinterpreted, and reconfigured as an essential part of the continuing constructive work, a new breed of pneumatological interpretations is also emerging, such as feminist and womanist, liberationist, sociopolitical, and ecological pneumatologies. True, none of these themes is absolutely new and untried in Christian theology; think only of the diversity in medieval interpretations of the Spirit. Yet, in a real sense, there is also much new in terms of the intensity, breadth, and depth of these so-called contextual views.

This section will first present and discuss the main theologico-ecclesiastical traditions in pneumatology from the oldest church, the Eastern Orthodox Church, to the newest group, the pentecostal/charismatic movements. Both denominational views and theologies of leading individual theologians will be discussed. The last part of this section will probe contextual interpretations, including the views of women and other liberationists as well those with political and ecological concerns.

CHAPTER 10

The Spirit in Eastern
Orthodox Theologies

Affirmation of Tradition:
Key Doctrinal Beliefs

A fitting introduction to the diverse and lively contemporary Eastern Orthodox pneumatological traditions is a concise statement from Rev. George Mastrantonis of the Greek Orthodox Archdiocese of America summarizing the fundamental teachings of the church, which stand on the long line of tradition.

From Rev. George Mastrantonis, "The Fundamental Teachings of the Eastern Orthodox Church," Greek Orthodox Archdiocese of America, http://www.goarch.org/en/ourfaith/articles/article7063.asp (accessed Mar. 18, 2008).

The Orthodox Church believes "in the Holy Ghost, the Lord, the Giver of life" (Nicene Creed). The Holy Spirit is the Third Person of the Holy Trinity, Who proceeds from the Father only (cf. John 15:26). The Church firmly opposed the opinion that the Holy Spirit was created by the Son, and pronounced the correct belief in the Nicene Creed at the Second Ecumenical Synod. The Orthodox Church does not use the phrase *filioque*, "and of the Son." According to the Scriptures, the Son Jesus Christ only sends the Holy Spirit in time, saying: "I will send unto you from the Father even the Spirit of truth which proceedeth from the Father" (John 15:26).

It is evident from the Scripture that the Holy Spirit proceeds from the Father only; this was the belief from the very beginning of the One Undivided Church. When the church in the West inserted the "*filioque*" phrase into the Creed, this innovation precipitated the Great Schism of the Undivided Church. The "*filioque*" phrase is an error. It is not found in the Scripture. It was not believed by the Undivided Church for eight centuries, including the church in the West. It introduces a strange teaching of a double procession of the Holy Spirit and refers to two origins of the Spirit's existence, thus denying the unity of the Godhead.

Known for its high regard of tradition, Greek Orthodoxy regards "the sacred tradition" as the work of the Holy Spirit.

From Anne K. Turley, "Articles on Aspects of Eastern Orthodox Christian Doctrine and Practices, Ecumenism, Contemporary Events, etc.," orig. pub. with the blessing of the Most Reverend Anthony Archbishop of Western American San Francisco, http://www.orthodox.net/articles/ heavenonearth.html (accessed Mar. 19, 2008).

Sacred Tradition

Just as the Grace of the Holy Spirit which descended on the Apostles at Pentecost flows in a living stream down through today's bishops and priests, so Sacred Tradition carries the spiritual life of the Church in an unbroken stream from the time of the Apostles down to Orthodox believers today. Sacred Tradition includes the unwritten acts and teachings of Christ and the Apostles which the Church preserves unchanged for us all (John 21:25; 2 Thess. 2:15; 2 Thess. 3:6). The power of Sacred Tradition is the power of the Holy Spirit as it influences Orthodox Christians in all ages. Through Sacred Tradition we are in communion with the spiritual life of all preceding generations back to the Apostles.

For Orthodox theology, the ultimate goal of all spiritual life is the reception of the Holy Spirit. While not limited to the religious, this aim is upheld especially in the monastic life, as the introduction to the Paracletos Greek Orthodox Monastery (Antreville, S.C.) indicates.

From "Paracletos Holy Spirit Monastery," http://www.greekorthodoxmonastery.org/MainPages/ HolySpirit.html (accessed Mar. 19, 2008).

Paracletos is the third person of the Holy Trinity. *"But when the Counselor comes, whom I shall send to you from the Father, even the Spirit of Truth, who proceeds from the Father, He will bear witness to Me"* (John 15:26). He appeared officially on the day of Pentecost, which is the birthday day of our Holy Church.

From that time, He continues to hold the Institution of the Church and to sanctify the faithful through His gifts. The purpose of our spiritual life is to obtain the Holy Spirit.

The purpose of the Monastic life is for the Monastics to be sanctified with the descent of the Holy Spirit, to receive His gifts and Comfort and to impart that to the contemporary suffering world.

Vladimir Lossky

Trinity, Incarnation, and the Spirit

Like several other exiled Russian Orthodox theologians, Vladimir Niko-laievich Lossky (d. 1958) spent the best days of his theological career in Paris, France. Famous for his *The Mystical Theology of the Eastern Church*, Lossky was dean of St. Denys Theological Institute, where he taught Orthodox dogmatics and philosophy. Here Lossky speaks of the mutual yet distinct work of the Spirit and Son in the Trinity.

From Vladimir Lossky, *Orthodox Theology: An Introduction*, trans. Ian and Ihita Kesarcodi-Watson (Crestwood, NY: St. Vladimir's Seminary Press, 1978), 47–48.

The Son and the Spirit thus appear, throughout the Gospel, as two divine persons sent into the world, the former to quicken our personal liberty, the latter to unite Itself with our nature and regenerate it. These two persons each have their proper relation to the Father (generation and procession); they also have between them a relationship of reciprocity: it is thanks to the purification of the Virgin by the Spirit that the Son could be given to men, as it is by the prayer of the Son ascended back to the right hand of the Father that the Spirit is dispensed to them ("the Protector Whom I will send you from the Father," John 15:26). . . . The Spirit leads us, through the Son, to the Father, where we discover the unity of the three. The Father, according to the terminology of St. Basil, reveals Himself through the Son in the Spirit. Here is affirmed a process, an order from which issues that of the three names: Father, Son and Holy Spirit.

Likewise all the divine names, which communicate to us the life common to the three, come to us from the Father through the Son in the Holy Spirit. The Father is the source, the Son the manifestation, the Spirit the force which manifests.

Against the "Filioque" Clause

Well known is the Orthodox opposition to the Western church's introduction of the *filioque* clause to the creeds. Here Lossky presents Orthodox theology's understanding of the proceeding of the Spirit in the Trinity.

From Vladimir Lossky, *The Mystical Theology of the Eastern Orthodox Church* (New York: St. Vladimir Seminary Press, 1976), 158–59.

Theologians have always insisted on the radical difference between the eternal procession of the Persons, which is, according to St. John Damascene, "the work of nature"—the very being of the Holy Trinity—and the temporal mission of the Son and of the Holy Spirit in the world, the work of the will which is common to the three hypostases. . . . On the level of the temporal mission, which is a work of the will belonging to the substance of the Trinity, the Son is sent by the Father and is incarnate by the Holy Spirit. . . . The same thing is true as to the mission of the Holy Spirit in the world. He performs the will which is common to the Three, being sent by the Father and imparted by the Son. . . .

Thus, just as the Son comes down to earth and accomplishes His work through the Spirit, so the Person of the Holy Spirit comes into the world, being sent by the Son: "the Comforter . . . whom I will send unto you from the Father, even the Spirit of truth, which proceedeth from the Father, he shall bear witness of me" (John xv, 26). Intimately linked as they are in the common work upon earth, the Son and the Holy Spirit remain nevertheless in this same work two persons independent the one of the other as to their hypostatic being. It is for this reason that the personal advent of the Holy Spirit does not have the character of a work which is subordinate, and in some sort functional, in relation to that of the Son. Pentecost is not a "continuation" of the Incarnation. It is its sequel, its result. The creature has become fit to receive the Holy Spirit and He descends into the world and fills with His presence the Church which has been redeemed, washed and purified by the blood of Christ.

Known for an apophatic approach to theology that advances via the negative, Orthodox theologians are keen on reminding of the mysterious, "hidden" nature of the third person of the Trinity.

Deification and Union

Lossky finds a parallel between the *kenosis* of the Son and that of the Spirit and links this idea with the Eastern church's view of salvation as union.

From Lossky, *Mystical Theology*, 169.

Quite distinct is the communication of the Holy Spirit at the time of His personal coming, when He appeared as a Person of the Trinity. . . . Then He appeared under the form of divided tongues of fire which rested upon *each one* of those who were present: upon each member of the body of Christ. This is no longer a communication of the Spirit to the Church considered corporately. This communication is far from being a function of unity. The Holy Spirit communicates Himself *to persons*, marking each member of the Church with a seal of personal and unique relationship to the Trinity, becoming present in each person. How does this come about? That remains a mystery—the mystery of the self-emptying, of the *kenosis* of the Holy Spirit's coming into the world. If in the *kenosis* of the Son the Person appeared to men while the Godhead remained hidden under the form of a servant, the Holy Spirit in His coming, while He manifests the common nature of the Trinity, leaves His own Person concealed beneath His Godhead. He remains unrevealed, hidden, so to speak, by the gift in order that this gift which He imparts may be fully ours, adapted to our persons.

In a remarkable way, Lossky speaks of the church as the place of union and deification.

From Lossky, *Mystical Theology*, 179, 181.

Some will be deified by the energies which they have acquired in the interior of their being; others will remain without, and for them the deifying fire of the Spirit will be an external flame, intolerable to all those whose will is opposed to God. The Church, then, is the sphere within which union with God takes place in this present life, the union which will be consummated in the age to come, after the resurrection of the dead.

All the conditions which are necessary that we may attain to union with God are given in the Church. This is why the Greek Fathers frequently liken it to the earthly paradise in which the first men were to have gained access to the state of deification. . . .

The Church surpasses the earthly paradise. The state of Christians is better than the condition of the first men. We no longer run the risk of losing irremediably our communion with God, for we are included in one body in which the blood of Christ circulates, purifying us from all sin and from every stain. The Word took flesh that we might receive the Holy Spirit. . . . In the Church and through the sacraments our nature enters into union with the divine nature in the hypostasis of the Son, the Head of His mystical body. Our humanity becomes consubstantial with the deified humanity, united with the person of Christ.

Pneumatological Ecclesiology

While Orthodox theology has not produced a full-scale ecclesiology, the tradition is known for the central role of the Spirit in the church. Lossky's favorite way of talking about that role is to refer to the Spirit and Christ as the dual foundation of the church.

From Lossky, *Mystical Theology*, 156–57.

A new reality came into the world, a body more perfect than the world—the Church, founded on a twofold divine economy: the work of Christ and the work of the Holy Spirit, the two persons of the Trinity sent into the world. The work of both persons forms the foundation of the Church. The work of both is requisite that we may attain to union with God.

If Christ is "Head of the Church which is his body," the Holy Spirit is He "that filleth all in all" (Eph. i, 23). Thus, the two definitions of the Church which St. Paul gives show two different poles within her which correspond to the two divine persons. The Church is *body* in so far as Christ is her head; she *is fullness* in so far as the Holy Spirit quickens her and fills her with divinity, for the Godhead dwells within her bodily as it dwelt in the deified humanity of Christ. We may say with Irenaeus: "where the Church is, there is the Spirit; where the Spirit is, there is the Church" (*Contra Haeres.*, III, 24, i, P.G., VII, 966 C).

In the church, the Holy Spirit works continually for her renewal and rejuvenation. Thus, the joint work of the Spirit and the Son results in a unity-in-diversity.

From Lossky, *Mystical Theology*, 167.

Thus, the work of Christ unifies; the work of the Holy Spirit diversifies. Yet, the one is impossible without the other. The unity of nature is realized in persons; and persons can only attain to perfection— become fully *personal*—within that unity of nature, in ceasing to be "individuals" living for themselves, having their separate individual nature and will. The work of Christ and the work of the Holy Spirit are therefore inseparable. Christ creates the unity of His mystical body through the Holy Spirit; the Holy Spirit communicates Himself to human persons through Christ. Indeed, it is possible to distinguish two communications of the Holy Spirit to the Church: one was effected by the breath of Christ when He appeared to His apostles on the evening of the day of His resurrection (John xx, 19–23); the other by the personal coming of the Holy Spirit on the day of Pentecost (Acts ii, 1–5).

The Spirit and the Sacraments

Eastern sacramental theology is highly pneumatological and christological.

From Lossky, *Mystical Theology*, 170–71.

For the mystical tradition of Eastern Christendom, Pentecost, which confers the presence of the Holy Spirit and the first-fruits of sanctification upon human persons, signifies both the end and final goal, and, at the same time, marks the commencement of the spiritual life. As He descended upon the disciples in tongues of fire, so the Holy Spirit descends invisibly upon the newly-baptized in the sacrament of the holy chrism. In the Eastern rite confirmation follows immediately upon baptism. The Holy Spirit is operative in both sacraments. He recreates our nature by purifying it and uniting it to the body of Christ. He also bestows deity—the common energy of the Holy Trinity which is divine grace—upon human persons. It is on account of this intimate connection between the two sacraments of baptism and confirmation that the uncreated and deifying gift, which the descent of the Holy Spirit confers upon the members of the Church, is frequently referred to as "baptismal grace." . . . This baptismal grace is so great, this source of life so necessary to man, that it is not withdrawn from a heretic until the hour of his death, until that day which Providence assigned to man to prove him during his life upon earth.

John Zizioulas

Proper Synthesis between Pneumatology and Christology

Along with Bishop Kallistos Diokleia (Timothy Ware), the titular metropolitan of Pergamon, Greece, John Zizioulas is the most well-known living Orthodox theologian in the West. His highly acclaimed *Being as Communion: Studies in Personhood and Church* of 1985 is a landmark theological work. While building on Orthodox tradition, both ancient and modern, Zizioulas is also critical of some of his own church's harsh criticism toward the alleged "Christomonism" of the Christian West.

From John Zizioulas, *Being as Communion: Studies in Personhood and Church* (Crestwood, NY: St. Vladimir's Seminary Press, 1985), 123–24.

One of the fundamental criticisms that Orthodox theologians expressed in connection with the ecclesiology of Vatican II concerned the place which the council gave to Pneumatology in its ecclesiology. In general, it was felt that in comparison with Christology, Pneumatology did not play an important role in the council's teaching on the Church. More particularly, it was observed that the Holy Spirit was brought into ecclesiology *after* the edifice of the

Church was constructed with Christological material alone. . . . This criticism may be on the whole a valid one, but when we come to the point of asking what its *positive* aspect is, namely what the Orthodox would in fact like to see the council do with Pneumatology in its ecclesiology, then we are confronted with problems. . . . [It is] clear . . . that Orthodox theology needs to do a great deal of reflection on the relationship between Christology and Pneumatology, and that the actual state of Orthodox theology in this respect is by no means satisfactory.

Having acknowledged the lack of a proper synthesis between Christology and pneumatology even in his own tradition, Zizioulas outlines a constructive proposal.

From Zizioulas, *Being as Communion*, 126–28, 130–32, 136.

What would a proper synthesis between Christology and Pneumatology have to include? This question must be asked before any attempt is made to tackle the problem of ecclesial institutions. . . . Few people if any would question the statement that Christology and Pneumatology belong together and cannot be separated. To speak of "Christomonism" in any part of the Christian tradition is to misunderstand or be unfair to this part of tradition. . . . The problem is not whether one accepts the importance of Pneumatology in Christology and vice versa; it arises in connection with the following two questions: (i) The question of *priority*: should Christology be made dependent on Pneumatology or should the order be the other way around? (ii) The question of *content*: when we speak of Christology and Pneumatology, what *particular* aspects of Christian doctrine— and Christian existence—do we have in mind?

First, the question of priority. That this is a *real* question and not the product of a theological construction is to be seen in the fact that not only the entire history of theology in what concerns the East-West relationship, but even the most primitive theology and liturgical practice we know of are conditioned by this problem. In the New Testament writings themselves we come across both the view that the Spirit is given *by* Christ, particularly the risen and ascended Christ . . . and the view that there is, so to say, *no Christ* until the Spirit is at work, not only as *a forerunner* announcing his coming, but also as the one who *constitutes his very identity as Christ*, either at his baptism (Mark) or at his very biological conception (Matthew and Luke). Both of these views could co-exist happily in one and the same Biblical writing, as is evident from a study of Luke (Gospel and Acts), John's Gospel, etc. . . . The most obvious thing to mention is that only the Son is incarnate. Both the Father and the Spirit are involved in history, but only the Son *becomes* history. . . . Now if *becoming* history is the particularity of the Son in the economy, what is the contribution of the Spirit? Well, precisely the opposite: it is to liberate the Son and the economy from the bondage of history. If the Son dies on the cross, thus succumbing to the bondage of historical existence, it is the Spirit that raises him from the dead (Romans 8:11). The Spirit is the *beyond* history, and when he acts in history he does so in order to bring into history the last days, the *eschaton*. Hence the first fundamental particularity of Pneumatology is its eschatological character. The Spirit makes of Christ an eschatological being, the "last Adam."

Another important contribution of the Holy Spirit to the Christ event is that, because of the involvement of the Holy Spirit in the economy, Christ is not just an individual, not "one" but "many." This "corporate personality" of Christ is impossible to conceive without Pneumatology. It is not insignificant that the Spirit has always, since the time of Paul, been associated with the notion of *communion* (Koinonia) (2 Corinthians 13:13). Pneumatology contributes to Christology this dimension of communion. And it is because of this function of Pneumatology that it is possible to speak of Christ as having a "body," i.e. to speak of ecclesiology, of the Church as the Body of Christ. . . .

It is not enough to speak of eschatology and communion as necessary aspects of Pneumatology and ecclesiology; it is necessary to make these aspects of Pneumatology *constitutive* of ecclesiology. What I mean by "constitutive" is that these aspects of Pneumatology must qualify the very ontology of the Church. The Spirit is not something that "animates" a Church which already somehow exists. The Spirit makes the Church *be*. Pneumatology does not refer to the well-being but to the very being of the Church. It is not about a dynamism which is added to the essence of the Church. It is the very essence of the Church. The Church is *constituted* in and through eschatology and communion.

Pneumatology is an ontological category in ecclesiology. . . . There is no "one" which is not at the same time "many"—is this not the same as the pneumatologically conditioned Christology, which we mentioned earlier? Pneumatology, by being constitutive of both Christology and ecclesiology, makes it impossible to think of Christ as an individual, i.e. of Christ without his Body, the "many," or to think of the Church as one without simultaneously thinking of her as "many."

Timothy Ware/Bishop Kallistos
of Diaklcia

Timothy Ware of England, a convert to Orthodoxy from Anglicanism, served for several decades as a lecturer at the University of Oxford, teaching Eastern Orthodox studies. In 1982 he was made the titular bishop of Diokleia. With Zizioulas, he is the most well-known and articulate spokesperson for and interpreter of Orthodox tradition to the Christian West. In keeping with the apophatic tradition of his church, Bishop Kallistos speaks of the Holy Spirit as something elusive.

From Kallistos Ware, *The Orthodox Way* (Crestwood, NY:
St. Vladimir's Seminary Press, 1979), 119.

There is a secret and hidden quality about the Holy Spirit, which makes it hard to speak or write about him. As St Symeon the New Theologian puts it:

He derives his name from the matter on which he rests,
For he has no distinctive name among men.

The bishop summarizes the essence of Orthodox spirituality and soteriology with the following sentence, which in this way or another has been said by many Eastern Fathers and teachers.

From Ware, *Orthodox Way*, 119.

The whole aim of the Christian life is to be a Spirit-bearer, to live in the Spirit of God, to breathe the Spirit of God.

The biggest complaint by the Orthodox tradition against the theology of the Christian West is the *filioque* ("and from the Son") addition to the creed. Bishop Kallistos explains here the reasons for their position.

From Ware, *Orthodox Way*, 122.

One of the chief reasons why the Orthodox Church rejects the Latin addition of the filioque to the Creed . . . as also the Western teaching about the "double procession" of the Spirit which lies behind this addition, is precisely our fear that such teaching might lead men to depersonalize and subordinate the Holy Spirit.

The coeternity and coequality of the Spirit is a recurrent theme in the Orthodox hymns for the Feast of Pentecost:

The Holy Spirit for ever was, and is, and shall be; He has neither beginning nor ending, But he is always joined and numbered with the

Father and the Son: Life and Giver of Life, Light and Bestower of Light,
Love itself and Source of Love: Through him the Father is made known,
Through him the Son is glorified and revealed to all. One is the power,
one is the structure, One is the worship of the Holy Trinity.

A recurring theme in Eastern theology is the mutuality of the Spirit and the Son, a genuine Spirit Christology or christological pneumatology.

From Ware, *Orthodox Way*, 123.

1. Incarnation. At the Annunciation the Holy Spirit descends upon the Virgin Mary, and she conceives the Logos: according to the Creed, Jesus Christ was "incarnate from the Holy Spirit and the Virgin Mary." Here it is the Spirit who is sending Christ into the world.

2. Baptism. The relationship is the same. As Jesus comes up from the waters of Jordan, the Spirit descends upon him in the form of a dove: so it is the Spirit that "commissions" Christ and sends him out to his public ministry. This is made abundantly clear in the incidents which follow immediately after the Baptism. The Spirit drives Christ into the wilderness (Mark 1:12), to undergo a forty-day period of testing before he begins to preach. When Christ returns at the end of this struggle, it is "in the power of the Spirit" (Luke 4:14). The very first words of his preaching allude directly to the fact that it is the Spirit who is sending him: he reads Isaiah 61:1, applying the text to himself, "The Spirit of the Lord is upon me, because he has anointed me to preach the Gospel to the poor" (Luke 4:18). His title "Christ" or "Messiah" signifies precisely that he is the one anointed by the Holy Spirit.

3. Transfiguration. Once more the Spirit descends upon Christ, this time not in the form of a dove but as a cloud of light. Just as the Spirit previously sent Jesus into the wilderness and then out to his public preaching, so now the Spirit sends him to his "exodus" or sacrificial death at Jerusalem (Luke 9:31).

The fact that the Eastern church describes its apostolic continuity and catholicity in terms of "fullness" and "wholeness" does not mean a confinement of the Spirit within the limits of the church.

From Kallistos Ware, *The Inner Kingdom*, vol. 1
(New York: St. Vladimir's Seminary Press, 2000), 8–9.

We are not to imagine that, because Orthodoxy possesses the fullness of Holy Tradition, the other Christian bodies possess nothing at all. Far from it; I have never been convinced by the rigorist claim that sacramental life and the grace of the Holy Spirit can exist only within the visible limits of the Orthodox Church.

Tradition is a highly valued aspect of Orthodox theology. The bishop explains what tradition means in this outlook.

From Ware, *Inner Kingdom*, 1:10.

As the life of the Holy Spirit within the Church, so I discovered, Tradition is all-embracing. In particular it includes the written word of the Bible, for there is no dichotomy between Scripture and Tradition. Scripture exists within Tradition, and by the same token Tradition is nothing else than the way in which Scripture has been understood and lived by the Church in every generation. Thus I came to see the Orthodox Church not only as "traditional" but also as Scriptural. It is not for nothing that the Book of the Gospels rests on the center of the Holy Table in every Orthodox place of worship. It is the Orthodox rather than the Protestants who are the true Evangelicals. (If only we Orthodox in practice studied the Bible as the Protestants do!)

Dumitru Staniloae

While not well known in the English-speaking world, the late Romanian bishop and theology professor Dumitru (or Dimitri) Staniloae is one of the most significant Orthodox theologians of the twentieth century. Staniloae was a Romanian translator of the *Philokalia*, his main work, and his multivolume *Orthodox Dogmatic Theology* is currently being translated into English.

The Spirit in Creation
Echoing the biblical teaching of the Spirit as the principle of life, Staniloae explains the nature and work of this divine energy in creation.

From Dumitru Staniloae, *The Experience of God: Orthodox Dogmatic Theology,* vol. 2 (Brookline, MA: Holy Cross Orthodox Press, 2000), 6, 16.

In fact, if the rational fabric of the world must have a subject who thinks it, a subject who is truly the one who knows and is master of the created world, this subject in communion is able to effect, even through created consciousness, the gathering together and transformation of matter into spirit. The creator Spirit who is the origin of the rationality of nature given material form and of the conscious subjects connected to it, is also their goal, a goal in which human subjects find their full unity in conjunction with that nature through which they communicate and which has itself been raised to a condition completely overwhelmed by spirit. . . .

The divine Spirit is able not only to produce modifications much greater than these upon the energy from which the forms of the world are made but also to produce this energy itself as an effect of his own spiritual energy, imprinting on it potentially the forms that will become actual in their own time.

The Romanian bishop introduces here a comprehensive pneumatology of nature.

From Staniloae, *Experience of God*, 2:60, 63.

Within the freedom of the divine Spirit there is provision both for the possibility of God's varied interventions in the world and for the power to render the effects of these interventions much more extensive, more sensible, and more efficacious than the interventions of human freedom. . . . If man can only exercise his free activity upon the world through the body, the divine Spirit, as infinitely more powerful, can work directly upon the world without generally impeding the operation of the factors within nature.

The Spirit is also at work through the incarnate spirit, which is our own being. In this way the working of the human person, made strong by the power of God, is at one and the same time an activity of the human person and of God, a synergic operation. Indeed synergy is the general formula for the working of God in the world. . . .

In the case of miracles, it is the human spirit strengthened by the divine Spirit, or the divine Spirit itself, that pervades nature more visibly with its power. And the more the spirit grows strong in human beings, the more it will pervade the entire medium that is nature, and within nature, first and foremost the bodies of human beings themselves.

Part of the pneumatology of nature is a theological anthropology developed pneumatologically.

From Staniloae, *Experience of God*, 2:67–68.

The soul is produced by the eternal conscious Spirit who, while conceiving the rational principles of matter and molding them into material form, also brings into existence in his own image a conscious soul. Such a soul stands over against these materialized principles but is connected to them and itself exists in order to conceive these principles and to make the material reality upon which they are stamped into a spiritual reality by means of its own union with the eternal conscious Spirit. . . .

This created image of the conscious eternal Spirit is brought into existence not simply as a rationality molded into material form and having a general and conceptual character, but as a factor which by itself—in the same manner as the Logos—is able to have itself as the object of its own thought, that is, to conceive itself and all other things besides. Here an interruption takes place within the creative action of the conscious eternal Spirit. It is not just through the simple conception and command of the creator Spirit that the conscious soul is brought into existence. Rather, since from the beginning it has the character of a subject, the soul is called into existence through a kind of reduplication of the creator Spirit on the created plane. The conscious supreme Spirit speaks with the created conscious spirit as with a kind of alter ego, though the latter remains created.

Sergius Bulgakov

In Eastern Orthodox apophatic theological tradition, theology comes in many ways, most often in other ways than in written academic treatises. Hence, a fitting preface to the pneumatology of Sergius Bulgakov, as chronicled in his *The Comforter*, is the eulogy by Metropolitan Evlogy. The exiled Russian-born Bulgakov, who taught theology in Paris, was trained as a political economist and embraced Marxism in his youth until in 1918 he was ordained into the Orthodox priesthood and became a significant shaper of twentieth-century immigrant Orthodox theology. Bulgakov passed away on July 12, 1944, in Paris.

From funeral homily by Metropolitan Evlogy, http://www.geocities.com/ sbulgakovsociety/ (accessed Aug. 25, 2008).

You were enlightened by the Holy Spirit, the Spirit of Wisdom, the Spirit of Understanding, the Comforter to Whom you dedicated your scholarly work. . . . He guided you to your last breath. Twenty-six years ago you partook of His gracious gifts in the sacrament of ordination and you bore the cross of priesthood in the Holy Spirit. It is significant that you received this gift on the day of the Holy Spirit—when He descended upon the holy apostles in tongues of fire. Thus you had a share in them. . . . It is significant too that you celebrated your last liturgy on earth on that very day of the Holy Spirit, the anniversary of your ordination as a priest.

Typical of Bulgakov's theology, he approaches pneumatology through the lens of Christology and vice versa.

From Sergius Bulgakov, *The Comforter*, trans. Boris Jakim
(Grand Rapids: Wm. B. Eerdmans Publishing Co., 2004), 220.

In the Divine life, the Holy Spirit realizes the fullness adequate to this life and plumbs the depths of God by a unique eternal act in creaturely being; the Holy Spirit is the force of being and the giver of life, but, according to the very concept of creation, this being and this life exist only as becoming, that is, not in fullness but only in the striving toward fullness.

The form of the kenosis of the Holy Spirit in the creaturely Sophia, or in creation, is the creative "let there be," the force of life and being, natural grace. The path followed by this natural grace is from the movement of the Spirit upon the face of the waters to the transfiguration of creation into a "new heaven and a new earth": "I make all things new" (Rev. 21:1, 5). This natural grace of the Holy Spirit, which constitutes the very foundation of the being of creation, exists in the very flesh of the world, in the matter of the world. It is the precondition for its sanctification through the reception of the Holy Spirit.

In keeping with his own theological tradition, Bulgakov explains the process of sanctification in pneumatological terms, using the terminology of "sophiology," the topic over which there was so much debate around this creative theologian.

From Bulgakov, *The Comforter*, 221–22.

In sanctification we have a descent of the Holy Spirit and a communication of His force to natural and spirit-bearing creation: the creaturely Sophia is united here with the Divine Sophia, the Holy Spirit with the spirit of God in creation. A mysterious "transmutation" of matter occurs here, not only in the Eucharist, but in all sacramental acts: matter is taken out of this world and borne into the world of grace of the future age, where God will be all in all. There occurs a mysterious, i.e., invisible, transfiguration of creation, in which the latter, while ontologically remaining itself, becomes transparent for the Spirit, receives the faculty of communion with God, is deified. Thus, in this permeability of matter for the Spirit and the resulting "communication of properties" or perichoresis (to use a term of christological theology), we have an inseparable and inconfusible unity of creaturely and divine life. In other words, a divine-humanity is being realized here, not in man himself but in the human world and in the world that is in the process of being humanized, a world that has its ontological center in man. This is the deification of creation, under the necessary condition of the conservation of its being.

CHAPTER 11

*The Spirit in Roman
Catholic Theologies*

Papal Insights into Pneumatology

The Roman Catholic Church more than any other church throughout the centuries has attempted to define its doctrine and spirituality by means of official documents. The following selections include three important papal encyclicals, then excerpts from four documents of the Second Vatican Council. The encyclical *Divinum illud munus* by Leo XIII (1897) is one of the precursors to the twentieth-century Catholic pneumatological renaissance. In keeping with the theology of the time, Christ is the head and the Holy Spirit is the soul of the church; the Spirit's role is to "animate" the structures and life of the church. In this passage, the salvific role of the Spirit in the church and liturgy is beautifully explained.

From *Divinum illud munus* [On the Holy Spirit], Encyclical
of Pope Leo XIII, May 9, 1897, http://www.vatican.va.

11. We ought to pray to and invoke the Holy Spirit, for each one of us greatly needs His protection and His help. The more a man is deficient in wisdom, weak in strength, borne down with trouble, prone to sin, so ought he the more to fly to Him who is the never-ceasing fount of light, strength, consolation, and holiness. And chiefly that first requisite of man, the forgiveness of sins, must be sought for from Him.

Another significant encyclical that helped Catholic theology rediscover the role of the Spirit in ecclesiology and spiritual life is the highly acclaimed writing by Pope Pius XII on the church during World War II.

From *Mystici Corporis Christi* [On the Mystical Body of Christ],
Pope Pius XII, June 29, 1943, http://www.vatican.va.

33. The Church which He founded by His Blood, He strengthened on the Day of Pentecost by a special power, given from heaven. For,

having solemnly installed in his exalted office him whom He had already nominated as His Vicar, He had ascended into Heaven; and sitting now at the right hand of the Father He wished to make known and proclaim His Spouse through the visible coming of the Holy Spirit with the sound of a mighty wind and tongues of fire.

By any standards, the encyclical on the Holy Spirit by the late John Paul II marks a milestone in contemporary Roman Catholic pneumatology. John Paul II saw reflection on the Holy Spirit mandated by the needs of the times: "In our own age, then, we are called anew by the ever ancient and ever new faith of the Church, to draw near to the Holy Spirit as the giver of life." Known for his strong christological stance, one of the main themes in the pope's mind was a Trinitarian Spirit Christology based on biblical teaching—both Old and New Testaments—and especially on the Augustinian tradition.

From *Dominum et vivificantem* [On the Holy Spirit in the Life of the Church and the World], John Paul II, August 5, 1986, http://www.vatican.va.

3. . . . . It is precisely this Spirit of truth whom Jesus calls the Paraclete—and *parakletos* means "counselor," and also "intercessor," or "advocate." And he says that the Paraclete is "another" Counselor, the second one, since he, Jesus himself, is the first Counselor, being the first bearer and giver of the Good News. The Holy Spirit comes after him and because of him, in order to continue in the world, through the Church, the work of the Good News of salvation. . . .

4. A little while after the prediction just mentioned Jesus adds: "But the Counselor, the Holy Spirit, whom the Father will send in my name, he will teach you all things, and bring to your remembrance all that I have said to you" [John 14:26]. The Holy Spirit will be the Counselor of the Apostles and the Church, always present in their midst—even though invisible—as the teacher of the same Good News that Christ proclaimed. The words "he will teach" and "bring to remembrance" mean not only that he, in his own particular way, will continue to inspire the spreading of the Gospel of salvation but also that he will help people to understand the correct meaning of the content of Christ's message; they mean that he will ensure continuity and identity of understanding in the midst of changing conditions and circumstances. The Holy Spirit, then, will ensure that in the Church there will always continue the same truth which the Apostles heard from their Master.

7. Between the Holy Spirit and Christ there thus subsists, in the economy of salvation, an intimate bond, whereby the Spirit works in human history as "another Counselor," permanently ensuring the

transmission and spreading of the Good News revealed by Jesus of Nazareth. Thus, in the Holy Spirit-Paraclete, who in the mystery and action of the Church unceasingly continues the historical presence on earth of the Redeemer and his saving work, the glory of Christ shines forth, as the following words of John attest: "He [the Spirit of truth] will glorify me, for he will take what is mine and declare it to you" [John 16:14].

10. In his intimate life, God "is love," the essential love shared by the three divine Persons: personal love is the Holy Spirit as the Spirit of the Father and the Son. Therefore he "searches even the depths of God" [1 Cor. 2:10], as uncreated Love-Gift. It can be said that in the Holy Spirit the intimate life of the Triune God becomes totally gift, an exchange of mutual love between the divine Persons and that through the Holy Spirit God exists in the mode of gift. It is the Holy Spirit who is the personal expression of this self-giving, of this being-love. He is Person-Love. He is Person-Gift. Here we have an inexhaustible treasure of the reality and an inexpressible deepening of the concept of person in God, which only divine Revelation makes known to us.

At the same time, the Holy Spirit, being consubstantial with the Father and the Son in divinity, is love and uncreated gift from which derives as from its source (*fons vivus*) all giving of gifts vis-a-vis creatures (created gift): the gift of existence to all things through creation; the gift of grace to human beings through the whole economy of salvation. As the Apostle Paul writes: "God's love has been poured into our hearts through the Holy Spirit which has been given to us" [Rom. 5:5].

The Holy Spirit in the Teaching of Vatican Council II

The decisive turn in Roman Catholic theology in general and in pneumatology in particular came with the Second Vatican Council (1962–1965), which not only was the single most important council of the Roman Catholic Church but also one of the historic watersheds of the whole Christian church. Pope John XXIII, when formally announcing the Council, wrote, "This getting together of all the bishops of the Church should be like a new Pentecost."[1] This council could

---

1. Germain Marc'hadour, "The Holy Spirit over the New World: II," *The Clergy Review* 59, no. 4 (1974): 247.

be called the "Council of the Holy Spirit," for as Pope Paul VI pointed out, the pages of the Council documents contain two hundred and fifty-eight references to the Holy Spirit.[2] Three theologians played a crucial role in initiating a fuller recovery of the doctrine of the Holy Spirit on the eve of Vatican II and afterwards: Yves Congar, Heribert Mühlen, and Karl Rahner. Since none of Mühlen's main writings are available in English, Congar's and Rahner's contributions to the Spirit, among other contemporary Catholic theologians, will be presented, following some key council documents. The Spirit's role in Scripture and revelation is discussed in one of the most important Vatican II documents, *Dei Verbum*, which presents the contemporary Catholic theology of revelation.

From *Dei Verbum* [The Dogmatic Constitution on Divine Revelation],
Second Vatican Council documents, http://www.vatican.va.

4. Jesus perfected revelation by fulfilling it through his whole work of making Himself present and manifesting Himself: through His words and deeds, His signs and wonders, but especially through His death and glorious resurrection from the dead and final sending of the Spirit of truth. . . .

5. "The obedience of faith" (Rom. 13:26; see 1:5; 2 Cor. 10:5–6) "is to be given to God who reveals, an obedience by which man commits his whole self freely to God, offering the full submission of intellect and will to God who reveals," and freely assenting to the truth revealed by Him. To make this act of faith, the grace of God and the interior help of the Holy Spirit must precede and assist, moving the heart and turning it to God, opening the eyes of the mind and giving "joy and ease to everyone in assenting to the truth and believing it." To bring about an ever deeper understanding of revelation the same Holy Spirit constantly brings faith to completion by His gifts.

Undoubtedly, the most important Vatican II document is the one on the church. *Lumen Gentium* is also one of the most important Christian statements on the church ever published. Authentically Trinitarian in its approach (as defined at the very beginning of the document, esp. nos. 1–4), it presents a Trinitarian pneumatology as the basis of contemporary Catholic theology of the church.

From *Lumen Gentium* [The Dogmatic Constitution on the Church],
Second Vatican Council documents, http://www.vatican.va.

4. When the work which the Father gave the Son to do on earth was accomplished, the Holy Spirit was sent on the day of Pentecost in

2. Ibid., 248.

order that He might continually sanctify the Church, and thus, all those who believe would have access through Christ in one Spirit to the Father. He is the Spirit of Life, a fountain of water springing up to life eternal. To men, dead in sin, the Father gives life through Him, until, in Christ, He brings to life their mortal bodies. The Spirit dwells in the Church and in the hearts of the faithful, as in a temple. In them He prays on their behalf and bears witness to the fact that they are adopted sons. The Church, which the Spirit guides in way of all truth and which He unified in communion and in works of ministry, He both equips and directs with hierarchical and charismatic gifts and adorns with His fruits. By the power of the Gospel He makes the Church keep the freshness of youth. Uninterruptedly He renews it and leads it to perfect union with its Spouse. The Spirit and the Bride both say to Jesus, the Lord, "Come!" Thus, the Church has been seen as "a people made one with the unity of the Father, the Son and the Holy Spirit."

7. . . . By communicating His Spirit, Christ made His brothers, called together from all nations, mystically the components of His own Body. In that Body the life of Christ is poured into the believers who, through the sacraments, are united in a hidden and real way to Christ who suffered and was glorified. Through Baptism we are formed in the likeness of Christ: "For in one Spirit we were all baptized into one body" [1 Cor. 12:13]. . . . In order that we might be unceasingly renewed in Him, He has shared with us His Spirit who, existing as one and the same being in the Head and in the members, gives life to, unifies and moves through the whole body. This He does in such a way that His work could be compared by the holy Fathers with the function which the principle of life, that is, the soul, fulfills in the human body.

One of the contributions of *Lumen Gentium* is to see the whole church, not only its hierarchy, as participating in the prophetic ministry of Christ in the power of the Spirit who dispenses various gifts, charisms to the faithful.

12. . . . The entire body of the faithful, anointed as they are by the Holy One, cannot err in matters of belief. They manifest this special property by means of the whole peoples' supernatural discernment in matters of faith when "from the Bishops down to the last of the lay faithful" they show universal agreement in matters of faith and morals. That discernment in matters of faith is aroused and sustained by the Spirit of truth. . . . It is not only through the sacraments and the ministries of the Church that the Holy Spirit sanctifies and leads the people of God and enriches it with virtues, but, "allotting his gifts to everyone according as He wills, He distributes special graces

among the faithful of every rank. By these gifts He makes them fit and ready to undertake the various tasks and offices which contribute toward the renewal and building up of the Church, according to the words of the Apostle: "The manifestation of the Spirit is given to everyone for profit" [1 Cor. 12:7]. These charisms, whether they be the more outstanding or the more simple and widely diffused, are to be received with thanksgiving and consolation for they are perfectly suited to and useful for the needs of the Church. Extraordinary gifts are not to be sought after, nor are the fruits of apostolic labor to be presumptuously expected from their use; but judgment as to their genuinity and proper use belongs to those who are appointed leaders in the Church, to whose special competence it belongs, not indeed to extinguish the Spirit, but to test all things and hold fast to that which is good.

In keeping with the current understanding, Vatican II defined the church as mission, rather than mission being merely a task assigned to the church. In the missionary life and activity, the Spirit is the guide and source of power.

From *Ad Gentes* [Decree on the Mission Activity of the Church], Second Vatican Council documents, http://www.vatican.va.

2. The pilgrim Church is missionary by her very nature, since it is from the mission of the Son and the mission of the Holy Spirit that she draws her origin, in accordance with the decree of God the Father. This decree, however, flows from the "fount-like love" or charity of God the Father who, being the "principle without principle" from whom the Son is begotten and Holy Spirit proceeds through the Son, freely creating us on account of His surpassing and merciful kindness and graciously calling us moreover to share with Him His life and His cry, has generously poured out, and does not cease to pour out still, His divine goodness.

One of the key concerns behind the convening of the Second Vatican Council was the need to respond to the challenges and needs of contemporary times. *Gaudium et Spes* is the document that tackles issues of secularism, atheism, technology, politics, and the like. Its approach is decidedly pneumatological as it sees the whole of humanity being united because of a common origin and destiny. In keeping with the contemporary Catholic theology of religions, according to which salvation in Christ through the Spirit is also available to people who have never heard the gospel (should they follow the light given in their own religion and pursue moral guidelines), paragraph 22 is a profound statement on the Spirit's role in making salvation available to people in other faiths.

From *Gaudium et Spes* [The Church in the Modern World],
Second Vatican Council documents, http://www.vatican.va.

22. . . . The Christian man, conformed to the likeness of that Son Who is the firstborn of many brothers, received "the first-fruits of the Spirit" (Rom. 8:23) by which he becomes capable of discharging the new law of love. Through this Spirit, who is "the pledge of our inheritance" (Eph. 1:14), the whole man is renewed from within, even to the achievement of "the redemption of the body" (Rom. 8:23): "If the Spirit of him who raised Jesus from the death dwells in you, then he who raised Jesus Christ from the dead will also bring to life your mortal bodies because of his Spirit who dwells in you" (Rom. 8:11). . . . All this holds true not only for Christians, but for all men of good will in whose hearts grace works in an unseen way. For, since Christ died for all men, and since the ultimate vocation of man is in fact one, and divine, we ought to believe that the Holy Spirit in a manner known only to God offers to every man the possibility of being associated with this paschal mystery.

Hans Urs von Balthasar

The Swiss "theologian of beauty," Hans Urs von Balthasar (d. 1988) is considered one of the most important Catholic writers of the twentieth century, with more than one hundred books and many, many more articles. The following excerpt comes from the last volume of the last work in his celebrated trilogy *The Glory of the Lord*, *Theo-Drama*, and *Theo-Logic*, in which he reflects on the nature and personhood of the Holy Spirit on the basis of the names given in Christian tradition. Such reflection is an exercise that, for example, St. Augustine also practiced.

From Hans Urs von Balthasar, *Theo-Logic*, vol. 3 of *The Spirit of Truth*,
trans. Graham Harrison (San Francisco: Ignatius Press, 2005), 223–34.

Three key words suggest themselves when we consider the ways in which the living God manifests himself in his mode of being as Holy Spirit: gift, freedom, and inward and outward testimony.

Gift, in the highest sense, means what God hands over to man and puts within him: "God's love has been poured into our hearts through the Holy Spirit who has been given to us" (Rom 5:5). . . . *Freedom*, likewise in the broadest possible sense: "Where the Spirit of the Lord is, there is freedom" (2 Cor 3:17). . . . *Testimony* is given by the Spirit both inwardly and outwardly: as "the Spirit of truth" he "bears witness" to Jesus (Jn 15:26). . . . All three concepts, particularly the third, but the second and first as well, refer equally to the operation of Father and Son; while specifically mentioning the Spirit, they always refer to the Son's salvific work, in which the Father's eternal "working" is manifested to the world (Jn 5:17). Nonetheless these three terms have a particular reference to the Spirit; . . . the terms are inseparable: they interpenetrate.

A rare combination of profound intellect and mystical spirituality, Balthasar's meditation in *The Conquest of the Bride* builds on long Catholic spiritual tradition and Bible exposition. Here the Lord of the Church is speaking to his people.

From Hans Urs von Balthasar, *The Conquest of the Bride*, http://catholiceducation.org/articles/religion/re0765.html, n.p. (accessed Aug. 25, 2008).

My kingdom is invisible, but I want to establish you, my Bride, before the eyes of men so visibly that no one will be able to overlook you. . . . It is not your love—that overcomes the world—which is a scandal to them; for that is a scandal which you should give! Their scandal, rather, is your luke-warmness and your unbridled lack of love. You were meant to be for men an image of the unity between me and the Father, and it was for this that I sent you our Holy Spirit, the bond of unifying love; for this it was that I established you on the all-embracing unity of baptism, doctrine, and the uninterrupted succession from Peter to John Paul II. . . . I have entered into you with my Spirit and, as your one heart, I move you towards unity from within. . . . Whoever stands closer to me, however, has been initiated into my mystery and, belonging to my Body, perceives the throbbing of my Heart as it resounds throughout the Body's internal vaulting: this person has received the Spirit and is, therefore, awake and able to choose freely.

Yves Congar

The French Dominican Yves Marie Joseph Congar (d. 1995) is generally recognized as one of the greatest and most influential Roman Catholic theologians of the twentieth century. A passionate ecumenist, alongside Hans Küng and Karl Rahner, he was a key advisor behind Vatican II. His pneumatological magnum opus, the three-volume *I Believe in the Holy Spirit*, has already established itself as a contemporary classic.

The Spirit and Theological Anthropology

The following selection presents a thoroughgoing pneumatological interpretation of the *imago Dei*.

From Yves Congar, *I Believe in the Holy Spirit*, trans. David Smith,
3 vols. (New York: Crossroad, 1997), 2:67–68.

He places beings outside himself in order to bring them back to himself, so that they can participate in what he is in his sovereign existence, in other words, in the beginning and the end of their existence. He places outside himself beings who are similar to himself. . . . Because they are like him, those beings are capable of knowing and loving freely, capable of giving themselves freely and returning to him equally freely. He animates them with a movement and therefore with a desire that is an echo in them of his own desire that he has revealed to us as his Spirit. . . . The Spirit is the principle of love and realizes our lives as children of God in the form of a Gift, fulfilling that quality in us. It was he who brought about in Mary the humanity of Jesus and anointed and sanctified him for his messianic activity. Through his resurrection and glorification, Jesus' humanity was made by the Spirit a humanity of (the Son of) God. During his life on earth, Jesus was the temple of the Holy Spirit, containing all men with the intention and the power to accept them as children of God. After the Lord's glorification, the Holy Spirit has that temple in us and in the Church and he is active in the same way in us, enabling us to be born *anothen* (from above and anew, see Jn 3:3) and to live as a member of the Body of Christ. He himself consummates this quality in our body, in the glory and freedom of children of God (see Rom 8:21–23). . . . Before the foundation of the world, the Father conceived his Son, the Word, as having to become human through the Holy Spirit and Mary, the daughter of Zion, and as having to assume a humanity that would begin again and at the same time complete the humanity that had come from Adam, because it would be a humanity of the "first-born of many brethren" (Rom 8:29).

The Spiritual Renewal of the Church

As is well known, Congar was a great champion of the renewal of the Catholic Church. His reading of Vatican II, especially its ecclesiological document *Lumen Gentium* [The Dogmatic Constitution on the Church], gives the highest approval to a renewed spiritual and charismatic life. Vatican II also sanctioned the Catholic charismatic renewal that was so quickly incorporated into the main church life.

From Congar, *I Believe in the Holy Spirit*, 2:151–52.

With regard to that Church, the Renewal has been concerned with maintaining the supernatural quality of the people of God at the base, with giving the charisms a stronger profile, without in any way monopolizing them, and with re-introducing into the ordinary life of the Church activities such as prophecy, in what we shall see later on to be a very modest sense, and healings not only spiritual—the sacrament of reconciliation has always contributed to this—but also physical. The Renewal has, at its own level and in its own way, certainly acted as a response to the pentecostal expectation expressed by John XXIII. Paul VI also declared that "the Church needs a perpetual Pentecost." And to say this is not to underestimate what has been coming to life, growing and even flourishing everywhere in the Church. . . . I know that it would be wrong to oppose charism and institution and to rewrite the history of the Church as a history of opposition between these two elements. The fact is that each of these two realities is the source of a different kind of order in the Church, with the result that they are often in a state of tension. That tension is normal and can even be beneficial. Grace has frequently gone beyond the fixed institutional forms of the Church. Both are required in the life of the Church. . . . The Renewal introduces the vitality of the charisms into the heart of the Church. It is a long way from having a monopoly of charisms, but it bears the label of "charismatic" and helps to make the "charismatic" theme more widely known. The movement is not a protest against the institution. Its aim is rather to infuse it with new life. It is neither a rejection nor a criticism of the institution, and the mere fact that it has developed within the institutional Church points to the Church's existence as something other than a great apparatus of grace or a juridical or even a sacramental institution.

Karl Rahner

The name of the German-Austrian Jesuit towers highest among the Catholic thinkers of the last decades of the second millennium. It simply is not possible to take any account of current Roman Catholic theology without acknowledging Rahner (d. 1984). Contrary to older scholastic theology "from above," Rahner set out to develop a genuinely Christian theology "from below," from the concrete historical particularity of human existence and the coming-to-humanity in the incarnation of the triune God. Thus, revelation for Rahner is nothing less than the self-communication of

God in Spirit to humanity, an observation that has profound implications for theological anthropology.

An Anthropological Approach to Theology

From Karl Rahner, *Foundations of Christian Faith: An Introduction to the Idea of Christianity*, trans. William V. Dych (New York: Crossroad, 2004), 116, 139.

[The human person, therefore is] the event of a free, unmerited and forgiving, and absolute self-communication of God. . . . God . . . has already communicated himself in his Holy Spirit always and everywhere and to every person as the innermost center of his existence.

From Karl Rahner, *Theological Investigations*, vol. 16, trans. David Morland (London: Darton, Longman & Todd, 1979), 57.

Revelation can only be grasped and understood for what it is through the grace of faith, which is nothing else than the self-communicating of God to the human spirit in the depths of its being.

If God has revealed himself in the depths of the human being through the Spirit, then it means that the Spirit is constantly at work to draw the world toward its God-set goal.

From Rahner, *Theological Investigations*, 16:204.

The world is drawn to its spiritual fulfilment by the Spirit of God, who directs the whole history of the world in all its length and breadth towards its proper goal. This means that every man, whatever his situation, can be saved.

Grace as God's Self-Giving

In scholastic theology of nature and grace, which laid the background for much of Catholic theology until the time of Rahner, grace was named "created" to indicate that the means by which humans conform to God's will, such as virtues, are God's salvific gifts but not God himself. The scholastic position was a departure from the patristic view, based on the New Testament orientations, in which grace is "uncreated" because God gave himself in the person of the Holy Spirit (who was named the Gift). Rahner helped rediscover this "intrinsic" view of grace according to which—differently from the views of the schoolmen—grace can be "experienced" and is indeed being experienced as the presence of God through the Holy Spirit. The following statement shows us in a dramatic way the extent to which Rahner takes his position.

From Rahner, *Foundations*, 139.

If God as he is in himself has already communicated himself in his Holy Spirit always and everywhere and to every person as the inner-most center of [the individual person's] existence, whether he wants it or not, whether he reflects upon it or not, whether he accepts it or not, and if the whole history of creation is already borne by God's self-communication in this very creation, then there does not seem to be anything else which can take place on God's part.

In his theological anthropology, Rahner had already established the fact that the human being is made "fit" to receive revelation and grace as the presence of God; thus, divinization, participation in God, is made available through God's self-giving.

From Rahner, *Foundations*, 120.

In grace, that is, in the self-communication of God's Holy Spirit, the event of immediacy to God as man's fulfillment is prepared for in such a way that we must say of man here and now that he participates in God's being; that he has been given the divine Spirit who fathoms the depths of God; that he is already God's son here and now, and what he already is must only become manifest.

The Charismatic Element in the Church

Always communion-driven in his theology, on the eve of Vatican II Rahner wrote a passionate appeal for openness to the Spirit titled "Do Not Stifle the Spirit," calling the Catholic Church to open up for the charismatic element in the church.

From Karl Rahner, "Do Not Stifle the Spirit," in *Theological Investigations*, vol. 7, trans. Cornelius Ernst (New York: Herder & Herder, 1971), 76.

It is a situation by a spirit which has been rather too hasty and too uncompromising in taking the dogmatic definition of the primacy of the pope in the Church as the bond of unity and the guarantee of truth, this attitude objectifying itself in a not inconsiderable degree of centralization of government in an ecclesiastical bureaucracy at Rome.

A couple of years later, while the Vatican Council II was still going on, he published another appeal for the charismatic in the church, titled *The Dynamic Element in the Church*. Rahner suggested that one must learn to perceive charismata when they first appear, rather than canonize charismatic persons after their death.

From Karl Rahner, *The Dynamic Element in the Church*
(New York: Herder & Herder, 1964), 82–83.

It is almost of greater importance to perceive such gifts of the Spirit on their first appearance, so that they may be furthered and not choked by the incomprehension and intellectual laziness, if not ill-will and hatred, of those around them, ecclesiastics included. . . . But the charismatic is essentially new and always surprising. To be sure it also stands in inner though hidden continuity with what came earlier in the Church. . . . Yet it is new and incalculable, and it is not immediately evident at first sight that everything is as it was in the enduring totality of the Church. . . . And so the charismatic feature, when it is new, and one might almost say it is only charismatic if it is so, has something shocking about it.

Kilian McDonnell, OSB

The Benedictine Fr. Kilian McDonnell is a leading Roman Catholic American pneumatologist. His magnum opus, released only a few years ago after decades of writings on the theology of the Spirit, is a landmark work titled *The Other Hand of God: The Holy Spirit as the Universal Touch and Goal*. In keeping with the current consensus, Fr. McDonnell underlines the ecclesial and liturgical significance of Trinitarian and pneumatological doctrine.

The Ecclesial and Liturgical Locus of Pneumatology

From Kilian McDonnell, OSB, *The Other Hand of God: The Holy Spirit as the Universal Touch and Goal* (Collegeville, MN: Liturgical Press, 2003), 30–31.

Neither the emergence of trinitarian doctrine, nor its defense, originated in pure theory or abstract speculation. Rather, their origins are to be found in hearing again the revealed word in the liturgical glorification of God in the ordinary Christian community as it expresses its simple faith. If we are looking for a way to construct a contemporary trinitarian theology reflecting these doxological and personalist themes, Basil's *On the Holy Spirit* and Richard's *On the Trinity* could serve as models. To use these models could not mean a simple return to the patristic/monastic theology of the early church and medieval period. Today it would have its own character, done in a contemporary mode, losing nothing of its philosophical discipline,

but cast in personalist, experiential, biblical, and doxological categories. This is a return to origins, to the original experience, that is, to
the praise and adoration in which the doxological community, the
church, gathers to hear the Word of God and celebrate the mysteries. Also it is a return to the liturgical praxis where the church first
experienced and recognized God as Father, Son, and Holy Spirit.

This reexperiencing of early ecclesial consciousness would enable
us to recover more of the biblical riches, sometimes lost because the
development of trinitarian doctrine was often determined by christological controversies dominated by a quite necessary technical
vocabulary. Would not retrieval of the biblical and liturgical experience of the early church help restore theology, especially trinitarian
Theology and pneumatology, to its role as a normal preparation for
contemplation? . . .

Could we . . . develop a new style of doing trinitarian theology,
including pneumatology, that would gather up the fruits of the long
history of trinitarian speculation—retaining philosophical categories and argumentation, but casting trinitarian thought also in aesthetic, hymnodic, and doxological images, so that one can pray and
preach and celebrate it? Doxology alone speaks the language of this
contemplative country. The very objectivity of most liturgical doxology signals an attempt to breach the border. The impersonal vocabulary tries to say into that unknowing night what cannot be said in the
knowing light.

The Spirit and Eschatology

One of the chapters in Fr. Kilian's pneumatological study is titled "To Do
Pneumatology Is to Do Eschatology." He argues that in the biblical account
the Spirit of God appears both in the beginning and the end of the story.

From McDonnell, *The Other Hand of God*, 34–37.

If spirit is to be found in the beginnings, so is eschatological awareness. Eschatology as a radical orientation to the future developed
early in Old Testament prophecy in conjunction with the patriarchal
promise, the monarchy, and the Sinai covenant. Though the spirit
in the Old Testament is not restricted to eschatology, whenever
ruach is associated with an outpouring it is always eschatological in
nature. From the beginning, Israel's faith was oriented to promise
and the future it contained. Chief among the proponents were the
prophets, though even when they hailed the coming of God upon
a new earth, rarely did their utterances concern a specifically messianic hope. In Joel 2:28–32 the message of hope in the midst of dev-
astation is manifested in a universal charismatic outpouring of the

spirit touching Israel's present and future. Isaiah (32:15) and Ezekiel (11:19; 36:26–27) link the spirit to Israel's glory, which is not in the past but in the future. . . .

Paul, who identified himself as "a Hebrew born of Hebrews" (Phil 3:5), was an heir and developer of this essentially Israelite reach to the future. . . . The apostolic proclamation of the gospel is not like other impartings of information, nor like any other announcement of prepositional truths, however exalted, but is made "in power and in the Holy Spirit and with full conviction" (1 Thess 1:5). The power comes from God (2:2, 4). Paul recognizes as the elect those in whom the power of the Spirit operates (1:4). In the relatively short period between the event of the resurrection and the return of Christ at the end of time together with the resurrection of the dead, the Spirit determines both the new existence of believers and the demands of holiness preparing them to meet with the Lord, the object of their hope (1:3; 3:13; 4:17). The whole of reality is sanctified in view of the move to the future.

In Paul's later epistles there is less talk of cosmic upheavals, and a recognition of the likelihood of personal death before the Lord returns, but Paul pays more attention to the present experience of union with Christ, who unites believers to him and makes them partakers of the Spirit. By linking the Spirit with the risen, exalted Lord, Paul orients the Spirit to the future. If the Spirit inaugurated and sustains the life of the resurrected Lord, then the Spirit will also inaugurate and sustain the life of believers in their resurrection. Paul sees in the resurrected Lord the realization of the believers' future. "The gospel concerning his Son, who was descended from David according to the flesh and was declared to be Son of God with power according to the spirit of holiness by resurrection from the dead, Jesus Christ" (Rom 1:3–4) may be a pre-Pauline formulation, making it the earliest witness to the resurrection. "Spirit" here is intrinsic to the resurrection, but in the Old Testament sense, where Ezekiel 37:14 attributes the resurrection of the whole of Israel—not of individuals—to the spirit of God.

CHAPTER 12

The Spirit in Protestant Traditions

Reformed Theologies

Karl Barth

Named the "church father of the twentieth century," the Swiss Reformed theologian Karl Barth (d. 1968) is by any account one of the most significant, if not *the* most significant, voice at the end of the second millennium. Raised in classical liberalism, he became an ardent opponent to everything that liberalism represented and attempted a return to orthodoxy without totally leaving behind modernity; thus his thinking is often labeled *neo*-orthodoxy. His theology in general and pneumatology in particular are characterized by an uncompromising dialectic between the divine and human.

"God the Holy Spirit"
Barth titles §12 "God the Holy Spirit" in the first part of the first volume of *Church Dogmatics.*

From Karl Barth, *Church Dogmatics*, I/1,
ed. Geoffrey W. Bromiley and Thomas F. Torrance
(Edinburgh: T. & T. Clark, 1975), 453.

1. The Spirit guarantees man what he cannot guarantee himself, his personal participation in revelation. The act of the Holy Ghost in revelation is the Yes to God's Word which is spoken by God Himself for us, yet not just to us, but also in us. This Yes spoken by God is the basis of the confidence with which a man may regard the revelation as applying to him. This Yes is the mystery of faith, the mystery of the knowledge of the Word of God, but also the mystery of the willing obedience that is well-pleasing to God. All these things, faith, knowledge and obedience, exist for man "in the Holy Spirit."

From Karl Barth, *Church Dogmatics*, III/1, ed. Geoffrey W. Bromiley and Thomas F. Torrance (Edinburgh: T. & T. Clark, 1975), 56–57.

Here as elsewhere what is true of the Father and the Son is also true of the Holy Spirit of the Father and the Son. The Holy Spirit is with the Father and the Son the true, eternal God in so far as, like the begetting Father and the begotten Son, He is the communion and self-impartation realised and consisting between both from all eternity; the principle of their mutual love proceeding from both and equal in essence; the eternal reality of their separateness, mutuality and convolution, of their distinctness and interconnexion. To this extent it may well be said that it is in the Holy Spirit that the mystery of God's trinitarian essence attains its full profundity and clarity. He is at once the innermost secret of God, and in God's relationship with man the great, bright and incontrovertible revelation of the unity and diversity of the Father and the Son. It is in the Holy Spirit that the commission of the Father and the obedience of the Son, the good pleasure of the Father and the glory of the Son, obviously coincide in the decree which is the intra-divine beginning of all things.

In this respect we may and must describe Him in His eternal, intra-divine reality as the "Spirit of the Lord," who is the "Spirit of wisdom and understanding, the Spirit of counsel and might, the Spirit of knowledge and of the fear of the Lord" (Is. 112f.). There pre-exists in Him (since He is the Spirit of the Father and the Son, and since the Father and the Son meet in Him in relation to the world and man), the whole reality of the fatherly compassion of God, His self-expression, His own glorification in His Son, the whole truth of the promise, the whole power of the Gospel, and therefore the whole order of the relation between God the Creator and His creatures. Because God is also the Holy Spirit in His will and activity toward and with the world and man, God becomes possible and supportable for the creature and the creature for God: God for the creature, so that it no longer entails its immediate destruction to be without and before God; and the creature for God, so that He can find in it something more and better than revolt and blasphemy and the violation of His glory. We may say in a word that it is in God the Holy Spirit that the creature as such pre-exists. That is to say, it is God the Holy Spirit who makes the existence of the creature as such possible, permitting it to exist, maintaining it in its existence, and forming the point of reference of its existence. For it is He who in that counsel anticipates and guarantees its reconciliation with God and redemption by Him in the union of the Father and the Son. It could not of course exist if, in relation to it, God had not been One with Himself from all eternity, if He had not been from all eternity the Holy Spirit of love, who in that agreement has willed its existence and assumed it on His own responsibility. For that reason it is only in the Holy Spirit that the creature can be sure that it can and may exist. For it is only in the Holy Spirit that there can be revealed to it that unity and agreement between the Father and the Son as that which makes it possible and legitimate. That this agreement exists and is valid is the work of the Holy Spirit in creation.

A central feature in Barth's theology in general and pneumatology in particular is freedom. The Holy Spirit is the One who establishes and guarantees freedom.

From Karl Barth, *Evangelical Theology: An Introduction*, trans. Foley Grover (Grand Rapids: Wm. B. Eerdmans Publishing Co., 1963), 53–54.

"Where the Spirit of the Lord is, there is freedom" (II Cor. 3:17). The freedom of which we talk is God's freedom to disclose himself to men, to make men accessible to himself, and so to make them on their part free for him. The one who does that is the Lord God, who is the Spirit. There are also other spirits, those created good by God, such as the spirit natural to man. Moreover, there are demonic, erring, and disruptive spirits of annihilation which deserve nothing else than to be driven out. But none of these are that sovereign power of which we speak. Of none of them, not even of the best among them, can it be said that where they are there is freedom. They must all be tested for the direction of their current, for their source from above or below. Above all, however, they must again and again be distinguished from the Spirit that, working in the ambiance of divine freedom, creates human freedom. In the Nicene Creed (as it was adopted by the Western Churches) the Spirit is called "the Holy One, the Lord and Giver of life," who "proceeds from the Father and from the Son, who together with the Father and the Son is adored and glorified." That is to say, the spirit is himself God, the same one God who is also the Father and the Son; he acts both as Creator and as Reconciler, as the Lord of the covenant. As this very Lord, however, he now dwells, has dwelt, and will dwell in men. He dwells not only *among* them but also *in* them by the enlightening power of his action. It is that flowing air and moving atmosphere in which men may live, think, and speak wholly and entirely freed from presuppositions—for they are men who know the spirit and are known by him, men called by him and obedient to him, his children begotten by his Word.

Faith, Love, and Hope

Faithful to his Reformed tradition, Barth highlights the role of the Holy Spirit in bringing about faith and the confession of the lordship of Christ, a main theme in Barth's theological vision.

From Karl Barth, *Church Dogmatics*, IV/1, ed. Geoffrey W. Bromiley and Thomas F. Torrance (Edinburgh: T. & T. Clark, 1956), 740, 748.

The Holy Spirit is the awakening power in which Jesus Christ summons a sinful man to His community and therefore as a Christian to believe in Him: to acknowledge and know and confess Him as the Lord who for him became a servant; to be sorry both on his own behalf and on that of the world in face of the victory over his pride and fall which has taken place in Him; and again on his own behalf and therefore on that of the world to be confident in face of the establishment of his new right and life which has taken place in Him. . . . The Holy Spirit is the power in which Jesus Christ the Son of God makes a man free, makes him genuinely free for this choice and therefore for faith. He is the power in which the object of faith is also its origin and basis, so that faith can know and confess itself only as His work and gift, as the human decision for this object, the human participation in it which he makes in his own free act but which he can only receive, which he can understand only as something which is received, which he can continually look for as something which is received again and which has to be confirmed in a new act.

Another Christian virtue, love is also the work of the Holy Spirit.

From Barth, *Church Dogmatics*, IV/2:727, 778–79.

The Holy Spirit is the quickening power in which Jesus Christ places a sinful man in His community and thus gives him the freedom, in active self-giving to God and his fellows as God's witness, to correspond to the love in which God has drawn him to Himself and raised him up, overcoming his sloth and misery. . . . In their fulfilment in which they become the basis of Christian love the act and work of God are the act and work of the Holy Spirit in whom man is called and drawn by the Father to the Son and the Son to the Father. This is the new creation of man, his liberation, his radical alteration by the established fellowship between God and himself. In this calling and drawing of the Father to the Son and the Son to the Father there takes place the divine love by which man too is made one who loves. But the power of this calling and drawing is the power of the Holy Spirit. . . . We now speak of the creative character of love in which it is the basis of human love. At this point we must be bold to make the direct equation that the love of God is the creative work of the Holy Spirit. As God is Spirit, the Spirit of the Father and the Son, as He gives Himself into human life as Spirit, and as He bears witness as Spirit to our spirit that we are His children (Rom. 8:16), God gives us to participate in the love in which as Father He loves the Son and as Son the Father, making our action a reflection of His eternal love, and ourselves those who may and will love. The fact that human action becomes the reflection, the creaturely similitude, of the divine can and must be described both as the work of God's love and also as the work of His Spirit. It is, in fact, both. As God loves man, giving Himself to him and for him, it comes about that the latter in his action can imitate the love of God, responding and corresponding to it. And it is the power of the Spirit, in which God gives Himself to man, to free him for this imitation, response and correspondence, and therefore to make his action the reflection of His own.

Hope, the third Christian virtue for Barth, is similarly pneumatologically conceived.

From Barth, Church Dogmatics, IV/2:902, 916, 942.

The Holy Spirit is the enlightening power in which Jesus Christ, overcoming the falsehood and condemnation of sinful man, causes him as a member of His community to become one who may move towards his final and yet also his immediate future in hope in Him, i.e., in confident, patient and cheerful expectation of His new coming to consummate the revelation of the will of God fulfilled in Him. ... The power of the Holy Spirit in which Jesus Christ is already near and present is not merely awakening and quickening but illuminating power in the fact that already, as the first glow of eternity, He shows and promises the dawn of this day, proclaiming it in His operation and already being to him the pledge and earnest of its coming (Rom. 8:23) and therefore of the nearness of His redemption.

The Holy Spirit is God in the power of His eternal and incarnate Logos, of His Word spoken in Jesus Christ. He is thus God in His power which enlightens the heart of man, which convicts his conscience, which persuades his understanding, which does not win him physically or metaphysically from without, but "logically" from within. Hence His work can only be man's freedom for life by Him and therefore for life in hope. Far from the Christian being mastered and taken out of himself when he is awakened to hope by the power of the Holy Spirit, it is in this life in hope awakened by the power of the Holy Spirit that he really comes to himself and may be himself. The man born of God or the Spirit, called to service and living in hope, is the man who is no longer self-alienated, and therefore he is real man.

The Spirit in the Church

Barth's ecclesiology is well grounded and directed by pneumatology, as indicated by the following excerpts from the paragraph titled "The Holy Spirit and the Gathering of the Christian Community."

From Barth, *Church Dogmatics*, IV/1:643.

The Holy Spirit is the awakening power in which Jesus Christ has formed and continually renews His body, i.e., His own earthly-historical form of existence, the one holy catholic and apostolic Church. This is Christendom, i.e., the gathering of the community of those whom already before all others He has made willing and ready for life under the divine verdict executed in His death and revealed in His resurrection from the dead. It is therefore the provisional representation of the whole world of humanity justified in Him.

Barth continues his pneumatological ecclesiology by focusing on the role of the Spirit of the resurrected Christ in the upbuilding of the community.

From Barth, *Church Dogmatics*, IV/2:614, 620, 651–52.

The powerful and living direction of the Resurrected, of the living Lord Jesus, and therefore the Holy Spirit, whom we have had to understand as the principle of sanctification, effects the upbuilding of the Christian community, and in and with it the eventuation of Christian love; the existence of Christendom, and in and with it the existence of individual Christians. . . .

The Holy Spirit is the power by which Jesus Christ fits His community to give a provisional representation of the sanctification of all humanity and human life as it has taken place in Him. . . .

In the thesis at the head of the section we have spoken of the Holy Spirit as the quickening power by which Christianity is built up as the true Church in the world. But as we made it clear it is Jesus the Lord who is at work in this quickening power of the Holy Spirit. And we must now take up again that which we have already said, and maintain that according to the normative view of the New Testament the Holy Spirit is the authentic and effective self-attestation of the risen and living Lord Jesus; His self-attestation as the Resurrected, the living One, the Lord, the exalted Son of Man, in whom there has already been attained the sanctification of all men, but also the particular, factual sanctification of Christians—their union with Him and therefore with one another. In the Holy Spirit as His self-attestation we know Him; which means again that we know Him as the Resurrected, the living One, the Lord, the exalted Son of Man, in whose exaltation all men are sanctified, and especially, factually and concretely Christians, who are distinguished in the first instance from all other men by His self-attestation and therefore by their knowledge. In the Holy Spirit as the self-attestation of Jesus they thus know themselves in and with Him; themselves in their union with Him, and also with one another, in the fellowship of faith and love and hope in which they express themselves as His and find self-awareness as this people which has a common descent. It is in this sense that the Holy Spirit as the self-attestation of Jesus is the quickening power by which Christianity is awakened and gathered and built up to a true Church in the world. As the self-attestation of Jesus the Holy Spirit achieves the *communio sanctorum* and causes it to grow (intensively and extensively). It lives by His power—from the very first and on all its way and ways in the realisation of the relationship of the *sancti* to the *sancta* right up to its goal at the end of all history when it will meet the eschaton which will be the eschaton of the cosmos. But to understand this in all its fulness of meaning we must be clear that the Holy Spirit by which the community lives and becomes and was and is and will be is the self-attestation of Jesus.

Hendrikus Berkhof

Long-time professor of theology at the University of Leiden in his homeland, the Netherlands, Hendrikus Berkhof attempted a powerful revision of traditional confessional Reformed theology in light of the heritage of classical liberalism and the new challenges of the twentieth-century context. In his 1964 work *The Doctrine of the Holy Spirit*, Berkhof puts forth a strongly modalistically oriented pneumatology in which the Spirit is hardly much more than an efficacy of God. Berkhof thus radicalizes the Barthian reluctance to speak of separate "persons" in the Trinity. The following citations clearly betray this orientation.

A Modalistic Pneumatology

From Hendrikus Berkhof, *The Doctrine of the Holy Spirit*
(Atlanta: John Knox Press, 1964), 116–17.

What we see before us in biblical revelation is a great divine movement, the movement of God as Spirit, moving toward the Son and out of the Son. It is a movement which urges us to utter three words: God-Christ-Spirit, or according to the order of our experience, as H. P. van Dusen did in his book: Spirit-Son-Father. These three names in their togetherness point to a movement of the one God, not to a static community of three persons. They are the description of an ongoing movement of condescendence, in which God reaches out deeper and deeper toward man in his sin and distress, until in the end he can touch the heart of the individual by his regenerating power in the Spirit of Christ. Then the Spirit leads man to Christ, and in Christ man finds God. So we must recognize a double movement: God stretches out his arm and his hand toward his fallen world and next draws man up toward himself, to press the prodigal son to his heart and to grant him the transformation according to the image of Christ.

In all this God is Person, acting in a personal way, seeking a personal encounter. The triune God does not embrace three Persons; he himself is Person, meeting us in the Son and in his Spirit. . . . And the Spirit is not a Person beside the Persons of God and Christ. In creation he is the acting Person of God, in re-creation he is the acting Person of Christ, who is no other than the acting Person of God. Therefore, we must reject all presentation of the Spirit as an impersonal force. The Spirit is Person because he is God, acting as a Person. However, we cannot say that the Spirit is a Person distinct from God the Father. He is a Person in relation to us, not in relation to God; for he is the personal God himself in relation to us. Therefore, the three names in the New Testament: God (Father)-Christ (Son)-Spirit are not meant to express a kind of tripartition in God, which would distinguish the Christian faith from Jewish monotheism (an old misunderstanding, still alive). On the contrary, in using these three names together the Apostles want to confess the unity of God, the fact that in the great movement of Spirit, Son, and Father we have not to do with three entities, but with one and the same acting and saving God. . . . To use the word *subsistentia* as meaning something between *persona* and *substantia* is no longer valid. The only expression which can satisfy us is *modus entis*, "mode of being," used by several theologians in the period of Reformed scholasticism. It is a modest word, which cannot create tritheistic misunderstandings, but at the same time, it makes clear that God does not exist in one way, but in different ways. He expresses the unity of his being in a diversity of ways.

Regeneration

Berkhof summarizes the soteriological work of the Spirit in the individual under the term "regeneration," which, he believes, best captures the all-inclusive, universal work of the Spirit.

From Berkhof, *Doctrine of the Holy Spirit*, 69–70.

I personally believe that the word which best expresses the unity and the totality of the Spirit's work is the word "regeneration." . . . The Spirit is the life-giver; he is God breathing the breath of life into man. That is the essence of his work in redemption as well as in creation. Redemption as the work of the Spirit means "rebirth." The heart of stone is replaced by a heart of flesh (Ezek. 36:26), breath comes into the dry bones (37:10). So we become children of God, not born of the will of man but of God (John 1:13). For "unless one is born anew, he cannot see the kingdom of God" (3:3). "Therefore, if any one is in Christ, he is a new creation" (2 Cor. 5:17). . . . These biblical references can easily be multiplied. They are in full agreement with the primitive and essential meaning of the Spirit as the living God who acts in order to transmit his life to his creatures.

Using regeneration as the key word in our context not only makes clear what the nature of the spiritual work in our lives is, but also implies a decision about its origin and its goal. To say first a word about the goal: The word "regeneration" points to conformity with Christ as the goal of the Spirit. Christ himself is our life. We are dead in our sins, but implanted by the Spirit into the life of him who is the firstborn from the dead. Our goal is that we may be glorified with him (Rom. 8:17), be changed into his likeness from one degree of glory to another by the Lord who is the Spirit (2 Cor. 3:18).

The word "regeneration" implies also a clear answer to the question of origin. It says that our transition from death to life, our being made alive with Christ, is entirely and exclusively the work of the Spirit. "For we are his workmanship, created in Christ Jesus for good works, which God prepared beforehand . . ." (Eph. 2:10; for the origin, nature, and goal of the Spirit's work, see the whole passage, Eph. 2:1–10). Here we find the main reason why the Reformed confession has such a preference for regeneration as a key word and why other confessions sometimes are so hesitant about emphasizing this word. If a man has to be born anew, he is merely passive; he cannot contribute in the least to his rebirth; he must wait for a miracle from above. All kinds of synergism are excluded. "So it depends not upon man's will or exertion, but upon God's mercy" (Rom. 9:16).

The Spirit's Universal Work

H. Berkhof points to the direction in which contemporary pneumatology has moved, namely, acknowledging and elaborating on the universal dimension of the work of the Spirit.

From Berkhof, *Doctrine of the Holy Spirit*, 95–96.

Now that we know God in his mighty acts in history, we can recognize his actions also in his work in creation and preservation. We understand that the same God in action, the same *ruach* working in the deeds of salvation, is also the secret of the entire created world. . . . We are inclined to begin with Genesis 1:2: ". . . the Spirit of God was moving over the face of the waters," but this translation is too doubtful to allow any consequences for our theme. The main pronouncements we find in Job and the Psalms. The fact that we often are inclined to translate *ruach* in these texts as "breath" does not diminish their pneumatological value. . . . For the faithful Israelite it was clear that "By the word of the lord the heavens were made, and all their host by the ruach of his mouth" (Ps. 33:6). Word and Spirit both describe God in action. God's Spirit creates and sustains the life of nature. . . . So intimate is the Spirit to man's life that we sometimes feel ourselves on the brink of pantheism. Job says that he has the Spirit of God in his nostrils [Job 33:4]. Nevertheless, in his immanence this Spirit remains strictly sovereign and transcendent. We cannot dispose of the Spirit within us. God gives his Spirit; he also takes him away, in which case man and nature die away. "If he should take back his spirit to himself, and gather to himself his breath, all flesh would perish together, and man would return to dust" [Job 34:15]. The Spirit of God also inspires man's culture. The Old Testament connects him with agriculture, architecture, jurisdiction, and politics (Cyrus as God's anointed one!). In general all human wisdom is the gift of God's Spirit. This relation between the Spirit and creation is much neglected in Christian thinking.

Echoing the ideas of Calvin, Kuyper, and the like, H. Berkhof further elaborates on the universal and public ministry of the Spirit by speaking of his work in the "secular" realm.

From Berkhof, *Doctrine of the Holy Spirit*, 104.

The work of the Spirit in our modern so-called secularized world reminds us of the fact that our exalted Lord is not only the Head of his church but also primarily the Head of the world. The Spirit is not locked up in the church. We know that his work in the world is ambiguous; but so is his work in the church. Nowhere do we find him on earth in heavenly purity. In the faithful he raises the conflict between Spirit and flesh, in the world that between Christonomy and autonomy.

. . . In spite of the deep shadows, the Spirit's work of humanizing men and their social structures is a parable, an analogy, and even a part of the great summorphia which has begun in Jesus Christ. It is a signpost toward the glorification of the universe, the conformity of mankind with its Head. As in the individual, it is not more than a small beginning. And this beginning is threatened by the fact that the majority of those who enjoy it do not know the center and the meaning of all this. They have the fruit without the root, the horizontal dimension without the vertical one. The church needs the instruction of the Spirit in world history in order to understand the cosmic consequences of her preaching. And the world needs the church to give meaning to its development, lest mankind's emancipation end in boredom and futility.

Jürgen Moltmann

A New Paradigm in Pneumatology
Widely regarded as the most significant and undoubtedly most widely debated living constructive theologian, the German Jürgen Moltmann first encountered living faith and theology as a prisoner of war in Scotland during World War II. Long-term professor of systematic theology at the University of Tübingen, Germany, Moltmann developed a powerful and creative theological vision during his publishing career, which stretched over four decades. While the Trinity and pneumatology have shaped all of his theology, his *The Spirit of Life* has been hailed as a landmark volume on the Holy Spirit in the twentieth century. This masterful work radiates with enthusiasm that was present in the preparation of the book, as testified by the author himself, as well as the desire to break new ground in the doctrine of the Spirit and salvation. One of the reasons for a new paradigm in pneumatology is the attempt by the church and theology to limit and control the Spirit.

> From Jürgen Moltmann, *The Spirit of Life: A Universal Affirmation*,
> trans. Margaret Kohl (Minneapolis: Fortress Press, 1992), 2–3.

It was the established churches' fear of the religious, as well as the irreligious, "free thinking" of the modern world which led to more and more reserve in the doctrine of the Holy Spirit. In reaction against the spirit of the new liberty—freedom of belief, freedom of religion, freedom of conscience and free churches—the only Spirit that was declared holy was the Spirit that is bound to the ecclesiastical institution for mediating grace, and to the preaching of the official "spiritual pastors and teachers." The Spirit which people experience personally in their own decision of faith, in believers' baptism, in the inner experience of faith in which "they feel their hearts strangely warmed" (as John Wesley put it), and in their own charismatic endowment, was declared "unholy" and "enthusiastic." Even today, in ecclesiastical discussions about the Holy Spirit, people like to turn first and foremost to "the criterion for discerning the spirits"—even when there do not seem to be any spirits to hand.

On the other hand, the continual assertion that God's Spirit is bound to the church, its word and sacraments, its authority, its institutions and ministries, impoverishes the congregations. It empties the churches, while the Spirit emigrates to the spontaneous groups and personal experience. Men and women are not being taken seriously as independent people if they are only supposed to be "in the Spirit" when they are recipients of the church's ministerial acts and its proclamation. God's Spirit is more than merely the being-revealed of his revelation in human beings, and more than simply the finding of faith in the heart through the proclaimed word. For the Spirit actually brings men and women to the beginning of a new life, and makes them the determining subjects of that new life in the fellowship of Christ. People do not only experience the Holy Spirit outwardly in the community of their church. They experience it to a much greater degree inwardly, in self-encounter—as the experience that "God's love has been poured into our hearts through the Holy Spirit" (Rom. 5.5).

Not only has there been a tendency to imprison the Spirit within church and its authority but also to limit the scope of pneumatology to the religious sphere.

From Moltmann, *Spirit of Life*, 8–9.

In both Protestant and Catholic theology and devotion, there is a tendency to view the Holy Spirit solely as *the Spirit of redemption*. Its place is the church, and it gives men and women the assurance of the eternal blessedness of their souls. This redemptive Spirit is cut off both from bodily life and from the life of nature. It makes people turn away from "this world" and hope for a better world beyond. They then seek and experience in the Spirit of Christ a power that is different from the divine energy of life, which according to the Old Testament ideas interpenetrates all the living. The theological textbooks therefore talk about the Holy Spirit in connection with God, faith, the Christian life, the church and prayer, but seldom in connection with the body and nature. In Yves Congar's great book on the Holy Spirit [*I Believe in the Holy Spirit*], he has almost nothing to say about the Spirit of creation, or the Spirit of the new creation of all things. It would seem as if the Spirit of God is simply and solely the Spirit of the church, and the Spirit of faith. But this would restrict "the fellowship of the Holy Spirit," and make it impossible for the church to communicate its experience of the Spirit to the world. Some theologians have discovered a new love for the charismatic movements; but this can also be an escape, a flight from the politics and ecology of the Spirit in the world of today.

. . . This has meant that the Holy Spirit has come to be understood solely as "the Spirit of Christ," and not at the same time as "the Spirit of the Father." As *the Spirit of Christ* it is *the redemptive Spirit*. But the work of creation too is ascribed to the Father, so *the Spirit of the Father* is also *the Spirit of creation*. If redemption is placed in radical discontinuity to creation, then "the Spirit of Christ" has no longer anything to do with Yahweh's *ruach*.

The Spirit of Life

In Moltmann's pneumatology in general and his main book on the topic, the leading idea is to consider God's Spirit as the Spirit of Life. This goes back to the biblical teaching of the Spirit as the Spirit of Life.

From Moltmann, *Spirit of Life*, 40.

If we wish to understand the Old Testament word we must forget the word "spirit," which belongs to Western culture. The Greek word *pneuma*, the Latin *spiritus*, and the Germanic *Geist/ghost* were always conceived as antitheses to matter and body. They mean something immaterial. Whether we are talking Greek, Latin, German or English, by the Spirit of God we then mean something disembodied, supersensory and supernatural. But if we talk in Hebrew about Yahweh's *ruach*, we are saying: God is a tempest, a storm, a force in body and soul, humanity and nature. The Western cleavage between spirit and body, spirituality and sensuousness is so deeply rooted in our languages that we must have recourse to other translations if we want to arrive at a more or less adequate rendering of the word *ruach*.

One way to define the essence of the "Spirit of Life" is to define it in terms of vitality as love of life.

From Moltmann, *Spirit of Life*, 86.

Here we shall interpret vitality as *love of life*. This love of life links human beings with all other living things, which are not merely alive but want to live. And yet it challenges human beings in their strange liberty towards life; for life which can be deliberately denied, has to be affirmed before it can be lived. Love for life says "yes" to life in spite of its sicknesses, handicaps and infirmities and opens the door to a "life against death."

Spirit and Christ/Christ and Spirit

A distinctive feature of Moltmann's theology is Christology that is deeply pneumatological and pneumatology that is deeply christological, as the two citations from his books on Christology and pneumatology, respectively, clearly show.

From Jürgen Moltmann, *The Way of Jesus Christ: Christology in Messianic Dimensions* (Minneapolis: Fortress Press, 1993), 73–74, 77.

Jesus' history as the Christ does not begin with Jesus himself. It begins with the *ruach*/the Holy Spirit. It is the coming of the Spirit, the creative breath of God: in this Jesus comes forward as "the anointed one" (*masiah, christos*), proclaims the gospel of the kingdom with power, and convinces many with the signs of the new creation. It is the power of the creative Spirit: through this he brings health and liberty for enslaved men and women into this sick world. It is in the presence of the Spirit that God reveals himself to him with the name "Abba," that Jesus discovers that he is the "Son" of this Father, and that he lives out this intimate relationship in his community of prayer with God. The Spirit "leads" him into the temptations in the desert. The Spirit thrusts him along the path from Galilee to Jerusalem. "Through the eternal Spirit" (Heb 9:14) he surrenders himself to death on the Roman cross. By the power of the Spirit, who gives new birth and new creation, God raises him from the dead. . . . When we are considering the New Testament testimony about the theological history of Jesus, it is impossible to talk about Jesus without talking about the workings of the Spirit in him, and about his relationship to the God whom he called "Abba," my Father. . . .

The experience of the Spirit evidently provides a differently supported logic of correspondence between the experience of Christ's presence and the remembrance of his history. If Christ is present now in the eternal Spirit of God, then his history must have been determined by this Spirit from the very beginning.

Revising Soteriological Concepts

One of the distinctive features of Moltmann's magnum opus on pneumatology is a creative, at times revisionist, reworking of typical *ordo salutis*. While building on tradition, this German theologian also expands and reformulates soteriological topics.

One way to revise the traditional doctrine of salvation is to cast the notion of "justification" in a wider context of "justice."

From Moltmann, *Spirit of Life*, 128, 142–43.

The Protestant doctrine about the justification of sinners, and today's theology about the liberation of the oppressed, do not have to be antitheses. They can correct and enrich one another mutually. The full and complete Protestant doctrine of justification is a liberation theology: it is about the liberation of people deprived of justice, *and* about the liberation of the unjust, so that they may all be freed for a just society. The one-sided limitation to the perpetrators, and the forgiveness of their active sins, has made Protestantism blind to the sufferings of the victims, and to God's saving "option for the poor." Protestantism has underrated the importance of "structural sin" by looking too exclusively at individuals. But this is a one-sided approach.

We have talked about establishing rights for people deprived of them, and about the justifying of the unjust, and the rectifying of their relations and circumstances. So who, then, is the Holy Spirit?

(a) *In negative terms*, he is the Spirit of righteousness and justice who can be sensed in *the pain of people without rights* over their deprivations. Without a feeling for justice this pain would not exist. Without the pain there would not be the struggle for the justice of which they have been robbed.

In negative terms, he is the Spirit of righteousness and justice who speaks in *the guilty conscience* of the people who commit violence. The "guilty conscience" does not necessarily mean a conscious sense of guilt. It can also provoke inner uncertainty, fear of one's own self and aggression towards oneself and other people. "The godless know no peace." That is to say, the people who commit violence have lost their inner identity and try to compensate by inhuman acts of this kind.

In negative terms, this divine justice is shown in world history by *the instability of unjust conditions*, which have to be kept on an even keel by more and more violence, more and more police, more and more military control. Peace is a fruit of justice. This is true of social peace in a society too, and it is no less true of peace between nations. All that grows on the foundation of injustice is organized peacelessness. So unjust systems have feet of clay. They have no lasting development. The hidden presence in world history of the divine justice in God's Spirit "destabilizes," so to speak, human systems of injustice, and sees to it that they cannot last.

(b) *In positive terms*, the Spirit of God is *the presence of Christ* among and in the victims of violence: Christ is their brother—they are his family and the community of his people, whether they know it or not. The Spirit is Christ's solidarity with them.

In positive terms, the Spirit of God is *the atoning power* of Christ's substitution among and in the perpetrators. Christ is "the God of sinners." The Spirit is Christ's atoning power for them and in them.

In positive terms, the fellowship of the Holy Spirit is *the divine love* which holds in life even self-destructive human communities in order to heal them. So the fellowship of the Holy Spirit is also the antitype of the human communities which are built up on injustice and violence, for the fellowship of the Holy Spirit gives to each his or her own. In the fellowship of the Holy Spirit, people accept one another mutually, and reciprocally recognize each other's dignity and rights. In the fellowship of the Holy Spirit compassion is alive. In that fellowship human socialities are as good as the fortunes of their weakest members.

(c) The Holy Spirit is the righteousness and justice of God which creates justice, justifies and rectifies. In the Spirit, lasting community with God, with other people and with nature becomes possible. That is why we can in this sense also call the Holy Spirit *the justification of life*. In the Spirit life again becomes worth loving. In the Spirit, human beings again become capable of loving life. In the Spirit life's intricate interactions again become fruitful. The rectifying Holy Spirit is God's "yes" in justice to the life of each and all of us, and the life of each with all of us.

Michael Welker

The same year that Moltmann's pneumatological magnum opus was released in English, the pneumatological work of another German theologian, Michael Welker, titled *God the Spirit*, was published in German. Professor of systematic theology at the University of Heidelberg, Welker focuses his study on a careful reading of the diversity of biblical testimonies for a postmodern and post-Enlightenment world. In what he calls a "realistic" theology of the Spirit, Welker wants to listen carefully to the diverse, pluriform testimonies about the presence and absence of the Spirit in the contemporary church and society as well as in the biblical canon.

What he resists is any "numinous," abstract, metaphysical notions of the Spirit, so prevalent in much of theology

A "Realistic" Theology of the Spirit
Welker's pneumatology seeks to locate itself and resolve the apparent tension between, on the one hand, the apparent feeling of the distance of God in the modern secular consciousness and, on the other hand, the enthusiastic embrace of the closeness of God in the rapidly growing charismatic churches.

From Michael Welker, *God the Spirit*, trans. John F. Hoffmeyer
(Minneapolis: Fortress Press, 1994), 1–2, 6, 7.

Without question, in our day people have experienced God's Spirit and continue to do so. Or are, for example, 300 million people—the current estimated size of the Charismatic Movement—in error? No one can exclude that possibility a priori. But if the members of the largest religious movement in history are not in error, is the so-called secular world, for whom the Spirit of God is to a large extent a Phantom, blind? Has this world, by means of its forms of experience, its language, and its construction of "reality" in the singular, obstructed the functioning of its capacity to perceive God's Spirit? Has this world immunized itself against the power with which God is present among human beings and acts on them? This possibility as well cannot simply be excluded. But is it meaningful to attempt to change the secular world's habitual forms of experience in the direction of a greater openness to experience of the Spirit, if we do not know with certainty that we can trust the experiences of persons who appeal to the Spirit of God?

Those who today want to overcome such uncertainties and doubts and to go beyond their own forms of experience and the religious experiences of our day cannot expect any easy answer. To set out on the path to a new intimacy with the reality of the Spirit, one must expose oneself to numerous different perceptions of, and attestations to, the Spirit. And one must expose oneself to helplessness and skepticism with regard to such attestations.

A view that does not arbitrarily block out these difficulties must note at the outset that the secular common sense of the West has great difficulty in gaining even a distant perception of anything approaching God's Spirit. While this everyday understanding presumably only "sees ghosts" in the doctrine of the Holy Spirit, members of the Charismatic Movement are not only ones who take seriously God's Spirit as a reality that unquestionably can be and is experienced. Many people in many lands can attribute the powerful spread of theologies of liberation in our world only to the action of God's Spirit. In societies that are dominated by individual, national, economic, and cultural forms of egotism, how could theologies of liberation develop into one of the most important forms of theology and piety? In massively patriarchal churches, how could feminist theologies make so much headway in barely two decades? How could this happen if not through God's Spirit, who, according to prophetic promise and Pentecostal confirmation, enables men and women, male and female slaves, old and young, local residents and people from other lands, intimates and strangers, to open God's reality with each other and for each other? How could this happen if a Spirit were not at work who—in accord with the prospect held out by the messianic promises of the Spirit—wills to make universal righteousness, mercy, and knowledge of God a reality?

Liberation and Empowerment of the Spirit

Reading Old Testament narratives of the Spirit, Welker finds striking the ministry of liberation and empowerment of the oppressed and weak. As a result, communities are being formed.

From Welker, *God the Spirit*, 56–57.

God's Spirit is neither a spirit of magic nor a spirit of war. This is true despite the fact that, according to the early testimonies, the Spirit's action can seem fantastic enough, and despite the fact that the Spirit is indirectly all too involved in militaristic actions. Yet nowhere is the claim made that this Spirit brings deliverance in an immediate, magical way. Nowhere is it said that the Spirit directly occasions militaristic actions. The texts do not say that the Spirit descended upon this or that human being—and the enemy fled. Nor does the enemy flee when Gideon blows his ram's horn or when Saul chops the oxen to pieces. There is no place where the Spirit of God immediately or directly causes a military conflict.

Instead the Spirit causes the people of Israel *to come out of* a situation *of insecurity, fear, paralysis, and mere complaint.* This happens by means of the persons upon whom the Spirit has come, and in concentration on these persons. In a situation of powerlessness, in a situation where it is to be expected that each individual person seek his or her welfare in flight, in a situation of perplexity and helplessness, the bearer of the Spirit—more precisely, God through the bearer of the Spirit—restores loyalty and a capacity for action among the people. This can, but it need not, move or even inspire people "to voluntary collaboration. . . . In all the early attestations to the experience of God's Spirit, what is initially and immediately at issue is the restoration of an internal order, at least of new commitment, solidarity, and loyalty. The direct result of the descent of God's Spirit is the gathering, the joining together of people who find themselves in distress. The support of their fellow persons is acquired; a new community, a new commitment is produced after the descent of the Spirit by the person upon whom the Spirit has come.

Lutheran Theologies

The Holy Spirit and Salvation in Current
Ecclesiastical Pronouncements
The first set of citations from the official Web site of the Evangelical Lutheran Church of America explains in a succinct way some of the leading Lutheran convictions about the Spirit and salvation.

From "Dig Deeper: The Holy Spirit." ELCA.org,
Evangelical Lutheran Church of America, http://www.elca.org/
holyspirit (accessed June 24, 2009).

Holy Spirit
"I believe that by my own reason or strength I cannot believe in Jesus Christ, my Lord, or come to him, but the Holy Spirit has called me through the Gospel, enlightened me with his gifts, and sanctified and preserved me in the true faith." . . . ELCA Lutherans believe that the Holy Spirit calls, gathers, enlightens and sanctifies us in the faith, and that all of this flows from what we understand to be the Holy Spirit's paramount work—to reveal and glorify Christ, and to strengthen the believer's faith. . . . The center of God's divine activity is the incarnate Son of God, Jesus the Christ. Yet, just as the Son performed the work of the Father who sent him, so the Spirit performs the work of the Son. The Spirit underscores the fulfillment of prophecy, witnessing to God revealed in Jesus. In carrying on Jesus' earthly ministry, the Spirit's ongoing work is to reveal truth, give life and strengthen faith (John 7:39, 14:26, 15:26, 16:7–15). . . .

ELCA Lutherans concur with Martin Luther that "the Holy Spirit is among humans in a twofold way":

"'First through a universal activity, by which [the Holy Spirit] preserves them as well as God's other creatures. . . .' (Thus, the Spirit's activity is not limited to the sphere of faith and the church, but that all activity in which God engages with reference to the world and humankind is mediated through the Spirit.)

"Secondly, the Holy Spirit 'is gift from Christ' to believers. One can establish the principle that, for Luther, a relationship with God is possible only through the Spirit—understood in the strict sense as a person of the Trinity. He believed that there is not a single theological doctrine in which the activity of the Spirit is not fundamental. The activities of the Spirit are personal in nature: speaking, bearing witness, and uniting believers with one another in one body. Apart from the Spirit there is no activity of God in the world or in human life, no living Word, no grace of Baptism, no real presence of the Lord in the Eucharist, no conversion or regeneration, no faith or fellowship in Christ. . . ."[1]

For Luther, the Spirit is the author of preaching the Gospel and, simultaneously, gift to humankind enclosed in the Word. He stressed both the Spirit as the creator of the new life and as indwelling witness. He professed that such things as, "Raising one's children, loving one's wife and obeying the magistrate are fruits of the Spirit."

At the same time, Luther taught and ELCA Lutherans profess that, within the church, the Spirit works through the Word and Sacraments, so ELCA Lutherans appreciate Word and the Sacraments as instruments of the Spirit which "feed" our faith.

"In binding the Spirit to the external means of Word and Sacrament, Luther did not deny the inner working of the Spirit. However, he did understand these to be safeguards against the excesses of subjectivism and emotionalism, a kind of romanticizing or ecstatic internalization of the Spirit. He disputed the (Reformation era) fanatics' right to appeal to special inspirations apart from revelation or Word and Sacrament . . . and noted that the Spirit's proper work is precisely a strengthening in faith."[2] As Luther put it in his explanation to the third article of the Apostles' Creed, still professed by ELCA Lutherans:

. . . the Holy Spirit has called me through the Gospel, enlightened me with his gifts, and sanctified and preserved me in true faith, just as he calls, gathers, enlightens, and sanctifies the whole Christian church on earth. . . . In this Christian church he daily and abundantly forgives all my sins, and the sins of all believers, and on the last day he will raise me and all the dead and will grant eternal life to me and to all who believe in Christ. This is most certainly true."

---

1. Bernhard Lohse, *Martin Luther's Theology*, trans. and ed. Roy A. Harrisville (Minneapolis: Fortress Press, 1999), 237–38, including citation of Luther's lectures on Galatians.

2. Ibid.

Wolfhart Pannenberg

The Spirit and the Word in Revelation
Not only the leading Lutheran theologian, alongside the Reformed Jürgen Moltmann, the German Lutheran Wolfhart Pannenberg is also one of the most significant constructive theologians of our times. Famous for his untiring call for theology to present its claims and rational argumentation in dialogue with the public sphere rather than with reference to inner piety and spiritual experiences, Pannenberg also demands that pneumatology do the same.

> From Wolfhart Pannenberg, "Insight and Faith," in *Basic Questions in Theology*, trans. George H. Kehm, vol. 2 (Philadelphia: Fortress, 1971), 43.

The Spirit of which the New Testament speaks is no "haven of ignorance" (*asylum ignorantiae*) for pious experience, which exempts one from all obligation to account for its contents. The Christian message will not regain its missionary power . . . unless this falsification of the Holy Spirit is set aside which has developed in the history of piety.

The book that launched Pannenberg as a young theologian into world fame was the 1961 collection of essays titled *Revelation as History*, to which he produced a programmatic writing. Pannenberg acknowledges that "one of the most hotly debated theses of Revelation as History was the claim that the revelation of God 'is open to anyone who has eyes to see' and does not need any supplementary inspired interpretation."[3] In defense of his view, the mature Pannenberg sets forth his understanding of a Spirit-filled apostolic proclamation.

> From Wolfhart Pannenberg, *Systematic Theology*, trans. Geoffrey W. Bromiley, 3 vols. (Grand Rapids: Wm. B. Eerdmans Publishing Co., 1991, 1994, 1998), 1:249–50.

The word of apostolic proclamation . . . does not supplement an event which is dumb and dull as such. It does not give radiance to the saving event. It simply spreads abroad the radiance that shines from Christ's own glory. It thus imparts the life-giving Spirit of God who consummates the event of the resurrection of the Crucified which is the content of the kerygma. . . . The word of the apostolic message is Spirit-filled in virtue of its content, and for this reason can impart the Spirit.

3. Wolfhart Pannenberg, *Systematic Theology*, trans. Geoffrey W. Bromiley, 3 vols. (Grand Rapids: Wm. B. Eerdmans Publishing Co., 1991), 1:249.

The thesis that we may know eschatological revelation without any supplementary inspiration is not directed against the function of the Word, the apostolic kerygma, relative to faith in the saving event of Christ's person and work, nor is it directed against the interrelation of Word and Spirit. On the contrary, it presupposes the relation of the Spirit to the Word in virtue of the latter's content. It is simply directed against views which regard the Spirit as outside the content of the Word and additional to it, as though the apostolic kerygma were not Spirit-filled in virtue of its content. The eschatological revelation of God does not need to be manifested by outside supplementary inspiration as a principle of interpretation, for the reality of the Risen Lord itself sheds forth the Spirit that makes him known as the fulfilment of the divine promises.

God as Spirit

From Pannenberg, *Systematic Theology*, 2:83.

Criticism of this traditional way of speaking about God as though the reference were to subjectivity (*nous* [reason]) led us to the insight (vol. I, 372ff.) that it is more in keeping with what the Bible says about God as Spirit, or about the Spirit of God, to view what is meant as a dynamic field that is structured in trinitarian fashion, so that the person of the Holy Spirit is one of the personal concretions of the essence of God as Spirit in distinction from the Father and the Son.

From Pannenberg, *Systematic Theology*, 1:383–84.

But the Spirit is not just the divine life that is common to both the Father and the Son. He also stands over against the Father and the Son as his own center of action. This makes sense if the Father and the Son have fellowship in the unity of the divine life only as they stand over against the person of the Spirit. Precisely because the common essence of the deity stands over against both—in different ways—in the form of the Spirit, they are related to one another by the unity of the Spirit.

Based on biblical teaching, Pannenberg "defines" God as love (1 John 4:8, 16) and Spirit (John 4:24; 3:8), which gives him opportunity to clarify the inner-Trinitarian relationships and the unity of the divine essence.

From Pannenberg, *Systematic Theology*, 1:428–30.

Each of the three persons is ec-statically related to one or both of the others and has its personal distinctiveness or selfhood in this relation. The Father is the Father only in relation to the Son, in the generation and sending of the Son. The Son is the Son only in obedience to the sending of the Father, which includes recognition of his fatherhood. The Spirit exists hypostatically as Spirit only as he glorifies the Father in the Son and the Son as sent by the Father. . . . In the person of the Father the sphere of the divine Spirit steps forth as the creative power of existence which takes form only through the relation to the Son. The divine mystery is expressible as a Thou, as the Thou of the Father, only through the Son and in fellowship with him. . . . The coming forth of the Son from the Father is the basic fulfilment through the creative dynamic of the Spirit who is the essence of Godhead, but on the Son's part as he knows that he has come forth and been sent, and as he thus distinguishes himself from the Father who is the divine origin of his existence, honoring him as the one God. On the Son's part, too, the Spirit always participates in what happens, though not in every respect as the hypostatic Spirit. The essence of the Godhead is indeed Spirit. It is Spirit as a dynamic field, and as its manifestation in the coming forth of the Son shows itself to be the work of the Father, the dynamic of the Spirit radiates from the Father, but in such a way that the Son receives it as gift, and it fills him and radiates back from him to the Father. . . . On the one side the Spirit and love constitute the common essence of deity; and on the other they come forth as a separate hypostasis in the Holy Spirit. . . .

The divine persons, then, are concretions of the divine reality as Spirit. They are individual aspects of the dynamic field of the eternal Godhead. This means that they do not exist for themselves but in ecstatic relation to the overarching field of deity which manifests itself in each of them and in their interrelations.

The Spirit in Creation
In Pannenberg's Trinitarian doctrine of creation, the Spirit plays an important role.

From Pannenberg, *Systematic Theology*, 2:31–33.

On the Christian view creation can be thought of as God's free act because it does not derive from a necessity that flows one-sidedly from the Father, nor from a mistake of the Pneuma but from the free agreement of the Son with the Father through the Spirit. . . . According to the biblical witnesses the Spirit was at work in creation (Gen. 1:2), especially as the origin of life in the creatures (Gen. 2:7; Ps. 104:29f.). On the one side the Spirit is the principle of the creative presence of the transcendent God with his creatures; on the other side he is the medium of the participation of the creatures in the divine life, and therefore in life as such. His working, then, is closely related to that of the Son, though also characteristically different. For the independence and distinction of the creatures relative to God goes back to the self-distinction of the Son, but the Spirit is the element of the fellowship of the creatures with God and their participation in his life, notwithstanding their distinction from him. To be sure, in the Son, too, self-distinction from God and union with him belong closely together, for self-distinction from the Father is the condition of fellowship with him. Nevertheless, we see there the indissoluble interrelation of the Son and Spirit. The Son is not the Son without the Spirit. . . . The bringing forth of the creature reaches fulfillment in the creature's continued independent existence, which is the goal of God's creative act. But continued creaturely existence is possible only by participation in God. For God alone has unrestricted duration. All limited duration derives from him. The creatures need participation in God not merely because their existence differs from that of God but also in their life's movement insofar as life finds fulfillment in transcendence of its own finitude. This life of creatures as participation in God that transcends their own finitude is the special work of the Spirit in creation—a work that is very closely related to that of the Son.

Holding on to the biblical teaching about the Spirit as the principle of life, Pannenberg seeks common ground between that and modern scientific explanations. He finds a clue in the field (or force-field) concept widely used in physics.

From Pannenberg, *Systematic Theology*, 2:76–77, 79–80, 83.

If we are to regard creatures in their plurality as the work of the Son both deriving from God and among one another, and if the Son, as the Logos of creation, is the principle of its order, by which all phenomena in their variety are related to one another, then, according to the biblical testimony, the Spirit of God is the life-giving principle, to which all creatures owe movement, and activity. This is particularly true of animals, plants, humans, of which Ps. 104:30 says: "Thou sendest forth thy Spirit; they created, and thou renewest the face of the ground." In keeping with this the second creation account, which says that God "formed man of dust from the ground, and breathed into his nostrils the breath of life, and man became a living being" (Gen. 2:7; cf. Job 33:4). Conversely, all life perishes when God withdraws his Spirit (Ps. 104:29; Job 34:14f.). The souls of all living things and the breath of all people are in the hands of the Spirit (Job 12:10).

At a first glance this biblical view of life is hard to reconcile with modern opinions. For modern biology, life is a function of the living cell or of the living creature as a self-sustaining (above all self-nourishing) and reproducing system, not the effect of a transcendent force that gives life. It might be suggested that the relevant biblical notions must be regarded merely as the expression of an archaic and outdated understanding of the world, like many other biblical views on natural phenomena. We will have to take up this point later. The direct symbolism of God breathing breath into creatures seems to us today to be more poetic than explanatory. The only question is whether the metaphor carries a deeper meaning that might be illuminating even for the modern understanding of natural processes. If so, it would be worth exploring. . . .

The description of forms of movement and moving forces is the central theme of physics today. To describe movement and change physics has developed the concept of force or energy working on bodies and thus producing movement. . . . The antireligious ramifications of the reduction of the concept of force to the body and its inert mass enable us to see at once the theological relevance of the changed relation between force and body resulting from the growing significance of field theories in modern physics from the time of Michael Faraday. Faraday regarded bodies themselves as forms of forces that for their part are no longer qualities of bodies but independent realities that are "givens" for bodily phenomena. . . .

The principal differences between the ways of describing reality in physics and in theology prohibit us from offering a direct theological interpretation of the field theories of physics. . . . These theories can be seen only as approximations to the reality that is also the subject of theological statements about creation. We see that the reality is the same because theological statements about the working of the Spirit of God in creation historically go back to the same philosophical root that by mathematical formalizing is also the source of the field theories of physics, and the different theories give evidence of the same emphases that we find in the underlying metaphysical intuitions. We also see that the reality is the same because the theological (as distinct from the scientific) development of the concept is in a position to find a place in its reflection for the different form of description in physics, for which there can be empirical demonstration, and in this way to confirm the coherence of its own statements about the reality of the world.

The relation, of course, is not merely an external one. If it were, we would simply have bad apologetics. Theology has to have its own material reasons for applying a basic scientific concept like field theory to its own philosophical rather than scientific presentation. Only then is it justified in developing such concepts in a way appropriate to its own themes and independently of scientific usage. Reasons for introducing the field concept into theology have been given in the context of the doctrine of God, namely, in interpreting the traditional description of God as Spirit. . . . It is more in keeping with what the Bible says about God as Spirit, or about the Spirit of God, to view what is meant as a dynamic field that is structured in trinitarian fashion, so that the person of the Holy Spirit is one of the personal concretions of the essence of God as Spirit in distinction from the Father and the Son.

The Spirit and Christ

While Pannenberg has also been critical of certain types of Spirit Christologies—for fear of adoptionism—his *Systematic Theology* offers a thoroughgoing, biblically based, Trinitarian Spirit Christology.

From Pannenberg, *Systematic Theology*, 1:266–67.

[In the New Testament] . . . the Spirit of God is either presupposed or expressly named as the medium of the communion of Jesus with the Father and the mediator of the participation of believers in Christ. According to Paul Jesus Christ was raised and instituted into divine sonship by the power of the Spirit (Rom. 1:4) and the God who raised up Jesus from the dead will by his Spirit, who dwells in believers, bring their mortal bodies also to eternal life (8:11). The Spirit of sonship who is given to Christians (8:13) is the Spirit who instituted Jesus into sonship. All sonship, then, rests on the working of the Spirit (8:14).

The Gospels, too, traced back the relationship of Jesus with the God whom he proclaimed to the presence and working of the Spirit within him. In the story of the baptism of Jesus by John the Spirit was imparted to him on this occasion (Mark 1:10 par.). The thought of adoption to sonship is also present. The infancy story in Luke, of course, traces back the sonship of Jesus to his birth and bases the description of Jesus as the Son of God on the operation of the divine Spirit, stating that he was conceived of the Spirit (1:35). John also bears witness that Jesus, whose words were spirit and life (6:63–64), was filled with the Spirit of God who enabled him to speak the words of God (3:33–34). If it is said later that during the earthly ministry of Jesus, before he was "glorified," the Spirit was not yet present (7:39), this applies only to believers to whom the Spirit was not to be given until later (14:16–17; cf. 15:26).

Among a growing number of contemporary theologians, Pannenberg opposes the *filioque* clause in defense of a genuinely Trinitarian theology. His judgment is balanced and ecumenically helpful.

From Pannenberg, *Systematic Theology*, 1:318–19.

In this question, which has played too fateful a role in the rift between Eastern and Western Christianity, the theology of the Christian West has good cause not merely to regret the one-sided addition of the *filioque* clause to the third article of the Creed of 381, and to withdraw it as uncanonical, but also to recognize that the Augustinian doctrine of the procession of the Spirit from both Father and Son is an inappropriate formulation of the fellowship of both Father and Son with the Spirit that Augustine rightly underscores. It is inappropriate because it describes the fellowship in the vocabulary of origin. It is not heretical, as many Eastern theologians have argued in excessive reaction. The mistaken formulation of Augustine points in fact to a defect which plagues the trinitarian language of both East and West, namely, that of seeing the relations among Father, Son, and Spirit exclusively as relations of origin. With this view one cannot do justice to the reciprocity in the relations.

The Spirit and Salvation

In this Trinitarian unfolding of the salvation plan of God, Pannenberg highlights the role of the Spirit in making Christ's reconciliation ours.

From Pannenberg, *Systematic Theology*, 2:450–53.

But how can others share in the reconciliation that was achieved in exemplary fashion by the incarnation and death of the Son in Jesus Christ? They can do so only as they are taken up into fellowship with the Father of the Son who became man in Jesus Christ (cf. Gal. 3:26f.; 4:5; Rom. 8:14f.). This taking up is not merely in the sense of something that happens to them from outside but as a liberation to their own identity, though not in their own power. This takes place through the Spirit. Through the Spirit reconciliation with God no longer comes upon us solely from outside. We ourselves enter into it.

As the self-offering of the Son the reconciliation of the world and his being offered up by the Father are one and the same event and form a single process, so we are to see the work of the exalted Christ and that of the Spirit in us as different aspects of one and same divine action for the reconciliation of the world. . . . The Spirit lifts us above our own finitude, so that in faith we share in him who is outside us, Jesus Christ, and in the event of reconciliation that God accomplished in his death. Believers are "ecstatic" i.e., outside themselves, as they are in Christ (Rom. 6:6, 11). . . . In "ecstatic" being with Christ, believers are not in bondage to another, for Jesus as the Son of the Father is for his part fully God and therefore the man who gives himself up for others. As believers through the Spirit are with Jesus, they participate in the filial relation of Jesus to the Father, in his acceptance of the world in virtue of the goodness of God as Creator, in his love for the world. Those who believe in Jesus are thus not estranged from themselves, for with Jesus they are with God, who is the origin of the finite existence of all creatures and their specific destiny. For this reason being outside the self through the Spirit and in faith in Jesus Christ means liberation, not merely in the sense of elevation above our own finitude, but also in the sense of attaining afresh by this elevation to our own existence as the Creator has affirmed it and reconciled it to himself. It means liberation from the bondage of the world, sin, and the devil for a life in the world in the power of the Spirit. . . .

By the Spirit, believers are capable of this self-distinction from Jesus, who is in person the eternal Son of the Father, for the Spirit himself differentiates himself from the Son by not openly glorifying himself but glorifying Jesus as the Son of the Father and the Father in the Son. The Spirit, who is himself God, brings with him fellowship with God, but only as he distinguishes himself from the Father and the Son, and with himself all those whose hearts he fills and lifts up to God. Even the "ecstatic" working of the Spirit does not mean that self-distinction from God is no longer a condition of fellowship with him. It makes it possible for us to rejoice in this distinction in peace with God.

The Spirit and the Church
Pneumatology is the way for Pannenberg to negotiate the ancient problem concerning the relationship between the one and many, in this case between the individual and community in the church. The implications, however, go beyond the church to society as well.

From Pannenberg, *Systematic Theology*, 3:130–31, 133–34.

The work of the Spirit releases and reconciles the tension between the fellowship and the individual in the concept of the church, and with it the underlying anthropological tension between society and individual freedom that in sign at least is meant to be experienced as

overcome in the church in anticipation of the future of God's kingdom. Along these lines the next section will deal with the general
basic form of the works of the Spirit in individual Christians by faith,
hope, and love, but in such a way that in the event we will also see the
place of individuals in the life of the church. The work of the Holy
Spirit lifts individuals ecstatically above their own particularity not
only to participation in the sonship of Christ but at the same time
also to experience of the fellowship in the body of Christ that unites
individual Christians to all other Christians. This is not just a matter
of lifting up the individuality of Christians into the social union of
the church. What will come to light is that raising up to existence
outside the self in Christ (*extra se in Christo*) does not simply assure
individuals of their freedom in Christ but in so doing brings them
to the place of believers' fellowship. Not just the individual but the
church, too, in its liturgical life has its existence outside itself in
Christ. In this way it shows itself to be a fellowship of the Spirit. . . .
The Spirit's work, then, is ecstatic not merely in individual Christians but also in the life of the church, leading to its center in worship
and then radiating out from there into everyday life. In the process
the relation to the Spirit does not mean that in every respect the
church is different from other forms of society for as God's Spirit is
at work in all living things, especially human souls, he is also at work
in social structures. The ecstatic nature of his work finds expression
in every society whose individual members are united by dedication
to a common cause. In this kind of common spirit, of course, the
creative Spirit of God is at work only in a more or less broken form.
The common cause that unites individuals may be most unholy.

According to Pannenberg, there is continuity between the Spirit's work
in creation and in bringing about the community of Christ, namely the
church, into being.

From Pannenberg, *Systematic Theology*, 3:1–2, 11–12.

The same Holy Spirit of God who is given to believers in a wholly
specific way, namely, so as to dwell in them (Rom. 5:9; 1 Cor. 3:16),
is none other than the Creator of all life in the whole range of natural
occurrence and also in the new creation of the resurrection of the
dead. Only when we see his imparting to believers in this comprehensive context can we judge what the event of the outpouring of
the Spirit means in truth. It involves much more than just cognitive
divine help in understanding an event of revelation that would otherwise be unintelligible. The work of the Spirit of God in his church

and in believers serves the consummating of his work in the world of creation. For the special mode of the presence of the divine Spirit in the gospel and by its proclamation, which shines out from the liturgical life of the church and *fills* believers, so that Paul can say of them that the Spirit "dwells" in them, is a pledge of the promise that the life which derives everywhere from the creative work of the Spirit will finally triumph over death, which is the price paid for the autonomy of creatures in their exorbitant clinging to their existence, in spite of its finitude, and over against its divine origin.

Theology has often neglected the relation between the soteriological operations of the Spirit in believers and his activity both as the Creator of all life and also in its eschatological new creation and consummation. This is particularly true of the theology of the Christian West, whose views of the work of the Spirit have concentrated mainly on his function as the source of grace or faith. . . .

The gift of the Spirit is not just for individual believers but aims at the building up of the fellowship of believers, at the founding and the constant giving of new life to the church. For by the link to the one Lord by which all believers receive a share in his sonship, and hence also in the Spirit of Christ, they are at the same time integrated into the fellowship of believers. Each by faith is related to the one Lord and hence to all other believers. By the Spirit each is lifted above individual particularity in order, "in Christ," to form with all other believers the fellowship of the church.

The story of Pentecost in Acts 2:1ff. gives expression to the fact that the Spirit does not simply assure each individual believer alone of fellowship with Jesus Christ, and therefore of a share in future salvation, but that thereby founds at the same time the fellowship of believers. For this story does at all events demonstrate that the Spirit was given to all the disciples in common and that therewith the church had its beginning.

The Spirit and the Eschaton

The principle of continuity between creation, the Christian life, including the church, and the eschatological consummation is perhaps the most characteristic feature of Pannenberg's Trinitarian pneumatology, which is unfolded in his massive systematic exposition of Christian doctrine.

From Pannenberg, *Systematic Theology*, 3:xiii, 2.

The doctrine of the Spirit as an eschatological gift . . . aims at the eschatological consummation of salvation. . . . The work of the Spirit of God in his church and in believers serves the consummating of this work in the world of creation.

From Pannenberg, *Systematic Theology*, 3:552–53.

It is from the Spirit of God, then, that the Christian world expects the eschatological fulfillment of believers, the changing of our mortal life into the new life of the resurrection of the dead (Rom. 8:11); and creation's waiting for the manifestation of the children of God (v. 19) suggests that its own corruptibility will be vanquished by the power of the life-creating Spirit as the world is transformed into the new creation of a new heaven and a new earth, just as the first creation already was created by the power of the Spirit (Gen. 1:2). We need hardly give special emphasis to the fact that this work of the Spirit is closely related to that of the Son. In the context of eschatology we shall bring this out specifically when we treat the theme of the return of Christ. That the subject of eschatology as a special relation to the work of the Spirit takes on plausibility when we consider that the Spirit is at work in both individuals and society. . . . Similarly, the redemptive work of the Spirit relates to both individuals and society. . . . By the Spirit the eschatological future is present already in the hearts of believers. His dynamic is the basis of anticipation of eschatological salvation already in the as yet incomplete history of the world. . . . Pneumatology and eschatology belong together because the eschatological consummation itself is ascribed to the Spirit, who as an end-time gift already governs the historical present of believers. . . . Thus we are to view the presence of the eschatological future by the Spirit as an inner element of the eschatological consummation itself, namely, as a proleptic manifestation of the Spirit who in the eschatological future will transform believers, and with them all creation, for participation in the glory of God.

Robert W. Jenson

In *Systematic Theology*, his two-volume magnum opus, leading American Lutheran theologian and ecumenist Robert W. Jenson, speaks of "The Pneumatological Problem" (vol. 1, chap. 9) and seeks to clarify the *filioque* question, among others. Jenson begins by attempting to clarify the issue of the Spirit's origin and relation to the Father.

Revisiting "Filioque"

From Robert W. Jenson, *Systematic Theology*, vol. 1: *The Triune God* (Oxford: Oxford University Press, 1997), 148.

What exactly *is* the relation by which the Spirit is an identity other than the Father? The question is, again, religiously weighty; if we cannot linguistically identify the Spirit by a specific unique relation of origin and if we posit in God only relations of origin, we cannot specifically invoke the Spirit, as the church in fact intends to do. The ancient recourse that the Spirit proceeds from the Father in a way *unknowably* different from that in which the Son proceeds from the Father only restates the difficulty; the concluding scholastic formula, that the Spirit's relation of origin is "anonymous," is mere resignation.

This reasoning takes the Lutheran theologian to the question of the *filioque.*

From Jenson, *Systematic Theology*, 1:149–50.

Finally we must come to the disputed *filioque* that has divided the Eastern and Western churches: the doctrine that the Spirit proceeds from the Father "*and the Son.*" That the Western church should not unilaterally have added this phrase to the text of an ecumenically dogmatized creed is now widely agreed, but the problems of order involved in redressing the fault are not here our concern. We are concerned with the phrase's theological function, in and out of the creed, and with the Eastern church's more strictly theological objections. The West's initial motive for the creedal insertion was not so much to say something about the Spirit as to say something about the Son. Against christological speculations originating in the Spanish church that were judged to mitigate the Son's deity, the Western church adopted the Augustinian theologoumenon to guarantee the Son's originality in deity with the Father: just as the Father breathes the Spirit, so does the Son. Whether this was necessary or effective may well be disputed.

But the *filioque* has also its own meaning, and this cannot be abandoned. In the biblical narrative, the Spirit indeed comes to us not only from the Father but also from the Son. We need note only one passage, decisive for John's understanding of the Resurrection: "He breathed on them and said. . . , 'Receive the Holy Spirit'" [John 20:22]. The *filioque* reads this giving into God himself, and just therefore must be maintained, however it is to be systematically integrated or whatever may be worked out about the creed. For it is the very function of trinitarian propositions to say that the relations that appear in the biblical narrative between Father, Son, and Spirit are the truth about God himself.

Jenson attempts a resolution to this ancient problem.

From Jenson, *Systematic Theology*, 1:158–59.

How can the Spirit be the love between the Father and the Son and still be a personal identity along with the Father and the Son? There is a problem only so long as we must put the question in that order. Let us instead look at the matter the other way around and say: the Spirit is himself one who intends love, who thus liberates and glorifies those on whom he "rests"; and *therefore* the immediate objects of his intention, the Father and the Son, love each other, with a love that is identical with the Spirit's gift of himself to each of them.

What is the relation by which the Spirit is other than the Father? There is only a problem if we are restricted to relations of origin. Freed from this restriction, we may say: the Spirit liberates God the Father from himself, to be in fact fatherly, to be the actual *arche* of deity; and so is indeed otherwise originated from that source than is the Son. Nor is the content of this "otherwise" ineffable, for we have just stated it: the Spirit so proceeds from the Father as himself to be the possibility of such processions, his own and the Son's.

So also the problem of the Spirit's personal distinction from the Son would have presented itself to Thomas [Aquinas] very differently, had he not been restricted to relations of origin. That only "opposed" relations can distinguish identities is obviously correct. But that, for example, the Spirit "glorifies" the Son because he "takes what belongs" to the Son and "declares" it[4] is just such a relation or complex of relations. Had Thomas been able to invoke any one of the plot lines Scripture suggests here, he would have had no need to resort to mere geometry, for he could have read the relation of Son and Spirit from the gospel narrative itself—as his Orthodox critics also have not done.

How, then, are we to understand "the *filioque*"? Theologians of the Eastern church sometimes describe ways in which they can affirm it. We may begin with one of these: only the Father is the source of the Spirit's *being*, of his sheer givenness as an other than the Father or the Son, but the Spirit's *energies*, his participation and agency in the triune life, come to him from the Father through the Son or, it can even be said, from the Father and the Son. For the whole divine life begins with the Father and is actual through the Son and is perfected in the Holy Spirit.

The Spirit does not derive his being from the Son, but does derive his energy from the Son. Within the construal of the divine life solely in terms of origin, and particularly within the Palamite framework from which it is advanced, this proposition would be as abstract as

4. John 16:14.

the Western and Eastern positions it modifies. But if the eschatological character of the gospel's plot line is recognized, the proposition can indeed state the necessary point: the life that the Spirit enables as the divine life has its plot from the Son's relations to the Father and to the Spirit; it is Christ who gives the Spirit to Israel and the church, that very Spirit who does *not* derive his being otherwise than from the Father and who is in himself the perfection, the liveliness, of the divine life. Here, too, the Cappadocians were ahead of their followers: according to them, the Spirit receives his *existence* from the Father, but *lives* eternally with and in the Son.

|

The Spirit in Anabaptist Perspective

|

"The Holy Spirit in the Life of the [Mennonite] Church"
In 1977 the Mennonite General Assembly adopted a statement titled "The Holy Spirit in the Life of the Church." Representing the global Anabaptist-Mennonite world communion, it is a thoughtful response to the charismatic movement among this Christian family. While prompted by the challenge and potential of the charismatic movements, the document goes beyond that particular case and offers valuable Anabaptist insights into the Holy Spirit.

> From Mennonite Church, "The Holy Spirit in the Life of the Church" (1977),
> *Global Anabaptist Mennonite Encyclopedia Online*, http://www.gameo.org/
> encyclopedia/contents/H6583.html (accessed June 13, 2007).

The range of the Spirit's work in the church is as broad as its life. The focus of this study is limited to issues related more or less closely to the charismatic movement. . . .

3. Some Biblical Guidelines
   A. The Spirit Is Fundamental to Existence of the Church
      1. The roots of the church go beyond Pentecost. But we cannot speak of the church in its full reality apart from the gift of the Spirit at Pentecost. The experiential mark of membership in the church for Jew and Gentile was the presence of the Spirit in them.
      2. Certain basic characteristics of the life of the church are directly related to the presence and work of the Spirit. Notable are the following:

a. The experience of fellowship that bound the early Christians together into a community of shared life and concern (Acts 2:44ff.; Acts 4:32ff.; 1 Corinthians 12:13).

b. The mood of holy joy and enthusiasm that pervaded their lives, inspiring worship and contagious witness (Acts 2:46–47; Romans 14:14; Ephesians 5:18–19).

c. The sense of power that was released in and through them for effective witness and service (Acts 1:8; Acts 2:43; Romans 15:18–19).

d. The awareness of a freedom that offered new possibilities for becoming the faithful people of God. This included freedom from the tyranny of sin and Satan; from bondage to long and powerful cultural and religious traditions; freedom to love, to serve, to live the more abundant life. There was victory in principle even over death. "Where the Spirit of the Lord is there is freedom" (2 Corinthians 3:17).

B. Significant Features of the New Testament Understanding of the Spirit

1. The Spirit indwells every Christian. To belong to Christ is to have the Spirit (Romans 8:9). It is not possible to distinguish between Christians on the basis of having or not having the Spirit.

2. The Spirit undergirds the whole range of Christian experience from beginning to end. This provides the broad basic framework for Paul's conception of spiritual gifts. Unlike the Corinthians, Paul did not limit the operations of the Spirit to the unusual and the spectacular.

3. The Spirit is closely tied to the person and mission of Christ. Although the dispensation of the Spirit follows the historical ministry of Jesus, it does not supersede it. The Spirit remains subject to Christ. The Spirit interprets Christ (John 14:16; 15:26; 16:13ff.) and the person and life of Christ is the norm for understanding who the Spirit is and what He does (1 Corinthians 12:3).

4. The Spirit was given that the church might truly be the body of Christ sharing in His life, faithfully manifesting His character, and being fruitful in every good work (Romans 8:29; Galatians 5:16–26). This is the basic evidence of the Spirit's presence and work. To stress the gifts of the Spirit at the expense of the ethical is not only to distort the gospel but also to invite judgment upon ourselves (Acts 8:18–24).

5. The Spirit was given to the church to empower it for the task of bearing witness to Christ (Acts 1:8). A powerful

evangelistic ministry in word and deed which is effective in making disciples among all nations is one of the most immediate and primary results of the Spirit's work since Pentecost.

6. In brief, it is the work of the Spirit so to interpret and vitalize the gospel in the lives of God's people in all its manifold and rich dimensions that the church, in turn, may become part of the good news of God's grace and purpose, commending its truth to the world.

C. Establishing and Maintaining a Relationship with the Spirit

1. The normal pattern for the reception of the Spirit is indicated at the close of Peter's sermon at Pentecost. "Repent and be baptized . . . in the name of Jesus Christ for the forgiveness of your sins and you shall receive the gift of the Holy Spirit" (Acts 2:38). Repentance involves a change of attitude from unbelief to faith in God's act in Christ. This new attitude publicly expressed in the symbolic rite of baptism is the basis upon which the Spirit is bestowed. Everyone meeting this condition may rightly claim the promised gift of the Spirit. . . .

D. The Fruit of the Spirit

1. This phrase occurs in the New Testament only in Galatians 5:22–23. The word "fruit" is a collective singular. It includes a variety (nine) of Christian graces such as love, joy, and peace. The model of Christian character that is sketched in this passage is drawn from the figure of Christ in the Gospels. It is God's purpose that we should "be conformed to the image of his Son" (Romans 8:29). All of these spiritual graces should be manifested in an ever-increasing measure in the life of every Christian as there is growth in the grace and knowledge of Christ (2 Peter 3:18).

2. The "fruit of the Spirit" is set in contrast to the "works of the flesh" (Galatians 5:19ff.). These are expressions of unredeemed human nature. It should be noted that the vices in this catalog are destructive of genuine community. The fruit of the Spirit, on the contrary, builds community.

3. The realization of these Christian virtues is tied to the indwelling presence of the Spirit in our lives. They are not produced by our unaided human effort. Neither are they the result of an automatic working of the Spirit apart from our efforts. They are brought to expression through the discipline of self-surrender and obedience to the Spirit whose will it is to reproduce the character of Christ in each of us.

4. The single occurrence of the phrase "the fruit of the Spirit" (vs. the repeated use of the "gift" terminology) should not obscure the fundamental importance of this aspect of the Spirit's work. The exhortations scattered throughout the New Testament emphasize this fact. Indeed, the meaning of the ultimate purpose of the gospel and the nature of Christian discipleship is in danger of distortion when this aspect of the Spirit's work is not kept steadily in view.

E. What Are Spiritual Gifts?

1. The "gifts of the Spirit" as a technical expression refers to service abilities given by the Spirit to Christians for the purpose of meeting needs in the life and ministry of the church. There are four catalogs of such gifts in Paul's letters—Romans 12:6–8; 1 Corinthians 12:8–10; 1 Corinthians 12:28; Ephesians 4:11—and a brief one in 1 Peter 4:10–11. The gifts are to be distinguished from the "fruit of the Spirit" (Galatians 5:22–23).

2. The lists of gifts vary in length and content, which suggest that they are representative rather than exhaustive in character. The gifts are God's response to the needs of the church on earth. As needs to some extent may vary, so also the gifts. Broadly viewed, the gifts fall into two groups, gifts of word and gifts of deed, corresponding to the two general areas of need in the life of the church.

3. Both ordinary and extraordinary abilities are included among the gifts. . . .

4. The gifts are sovereignly and diversely bestowed (1 Corinthians 12:7–11). . . .

5. The primary purpose for which the gifts are given is the edification of the church (1 Corinthians 12:7; Ephesians 4:11–16). The emphasis on love in connection with the discussion of the gifts in 1 Corinthians 12 to 14 is significant. Love prevents the selfish use of the gifts which so often disrupts rather than edifies the church. Furthermore, if gifts are given to edify the church, their presence in response to genuine needs in the contemporary church should be anticipated.

6. There is need for the congregation to test spiritual gifts. The primary tests for discerning whether gifts are genuine or false are: whether they conform to the person and life of Christ and whether they build the community in faith.

Thomas N. Finger

A leading Anabaptist theologian, Thomas N. Finger has recently released a massive book, *A Contemporary Anabaptist Theology*, that puts his own tradition in theological and ecumenical dialogue with other traditions. One of the ecumenical proposals Finger has suggested for years is an attempt to find common ground between an Anabaptist notion of salvation as discipleship and the Orthodox view of *theosis*.

The Spirit's Work in Discipleship and Divinization

> From Thomas N. Finger, *A Contemporary Anabaptist Theology: Biblical, Historical, Constructive* (Downers Grove, IL: InterVarsity Press, 2004), 150–51.

In sum, Orthodoxy's concept of divine energies can help Anabaptist theology characterize divinization and ontological transformation as not becoming a different, divine being, but as renewal of our thoroughly human being by the divine Being's direct action or touch. Christomorphism can help Anabaptists insist that this occurs through earthly following of and increasing conformity to Jesus and his way.

Biblical considerations. Is something like this historic Anabaptist notion, now sharpened by Orthodoxy, found in Scripture? Precise theological language of divinization appears only in 2 Peter 1:4, which Anabaptists often cited: we are becoming "participants of the divine nature." But something quite similar is conveyed by the Anabaptists' foremost biblical image, the new birth: we are born from the Word of truth (Jas 1:18), from imperishable seed through the living Word (1 Pet 1:23), through Jesus' resurrection (1 Pet 1:3–4), "from above of water and Spirit" (Jn 3:3, 5). Birth seems to indicate impartation of something of divine reality itself.

The Bible also attributes such a direct transformation to the Holy Spirit's work in and among us. This can operate below conscious levels (Rom 8:26–27; cf. Gal 4:6; 1 Cor 2:9–11). God's Spirit makes our bodies, personal and corporate, God's own temple (1 Cor 3:16–17; 6:17, 19; cf. 1 Cor 12:13; Eph 2:18, 22).The Spirit liberates us and transforms us into the divine glory (2 Cor 3:17–18; Rom 8:13–22, 1 Pet 4:13–14). . . .

The Johannine writings expressed the same realities. . . . We are also "born" of the Spirit (Jn 3:3–8), of the Son (1 Jn 2:29) and of God (1 Jn 3:9; 4:7, 12; 5:1, 18). Moreover, the Son and Father dwell in each other (Jn 14:10–11), and Christians dwell in both (Jn 14:20–23; 17:22–23), so that salvation involves participation in the trinitarian dynamic (Jn 14:16–17; 15:26; 16:13–16).

For various New Testament writers, then, salvation involved God's direct, personal transforming action within and among individuals.

The reason that divinization—a highly pneumatological concept—finds resonance with Anabaptist soteriology is the biblical Spirit Christology.

From Finger, *Contemporary Anabaptist Theology*, 358–59, 458.

Historic Anabaptists . . . underlined not only the specific features of Jesus' historical work but also its present, participatory character. Salvation, that is, was not only christomorphic but also divinization, bestowed by the risen Jesus. . . . We can best explore the latter biblically by examining, in greater detail . . . how Jesus' work was connected with the Holy Spirit's.

God's Spirit, who was credited with begetting Jesus, prepared the way for him and inaugurated his ministry at his baptism (Mk 1:10–11 and parallels). The Spirit then impelled Jesus into the wilderness encounter with Satan and back to Galilee (Mt 4:1; Mk 1:12; Lk 4:1, 14, 18). The Spirit continually guided and empowered Jesus, particularly his exorcisms. Indeed, Jesus may have become convinced that the kingdom was coming through his "awareness of otherly power working through him. . . . In his action God acted. . . . The sufferer was relieved, the prisoner freed, the evil departed. This could only be the power of God."[5] Jesus' exorcisms "by the Spirit" provided the main evidence that God's kingdom was plundering Satan's (Mt 12:28; cf. Mt 12:31–32; Lk 11:14–22). Then through the Spirit, Jesus offered himself to God on the cross (Heb 9:14). In turn the Father raised him through the Spirit (Rom 1:4, 8:11; 1 Tim 3:16; 1 Pet 3:18–19).

With this exaltation . . . Jesus entered a divine communion so full that he began bestowing the Spirit on others. This meant not that Jesus remained distant but that through the Spirit he came to them (Jn 14:16–19, 26; 16:13–15; 1 Jn 3:24; 4:13). A few texts nearly identified the work of Jesus and the Spirit (1 Cor 15:45; 2 Cor 3:17). In other texts the Spirit led humans into the divine. The same Spirit surged through the whole creation (esp. Rom 8:18–27). . . . Jesus' resurrection bestowed the Spirit who alone could clear out that channel, opening it toward God. . . .

The New Testament portrays Jesus not only as wholly led by the Spirit but more specifically as the second Adam who reversed the path by which the first had brought humans under death's reign, so that they might reign eternally in life (Rom 5:12–21; cf. 1 Cor 15:45–49).

5. James Dunn, *Christology in the Making* (Philadelphia: Westminster Press, 1980), 47.

After raising Jesus, being given by the Father to Jesus and then being poured out by him (Acts 2:33; cf. Jn 14:16; 15:26), the Spirit was often recognized as initiator of the saving process. The Holy Spirit was salvation's "guarantee" (*arrabon*, 2 Cor 1:22; 5:5) and "firstfruits" (*aparchē*, Rom 8:23)—not as an extrinsic sign but an intrinsic energy. The Spirit was central in salvation's early stages (Rom 7:6; 1 Cor 13; Gal 3:2–5) and guided salvation toward its goal (Gal 5:5, 16–25; 2 Thess 2:13). The Holy Spirit also bestowed "life" (*zōē*) directly: not biological longevity but divine energy that raised Jesus from death's dominion (Rom 1:4; 8:10–11; 1 Tim 3:16; 1 Pet 3:18). . . . This direct impartation was also expressed through the feminine metaphor of birth. . . . In the early church then Spirit, Son and Father were experienced as salvation's direct agents, sometimes operating in a threefold, interwoven dynamic.

The Spirit in the Ecumenical Movement

The Spirit, Mission, and Healing

May 6–19, 2005, the Commission of the World Mission and Evangelization (CWME) held its latest world conference, which takes place every seventh year, under the title "Come Holy Spirit, heal and reconcile—Called in Christ to be reconciling and healing communities." Its membership is wider than the WCC, including for the first time the official participation of the Roman Catholic Church, and a number of pentecostal-charismatic and other "nonecumenical" churches were represented. Out of many preparatory papers, two are selected here to highlight the pneumatological and salvific themes.

> From "The Healing Mission of the Church," Commission for World Mission and Evangelization, World Council of Churches, preparatory paper no. 11 for the May 2005 CWME Conference in Athens, "Come Holy Spirit, heal and reconcile—Called in Christ to be reconciling and healing communities," http://www.mission2005.org.

37. . . . In the power of the Holy Spirit, Jesus of Nazareth was a healer, exorcist, teacher, prophet, guide and inspirator. He brought and offered freedom from sin, evil, suffering, illness, sickness, brokenness, hatred and disunity (Luke 4:16ff, Matthew 11:2–6). . . . Jesus' healings always brought about a complete restoration of body and mind unlike what we normally experience in healings. . . .

40. In ecumenical missiology, the Holy Spirit, Lord and life-giving, is believed to be active in church and world. The ongoing work of the Holy Spirit in the whole of creation initiating signs and foretastes of the new creation (2 Cor. 5:17) affirms that the healing power of God transcends all limits of places and times and is at work inside as well as outside the Christian church transforming humanity and creation in the perspective of the world to come.

God the Holy Spirit is the fountain of life for Christian individual and community life (John 7:37–39). The Spirit enables the church for mission and equips her with manifold charisms, including (e.g.) the one to heal (cure) by prayer and imposition of hands, the gift of consolation and pastoral care for those whose suffering seems without end, the charism of exorcism to cast out evil spirits, the authority of prophecy to denounce the structural sins responsible for injustice and death, and the charism of wisdom and knowledge essential to scientific research and the exercise of medical professions. But God the Holy Spirit also empowers the Christian community to forgive, share, heal wounds, overcome divisions and so journey towards full communion. The Spirit pursues thus, widens and universalises Christ's healing and reconciling mission.

Groaning in church and creation (Rom. 8), the Spirit also actualises Christ's solidarity with the suffering and so witnesses to the power of God's grace that may also manifest itself paradoxically in weakness or illness (II Cor. 12:9).

41. The Spirit fills the church with the transforming authority of the resurrected Lord who heals and liberates from evil, and with the compassion of the suffering Servant who dies for the world's sin and consoles the downtrodden. A Spirit-led healing mission encompasses both bold witness and humble presence.

The Spirit and Reconciliation

One of the preparatory documents of the conference speaks of the Spirit's role in reconciliation.

> From preparatory paper no. 4 for the May 2005 CWME Conference in Athens, "Come Holy Spirit, heal and reconcile—Called in Christ to be reconciling and healing communities," http://www.mission2005.org.

The Holy Spirit calls us to a ministry of reconciliation and to express this in both the spirituality and strategies of our mission and evangelism. . . . We look to the Spirit of God to lead us and all creation in integrity and wholeness and empower our reconciliation with God and one another. However, exposed to the strength and vicissitudes of global forces, the difficulties of discerning the Holy Spirit among the complexities of the world have never been greater as we are faced with difficult personal and strategic choices in mission. . . . Since Pentecost the Holy Spirit has inspired the church to proclaim Jesus Christ and we continue to be obedient to the command to preach the gospel in all the world. The Holy Spirit anointed the Son of God to bring good news to the poor and we seek to continue his liberating mission through the struggle for justice on the side of the oppressed and marginalized. Recognising that the Spirit of God has been present in creation since the beginning and goes before us in our mission and evangelism, we have also affirmed the Spirit's creativity expressed in diverse cultures and we have entered into dialogue with people of other faiths.

. . . The Holy Spirit empowers the church to participate in this work of reconciliation as the document "Mission and Evangelism in Unity" states: "The mission of God (*missio Dei*) is the source of and basis for the mission of the church, the body of Christ. Through Christ in the Holy Spirit, God indwells the church, empowering and energizing its members." The ministry of the Spirit (2 Cor. 3:8) is a ministry of reconciliation, made possible through Christ and entrusted to us (2 Cor. 5:18–19).

In the power of the Spirit, the church as *koinonia*—the communion of the Holy Spirit (2 Cor. 13:13)—continually grows into a healing and reconciling community that shares the joys and sorrows of her members and reaches out to those in need of forgiveness and reconciliation. According to the book of Acts (2:44–45; 4:32–37), the early church, having been born on the day of Pentecost, shared its goods among her members, pointing to the interrelatedness of "spiritual" and "material" concerns in Christian mission and church life. One aspect of the empowering ministry of the Holy Spirit is to endow Christians and Christian communities with charismatic gifts, which include healing (1 Cor. 12:9; Acts 3).

The Spirit among Religions

One of the themes widely studied and debated in the WCC has to do with Christianity's relation to other religions. Several meetings and consultations, including the above-mentioned Athens Conference as well as a meeting in June 2005 involving some 130 participants of different faiths, have participated in the preparation and continuing refinement of a major document that would set forth an authentic Christian response to religions. The newest published version is titled "Religious Plurality and Christian Self-Understanding." The following excerpts highlight the ministry and role of the Spirit in the theology of religions.

From "Religious Plurality and Christian Self-Understanding," *Current Dialogue* 45 (July 2005), http://www.wcc-coe.org/wcc/what/interreligious/cd45-01.html.

32. The Holy Spirit helps us to live out Christ's openness to others. The person of the Holy Spirit moved and still moves over the face of the earth to create, nurture and sustain, to challenge, renew and transform. We confess that the activity of the Spirit passes beyond our definitions, descriptions, and limitations in the manner of the wind that "blows where it wills" (John 3:8). Our hope and expectancy are rooted in our belief that the "economy" of the Spirit relates to the whole creation. We discern the Spirit of God moving in ways that we cannot predict. We see the nurturing power of the Holy Spirit working within, inspiring human beings in their universal longing for, and seeking after, truth, peace and justice (Rom. 8:18–27). "Love, joy, peace, patience, kindness, goodness, faithfulness, gentleness, self-control," wherever they are found, are the fruit of the Spirit (Gal. 5:22–23, cf. Rom. 14:17).

33. We believe that this encompassing work of the Holy Spirit is also present in the life and traditions of peoples of living faith. People have at all times and in all places responded to the presence and activity of God among them, and have given their witness to their encounters with the living God. In this testimony they speak both of seeking and of having found wholeness, or enlightenment, or divine guidance, or rest, or liberation. This is the context in which we as Christians testify to the salvation we have experienced through Christ. This ministry of witness among our neighbours of other faiths must presuppose an "affirmation of what God has done and is doing among them" (CWME San Antonio 1989).

45. Extending such hospitality is dependant on a theology that is hospitable to the "other." Our reflections on the nature of the biblical witness to God, what we believe God to have done in Christ, and the work of the Spirit shows that at the heart of the Christian faith lies an attitude of hospitality that embraces the "other" in their otherness. It is this spirit that needs to inspire the theology of religions in a world that needs healing and reconciliation. And it is this spirit that may also bring about our solidarity with all who, irrespective of their religious beliefs, have been pushed to the margins of society.

CHAPTER 13

*The Spirit in "Evangelical"
and Pentecostal/
Charismatic Traditions*

The Spirit in "Evangelical" Theologies

In recent decades the term *evangelical* in North American parlance (and by extension in the wider English-speaking world, including the British Isles) has become a technical term referring to a conservative segment of Christian churches who want to hold on to biblical authority and classical Christianity as explicated in the ancient creeds and Protestant Reformation. This is, of course, a significant departure from its original meaning, in which "evangelical" denoted Protestant theology as opposed to Catholic theology—thus, for example, the "Evangelical-Lutheran Church" or "evangelical theological faculty." While critical of "liberal theology," the evangelical movement, which is transdenominational and global, representing not only all sorts of Protestants from Lutherans to Presbyterians to Baptists to Pentecostals but also Anglicans, has distanced itself from the more reactionary fundamentalism (even though most fundamentalists claim to be the "true" evangelicals). Before presenting contributions of some leading evangelical theologians, we will discuss a key document produced by the worldwide movement.

The Lausanne Covenant
The International Congress on World Evangelization was held in Lausanne, Switzerland, in 1974. This gathering was organized by a committee headed by Rev. Billy Graham and drew more than 2,300 evangelical leaders from 150 countries. Lausanne I, as it is called, produced a significant theological statement, the *Lausanne Covenant*, that focused on mission, evangelism, and social concern. The following citations are from that document.

From *Lausanne Covenant*, by the Lausanne Movement, http://www.lausanne.org/
lausanne-1974/lausanne-covenant.html (accessed June 12, 2008).

2. The Authority and Power of the Bible
We affirm the divine inspiration, truthfulness and authority of both Old and New Testament . . . for God's revelation in Christ and in

Scripture is unchangeable. Through it the Holy Spirit still speaks today. He illumines the minds of God's people in every culture to perceive its truth freshly through their own eyes and thus discloses to the whole Church ever more of the many-colored wisdom of God. . . .

4. The Nature of Evangelism
To evangelize is to spread the good news that Jesus Christ died for our sins and was raised from the dead according to the Scriptures, and that as the reigning Lord he now offers the forgiveness of sins and the liberating gifts of the Spirit to all who repent and believe. . . .

12. Spiritual Conflict
We believe that we are engaged in constant spiritual warfare with the principalities and powers of evil, who are seeking to overthrow the Church and frustrate its task of world evangelization. We know our need to equip ourselves with God's armour and to fight this battle with the spiritual weapons of truth and prayer. For we detect the activity of our enemy, not only in false ideologies outside the Church, but also inside it in false gospels which twist Scripture and put people in the place of God. . . . The Church must be in the world; the world must not be in the Church. . . .

14. The Power of the Holy Spirit
We believe in the power of the Holy Spirit. The Father sent his Spirit to bear witness to his Son; without his witness ours is futile. Conviction of sin, faith in Christ, new birth and Christian growth are all his work. Further, the Holy Spirit is a missionary spirit; thus evangelism should arise spontaneously from a Spirit-filled church. A church that is not a missionary church is contradicting itself and quenching the Spirit. Worldwide evangelization will become a realistic possibility only when the Spirit renews the Church in truth and wisdom, faith, holiness, love and power. We therefore call upon all Christians to pray for such a visitation of the sovereign Spirit of God that all his fruit may appear in all his people and that all his gifts may enrich the body of Christ. Only then will the whole church become a fit instrument in his hands, that the whole earth may hear his voice.

Stanley J. Grenz

The late Canadian Stanley J. Grenz, Baptist by denomination and student of W. Pannenberg, was a leading constructive evangelical scholar who dialogued widely with mainstream Protestant and Roman Catholic theologies. His totally unexpected, sudden death a few years ago hindered him from redeeming the promises of producing the first full-scale evangelical Matrix of Christian Theology for the postmodern world; only the first two works in this projected six-volume series came to light. The first set of citations from his widely used one-volume *Theology for the Community of God* highlight the integral role of the Spirit in revelation and Scripture.

The Spirit, Scripture, and Revelation

From Stanley J. Grenz, *Theology for the Community of God* (Grand Rapids: Wm. B. Eerdmans Publishing Co., 2000), 380–83.

In acknowledging the Bible, we are actually looking to the Holy Spirit who addresses us through its pages.

The close connection between the Spirit and the Bible as his instrumentality is explicitly stated in what Bernard Ramm calls the "Protestant principle of authority." . . . This principle is not the sole possession of Protestants, for it belongs to the common heritage shared by Christians. . . . In short, Scripture is authoritative in that it is the vehicle through which the Spirit chooses to speak. . . .

The Concept of Inspiration.

Inspiration has played a central role in bibliology. Theologians do not agree, however, as to what the term means.

Some theologians understand the word as referring to the Spirit's activity in the lives of the authors of Scripture. They define "inspiration" as his activity in "superintending" the lives of prophets, apostles, and other authors so that what they came to write is Scripture. For the foundation of this understanding, proponents appeal to texts which speak of God's prophets receiving messages from the Lord which they subsequently wrote down (Jer. 36:1, 2; Ezek. 11:5; Mic. 3:8; 2 Pet. 1:21). Consequently, this view is often known as the prophetic model. . . .

Other theologians build from the Pauline declaration, "All Scripture is God-breathed" (2 Tim. 3:16). On this basis, they assert that "inspiration" refers to a quality of the biblical writings themselves.

These two positions are not mutually exclusive. We could construct a mediating position by simply affirming the central element in each alternative. . . . We may define "inspiration" as primarily an activity and secondarily a deposit. It is that work of the Holy Spirit in influencing the authors and compilers of Scripture to produce writings which adequately reflect what God desired to communicate to us. . . .

The Concept of Illumination.
The Spirit's work within Scripture did not end in the distant past. . . .
Illumination . . . belongs to the mission of the Spirit. He makes the
Bible "come alive," as he causes the people of God to understand the
significance of the biblical texts for life in the present. . . . Contrary
to what seems to be a clear historical and logical progression from
inspiration to illumination, the two are actually intertwined.

The Spirit and the Process of Salvation

In keeping with the typical evangelical order, Grenz discusses pneumatology widely in the context of soteriology when speaking of the subjective
application of Christ's objective work. He prefaces his discussion of *ordo
salutis* with a note on the mysterious nature of the person and work of the
Holy Spirit. He speaks next of the Spirit's role in the beginning stages of
the process of salvation.

From Grenz, *Theology for the Community of God*, 433–34, 436, 438.

We may understand the Spirit's application of the work of Christ
in the context of a metaphor drawn from interpersonal relations.
Seen from this perspective, in conversion the Spirit effects *regeneration*. In the miraculous transaction that marks the beginning of our
Christian experience, he authors in us new spiritual life. In this manner, we become members of the family of God and enjoy restored
fellowship with our Creator. . . . Regeneration refers to our spiritual
birth, the transaction that brings us into intimate relationship with
God as his children. Just as physical birth endows the newborn with
a special relationship with his or her parents, so also our spiritual
birth means that we are sons or daughters of God and members of
his family. Through regeneration, we now participate in the divine
family as God's spiritual children. . . . We may also draw from a legal
metaphor in seeking to comprehend the Spirit's work of applying the
provision of Christ. Viewed in this manner, through conversion the
Spirit effects *justification*. The grand transaction is the Spirit's work
in granting us a new standing before God. We are now treated as
righteous in God's sight. . . .

The third metaphor we use in understanding the work of the
Spirit arises from the cosmic drama of the conflict between God
and the powers of evil. In conversion the Spirit effects our *liberation* from enslavement to hostile forces. His presence mediates to
us freedom—the ability to reject sin and choose God's will. . . . The
final motif through which we may view the Spirit's application of
Christ's provision in salvation is that of *empowerment*. In conversion
the Spirit bestows on us power for service.

The following selections highlight the continuation of the process of salvation from sanctification to glorification.

From Grenz, *Theology for the Community
of God*, 440, 444, 446–47.

The saving work of the Holy Spirit in an individual does not end at conversion. This event is only the beginning of a process of transformation into Christ-likeness which extends throughout our days. We speak of this ongoing process as "sanctification." In the strict theological sense sanctification is the Holy Spirit accomplishing God's purpose in us as Christian life proceeds. Or viewed from the human perspective, it is our cooperation with the Spirit in living out in daily life the regeneration, justification, freedom, and power which is ours through conversion, so that we grow in Christlikeness and service to God. . . .

Of utmost significance in the process of sanctification, of course, is the working of God's Spirit. Paul reminded his readers that the Spirit carries on a war with old sinful nature (Gal. 5:17). Likewise, this Spirit provides the necessary power for overcoming temptation (1 Cor. 10:13) and sin (Rom. 8:12–14).

While the ultimate agent of sanctification is the Holy Spirit, in this process he requires our personal cooperation. In fact, we must diligently apply ourselves to the task (2 Pet. 1:5–11). Foundational to our involvement in the battle against our opponent is the utilization of the provision God has given us (2 Pet. 1:3), including our spiritual weaponry (Eph. 6:10–17). Important as well is fervent prayer (Eph. 6:18; Matt. 26:41). But above all, we must love one another (1 Pet. 4:8). . . . The lifelong nature of the sanctification process leads us to anticipate a final aspect of our experience of the Holy Spirit's work in personal salvation. We call this final experience glorification. Simply stated, glorification refers to the Spirit's eschatological completion of our salvation, when he brings us to reflect perfectly the goal of our conversion and sanctification. . . . The agent at work in this dimension of our salvation is the same Holy Spirit who facilitates every step of the divine project. . . .

The effects of glorification will not be limited to the so-called spiritual dimension of our existence, however. Rather, the Christlikeness which the Spirit will cause us to share will extend to our physical bodies as well. Paul declared that "he who raised Christ from the dead will also give life to your mortal bodies through his Spirit who lives in you" (Rom. 8:11). Hence, we can take quite literally John's vision of the new order: "There will be no more death or mourning or crying or pain, for the old order of things has passed away" (Rev. 21:4). Our bodies will no longer be subject to decay, sickness, disease, or death. They will be made perfect, in accordance with the pattern of the glorified body of our risen Lord. Indeed he is the firstfruits of those who will attain to the resurrection (1 Cor. 15:20, 23).

Although it occurs as the culmination of the salvation of the individual believer, glorification is a corporate reality. Rather than happening to each of us alone, the resurrection which facilitates our glorification occurs only as we are participants in the one body of Christ.

Donald Bloesch

The senior evangelical scholar Donald Bloesch, professor emeritus of the University of Dubuque Theological Seminary (Dubuque, Iowa), has published actively during the past four decades, trying to find a middle course between conservative Protestant traditions and mainstream theological thought. One of the seven volumes in his magnum-opus Christian Foundations Series is devoted to the Holy Spirit. While a minister of the United Church of Christ, he did his life work in the Reformed seminary and is thus known for a Reformed-based, especially Barthian-flavored, evangelical theology.

Spirit-Word Theology

In his main pneumatological work, *The Holy Spirit: Works and Gifts*, in keeping with his overall theological method, Bloesch clarifies the meaning of his "Spirit-Word" orientation in the midst of a bewildering diversity of current theological proposals.

From Donald G. Bloesch, introduction to *The Holy Spirit: Works and Gifts*, Christian Foundations Series (Downers Grove, IL: InterVarsity Press, 2000), n.p.

There is a theology of Word and Spirit, which I also call a theology of divine-human encounter or a theology of crisis in that its focus is on the divine judgment over human history. It does not claim to set forth a revealed metaphysic, but at the same time it does not shrink from engaging in metaphysical speculation, for the revelation in Scripture has profound metaphysical implications. In this theology the Bible is not fundamentally a narrative history, though it assuredly contains narrative. Neither is it a handbook of revealed propositions or irreformable truths. Instead it is the mirror of God's self-condescension in Jesus Christ. Narrative is the preponderant form of revelation but not the content. The content is the gospel and the law, a transcendent structure of meaning that is revealed by the Spirit through an encounter with the apostolic proclamation in Scripture and the church.

In keeping with the richness of the ways the biblical narrative describes the Spirit, the Spirit also has a diversity of functions.

From Bloesch, *Holy Spirit*, 73.

The Spirit of God has various roles, and it is a mistake to magnify one of these over all the others. The Spirit is active in creation, as is also the Word or Logos. He is at work in revelation, opening our eyes to the significance of what God has accomplished for us in Jesus Christ. He is the principal agent in our regeneration by which we are born anew into a life of service and freedom (cf. Ezek 36:25–27; Jn 3:1–15; 2 Cor 3:17). He preserves the people of God and indeed all of humanity from the destroying powers of sin, death and hell. He convicts people of their sins and drives them to Christ for mercy and consolation. He empowers the people of God to bear witness to Christ and triumph over the principalities of the world. Together with the other members of the Trinity the Spirit is responsible for the incarnation of God in Jesus Christ. In addition he plays a unique role in the inspiration or supervision of the writing that bears testimony to God's saving act in Christ, the writing that now forms the canon of Holy Scripture (2 Tim 3:16–17; 2 Pet 1:20–21). The Spirit is also the source of the gifts that equip Christians for their holy vocation to be witnesses and ambassadors of the Lord Jesus Christ (cf. Is 11:2; 1 Cor 12, 14; Heb 2:4).

The Spirit and Salvation
Again, Bloesch's preference for "both-and" rather than "either-or" becomes manifest in his discussion of the role of the divine and human with regard to salvation.

From Bloesch, *Holy Spirit*, 322–23, 325–26.

Salvation is comprised not of two levels but of two moments: conversion to Christ and conversion to the world. We not only turn to Christ in faith and repentance, but we also turn to the world with the message of Christ, empowered by his Spirit to witness to his victory over evil. In faith we are baptized into the passion of Christ and rise with him to battle the powers of evil. The baptism of the Spirit does not transport us out of the world but sends us into the midst of the world's affliction and tribulation with a message that can heal and

redeem. . . . The Holy Spirit alone makes our witness spiritually fruitful, but he does not witness for us. He speaks with us and through us
as we speak and pray in obedience to the divine imperative of being
a disciple and herald of the Lord Jesus Christ. . . . Our progress in
holiness is due to the sanctifying work of the Spirit within us, but
the way in which we live our lives testifies to the authenticity of our
faith in Christ. . . . Self-examination and self-mortification do not
gain us access to the Spirit of God, but they proceed from the Spirit's
first grasping us and turning us toward Jesus Christ. The knowledge
of God's love in Christ is prior to the knowledge of our sin. The outpouring of the Spirit precedes mortification and confession. . . .

Against decisionism I contend that the decision of faith does not
procure our salvation but ratifies and confirms it. It does not make
us acceptable before God but certifies that God has accepted us in
Jesus Christ. The decision of faith is both an instrument by which
the Spirit seals the love of Christ within us and a confirmation of
God's undeserved mercy extended to us in Christ. It is also an evidence that the Spirit is at work in our lives. It does not induce God
to grant us his salvation, but it carries salvation forward in our lives.
Our decision and our subsequent obedience contribute to the efficacy of Christ's saving work in our faith pilgrimage. . . . Conversion
is both an event and a continuous process. It begins in the baptism of
the Spirit, who engrafts us into the mystical body of Christ through
faith and repentance. It continues as the Spirit fills us and directs
us in the arduous task of living out our faith. If we fall away from
the faith we need to be engrafted once more into the body of Christ
and experience a new baptism of the Spirit. It is possible to believe
and yet quench and grieve the Spirit by not committing ourselves
unreservedly to Christ. We must then pray that the Spirit's baptizing
work might be made complete in our lives through the obedience
of faith and works of love. . . . All Christians, indeed all mortals, are
called to be saints (cf. Rom 1:7; 1 Cor 1:2), but this mandate cannot
be fulfilled without the outpouring of the Holy Spirit. The Holy Spirit
himself is indeed the sanctifier, the one who works sanctity within
us. But we too have a role—not in the creation of sanctity but in its
manifestation and proclamation. Theologians often err by overem-
phasizing divine sovereignty and minimizing human responsibility
in salvation.

Salvation is not only a gift to be received but also a task to be
performed. It is not only a privilege to be conferred but also a race
to be won, a crown to be gained (1 Cor 9:24; Heb 12:1; 2 Tim 4:8).
Lutherans are often better than Calvinists in affirming the paradox
of divine agency in the procuring of salvation and human responsibility for the loss of salvation. . . .

God is sovereignly free not only in imparting grace but in using means to prepare us for grace and confirm us in grace. Faith comes by hearing, and hearing comes by preaching (Rom 10:17), but it is the Holy Spirit who converts the words of the preacher into the Word of life and who renders the sacrament of baptism efficacious as the vehicle of the water of life. The hope for redemption rests finally on God, on his work of reconciliation in Jesus Christ, on the sending forth of his Spirit at Pentecost. Our task is to celebrate and proclaim the good news that Christ has overcome the powers of sin and death and that he continues to overcome through the Holy Spirit who works within us and upon us as we go forward in the life of faith.

Clark Pinnock

If Grenz represents a "mainstream" evangelical position and Bloesch, the "dialogical" one, then the other senior theological evangelical statesman, the Canadian Clark Pinnock, is to be regarded as both the "revisionist" and charismatically sympathetic theologian in the camp. Throughout his long career, this Baptist professor emeritus of McMaster Divinity College (Hamilton, Ontario, Canada) has challenged his fellow evangelicals to reconsider their positions concerning the doctrine of Scripture, election, God, and theology of religions, to name the most well-known cases. His 1996 *Flame of Love: A Theology of the Holy Spirit* may be the most significant pneumatological work by a contemporary evangelical.

The Spirit Experienced
The way Pinnock opens his pneumatological magnum opus tells a lot about his approach, which is experientially oriented.

From Clark H. Pinnock, *Flame of Love: A Theology of the Holy Spirit*
(Downers Grove, IL: InterVarsity Press, 1996), 12–14.

The Spirit is elusive but profound and worthy of adoration. If Father points to ultimate reality and Son supplies the clue to the divine mystery, Spirit epitomizes the nearness of the power and presence of God. . . . Though this is not a testimony book, I hope the reader will sense how in love with God I am and how much practical usefulness there is in improved theology. Poor theology can hurt us, for we will miss certain stirrings of the Spirit where we are not expecting them and are not open to them owing to an inadequate doctrinal map. If, on the other hand, places and situations are identified where we ought to be expecting the Spirit to be at work, our eyes may be opened to new possibilities. A person who does not expect the Spirit to be at work in the natural order, for example, will not be attentive to such activities in nature and will be impoverished as a result. Similarly, a person unaware of the full range of spiritual gifts that are available will not be open to receive them or may not value certain gifts. . . . To know the Spirit we must become persons of prayer who are willing to yield in complete openness to God. Waiting in silence and patient receptivity will cultivate a heart-knowledge of our Life-giver. Theology must always be more than rational, especially in this case. For we are speaking of a reality that is active in our lives and that cannot be captured altogether in cognitive ways. There are depths of the mystery that cannot be accessed by reason alone. . . . The heart dimension comes into play immediately. For of all theological topics, Spirit is one of the most elusive. . . . The Spirit is experiential, and the topic is oriented toward transformation more than information.

The Principle of Continuity

A distinctive feature of Pinnock's theology of the Spirit highlights the principle of continuity: the same Spirit that was instrumental in creation is also instrumental in new creation.

From Pinnock, *Flame of Love*, 54, 61.

Only the Spirit who brought life to the world in the first place can bring new life to it. Redemption does not leave the world behind but lifts creation to a higher level. The Spirit has been implementing God's purposes for creation from day one and is committed to seeing to it that they issue in restoration. Creator Spirit inspires hope for a world beyond the reach of humanity, in which God's power raises the dead and makes everything new. The prophet asks, "Can these bones live?" and God tells him to say, "I will cause breath [my Spirit] to enter you, and you shall live" (Ezek 37:1–6). Another prophet says that creation will be desolate "until a spirit from on high is poured out on us, and the wilderness becomes a fruitful field" (Is 32:15). They can speak of the Spirit in this way only because he is the power of creation. . . . Spirit challenges everyone to relate to God by means of his self-disclosure to every nation in the course of history. God is revealed in the beauty and order of the natural world and is the prevenient grace that benefits every person.

Logos and Spirit Christologies

While Pinnock is not recommending that theology should replace the Logos (Word) Christology with Spirit Christology, he is calling for a balance. One of the main reasons for this call is the prevalence of the references to the Spirit in relation to Jesus Christ in the Gospels.

From Pinnock, *Flame of Love*, 79–82, 85.

Anointing by the Spirit is central for understanding the person and work of Jesus—more central than theology has normally made it. Christology must not lack for pneumatology. The Gospel narratives portray the Spirit as working actively in every phase of Jesus' life and mission. The title "Christ" itself signifies anointing—in this case by the Spirit. Jesus is the Christ, the Anointed One, and therefore he said when inaugurating his mission in Nazareth, "The Spirit of the Lord is upon me, because he has anointed me to bring good news to the poor" (Lk 4:18). Jesus was a man of the Spirit. . . . It may be that if this truth is given its due, we will gain insight into the Person and work of Christ. . . .

Just as there has been neglect of the Spirit as Creator, there has been neglect concerning the work of the Spirit in relation to Christ. The effect of such neglect has been to exalt Christ above Spirit and direct attention away from certain aspects of Christ's work as the last Adam, representative of the human race. . . . I am not suggesting a rejection of Logos Christology, only contesting its dominance over other models. . . . Jesus was ontologically Son of God from the moment of conception, but he became Christ by the power of the Spirit. When Satan tempted him to misuse his powers, the Son refused, choosing the path of dependence on the Spirit.

The Almighty has inserted himself into history and humanity in Jesus—as weak, powerless and dependent on the Spirit—in order to become what we were meant to be, the communion of God and humanity. By the Spirit he has also become through resurrection the firstfruits of a new humanity. As a result of his assuming our human nature as last Adam, Jesus has created a new human situation ("there is a new creation," 2 Cor 5:17). As a result, we all in union with Christ by the power of the Spirit are enabled to participate in divine life. . . . The point to stress here is that the Spirit is more central to the story of Jesus than theology has usually acknowledged. It was by the Spirit that Jesus was conceived, anointed, empowered, commissioned, directed and raised up. . . . The Gospels present Jesus as dependent on the Spirit. They depict the Spirit as helping him trace out his human path. Spirit prepared for his coming, was instrumental in his birth, guided him through life and by his death and resurrection opened up the door to salvation for everyone.

The Spirit is also the key for understanding the *kenosis*, self-emptying, of Jesus.

The Spirit and Union

A robust Spirit Christology is also the basis for an equally robust pneumatological theology of salvation in which Pinnock borrows from the Orthodox notion of *theosis* with the stated intention of balancing and enriching the typical Western notion of justification.

From Pinnock, *Flame of Love*, 149–51, 155.

When we look at salvation from the standpoint of the Spirit, we view it in relational, affective terms. Every religion on earth has its idea about the goal of life. Martin Luther's experience of salvation as justification has skewed the Christian understanding somewhat toward legal terms. Emphasis has been placed on the sinner's change of status, from guilty to not guilty, rather than on personal union with God. While Luther caught an aspect of the truth, a more relational model is required. Spirit is leading us to union—to transforming, personal, intimate relationship with the triune God. "This is eternal life, that they may know you, the only true God, and Jesus Christ whom you have sent" (Jn 17:3). Jesus adds, "That the love with which you have loved me may be in them, and I in them" (v. 26). As the psalmist says, "Lord, you have been our dwelling place in all generations" (Ps 90:1). Let us explore salvation now as the beatific vision, as the embrace of God. . . . Salvation is directed toward the loving embrace of God. . . . The Spirit summons us to a transforming friendship with God that leads to sharing in the triune. Thanks to the grace of Christ and the love of God, the Spirit dwells in and unites us to the corporate triune fellowship (2 Cor 13:13). . . . Peter gives it classic expression: Christians are becoming "participants of the divine nature" (2 Pet 1:4). The destiny of the community is to be embraced in triune life as its final condition. . . . What we call union (theosis or divinization) is not pantheism—there is no absorption of the person in God. By the grace of God and as creatures we participate in him. United to Christ without becoming Christ, we are also united to God without becoming God. It is a personal union in which the distinction between Creator and creature is maintained. We enter the dance of the Trinity not as equals but as adopted partners. When Peter says we participate in the divine nature, he is indicating not ontological union but union in resurrected bodies. This is a personal union, not an ontological union. It does not deny the distinction between God and creature or make God the only reality. As the Persons of the Trinity dwell in and with one another, so we, created in the image of God, dwell in and with God, sharing the life of the Trinity and experiencing movements of love passing between the Persons.

The Spirit and Universality

Differently from most evangelicals, Pinnock speaks boldly for the "wideness in God's mercy"—as the title of one of his well-known books puts it—in relation to other religions. He interprets this pneumatologically and argues that salvation through the Spirit's ministry may be available to many more than traditional Christians and contemporary conservatives have believed.

From Pinnock, Flame of Love, 188, 192–95.

Access to grace is less of a problem for theology when we consider it from the standpoint of the Spirit, because whereas Jesus bespeaks particularity, Spirit bespeaks universality. The incarnation occurred in a thin slice of land in Palestine, but its implications touch the farthest star. Spirit helps theology break free of attitudes that diminish grace and create helplessness. . . . Recognizing the cosmic breadth of Spirit activities can help us understand the divine universality, since God's breath is everywhere, reaching out and touching people. The bond of love of the Trinity is the power of God in the world, ceaselessly pouring out love and creating hope. The Spirit has a thousand ways of passing by and gracing people. . . .

There is a tension inherent in the Christian faith between universality and particularity, a tension between the belief that God loves the whole world (universality) and the belief that Jesus is the only way to God (particularity). It challenges skills of theological interpretation to explain how they both can be true. Does God love the whole world or not? . . . I believe it would help us if we recognized the twin, interdependent missions of Son and Spirit. It reduces tension between universality and particularity and fosters a sense that they are complementary rather than contradictory. The two poles turn out to be both-and, not either-or.

Here is the scenario. Christ, the only mediator, sustains particularity, while Spirit, the presence of God everywhere, safeguards universality. Christ represents particularity by being the only mediator between God and humanity (1 Tim 2:5–6), while Spirit upholds universality because no soul is beyond the sphere of the Spirit's operations. Spirit is not confined to the church but is present everywhere, giving life and creating community. Hovering over the waters of creation, Spirit is present also in the search for meaning and the struggle against sin and death. Because inspiration is ubiquitous and works everywhere in unseen ways, Spirit is in a position to offer grace to every person. Because Spirit works everywhere in advance of the church's mission, preparing the way for Christ, God's will can be truly and credibly universal. The life-giving Spirit, breathed out by the Father, works in the world and in all of history. The Spirit renews the face of the ground, gives life to every creature and bestows insight. God's Spirit and wisdom are at work everywhere— their action pervaded history from the beginning and continue to do so. . . . God's empowered presence graces the world, giving life and hope. It is the source of movement in the world and is present wherever reality reaches out to God. Spirit is not an esoteric "ghost" but an empirical power that breaks forth in perceptible ways. This is the power that called forth life from nonlife and the power drawing humanity to God. . . . Spirit works ceaselessly to persuade human beings to trust and open themselves up to love. Those with eyes to see can discern the Spirit's activity in human culture and religion, as God everywhere draws people to friendship. . . . Humanity was made to live in fellowship with God, and Spirit everywhere woos sinners to come home. The incarnation should not be viewed as a negation of universality but as the fulfillment of what Spirit had been doing all along. The birth of Jesus by the Spirit was the climax of a universal set of operations. Hovering over Mary, Spirit was engaged in new creation. The incarnation marked a new stage in Spirit's universal operations. Spirit, everywhere at work in the whole of history, was now at work in Jesus to make him the head of a new humanity. Throughout history the Spirit has been seeking to create such an impression of God's true self in human beings and hear the response to God that would delight his heart. This is what happened in Jesus by the Spirit.

Pentecostal and Charismatic Testimonies

Pentecostal Testimonies
While pentecostal and charismatic movements represent a highly diverse and fluid constellation of churches, movements, and groups, a scholarly typology is emerging. *The New International Dictionary of Pentecostal and Charismatic Movements*[1] makes a threefold distinction: (1) (classical)

---

1. Stanley M. Burgess and Eduard M. van der Maas, eds., *The New International Dictionary of Pentecostal and Charismatic Movements,* rev. and exp. ed. (Grand Rapids: Zondervan, 2002).

pentecostal denominations such as Assemblies of God or Foursquare Gospel, which owe their existence to the famous Azusa Revival in the beginning of the twentieth century in Los Angeles, California; (2) charismatic pentecostal-type spiritual movements within the established churches (the largest of which is the Roman Catholic charismatic renewal); and (3) neo-charismatic movements, some of the most notable of which are the Vineyard Fellowship in the United States, African initiated churches, and the China house church movement, as well as an innumerable number of independent churches and groups all over the world. In membership, the charismatic movements (about 200 million) and neo-charismatics (200–300 million) well outnumber classical Pentecostals (75–125 million). Some distinctive pentecostal contributions to pneumatology will be first presented, to be followed by a more extensive discussion of Spirit baptism and spiritual gifts, the most distinctive concept among Pentecostals and charismatic Christians. The distinctive contributions from charismatic movements will be introduced in that section as well.

In Search of Pentecostalism

A key debate in pentecostal studies is the question of definition, which of course has everything to do with what can be regarded as pentecostal pneumatology. The following is a short, inclusive definition.

From Allan Anderson, *An Introduction to Pentecostalism:
Global Charismatic Christianity* (Cambridge: Cambridge
University Press, 2004), 13–14, 187, 196.

I think that the term "Pentecostal" is appropriate for describing globally all churches and movements that emphasize the working of the gifts of the Spirit, both on phenomenological and on theological grounds—although not without qualification. A broader definition should emphasize Pentecostalism's ability to "incarnate" the gospel in different cultural forms. . . . The debate about the meaning of "Pentecostal" and "Pentecostalism" must conclude that it is a definition that cannot be prescribed. . . .

If there is one central and distinctive theme in Pentecostal and Charismatic theology, then it is the work of the Holy Spirit. The history sketched in this book has shown that all the various expressions of Pentecostalism have one common experience, that is a personal encounter with the Spirit of God enabling and empowering people for service. Pentecostals often declare that "signs and wonders" accompany this encounter, certain evidence of "God with us." Through their experience of the Spirit, Pentecostals and Charismatics make the immanence of God tangible. . . .

The starting point for Pentecostal theology is its distinctive spirituality: "the Holy" Spirit who is "God with us." The central Pentecostal concern is "to emphasise the lived reality of the faith, the life and service of the people of God who are organically constituted as the body of Christ by the indwelling of the Holy Spirit." At the heart of this spirituality is prayer, through which people respond to God's revelation. . . . The experience of the fullness of the Spirit is the essence of Pentecostal and Charismatic theology.

Pentecostals consider the outpouring of the Spirit on the Day of Pentecost the event that constituted the church as an eschatological community. Pentecostals see themselves as heirs of that charismatic event.

> From Steven J. Land, *Pentecostal Spirituality: A Passion for the*
> *Kingdom*, Journal of Pentecostal Theology Supplement Series 1
> (Sheffield: Sheffield Academic Press, 1993), 60–61, 64.

Thus, the outpouring of the Spirit at Pentecost constituted the church as an eschatological community of universal mission in the power and demonstration of the Spirit. The tongues at Pentecost and Peter's subsequent sermon meant that the church in general and each Spirit-filled individual are to be and to give a witness to the mighty acts of God in saving humanity. This witness centers in Jesus Christ and must therefore be given in the power of the Spirit if it is to have continuity with his ministry and fulfill the promise of the Father through Christ. The "full gospel" of the Jesus who is Savior, Sanctifier, Healer, Baptizer in the Holy Spirit and coming King can and should be proclaimed in the fullness of the Spirit so that the kingdom will be manifested in the midst of the world in words and deeds. . . . The outpouring of the Spirit in the post-Easter community created and sustained that eschatological tension and vision which characterized the early church and the early Pentecostals. Now everything was considered from the standpoint of the imminent parousia. In the transcendent presence of God categories of time and space were fused; and, since Jesus was near, so was the end. The Spirit who raised Jesus, made him present in salvation, signs and wonders, and showed things to come. The Spirit who burned as intense hope and energized witness, superintended the ongoing mission. To live in the Spirit was to live in the kingdom. Where the Spirit was present in eschatological power, there was the church of Pentecost.

The Singaporean Pentecostalist Tan-Chow May Ling issues another challenge to pentecostal pneumatology, namely, a more robust christological and Trinitarian focus.

From Tan-Chow May Ling, *Pentecostal Theology for the Twenty-First Century: Engaging with Multi-Faith Singapore*, Ashgate New Critical Thinking in Religion, Theology and Biblical Studies (Aldershot, England: Ashgate, 2007), 102–3.

The fundamental fragility in the empirical Pentecostal conception of the Spirit lies in its inability to connect adequately the inextricable relationship between the empowering work of the Spirit and the life, death and resurrection of Christ. Calvary and Pentecost are regarded as two successive stages of God's activity. . . . It is not that Pentecostalism denies the centrality of the Christ event; conversely, this is its explicit teaching. The problem lies in bifurcating the events of the cross and Pentecost into the "pardon department" and the "power department." The attending danger with such compartmentalisation is the privileging of the experiential (power of the Spirit), and often the experiential becomes disconnected from the life, death and resurrection of Christ. Herein is the fragility inherent in the promise of Pentecostalism . . .—a facile alternative of the either/or, *theologia crucis* or *theologia gloriae*. However, this dangerous bifurcation is neither inevitable nor incorrigible. As Macchia highlights, a consistent Pentecostal theology of the Spirit's empowerment is not viewed as a journey away from the cross or a "journey 'beyond' the figure of Christ"; rather, it is an *intensification* of an involvement of the "prophetic ministry of Jesus for all creation" (italics mine).[2] Passion and Pentecost are not antithetical realities. Pentecost is not about the Spirit's independent agency and autonomous freedom to operate in isolation from the other Persons of the Trinity. Rather, Pentecost reveals how intricately interconnected both they and the events are. Instead of a sequence of disconnected events, the cross and Pentecost are in fact deeply interwoven, as narrated in Luke, John and Paul's writings.

Spirituality as the Bedrock

While the chapters on African, Asian, and Latin American pneumatologies will include pentecostal testimonies, the focus here is on Euro-American testimonies and insights. In general, Pentecostals have not contributed significantly to pneumatology until the last two decades or so when academically trained Pentecostals have joined in academic research and writing. By and large, Pentecostals used to borrow much of their pneumatology from other Christians, especially from the Reformed tradition—and in some cases, depending on the location, from Roman Catholics (Italy and

2. F. D. Macchia, "The Struggle for Global Witness: Shifting Paradigms in Pentecostal Theology," in *The Globalization of Pentecostalism: A Religion Made to Travel*, ed. M. W. Dempster, B. D. Klaus, and D. Petersen (Oxford: Regnum, 1999), 15–16.

France) or Lutherans (Scandinavia)—and just add their distinctive views of Spirit baptism and spiritual gifts. In the beginning of the international Roman Catholic-Pentecostal dialogue, a statement called "Essence of Pentecostalism" was issued that sought to define the basic identity of Pentecostalism in terms of its spirituality.

> From "Essence of Pentecostalism," Statement by the Pentecostal Team at the International Dialogue between the Roman Catholics and Pentecostals at Horgen, Switzerland, 1972, cited in V.-M. Kärkkäinen, *Spiritus ubi vult spirat: Pneumatology in Roman Catholic-Pentecostal Dialogue (1972–1989)*, Schriften der Luther-Agricola-Gesellschaft 42 (Helsinki: Luther-Agricola Society, 1998), 50–51.

It is the personal and direct awareness and experiencing of the indwelling of the Holy Spirit by which the risen and glorified Christ is revealed and the believer is empowered to witness and worship with the abundance of life as described in Acts and the Epistles. The Pentecostal experience is not a goal to be reached, not a place to stand, but a door through which to go into a greater fullness of life in the Spirit. It is an event which becomes a way of life in which often charismatic manifestations have a place. Characteristic of this way of life is a love of the Word of God, fervency in prayer and witness in the world and to the world, and a concern to live by the power of the Holy Spirit.

Whatever the pentecostal contributions are, nearly every scholar agrees that a distinctive charismatic spirituality lies behind and beneath Pentecostalism. Harvey J. Cox, a sympathetic observer of the global movement, helps set the stage. Cox identifies pentecostal spirituality as "elemental" or "primal" spirituality, with three components.

> From Harvey Cox, *Fire from Heaven: The Rise of Pentecostal Spirituality and the Reshaping of Religion in the Twenty-first Century* (Reading, MA: Addison-Wesley, 1995), 82–83.

The first, *primal speech*, pinpoints the spiritual import of what scholars of religion sometimes call "ecstatic utterance" or glossolalia, what the earliest pentecostals called "speaking in tongues," and what many now refer to as "praying in the Spirit." In an age of bombast, hype, and doublespeak, when ultraspecialized terminologies and contrived rhetoric seem to have emptied and pulverized language, the first pentecostals learned to speak—and their successors still speak—with another voice, a language of the heart.

A second dimension, *primal piety*, touches on the resurgence in pentecostalism of trance, vision, healing, dreams, dance, and other archetypal religious expressions. These primeval modes of praise and supplication recall what the great French sociologist Emile Durkheim once called the "elementary forms" of religious life, by which he meant the foundations of human religiosity. Perhaps they also represent a kind of universal spiritual syntax, resembling the "universal grammar" that such structural linguists as Noam Chomsky claim underlies all human languages, however diverse. . . .

The third, *primal hope*, points to pentecostalism's millennial outlook—its insistence that a radically new world age is about to dawn. This is the kind of hope that transcends any particular content. . . . It is what the Epistle to the Hebrews calls the "evidence of things not seen," and because it is more an orientation to the future than a detailed scheme, it persists despite the failure of particular hopes to materialize. Thus despite the fact that the early pentecostals' belief in the imminent and visible Second Coming of Christ seemed to be controverted at one level, the tenacity of primal hope has made their message more contemporary with every passing year.

Holistic Salvation

The Asian American Pentecostal theologian Amos Yong argues that what makes the Pentecostal vision of salvation unique among theological traditions is its pneumatological orientation.

> From Amos Yong, *The Spirit Poured Out on All Flesh: Pentecostalism and the Possibility of Global Theology* (Grand Rapids: Baker Academic, 2005), 82.

A world pentecostal perspective on the doctrine of salvation therefore leads to a pneumatological soteriology. This would be in contrast to soteriologies that tend to bifurcate the work of Christ and of the Spirit, such as those articulated by Protestant scholasticism. In that framework, Christ provides salvation objectively (e.g., in justification) and the Spirit accomplishes salvation subjectively (e.g., in sanctification). Hence the soteriological work of the Spirit is subsequent to and subordinated to the work of Christ. In response, a pneumatological soteriology understands salvation to be the work of both Christ and the Spirit from beginning to end. To use Pauline language: the Holy Spirit enables the proclamation, hearing, and understanding of the gospel, justifies through the resurrection of Christ, provides for the adoption of believers, accomplishes rebirth and renewal, sanctifies hearts and lives, and provides the down payment for eschatological transformation. In all of this, the Spirit is not an appendage to Christ in the process of salvation but saves with Christ throughout.

From the beginning Pentecostals have insisted on the "Full Gospel" in which salvation is expected to compass not only the spiritual but also the physical needs of men and women.

From Vernon Purdy, "Divine Healing," in *Systematic Theology: A Pentecostal Perspective*, ed. Stanley M. Horton (Springfield, MO: Logion Press, 1999), 508–9.

Critics of the biblical doctrine of divine healing do not understand the full extent and significance of Christ's atoning work. Jesus' suffering was for us, in our stead and on our behalf. In Isaiah 53, the Servant of Yahweh experiences rejection and suffering. . . . What is the result? It effects the healing of God's people through "his stripes." The affirmation that the sufferings of Jesus bring healing to those who suffer stands on firm theological ground. The fact that God has healed the sick in the past and that He heals the sick today is evidence of His promised redemption of our bodies (Romans 8:23). When we observe a manifestation of God's power to heal it reminds us that some day, when Christ returns, His people will be delivered completely from the pangs of a fallen world. Even when we are not healed ourselves in the present, the healing of another need not serve as an irresolvable quandary but rather as a divine testimony that we too—if not now, then—shall be made whole. Divine healing is actually an inbreaking of the power of the coming ages. This is how the author of the epistle to the Hebrews understood the signs and wonders that he beheld. They were confirmations of the salvation promised (see Heb. 2:3–4), signs of the "powers of the coming age" (Heb. 6:5). . . . At the same time, divine healing is temporary in this age, . . . serving notice of the impending judgment of God on the kingdoms of this world as well as the establishment in this world of God's righteous rule. That is, healing is a very tangible expression of God's enduring love for His creation.

The healings that Christ performed in the power of the Spirit were signs that the kingdom of God was near (see Matt. 10:7–8). The healing of the sick was understood by Christ and the gospel writers to be an expression of God's future victory, to be consummated when Jesus comes back to earth again. . . . Every time a sick person is healed through prayer and faith in Christ a witness is proclaimed concerning His promised return. It is a testimony of God's faithfulness. Thus, the healings that we experience today are just a first installment of the future redemption of our bodies.

From Yong, *The Spirit Poured Out*, 38–39.

Pentecostals in Latin America are becoming increasingly engaged in social and political activities. Second, such engagement shows an emerging awareness that salvation is not only an otherworldly anticipation but also a this-worldly experience, manifest in the material, economic, social, and political dimensions of human existence. Third, pentecostal leaders and laypersons are realizing more than ever that the outpouring of the Spirit and the saving work of God do not preclude but include these various dimensions. Here the early modern pentecostal conviction that the presence and activity of the Spirit meant the healing of the body or the provision of the material needs of the believer is extended to encompass the sociopolitical sphere.

In the international dialogue between Pentecostals and Roman Catholics, the community-forming power of the Spirit was seen as the key to social concern.

From "Evangelization, Proselytism and Common Witness: Final Report of the Dialogue (1990–1997)," no. 43 in *Information Service* 97 (1998/I–II): 38–56.

In the life of the community, Pentecostals have found a new sense of dignity and purpose in life. Their solidarity creates affective ties, giving them a sense of equality. These communities have functioned as social alternatives that protest against the oppressive structures of the society at large. Along with some social critics, Pentecostals have discovered that effective social change often takes place at the communal and micro-structural level, not at the macro-structural level.

The Spirit in Pentecostal Hermeneutics

Understandably, hermeneutics among Pentecostals is Spirit driven, as several South African Pentecostalists explain.

From Matthew S. Clark, Henry I. Lederle, et al., *What Is Distinctive about Pentecostal Theology?* (Pretoria: University of South Africa, 1989), 101.

Pentecostal use of the Bible is conducted according to a basic hermeneutical model which is distinctively Pentecostal. Although lip-service is often given to non-Pentecostal models, particularly in much of modern Pentecostal training for ministry, in homiletical and teaching practice the Pentecostal model still comes to the fore. In this model the reader of Scripture can identify with the writer by virtue of common spiritual experience. The Bible itself is not used primarily as a source-book of Christian doctrine. It may be rather daring to aver that in Pentecost the role of Scripture is to serve as confirmation and guideline to the dynamic of the Spirit, while at the same time the obvious moving of the Spirit serves as confirmation and guideline to the proclamation of the witness of the Scriptures, since if the context of the statement (a Pentecostal community) is misunderstood, a totally erroneous impression of subjective appropriation of Scripture may be conveyed. However, this is the way it generally works in Pentecost, where the Bible is associated with activity and experience rather than viewed as a text-book of doctrine. Experience after the Biblical pattern takes precedence over confession according to the supposed theological content of Scripture. For instance, trinitarian and non-trinitarian Pentecostals are immediately recognisable as Pentecostal, although in confessional disputes the fur might fly!

Spirit Baptism as an Ecumenical Question

"Sacramental" and "Pentecostal" Interpretations

A distinctive theological category among Pentecostals and charismatic Christians is Spirit baptism. The New Testament scholar J. D. G. Dunn has been one of the instrumental figures in turning contemporary theologians' attention to this concept. Before delving into a more detailed consideration of theological interpretations of Spirit baptism, it is helpful to look at Dunn's broad, twofold typology: what he names "sacramental" and "Pentecostal."

From James D. G. Dunn, *Baptism in the Holy Spirit*
(London: SCM Press, 1975), 21–22, 54.

We can . . . summarize our findings so far as they bear on our debate with Pentecostal and sacramentalist. The former must note that in the initial formulation of his favourite metaphor any idea of a baptism in the Spirit as something which those already in the Kingdom might yet be without is totally excluded. The baptism in the Spirit was not something distinct from and subsequent to entry into the Kingdom; it was only by means of the baptism in Spirit that one could enter at all.

To the sacramentalist we must make two points. First, the baptism in Spirit does not refer to water-baptism. It is simply a metaphor which was drawn from John's water-rite and which was chosen primarily with a view to bringing out the contrast with the water-rite most sharply. In the preaching of the Baptist water-baptism had no part in the future messianic baptism beyond symbolizing it and preparing for it. Second, it is a mistake to say that John's baptism gave or conveyed forgiveness. It is even imprecise and misleading to say that John's baptism resulted in forgiveness. It is the repentance expressed in the baptism which resulted in forgiveness, and it was God who himself conveyed the forgiveness directly to the heart of the repentant. Baptism was the means John used to stimulate repentance and to give it occasion for full and public expression—he may even have regarded baptism as the necessary form for expressing repentance—but that God conveyed the forgiveness through baptism we cannot say on either grammatical or theological grounds.

As in the case of Jesus' experience at Jordan the Pentecostals are quite right to emphasize that Pentecost was an experience of empowering (Luke 24.49; Acts 1.8). However, they, and by no means only they, are again wrong in making Pentecost only and primarily an experience of empowering. On the contrary, the Baptism in the Spirit, as always, is primarily initiatory, and only secondarily an empowering. The fact is that the phrase "baptism in Spirit" is never directly associated with the promise of power, but is always associated with entry into the messianic age or the Body of Christ.

The positive value of the Pentecostal's emphasis is his highlighting of the dramatic nature of the initiating Spirit-baptism: the Spirit not only renews, he also equips for service and witness. Yet, however correct Pentecostals are to point to a fresh empowering of the Spirit as the answer to the Church's sickness, they are quite wrong to call it "the baptism in the Spirit." One does not enter the new age or the Christian life more than once, but one may be empowered by or filled with the Spirit many times (Acts 2.4; 4.8, 31; 9.17; 13.9; Eph. 5.18).

Spirit Baptism in the Wider Christian Tradition

The way John of Damascus subsumes Spirit baptism under the idea of "baptism" of purification or cleansing is typical of mainline Christian tradition.

From John of Damascus, *Exposition of the Orthodox Faith*, trans. S. D. F. Salmond, *NPNF*[2] 9, bk. 4, chap. 9, p. 78, http://www.ccel.org.

For since man's nature is twofold, consisting of soul and body, He bestowed on us a twofold purification, of water and of the Spirit: the Spirit renewing that part in us which is after His image and likeness, and the water by the grace of the Spirit cleansing the body from sin and delivering it from corruption, the water indeed expressing the image of death, but the Spirit affording the earnest of life. . . . The remission of sins, therefore, is granted alike to all through baptism: but the grace of the Spirit is proportional to the faith and previous purification. Now, indeed, we receive the firstfruits of the Holy Spirit through baptism, and the second birth is for us the beginning and seal and security and illumination of another life.

John Calvin represents a majority view among Protestants when it comes to the interpretation of Spirit baptism. He simply identifies baptism in the Holy Spirit with the work of regeneration.

From John Calvin, *Inst.* 3.1.4.

Therefore, as we have said that salvation is perfected in the person of Christ, so, in order to make us partakers of it, he baptizes us "with the Holy Spirit and with fire," (Luke 3:16), enlightening us into the faith of his Gospel, and so regenerating us to be new creatures. Thus cleansed from all pollution, he dedicates us as holy temples to the Lord.

Luther hardly uses the term Spirit baptism. He comes closest to it in his exposition of Titus 3:5 and follows tradition.

From Martin Luther, *Lectures on Titus, Philemon, Hebrews* (on Titus 3:5), trans. and ed. Jaroslav Pelikan and Walter A. Hansen, in *Luther's Works*, vol. 29 (St. Louis: Concordia Publishing House, 1968), 81–82, 84.

Therefore do not neglect it and give yourself over to speculation. *Not because of deeds [done by us in righteousness but in virtue of His own mercy by] the washing [of regeneration and renewal in the Holy Spirit].* You have here a commendation of Baptism such as I can hardly find anywhere else in the New Testament. The enemies of the grace of God, under the pretext of love, have preceded us and distorted all those other passages. Therefore this passage summarizes those. *By mercy*, he says, *we are saved.* But by what road does mercy come to us? *By washing.* They say: "Washing can refer to the Word, the Gospel, the Holy Spirit, namely, that we are baptized in the Spirit. If He is conferred, then Baptism is a washing of regeneration, that is, it is a sign of those who are regenerated. In other words, the washing of regeneration is bestowed on those who have already been regenerated through the Holy Spirit." If we say: "By what authority do you establish this as the meaning?" there is no one at home. Therefore they say that no outward thing justifies or profits a person. But

Baptism with water is such a thing; and therefore wherever it is said of Baptism that it justifies, they add a gloss, as, for example, in the passage from Peter (1 Peter 3:21), which they take to mean: "You have had a seal impressed upon you by which it is declared that you have been baptized through the Holy Spirit." . . . This is a washing *of the Holy Spirit*. He is the one who bathes you in this washing. It is a glorious commendation that He is present in Baptism, but this is also the warmth that transforms the heart, the anointing, the heat of the fire, and the renewal which renews in such a way.

Whereas mainline Christian tradition has either not made much of Spirit baptism as a separate category or subsumed it under the (sacramental) Christian initiation, two Roman Catholic theologians, the New Testament scholar George Montague and the patristic-systematic theologian Kilian McDonnell, OSB, have argued vocally that during the first eight centuries of Christian history all over the then-Christian world, Spirit baptism played a significant role as part of the extended initiation process often lasting for years because of the catechumenate. In the following, Fr. McDonnell summarizes the main results of his historical study based on extensive research into Latin, Greek, and Syrian traditions all around the Mediterranean seaboard, including a number of key theologians from Tertullian to Hilary to Cyril to the Cappadocians, many of whom are doctors of the church.

> From Kilian McDonnell, OSB, and George T. Montague, *Christian Initiation and Baptism in the Holy Spirit: Evidence from the First Eight Centuries* (Collegeville, MN: Liturgical Press, 1991), 315, 334–35.

I have been looking for three elements in the authors studied: (1) a sign of the prayer for the descent of the Spirit, usually the imposition of hands, but also anointing, (2) praying for the descent of the Spirit, (3) an expectation that the charisms will be manifested, and/or the actual manifestation. These three elements are not the baptism in the Spirit itself, but are signs usually associated with the baptism in the Holy Spirit. The baptism in the Spirit is the whole rite of initiation. . . . If the baptism in the Holy Spirit is integral to Christian initiation, to the constitutive sacraments, then it belongs not to private piety but to public liturgy, to the official worship of the church. Therefore the baptism in the Spirit is not special grace for some but common grace for all. . . . If the baptism in the Spirit is integral to Christian initiation, it is also integral to the paradigm for social transformation. Initiation equips one to do what Jesus did: to preach the good news to the poor, to proclaim liberty to the captives, to restore sight to the blind, to let the oppressed go free (Luke 4:18).

On the basis of their research, the two Catholic theologians challenge the whole church to reconsider the importance and meaning of Spirit baptism.

From McDonnell and Montague, *Christian Initiation and Baptism*, 337, 339-40.

What we have found there indeed presents, we believe, a major challenge to the church today. The energizing power of the Holy Spirit, manifesting itself in a variety of charisms, is not religious fluff. Nor is it—as viewed by many today—an optional spirituality in the church such as, among Catholics, the devotion to the Sacred Heart or the stations of the cross. The baptism in the Holy Spirit does not belong to private piety, but, as we have demonstrated, to the public official liturgy of the church. It is the spirituality of the church. By that account it is not—let it be said clearly—the property of the charismatic renewal. The unique gift which the charismatic renewal brings to the church is the awareness of the baptism in the Holy Spirit. This is all the more reason why the baptism in the Holy Spirit is not to be identified with any group or movement. Because it belongs to the church as an integral element of Christian initiation, it must be taken with ultimate seriousness. Indeed, the baptism in the Spirit is normative. . . . If early church practice, witnessed both by scripture and tradition, is normative, then the baptism in the Holy Spirit with the full expectation of charisms, should be the effect and the expectation of every adult baptism. For a church which has infant baptism, the baptism in the Spirit is a new actualization, a new level of one's awareness and experience, as a responsible . . . person, of what was received at baptism through the sovereign act of Jesus who is the Baptizer.

Contemporary Catholic and Protestant Interpretations

Before looking at the distinctively charismatic and pentecostal interpretations of Spirit baptism that have challenged the traditional view, especially the sacramental view according to which Spirit baptism is but another name or another facet to the giving of the Spirit at the moment of Christian initiation in water baptism, we will take a look at Roman Catholic and Protestant views in mainline theologies. A profitable way to begin this account is to look at the joint statement by the Lutheran A. Bittlinger and Roman Catholic K. McDonnell, OSB, in a significant work titled *The Baptism in the Holy Spirit as an Ecumenical Problem*. While both theologians have worked extensively with the Lutheran and charismatic renewals, respectively, their formulation here does not reflect distinctively charismatic interpretation but rather a typical sacramental theology.

From Kilian McDonnell, OSB, and Arnold Bittlinger,
The Baptism in the Holy Spirit as an Ecumenical Problem
(Notre Dame, IN: Charismatic Renewal Services, 1972), 6.

In Christian baptism the determining factor is the receiving of the Holy Spirit (repentance and forgiveness of sins were already present in the baptism of John). The promise of John the Baptist, that all shall be baptized with the Spirit, which is mentioned in all four gospels, was fulfilled at Pentecost and since then holds for every Christian baptism. If the baptism is not connected with the receiving of the Holy Spirit, then something very important is missing. John's baptism as well as Christian baptism is only a genuine baptism if it is connected with receiving the Spirit (Acts 8:14–17, Acts 19:2–7). Therefore, the gift of the Holy Spirit is not just an aspect of baptism, but it is the basic element of Christian baptism. Christian baptism is always a baptism with water and with Spirit.

Yves Congar represents the Roman Catholic teaching.

From Yves Congar, *I Believe in the Holy Spirit*, trans. David Smith,
3 vols. (New York: Herder & Herder, 1997), 218, 222–23.

Christian baptism is, of course, baptism in the Spirit (Mk 1:8; Jn 1:33; 1 Cor 6:11; 12:13; Tit 3:5). It confers regeneration or rebirth and introduces the recipient into the life of Christ himself, that is, into his body (Rom 6:4ff.; 1 Cor 12:13; Gal 3:27). This is certainly stated in the Church's liturgies and the writings of the earliest Fathers. . . . Jesus entered the water, identifying himself with those who repent, and, while he was praying, the Spirit came down on him. In the same way, Christians are plunged into the water as into his death (Rom 6:3) and the Spirit is given. This is a baptism of water and the Spirit, introducing the believer into the body which is the Body of Christ (1 Cor 12:12–13; see also Volume II, pp. 189–195). In the one single process of initiation, which is consummated in the sacrament of the body and blood of the Lord, a symbolic aspect, which completes the act of baptism and seals the gift received in it, the sacrament of the "seal of the gift of the Spirit," has been distinguished from the baptism strictly so called. I believe that this is the liturgical expression of the two missions of the Word, the Son, and of the Holy Spirit, who are closely associated in the task of accomplishing the same work.

Walter J. Kaiser Jr. introduces the contemporary Reformed perspective on Spirit baptism.

From Walter J. Kaiser Jr., "A Reformed Perspective," in
Perspectives on Spirit Baptism: Five Views, ed. Chad Owen
Brand (Nashville: Broadman & Holman, 2004), 35–36.

We agree that Spirit baptism is a separate work of the Holy Spirit from the fruit of the Spirit or the filling of the Spirit. As we have already argued, the Holy Spirit's baptism is that work, which first came for the Jews at Pentecost in Acts 2, the Samaritans in Acts 8, and the Gentiles in Acts 10, and then for all subsequent believers when they experience new birth in Christ, that incorporates all who believe into one body of Christ so that we all drink of one Spirit. In that sense, then, the two works of the Spirit are correctly separated. . . . But to argue that Luke and Paul speak of two dimensions of the Holy Spirit so that one is power for prophetic inspiration (Luke) and the other is soteriological (Paul) is to erect barriers where they do not exist.

The major line of demarcation in our two positions, that are otherwise so closely related, is that Luke's work of the Spirit is placed outside of the salvation process and made to be a separate use of the same term that Paul shares with Luke, *namely*, being "baptized in the Holy Spirit." . . . The conclusion we come to is this: each believer, subsequent to the three "Pentecosts" mentioned in the book of Acts, is automatically placed in the body of Christ and made to drink/ participate in the Holy Spirit by being "baptized in the Holy Spirit." It is this same Holy Spirit who also is available to "fill" believers and who produces the "fruit of the Spirit" in those who walk by faith and obedience to their Lord.

Spirit Baptism in Pentecostal Theologies

The term "pentecostal" refers to so-called classical pentecostal denominations such as the Assemblies of God, Church of God (Cleveland, TN), or Church of God in Christ that owe their beginnings to the famous revival at Azusa Street, Los Angeles, California, in the beginning of the twentieth century. The statement on Spirit baptism from the U.S. Assemblies of God, one of the oldest and most significant classical pentecostal movements, defines clearly and unambiguously the pentecostal view in which Spirit baptism is subsequent to new birth and accompanied with the "evidence" of a particular spiritual gift, namely, speaking in tongues.

From "The Four Defining Truths of the Assemblies of God,"
http://ag.org/top/Beliefs/index.cfm (accessed Aug. 28, 2008).

All believers are entitled to receive the baptism in the Holy Spirit, and therefore should expect and earnestly seek the promise of the

Father, according to the command of our Lord Jesus Christ. This was the normal experience of all believers in the early Christian church. With the experience comes the provision of power for victorious Christian living and productive service. It also provides believers with specific spiritual gifts for more effective ministry. The baptism of Christians in the Holy Spirit is accompanied by the initial physical sign of speaking in other tongues (unlearned languages) as the Spirit of God gives them audible expression (Luke 24:49; Acts 1:4, 8; 2:4; 8:12–17; 10:44–46; 11:14–16; 15:7–9; 1 Cor. 12:1–31).

E. S. Williams was a leading pentecostal theologian and Bible teacher who authored a multivolume *Systematic Theology*, one of the few penned by a representative of the movement. In keeping with the pentecostal view, Williams distinguishes Spirit baptism from the new birth as well as from the "filling with the Holy Spirit": while the believer can only be baptized in the Spirit once after his or her regeneration, filling with the Spirit is supposed to be a daily continuation of empowerment.

From Ernst Swing Williams, *Systematic Theology*,
vol. 3: *Pneumatology, Ecclesiology, Eschatology* (Springfield,
MO: Gospel Publishing House), 40–42.

Are the Baptism and the New Birth the Same?
The Scofield Bible speaks for many when it says—"one baptism, many fillings." The New Testament distinguishes between having the Spirit, which is true of all believers, and being filled with the Spirit. Every believer is born of the Spirit and indwelt by the Spirit, whose presence makes the believer's body a temple, and baptized by the Spirit, thus sealing him for God.—Note on Acts 2:4. The Scofield Bible also recognizes "many infillings." This is a truth which many overlook. It distinguishes between having the Spirit and being filled with the Spirit. While the Scofield Bible does not teach, neither is its comment intended to teach, a definite subsequent infilling of the Spirit, we are sure that its author would welcome special visitations from the presence of the Lord among the people of God. Such an open door for special infillings would not be welcomed by some. To them the work of salvation seems the end of the Spirit's activities. . . .

The Baptism with the Spirit Defined
The Baptism with the Holy Spirit is a definite experience. It was definite in the time of the early Church, it ought to be definite today. Too much is too often taken for granted. Seekers are told to take the Spirit by faith. Unfortunately, in too many instances, all they take is a consent to truth. The Holy Spirit is life and power. . . .

The Baptism with the Spirit Subsequent to Regeneration

If we are to be guided by the record in the New Testament, the Baptism with the Spirit is subsequent to conversion. There is plentiful evidence that the disciples who received the Spirit at Pentecost were already in a saved state. This truth cannot be easily dismissed by saying the days of the ministry of Jesus on earth were in a transition period between the Old and the New Testament times. Whatever a person may think concerning this, the evidence shows that the disciples were not of the world even as Christ was not of the world (John 17:14). Their names were written in heaven (Luke 10:20). They were spiritually clean (John 15:3) and were acknowleged by Jesus as united to Him as a branch is to the vine (John 15:4, 5). Yet they had not received the Baptism with the Holy Spirit. The Baptism came to them "*when the day of Pentecost was fully come*" (Acts 2:1–4).

Spirit Baptism in Charismatic Theologies

"Charismatic" theologies refer to the views of the charismatic movements that can be found within the established churches, such as the Roman Catholic, Lutheran, Orthodox, and Baptist churches. This is distinct from classical pentecostal churches, which comprise their own movement. While close to their own respective traditions in their theologies, the charismatic movements—say, the Roman Catholic and Lutheran movements— also betray distinctive features that owe to their spiritual experiences and subsequent theological reflection on them. Some charismatic movements are sacramental (e.g., Roman Catholic) while others are not (e.g., Baptist). This has an effect on how they conceive the relation of Spirit baptism to Christian initiation and the sacraments.

The Roman Catholic Donald L. Gelpi, at one time a participant in and a leading theologian of the Catholic charismatic movement, presents a sacramental view of Spirit baptism in a way that does not limit the giving or the operations of the Spirit solely to the sacraments.

From Donald L. Gelpi, *Charism and Sacrament: A Theology of Christian Conversion* (New York: Paulist Press, 1976), 142, 149–51.

The sacraments, as we have just seen, cause grace by signifying it. As rituals, moreover, their meaning is in part a function of the life situation which they address. Baptism is a rite of acceptance into the Church universal. And it speaks to the commitment that is demanded of any person publicly decided to live in the name and image of Jesus. The complete rite of Christian initiation has a double focus: belief in Jesus and belief in the transforming power of the Spirit. This is only appropriate; for the God whom Christians adore takes experiential shape in the twofold mission of the Son and of the Spirit. . . . The graces of any sacrament can, of course, be given outside the sacramental system. The Spirit is not bound by ritual. But the mere fact that a grace is so given is no proof that it ought to be. For one cannot respond authentically in love to a grace that binds one in covenant to the Christian community while repudiating the ritual which embodies such a commitment. To consent to the gifts of service but remain closed to some legitimate sacramental sealing of that consent is, then, to introduce some element of inauthenticity into one's personal response to God. . . . The phrase "the baptism in the Holy Spirit" is also somewhat theologically abrasive. The problem is not with "baptism in the Holy Spirit" but with the article "the." For the article seems to tie Spirit-baptism to a single moment in human experience. In point of fact, Spirit-baptism is a lifetime process. It cannot be equated with any single graced experience, much less with the reception of any single service gift, like tongues. Jesus Himself did not enter into relationship with the Spirit for the first time on the Jordan. The virginal conception of Jesus proclaimed in the infancy gospels, whatever its full exegetical meaning, is in part an attempt by the evangelists to affirm that from the very first moment of conception, Jesus stood in a positive relationship with the Holy Spirit. Moreover, even after His Jordan experience, Jesus could say: "There is a baptism I must still receive, and how great is my distress until it is over!" [Luke 12:50]. If, then, the Spirit comes in order to conform us to Jesus, Catholic charismatics should be sensitive not to speak as though they enjoyed pneumatic privileges which Jesus Himself lacked. Jesus' Spirit-baptism was a lifelong transformation in the Spirit, culminating in His glorification. But He experienced a moment of decisive "charismatic" breakthrough in His messianic anointing. Every Christian is called to a Pentecostal moment analogous to Jesus' Jordan anointing. It consists in the initial reception of one or more of the service gifts. It effects the intensification and personalization of baptismal faith. It may be reached gradually or suddenly. But when it occurs it ought to change visibly a person's life into a public act of witness to Jesus. Such a moment may also be legitimately designated "a baptism in the Holy Spirit," that is, a deeper plunging into the Spirit received in baptism. It may be called "an experience of Spirit-baptism." But it may not be called "*the* baptism in the Holy Spirit," for the simple reason that there is much more to "Spirit-baptism" than the experience of a Pentecostal breakthrough. The phrase "a fuller release of the gifts of the Spirit" may, however, be used to describe the Pentecostal moment in personal religious development, provided one does not imagine that all of the gifts of the Spirit lie latent in each believer waiting to be triggered.

Similarly, Catholic charismatics must stop using the term "Spirit-filled" or "Christian" in a restrictive sense. The only person who possessed the plentitude of the Spirit was Jesus; only He, then, was truly "Spirit-filled."

In the mid-1980s a number of Lutheran theologians from all over the world gathered together for a theological symposium in order to clarify the meaning of the charismatic renewal and Spirit baptism for Lutheran theology. As a result, a working group produced a major statement, a book titled *Welcome, Holy Spirit.*

From Larry Christenson, ed., *Welcome, Holy Spirit: A Study of Charismatic Renewal in the Church* (Minneapolis: Augsburg Fortress, 1987), 82–83.

If we consider baptism with the Spirit strategically, it seems to answer to the need for an outpouring of the Spirit's power to initiate or renew witness and ministry. In the book of Acts, both times the term occurs it describes a dramatic initial outpouring of the Spirit. The history of the Pentecostal and charismatic movements tends to echo this: a key factor in the spread of the movements has been the widely shared personal experience of an outpouring of the Spirit. For many, perhaps most, this has initiated a new sense of the Spirit's presence and power for life and ministry.

The experience of baptism with the Holy Spirit has commonly been accompanied by a manifest demonstration of the Spirit's presence through charismatic gifts, and this is also consistent with the scriptural witness. In the theology of Luke, the experience of being filled with the Holy Spirit consistently results in a manifest demonstration of the Spirit's presence, usually in the form of exalted speech—they spoke in tongues (Acts 2:4; 10:46; 19:6), prophesied (Acts 19:6), extolled God (Acts 10:46), and spoke the Word of God with boldness (Acts 4:31); or it was accompanied by a supernatural sign—a healing (Acts 9:17–18), a divine judgment (Acts 13:9–11), or a rapturous vision (Acts 7:55).

CHAPTER 14

Contextually Oriented Interpretations

|
Women's Pneumatologies
|

Mary Ann Fatula

Sister Mary Ann Fatula, OP, is professor of theology at Ohio Dominican University, Columbus, Ohio. She has published on spirituality, the Trinity, and pneumatology, among other topics. The way she brings a woman's perspective on the theology of the Spirit and salvation is different from feminists and other women activists. Rather than engaging the debate about sexism, she proactively writes about theology in a way that complements and corrects the male-dominated game.

Silhouettes of the Holy Spirit
Fatula writes almost in a devotional and artistic way when she describes with many metaphors and pictures the nature and personhood of the Spirit, many taken from the biblical testimonies.

From Mary Ann Fatula, OP, *The Holy Spirit: Unbounded Gift of Joy* (Collegeville, MN: Liturgical Press, 1998), 2–3.

To speak of the Holy Spirit, the Scriptures often use lovely but impersonal images such as breath (John 20:22), wind (Acts 2:2), water (John 7:38–39), tongues of fire (Acts 2:3), anointing (1 John 2:27, Acts 10:38), finger of God (Luke 11:20), dove (Luke 3:22), seal (Eph 4:30), gift (Acts 11:17), peace (John 20:21–22), and love (Rom 5:5). Yet early Christians recognized in faith that these impersonal images suggest the unfathomable beauty of the Holy Spirit precisely as Someone. The Holy Spirit is the third divine person whose tenderness we experience like a gentle breeze caressing our face, like the sun bathing us in warmth, like love itself deep within us. And just as we cannot live without breath or water, without freedom or love, we cannot live without the sweet joy of the Spirit.

Intimacy with the Spirit

Fatula's devotional theology invites us to experience a close, intimate relationship with the Holy Spirit.

From Fatula, *Holy Spirit*, 2, 5, 22.

We ourselves know this Spirit, just as we intuitively know the air we breathe and without which we cannot live, for the Spirit lives with us and *is* deep within us (John 14:17). Though we may not always realize it, we experience the Holy Spirit's closeness when we are near our loved ones and our life feels good and sweet to us. We feel the Spirit's joy, too, as we savor the perfumes of springtime, when nature all around us bursts into bloom. Even hard times bring us the Holy Spirit's fragrance, for all that the Spirit touches is anointed with joy (1 Thess 1:5–6). . . . Nothing created—not even the greatest ecstasy nor the most exquisite tenderness—can describe this happiness which the Holy Spirit *is* at the heart of the Trinity. . . . The Holy Spirit of love . . . dwells in us as our inseparable and intimate friend, our beloved "Paraclete" and counselor, our advocate and helper, our comfort and consoler. This Spirit at the depths of the Trinity (1 Cor 2:10) comes to live in us not in a shallow or superficial way, but permanently and in our inmost depths: "I will put my spirit within you" (Ezek 36:27, 37:14). Through thick and thin, the Spirit abides with us always (1 Cor 3:16; 1 Cor 6:19; Rom 8:9, 11; John 14:16–17; 1 John 4:13). Dwelling in us more deeply than we ourselves do, the Holy Spirit draws us to our own heart, to find within us the contentment we seek outside ourselves. As we experience the Holy Spirit's closeness, we begin to take joy in our own company, for we know that we are not alone. Enveloped by the person who is the Father's and Son's own love, we discover that even our bodies are the temple of this sweet Spirit (1 Cor 6:19). . . .

The Spirit unites us so intimately with Jesus that we now have a radically new power to pray (Rom 8:26), and to address the first divine person with the same intimate name which Jesus himself used when praying, *"Abba"* (Gal 4:6). No longer strangers and slaves filled with the spirit of fear, we are sons and daughters of the Father, filled with the Holy Spirit of God (Rom 8:15–16). This Spirit does not form us into isolated individuals but into a community of people in loving relationship, living in the "communion" (*koinonia*) of the Holy Spirit with the triune God and one another (2 Cor 13:14). We enter into this communion by drinking of the one Spirit, that is, by being baptized into the one body of Christ, the Church (1 Cor 12:13).

The Beauty of Pentecost

With beautiful rhetoric, Sister Fatula paints a picture of the Day of Pentecost.

From Fatula, Holy Spirit, 33–34.

In the midst of the lavish beauty of spring we celebrate Pentecost as "the last and great day," the beginning and culmination of our redemption. During the brilliance of springtime, the myriad voices of nature break out in the joy of living to announce this feast of the Spirit, great distributor of life.[1] . . .

Spring itself is the irrepressible feast of life. Who can resist its bounty, its beauty? Against all odds, delicate buds blossom forth, pushing their tender way through hard ground, from in between rocks, and in desert land. Everywhere, winter's cold night is conquered by glorious life. All three divine persons create this life, but earth's beauty is accomplished in a special way by the Spirit of life who adorns all of creation with loveliness. Not simply a few flowers, nor even a few kinds of flowers spring to life, but myriads of them, every one of them different. Glorious colors and intoxicating fragrances perfume the air with profusion and plenitude—gorgeous daffodils and hyacinths, lilies of the valley and violets, splendid magnolias and delicate apple blossoms. The mark of springtime is the casting off of restraint.

Elizabeth Johnson

Another Roman Catholic woman theologian, Elizabeth Johnson, engages the women's issue debate but does so in a moderate way. Unlike radical feminists and other liberationists, she believes it is possible to redeem Christian tradition and make it more inclusive.

Spirit Sophia

One of the complementary names for the Holy Spirit that Johnson takes from Christian tradition is Spirit Sophia. It helps highlight many of the features of the Holy Spirit otherwise in danger of neglect. Says Johnson in *She Who Is*, "In sum, The deeds of Spirit-Sophia encompass the breadth, depth, and historical length of the whole world."[2]

---

1. Anne Fatula owes this phrase ("great distributor of life") to Karl Adam (*Christ Our Brother* [London: Sheed & Ward, 1937], 145), e-mail communication March 23, 2009.

2. Elizabeth Johnson, *She Who Is: The Mystery of God in Feminist Theological Discourse* (New York: Crossroad, 1992), 141.

From Elizabeth Johnson, *She Who Is: The Mystery of God in Feminist Theological Discourse* (New York: Crossroad, 1992), 124–27.

At the root of all religious imagery and its doctrinal elaboration lies an experience of the mystery of God. Since what people call God is not one being among other beings, not even a discrete Supreme Being, but mystery which transcends and enfolds all that is, like the horizon and yet circling all horizons, this human encounter with the presence and absence of the living God occurs through the mediation of history itself in its whole vast range of happenings. To this movement of the living God that can be traced in and through experience of the world, Christian speech traditionally gives the name Spirit.

If we ask more precisely which moments or events mediate God's Spirit, the answer can only be potentially *all* experience, the whole world. There is no exclusive zone, no special realm, which alone may be called religious. Rather, since Spirit is the creator and giver of life, life itself with all its complexities, abundance, threat, misery, and joy becomes a primary mediation of the dialectic of presence and absence of divine mystery. The historical world becomes a sacrament of divine presence and activity, even if only as a fragile possibility. The complexities of the experience of Spirit therefore, are cogiven in and through the world's history: negative, positive, and ambiguous; orderly and chaotic; solitary and communal; successful and disastrous; personal and political; dark and luminous; ordinary and extraordinary; cosmic, social, and individual. Wherever we encounter the world and ourselves as held by, open to, gifted by, mourning the absence of, or yearning for something ineffably more than immediately appears, whether that "more" be mediated by beauty and joy or in contrast to powers that crush, there the experience of the Spirit transpires. Within this wide horizon of historical experience language about the Spirit of God finds its origin and home. The breadth and depth of experience that may mediate holy mystery is genuinely inclusive. It embraces not only, and in many instances not even primarily, events associated with explicitly religious meaning such as church, word, sacraments, and prayer, although these are obviously intended as mediations of the divine. But since the mystery of God undergirds the whole world, the wide range of what is considered secular or just plain ordinary human life can be grist for the mill of experience of Spirit-Sophia, drawing near and passing by. Consider at least three historical mediations:

1. The natural world mediates the presence and absence of Spirit. . . . Until recently there has been little sustained reflection on what J. B. Metz has informally called "the Alps experience," a moment of

wonder when we are overtaken by the grandeur of the natural world as it exists beyond us and without us, simply there in its own givenness and beauty, fragility and threatened state. . . . Anyone who has ever resisted or mourned the destruction of the earth or the demise of one of its living species, or has wondered at the beauty of a sunrise, the awesome power of a storm, the vastness of prairie or mountain or ocean, the greening of the earth after periods of dryness or cold, the fruitfulness of a harvest, the unique ways of wild or domesticated animals, or any of the other myriad phenomena of this planet and its skies has potentially brushed up against an experience of the creative power of the mystery of God, Creator Spirit.

2. Personal and interpersonal experience likewise mediates the presence and absence of Spirit to human life. As the Bible's love songs show, the love of God for the world is revealed through the depths of love human beings can feel for one another. We seek and are found by Spirit in the person-creating give and take of loving relationships, in each fresh, particular discovery of the other's beauty, in the strength of ongoing fidelity. The anguish of broken relationships, by contrast, mediates traces of divine absence and, perhaps, divine compassion. Moreover, the dynamism of questioning, of arriving at insight in clarity or darkness, of imagining new possibilities, of artistic and scientific creation conveys the fire of the intelligent Spirit, source of all creativity. . . .

3. On the level of the macro systems that structure human beings as groups, profoundly affecting consciousness and patterns of relationship, experience of the Spirit is also mediated. Whenever a human community resists its own destruction or works for its own renewal; when structural changes serve the liberation of oppressed peoples; when law subverts sexism, racism, poverty, and militarism; when swords are beaten into ploughshares or bombs into food for the starving; when the sores of old injustices are healed; when enemies are reconciled once violence and domination have ceased; whenever the lies and the raping and the killing stop; wherever diversity is sustained in *koinonia*; wherever justice and peace and freedom gain a transformative foothold—there the living presence of powerful, blessing mystery amid the brokenness of the world is mediated. . . .

So universal in scope is the compassionate, liberating power of Spirit, so broad the outreach of what Scripture calls the finger of God and early Christian theologians call the hand of God, that there is virtually no nook or cranny of reality potentially untouched. The Spirit's presence through the praxis of freedom is mediated amid profound ambiguity, often apprehended more in darkness than in light. It is thwarted and violated by human antagonism and systems of collective evil. . . . Within the tradition of Jewish and Christian faith, the Spirit's saving presence in the conflictual world is recognized to be everywhere, somehow, always drawing near and passing by, shaping fresh starts of vitality and freedom.

"Divine Emancipation of Women"

This title of a chapter in a book written by a feminist theologian expresses the desire of many woman theologians to discover in the person of the Holy Spirit and pneumatology resources to fight for sexual equality and liberation for women. This citation bespeaks the liberating power of Pentecost when the Spirit was poured out.

> From Victoria B. Demarest, *Sex and Spirit: God, Woman and Ministry*
> (St. Petersburg, FL: Sacred Arts International, 1977), 38–39.

The most significant commission to women as prophets occurred on the day of Pentecost, the birthday of the church, when 120 men *and women*, including Mary, the Mother of Jesus, were assembled. All of them were waiting for the baptism of the Holy Spirit, as Jesus had instructed them to do. And when the Holy Spirit descended all of them began to prophesy.

The people who were watching started mocking, accusing them of being drunk. This evoked Peter's great declaration which signified the Holy Spirit's emancipation of women and settled once and for all the question of woman's equal right, with man, to preach the Gospel.

Quoting the prophet Joel, Peter said, "In the last days I will pour out of my spirit upon all flesh: and your sons and *your daughters* shall prophesy . . . on my servants and on my *handmaidens* I will pour out in those days of my spirit: and *they shall prophesy*" [Acts 2:17–19 KJV, italics mine].

. . . If the baptism of the Holy Spirit and the gift of prophecy had been intended for men alone, if the women had been sent home and only the men had remained, there would have been a false note in Peter's declaration, which was the founding block of the church. Would this not have done an injustice to the Holy Spirit?

Throughout the New Testament God is spoken of sometimes as *Father*, sometimes as *Christ*, and sometimes as *Holy Spirit*. . . . Christian believers . . . knew God [also] as *Holy Spirit*—through his divine power in their lives.

. . . On the day of Pentecost flames of fire (symbolical of the Holy Spirit) were seen to light on the heads of all the disciples, men and women. This fire of God is the fire of love ("God is love") without which the many gifts of the Spirit, including that of prophetic preaching, Paul tells us are without value. On that day the fire of LOVE—

for God, for each other, for all men, even for their enemies—fell on the disciples, women as well as men.

A leading radical Christian feminist, Rosemary R. Ruether seeks to rediscover resources in Christian religious history to make God-talk more balanced by highlighting the feminine dimensions of the Holy Spirit and the Trinity.

From Rosemary R. Ruether, *Goddesses and Divine Feminine: A Wisdom Religious History* (Berkeley: University of California Press, 2005), 132–37.

The identification of the roles of Wisdom with a masculine Logos-Christ largely repressed any development of a female personification of the divine, based on the figure of Wisdom, in the writings of church fathers. But the Wisdom literature of Hebrew scripture, including books such as the Wisdom of Jesus ben Sirach and the Wisdom of Solomon, was included in the Christian Bible. . . .

The father-son metaphor for the relation of God to the Word of God generally fixed the two poles of the Christian Trinity as male-male, but the Holy Spirit remained fluid. Imaged as a dove, it was not fixed in any gendered personification. . . . The most lush development of female images for the Spirit is found in the second-century Syriac hymns the *Odes of Solomon*. The language of these hymns is poetic, not philosophical, and explores a plurality of images for the believer's transformed life through communion with the divine. Feminine images cluster around the Spirit, as the Syriac word for spirit, *ruha'*, is itself feminine. But the Father and the Word can also be imaged in feminine terms. Here, the source of the metaphors is not simply grammatical gender but the images themselves, such as milk and birth, that suggest the female activities of carrying a child in the womb, giving birth, and suckling.

A well-known Roman Catholic Trinitarian theologian and theological advocate of equality, the late Catherine Mowry LaCugna reminds us that as person the Holy Spirit is the "contact" point between humanity and the triune God; thus, the Spirit removes obstacles and liberates humanity.

From Catherine Mowry LaCugna, *God for Us: The Trinity and Christian Life* (San Francisco: HarperSanFrancisco, 1993), 362.

The Spirit is involved in every operation of God in the economy. Spirit hovered over the waters at creation; the Spirit spoke through the prophets. Jesus was conceived, anointed, led, accompanied, inspired by the Spirit. Only in the Spirit can we confess Jesus as Lord; the Spirit makes us holy and enables our praise of God. The Spirit gathers together what has been sundered—races, nations, persons. The Spirit is God's power active in creation, history, personality. The Spirit who animates the praise of God incorporates persons into the deepest regions of divine life. We must continually remind ourselves that this divine life is bestowed and active in history and human personality, not locked up in itself.

The Spirit, Nature, and the Environment

While Christian tradition has never limited the sphere of the Holy Spirit to the religious alone, a growing number of contemporary theologians are exploring the many ways biblical teaching about the Holy Spirit as the "Spirit of Life" could inform our understanding of and responsibility for the environment.

Spirit Sophia as Sustainer and Giver of Life
The moderate, Catholic, feminist theologian Elizabeth Johnson expands her idea of the Holy Spirit as Spirit Sophia in relation to nature and, along with a number of contemporary theologians, moves towards panentheism.

From Elizabeth Johnson, *Women, Earth and Creator Spirit* (Mahwah, NJ: Paulist Press, 1993), 42–44.

Of all the activities that theology attributes to the Spirit, the most significant is this: the Spirit is the creative origin of all life. In the words of the Nicene Creed, the Spirit is *vivificantem*, vivifier or life-giver. This designation refers to creation not just at the beginning of time but continuously: the Spirit is the unceasing, dynamic flow of divine power that sustains the universe, bringing forth life. From this primordial religious intuition, three other insights reverberate. First, as the continuous creative origin of life the Creator Spirit is immanent in the historical world. "Where can I go from your presence," sings the psalmist, "and from your Spirit where can I flee?" The Spirit is in the highest sky, the deepest hole, the darkest night, farther east than the sunrise, over every next horizon (Ps 139:7–12). The Spirit fills the world and is in all things. Since the Spirit is also transcendent over the world, divine indwelling circles round to embrace the whole world, which thereby dwells within the sphere of the divine. Technically this is known as panentheism or the existence of all things in God. Distinct from classical theism which separates God and the world, and also different from pantheism which merges God and the world, panentheism holds that the universe, both matter and spirit, is encompassed by the Matrix of the living God in an encircling that generates freedom, self-transcendence, and the future, all in the context of the interconnected whole. The relationship created by this mutual indwelling, while non-hierarchical and reciprocal, is not strictly symmetrical, for the world is dependent on God in a way that God is not on the world. Yet the Spirit's encircling indwelling weaves a genuine solidarity among all creatures and between God and the world. Second, when things get broken, which can happen so easily, this divine creative power assumes the shape of a rejuvenating energy that renews the face of the earth (Ps 104:30). The damaged earth, violent and unjust social structures, the lonely and broken heart—all cry out for a fresh start. In the midst of this suffering the Creator Spirit, through the mediation of created powers, comes, as the Pentecost sequence sings, to wash what is unclean; to pour water upon what is drought-stricken; to heal what is hurt; to loosen up what is rigid; to warm what is freezing; to straighten out what is crooked and bent. When Jesus reads from the scroll of Isaiah in the Nazareth synagogue, he highlights this point with explicit examples. The Spirit who was upon him had sent him to bring good news to the poor, to proclaim release to captives, sight to the blind, and liberty to the oppressed (Lk 4:16–20). The resurrection of Jesus from the dead into the new life of glory is but the most surprising revelation of this characteristic of the Creator Spirit. Precisely as the giver of life the creative Spirit cherishes what has been made and renews it in myriad ways.

Third, the continuous changing of historical life reveals that the Spirit moves. From the beginning of the cosmos, when the Spirit moves over the waters (Gen 1:2), to the end, when God will make all things new (Rev 21:5), standing still is an unknown stance. The long and unfinished development known as evolution testifies to just how much novelty, just how much surprise, the universe is capable of spawning out of pre-given order or chaos. In every instance the living Spirit empowers, lures, prods, dances on ahead. Throughout the process, the Spirit characteristically sets up bonds of kinship among all creatures, human and non-human alike, all of whom are energized by this one Source. A Christian liturgical greeting expresses this very beautifully: "The grace of our Lord Jesus Christ, and the love of God, and the fellowship of the Holy Spirit be with you all." Fellowship, community, koinonia is the primordial design of exis tence, as all creatures are connected through the indwelling, renewing, moving Creator Spirit. The fundamental insight that the Spirit is the giver of life with its three corollaries of the Spirit's renewing, indwelling, and moving power cry out for concrete, imaginative expression. How shall we speak of Creator Spirit? If we search the scriptures with our major thesis in mind we find a small collection of cosmic and female symbols of the Spirit, most of which are marginalized by a patriarchal imagination. Remembering these texts can give us the beginnings of a vocabulary for an ecological ethic and spirituality.

A "Green" Pneumatology

One of the most creative constructive theologians in the emerging "Green" pneumatologies is Mark I. Wallace.

> From Mark I. Wallace, *Finding God in the Singing River*
> (Minneapolis: Augsburg Fortress, 2005), 6, 8–9.

I want to retrieve a central but neglected Christian theme—the idea of God as carnal Spirit who imbues all things—as the linchpin for forging a green spirituality responsive to the environmental needs of our time. Theologically speaking, I believe that hope for a renewed earth is best founded on belief in God as Earth Spirit, the compassionate, all-encompassing divine force within the biosphere who inhabits earth community and continually works to maintain the integrity of all forms of life. Like the river deity I encountered in the Singing River as a boy, in green spirituality God is the *Earth God* who indwells the land and invigorates and flows with natural processes, not the invisible *Sky God* who exists in a heavenly realm far removed from earthly concerns. . . .

In particular, on the topic of the Spirit, not only do the scriptural texts not divorce the spiritual from the earthly, but, moreover, they figure the Spirit as a creaturely life-form interpenetrated by the material world. Indeed, images of the Spirit drawn directly from nature are the defining motif in biblical notions of Spirit. Consider the following metaphors and descriptions of the Spirit within the Bible: the *animating breath* that brings life and vigor to all things (Genesis 1:2; Psalms 104:29–30); the *healing wind* that conveys power and a new sense of community to those it in-dwells (Judges 6:34; John 3:6; Acts 2:1–4); the *living water* that vivifies and refreshes all who drink from its eternal springs (John 4:14; 7:37–38); the *cleansing fire* that

alternately judges wrongdoers and ignites the prophetic mission of
the early church (Acts 2:1–4; Matthew 3:11–12); and the *divine dove*,
a fully embodied earth creature, who births creation into existence,
and, with an olive branch in its mouth, brings peace and renewal to
a broken and divided world; this same bird God hovers over Jesus at
his baptism to inaugurate his public ministry (Genesis 1:1–3; 8:11;
Matthew 3:16; John 1:32). The Spirit is an earthen reality who is biblically figured according to the four primitive, cardinal elements—
earth, wind, water, fire—that are the key components of embodied
life as we know it. In these scriptural texts, the Spirit is pictured as
a wholly enfleshed life-form who engenders healing and renewal
throughout the abiotic and biotic orders.

As I perform a retrieval of the Spirit's *earthen* identity . . . , I also
hope to recover the Spirit's female identity. As God's indwelling,
corporeal presence within the created order, the Spirit is variously
identified with feminine and maternal characteristics in the biblical
witness. In the Bible the Spirit is envisioned as God's helping, nurturing, inspiring, and birthing presence in creation. The mother Spirit
Bird in the opening creation song of Genesis, like a giant hen sitting
on her cosmic nest egg, broods over the earth and brings all things
into life and fruition. In turn, this same hovering Spirit Bird, as a
dove that alights on Jesus as he comes up through the waters of his
baptism, appears in all four of the Gospels to signal God's approval
of Jesus' public work. The maternal, avian Spirit of Genesis and the
Gospels is the nursing mother of creation *and* Jesus' ministry who
protects and sustains the well-being of all things in the cosmic web
of life. Early Christian communities in the Middle East consistently
spoke of the Spirit as the motherly, regenerative breath and power
of God within creation. These early Christians believed that the
Hebrew feminine grammatical name of the Spirit—*ruach*—was a
linguistic clue to certain woman-specific characteristics of God as
Spirit. As these early Christians rightly understood that God transcends sex and gender, their point was not that God was a female
deity, but that it is appropriate alternately to refer to God's mystery,
love, and power in "male" *and* "female" terms. In this book I will
take the liberty of referring to the Spirit as "she" in order to recapture
something of the biblical understanding of God as feminine Spirit
within the created order.

While issuing a warning to all inhabitants of the earth with regard to the
ecological catastrophe, as a theologian Wallace develops his pneumatology towards a radical panentheism in which God the Spirit not only suf-
fers with the endangered earth, but the danger of the "death" of God is on
the horizon.

From Mark I. Wallace, *Fragments of the Spirit:*
Nature, Violence, and the Renewal of Creation
(New York: Continuum, 1996), 136, 138.

I maintain that the most adequate response to the current crisis lies in a recovery of the Holy Spirit as a natural, living being who indwells and sustains all life-forms. The point is not that the Spirit is simply *in* nature as its interanimating force, as important as that is, but that the Spirit *is* a natural being who leads all creation into a peaceable relationship with itself. Spirit and earth internally condition and permeate each other; both modes of being coinhere through and with each other without collapsing into undifferentiated sameness or equivalence. Insofar as the Spirit abides in and with all living things, Spirit and earth are *inseparable* and yet at the same time *distinguishable*. Spirit and earth are internally indivisible because both modes of being are living realities with the common goal of sustaining other life-forms. But Spirit and earth also possess their own distinctive identities insofar as the Spirit is the unseen power who vivifies and sustains all living things, while the earth is the visible agent of the life that pulsates throughout creation. The Spirit inhabits the earth as its invisible and life-giving breath (*ruah*), and the earth (*gaia*) is the outward manifestation of the Spirit's presence within, and maintenance of, all life-forms. . . .

To reconceive the Spirit as a natural entity—as a living, breathing organism like a dove or an inanimate life-form such as wind or fire—is to emphasize the coinherence of the Spirit and the natural world. This model, however, presents an extraordinary challenge to the traditional doctrine of God. One intriguing but troubling implication of an ecological pneumatology of internal relatedness is that it places the divine life at risk in a manner that an extrinsic doctrine of the Spirit vis-à-vis the earth does not. *If Spirit and earth mutually indwell each other, then God as Spirit is vulnerable to loss and destruction insofar as the earth is abused and despoiled.* While this association is beginning to be felt by many people today, most theologians are hesitant to postulate that ecologically toxic relationships with other life-forms places the presence of the Spirit in the world in fundamental jeopardy.

The Spirit and Science

An Anglican clergyman and particle physicist from England, John Polkinghorne has for years reflected on the relationship between science and faith. He speaks of the hidden presence of the Spirit of God in the world created by God.

From John Polkinghorne, "The Hidden Spirit and the Cosmos," in
The Work of the Spirit: Pneumatology and Pentecostalism, ed. Michael Welker
(Grand Rapids: Wm. B. Eerdmans Publishing Co., 2006), 171, 173.

According to this understanding, the sanctifying work of the Spirit is a continuing activity that awaits its final completion in the creation of the community of the redeemed, a consummation that will be manifested fully only at the eschaton. Of the Persons of the Trinity we can appropriate most specifically to the Spirit the title of *deus absconditus*, the hidden God.

The expectation of a degree of harmonious congruence between the insights of science and the insights of theology is increased by an understanding that the Spirit is "the Spirit of truth" (John 15:26), and so the *Paraclete* is expected to be hiddenly at work within all truth-seeking communities, including the community of science. This expectation accords with the affiliation found in the New Testament writings between "Spirit" and "truth," to which Michael Welker draws our attention in his chapter. In scripture, the Spirit is the carrier of the divine gift of wisdom. Concerning that gift, the author of the Wisdom of Solomon wrote that "it is he who gave me unerring knowledge of what exists, to know the structure of the world and the activity of the elements; the beginning and the end of times" (Wis. 7:17–18). The inspiration of the pursuit of science lies within the realm of the Spirit's hidden work. It is a well-documented experience in science that after intense but fruitless engagement with a profound problem, a period of mental rest in which the task is set aside for a while can then be followed by the sudden emergence into consciousness of the sought-for solution, fully formed and articulated. Psychologists will speak of the activity of the unconscious mind, but theologians may well believe that the hidden guidance of the Spirit, received and appropriated in those unconscious depths, has also played a part. Profound thinkers and creative artists also often speak of achievements that have about them the character of a gift received.

The Spirit in the Sociopolitical Arena

We now take a brief look at European and North American pneumatological sources that have to do with liberation, social and political justice, and other public issues. The Yugoslavian-born Yale theologian Miroslav Volf, who has written extensively on peace

and reconciliation, among other political issues, has developed a pneumatological approach to work.

The Spirit and Work

From Miroslav Volf, *Work in the Spirit: Toward a Theology of Work*
(New York: Oxford University Press, 1991), 102, 114–15.

One cannot talk about the new creation without referring to the
Spirit of God. For the Spirit, as Paul says, is the "firstfruits" or the
"down payment" of the future salvation (see Rom. 8:23; 2 Cor. 1:22)
and the present power of eschatological transformation in them. In
the Gospels, too, Spirit is the agent through which the future new
creation is anticipated in the present (see Matt. 12:28). Without the
Spirit there is no experience of the new creation! A theology of work
that seeks to understand work as active anticipation of the *transformatio mundi* must, therefore, be a *pneumatological* theology of
work. . . . If Christian mundane work is work in the Spirit, then it
must be understood as *cooperation with God*. *Charisma* is not just a
call by which God bids us to perform a particular task, but is also an
inspiration and a gifting to accomplish the task. Even when *charisma*
is exercised by using the so-called natural capabilities, it would be
incorrect to say that a person is "enabled" irrespective of God's relation to him. Rather, the enabling depends on the presence and activity of the Spirit. It is impossible to separate the gift of the Spirit from
the enabling power of the Spirit. When people work exhibiting the
values of the new creation (as expressed in what Paul calls the "fruit
of the Spirit") then the Spirit works in them and through them.

The understanding of work as cooperation with God is implied
in the New Testament view of Christian life in general. Putting forward his own Christian experience as a paradigm of Christian life,
Paul said: "it is no longer I who live, but Christ who lives in me; and
the life I now live in the flesh I live by faith in the Son of God" (Gal.
2:20). That Paul can in the same breath make such seemingly contradictory statements about the acting agent of Christian life ("I no
longer live, *Christ lives* in me" and "*I live* my life in the flesh") testifies
unmistakably that the whole Christian life is a life of cooperation
with God through the presence of the Spirit. A Christian's mundane
work is no exception. Here, too, one must say: I work, and the Spirit
of the resurrected Christ works through me.

Since the Spirit who imparts gifts and acts through them is "a
guarantee" (2 Cor. 1:22; cf. Rom. 8:23) of the realization of the
eschatological new creation, cooperation with God in work is proleptic cooperation with God in God's eschatological *transformatio
mundi*. As the glorified Lord, Jesus Christ is "present in his gifts and

in the services that both manifest these gifts and are made possible by them." Although his reign is still contested by the power of evil, he is realizing through those gifts his rule of love in the world. As Christians do their mundane work, the Spirit enables them to cooperate with God in the kingdom of God that "completes creation and renews heaven and earth."

The Spirit and Public Issues

Geiko Müller-Fahrenholz, a German clergyman and theologian who has also worked for years in Latin America, has constructed a politically sensitive and responsible pneumatology. The first citations talk about the prayer for the coming of the Spirit and how it ties in with a pneumatological creation theology.

From Geiko Müller-Fahrenholz, *God's Spirit: Transforming a World in Crisis* (New York: Continuum; Geneva: WCC Publications, 1995), 2, 4, 26–27.

"Veni, Creator Spiritus!" These are the first three words of a well-known Pentecost hymn by Rabanus Maurus (776–856). But "Come, Creator Spirit!" is not just the first line of a hymn. It is a cry: an exclamation of longing and an appeal.

This appeal recalls the entreaty of the first Christians: "*Maranatha*," "Our Lord, come!" (1 Cor. 16:22; cf. Rev. 22:20). Neither in Paul nor in the Apocalypse of John is this petition a mere pious refrain. It is a vital expression of all the suffering of communities living under persecution.

Over the centuries, whenever persecution or death has threatened to overwhelm believers, they have concentrated all their need and all their hope in this cry for the presence of the Lord Jesus and his *pneuma*. Amidst the afflictions of our own age, then, it was quite appropriate for the World Council of Churches to choose "Come, Holy Spirit—renew the whole creation!" as the theme of its seventh assembly (Canberra 1991). The voices heard in Canberra did reveal unmistakably the painful face of our day, even if the assembly, in the short time available to it, was unable to elicit the full implications of this prayer because of the quite diverse circumstances and convictions that delegates brought with them and the profound disorientation that the Gulf war cast over the meeting.

The meaning of this appeal is still urgently with us. "Come, Creator Spirit!" remains our petition.

It is the lament of people whose consciences are haunted by nightmarish images of millions of starving human beings and of so many children dying in torment. . . .

We make these petitions in the hope that beneath our entreaties an appropriate answer is already taking shape and that in our very appeal to the Spirit, the Spirit is already moving out towards us. It is not a matter of invoking a transcendent power to deliver *us from* this or that affliction or distress—that would be to instrumentalize the *pneuma*—but of experiencing the "encounter" in which all real life is rooted and the sometimes only momentarily apparent presence of the Spirit *in* our need. Whenever this happens we are touched by the most precious of all things: by *superna gratia,* by *charis,* by grace as if from another world. In such moments our lamentation becomes thanksgiving and our mouth is "filled with laughter" (Ps. 126:2). Then we sing and celebrate our gratitude, culminating in the eucharist, the feast of thanksgiving.

But it sometimes happens that we have to hold on to this cry and remain within the realm of complaint, lamentation, disappointment and anger. Even then we retain a quiet hope that perhaps the breath of God is waiting to come, interceding for us "with sighs too deep for words" (Rom. 8:26).

Prayer typically consists of a series of interwoven assertions of various kinds—petition, assurance, complaint, consolation. The basic reason for this is that God's breath, God's *pneuma,* communicates itself in our own breath, so that our appeal for God's nearness already takes place in the medium of the *pneuma.* Even so, we want to understand this kind of communication better. What are we really doing when we pray? . . .

By praying "Come, Holy Spirit" we seek to restore the association between creation and salvation. This prayer implicitly acknowledges our belief that no demiurge or alien spirit is at work in the world. The motherly *ruah* sustains all created things with its loving energy and thus unites the work of creation and the work of redemption. . . . God's *ruah* is the inexhaustible power which as the soul of the world bestows breath and order, energy and love of life on all things. It is the divine power that maintains creation, not in the way that an automobile has to be serviced regularly, but as the power that prompts the creation onwards because it has not yet reached its goal. . . . *God-ruah* enlivens, ensouls and wholly governs everything that is. Accordingly, all things live by the original blessing of that abundant fertility which has its times and its occasions. Where the *ruah* draws in her breath, apathy and death prevail. Where the *ruah* is absent or concealed, we feel that profound fear which always assails us when the ground is taken from under our feet—a sense of terror familiar to people in earthquake zones. But where *God-ruah* issues forth with new strength the face of the earth is renewed.

Introduction: Theologies from the Global South

One of the most exciting features of more recent theological reflection in general and pneumatology and the doctrine of salvation in particular is the emergence of rich, diverse, and dynamic voices and testimonies from all around the world. The majority of Christians can now be found outside Europe and North America (conveniently called the Global North) in Asia, Africa, and Latin America, or what is often called the Global South. In keeping with this dramatic change in the makeup of the Christian church, theological diversity in the beginning of the third millennium is no longer limited to denominational or ecclesiastical diversity but also includes contributions from various regions of our globe as well as from different agendas, such as liberationist and feminist. While past academic theology was done predominantly by white male theologians from Europe and North America, in today's world African, Asian, Latin American, and other non-Northerners are joining in and producing a most exciting variety of insights into the Spirit and salvation.

Mapping out and giving a fair hearing to this global diversity is a daunting task. Every theologian, including myself as the editor of this volume, is necessarily bound by one's own context, and as an individual theologian my knowledge of the global diversity of theological reflections is limited. Although I have lived, studied, and taught theology on three different continents—Europe, Asia, and North America—it is no guarantee that the choices I made for this part of the book are the best and most appropriate representatives of particular local contexts. On the other hand, the fact that this volume makes an intentional effort to give a hearing to pneumatological and soteriological testimonies from African, Asian, and Latin American contexts points the way to how Christian theology should be done in the third millennium. This part of the book, therefore, simply consists of insights into and testimonies to the Spirit and salvation from Asia, Africa, and Latin America across the ecumenical and denominational spectrum.

CHAPTER 15

Testimonies from Africa

Introduction to the African Context

Similarly to both Asian and Latin American contexts, African religion permeates all of life. In the words of the premier Kenyan theologian John Mbiti, "There is no formal distinction between the sacred and the secular" or between "the spiritual and material areas of life."[1] For Africans, the world of the spirits is as real as the visible world, perhaps even more real. The visible world is "enveloped in the invisible spirit world."[2] Consequently—and differently from U.S. and European perspectives—life and world are believed to be governed by God, the ancestors, and (other) spirits.

In many African cultures, the spirits, including ancestors, live in close relationship to God. Called by various names, these are real powers, created by God to mediate his power. Ancestral spirits that live closer to the living community are also a central feature of all African religiosity.

While thoroughly religious, much of the African worldview has a "this-worldly" orientation that does not exclude the other-worldly reality; rather, religions are brought to bear on the lives of a particular people.[3] Conversion, thus, is often understood as an encounter between two, or several, systems of salvation, a kind of power encounter. The God who is believed to be the strongest is given allegiance.[4]

This religious orientation and many other cultural features shape the way theology in general and pneumatology and soteriology in particular are being done on the African continent. Perhaps the most striking feature to most African cultures is the primacy of community over individuals.

---

1. John S. Mbiti, *African Religions and Philosophy* (London: Heinemann, 1969), 2.

2. Tokunboh Adeyemo, "Unapproachable God: The High God of African Traditional Religion," in *The Global God: Multicultural Evangelical Views of God*, ed. Aida Besancon Spencer and William David Spencer (Grand Rapids: Baker, 1998), 130–31.

3. See further, Cyril C. Okorocha, "Religious Conversion in Africa: Its Missiological Implications," *Mission Studies* 9.2, no. 18 (1992): 168–81.

4. See further, Cyril Okorocha, "The Meaning of Salvation: An African Perspective," in *Emerging Voices in Global Christian Theology*, ed. William A. Dyrness (Grand Rapids: Zondervan, 1994), 59–92.

The well-being of the community is a value taken for granted, and life is perceived as lived in relationship to significant others. To quote the famous saying of Mbiti, "I am because we are, and since we are, therefore I am."[5]

Distinctive Features of the African Worldview
as the Context for Pneumatology and Soteriology

As previously mentioned, one of the key differences between the Western and African worldviews is the latter's focus on spirit, the invisible reality, and spirituality. The most widely known African theologian, churchman and ecumenist John Mbiti, outlines some key features of the spiritual worldview among many African peoples. In the selection that follows Mbiti's, note how the Nigerian theologian Osadolor Imasogie similarly describes the differences between African and Western worldviews and conceptions of the spiritual.

From John S. Mbiti, *Introduction to African Religion*
(London: Heinemann Educational, 1975), 70.

According to African views, the universe is composed of visible and invisible parts. It is commonly believed that besides God and human beings there are other beings who populate the universe. These are the spirits. There are many types of spirits. God is their Creator, just as he is the Creator of all things. The spirits have a status between God and men, and are not identical with either. But people often speak about them in human terms, or treat them as though they had human characteristics such as thinking, speaking, intelligence and the possession of power which they can use as they will. Because the spirits are created by God, they are subordinate to him and dependent on him, and some of them may be used by God to do certain things.

From Osadolor Imasogie, *Guidelines for Christian Theology in Africa*
(Achimota, Ghana: Africa Christian Press, 1993), 83.

The spiritual world is real for the African. He is open to active communion with spiritual forces as he faces the riddles of life. He needs the assurance of solidarity with his human as well as his spiritual communities which, in his traditional world view, are held together

---

5. Mbiti, *African Religions and Philosophy,* 106.

by ancestral spirits. In the Christian context, our solidarity with our human and spiritual communities inheres in the Living Christ as mediated by the Holy Spirit. That is to say that Christ, through the Holy Spirit upholds and guides his Church which is his community.

Under the subheading "A New Emphasis on the Role of the Holy Spirit and the Present Mediatory Efficacy of the Living Christ," Imasogie elaborates on the importance of the category of the spiritual to relevant theology in Africa, including ecclesiology, the doctrine of the church.

From Imasogie, *Guidelines for Christian Theology*, 81.

If the African finds his fulfillment only in relation to human and spiritual communities, then for him to feel at home in Christianity he must come to a vital appreciation of the role of the Holy Spirit as the unifying force in the Christian community. The solidarity of the Christian community inheres in the power of the Holy Spirit who unites all Christians with God and one another.

The Church is the community brought into being by the Holy Spirit by virtue of his indwelling presence in all who are incorporated into Christ As the one who walks alongside the Christian, the Holy Spirit guides him into all truth, comforts him in times of difficulties, and directs his thoughts as he grapples with the knotty problems of life's decisions.

Features of the African Spirit World

Here are descriptions of the rich and complicated spirit world as perceived in African cultures—perceptions that have bearing on their understanding of the Spirit of God.

From John S. Mbiti, *African Religions and Philosophy*
(New York: A. Prager, 1969), 78–81.

Myriads of spirits are reported from every African people, but they defy description almost as much as they defy the scientist's test tubes in the laboratory. Written sources are equally confusing. We have tried to include under the term "divinity" those spiritual beings of a relatively high status. If we pursue the hierarchical consideration, we can say that the spirits are the "common" spiritual beings beneath the status of divinities, and above the status of men. They are the "common populace" of spiritual beings. As for the origin of spirits, there is no clear information what African peoples say or think about it. Some spirits are considered to have been created as a "race" by themselves. These, like other living creatures, have continued to reproduce themselves and add to their numbers. Most peoples, however, seem to believe that the spirits are what remains of human beings when they die physically. This then becomes the ultimate status of men, the point of change or development beyond which men cannot go apart from a few national heroes who might become deified. Spirits are the destiny of man, and beyond them is God. Societies that recognize divinities regard them as a further group in the ontological hierarchy between spirits and God. Man does not, and need not, hope to become a spirit: he is inevitably to become one, just as a child will automatically grow to become an adult, under normal circumstances. A few societies have an additional source of the spirits, believing that animals also have spirits which continue to live in the spirit world together with human and other spirits.

Spirits are invisible, but may make themselves visible to human beings. In reality, however, they have sunk beyond the horizon of the Zamani period, so that human beings do not see them either physically or mentally. Memory of them has slipped off. They are "seen" in the corporate belief in their existence. Yet, people experience their activities, and many folk stories tell of spirits described in human form, activities and personalities, even if an element of exaggeration is an essential part of that description. Because they are invisible, they are thought to be ubiquitous, so that a person is never sure where they are or are not. . . . Spirits as a group have more power than men, just as in a physical sense the lions do. Yet, in some ways men are better off and the right human specialists can manipulate or control the spirits as they wish. Men paradoxically may fear, or dread, the spirits and yet they can drive the same spirits away or use them to human advantage. In some societies only the major spirits (presumably in the category of divinities) are recognized, and often these are associated with natural phenomena or objects.

Although the spirits are ubiquitous, men designate different regions as their places of abode. Among some societies like the Abaluyia, Banyarwanda and Igbo, it is thought that the spirits dwell in the underground, netherworld or the subterranean regions. The Banyarwanda say, for example, that this region is ruled by "the one with whom one is forgotten"; and the Igbo consider it to be ruled by a queen. . . . A few societies like some Ewe, some Bushmen and the Mamvu-Mangutu, situate the land of the spirits above the earth, in the air, the sun, moon or stars.

The majority of peoples hold that the spirits dwell in the woods, bush forest, rivers, mountains or just around the villages. Thus, the spirits are in the same geographical region as men. This is partly the result of human self-protection and partly because man may not want to imagine himself in an entirely strange environment when he becomes a spirit. There is a sense in which man is too anthropocentric to get away from himself and his natural, social, political and economic surroundings. This then makes the spirits men's contemporaries: they are ever with men, and man would feel uncomfortable if the ontological mode of the spirits were too distant from his own. This would mean upsetting the balance of existence, and if that balance is upset, then men make sacrifices, offerings and prayers, to try and restore it. . . . In many African societies the spirits and the livingdead act as intermediaries who convey human sacrifices or prayers to God, and may relay His reply to men. We have also seen that in some societies it is believed that God has servants or agents whom He employs to carry out His intentions in the universe. The spirits fill up the ontological region of the Zamani between God and man's *Sasa*. The ontological transcendence of God is bridged by the spirit mode of existence. Man is forever a creature, but he does not remain forever man, and these are his two polarities of existence. Individual spirits may or may not remain for ever, but the class of the spirits is an essential and integral part of African ontology.

Mbiti further explains about the interaction between the spirits and humans.

From Mbiti, *African Religions*, 82–83.

Human relationships with the spirits vary from society to society. It is however, a real, active and powerful relationship, especially with the spin of those who have recently died—whom we have called the livingdead. Various rites are performed to keep this contact, involving the placing of food and other articles, or the pouring of libation of beer, milk, water or even tea or coffee (for the spirits who have been "modernized"). In some societies this is done daily, but most African peoples do it less often. Suci offerings are given to the oldest member of the departed, who may still be a livingdead, or may be remembered only in genealogies. This is done with the understanding that he will share the food or beverage with the other spirits of the family group. Words may or may not accompany such offerings, in form of prayers, invocations or instructions to the departed. These words are the bridge of communion, and people's witness that they recognize the departed to be still alive. Failure to observe these acts means in effect that human beings have completely broken off their links with the departed, and have therefore forgotten the spirits. This is regarded extremely dangerous and disturbing to the social and individual conscience. People are then likely to feel that any misfortune that befalls them is the logical result of their neglect of the spirits, if not caused by magic and witchcraft.

For spirits which are not associated with a particular family, offerings may be placed in spirit shrines where these exist. Such shrines belong to the community, and may be cared for by priests. Some of the spirits who are accorded this honour are venerated according to their functions, for example the spirits of the water may receive offerings when people want to fish or sail in the water; and the spirits of the forests may be consulted when people want to cut down the forest and make new fields. Here we merge with the category of the divinities, which we have already described above.

|

Toward an Authentic African Theology
of the Spirit and Salvation

|

Several African theologians have lamented the lack of an authentic African approach to theology and called for the rediscovery of the Spirit and spirituality.

From Gwinyai H. Muzorewa, *The Origins and Development of African Theology* (Maryknoll, NY: Orbis Books, 1985), 84.

The structure of African traditional theology is determined by an African cultural *modus operandi*, over against the Western or Eastern method. Africans differ from non-Africans in their culture more than anything else, and one's method of thinking (reflection) is influenced more than anything else by one's culture. What distinguishes Africans' culture from that of others must also make their traditional theology different from theologies of and for other cultures and religions. When these two criteria are satisfied, it may be possible to construct an African traditional theology that will make a significant contribution to Christendom. . . . I believe that in order for traditional theology to be a genuine African product, it should be faithful to the African way of thinking, which is based on a prescientific cosmology. Only an African epistemology will yield a distinct African traditional theology. From time immemorial, Africans have had their religious ways of knowing. A traditional theologian must first recapture this epistemology before she or he starts doing traditional theology for a prescientific mentality in a post-scientific world.

From Imasogie, *Guidelines for Christian Theology*, 81.

It is no exaggeration to say that the role of the Holy Spirit has been neglected in Christian theologizing in Africa. This is so partly because the secularized Western theologian is not thoroughly convinced of the reality and hence relevance of the Holy Spirit. He has more faith in psychological guidance than in spiritual guidance for the Christian. The typical African, on the other hand, comes from a world view that lays in store in spiritual guidance which is sought through divination, dreams and sooth-saying. The almost irresistible attraction of the modern pentecostal movement as represented in the Independent Churches in Africa is not unconnected with their emphasis on the place of the Holy Spirit in the life of the Christian. It is not enough to condemn the excesses and the obvious mercenary tendencies of some of these Churches. We must also confess that the failure of the orthodox Christian theologian to put the right emphasis on this veritable biblical doctrine is responsible for the aberration in its current expression.

An African Spirit Christology

An authentically African theology would need to develop not only pneumatology but also Christology and soteriology in keeping with the cultural and religious context. Briefly stated, African Christology is pneumatic Christology, as the selection by Ghanaian Kwame Bediako summarizes. In the second selection, an example of a relevant Spirit Christology to that effect is offered by the Roman Catholic Donald J. Goergen, OP.

From Kwame Bediako, *Christianity in Africa:*
The Renewal of a Non-Western Religion (Edinburgh:
Edinburgh University Press, 1995), 176.

It is hardly surprising that the Christologies that have emerged in African theology so far are predominantly "pneumatic," presenting a Christ who is a living power in the realm of spirit.

From Donald J. Goergen, "Quest for the Christ of
Africa," *African Christian Studies* 17, no. 1 (March 2001),
http://www.sedos.org/english/goergen.htm
(accessed May 29, 2007), n.p.

Risen Jesus, Giver of the Spirit, Lord of the Spirits

The centrality of "life-force" in African cultures is equalled only by
the theme of the spirit-world. There is no dichotomy or antagonism
between matter and spirit as in some Western philosophies. Rather
the spiritual and material form one interconnected organic and cosmic whole in which there is a continuity between this world, the
living dead, the ancestral spirits, and God. In an African view of the
world, the Holy Spirit is at home. The Holy Spirit is promised by
Jesus and given by the risen Christ. An African christology ought
to be a pneumatic or Spirit Christology which shows Jesus' power
over the world of spirits and his connectedness to the Holy Spirit.
. . . The Holy Spirit is Jesus' supreme gift to those who are his disciples. This is again a particularly Johannine theology, but the Holy
Spirit also plays a prominent role in the Lucan and Pauline writings. Following are some texts from the Gospel of John: "And I will
pray the Father, and he will give you another Counselor, to be with
you for ever" (14:16). "But the Counselor, the Holy Spirit, whom the
Father will send in my name, he will teach you all things, and bring
to your remembrance all that I have said to you" (14:26). "But when
the Counselor comes, whom I shall send to you from the Father,
even the Spirit of truth, who proceeds from the Father, he will bear
witness to me" (15:26). "Nevertheless, I tell you the truth: it is to
your advantage that I go away, for if I do not go away, the Counselor
will not come to you; but if I go, I will send him to you" (16:7). "And
when he [the risen Jesus] had said this, he breathed on them, and
said to them, 'Receive the Holy Spirit'"(20:22). Christology is always
interwoven with pneumatology and *vice-versa*. It was the Holy Spirit
who was already present in Africa and African religions before the
arrival of Christian missionaries. It is the same Spirit who animates
African religion and African Christianity. Yet this Spirit who was
active in the world even before the Christian Era comes to us from
the Father through the Son. He is Jesus' Spirit as well as God's Spirit.
Thus, he is seen as Jesus' gift to us.

A Holistic Salvation and Healing

Healing and deliverance are integral parts of African spirituality and theology.

From Muzorewa, *Origins and Development of African Theology*, 85–86.

Another traditional Christian concept that will need reinterpretation is the doctrine of salvation. If we concede that the African Trinity implies the presence of Christ within the African culture, one may say that salvation is a built-in concept there as well. Since the idea of survival dominates in African culture, I submit that salvation is the African mode of *being* that makes survival happen. In traditional religious beliefs, any life-saving act is ultimately attributable to God.

Salvation is an African spiritual mechanism that works through any agent, including historical reality, to rescue or save an endangered life. For instance, a man who is washed away by a flood may be thrown on a tree trunk lying across the flooded river. If his life is saved by that log, he can say: "Were it not for that log, I would have perished." He rejoices that he has been saved from physical destruction. Salvation is not only spiritual; in the African context, salvation must be holistic. The African traditional theologian knows that that log has no "intention" to "save" anyone, but God uses that log to physically save a creature. Most Africans who find themselves rescued from this kind of danger would attribute such a salvation to their ancestral spirit. It is through the spirit that one is saved, or rescued, or redeemed; but the total event of salvation is God's plan.

For Africans, salvation is not only spiritual; it touches all aspects of the person's—and community's—life and well-being.

From Goergen, "Quest for the Christ of Africa," n.p.

It is difficult to determine which expression we should prefer [of Jesus], whether healer, diviner, medicine man, or witchdoctor. We are dealing with the African concept of *nganga*.

Among Christians, and in the West, some may find "witchdoctor" too strong given negative associations with the word "witch." Yet "witchdoctor" itself is not a negative word, anymore than doctor is. The witchdoctor is a doctor who treats witches, whose expertise is knowledge of witchcraft and how to deal with it. He is not a sorcerer.

In contemporary terms, he practices alternative medicine. The causes of disease, physical and mental, as they were understood in the first century world of Jesus were not so dissimilar to those in traditional African religion. Indeed, an African or Africanist can at times more easily understand the world of the Bible than a modern Westerner can. Hence Jesus the Witchdoctor is as good an expression as Jesus the Healer. . . . There are many positive aspects to this way of naming Jesus in Africa, and it is surprising that this approach to African christology has not received even more attention. The title resonates well with what we know about the Jesus of the Gospels. Although post-Enlightenment skepticism has dismissed most of Jesus' miracles, healing was a significant dimension of Jesus' ministry. Jesus, preacher and teacher, prophet and sage, is often given greater attention today. But healings and exorcisms are widely attested in the New Testament, and in material that meet modern critical biblical criteria. Nor should the healings and exorcisms be separated from the preaching. They were preaching—preaching in deeds rather than words. The symbolic actions in Jesus' ministry were as important as the parabolic stories. Both reflect Jesus the healer—healing in words and in deed—the two always being integrated in Jesus for whom praxis was never separated from proclamation.

The Spirit and Salvation among African Indigenous Churches

"Folk Theology"

The Roman Catholic missiologist and theologian Philip Knights offers helpful reflections on the nature of "folk theology" as evident among the African instituted (or African indigenous) churches, which constitute tens of millions of Christians, many of them somewhat syncretistic.

From Philip Knights, "MIL 4002 Lecture 8 *Missio Dei* 2—The Sending of the Spirit" in "Theological Foundations of Mission, Justice and Peace," http://www.home.freeuk.com/knights/MJP/MIL4002-8.htm (accessed August 24, 2009), n.p.

Again . . . we must make a distinction here between folk theology: what the people do, how they worship and academic theology. Most AICs [African Instituted Churches], indeed most African Christians, have little formal theology, but this is not the same as no theology. In their folk theology they celebrate their living experience of divine involvement through the pervading Spirit. This living experience of the Spirit is manifested in possession experiences, in speaking in tongues, in prophecy and perhaps above all in healing. This healing is fundamentally healing of conditions largely beyond western biomedicine: bad luck, infidelity of husbands, barrenness in women, witchcraft, possession of stranger spirits and so forth.

These experiences can be seen in two lights: they can be seen as parallel to the experiences of Pentecostalism and Charismatic Renewal in other Christian Churches, or they can be seen as a continuity with African traditional religion. Thirty or forty years ago most workers in the field tended to dismiss AICs as syncretistic and their worship patterns as heretical or pagan. However, most recent scholarship, including many notable changes of mind, has been much more sympathetic and willing to see AICs as Christian. It is clear that AICs tend to see themselves as different from traditional religion and attack traditional practices and diviners with greater vigour than mainstream Christianity. They see themselves as addressing the life experiences of Africans but with greater power than pre-Christian traditional religion. I think there is a definite tension here, a tension of continuity or discontinuity. Continuity with African traditions, and continuity with Christian theology as well as discontinuity with African traditions and discontinuities with Christian experience. All I can say is that most AICs want to see themselves as Christian. Christian mission must be in a dialogue with these experiences which recognises that which is of God, but also able to offer genuine criticism. Neither outright rejection nor complete absolute acceptance will be satisfactory. A proper respect for and Christian analysis of these phenomena is called for. The line between error laden syncretism and proper inculturation can be a very fine one.

Different Approaches to Pneumatology in Western and Indigenous African Theologies

The Yoruba in Western Nigeria are a group of semi-independent peoples loosely linked by geography, language, history, and religion, numbering over ten million people. The Yoruba land has been fertile with traditional religions, and Christianity has also infiltrated these peoples in a significant way. The Nigerian theologian Caleb O. Oladipo, who teaches in the United States, has published a major study on the Yoruba view of the Spirit and salvation. Oladipo outlines the main differences between the pneumatologies of the West and those from the African context. While in the West salvation has been understood individualistically and the work of the Spirit has been part of soteriology and the doctrine of the Word of God, in Africa there is a holistic and communal approach.

From Caleb Oluremi Oladipo, *The Development of the
Doctrine of the Holy Spirit in the Yoruba (African) Indigenous
Christian Movement*, American University Studies, Series 2, Theology
and Religion, vol. 185 (Frankfurt: Peter Lang, 1996), 100–101.

The term Holy Spirit is the strangest of the strange terms that appear among Christian symbols. . . . [The] use of the term Holy Ghost produces an impression of great remoteness from our way of speaking and thinking. But spiritual experience is a reality for everyone, as actual as the experience of being loved or the breathing of air. Therefore, we should not shy away from the word spirit. We should become fully aware of the Spiritual Presence, around us and in us. . . . This is what Divine Spirit means: God present to our spirit. Spirit is not a mysterious substance: it is not a part of God. It is God Himself.

With this understanding of the Holy Spirit, creation, redemption, and sanctification are not different actions of the Father, Son, and Holy Spirit in sequence. Creation does not mean that God set things going at the beginning of time. Rather, creation is an ongoing activity of God. By reconciliation and redemption, Christians mean that the creative activities of God [are] also a continuous process whereby the disorderliness of existence are healed, its imbalances redressed, and its alienation bridged over. Sanctification is also a continuous activity of God whereby he brings creation to its perfection. . . .

In traditional Western Christian thought, the Holy Spirit is understood from the point of view of salvation. Saving faith is accomplished by the Holy Spirit through the Word of God. Salvation is thus a gift bestowed by the grace of God. The Reformed theologians of the sixteenth-century like Martin Luther (1483–1546) and John Calvin (1509–1564) maintained that the Word (or the Gospel) as preached is primarily the efficacious Word of God after the Holy Spirit works upon the hearts of the hearers. They believed that no one can rightly understand the Scripture without the working of the Spirit. . . . In general, Pneumatology in traditional Western Christian thought seems to lay particular emphasis on the function of the Holy Spirit in the economy of salvation and on the nature of the Holy Spirit in trinitarian understanding of the divine Godhead. . . .

The understanding of the Holy Spirit in Western theological thought still leaves some important questions unanswered and two of these questions are particularly important. First, the Holy Spirit is God's coming to humanity in an inward way to enlighten and strengthen humanity. But salvation of an individual implies a polarity of that particular individual and communal aspects of everything else that is existing and under God's dominion. As it was demonstrated in the previous chapter, the conception of those who are devoted to African Traditional Religions is that humanity is a social being and one cannot separate [an individual's] salvation from all other aspects of his existence. The Yoruba people particularly understand salvation to be more communal. This means that salvation is seen in terms of a *corporate personality*.

The Holy Spirit in Ancestor Metaphors

African Christology has for a long time utilized metaphors from the rich reservoir of ancestor worship; here is an example of the use of those metaphors in pneumatology.

From Oladipo, *Development of the Doctrine of the Holy Spirit*, 102, 105.

During the past few decades, the Indigenous Christian movements in Yorubaland have taken seriously the trinitarian understanding of God as articulated by Western Christian theologians. Many theologians in Africa have made serious attempts to forge genuine contacts between African Traditional Religion and the trinitarian theology of the West. As a result of theological efforts, the Christian experience among the Yoruba people has acquired, out of necessity, a new form of characterization. The Yoruba people now view God the Father as "the Great ancestor," God the Son as "the Proto-ancestor," and God the Holy Spirit as "the Grand ancestor." There is a recognition that these models are characterizations of the Christian experience in Yorubaland, and the models are not peculiar to the Yoruba people alone. . . .

There are two layers of the concept of God in Yorubaland. First, there is the concept of God as the essence of cosmic totality, and, second, there is the concept of God as the Great Ancestor. The latter is, perhaps, the more widely held concept. *Olodu mare*, as the essence of cosmic totality, fulfills the requirement as the Great Ancestor. He is the begetter of the lesser divinities as well as of all creation. In his role as the progenitor of all creation, he is appropriately conceived by the Yoruba people as the Great Ancestor. *Olodu mare* is the father and mother of all people, and therefore the Grand Ancestor. *Olodu mare* is not said to have ruled as a King, but he is said to be the divine ancestor because He created all things. His "divine nature" is embodied in the human kings in whom he is incarnated. For the Yoruba people therefore, God is "the Great Ancestor," and the Great Progenitor of all divinities.

Having laid out the ancestral interpretation of the doctrine of the Trinity, Oladipo elaborates on the notion of the Holy Spirit as the "Grand Ancestor."

From Oladipo, *Development of the Doctrine of the Holy Spirit*, 104, 107–8.

The Holy Spirit is the Grand ancestor because of the specific role he plays in sustaining the Yoruba people. Like the ancestors, the Holy Spirit is with the Yoruba people for spiritual guidance, and they direct their spiritual destiny through him. This role of the Holy Spirit is seen by the Yoruba people as an important role in the lives of the believers. Hence, the Holy Spirit is considered the Grand ancestor. This trinitarian understanding may well be one of the most important contacts the Yoruba Christians have made with the traditional Western Christian thought, and it is important to examine these models one by one. . . .

In traditional Yoruba religion, ancestors are strictly considered mediators and intermediaries. They are taken to be the guarantors of solidarity, stability and progress of the community of the living, who have "a real communion of life with their ancestors." In all ramifications, therefore, the major function of the ancestors is to maintain a peaceful and stable society in so far as this will result in achieving the expected spiritual destiny of the Yoruba people. When this view is translated into the Christian context, one can state that the Holy Spirit is the ancestor par excellence because the Spirit plays the role of an intercessor, and also because he is in unity with *Olodu mare* and with Jesus Christ. As the ancestor par excellence, the Holy Spirit is the source of a new life, and the fountainhead of Christian living. The Holy Spirit, by virtue of his ancestorship, sustains the entire line of humanity by embracing the beginning as well as the end of human spiritual destiny. The Holy Spirit assumes the legitimate aspiration of African ancestors by his authentic relationship with divine reality. Thus, the "mystery of the Holy Spirit" is that he is the unique ancestor. This means that the eminent assumption of the spiritual destiny which African ancestors seek to guarantee to their earthly descendants is obtainable through an indigenous Christian definition of the Holy Spirit. The aspiration of the ancestors is efficacious through the Holy Spirit and through Jesus Christ. The spiritual destiny of the Yoruba people is now fully guaranteed by the outpouring of this Holy Spirit. In this way, the efflorescence of the Holy Spirit enables the Yoruba people to see the Holy Spirit as the "Grand-Ancestor."

Just as Jesus Christ is the locus of a total encounter with God from Christian perspectives, the Holy Spirit is the locus where the living can encounter the God of salvation. This conception of the Holy Spirit as the "Grand Ancestor" has the theological advantage of being more meaningful and relevant to the Yoruba people than the alien idea of the *logos* or *kyrios* that has been forced upon Yoruba Christians. This also makes it possible for anthropocentric spirituality (human-centered spirituality) to be the source and fountainhead of African Christian experience and practice—a kind of pneumatology from below based on religious existentialism.

Notwithstanding the many similarities, there are also differences that need to be acknowledged.

From Oladipo, *Development of the Doctrine of the Holy Spirit*, 110–11.

The first fundamental difference between the Holy Spirit and the ancestors is that the Holy Spirit does not acquire his status after death like the ancestors. The Holy Spirit is related to believers because of his supernatural relation with God the Father and God the Son. This view is in accord with historic Christian teaching in the West, and many Yoruba Christians are also aware of this. Thus, the relationship between the Holy Spirit and believers transcends all family ties and relations. In this regard, the Holy Spirit does not acquire tribal qualification before achieving his status. It is by his hypostatic union that he established his intercession between God and humanity. . . .

Second, it can be said that the Holy Spirit is more infinitely perfect as the guidance and source of Christian living than the Yoruba ancestors can ever be. The Holy Spirit is more than the external prototype of Christian conduct for believers, because he is the inner source and vital principle of Christian life. In this regard, the Holy Spirit is much more than ancestors who can only be external exemplars of the behavior of their living descendants. Whereas the relatives can still be kin to the ancestors apart from the literal influence of the ancestors, Christians literally cannot do anything apart from the Holy Spirit. The Holy Spirit is an inner principle and it is only through him that believers can receive both divine guidance and their source of stability in their Christian journey. Being rooted in him, Christians can never change in their fundamental affirmation of the Christian tradition. It should be recognized, however, that it is the responsibility of Christians in Yorubaland to determine ultimately what is more in the Holy Spirit, and the significance of this *more* for Christians, and how this significance relates to the universal claim of the Christian message.

Third, there is a vast difference between the supernatural communication of the Yoruba conception of the Holy Spirit and that of the Yoruba ancestors. The Holy Spirit, as Yoruba people maintained, communicates to believers not only in material blessings but also in establishing within the believers what the Apostle Paul called the *fruits of the Spirit*. It is by this that believers are transformed and united intimately in relationship with God the Father.

It is for reasons such as this one that Jesus Christ came to redeem God's creation. This being the case, a neglect of fellowship with God the Father in the Holy Spirit through Jesus Christ is infinitely and qualitatively worse than an offence against the Yoruba ancestors. No one can appease God from such an offence by merely outward rituals. Only a sincere expression of sorrow and total conversion of heart towards the Spirit of God is efficacious in appeasing a severed relationship with God.

"The Pentecostalization of Africa"

There is no way to give any kind of survey of African pneumatologies without reference to the largest segment of the African churches and spirituality, namely, the pentecostal/charismatic movements. Even those churches that do not identify themselves formally with pentecostal/charismatic movements often reflect the kind of spirituality that has been associated with those movements. The leading researcher of African Pentecostalism and independent churches, Allan H. Anderson of South Africa, sets the stage in a very helpful way.

From Allan H. Anderson, "African Pentecostal Churches and Concepts of Power," http://artsweb.bham.ac.uk/aanderson/Publications/apcs_ and_concepts_of_power.htm, n.d., n.p. (accessed May 29, 2007).

A large number of African initiated churches have been variously described as "independent African Pentecostal churches" . . . "spiritual churches" . . . , "prophet-healing churches" . . . and "Spirit-type churches." . . . They constitute today the majority of so-called African independent churches (AICs). Because of the connection between these movements and pentecostal churches of western origin . . . , I refer to them simply as "African pentecostal churches." This term is intentionally wide and any generalisations made do not apply to every "pentecostal" church. These churches are now a prominent part of African Christianity and yet, for various reasons, their voice is virtually unheard in ecumenical circles. They emerged in a situation where they were denied socio-economic and religious "power," whilst mission churches dominated by Europeans often represented colonial oppression. This was especially true in South Africa, where until comparatively recently, churches were segregated, white church leaders exercised paternalistic control at every administrative level.

Anderson argues that Pentecostalism has been capable of incorporating into its spirituality various kinds of local customs, beliefs, and rituals. African Pentecostalism, which is in constant interaction with the African spirit world, has radically changed the face of Christianity simply because it has proclaimed a holistic gospel of salvation that includes deliverance from all types of oppression, such as sickness, sorcery, evil spirits, and poverty.

From Allan H. Anderson, "Gospel and Culture in Pentecostal
Mission in the Third World," paper presented at the 11th Meeting of the
European-Pentecostal Charismatic Association at Missionsakademi of the
University of Hamburg, Germany, July 13–17, 1999, 11.

All the widely differing Pentecostal movements have important common features: they proclaim and celebrate a salvation (or "healing") that encompasses all of life's experiences and afflictions, and they offer an empowerment which provides a sense of dignity and a coping mechanism for life, and all this drives their messengers forward into a unique mission.

The concept of "power" is essential to Pentecostal and independent churches in Africa.

Anderson, "African Pentecostal Churches and Concepts of Power," n.p.

African pentecostal churches have been criticised for their emphasis on the "power" of the Holy Spirit. . . . In keeping with ideas of power in African religion, some have alleged that this force or "power" is tangibly perceived and manipulable, and that some people may have more of it than others. In fact, African pentecostals do not see the Holy Spirit as an impersonal manipulable force, and the Bible furnishes abundant evidence of tangible manifestations of the Holy Spirit's power. Negative evaluations sometimes stem from an overemphasis on theological theory (as seen by westerners), and a disparaging of African experience. The "power" made available to Christian believers through the Spirit may be closer to the African concept of "vital force" . . . than westerners might admit. Life and human existence are inextricably tied up with power. To live is to have power; to be sick, to die, to be poor or oppressed is to have less of it. Whenever problems came to an African society, or even when there was a foreboding of trouble, it was often necessary for the afflicted to consult the specialists, the traditional diviners and healers. They had special power to discern the wishes of the ancestors and to act as protectors of society. Very often the unseen evil force of witches or sorcerers also needed to be counteracted with a more powerful force. Sorcerers could only succeed with their evil intent if some kind of access to the victim was gained through the latter's protective ancestors. For this reason people turned to diviners who were able to diagnose the cause of affliction, and usually prescribed some ritual or gave protective medicines and charms to overcome the evil force. In much of western Christianity exported to Africa no alternative solution was offered to the real fears and problems encountered by Africans. . . . An African theology and practice concerning the Holy Spirit that is both biblical and contextualised, such as is found in African pentecostal churches, provides a dynamic Christianity that attempts to meet Africa's needs in this realm. . . .

The promise of "power from on high" (Luke 24:49) means that God has granted to the black person dignity, power and liberation that is realised through the pentecostal experience. This liberation is a holistic liberation from everything that oppresses and demeans personal dignity, empowering people to take their places in equality and leadership among God's people. As Lovett (1975:140) remarks "Black pentecostalism affirms with dogmatic insistence that liberation is always the consequence of the presence of the Spirit. . . . No man can genuinely experience the fullness of the Spirit and remain a *bona fide* racist." The God who forgives sin is also deeply concerned about powerlessness manifested in poverty, oppression and (especially) in liberation from all of people's physical afflictions. It is this message of physical liberation that makes the pentecostal churches so attractive to Africans. Even though sometimes African pentecostals have little formal theology (a factor which is now changing), an implicit theology is exhibited in their practices and in their interpretation of the working of the Holy Spirit in daily life. . . .

An understanding of power concepts places us in a better position to appreciate the attempt made by the African pentecostal churches to fill the gap between these concepts with their seemingly inherent inadequacies, and the somewhat sterile western theology imported to Africa. The message that African pentecostal churches proclaimed was the power of the Spirit given to people permanently and unconditionally. . . . The message of the receiving of the power of the Holy Spirit, a power greater than any of the powers that threaten human existence, is good news indeed! Clearly, African pentecostal churches are founded on an emphasis on the power of the Holy Spirit, an emphasis which in their own estimation distinguishes them from most other churches. The Holy Spirit is unanimously associated with power—whether physical, moral, or spiritual—the all-embracing, pervading power of God. A demonstration of God's power through his Spirit will often convince Africans that God is indeed more powerful than surrounding evil forces, and therefore is worthy of worship, faith and service. In Africa God is indeed all-powerful, and this omnipotent God manifests his presence through the Holy Spirit working graciously and actively in the church.

CHAPTER 16

Testimonies from Asia

Introduction to the Asian Context

According to the Korean-born theologian Jung Young Lee, the "cultural and historical context of the West is so very distinct from that of the East that they seem opposite to each other." However, he adds, "their difference should be regarded not as a source of conflict but as a basis for mutual fulfillment. Their contextual difference will enrich a holistic understanding of the Christian faith."[1] While Christianity has not made inroads evenly into that part of the world[2]—the continent inhabited by more than half the world's population—we must not underrate the significance of Christian faith there. After all, the presence of the Christian church claims an ancient pedigree—from the missionary work of the apostle Thomas in the Middle East and the western and southern coast of India, to the vital Catholic missionary influence after the discovery of the sea route to India and the rest of Asia in the later Middle Ages, to the modern missionary movement of European (and later American) origin, which has been mainly Protestant.[3]

What would a "theology from the womb of Asia," to cite the title of the book by the Taiwanese Choan-Seng Song,[4] look like? The words of the Sri Lankan Roman Catholic liberationist Aloysius Pieris succinctly summarize the two defining features of this vast continent: "The Asian context can be described as a blend of a profound religiosity (which is perhaps Asia's greatest wealth) and an overwhelming poverty."[5] Asian religiosity is

---

1. Jung Young Lee, *The Trinity in Asian Perspective* (Nashville: Abingdon Press, 1996), 17.

2. Statistically, the number of Christians in Asia range all the way from less than one percent (Japan, Thailand, among others) to a few percent at most, with the exception of the predominantly Roman Catholic Philippines (about 85 percent Christian) and more recently South Korea (less than a third Christian) and China (estimations vary widely from 50–70 million or so).

3. See further George Gispert-Sauch, SJ, "Asian Theology," in *The Modern Theologians: An Introduction to Christian Theology in the Twentieth Century*, ed. D. F. Ford, 2nd ed. (Cambridge: Blackwell, 1997), 455.

4. Choan-Seng Song, *Theology from the Womb of Asia* (Maryknoll, NY: Orbis Books, 1986).

5. Aloysius Pieris, "Western Christianity and Asian Buddhism," in *Dialogue* 7 (May–August 1980): 61–62.

rich and variegated and touches all aspects of life; in contrast to the Western modernist dualism between the sacred and secular, for most Asians religion is an irreducible part of all life and undergirds beliefs, decisions, and behavior of everyday life. Even with rapid developments in technology and education, Hinduism, Buddhism, Confucianism, and a host of other religions, most of them manifested in forms that used to be called "animistic" (having to do with spirits), permeate all of life. Similarly to Africa but differently from Europe and the United States, religion is visible and part of everyday life. Thus, talk about God/gods can be carried on everywhere, from the street markets to luxurious hotels to desperate slums to exotic restaurants.

The Spirit in the Asian Context

Similarly to the discussion of pneumatology and soteriology in the African context, it is appropriate to begin this section by looking at the ways Spirit is perceived in Asia.

From Yeow Choo Lak, preface to *Doing Theology with the Spirit's Movement in Asia*, ed. John C. England and Alan J. Torrance (Singapore: ATESEA, 1991), vi.

The spirit-world is alive and is doing well in Asia. Seemingly, education (eastern or western) has done little to dampen the influence of the spirit-world. Whilst writing these few lines, a neighbour is having his front yard done up. He is highly educated and is doing well in the corporate world. Yet, before the workmen started digging up his garden he was burning joss papers and joss sticks. That was his way of ensuring success and prosperity in this venture. One cannot say that he is uneducated and uninformed. In spite of his high education he is still very much influenced by the spirit-world.

From Zhihua Yao, "In the Power of the Spirit," *Tripod* 91 (Jan.–Feb. 1996): 28.

The lands of Asia, rich in color and resources, conceived most of the great civilizations that survive today. Most of the world's religions also originated in Asia; this includes the so-called Western religions: Christianity and Judaism. While the huge populations of Islam, Hinduism, Buddhism and Confucianism in Asia make the missionary work of Christianity exceedingly difficult, they also provide Christianity with a wealth of resources with which it can enrich itself.

Asian culture is replete with religious traditions and many Asian theologians search for a theology that cuts across the boundaries of culture, religion and history, a theology that focuses on compassion at the heart of religion. . . . To this end they find interfaith dialogue useful. To my knowledge, there are two major lines in the development to this dialogue: one is *theocentric*; the other is *spirit-centred*. In the first, God reveals the divine self to all nations; in the second the stress is on the Holy Spirit who works in the peoples. But in both of these lines, each nation has a different understanding of this revelation within the framework of its cultural context. Both of these positions try to replace the central position of Jesus Christ in Christianity.

From *The Spirit at Work in Asia Today: A Document of the Office of Theological Concerns of the Federation of the Asian Bishops' Conferences*, FABC Papers no. 81 (1998), 1–2.

"Come, Oh Creator Spirit" (Veni Creator Spiritus) today is a hymn that swells up from the heart of Asia and finds expression on the lips of millions of its daughters and sons. As we Asians are facing the marvellous new things unfolding before our eyes today in every realm of life, we experience the irresistible power of that Spirit "blowing where it wills" crossing in one divine sweep, across all kinds of barriers and boundaries. The Spirit moves on, and in its movement it wants us to follow it, so that we may see, experience and savour the sublimity of the divine realities for which Asia has always been longing. It leads us, at the same time, to the arcane mysteries of all life in its every shade and form, filling our quest for the human and the cosmic with a new vigour and force.

On the face of the Spirit, coming fresh upon us today, we recognise the power with which generations of our foremothers and fathers have been familiar during the millennial history of this continent. It is especially, the life and experience of the poor and the marginalised peoples of Asia that has been much attuned to the world of the Spirit as we find in their many religio-cultural beliefs, rites and expression. The Spirit binds us in a marvellous way with all those who have left the indelible imprint of their spirit, heart and mind in innumerable forms on our cultures and on our traditions. It is the same Spirit of God that Asia wants to rely on in shaping its future destiny. At the threshold of a new millennium, our Asian local Churches invoke the Spirit, knowing that its transformative and creative power is what we need most to be able to respond to the new and unprecedented challenges the continent is facing, and thus become truly Churches of the Spirit.

"Spiritual" Cosmos

One difference between a Western and an Asian outlook on life is that for the Asian nature and cosmos are more "spirited." The distinction between "material" and "spiritual" is far less categorical. In typical Asian views of life—if there is anything "typical" in such a vast continent—what is spiritual is primary while the material world is secondary, a feature that runs contrary to much in the West.

From Jung Young Lee, *The Theology of Change: A Christian Concept of God in an Eastern Perspective* (Maryknoll, NY: Orbis Books, 1979), 105–6, 110.

The Bhagavad Gita, one of Hinduism's most popular scriptures, affirms the interdependence of the spiritual and material nature, depicting Brahman as the womb of all things: "My womb is the great Brahman; in it I plant the germ. Thence comes the origin of all beings." . . . It is God's own, whose essence is the spirit. Thus the whole material universe is regarded as the manifestation of his spiritual nature, which sustains the material nature. Since God is ultimately one, his material nature is simultaneously his spiritual nature. In the highest reality the two natures are identical. According to the Heart Sutra of Mahayana Buddhism, nirvana and samsara, or the spiritual and material natures, are identical. Ignorance and illusion result from the false dualism that separates matter from spirit. In God one is in all and all is in one. . . .

The Holy Spirit is in this respect analogous to the Taoist tao, which is characterized by the receptiveness of change. Like the Holy Spirit, tao is patient and yielding. It changes, without intent, like buds opening. It accomplishes everything by inaction.

Another typically Asian way of looking at reality and thus at topics such as the Spirit is the complementary pair of *yin* and *yang*. The cosmology of East Asian people is encapsulated in the bipolarity of nature, which operates cyclically in terms of growth and decline, or the waxing and waning of the moon. The opposites are necessary and also complementary. Thus, the organizing principle of the cosmos is *yin* and *yang*, such as day and night, big and small. While opposite, they are also united together. They are "both-and" rather than "either-or."

From Jung Young Lee, *Trinity in Asian Perspective*
(Nashville: Abingdon Press, 1996), 95–98.

The Spirit, according to Asian trinitarian thinking, is known as "she," the Mother, who complements the Father. The Spirit as the image of Mother, as a feminine member of the Trinity, is important for today's women who are conscious of their place in the world. The abstruseness of the Spirit in the Trinity has to do with her pervasiveness. She is present everywhere and at all times, and is known in both personal and impersonal categories. The Spirit is not only natural phenomena, such as wind, but also a personal being, such as the Advocate, who is sent in Jesus' name (John 14:26). The reconciliation between personal and nonpersonal manifestations of the Spirit is possible in yin-yang thinking, which is also "both-and" thinking. The inclusivity of the Spirit is known in East Asia as "*ch'i*," the activity of yin and yang, which is the essence and the animating energy of all existence. In the concept of *ch'i*, the problem of personal and nonpersonal categories is easily resolved, for *ch'i* must be considered in terms of cosmo-anthropology.

The cosmic dimension of spirit is expressed in the idea of *ch'i*, the vital energy which is the animating power and essence of the material body. *Ch'i* (or *ki* in Korean) is almost identical with "spirit," *ruach* in Hebrew and *pneuma* in Greek, both of which are often translated as "wind" or "breath." . . . *Ch'i*, as the Spirit, is the activity of yin and yang, which changes and transforms all things in the world.

Let me now recapture the idea of spirit and incorporate two different manifestations of spirit. If "ruach" in Hebrew and "pneuma" in Greek are translated "spirit" in the Old and New Testaments, the Spirit is also both wind in nature and breath in the living. In other words, wind symbolizes the power of life in nature, while breath symbolizes the power of life in the living. Both wind and breath are power, because they represent the movements of yin and yang. Yin-yang movements are none other than *ch'i*, because the single *ch'i* embraces the modes of yin and yang activities. Because yin and yang are ubiquitous, the Spirit, as wind and breath, is also present everywhere and all the time. According to Chang Tsai's cosmology, *ch'i* is not only all-pervasive reality but also undifferentiated singleness. According to this concept of *ch'i*, the distinction between wind and breath is simply one of modes of manifestation. *Ch'i* is the essence of all life and all existence, which includes the living as well as the nonliving. Without *ch'i* life does not exist. . . . The concept of *ch'i* helps us understand the cosmological implication of the Spirit and her inclusive presence in all existence. Earth is a living organism because of *ch'i* in the ground, and heaven is alive because of *ch'i* in the sky. It is the Spirit as *ch'i* that assists us in reaffirming the idea of divine immanence or immanuel.

If all things exist because of the Spirit as *ch'i*, nothing that exists is real without the Spirit. The Spirit is then the essence of all things, and without her everything is a mirage. Moreover, creativity is an act of *ch'i* as the Spirit. In the story of creation, we find the creativity of *ch'i* or Spirit: "In the beginning when God created the heavens and the earth, the earth was a formless void and darkness covered the face of the deep, while a wind from God swept over the face of the waters" (Gen. 1:1, 2). Here, "a wind from God" or the Spirit of God seems to be closely related with the speech or words that act as the power of creation. . . . Because of the Spirit as *ch'i*, everything that exists is creative and alive. It is, therefore, impossible to separate spirit from matter. In other words, spirit is inseparable from matter, for they are essentially one but have two modes of existence. Because they are inseparable, thinking of matter alone without spirit or spirit alone without matter is illusory. This idea is applicable not only to the East Asian notion of *ch'i* but also to the Hindu notion of "prana." In Hinduism, the world of matter separated from the Spirit of Brahman, or *reality*, is considered illusory, and this illusory world is commonly called maysa. *Ch'i* as the Spirit of God can also be symbolized by the womb of the world, for all things in the world have their origins in the Spirit. . . . If *ch'i*, as the most pervasive and the all-embracing essence of life, manifests itself in concrete forms, the Spirit, which cannot be separated from *ch'i*, must also manifest herself in all different forms. She must be in trees, rocks, insects, animals, and human beings. She must also be active in all things and in all activities in our lives. This seems to make Christianity not only an animistic but a panentheistic religion. However, Christianity is more than animistic or panentheistic, because the Spirit is not only *ch'i* but also more than *ch'i*. She is more than *ch'i*, because she is also God. Moreover, the God of Christianity is not only the Spirit, but also more than the Spirit because of the divine Trinity. The Spirit is also in the Father and in the Son, who make Christianity a religion that transcends animistic and panentheistic tendencies.

Salvation in Nature

Kosuke Koyama elaborates on these features by reflecting on the topic, familiar to an Asian mind-set, of finding "salvation" in nature.

From Kosuke Koyama, *Mount Fuji and Mount Sinai: A Critique of Idols* (Maryknoll, NY: Orbis Books, 1985), 74.

"Heaven and earth" is not a totality created by One who is beyond it. The gods and buddhas are within heaven and earth. This position is neither atheistic nor humanistic. It does not define itself in philosophical terms. It is quite free from such arguments. It simply states the feeling of salvation we have when we are embraced by the totality of nature, "heaven and earth." This feeling is not concerned with scientific preciseness. It is poetic rather than propositional. It does not seek to understand the social existence of humanity in terms of social analysis and criticism. In the perspective of this "pop spirituality" sociological and theological debates disappear as we ourselves disappear into the bosom of the cosmic embrace. "My help comes from nature."

The word "totality" is used here in a symbolic, not a scientific sense. The symbol of totality has a healing effect upon the human soul. It can give us our needed self-identity, showing us where we are between creation and destruction, life and death, and good and evil. The words "heaven and earth" carry a therapeutic message because it will give us an image of "all things." Nature surrounds us. We come from nature and we go back to nature.

Metaphors of the Holy Spirit
Drawn from Asian Soil

The Asian cultural heritage possesses a rich tapestry of metaphors and symbols of the Holy Spirit.

Lee, *Trinity in Asian Perspective*, 104.

Cloth as a metaphor of the Spirit protects and sustains all things on earth. Unlike the shield, a masculine metaphor of protection, it is closely associated with a feminine image in Asia. Women weave cloth and use it for the protection and decoration of the body. The Spirit as *ch'i* also weaves through the entire cosmos and gives life. The Spirit is a weaver and a protector of all things on earth, for cloth is the symbol of her presence. . . . By the very nature of being a mother, she protects her young, as "a hen gathers her brood under her wings" (Luke 13:34). The Spirit as the mother can be best described as the sustainer of the world. . . . The kettle is another metaphor that belongs to the mother. In most countries, the mother is responsible for preparing food for her family. The kettle is for cooking, and is the symbol of nourishment. The kettle here is regarded as an image of spiritual nourishment. Here, spiritual nurture is not separate from the nourishment of the body. In fact, the Spirit as *ch'i* is the vitality of the material principle, and the nourishment of soul is, in fact, the nourishment of the body.

"God is Rice." Food is the source of both spiritual and material life. "This [food or bread] is my body that is [given] for you" (1 Cor.

11:24). The kettle, therefore, as a symbol of food, becomes the source of life for trees, grass, animals, human beings, and other things, for it is also the symbol of spirit as mother. Because food is cooked in the kettle, the kettle represents the nurture and transformation of all things. The animating and nurturing power of the Spirit is, therefore, symbolized in the kettle.

. . . Asians tend to seek their divinity in a warm-hearted mother rather than a stern father. . . . For Asians, God as the image of a gentle mother, God as the Spirit, is more attractive than God as the image of a stern father. This gentle Spirit, therefore, does not force us to heed her way, but rather through her presence patiently waits for us to do her will. Her voice is not like an earthquake but like the sound of sheer silence (1 Kings 19:12). Her power is not found in our strength but found in our weakness (2 Cor. 12:10), because her gentleness attracts the weak. According to Eastern wisdom, gentleness is not only the quality of the mother but also the basic characteristic of the yin. According to the *Book of Change*, a yin line or divided line (- - -) is called a *jou hsiao*, a soft or tender line, because tenderness is the essential nature of the yin. On the other hand, a yang line or undivided line (----) is called a *kang hsiao*, a hard line.

The softness of the yin, or the gentleness of the mother, is best symbolized by water that seeks the level. Thus, the Spirit, as the feminine member of the Trinity, is impartial, for the level represents evenness. As a mother loves all her children, the Spirit does not show partiality. Like water, she penetrates all; like wind, she blows everywhere; and like darkness, she covers all corners of the earth. . . .

The Spirit as a feminine principle is similar to form or the empty canvas, which is not apparent but is essential for things to exist. This is why the Spirit is often known as the anonymous member of the Trinity. She is behind the picture, behind the stage, and behind the action taking place in the world was the activity of the Spirit, and behind the creative work of the Father was the presence of the Spirit. The Spirit is the image of an empty form which can contain all, but in itself is nothing. Because she contains all, her nothingness is also the background and essence of all things. Thus, in Asian tradition, nothingness or emptiness is often valued more than "thingness." The Spirit, the image of nothingness or an empty form, was embodied in the mother I knew. She did everything for her family members. She held her family together. She helped my father to succeed but she never received credit for it. She gave everything for her children. She became an empty form by emptying herself for the sake of her family. She was truly an image of the Spirit, who held her trinitarian family together by becoming the background of trinitarian activities.

Kirsteen Kim, a British theologian with wide experience in Asian spiritualities and pneumatologies, makes the important point that using the dove, a bird, as a metaphor of the Spirit, the Bible joins in with an ancient religious tradition.

From Kirsteen Kim, *The Holy Spirit in the World: A Global Conversation* (Maryknoll, NY: Orbis Books, 2007), 181.

In many religious traditions, including Christianity, birds symbolize divine presence. . . . The reason is not hard to find: birds come down from heaven and rise up there again. Like the Spirit of God, birds are go-betweens, connecting heaven and earth. They appear as messengers of God, like the angels. The descent of the dove on Jesus at his baptism is a reminder that, in Christ, God is reconciling the world (2 Cor 5:19) and that, in the Spirit, heaven and earth are connected. Participating in God's mission is catching onto—and being caught up by—the wings of the Spirit as she moves in the world. However, the heavenly bird is not limited in the biblical record to the dove, nor is the imagery of the Holy Spirit restricted to the dove. . . . Nor is reconciliation the only paradigm of mission. David Bosch was right when he described a multiplicity of entry points to mission, from evangelism to common witness, from action for Justice to being with others. . . . We have seen in this book that the mission of the Spirit encompasses the whole breadth and depth of God's purposes in the world. I do not feel the need, as a result of this research, to come to some overarching definition of that mission, which would in any case be impossible. Nor can we arrive at unanimous expressions of Christian doctrines or theologies of how the Holy Spirit relates to the other spirits in the world. However, we need to keep up the global conversation on these matters, and Christians must continue to confess that, wherever and however the Spirit is present and active, the Spirit leads to Jesus Christ, the Son who reveals the Father, the origin of all things.

Han and *Dan*: Suffering and Salvation in Minjung Theology

In the Korean context, the two defining religious terms are *han* and *minjung*. The term *han* has several meanings, ranging from the experience of oppression to a sense of unresolved resentment to people's "root experience," which "comes from the sinful interconnectedness of classism, racism, [and] sexism."[6] The so-called *minjung* theology is a Korean and more widely, an Asian, liberation theology which works for the liberation of the oppressed, the poor, and other marginalized. *Minjung* is a combination of the two Chinese characters *min* (people) and *jung* (the mass); thus, literally "the mass of the people" or more simply "mass."

From J. Y. Lee, *An Emerging Theology in World Perspective: Commentary of Korean Minjung Theology* (New London, CT: Twenty-Third Publications, 1988), 8–10.

One of the distinctive characteristics of the minjung experience is a particular form of suffering known as "*han*." *Han*, like minjung, is difficult to define. It is more than suffering; it is the cluster of suffering experiences. It is the repressive feeling of unjust suffering which seeks just retaliation. . . . *Han* is the outgrowth of innocent suffering. Han is the experience of the minjung. . . . Minjung theology is, then, the theology of *han*. Christian ministry is the ministry of *han*, and Christ came to relieve the minjung from their *han*. By releasing the power of *han*, the minjung find liberation. The method of resolving *han* is known as *dan*, "cutting off"—cutting off the vicious cycle of *han*. . . . Since *han* is the crystallization of suffering and unresolved feelings owing to injustice, minjung theologians work to resolve the *han* of minjung. They are, in a sense, the "priests" of *han*. *Han*, however, is not sin as most Christians understand it. *Han* results from sins, the sins of the ruling group; therefore, resolving *han* is different from the forgiveness of sin or salvation in the traditional sense. *Han* cannot be resolved without justice. As long as injustice exists, *han* cannot be irradicated. In other words, to resolve *han* means to restore justice; therefore, for minjung theology, justice seems more important than forgiveness and love. Without justice there is no peace, no forgiveness, and no love. Justice alone heals the wound of *han* and restores the minjung to their rightful place. *Dan* means to resolve *han*. It is to cut off the chain of *han* that creates vicious circles of violence and repression.

6. Chung Hyun Kyung, "'Han-pu-ri': Doing Theology from Korean Women's Perspective," in *We Dare to Dream: Doing Theology as Asian Women,* ed. Virginia Fabella and Sun Ai Lee Park (Kowloon, Hong Kong: Asian Women's Resource Centre for Culture and Theology, 1989), 138.

The Holy Spirit and Other Faiths:
A Burning Issue for Asian Christians

Stanley J. Samartha, Indian theologian and ecumenist and former director of the World Council of Churches' Interfaith Department, speaks of the Holy Spirit in the pluralistic Asian context.

From Stanley J. Samartha, *Between Two Cultures: Ecumenical Ministry in a Pluralist World* (Geneva: WCC Publications, 1996), 187.

To most Christians the Holy Spirit is associated not so much with doctrine as with life. It is in the unwrapping of the gift of God in Jesus Christ that the Spirit becomes alive in the hearts and minds of Christians. The Spirit inwardly nourishes the new life in Christ and guides the community of believers in their acts of witness and service in the world. The Spirit makes the *koinonia* in Christ real to the believers. This may be one of the reasons why the question of the relation of the Spirit to people of other faiths would not even occur to most Christians, including those who live in multi-religious societies.

This is true in the history of the church as well. The early church did have to take into account the religions in the Roman empire, later it had to contend with Islam, still later with other religions in Asia and Africa. But in the major debates of the councils which touched the Spirit the main concern was to guard the purity of doctrine and preserve the unity of the church. Except as objects of Christian mission, people of other faiths did not seriously enter into the theological agenda of the church. This situation has drastically changed in the decades since the second world war.

The question of the Spirit and people of other faiths is therefore a new question that has somewhat aggressively thrust itself on the theological consciousness of the church only in recent years. Facing it has become both a historical demand and a theological imperative for the church living in a religiously plural world. Perhaps the discussion needs to be shifted from the ecclesiological to the theological context. And because it is a new question, it demands a new theological framework, new methodologies and new perceptions of the decisively changed historical context in which Christians live and work together with people of other faiths and ideological convictions in the world today.

Another leading Chinese theologian, C.-S. Song, similarly believes that the Spirit has always been at work among religions of his continent and that Christian theology better take notice of that.

From Choan-Seng Song, *Third Eye Theology: Theology in Asian Settings*, rev. ed. (Maryknoll, NY: Orbis Books, 1991), 13.

Doing Christian theology of history in this dialogic manner exposes us to the movements of the Spirit in the life and history of the nations and peoples of Asia. It is a liberating experience of exploring our own history theologically. Did not Jesus, according to John the Evangelist, say to Nicodemus: "the Spirit (or wind) blows where it wills; you hear the sound of it. But you do not know where it comes from, or where it is going" (John 3:8)? The same Spirit must have been blowing where it wills in Asia as well as in the rest of the world, enabling men and women there to shape their own histories and empowering them to hope in the midst of suffering, pain, and death. To regain our faith in God as the Lord of history, we have learned to see how our people, empowered by the Spirit, rise from the ashes of destruction again and again from one generation to the next. Our theology of history is no longer a theological discourse on the "divine economy" of salvation for the world with the Christian church playing the central and privileged role, but an account of the power of the Spirit at work in men and women of Asia who build their life and history for themselves and for the generations to come.

The Indian-born cosmopolitan Raimundo Panikkar, a leading Asian theologian and scholar of religions, lays out his view of an interfaith encounter with reference to the Spirit.

From Raimundo Panikkar, *The Unknown Christ of Hinduism*
(London: Darton, Longman & Todd, 1968), 26.

Spiritualities are not there to be "studied"—they cannot be properly "studied"—but to be lived, or, we could add, to be experienced, if the word is kept free from any idea of artificial "experimentation." I repeat that the meeting of religions is a *religious* act—an act of incarnation and redemption. . . .

In supernatural *Love* the encounter is not only implicit, but explicit. The Christian does not only share the same hope, or embrace others in his faith, he actually meets Christ and communicates with him in the person of his brethren, the men in earth, without distinction of race, creed or condition. If he really loves, he discovers Christ already there. It is Christ himself who has awakened that love, and the Christian himself will not be able to explain how he came to possess it and be inflamed by it. Love unifies and makes one.

The Christian encounter is really much more than the meeting of two friends, it is the Communion in being, in one Being which is much more intimate to both of them, than they themselves are; it is the communion not only in Christ, but of Christ. Nothing of condescension, nothing of paternalism or of superiority is to be found in the supernatural love of a Christian encounter.

The Holy Spirit and Salvation among Religions

Asian theologians have a lot to say about the role of the Spirit and salvation among particular religious traditions of the East. The first quotation applies to the "animistic" context, as it used to be called in the past.

Asian Folk and Primal Religions

From James Haire, "Stories in Animism and Christian Pneumatology,"
in *Doing Theology with the Spirit's Movement in Asia*, ed. John C. England
and Alan J. Torrance (Singapore: ATESEA, 1991), 122.

From what we have seen, it can be observed that in the pre-literary religious understanding of the North Moluccans the security-creating harmony most closely related to the Christian concept of salvation concerns protection from the village-spirits, the correct relationship with other creatures and nature, the right ties with the gomanga and the hoped-for respect to guarantee one's own future gomanga-status.

From *The Spirit at Work in Asia Today*, 23.

The cult of the spirits and cosmic forces as the Bons (Tibet), Devas (South-Asia), Nats (Burma), Phis (Thailand, Laos, Cambodia), the ancestral spirits (in the Confucian cultures of China, Korea, Vietnam, the Kalash in Pakistan) and the Kami (Japan) are an essential element of the spirituality of primal religions. The most persistent influence of primal religions on religious ideas and popular religious practices can be found in the many expressions of ancestor worship or veneration in the various Asian countries. The attitudes towards life and death are heavily influenced by beliefs which stress the permanent relationship of the living with the dead and the many obligations which result from it. The belief that the dead ancestors are actively influencing the fate of their living descendants can be seen in the many forms of burying the dead and caring for the upkeep of their graves which have to be selected in strict observance to prescriptions deriving from geomancy (fengshui). In the home the altars with the name-tablets of dead ancestors and/or the urns with some of their bones have a place of honour, and on special days and occasions gifts of food and incense are made to them. Major events in the lives of the descendants are reported to the ancestors, and during the feast of the dead (O-Bon-Festival, Spring Festival) their temporal presence is noted with reverence and fear. The influence of ancestor veneration can be seen as a work of the Holy Spirit in as far as it fosters the sense of honouring the parents, of gratitude to former generations who have made their contributions to the prosperity of their descendants. The insight that every generation depends on the achievements of the preceding one is a good simile for the lasting dependence on the grace of God and the Holy Spirit which is at the essence of Christianity. On the other hand there are negative elements in ancestor worship which can enslave people to a conservative outlook on life and bring them into opposition to the stirring of the Holy Spirit to new forms of life and constant change. In the history of the Christian mission in Asia the controversy about ancestor worship has been a major hindering influence, because of the decision taken by the major authorities in the Church to consider all forms of ancestor worship as belonging to the realm of superstitious and idolatrous practices, condemned by the Church as idol worship. The negative decision regarding the problem of rites and ancestor worship was revised only in the thirties of our century. The Roman authorities gave permission to Catholics in Japan and Korea to take part in burial ceremonies and ancestral rituals, as long as these could be considered as civil ceremonies, common in the cultural society to express respect and gratitude to the ancestors.

Hinduism

From *The Spirit at Work in Asia Today*, 3, 6.

We briefly review concepts that are very much part of Hindu belief and practice and which at the same time evoke resonances with the understanding of the Holy Spirit in Christianity.

. . . *Atman*: In Hinduism *atman* means "the Self, "the ultimate Divine subject." Some point to the meaning of breath contained in *atman*. This Hindu concept of *atman* rooted in the Vedas, but mostly Upanishadic and Vedantic, signifies the ultimate Reality, the Absolute, and hence does not resonate with our understanding of the Holy Spirit in Christian faith. However, it is interesting to note that Indian Christians, especially in North India, have used the Hindu term *atman*, with the adjective *pavitra*, for the Holy Spirit.

. . . *Prana* (Breath): This is an interesting concept that reminds us of the Hebrew idea of *ru'ah* which literally means breath and *pneuma* in Greek signifying the same. In the Bible, the latter two terms are used for the spirit. *Prana* (used both as singular and plural) means "breath of life." It is pre-upanishadic in origin and signifies life. In early Hinduism its meaning is metaphysical. It is identified with life. Later *prana* is used in its literal sense in the yoga exercise pranayama—control of breath. The earlier metaphysical meaning gets lost. There is another word for *prana*, namely *asu*. In its earlier meaning *prana* evokes resonance with the biblical meaning of the Holy spirit as breath and as breath of life or life itself. It is strange that Indian Christian theology did not consider this term in the theology of the Holy Spirit. . . . However, one can ask: was the Spirit (apart from concepts congenial with the Spirit) present in the Indian Tradition? Yes. If we are able to discern the signs of the Spirit we can read the history of Hinduism as a Holy history, where the Spirit has led our brothers and sisters to the depths of the mystery of God and leads them towards Christ. The Second Vatican council in Nostra Aetate no. 2. speaks of "that hidden power which hovers over the course of things and over the events of human life." . . . The early nature symbolism and apparent polytheism of the Vedas becomes purified by the strong affirmation in the Upanishads of the above without a second (*ekam eva advitiyam*). The metaphysical depth is imbued by an ethical concern and a spirit of detachment characteristic of Buddhism and Jainism. Out of this encounter the monotheistic creeds of a personal God (Vaisnavism and Saivism) emerge, with a relation of love to the world. The devotional trend and the monotheistic faith are strengthened by the arrival of Islam and the later bhakti trends. Meanwhile the knowledge and love of the name of Jesus was present in India from the earliest century: That name is received with devotion by the Hindu tradition in the Renaissance of the 19th and 20th centuries. The actual teaching of Jesus enters, more and more, the centre of the Hindu and national consciousness and finds an articulation in the Preamble of the Indian Constitution where the people of India affirm their faith in justice, freedom, equality and fraternity of all citizens.

From Helmuth Glasenapp, *Immortality and Salvation in Indian Religions* (Calcutta: Susil Gupta India, 1963), 60–61.

The Indian theories of salvation have their parallels in the West. Individual mystics of the most different periods down to Schopenhauer have taught "that man can obtain salvation from his own strength by virtue of his knowledge." The Christian churches, on the other hand, have always maintained the standpoint that man can be saved only through God's grace (Romans 3, 23f.). The parallels existing between the Indian theists' doctrine of grace and that of Christianity are obvious, and they have been dealt with on many occasions. But however great the analogies that exist in particular as regards the decisive controversial questions of monergism and synergism, the Indian doctrine of grace is, nevertheless, fundamentally different from the Christian in a number of essential points. For the Christian, salvation is the deliverance of mankind from the sin that took its origin in the disobedience to God of the first human pair. On the other hand, the Indians see in salvation the deliverance of the individual being entangled in beginningless Samsara and suffering from the restlessness and want of freedom conditioned thereby. For the Christian, salvation has generally been made possible only by a free act of divine mercy; by the incarnation of Christ the Son of God; by his dying as an expiatory offering, Christ redeemed mankind from sin, and earned for it salvation. This objective salvation becomes a subjective salvation of the individual man only when he enters (through faith or sacraments) into a special spiritual connexion with Christ. The Indian theists also see in salvation an act of divine mercy, but this act is directly of benefit to the individual. The idea of a universal atonement of mankind, that had through a fall lapsed from its originally pure state of life, through the vicarious sacrificial death of a divine incarnation is to them, however, just as foreign as the view that the eternal salvation of each person is connected with the belief in an event isolated in the course of the whole world process.

However differently in detail the Western and Indian doctrines of salvation judge of salvation and of the ways leading thereto, they all agree in one thing, namely, in the belief that man cannot become blessed so long as he is attached to the real and substantial, and that only his growing beyond his innate natural limitedness can bring about salvation. For salvation is something supramundane that is indeed elucidated by expressions like "illumination" and "grace," but is not adequately described or rendered intelligible.

Buddhism

From *The Spirit at Work in Asia Today*, 6–7.

One cannot talk about a concept of the "Spirit" in Buddhism and any attempt to do so, or to try to "find the idea of the Spirit in Buddhism," would be an exercise in distortion of the very essence of Buddhism. . . . *Dharma* is a vehicle of emancipation. It has been compared to a raft that ferries one across of the waters of birth-and-death to the farther shore of *Nirvana*, a vehicle which carries one across to the transcendent. Hence *Dharma* is something that must be experienced rather than studied. Ultimately to understand what Buddhism is all about one must walk the way, one must experience. . . . If one sets out to "find God" in Buddhism, the result will be either frustrated disappointment or distortion of the tradition.

Where then is the meeting point? Not on the level of these concepts, but rather on the level of experience of human life and the human quest for the transcendent. The fact that a Christian also belongs to a tradition which affirms the transcendent, the existence of a spiritual world beyond the world of physical senses and the rational mind, should make the Christian open to a different conception and experience of that reality. A Christian should be willing to give consideration to the Buddha's claim that he had achieved an experience of the transcendent himself and that by following his teaching others too might achieve it. The meeting point will be beyond concepts, dogmas, symbols and rituals at the level of experience.

From N. Callaway Tucker, *Japanese Buddhism and Christianity: A Comparison of the Christian Doctrine of Salvation with that of Some Major Sects of Japanese Buddhism* (Tokyo: Shinkyo Shuppansha, 1957), 199–203.

Buddhism and Christianity agree that salvation is primarily an experience rather than the rational understanding of a set of doctrines. Christians can assent to *Zen's* affirmation that words and concepts are, like a finger pointing at the moon, of value only to the extent that they turn the attention from themselves to the realities they represent. Christians believe a man could memorize the Bible, become familiar with the ideas of all theologians, and still be without salvation. They believe, on the other hand, that the unlettered, even children, can experience salvation. Though the two religions agree that salvation is an experience, they are, however, in complete disagreement regarding the nature of that experience . . . Buddhism . . . interpret[s] salvation as enlightenment. . . . The need for this salvation arises out of the fact that men erroneously suppose that the things and persons of their experience have objective reality. . . . Christianity, on the other hand, thinks of salvation as an experience of deliverance from sin. Sin is essentially the individual creature's defiance of the will of his Creator. It is disobedience to God. . . . On the ground of what has been said, the utter contradiction between the Buddhist and the Christian concept of salvation is clear. Buddhists hold the position that there are no objectively real individuals. For Buddhists, salvation consists of realizing the truth of such doctrines as *muga* and *kuu*. Buddhist salvation is to know that personalities do not exist except as ideas in the all-inclusive *busshin*. Christian salvation, on the other hand, means the perfecting of individual personalities through the activity of the divine Personality.

Islam

From *The Spirit at Work in Asia*, 25–26, 28.

The Divine Spirit, who works unceasingly to renew the face of the universe, is also active in the religion of Islam to produce the Spirit's inimitable fruits in the lives of Muslims. In recognising the signs of the Spirit's activity in Islam, as elsewhere, Christians praise and glorify the Holy Spirit for its wondrous works. . . . A study of the Qur'an, the Sacred Book of Islam, shows a constant effort to sow in the lives of believing Muslims those qualities that Christians recognise as the fruits of the Spirit. In the Qur'an, love is *mahabha*. Joy is *sara'*, patience is *sabr*, and *musabara* is long-suffering endurance. Kindness is *ihsan*, faithfulness is *sidq*, and so on. A few examples of Qur'anic teaching must suffice. . . .

Another point of departure for discerning the action of the Spirit in Islam is the words of Christ in the parable of the Last Judgement: "When I was hungry, you gave me to eat" [Matt. 25:35] etc. It is significant that in the Gospel parable both those who accepted Jesus and those who rejected him are unaware that it was He whom they have met. It is not correct to say that some people have never met Christ, for everyone meets him repeatedly in the person of the neighbour in need. In each encounter, Christ offers the grace of salvation, which each person either accepts or refuses, depending on one's response to the neighbour. Applying this criterion to Islam, we must ask, first, whether Muslims respond in love and service to the neighbour in need and, secondly, whether it is their Islamic faith that prompts them to do so. Throughout Asia, one can point to countless examples of Muslims who, in response to the exhortations of the Qur'an, have expended their energies and material goods for the welfare of those in need.

Chinese Religions

From Zhihua Yao, "In the Power of the Spirit," *Tripod* 91 (Jan.–Feb. 1996): 29–30.

Spirit and *Qi*

In Christianity the Spirit is God permeating God's own creation. According to the creation study in the Hebrew Scriptures, "a wind [spirit] from God swept over the face of the waters" in the beginning of creation (Gen. 1:2). . . . Hence, the primary mission of the Spirit has to do with life, creating it, sustaining it and directing it towards its future destiny. The Spirit is the source of life, not only of the present life but of eternal life as well. The Sprit is within creation, but is not conditioned by creation.

Chinese theologians Chang Chun-shen and C. S. Song suggest that this Spirit is what the Chinese would call *qi*—air, breath and spirit. According to the teachings of Confucianism and Taoism, *qi* is the material origin of all things; it is at the same time the origin of the life-force and energy moving into action. Or rather it is in itself equipped with life-giving properties and energy for action. The following is a standard expression of *qi*:

Ch'i [*qi*] fills the space between heaven and earth. Heaven and earth themselves, all things between heaven and earth, are all constituted by ch'i. Because of ch'i everything between heaven and earth moves, changes, and functions. It itself moves and moves all things. It is the subject of changes and movements and the origin that causes them. Human beings and animal-plant life also consist of ch'i. The human body is filled with ch'i which comes and goes. The ch'i within the human body and the ch'i outside it are the same ch'i and interpenetrate one another.

. . . The *qi* must have something to do with the *pneuma* mentioned by Jesus "The *pneuma* [air, wind or spirit] blows where it chooses, and you hear the sound of it, but you do not know where it comes from or where it goes" (Jn. 3:8). This is the mystery of *pneuma* and *qi*. It is wind as well as spirit. It moves and works like wind, blowing where it wills. This actually is similar to the Old Testament concepts of "soul" and "breath," and "soul" and "blood." In Chinese spirituality the "heart" rather than the "head" is considered the center of the whole person. Christian prayer also uses the heart to sing, to thank God and to love. This is one reason that Christianity is called the religion of love.

Japanese Religions

The Japanese theologian Takenaka summarizes key ideas gathered by a group of Christians focusing on the religious context of Japan in a WCC-sponsored consultation in the early 1970s.

From Masao Takenaka, "Salvation: A Japanese Discussion," *International Review of Mission* 61, no. 241 (Geneva: WCC Publications, 1972): 82–84.

Salvation in the Japanese language is "sukui" which means literally "to make an effort to get out of a critical situation." . . . There is no requirement other than to recite the Nembutsu (the repetition of the sacred name of Amida) which is a simple expression of faith. This is rather close to the Reformer's doctrine of justification by faith. It recognizes the saving grace which embraces every living creature. Beyond every relative good and evil, there is an operation of mercy. The Christian faith also affirms the universal work of grace and transforming power in all places and periods. The Christian faith accepts the truth through the decisive disclosure of God in the event of Jesus Christ. This historic particular revelation should not be understood in such a way as to establish an exclusive and special domain in which grace works but through the particular revelation we should see the universal embrace of transforming grace. Only because we return to the centre do we meet with others in the frontier.

On the other hand, many Japanese are still under the influence of the other aspect of traditional religion. It was not nationalistic Shintoism which was the dominating force during the Second World War, centring upon the divinity of the Emperor. It was rather a naturalistic folk religion which is still influential among ordinary Japanese people today. It can be regarded as a shamanistic popular religion which is still actively running through Japanese society as a civil religion. Salvation according to such naturalistic Shinto and folk religions is understood as attaining the status of purification (*Kiyome*). One needs to obtain purification from dirty, evil and demonic spirits. There are many acts of purification and exorcism still remaining in ordinary Japanese social life: at the time of birth and death, at the time of sowing seed, at the time of sickness and at the time of building one's house. Even the highly technically advanced factories hire local Shinto priests to perform the act of purification in order to eliminate accidents. In this sense, the ordinary Japanese find a natural familiarity in the stories of exorcism appearing in the Bible, such as Jesus casting out the unclean spirit from a ruined man (Mark 5:1–13). The acts of purification and exorcism are quite popular in many religions, particularly the primitive ones. Many of the new Japanese religions take this aspect of traditional religion positively and put it into modern expression and form. . . .

Perhaps one of the most wide-spread ethical impacts in Japanese life comes from Confucianism. It was Confucianism which provided the ethical teaching to train the virtues of hard work, patience, loyalty and perseverance. Some wonder how the Japanese could proceed so quickly in the process of modernization without puritanism. It was Confucian ethical teaching which played a role similar to the role played by Calvinistic ethics in the course of the rise of capitalism. Confucianism understood salvation in terms of the attainment of the middle way. It was not to achieve a compromise nor to reach a mechanical middle road. Rather it was to maintain the integrity and balance befitting the path each one walks. The Samurai who was trained according to Confucian teaching was instructed to discipline himself to walk his road according to the demands of the way. To be sure, this way was not specifically defined but was left quite open. Many of the early Japanese Christians who came from Samurai backgrounds interpreted the way as it was revealed in Jesus Christ and they found special significance in Jesus' words, "I am the Way, the Truth and the Life" (John 14:6).

Asian Evangelical Voices

One of the most hotly contested issues in Christology and soteriology in general and in the Asian context in particular is the extent of salvation—in other words, the question of whether "salvation in Christ" extends to those who never heard of the gospel or did not hear it in a meaningful way. The following quotations from more "pluralistic" traditions move towards universalism, whereas the opinions of those called evangelicals tend to be more restrictive. The first citations come from a collection of essays that represent a number of leading Asian evangelicals, from Hindu, Buddhist, Chinese, and other contexts.

From Ken R. Gnanakan, ed., *Salvation: Some Asian Perspectives*
(Bangalore, India: Asia Theological Association, 1992), 30–31.

The Buddhist, the Hindu, the Muslim who does not know the name of Jesus Christ will not be saved unless God reveals Himself to him. . . . There is only one ground for the salvation of all who will be saved, whether they lived before Christ or after, whether they have an explicit knowledge of the name of Christ or not, and that is the cross. . . . It is not surprising that people of other faiths find the claims to the finality of the cross incomprehensible. . . . [The] essence of the Hindu mind . . . sees the events of the phenomenal world as relative, as less than ultimately real so that no event in time could have eternal significance. The cross is reduced to a level of subjective experience for there is no ultimate objectivity. This is the unitary principle which is fundamental to all forms of universalism. . . . It is the denial of God the Creator and of the truth of the incarnation and the resurrection. History is reduced to suprahistory, the objective to the subjective.

We affirm that Christ died as an atonement for all yet the benefits of the atonement are only received by those whom God elects to salvation. Apart from the divine initiative no one would be saved. Apart from divine grace there is no salvation and apart from faith, which is also a gift of God there is no response acceptable to God.

From Gnanakan, *Salvation*, 115.

Salvation by faith in the biblical sense is a message that can win a hearing among the Muslims. The emphasis, however, should strongly be on the side of divine acts based upon Allah's sovereign and gracious nature. Man should respond by faith. The object and content of faith should be clearly elaborated because of the extreme difference between Christian faith and Islamic faith. The point they reject is the death of Christ for the atonement of sin applicable to all mankind. With solid historical facts to back up the message, we should finally come to terms with the Muslims.

Finally, however, after all attempts have been made to present clear, relevant, challenging, unique, superior and biblical messages about Christ, whose death on the cross paid the penalty for sin, to enable God to save believing sinners, one must sit back and wait to observe the working of the Holy Spirit in convicting and redeeming those whom God "in love . . . has predestined to adoption of sons . . . to the praise of the glory of His grace" (Eph. 1:5, 6 NASV). Total dependence upon the work of the Spirit to convict, to anoint and to regenerate the lost Muslims is indispensable.

Pentecostal Experiences in Asia

While the number of Christians in Asia—with the exception of some countries such as the Philippines, South Korea, and China—is relatively small, pentecostal movements are growing rapidly in many parts of the continent. In India alone, it is estimated that almost 40 million Pentecostals can be found. In the first selection, Chin Khua Khan explains the practices and characteristics of Pentecostalism in Myanmar, formerly known as Burma.

From Chin Khua Khan, "Pentecostalism in Myanmar: An Overview,"
Asian Journal of Pentecostal Studies 5, no. 1 (Jan. 2002): 63–64.

The emphasis on speaking in tongues (glossolalia) as a sign of the baptism of the Holy Spirit was a dynamic factor of the Pentecostal renewal. As Pentecostalism developed into a movement in the late 1970s, believers were urged to seek the baptism of the Holy Spirit, also known as being filled with the Holy Spirit, as subsequent to the bom-again experience. . . .

The Pentecostals were evangelical in their basic tenant of faith and practice. They strictly emphasized the authority of Scripture, salvation of Christ by faith through grace, the urgency of Christ's coming, and the need for immediate response to the invitation for salvation. Doctrinally, they were distinct from the mainline evangelical bodies only in terms of their emphasis on the charismatic gifts and functions. Traditionally, they have put their overall theological emphasis precisely where other evangelicals do on the person and work of Christ. Nonetheless, the public expression of tongues, which has so often characterized Pentecostal worship, has also served as much as anything else to distinguish Pentecostals. . . . Moreover, Pentecostals preach and teach subjects on the full gospel message, living a holy life and the imminent return of Christ-messages that have helped many to deeper commitment. Their message of liberation from poverty and self-lowliness, and toward positive attitude have helped people to improve their low self-images. The subject of holy living emphasizes that believers are the temples of the Holy Spirit, urging them to keep themselves holy, and to be separated from worldly manners.

As a result, believers abstained from their old habits of drinking, smoking, singing secular songs, reading novels, watching movies and anything that would affect their spiritual growth. Also believers always look forward to the rapture of the church in their lifetimes.

Pentecostal worship is a great pattern for transformation. Worship is an essential part of being Christians, and corporate worship is a compelling need among believers. Pentecostal worship services are very different from those of the traditional style of worship. The enthusiasm of modern praise and worship choruses and musical instruments in addition to corporate prayer makes worship services exciting and joyful. Praise and worship with choruses and a few hymns, led with musical accompaniment, and clapping hands are seen in most born-again churches. Solos, duets, trios, group singers and action singers attractively and persuasively support the worship. Choruses composed within their own contexts that convey deep relationship with the Lord, developing theological insight that has helped people focus on deeper worship and praise.

The Korean missiologist and educator Julie Ma, who has worked for more than two decades in the Philippines, has studied the life of Jashil Choi, the mother-in-law of the world's most famous pentecostal preacher, Yonggi Choi, and her experience of "spiritual warfare," a topic common among Pentecostals in Asia.

From Julie C. Ma, "Korean Pentecostal Spirituality:
A Case Study of Jashil Choi," *Asian Journal of
Pentecostal Studies* 5, no. 2 (July 2002): 245–47.

Throughout her ministry, Choi encountered many demon-possession cases. After a Sunday worship service, a member from a neighboring church rushed asking Choi to visit her friend who had been tormented by a terrible sickness. The sick woman was not a Christian and she was always referred to shamans for healing and advice. One day the shaman gave a striking "revelation": if she fails to become a shaman through a special ritual, she would die soon. Upon hearing such a dreadful verdict, her family fiercely opposed the idea. She out of great anxiety shared her problem with her Christian friend. It proves that Choi was quite well known in the area as a woman filled with the Spirit as she had an earnest desire to minister to people who were going through difficulties. . . .

Choi and her ministry partner Yonggi Cho were brought to the house of the sick woman. When they entered the room, she suddenly sat down and stared at them like an angry rooster. Choi and the accompanying members quietly sat on the floor and began to sing hymns. Choi instantaneously knew that Satan attempted to attack. Ephesians 6:10–20 well states such a spiritual struggle. Believers are caught in the idea of eschatological tension that is "already, but not yet." Apostle Paul was well aware of two different realms of power: God and the devil. It is also obvious that the world as the dominion of darkness is on one side, while Christ, Christians, the power and authority of God on the other. With this understanding, Choi and her group sang continually and rebuked the evil spirit in the woman with the authority of Christ. In the middle of singing and prayer, the woman abruptly uttered in Japanese, "Let's go. Let's go to Japan." (Choi spoke Japanese like many Koreans who received Japanese occupation.) Then she seemed to be back to normal.

The Japanese language was spoken not by the woman but by Satan. According to the woman, she had gone to Japan for study when she was a young girl and had stayed there for several years. During this period she became a member of a religious group. Then she returned to Korea and married a man. When she was pregnant with a first child, she was terribly ill and the sickness continued until

Choi's ministry. Through the power of God displayed in prayer, the woman was delivered from her bondage. Such manifestation of God's power led her entire family and relatives to the Lord.

Power encounter is a regular part of Christian spiritual life especially among Pentecostals. Thus, the concept has been used among Asian Christians without question. But some believers feel reluctant to use such a term because of its military connotation. This term was first used by Alan Tippett to refer to a conflict between the kingdom of God and the kingdom of Satan. It frequently takes place especially among tribal groups who believe in the spiritual world, and the involvement of the spirits in their life. During the ministry of Jesus, he drove out many demons from people. The demonstration of God's power was also frequent in the Old Testament. One of the outstanding instances is the story of Elijah, confronting the four hundred and fifty prophets of Baal on Mount Carmel (I Kings 18:16–45). Oscar Cullmann notes that Satan still has great power, power that can destroy any human being and his or her plan if they remained without encumbrance. Thus, divine power and authority is essential for effective work in God's kingdom. . . . In the Book of Acts, when believers came together in one accord, the power of God was manifested.

It is well noted that Choi's spiritual exercise with prayer and fasting played a significant role in her successful evangelistic ministry.

CHAPTER 17

Testimonies from
Latin America

Introduction to the Latin American Context

There is much truth in the saying that whereas Africa theology begins with a shout of joy, in Latin America theological reflection starts from a cry of despair. The theme of liberation is the driving force in much of Latin American theology, including the immigrant theologies written by Hispanic theologians in the United States. The many reasons that liberation has arisen as the key theme in much of Latin America's theology include massive poverty, injustice, oppression and colonization, the imposition of alien languages on the "natives" (Spanish or Portuguese) or immigrants (English), and the denigration of indigenous cultures. Furthermore, unlike European and North American societies— but similarly to most societies in Africa and Asia—Latin American people value community and communalism: "The best theology is a communal enterprise. This is a contribution that Hispanics can bring to theology. Western theology—especially that which takes place in academic circles— has long suffered from an exaggerated individualism."[1]

Other features central to many Latin American contexts that help shape their pneumatology and soteriology are the importance of folk religions and their influence on Catholic piety, as well as the transforming significance of the rapidly growing pentecostal and charismatic movements in all Hispanic Christian communities, including the Roman Catholic Church. While Latin American and Hispanic Pentecostals have not produced much academic theology, there is a growing body of literature, particularly in Spanish, that records the experiences of the Spirit in that continent. English literature on this topic is more scarce.

---

1. Justo L. González, *Mañana: Christian Theology from a Hispanic Perspective* (Nashville: Abingdon Press, 1990), 29–30.

The Feast of the *Espírito Santo*

Well known for feasts and parties, the Latin American continent has a number of ways of celebrating significant religious and cultural events. Not surprisingly, the Holy Spirit is the theme of one of the ancient feasts. It is thus appropriate to begin the Latin American reflection on the Spirit and salvation by pointing to the theological and religious significance of the Feast of the Holy Spirit.

From Almir C. Bruneti, "The Feast of the Holy Spirit,"
http://lal.tulane.edu/programs/exhibits/feast.htm
(accessed Nov. 1, 2007).

The Feast of the Holy Spirit, or Espírito Santo, is a devotion that has been popular in the Lusophone world (Europe, Asia, Africa, South and North America) for centuries. It is a communal type of celebration for which the whole population contributes money and foodstuffs. The main ceremony includes the coronation of a child as "Emperor and/or Empress of the Holy Spirit" who then presides over a banquet of which all partake.

In the olden days, before the banquet the emperor would go to the prisons and release all prisoners who had not committed any violent crimes. The origins of the celebrations seem to be connected with the ideas of Joachim of Fiore (c. 1135–1202), a Calabrian monk who believed that the history of the world would end around 1260 with the beginning of the "Age of the Holy Spirit" when a spiritualized humanity would start to live in an era of peace and abundance. These ideas were disseminated throughout Europe by various heterodox thinkers who were at odds with the papacy. . . .

As in traditional iconography, the Holy Spirit is symbolized by a dove, sometimes depicted as having an eagle's beak. There is always food associated with the Feast, and most cycles culminate with a procession at the end of which bread, meat, wine, etc., are distributed among the poor who also participate in the communal banquet.

A number of contemporary theologians in various parts of the world have lamented the neglect of the Spirit in theology and church life. The Portuguese (and Indian) Jesuit Luis M. Bermejo speaks of the need to rediscover interest in the Holy Spirit.

From Luis M. Bermejo, introduction to *The Spirit
of Life: The Holy Spirit in the Life of the Christian*
(Anand, Gujarat: X. Diaz del Rio, 1987), n.p.

As compared to this myriad of christological reminiscences and
signs of our all-pervading attachment to Jesus Christ, what does the
Holy Spirit mean to most of us? The Spirit seems to be nothing but
an impersonal abstraction, either wrongly identified with the mentality, frame of mind and values of Jesus of Nazareth, or turned into
an abstract belief of only academic interest. We all know, of course,
every catechism kid does, that there are three persons in God, but
has the reality of the Holy Spirit gone beyond the realm of a merely
theoretical tenet of our Christian faith? Do we value and loudly proclaim the person and activity of the Holy Spirit as a positive and distinct force in our Christian life to be reckoned with? Briefly stated:
in our religious enterprise the lion's share goes surely to Jesus, with
only a passing nod, if at all, to Holy Spirit. We seem to forget that the
Spirit is the supreme gift of Easter, that the pentecostal outpouring of
the Holy Spirit is but the fruit of Christ's death and resurrection, that
if the Spirit is the gift the glorified Jesus is the giver, and to leave a gift
untouched and unappreciated is an insult to the giver himself.

Spiritual Experience

Several leading Latin American lib-
eration theologians speak for many pneumatologists when they call for
the primacy of spiritual experience over doctrine and theology.

From Gustavo Gutiérrez, *We Drink from Our Own Wells: The Spiritual
Journey of a People* (Maryknoll, NY: Orbis Books, 2003), 36–37, 70.

The solidity and energy of theological thought depend precisely on
the spiritual experience that supports it. This experience takes the
form, first and foremost, of a profound encounter with God and
God's will. Any discourse on faith starts from, and takes its bearings
from, the Christian life of the community. Any reflection that does
not help in living according to the Spirit is not a Christian theology.
When all is said and done, then, all authentic theology is spiritual
theology. This fact does not weaken the rigorously scientific character of the theology; it does, however, properly situate it. . . .

At the root of every spirituality there is a particular experience that is had by concrete persons living at a particular time. The experience is both proper to them and yet communicable to others. . . . St. Bernard of Clairvaux . . . says that in these matters all people should drink from their own well. The great spiritualities in the life of the church continue to exist because they keep sending their followers back to the sources.

A spirituality, which is a way of being a Christian, has as its foundation an advance through death, sin, and slavery, in accordance with the Spirit, who is the life-giving power that sets the human person free. To be a Christian is to be free of all external coercion: "Where the Spirit of the Lord is, there is freedom" (2 Cor. 3:17), a freedom put at the service of God and neighbor. To reject the power of the flesh does not mean to have contempt for the body. On the contrary, Christian spirituality consists in *embracing the liberated body* and thus being able both to pray "Abba, Father!" and to enter into a comradely communion with others.

From José Comblin, *The Holy Spirit and Liberation*, trans.
Paul Burns (Maryknoll, NY: Orbis Books, 1989), xii.

To know God the Father and his Son Jesus Christ who revealed him, we have to start from a spiritual experience, which means an experience provided and guided by the Holy Spirit, a specific and practical experience.

This is because, as Jesus says in the fourth Gospel, "God is spirit" (John 4:24). Jesus is not saying merely that God has no body; this would be too trivial, and besides, spirit does not mean noncorporeal. What Jesus means is that the Father can be found only through a spiritual experience; and we have to understand this in the strongest sense: an experience in the Holy Spirit. Jesus is not trying to give a definition of God; God cannot be defined. He is showing us the place where God can be met.

St Paul, too, says: "This Lord is the Spirit" (2 Cor. 3:17). He does not mean that Jesus and the Holy Spirit are the same person, but that the place where we meet the Lord is the Holy Spirit. Only the Spirit can lead us to Jesus the Christ. Without passing through the experience of the Spirit, in this case the experience of freedom, we cannot possibly know the true Christ.

The Holy Spirit as "Mother"

While not unknown in Christian history, several Latin American liberationists' way of referring to the Spirit as mother is a profound statement about the equality of men and women.

From Leonardo Boff, *Holy Trinity: Perfect Community*
(Maryknoll, NY: Orbis Books, 2000), 92.

Theological reflection saw the feminine dimensions in the Holy Spirit very early, more so than with reference to the Father and the Son—beginning with the name Holy Spirit, which in Hebrew is feminine. In the scriptures the Spirit is always associated with the function of generation and with the mystery of life. St. John's gospel delineates the activity of the Holy Spirit in characteristically feminine terminology. The Spirit consoles us as Paraclete, exhorts and teaches (Jn 14:26, 16:13) as mothers do with their little children; does not leave us orphans (Jn 14:18); teaches us to stammer the true name of God, *Abba*; and passes on to us the secret name of Jesus, which is Lord (1 Cor 12:3). Finally, as mothers also do, the Spirit educates us in prayer and in the way to ask for the right things (Rom 8:26).

In the Hebrew scriptures the Spirit also is associated with feminine functions. The very hovering of the Spirit over the waters of the primitive chaos of creation before the arrival of order seems to symbolize, according to interpreters, the incubation entailed in any kind of life. In the wisdom literature, as is widely known, Wisdom is loved as a woman (Sir 14:20–27) and is presented as wife and mother (Sir 15:2), sometimes identified with the Spirit (Wis 9:17). In some representations of the Trinity, the Holy Spirit is placed between the Father and the Son in the form of a woman. In the Odes of Solomon, a text from Syrian Christianity, the dove at the baptism of Jesus, which is one of the representations of the Holy Spirit, is called Mother. Some church fathers have called the Holy Spirit the divine Mother of the man Jesus, because the conception in the womb of the Virgin Mary took place by the work and grace of the Spirit (Mt 1:18).

The Work of the Spirit on Earth

Based on the Irenean idea of the Son and Spirit as the "two hands" of the Father, Boff highlights the distinctive tasks of the Spirit in the world.

From Boff, *Holy Trinity*, 22–23, 87, 93–95.

The Holy Spirit is the second hand by which the Father reaches out to us and embraces us. Father and Son have sent the Holy Spirit into the world. First, the Spirit is ever acting on earth, motivating life, bolstering the courage of the prophets, and inspiring wisdom for human actions. The Spirit's great work has been to come down upon Mary to form in her womb the sacred humanity of the Son incarnate in Jesus; the Spirit descended upon Jesus when he was baptized by John; in the strength of the Spirit, Christ performs signs that liberate from human ills. Jesus himself says, "If it is by the Spirit of God that I cast out demons, then the kingdom of God has come to you" (Mt 12:28). After the ascension of Jesus into heaven, it is the Spirit who deepens and spreads Christ's message, brings us to accept with faith and love the Person of the Son, and teaches us to pray: Abba, our Father!

The revelation of the Spirit takes place in four privileged places. The first is the Virgin Mary. The Spirit dwelled in her and raised her to the height of the divine. Hence he who is born of Mary, as St. Luke says, shall be called Son of God (Lk 1:35). The feminine has been touched by the Divine and also made eternal. Woman has her place in God.

The second place is Christ. He was filled with the Spirit. Hence, he was the new human, fully free, and liberated from the age-old bonds. In the power of the Spirit, he launches his messianic program of complete liberation (Lk 4:18–21). The Spirit and Christ will ever be united to lead creation back to the bosom of the Blessed Trinity.

The third place is mission. The Spirit descends upon the apostles at Pentecost, removes their fear, and sends them to spread Christ's message among all peoples. It is the Spirit who in mission makes it possible to see and achieve unity amid the variety of nations and languages. Variety need not mean confusion but can mean the wealth of unity.

The fourth place is human and church community, in human community many services and capabilities come to the fore. Some people are able to console, others to coordinate, others to write, still others to build. Likewise in the Christian community there exists every kind of service and ministry, whether for the good of the community or the good of society, often breaking patterns and starting something new. Everything comes from the Spirit. Christians have meditated on all these manifestations and have concluded that the Spirit is also God, together with the Father and the Son. They are not three gods, but one God in communion of Persons. . . .

The Spirit has been poured forth over us and dwells in the hearts of people, granting them enthusiasm, courage, and determination. It consoles the afflicted, keeps utopia alive in human minds and in the social imagination—the utopia of a fully redeemed humankind—and gives strength to anticipate it, even through revolutions in history. The Spirit is a divine Person together with the Son and the Father, emerging simultaneously with them and being essentially united to them through love, communion, and the divine life itself. . . .

The action of the Holy Spirit in history is a reflection of its action within the Trinity, where the Spirit is the principle of diversity and of union between those who are distinct (Father and Son). Hence the Spirit is love and communion par excellence, even though each divine Person is communion and love. Whenever in history we encounter driving forces that build up love, that conciliate where differences live together in harmony, there we discern the ineffable presence of the Holy Spirit's action. The Spirit is linked to transforming and innovating action. The Spirit's action permeates human acts, making them bring about the design of the Trinity. In particular, actors in history, charismatic leaders, those who provide new horizons, those who clear new paths, are expressions of the power of the Holy Spirit. More particularly, when the poor resist oppression, when they organize to seek life, bread, and freedom, when in the midst of struggle they maintain faith and tenderness toward others, they are the great historic sacraments of the active presence of the Holy Spirit. . . . The Holy Spirit makes present the message of Jesus and does not let the spirit of authoritarianism prevail in the community, or ritualism dominate in celebrations, or Christian thinking fall into boring repetition of formulas The saving efficacy of the Spirit is evidenced in the sacraments, particularly in the eucharist. The Spirit comes as grace that divinizes our life; through the Spirit's activity the words of Christ who instituted the sacrament of the eucharist become effective and bring the sacred humanity of Christ into our midst, under the form of bread and wine.

The Spirit's Work in the Human Being

An important aspect of the Spirit's work on earth has to do with human beings having been created in the image of God. Gutiérrez outlines here a theological anthropology from a pneumatological perspective.

From Gutiérrez, *We Drink from Our Own Wells*, 62.

The dynamism and vitality expressed by "spirit" are accentuated when the human person is considered from the standpoint of God's action on it. Spirit and its derivates signify a life that is in accordance with God's will—that is, a life in accordance with the gift of divine filiation that finds expression in human fellowship.

In this context the spirit is the subject that receives the gifts of God: "The grace of the Lord Jesus Christ be with your spirit, brethren" (Gal. 6:18)—that is, with you (as we saw above), but with the connotation of you-as-receptive to divine grace (cf. Phil. 4:23). The first of these gifts of the Spirit is love (*agape*). "The fruit of the Spirit is love, joy, peace, patience, kindness, goodness, faithfulness, gentleness, self-control; against such there is no law" (Gal. 5:22–23). This fruit (*karpos*) of the Spirit is the opposite of the works (*erga*) of the flesh that we saw reviewed in the previous section.

Love is the central gift and in a way contains all the others: "I appeal to you, brethren, by our Lord Jesus Christ and by the love of the Spirit, to strive together with me in your prayers to God on my behalf" (Rom. 15:30). Love alone will remain (1 Cor. 13) and for this reason is the first gift that should be sought: "Make love your aim, and earnestly desire the spiritual gifts, especially that you may prophesy" (1 Cor. 14:1)

Bermejo reminds us of the obvious biblical insight that Christians are temples of the Holy Spirit.

From Bermejo, *Spirit of Life*, 72–73.

According to the New Testament we are all temples of the Holy Spirit rather than temples of Christ. It is the Holy Spirit that substantially and almost physically dwells in us, not Jesus of Nazareth with his glorified humanity. As a rule and with only one exception (Eph 3,17) Paul never says that Christ dwells in the Christian; this function is reserved to the Spirit, and we would do well to follow Paul. . . . The Spirit dwells in us as in a temple because we are immanent in Christ, rather than the other way around. Jesus proclaimed in the Jerusalem Temple, as we saw above, "If any man is thirsty, let him come to me and drink. This he said of the Spirit" (Jn 7, 37). The Christian . . . comes to Jesus through living faith and receives from him the bountiful outpouring of the Holy Spirit. The indwelling of the Spirit is but the natural result, the fruit, of our immanence in the glorified Christ.

The implication of the Spirit's indwelling is that the Spirit is not far away from the human person.

The Holy Spirit and Liberation
José Comblin has produced a major pneumatological program from the perspective of Latin American Liberation theology.

From Comblin, *Holy Spirit and Liberation*, xi, xiii.

The experience of God found in the new Christian communities of Latin America can properly be called experience of the Holy Spirit.

. . . Most of the Christians who make up these communities do not know that this is their experience; because of their religious upbringing, the Holy Spirit is still the great unknown for them. The fact is that, virtually from its beginnings, Western theology lost interest in the Holy Spirit, and the traditional liturgy of the West, particularly that of the Roman Missal, also left the Spirit out of account. The lack of interest shown by Christians reflects the lack of interest shown by theology. But now, the new experience Christians are finding in those communities that aspire to the integral liberation of the peoples of the continent of Latin America is precisely an experience of the Holy Spirit.

Once again we are discovering that the way we approach God, according to the Bible and true Christian tradition, is not through discursive reason, or our experience of creation, or through meditating on our inner being, but through a living experience of the Holy Spirit and its gifts. Only a spiritual experience, one of the Holy Spirit active in the community, can lead to the true God—the God of Jesus Christ, not a God of philosophers. . . . What is evident is that experience of the Spirit comes about principally in poor communities. There is nothing surprising in the fact that experience of the Spirit regains its value and esteem in the churches precisely when they come to rediscover the meaning of the preferential option for the poor.

In the following, Comblin unpacks some of the features of the liberating work of the Holy Spirit evident in Latin American contexts and churches.

From Comblin, *Holy Spirit and Liberation*, 61–67.

The action of the Holy Spirit on humanity and through the new humanity is at once simple and complex. It can be avoided through five key concepts . . . that everyone knows but which are neglected by the social sciences, which do not know how to deal with them. The Holy Spirit produces freedom, speech, action, community and life. . . . There is no separation between what the Spirit does and what human beings do, despite the fact that far from everything that they do proceeds from the Spirit—very much to the contrary.

(a) The Spirit and Freedom

. . . The freedom experienced in Christian communities today forces our attention on the good news of freedom as preached by St Paul, though this news is not exclusive to him; the whole New Testament proclaims the coming of a new age for humanity. Paul, however, gives expression to consciousness of the coming of a freedom that is something radically new in both its conception and its realization. . . . "Where the Spirit of the Lord is, there is freedom" (2 Cor 3:17). This freedom applies also and indeed above all to the religious sphere and our relationship with God. . . . The Spirit guides the new humanity from within, replacing obedience with spontaneity. . . . This freedom is a gift of the Spirit, the effect of the Spirit's presence in men and women. But as a gift of the Spirit it is also a human work, since the property of the Spirit is not to act of itself but to tell creatures what to do, or to work through what they do. This is why the gift of freedom is also a calling; the gift of the Spirit is the call to be able and obliged to win freedom. . . . The Spirit is the power that acts through appeal, through attraction, not through constraint: through maternal, not paternal authority. God acts among human beings as a mother; the direction of the whole of human history demonstrates the motherhood of the Spirit. . . .

(b) The Spirit and Speech

Human beings speak. They were created in this way so as to give names to things and tell these to others. In the beginning human beings received a power of speech that now has to do with the Spirit. Yet not all speech comes from the Spirit; not all words indicate the Spirit. The coming of the Spirit brings new words which proceed directly from it. . . . With the gospel, the Spirit makes the words of the poor resound through the world. We need to get rid of the presumption of the formalism and formulations in which the vocabulary relating to the word of God and the gospel has been wrapped up for centuries. Such words end by covering over hateful things. The poor are now enabling us to rediscover the newness these words originally possessed.

The poor speak in public, and say different things. They speak not to confirm or consolidate the established system, nor to justify or explain it. They speak to announce something new, speaking out before tribunals and authorities. Such was and is the miracle of the Holy Spirit. St Luke describes the poor speaking like this symbolically in his account of Pentecost: all these uncultured persons spoke all the languages of the world. Later the Twelve were to appear before the Sanhedrin, and they spoke out openly, boldly: "They were astonished at the assurance shown by Peter and John, considering they were uneducated laymen" (Acts 4:13).

Echoing the "life-pneumatology" of Jürgen Moltmann, Boff speaks of the Spirit in relation to love and dignity of life. Everywhere in his writings, Boff also emphasizes the need for Christians to consider the importance of Trinity as communion, a paradigm for human communities.

From Boff, *Holy Trinity*, 47–48.

The Christian God is eternal communion of the divine Three—Father, Son, and Holy Spirit. They are eternally pouring forth, one toward the other, so much so that they build a single movement of love, communication, and encounter. How can we better understand this? It is not a matter of removing the veil from the mystery of God, but rather of grasping the divine movement so that we may better experience the presence and activity of the Blessed Trinity in the world and in our own personal journey. Biblical theology has found a word to express this divine thrust: *life*. God is understood as a living activity that is eternal, life-giving, and protective of all life that is threatened, such as that of the poor and those who suffer injustice. Jesus himself, the incarnate Son, presented himself as one who came to bring life and life in abundance (Jn 10:10). If we briefly consider what life is about, we will better grasp the communion of the divine Three.

Life is a mystery of spontaneity, an inexhaustible process of giving and receiving, assimilating, incorporating, and surrendering one's own life in communion with other life. The phenomenon of life entails expansion and presence. A living being is not present as a stone is present. A living being has presence, which means an intensification of existence.

The Spirit and the Church in Latin America
Pope Benedict XVI, when speaking recently to the Latin American bishops, emphasized the integral role of the Spirit in the church.

From Pope Benedict XVI, Homily at the Inauguration of the Fifth General Conference of the Bishops of Latin America and the Caribbean at the square in front of the Shrine of Aparecida, Sixth Sunday of Easter, May 13, 2007, http://www.vatican.va/ holy_father_benedict_XVI/homilies/2007 (accessed Nov. 1, 2007).

"To the Holy Spirit and to us." This is the Church: *we*, the community of believers, the People of God, with its Pastors who are called to lead the way; together with the *Holy Spirit*, the Spirit of the Father, sent in the name of his Son Jesus, the Spirit of the one who is "greater" than all, given to us through Christ, who became "small" for our sake. The Paraclete Spirit, our *Ad-vocatus*, Defender and Consoler, makes us live in God's presence, as hearers of his word, freed from all anxiety and fear, bearing in our hearts the peace which Jesus left us, the peace that the world cannot give (cf. Jn 14:26–27). The Spirit accompanies the Church on her long pilgrimage between Christ's first and second coming. "I go away, and I will come to you" (Jn

14:28), Jesus tells his Apostles. Between Christ's "going away" and his "return" is the time of the Church, his Body. Two thousand years have passed so far, including these five centuries and more in which the Church has made her pilgrim way on the American Continent, filling believers with Christ's life through the sacraments and sowing in these lands the good seed of the Gospel, which has yielded thirty, sixty and a hundredfold. *The time of the Church, the time of the Spirit:* the Spirit is the Teacher who trains *disciples:* he teaches them to love Jesus; he trains them to hear his word and to contemplate his countenance; he conforms them to Christ's sacred humanity, a humanity which is poor in spirit, afflicted, meek, hungry for justice, merciful, pure in heart, peacemaking, persecuted for justice's sake (cf. Mt 5:3–10). *By the working of the Holy Spirit, Jesus becomes the "Way" along which the disciple walks.* "If a man loves me, he will keep my word," Jesus says at the beginning of today's Gospel. "The word which you hear is not mine but the Father's who sent me" (Jn 14:23–24). Just as Jesus makes known the words of the Father, so the Spirit reminds the Church of Christ's own words (cf. Jn 14:26). And just as love of the Father led Jesus to feed on his will, so our love for Jesus is shown by our obedience to his words. Jesus' fidelity to the Father's will can be communicated to his disciples through the Holy Spirit, who pours the love of God into their hearts (cf. Rom 5:5).

According to Comblin, the church's coming into existence is a function of the Spirit.

From Comblin, *Holy Spirit and Liberation,* 77, 79–80.

The Holy Spirit was not sent to an already formed church; it was the sending of the Spirit that formed the church. The church exists because the Holy Spirit was sent to form it; the gift of the Spirit is the basis of its existence. So the church is neither before nor outside the Holy Spirit. There was first a sending of the Spirit to the whole of creation, to call it into being. The church arose and exists as part of this general mission.

This statement is important; it shows that the action of the Spirit is not determined by the action of the church. It is not for the church to tell where the Spirit blows. The reverse is the case: the church must follow—and exists only in following—where the Spirit blows. The Spirit makes the church its instrument and means of acting in the world—one of its instruments and means, though a special one. . . .

In Luke's theology, the Spirit comes first. The Spirit makes the Apostles, and through them, makes communities; in each community is the church. The same people of God is in the communities and in the missionary movement that brings them together in a dynamic unity. This creative presence of the Spirit has to be understood in its most complete sense. It is not a stamp of approval put from outside on a human process: the communities are really born from their experience of the Spirit.

Comblin connects the classical marks of the church with the Spirit as well. A church in the liberationist vision is the church of and for the poor.

From Comblin, *Holy Spirit and Liberation*, 94–95, 99.

Those who conform to the movement of the Spirit by forming communities made up of friends meeting in people's houses are the poor. Paul saw this happening in Corinth, and the same can be observed today. The ruling classes want a church organized from the top down; the poor want a church built from the bottom up: they are the ones in conformity with the will of the Spirit.

Structures and organizations are valid as a means of helping ministry in the church, but provided they are there to serve and not to be served. Structures follow sociological laws and become ends in themselves, forgetting the intentions of their founder. The Spirit works by founding new base communities, from which springs new life. . . .

The clamour of the poor, the cry of the oppressed, rises up from them, and the Spirit is at the source of the cry of the poor (cf Rom. 8:18–27). The church is the huge caravan of the rejected of the earth who call out, cry for justice, invoke a Liberator whose name is often unknown to them. . . .

The Spirit is the one who gathers the poor together so as to make them a new people who will challenge all the powers of the earth. The Spirit is the strength of the people of the poor, the strength of those who are weak. Without the Spirit, the poor would not raise their voices and conflict would not raise its head. The antagonism between the people of the oppressed and the powers of this world (cf Eph. 1:13–14; Rom. 8:18–27) exists because the poor exist as a people. The people of the poor cries out for its liberation.

The Pentecostal Experience

As is well documented nowadays, Pentecostalism and independent charismatic movements are the most rapidly growing Christian force in Latin America. At the same time, Pentecostalism is also widely influencing the Roman Catholic Church as well as most Protestant churches. In a vast continent such as Latin America, Pentecostalism exhibits as much diversity as it does anywhere else, such as in Africa or North America. The following citation speaks of one Latin American pentecostal experience, that of Chilean Pentecostalism. While showing off many features characteristic of global Pentecostalism, Chilean Pentecostalism also reflects some unique traits, as described by Chilean pentecostal pastor and theologian Juan Sepulveda.

From Juan Sepulveda, "Theological Characteristics of an Indigenous Pentecostalism: Chile," in *In the Power of the Spirit*, ed. Dennis A. Smith and B. F. Gutierrez, trans. Peter Kemmerle (Presbyterian Church (U.S.A.) and AIPRAL/CELEP, 1996, n.p.), http://www.religion-online.org/showchapter.asp?title=374&C=9 (accessed Nov. 2, 2007).

Distinguishing Features of Pentecostal Theology

To understand the specificity of Chilean Pentecostalism, one must first identify the theological features of Pentecostalism the world over. This is not an easy task since Pentecostalism has roots in various confessional traditions.

It seems that the single aspect that is absolutely unique to Pentecostalism is the "baptism of the Holy Spirit." A Norwegian pastor, cited by Beatriz Muñiz de Souza, wrote: "With respect to salvation through justification by the faith we are Lutherans. In our form of baptism by water we are Baptists. With respect to sanctification, we are Methodists. In our aggressive evangelism we're like the Salvation Army. But in relation to the Baptism of the Holy Spirit, we are Pentecostals."

The well-known specialist in Pentecostal origins, Donald Dayton, thinks that the common and distinctive traits of Pentecostalism can be summed up in the four theological affirmations of the Foursquare Gospel Church: salvation, the baptism of the Holy Spirit, healing, and the second coming of Christ.

Pastor Gabriel Vaccaro proposed the following elements as constitutive of the Pentecostal theological identity: 1) evangelization oriented to conversion (understood as a change in life); 2) baptism of the Holy Spirit (speaking in tongues); 3) the church as a charismatic and healing community; 4) and belief in a spiritual world. Vaccaro's view complements rather than contradicts Dayton's. Both describe speaking in tongues, or glossolalia, as the key manifestation of the baptism of the Holy Spirit.

In Pentecostal theology in general and Latin American Pentecostalism in particular, the notion of salvation is closely connected with healing, whether physical or mental.

From Sepulveda, "Theological Characteristics," n.p.

Healing and Salvation

As in mainstream Pentecostalism, faith in God's healing power plays an important role in the life of the Chilean Pentecostal communities. Considering how little access poor Chileans had to the benefits of modern medicine during the first decades of this century, experiences of divine healing occupy a privileged place in the conversion testimonies of the first generations of Chilean Pentecostals. . . .

In Chilean Pentecostalism, many testimonies blend healing and conversion into a single experience; yet we must not confuse the two. Conversion ("giving oneself up to God" or accepting Jesus Christ as personal savior) is understood as a joyful response to God's love, which can be expressed in healing. However, people can be healed and not converted, and people who have been converted have not necessarily experienced physical healing.

While the mass healing campaigns (including the more recent televised versions) emphasize the marvel of individual healing, Chilean Pentecostalism emphasizes the everyday life of the faith communities. The healing power of God is manifested in the warm welcome given to newcomers, in caring for the sick, in community prayer, and in perseverance in care and visitation. It is the community that heals. If, for reasons known only to God, there is no physical cure, there is always God's power manifest in the community, which gives the afflicted strength to confront adversity with hope, and even with joy.

Healing ministry is, thus, an integral part of the pentecostal church life.

From Daniel Chiquete, "Healing, Salvation, and Mission: The Ministry of Healing in Latin American Pentecostalism," *International Review of Mission* 93, nos. 370–371 (Geneva: WCC Publications, 2004): 479–80.

The importance of the ministry of healing makes itself felt in various facets of the life of Pentecostal communities, most notably in worship, in teaching and in mission. Experiences of healing are central in the Pentecostal understanding of the church and mission. Pentecostals see the church as a living organism and hold it in high esteem as the "community of saints" and as a place where the presence of the Holy Spirit is felt in a special way (1 Cor. 3:16; 6:15, 19; 12:12f; Rom. 12:3f). They see a direct relationship between holiness and health. They argue implicitly that if God sanctifies people through the presence of the Holy Spirit, and if we believe that where God's Spirit is there is complete freedom and liberation, including freedom from disease, then we have to conclude that it is not God's will that there should be sick people in the church, which is the body of Christ. In this way they establish a fundamental religious premise: the presence of God's Spirit in the community and in each one of the believers generates health/healing and salvation. This view is a central motive for the attempts at healing that are carried out in the worshipping community and in home visits and other group activities organized for the purpose of evangelizing. The same healing concern is also expressed in preaching, in testimonies, thanksgiving, prayers, singing and, often, the celebration of the Lord's Supper. It is therefore easy to understand the power of attraction that the Pentecostal communities may exert among social groups where disease is rife.

In general the Pentecostal communities can become effective spaces of healing, also on an emotional level. They are able to establish strong emotional ties and solidarity where people can find support and advice to help them cope with daily problems that often have to do with illness. This welcoming, empathizing capacity, plus the attractiveness of its worship services and its religious message, are essential to understanding the success and expansion of Pentecostalism. What makes it attractive to so many people is not its orthodoxy or its systematic theology, but the emotional and spiritual strength that radiates from its communities.

Permissions

Anselm of Canterbury, *Monologion* and *The Procession of the Holy Spirit*, in *Anselm of Canterbury*, vols. 1 and 3, ed. and trans. Jasper Hopkins and Herbert Richardson (New York: Edwin Mellen, 1974). Reprinted by permission.

Johann Arndt, *True Christianity*, translation and introduction by Peter Erb. Copyright © 1979 by The Missionary Society of St. Paul the Apostle in the State of New York. Paulist Press, Inc., New York/Mahwah, NJ. Reprinted by permission of Paulist Press, Inc. www.paulistpress.com.

Athanasius, *Letters to Serapion Concerning the Holy Spirit*, in *Athanasius*, trans. and ed. Khaled Anatolios (London: Routledge, 2004). Reprinted by permission.

Blessed John of Avila, *The Holy Ghost* (Chicago: Scepter, 1959). Reprinted by permission.

Karl Barth, *Church Dogmatics*, ed. Geoffrey W. Bromiley and Thomas F. Torrance, vols. 1, 3, and 4 (Edinburgh: T. & T. Clark, 1956, 1975). Reproduced by kind permission of Continuum International Publishing Group.

Karl Barth, *Evangelical Theology: An Introduction*, trans. Foley Grover (Grand Rapids: Wm. B. Eerdmans Publishing Co., 1963). Reprinted by permission.

Hendrikus Berkhof, *The Doctrine of the Holy Spirit* (Atlanta: John Knox Press, 1964). Reprinted by permission.

Luis M. Bermejo, introduction to *The Spirit of Life: The Holy Spirit in the Life of the Christian* (Anand, Gujarat: X. Diaz del Rio, 1987). Reprinted by permission.

Bernard of Clairvaux, *On the Song of Songs* and *The Steps of Humility and Praise*, in *The Works of Bernard of Clairvaux*, vol. 2, trans. Kilian Walsh, OCSO, and Irene M. Edmonds (Kalamazoo, MI: Cistercian Publications, 1976). Copyright 1976 by Cistercian Publications. Published by Liturgical Press, Collegeville, Minnesota. Reprinted with permission.

Bernard of Clairvaux, *The Steps of Humility and Pride*, in *The Works of Bernard of Clairvaux*, vol. 5, Treatises II, trans. The Order of Cistercians (Washington, DC: Cistercian Publications Consortium Press, 1974). Copyright 1974 by Cistercian Publications. Published by Liturgical Press, Collegeville, Minnesota. Reprinted with permission

Donald G. Bloesch, *The Holy Spirit: Works and Gifts*. Christian Foundations Series (Downers Grove, IL: InterVarsity Press, 2000). Reprinted by permission.

Leonardo Boff, *Holy Trinity: Perfect Community* (Maryknoll, NY: Orbis Books, 2000). Reprinted by permission.

Bonaventure, *The Soul's Journey into God; The Tree of Life; The Life of St. Francis*, translation and introduction by Ewert Cousins. Copyright © 1978 by Paulist Press. Paulist Press, Inc., New York/Mahwah, NJ. Reprinted by permission of Paulist Press, Inc. wwww.paulistpress.com.

Bonaventure, *Works of St. Bonaventure: Breviloquium*, trans. Dominic V. Monti, OFM (St. Bonaventure, NY: Franciscan Institute Publications, 2005). Reprinted by permission.

Robert C. Broderick, ed., *The Catholic Encyclopedia* (Nashville: Thomas Nelson, 1975). Reprinted by permission.

Sergius Bulgakov, *The Comforter*, trans. Boris Jakim (Grand Rapids: Wm. B. Eerdmans Publishing Co., 2004). Reprinted by permission.

Daniel Chiquete, "Healing, Salvation, and Mission: The Ministry of Healing in Latin American Pentecostalism," *International Review of Mission* 93, nos. 370–371 (Geneva: WCC Publications, 2004). Founded in 1948, the World Council of Churches is now a fellowship of more than 340 Christian churches confessing together "the Lord Jesus Christ according to the scriptures" and seeking "to fulfill together their common calling to the glory of the one God, Father, Son and Holy Spirit." Tracing its origins to international movements dedicated to world mission and evangelism, life and work, faith and order, Christian education and church unity, the World Council is made up primarily of Protestant and Orthodox churches. The Roman Catholic Church is not a member church but participates with the World Council of Churches and its member communions in a variety of activities and dialogues. Reprinted by permission.

José Comblin, *The Holy Spirit and Liberation*, trans. Paul Burns (Maryknoll, NY: Orbis Books, 1989). Reprinted by permission of Continuum International Publishing Group.

Yves Congar, *I Believe in the Holy Spirit*, trans. David Smith, 3 vols. (New York: Crossroad, 1997). Reprinted by permission.

Jonathan Edwards, *Works of Jonathan Edwards Online*, ed. Harry S. Stout, Kenneth P. Minkema, Caleb J. D. Maskell (2005–), http://edwards.yale.edu/archive. Reprinted by permission.

Vernard Eller, ed., *Thy Kingdom Come. A Blumhardt Reader* (Grand Rapids: Wm. B. Eerdmans Publishing Co., 1980). Reprinted by permission.

Evangelical Lutheran Church of America, "Dig Deeper: The Holy Spirit," ELCA.org, http://www.elca.org/holyspirit. Reprinted by permission.

Mary Ann Fatula, OP, *The Holy Spirit: Unbounded Gift of Joy* (Collegeville, MN: Liturgical Press, 1998). Reprinted by permission.

Thomas N. Finger, *A Contemporary Anabaptist Theology: Biblical, Historical, Constructive* (Downers Grove, IL: InterVarsity Press, 2004). Copyright © 2004 by Thomas N. Finger. Used by permission of InterVarsity Press, P.O. Box 1400, Downers Grove, IL 60515. www.ivpress.com.

Donald L. Gelpi, *Charism and Sacrament: A Theology of Christian Conversion* by Donald L. Gelpi, SJ. Copyright © 1976 by The Missionary Society of St. Paul the Apostle in the State of New Your. Paulist Press, Inc., New York/Mahwah, NJ. Reprinted by permission of Paulist Press, Inc. www.paulistpress.com.

Ken R. Gnanakan ed. *Salvation: Some Asian Perspectives* (Bangalore, India: Asia Theological Association, 1992). Reprinted by permission.

St. Gregory of Sinai, *Texts on Commandments and Dogmas*, in *Writings from the Philokalia on Prayer of the Heart*, trans. E. Kadloubovsky and G. E. H. Palmer (London: Faber & Faber, n.d.). Reprinted by permission.

Stanley J. Grenz, *Theology for the Community of God* (Grand Rapids: Wm. B. Eerdmans Publishing Co., 2000). Reprinted by permission.

Gustavo Gutiérrez, *We Drink from Our Own Wells: The Spiritual Journey of a People* (Maryknoll, NY: Orbis Books, 2003). Reprinted by permission.

G. W. F. Hegel, "The Divine in a Particular Shape," *Early Theological Writings (1793–1800)*, in *G. W. F. Hegel: Theologian of the Spirit*, ed. Peter C. Hodgson, The Making of Modern Theology, Nineteenth and Twentieth Century Texts (Minneapolis: Fortress Press, 1997). Reprinted by permission.

Hippolytus, *The Apostolic Tradition*, in *The Apostolic Tradition of Hippolytus*, ed. and trans. Burton Scott Easton (Cambridge: Cambridge University Press, 1934). Copyright 1934 Cambridge University Press. Reprinted with the permission of Cambridge University Press.

A. A. Hodge, *Outlines of Theology*, rev. and enlarg. (Grand Rapids: Wm. B. Eerdmans, 1949). Reprinted by permission.

Robert W. Jenson, *Systematic Theology*, vol. 1: *The Triune God* (Oxford: Oxford University Press, 1997). © 1997 by Robert Jenson. Reprinted by permission.

John of the Cross, *The Living Flame of Love, Versions A and B*, edited by Jane Ackerman. MRTS Volume 135, Tempe, AZ, 1997. Copyright Arizona Board of Regents for Arizona State University. Reprinted with permission.

Elizabeth Johnson, *She Who Is: The Mystery of God in Feminist Theological Discourse* (New York: Crossroad, 1992). Reprinted by permission.

Elizabeth Johnson, *Women, Earth and Creator Spirit*. Copyright 1993 by Saint Mary's College, Notre Dame, Ind. Paulist Press, Inc., New York/Mahwah, NJ. Reprinted by permission of Paulist Press, Inc. www.paulistpress.com.

Chin Khua Khan, "Pentecostalism in Myanmar: An Overview," *Asian Journal of Pentecostal Studies* 5, no. 1 (Jan. 2002). Reprinted by permission.

Kosuke Koyama, *Mount Fuji and Mount Sinai: A Critique of Idols* (Maryknoll, NY: Orbis Books, 1985). Reprinted by permission.

Abraham Kuyper, "Common Grace," in *Abraham Kuyper: A Centennial Reader*, ed. James D. Bratt (Grand Rapids: Wm. B. Eerdmans Publishing Co., 1998). Reprinted by permission.

Jung Young Lee, *Trinity in Asian Perspective* (Nashville: Abingdon Press, 1996). Reprinted by permission.

Vladimir Lossky, *Orthodox Theology: An Introduction*, trans. Ian and Ihita Kesarcodi-Watson (Crestwood, NY: St. Vladimir's Seminary Press, 1978). Reprinted by permission.

Julie C. Ma, "Korean Pentecostal Spirituality: A Case Study of Jashil Choi," *Asian Journal of Pentecostal Studies* 5, no. 2 (July 2002). Reprinted by permission.

Lawrence T. Martin, translation and introduction, *The Venerable Bede, Commentary on the Acts of the Apostles* (Kalamazoo, MI: Cistercian Publications, 1989). Reprinted by permission.

Maximus the Confessor, *First Century on Various Texts* 72–73, in *The Philokalia: The Complete Text*, vol. 2, comp. by St. Nikodimos of the Holy Mountain and St. Makarios of Corinth; trans. and ed. by G. E. H. Palmer, Philip Sherrard, Kallistos Ware, and Holy Transfiguration Monastery et al. (London; Boston: Faber & Faber, 1979). Translation copyright © 1981 by the Eling Trust. Reprinted by permission.

Maximus the Confessor, *Maximus Confessor: Selected Writings*, translation and notes by George C. Berthold. Copyright © 1985 by George Berthold. Paulist Press,

Inc., New York/Mahwah, NJ. Reprinted by permission of Paulist Press, Inc. www.paulistpress.com.

John S. Mbiti, *African Religions and Philosophy* (New York: A. Prager, 1969). Reprinted by permission.

Kilian McDonnell, OSB, and George T. Montague, *Christian Initiation and Baptism in the Holy Spirit: Evidence from the First Eight Centuries* (Collegeville, MN: Liturgical Press, 1991). Copyright 1991 by the Order of Saint Benedict, Inc. Published by Liturgical Press, Collegeville, Minnesota. Reprinted with permission.

Kilian McDonnell, OSB, *The Other Hand of God: The Holy Spirit as the Universal Touch and Goal* (Collegeville, MN: Liturgical Press, 2003). Reprinted by permission.

Mennonite Church, "The Holy Spirit in the Life of the Church" (1977), *Global Anabaptist Mennonite Encyclopedia Online*, http://www.gameo.org/encyclopedia/contents/H6583.html. Reprinted by permission.

John Meyendorff, ed. with introduction, *The Triads of Gregory Palamas*, trans. Nicholas Gendle (New York: Paulist Press, 1983). Reprinted by permission.

Jürgen Moltmann, *The Spirit of Life: A Universal Affirmation*, trans. Margaret Kohl (Minneapolis: Fortress Press, 1992). Reprinted by permission.

Geiko Müller-Fahrenholz, *God's Spirit: Transforming a World in Crisis* (New York: Continuum; Geneva: WCC Publications, 1995). Reprinted by permission.

Gwinyai H. Muzorewa, *The Origins and Development of African Theology* (Maryknoll, NY: Orbis Books, 1985). Reprinted by permission.

Caleb Oluremi Oladipo, *The Development of the Doctrine of the Holy Spirit in the Yoruba (African) Indigenous Christian Movement*, American University Studies, Series 2, Theology and Religion, vol. 185 (Frankfurt: Peter Lang, 1996). Reprinted by permission.

Wolfhart Pannenberg, *Systematic Theology*, trans. Geoffrey W. Bromiley, 3 vols. (Grand Rapids: Wm. B. Eerdmans Publishing Co., 1991, 1994, 1998). Reprinted by permission.

Sister Jane Patricia, *The Hymns of Abelard in English Verse* (Lanham, MD: University Press of America, 1986). Reprinted by permission.

Jaroslav Pelikan and Helmut T. Lehman, eds., *Luther's Works*, American ed. (Libronix Digital Library), 55 vols. (Minneapolis: Fortress Press, 2002). Reprinted by permission of Augsburg Fortress and Concordia Publishing House.

Jaroslav Pelikan and Helmut T. Lehman, eds., *Luther's Works*, vol. 1 © 1958. 1986 Concordia Publishing House. Used with permission. All rights reserved.

Jaroslav Pelikan and Helmut T. Lehman, eds., *Luther's Works*, vol. 14 © 1958. 1986 Concordia Publishing House. Used with permission. All rights reserved.

Jaroslav Pelikan and Helmut T. Lehman, eds., *Luther's Works*, vol. 25 © 1972 Concordia Publishing House. Used with permission. All rights reserved.

Jaroslav Pelikan and Helmut T. Lehman, eds., *Luther's Works*, vol. 27 © 1964. 1992 Concordia Publishing House. Used with permission. All rights reserved.

Clark H. Pinnock, *Flame of Love: A Theology of the Holy Spirit* (Downers Grove, IL: InterVarsity Press, 1996). Reprinted by permission.

Pseudo-Macarius, *The Fifty Spiritual Homilies and the Great Letter*, translated and edited by George A. Maloney, SJ. Copyright © 1992 by George A. Maloney, SJ. Paulist Press, Inc., New York/Mahwah, NJ. Reprinted by permission of Paulist Press, Inc. www.paulistpress.com.

F. D. E. Schleiermacher, *The Christian Faith*, ed. H. R. Mackintosh and J. S. Stewart (London/New York: T. & T. Clark, 1999). Republished by kind permission of Continuum International Publishing Group.

Dumitru Staniloae, *The Experience of God: Orthodox Dogmatic Theology*, vol. 2 (Brookline, MA: Holy Cross Orthodox Press, 2000). Reprinted by permission.

Symeon the New Theologian, *The Discourses*, translated by C. J. deCatanzaro. Copyright © 1980 by The Missionary Society of St. Paul the Apostle in the State of New York. Paulist Press, Inc., New York/Mahwah, NJ. Reprinted by permission of Paulist Press, Inc. www.paulistpress.com.

Masao Takenaka, "Salvation: A Japanese Discussion," *International Review of Mission* 61, no. 241 (Geneva: WCC Publications, 1972). Founded in 1948, the World Council of Churches is now a fellowship of more than 340 Christian churches confessing together "the Lord Jesus Christ according to the scriptures" and seeking "to fulfill together their common calling to the glory of the one God, Father, Son and Holy Spirit." Tracing its origins to international movements dedicated to world mission and evangelism, life and work, faith and order, Christian education and church unity, the World Council is made up primarily of Protestant and Orthodox churches. The Roman Catholic Church is not a member church but participates with the World Council of Churches and its member communions in a variety of activities and dialogues. Reprinted by permission.

Theodore G. Tappert, trans. and ed., *Book of Concord: The Confessions of the Evangelical Lutheran Church*. With Jaroslav Pelikan, Robert W. Fischer, and Arthur C. Piepkorn (Philadelphia: Fortress Press, 1959). Reprinted by permission.

Miroslav Volf, *Work in the Spirit: Toward a Theology of Work* (New York: Oxford University Press, 1991). Reprinted by permission.

Mark I. Wallace, *Fragments of the Spirit: Nature, Violence, and the Renewal of Creation* (New York: Continuum, 1996). Reprinted by permission.

Michael Welker, *God the Spirit*, trans. John F. Hoffmeyer (Minneapolis: Fortress Press, 1994). Reprinted by permission.

World Council of Churches, "The Healing Mission of the Church," Commission for World Mission and Evangelization, World Council of Churches, preparatory paper nos. 4 and 11 for the May 2005 CWME Conference in Athens, "Come Holy Spirit, heal and reconcile—Called in Christ to be reconciling and healing communities," http://www.mission2005.org. Reprinted by permission.

World Council of Churches, "Religious Plurality and Christian Self-Understanding," *Current Dialogue* 45 (July 2005), http://www.wcc-coe.org/wcc/what/interreligious/cd45-01.html. Reprinted by permission.

Zhihua Yao, "In the Power of the Spirit," *Tripod* 91 (Jan.–Feb. 1996). Reprinted by permission.

John Zizioulas, *Being as Communion: Studies in Personhood and Church* (Crestwood, NY: St. Vladimir's Seminary Press, 1985). Reprinted by permission.

Huldrych Zwingli, *Huldrych Zwingli Writings: The Defense of the Reformed Faith*, vol. 1, trans. E. J. Furcha (Allison Park, PA: Pickwick Publications, 1984). Reprinted by permission.

Suggestions for Further Reading

Biblical Perspectives

Dunn, James D. G. *Baptism in the Holy Spirit*. London: SCM Press, 1970.

——. *Jesus and the Spirit*. London: SCM Press, 1975.

Ewert, David. *The Holy Spirit in the New Testament*. Scottsdale, PA: Herald, 1983.

Fee, Gordon. *God's Empowering Presence: The Holy Spirit in the Letters of Paul*. Peabody, MA: Hendrickson, 1994.

Hawthorne, Gerald F. *The Presence and the Power: The Significance of the Holy Spirit in the Life and Ministry of Jesus*. Dallas: Word, 1991.

Levison, John R. *The Spirit in First Century Judaism*. Leiden: E. J. Brill, 1997.

Martin, Ralph P. *The Spirit and the Congregation: Studies in 1 Corinthians 12–15*. Grand Rapids: Wm. B. Eerdmans Publishing Co., 1984.

Montague, George. *The Holy Spirit: Growth of a Biblical Tradition*. Peabody, MA: Hendrickson, 1994.

Penney, John M. *The Missionary Emphasis of Lukan Pneumatology*. Sheffield: Sheffield Academic Press, 1997.

Schweizer, Eduard. *The Holy Spirit*. London: SCM Press, 1980.

Turner, Max. *Power from on High: The Spirit of Prophecy in Luke-Acts*. Sheffield: Sheffield Academic Press, 1997.

Historical Perspectives

Burgess, Stanley M. *The Holy Spirit: Ancient Christian Traditions*. Peabody, MA: Hendrickson, 1984.

——. *The Holy Spirit: Eastern Christian Traditions*. Peabody, MA: Hendrickson, 1989.

——. *The Holy Spirit: Medieval Roman Catholic and Reformation Traditions*. Peabody, MA: Hendrickson, 1997.

Congar, Yves. *I Believe in the Holy Spirit*. 3 vols. New York: Herder & Herder, 1997.

De Klerk, Peter, ed. *Calvin and the Holy Spirit: Papers and Responses Presented at the Sixth Colloquium on Calvin and Calvin Studies*. Grand Rapids: Calvin Studies Society, 1989.

McDonnell, Kilian, and George T. Montague. *Christian Initiation and Baptism in the Holy Spirit: Evidence from the First Eight Centuries*. Collegeville, MN: Liturgical Press, 1991.

Opsahl, Paul D., ed. *The Holy Spirit in the Life of the Church from Biblical Times to the Present*. Minneapolis: Augsburg, 1978.

Watkin-Jones, Howard. *The Holy Spirit from Arminius to Wesley*. London: Epworth, 1929.

——. *The Holy Spirit in the Medieval Church*. London: Epworth, 1922.

Contemporary Pneumatologies

Anderson, Allan H. *Moya: The Holy Spirit from an African Perspective*. Pretoria: University of South Africa Press, 1994.

Badcock, Gary D. *Light of Truth and Fire of Love: A Theology of the Holy Spirit*. Grand Rapids: Wm. B. Eerdmans Publishing Co., 1997.

Balthasar, Hans Urs von. *Explorations in Theology*. Vol. 3: *Creator Spirit*. San Francisco: Ignatius Press, 1993, orig. 1967.

Bergmann, Sigurd. *Creation Set Free: The Spirit as Liberator of Nature*. Grand Rapids: Wm. B. Eerdmans Publishing Co., 2005.

Berkhof, Hendrikus. *The Doctrine of the Holy Spirit*. Atlanta: John Knox Press, 1964.

Boff, Leonardo. *Church, Charism, and Power*. New York: Crossroad, 1985.

Bruner, Frederick D., and William Hordern. *The Holy Spirit: Shy Member of the Trinity*. Minneapolis: Augsburg, 1984.

Bulgakov, Sergius. *The Comforter*. Translated by Boris Jakim. Grand Rapids: Wm. B. Eerdmans Publishing Co., 2004.

Christenson, Larry, ed. *Welcome Holy Spirit: A Study of Charismatic Renewal in the Church*. Minneapolis: Augsburg, 1987.

Coffey, David. *Grace: The Gift of the Holy Spirit*. Manly, Australia: Catholic Institute of Sydney, 1979.

Del Colle, R. *Christ and the Spirit: Spirit Christology in Trinitarian Perspective*. Oxford: Oxford University Press 1994.

Durrwell, F.-X. *Holy Spirit of God*. London: Geoffrey Chapman, 1986.

Fatula, Mary Ann. *The Holy Spirit: Unbounded Gift of Joy*. Collegeville, MN: Liturgical Press, 1998.

Comblin, J. *The Holy Spirit and Liberation*. Maryknoll, NY: Orbis Books, 1989.

Hendry, George S. *The Holy Spirit in Christian Theology*. Philadelphia: Westminster Press, 1956.

Heron, Alasdair I. C. *The Holy Spirit*. Philadelphia: Westminster Press, 1983.

Hollenweger, Walter J. *Pentecostalism: Origins and Developments Worldwide*. Peabody, MA: Hendrickson, 1997.

Johnson, Elisabeth. *She Who Is: The Mystery of God in Feminist Theological Discourse*. New York: Crossroad, 1992.

———. *Women, Earth, and Creator Spirit*. New York/Mahwah: Paulist Press, 1993.

Jones, James W. *The Spirit and the World*. New York: Hawthorn Books, 1975.

Kim, Kirsteen. *The Holy Spirit in the World: A Global Conversation*. Maryknoll, NY: Orbis Books, 2007.

Kärkkäinen, Veli-Matti. *Pneumatology: The Holy Spirit in Ecumenical, International, and Contextual Perspectives*. Grand Rapids: Baker Academic, 2002.

Küng, Hans, and Jürgen Moltmann, eds. *Conflicts about the Holy Spirit*. New York: Seabury, 1979.

Kuyper, Abraham. *The Work of the Holy Spirit*. Grand Rapids: Wm. B. Eerdmans Publishing Co., 1973.

Lossky, Vladimir. *The Mystical Theology of the Eastern Church*. Crestwood, NY: St. Vladimir's Seminary Press, 1998.

Macchia, Frank. *Baptized in the Spirit: A Global Pentecostal Theology*. Grand Rapids: Zondervan, 2006.

McDonnell, Kilian, OSB. *The Other Hand of God: The Holy Spirit as the Universal Touch and Goal*. Collegeville, MN: Liturgical Press, 2003.

McIntyre, John. *The Shape of Pneumatology: Studies in the Doctrine of the Holy Spirit*. Edinburgh: T.&T. Clark, 1997.

Mills, Edward. *The Holy Spirit: A Bibliography*. Peabody, MA: Hendrickson, 1988.

Moltmann, Jürgen. *The Spirit of Life: A Universal Affirmation*. Translated by Margaret Kohl. Minneapolis: Fortress Press, 1992.

———. *The Source of Life: The Holy Spirit and the Theology of Life*. Translated by Margaret Kohl. Minneapolis: Fortress Press, 1997.

Müller-Fahrenholz, Geiko. *God's Spirit: Transforming a World in Crisis*. New York: Continuum, 1995.

O'Carroll, Michael. *Veni Creator Spiritus: A Theological Encyclopedia of the Holy Spirit*. Collegeville, MN: Liturgical Press, 1990.

Pannenberg, Wolfhart. *Systematic Theology*. 3 vols. Translated by G. Bromiley. Grand Rapids: Wm. B. Eerdmans Publishing Co., 1991–97.

Pinnock, Clark H. *Flame of Love: A Theology of the Holy Spirit*. Downers Grove, IL: InterVarsity Press, 1996.

Pope John Paul II. *Celebrate 2000! Reflections on the Holy Spirit*. Ann Arbor: Servant Publishers, 1997.

Prenter, Regin. *Spiritus Creator: Studies in Luther's Theology*. Translated by John M. Jensen. Philadelphia: Muhlenberg, 1953.

Prichard, Rebecca Button. *Sensing the Spirit: The Holy Spirit in Feminist Perspective*. St. Louis: Chalice Press, 1999.

Rahner, Karl. *The Dynamic Element in the Church*. New York: Herder & Herder, 1964.

———. *Experience of the Spirit: Source of Theology*. Theological Investigations 16. New York: Crossroad, 1981.

Reynolds, Blair. *Toward a Process Pneumatology*. London: Associated University Presses, 1990.

Rosato, Philip J. *The Spirit as Lord: The Pneumatology of Karl Barth*. Edinburgh: T.&T. Clark, 1981.

Shults, F. Leron, and Andrea Hollingsworth. *The Holy Spirit*. Guides to Theology. Grand Rapids: Wm. B. Eerdmans Publishing Co., 2008.

Taylor, John V. *The Go-Between God: The Holy Spirit and Christian Mission*. London: SCM Press, 1973.

Tillich, Paul. "Life and the Spirit." In *Systematic Theology*. Vol. 3 (Chicago: University of Chicago Press, 1963), 11–294.

Vandervelde, George, ed. *The Holy Spirit: Renewing and Empowering Presence*. Winfield, BC: Wood Lake Books, 1988.

Wallace, Mark I. *Fragments of the Spirit: Nature, Violence, and the Renewal of Creation*. New York: Continuum, 1996.

Welker, M. *God the Spirit*. Minneapolis: Fortress Press, 1994.

———, ed. *The Work of the Spirit: Pneumatology and Pentecostalism*. Grand Rapids: Wm. B. Eerdmans Publishing Co., 2006.

Yong, Amos. *Beyond the Impasse: Toward a Pneumatological Theology of Religions*. Grand Rapids: Baker Academic, 2003.

———. *The Spirit Poured Out on All Flesh: Pentecostalism and the Possibility of Global Theology*. Grand Rapids: Baker Academic, 2005.

Index